A Man and His Presidents

ALSO BY ALVIN S. FELZENBERG

The Leaders We Deserved (and a Few We Didn't): Rethinking the Presidential Rating Game (2010, 2008)

Governor Tom Kean: From the New Jersey Statehouse to the 9-11 Commission (2006)

The Keys to a Successful Presidency, editor (2000)

Evolution of the Modern Presidency: A Bibliographical Survey, with Fred I. Greenstein and Larry Berman (1977)

A Man and His Presidents

The Political Odyssey of William F. Buckley Jr.

Alvin S. Felzenberg

Yale
UNIVERSITY
PRESS
New Haven & London

Published with assistance from the Mary Cady Tew Memorial Fund.

Yale University Press books may be purchased in quantity for educational, business, or promotional use. For information, please e-mail sales.press@yale.edu (U.S. office) or sales@yaleup.co.uk (U.K. office).

Set in PostScript Electra and Trajan type by IDS Infotech Ltd.
Printed in the United States of America.

Library of Congress Control Number: 2016953816
ISBN 978-0-300-16384-1 (hardcover : alk. paper)

A catalogue record for this book is available from the British Library.

This paper meets the requirements of ANSI/NISO Z39.48-1992 (Permanence of Paper).

10 9 8 7 6 5 4 3 2 1

To the memory of Paul E. Sigmund Sr., 1929–2014
Professor of Politics, Princeton University, 1964–2014
In gratitude

Contents

Preface

When friends, colleagues, and relatives learned that I was writing a book about William F. Buckley Jr., they almost universally had the same response: "Oh, what fun!" *Fun* was a word often associated with Buckley. On November 3, 1967, during my first semester in college, he made the cover of *Time*. Beneath a David Levine drawing of him appeared the words: "William Buckley/ Conservatism Can Be Fun." (Weeks prior to that he had been the freshman orientation speaker at the university I was attending.)

Buckley had come into my life just two years earlier, in 1965. I was sixteen and a sophomore at Irvington High School in New Jersey; Buckley was running for Mayor of New York City. Already interested in politics, I was enthralled by the mayoral debates that had become a major component in the campaign taking place across the Hudson River. There was Republican Congressman John V. Lindsay—"the next John F. Kennedy," according to some press accounts. Lindsay was young, handsome, tall, and said to be in the race because he needed a bigger office from which to run for President. There was the City Comptroller, the older, shorter, silver-haired Democrat Abraham D. Beame, a man very much of the clubhouse. He had been on the city payroll since 1946 and had the demeanor of a man running for Mayor primarily to augment his city pension.

Then there was Buckley. He was articulate, knowledgeable, witty, and urbane—hardly attributes people associated with "conservatives." He used multisyllabic words I could not comprehend. He made no attempt to conceal his contempt for his opponents' intellects—or his boredom when they recited platitudes. Lindsay was serious and sanctimonious and Beame self-disciplined and polite. Only Buckley appeared to be enjoying both the campaign and the spotlight. Buckley had "a smile that could light up an auditorium," as George

F. Will noted in a column after Buckley's passing in 2008. And that attribute of his was much on display in the fall of 1965.

Buckley was clearly not in the race to win or to improve his chances of attaining another post later on. He had a broader goal in mind: to turn the Republican Party into the natural political home for conservatives and to offer up alternative solutions to problems in a city that seemed in perpetual "crisis" after decades of New Deal liberalism—and about to receive a new dose of it from Lyndon Johnson's Great Society, which was just taking hold. All this seemed a tall order, given that just a year before Buckley ran for Mayor in a city that saw itself as the capital of American liberalism, the nation's most prominent conservative, Barry Goldwater, had lost the presidential election to LBJ in an overwhelming landslide.

Because a strike had shut down the city's newspapers for much of the campaign, television and radio became the primary means through which people could follow the mayoral race. I tuned in to the multiple debates primarily to hear Buckley's latest one-liners. Lindsay and Beame learned early on not to tangle with him. (I discovered only later that Buckley had been a champion debater at Yale.) The unconventional solutions he offered to the city's problems were, for me, almost an afterthought. Yet, they struck me as reasonable. Why had they not been tried years ago?

Eventually, I learned that I was not alone in my discovery of this new phenomenon that went by the name "Buckley." A year after the election, while on my way to class, I ran into a friend I had known since the first grade. She was carrying a copy of Buckley's recently published memoir of the campaign, *The Unmaking of a Mayor.* "Were you following the election for Mayor of New York last fall?" she asked. I had indeed. "Isn't he a riot?" She did not need to mention Buckley's name. Buckleymania had arrived in, of all places, the overwhelmingly Democratic Irvington. Who would have thought?

I began following Buckley's column in the *Newark Evening News.* In an age before professional SAT tutors had turned themselves into an industry, I prepared for the test, in part, by devouring Buckley's writings. His columns were about the same length as the essays in the reading comprehension section. Surely some of the multisyllabic words he was introducing me to would appear on the vocabulary component. (Many did.)

I also began to pay closer attention to what Buckley was actually saying. Before I encountered him, the only book by a contemporary self-identified conservative I had read was Barry Goldwater's *Conscience of a Conservative.* (I later learned that Brent Bozell, Buckley's brother-in-law, had ghosted it.) I discovered that Buckley was about more than fun. He was both what Christopher

Hitchens (in a tribute in the *Weekly Standard*) called "a man of incessant labor" and what the French have in mind when they speak of *un homme sérieux*.

Buckley used his wit to attract the attention of the uninitiated to what he had to say. I could always count on him to offer a perspective different from that of most other commentators. Most of them saw their mission as passing along the conventional wisdom of the times, which was decidedly liberal. I began to seek out Buckley's books. The first one I read was *The Unmaking of a Mayor.* Next came *Up from Liberalism* and *Rumbles Left and Right.* (I did not pick up *God and Man at Yale* until I was well along in college, where I also delved into back issues of *National Review.*) Buckley's television program *Firing Line* premiered during my junior year in high school. By the time I graduated, I was hooked.

At the time, I had no idea how much of Goldwater's firepower and, later, that of Ronald Reagan, who was elected California's Governor a year after Buckley ran for Mayor, originated in the mind of a man who operated out of a cluttered office on East 35th Street, played the harpsichord, sailed the great oceans, spoke with a sort-of-British accent, and so worshipped gadgetry that he once devoted an entire column to the metallic balls that came with his IBM Selectric typewriter. ("You can actually change the font!") A picture of Buckley pecking away at that machine adorned the cover of his book *Execution Eve and Other Contemporary Ballads* (1975).

In college, I found Buckley's writings a useful alternative to the standard explanations of the recent and distant past that adorned the syllabi of American history courses. One thing Arthur M. Schlesinger Jr., Henry Steele Commager, Richard Hofstadter, and other staples did not provide their readers were opinions or interpretations of events different from those offered by their peers. As Buckley himself joked, that was because they did not think there *were* any opinions other than those offered up by orthodox liberals.

It took me a while, though, to understand why Buckley had been more critical of the Eisenhower presidency than most Democrats were. To me, Ike was the epitome of a conservative, as I thought I understood the term. One professor tried to discourage me from writing my senior thesis about the thirty-fourth President, on the grounds that Eisenhower was "old, stodgy, boring," and—worst of all—"went against the activist grain of his two Democratic predecessors." This had not been sufficient for Buckley. He had wanted more after the election of 1952 than a mere slowing of the pace of government expansion. He wanted to repeal most domestic programs FDR and Truman had left in their wake. Ike did not think the public would tolerate that. Neither had some of Buckley's colleagues and mentors, I would discover. I ignored my professor's advice and pressed on, with Buckley as my invisible and anonymous thesis adviser. (I still think of Ike's administration as the prototype of prudent, constitutional, and conservative governance, but not to worry!)

In 1969, during my sophomore year, I finally ginned up the nerve to write Buckley from time to time, asking him a question or two about something he had written or said. He always answered. Before long I was pestering his scheduler, Frances Bronson, for an appointment to meet him. It was a long slog, but permission was eventually granted. Years later, while going through Buckley's papers at Yale University I came across one of the requests I had sent him. Frances wrote in pencil across the top, "Persistent, isn't he? Five minutes?" She had left room for Buckley to check "yes" or "no."

In the appropriate box, he had checked "yes." I was invited to sit in on a meeting at which Buckley and his fellow editors put the latest issue of *National Review* "to bed." It happened to be the day that Buckley's representatives had successfully served the playwright and novelist Gore Vidal with a subpoena in conjunction with the lawsuit Buckley had filed against him for libel, slander, and defamation. The office was in a festive mood. More letters, meetings, and telephone calls followed over the next four decades. While we were not close friends and I was never officially a part of Buckley's orbit, we maintained what I would term an "active acquaintanceship."

Bill always found time. His notes, often just one line long, always included a quip, a joke, or a reference discernible only to the recipient. He was the same in our telephone conversations and in our brief personal encounters. In failing health, he graciously supplied a blurb for one of my books. There was no mistaking his style for anyone else's. Although many people impersonated Buckley on television, in private, and sometimes right in front of him, no one could ghost for him.

Only after he had passed from the scene did I learn of the impact he had on other teenagers when they were politically coming of age. In a March 3, 2008, column for the *New York Times*, William Kristol related that his high school yearbook bears a photograph in which he is wearing a button that reads: "Don't let them immanentize the eschaton." The quotation was Buckley's distillation of Eric Voegelin's political philosophy. It warns readers not to allow ideologues to try to create heaven on earth. When they do, bad things happen: gulags, death camps, cultural revolutions, planes turned into missiles and flown into buildings, and beheadings. One could always count on Buckley to sound the alarm.

Kristol, of course, knew Buckley as a family friend. Around the time the young Kristol sported the above-mentioned button, his father, Irving, wrote

Buckley apologizing for his tardy response to a request for feedback on one of Buckley's articles. The founder of the neoconservative movement explained that he had tried and failed to wrestle that particular issue of *National Review* away from his sixteen-year-old son and that he had solved the problem by taking out a second subscription.

Buckley always attracted young readers. One day in the mid-1980s, I stopped in a bookstore across from New York's Penn Station to pass the time before boarding the train back to Princeton, New Jersey. Two tables away from me was a teenager in a jacket sporting the insignia of a regional Catholic high school. He was around the age Kristol was when the photograph he described appeared in his high school yearbook. The young man picked up a copy of Buckley's *Right Reason* (1986) and began waving it at friend a few yards away. The two started chanting in muted voices, "Will-iam F.! Will-iam F.!" I wonder what they are now and whether they followed their role model into the worlds of writing and politics.

One of the challenges in writing this book was to re-create Buckley's radiance, brilliance, wit, love of life, and appreciation of the human condition for people whose personal memory of him is at best dim, and more likely nonexistent. My students, most of them born during the 1990s, have little memory of him. Some recall the tremendous media coverage his passing received. They have a sense that such attention is bestowed primarily upon the extraordinary. And Buckley was nothing short of extraordinary.

In this book, which covers Buckley's entire career, I place my emphasis on how Buckley functioned behind the scenes as a political strategist and adviser to the principal center-right political actors of his era. This has been one of the least explored aspects of his career. In his more than half century on the public stage, Buckley operated on multiple platforms: the printed page, television, radio, speeches, public debates, and sponsorship of campus political groups and conservative organizations. He also functioned as an informal adviser to leading public figures of his times. Some, like Ronald Reagan, came to regard Buckley as more than an ideological comrade in arms—but as a personal friend, tutor, confidant, enabler, adviser, and protector.

Most discussions of Buckley focus on his role as founder of the post–World War II American conservative movement. They should. If not for Buckley's inexhaustible energy, radiant personality, organizational skills, and gift for publicizing and promulgating what he saw as time-tested truths through multiple forums, ideas that have come to be characterized as "conservative" might have remained confined to the remote reaches of library shelves. That they did not attests to another Buckley attribute: his skills as a political strategist and activist, behind-the-scenes operator, and networker par excellence. As one of his friends, the late Frank Shakespeare, remarked to me, "Bill Buckley knew almost everybody—and how to get to anybody."

That this side of his story has been largely underexamined is understandable, given that Buckley produced more than fifty books, in excess of a thousand taped televised programs, fifty-six hundred newspaper columns, and assorted other writings—to say nothing of the magazine he founded and whose editorial stance he controlled for decades; not to mention the secondary literature about him that appeared in the popular press and previous books and the voluminous correspondence he left behind. Even more exists in the files of his contemporaries, the memories of associates, and documentary and other evidence of his activities. Such a treasure trove will keep scholars studying the second half of the twentieth century and the opening years of the twenty-first amply occupied.

Through their sheer volume, Buckley's works leave hidden the extent to which he was as much a politician as he was a writer, and an activist as well as a commentator on events. Most magazine editors and newspaper columnists do not found ad hoc organizations to protest certain occurrences, be they Khrushchev's visit to the United States in 1959 or a Supreme Court decree that banned prayer in public schools. They do not found organizations intended to bring young people into political movements or assemble an army of young intellectuals upon whom policy makers might rely. They do not dangle party nominations before a sitting Governor seeking reelection in a major state. They do not advise presidents behind the scenes on policy or influence the course administrations might take by actively promoting candidates for key positions. Buckley did all of this, while simultaneously churning out three syndicated columns each week, hosting a weekly television program, editing a biweekly magazine, and making more than seventy public appearances a year.

The title of this book seemed a good way to emphasize these aspects of Buckley's career. Even as a boy, William F. Buckley Jr. presumed to tell heads of state what to do. At the age of six (according to his father's account; his mother said he was seven), Billy Buckley wrote King George V of England demanding immediate repayment of the debt the United Kingdom owed the United States after the Great War. As an adolescent, he joined the America First Committee and criticized Franklin D. Roosevelt's plans to provide assistance to war-torn Britain. While Chairman of the *Yale Daily News*, he hectored Harry Truman on economics, labor unions, and corruption. His first book took as its mission nothing less than revising the curricula and restructuring the governance of the university from which he had recently graduated. Before he was thirty, Buckley vowed to "read" Dwight Eisenhower out of the conservative movement—which barely existed at the time.

As the vehicle through which to move ideas once thought to be on the fringe into the respectable range of public opinion, Buckley founded *National Review*, a journal "of fact" and opinion to which conservatives of many stripes could turn to find out what other conservatives were thinking and where readers might find validation for their opinions. He insisted that, as a periodical that appealed to opinion leaders, *National Review* display its own distinctive style and be laden with wit. To transform the GOP into a party that presented a genuine alternative to the liberalism that was then dominant within both major parties, he settled on Barry Goldwater as the public face through which conservative ideas could receive a hearing by the broad general public. With Goldwater as the Republicans' presidential standard-bearer in 1964, Buckley's *National Review* functioned as the candidate's unofficial headquarters and policy shop.

So great was Eisenhower's hold on the affections of the American people, and so absent were conservatives from positions of influence in *National Review*'s early days that Ike could afford to ignore Buckley, his magazine, and their criticisms of his administration in Washington. John and Robert Kennedy, master communicators in their own right—and the latter a talented political organizer—recognized the threat Buckley and his followers posed to the liberal consensus that then dominated American politics. They and their allies took steps to weaken what they perceived to be a growing political movement.

Lyndon Johnson, at first, found in the pages of *National Review* more support for the war in Vietnam than he received from liberal intellectuals or liberal Democratic politicians. That was not to last, as Johnson settled on a policy of "gradualism" and made negotiations rather than victory the primary objective of his Vietnam policies. On the domestic front, Buckley offered alternatives to Johnson's brand of liberalism, with its inherent heavy imprint from the federal government characterized by "one size fits all" remedies administered through bureaucracies. Most were incentive based and included elements of competition contained in the works of economist Milton Friedman and later popularized by "Bleeding Heart Conservative" Jack Kemp. Buckley decided to air those ideas in a quixotic campaign for Mayor in liberal New York City, where he also sought to deliver the death knell to liberal Republicanism where it flourished.

Aware of Buckley's growing influence and following, Richard Nixon, in 1968, found Buckley a useful vehicle through which to bolster the former Vice President's standing, first among party conservatives and later as the only true conservative in a three-party race in which Alabama Governor George Wallace also tried to lay claim to the "conservative" label. After the election, Buckley brought to Nixon's attention several persons of talent, beginning with Henry A. Kissinger, who became National Security Adviser and eventually Secretary of State. With Nixon's tacit assistance, Buckley's brother James won election as U.S. Senator from New York after Buckley negotiated a nonaggression pact with some of the very Republicans with whom he had been battling for more than a decade. Later, during Nixon's tenure, Buckley helped pry loose from the President's coalition much of the conservative movement he had once pushed in Nixon's direction.

Aware of his own drawing power as a public figure and of his skills as a political tactician, Buckley once considered a run for the presidency. He declined to pursue an intermediate office he could win because he thought the odds were too long against his going all the way. That being the case, already exercising greater influence over politics and policy than did most members of Congress and governors, he worked to advance the political prospects of others and stood guard over the movement he founded and—in what he called his greatest achievement—kept it free where he could of extremists, bigots, kooks, anti-Semites, and racists.

With the election of Ronald Reagan as President, Buckley's role changed from that of plitical commentator, go-between, and even political broker to that of unofficial participant in the administration's inner sanctum. Having helped guide Reagan on the path he traveled from liberal Democrat to conservative Republican (both men, at different times, would describe Reagan as Buckley's "pupil"), Buckley acted as an unofficial minister without portfolio for both Ronald and Nancy Reagan, a role he had already been playing for several years. "The word is out that Ronnie needs help," Buckley wrote Nancy Reagan early in her husband's tenure as Governor of California. Buckley helped the Reagans attract able staff in both Sacramento and Washington, DC. Some he recommended to Reagan when he was in the White House proved critical in helping the President advance his vision for the nation and the world. Tony Dolan and Peter Robinson, writers of Reagan's most memorable phrases, were both Buckley protégés. (Dolan drafted Reagan's "evil empire" speech; Robinson, his "Tear Down This Wall" address.) Time and time again, the Reagans sought Buckley's assistance in extricating the President from difficult or embarrassing situations or making the administration's case before opinion leaders and the public. He also proved a constant source of emotional support to Ronald and Nancy Reagan. On the few occasions when Buckley and Reagan disagreed over policy, sometimes strongly, their friendship never frayed.

For Buckley, Reagan's presidency represented the culmination of what he had hoped the conservative movement would attain and achieve. George F.

Will described the trajectory that movement had taken in the course of Buckley's career:

> Before there could be Ronald Reagan's presidency, there had to be Barry Goldwater's candidacy. It made conservatism confident and placed the Republican Party in the hands of its adherents.
>
> Before there could be Goldwater's insurgency, there had to be *National Review* magazine. From the creative clutter of its Manhattan offices flowed the ideological electricity that powered the transformation of American conservatism from a mere sensibility into a fighting faith and blueprint for governance.
>
> Before there was *National Review,* there was Buckley, spoiling for a philosophic fight.

Buckley began that fight with the publication of his first book, *God and Man at Yale,* in 1951. A year earlier, Lionel Trilling had declared in *The Liberal Imagination,* "In the United States at this time Liberalism is not only the dominant but even the sole intellectual tradition. For it is the plain fact that nowadays there are no conservative or reactionary ideas in general circulation." Conservative impulses, according to Trilling, expressed themselves not in ideas but in "irritable mental gestures" that sought to resemble ideas.

Buckley made it his life's work both to change this and to make conservatism a respectable alternative to the liberal orthodoxy. "Standing athwart history yelling stop," the mission he proclaimed for *National Review* in its first issue, became for Buckley as much a political agenda as an intellectual one. It included nothing less than reversing the steady centralization of power in the United States from the states to the federal government and from the legislative to the executive branch that began with the arrival of the New Deal in 1933. On the international scene, it rejected the dominant strategy of containment of the Soviet Union and made victory in what John F. Kennedy called "that long twilight struggle" its primary objective.

The goal Buckley set for his undertaking was as audacious as that which another young man, more than a century earlier, ascribed to another movement that leaders of public opinion in his day had also thought would have little chance of succeeding. In the first issue of his publication the *Liberator,* abolitionist William Lloyd Garrison proclaimed: "I am in earnest—I will not equivocate—I will not excuse—I will not retreat a single inch—and I will be heard." In the course of his eighty-one years, William F. Buckley Jr. was not known to retreat on many things. On the few on which he did, he also exerted his influence. And he certainly made himself heard.

In his quest to reverse the advance of socialist impulses at home and roll back Communism abroad, Buckley displayed an unwavering hostility toward "moral equivalence." He worked for decades to elect a President who shared his view that the struggle between East and West was more than one between different economic and political systems—it was a contest between good and evil. After Reagan left the political stage, Buckley reverted to the role he had earlier carved out for himself, as "tablet keeper" for his movement. He spent the last two decades of his life largely in opposition to the incumbent President, whether Republican or Democrat.

His personal friendship with George H. W. Bush notwithstanding, Buckley parted political company with him after Bush went back on his promise not to raise taxes without so much as offering a reasonable explanation for his action. He differed with Clinton less over policy than over character defects Buckley considered disqualifying in a President. In George W. Bush, Buckley also detected a lack of discipline but of a different kind than he saw in Clinton. He found the forty-third President wanting in fiscal restraint at home and blind to limitations upon the capacity of the United States to reorder much of the world.

When Buckley began his life journey in 1925, at the height of Calvin Coolidge's presidency, few could have imagined that by the time he entered college, the laissez-faire economics that had guided American domestic policy for most of its history and the isolationism that had undergirded its approach to foreign affairs in the years preceding and following the First World War would have given way as the United States endured the twin cataclysmic upheavals of the Great Depression and the Second World War. When he launched *National Review* at the age of twenty-nine, few, even among Buckley's backers, foresaw a time when the prevailing assumptions that were presumed to be so permanent in the days of FDR, Harry Truman, and Dwight Eisenhower would also give way. Buckley helped bring that about. What follows is the story of how he did it and, yes, of the fun he had along the way.

A Man and His Presidents

1

In the Shadow of Woodrow, Lindbergh, and Franklin D.

William F. Buckley Jr. came into the world on November 24, 1925, in New York City. The sixth of ten children and the third son born to William F. Buckley Sr. and Aloise Steiner Buckley, Billy—so called to distinguish him from his father, Will—grew up in a secure, serene, and privileged environment. His father was forty-four years old and a successful entrepreneur and wildcat oilman when Billy was born; his mother was thirty. Billy grew up in comfort, but his older siblings would remember more precarious times when their father accumulated and lost more than one fortune. Will's youngest son, Reid, described his father as a "risk taker" and even a "gambler" in his business ventures.[1]

Those who knew the family well said that William F. Buckley Jr. inherited his most notable attributes from his father: his political views, the certitude with which he defended them, the causes he took on, his love of books, his dexterity with words, his use of sarcasm in making his points, and his quick wit. William F. Buckley Sr. believed that societies should be governed in accordance with eternal, time-tested, universal truths, all enshrined within the tenets of the Roman Catholic Church, and he impressed this worldview on his children. Family friends and outside observers attributed Billy's genial disposition, ingratiating manner, easy charm, and ready demonstrations of affection and empathy to the influence of his mother, to whom he bore a striking physical resemblance.

Although others would play important roles in his intellectual development, none did more to shape the man Billy would become than his father. As a child and young man, Billy made winning his father's approval his highest priority. Having obtained it at an early age, he grew up fully cognizant that the ideas he advanced would not meet with universal acclaim. Nor did they need to. He went out into the world knowing he had the support of the only people whose opinions mattered to him, his parents and his siblings.

The Buckleys formed their own social system, with its own norms and expectations, and even its own newspaper (more on this below). They often found themselves at odds with the political opinions and social values of their neighbors in whatever community they happened to reside. Billy's brother Reid joked that the family's neighbors in Connecticut, where they lived for more than half the year, regarded them as "southerners," whereas those in South Carolina, where they had a winter home, considered them Yankees.[2] Wealthy, multilingual, and cosmopolitan, the Buckleys came to lead a movement that grew increasingly anti-elitist and populist in its appeal and orientation. Yet they helped form a new elite that defined that movement. Within the literary and intellectual universe to which they gravitated, they were conservatives in a world dominated by liberals.

Within their orbit, whatever any Buckley undertook became a family enterprise. Will's sister worked to help finance his and his younger siblings' college educations. Two of Will's brothers worked in the law firm he founded. All of Will's children joined in their father's various political crusades, as they would later in their brothers' political campaigns. Most of the children of Will and Aloise, whether as writers, editors, staffers, or contributors, played some role at *National Review*, the magazine Bill founded and edited. The Buckleys were exceptionally loyal to one another. As one made clear, "Buckleys tolerate disparagement of Buckleys only from Buckleys—and only from Buckleys within the same degree of consanguinity."[3]

On his father's side, Bill descended from Irish immigrants. His great-grandfather John Buckley, a Protestant, hailed from heavily Catholic County Cork. The family name is an anglicized version of O Buachalla, a common surname in Ireland. In the 1840s, John Buckley married Elinor Doran, a Catholic. Will told his children that his grandfather, out of respect for his Catholic bride, asked the organizers of the annual Orangeman's Day Parade to bypass his property.[4] When marchers disregarded his request, John, according to family lore, took a plowshare to the head of the first trespasser.[5] John was arrested and held, pending the ultimate fate of his victim. After the man he had assaulted recovered, John was fined and released.[6]

In 1845 John and Elinor departed for Canada. Given that he arrived in the New World with sufficient resources to purchase a farm, it is unlikely that he had suffered severely from the effects of the potato famine, which began in the year he and Elinor set sail. A more likely explanation for his decision to emigrate was a desire to start anew in a place where religious differences played less of a role in community life. John and Elinor lived in Quebec for a time before settling in Hamilton, Ontario.

Will's recollections of his grandfather attest to the man's independence, stubbornness, loyalty to loved ones, and adherence to principle—all traits future generations of Buckleys would exhibit. Will passed along another story about his grandfather that makes similar points. When Elinor informed Will's father that, on his deathbed, John received the last sacraments of the Catholic Church, Will's father whispered to him that the old man "must have been unconscious."[7]

Will's father, also named John, married into a family much like his own. His wife, Mary Ann Langford, was the daughter of Charles and Hanna Lane Langford, who had arrived in Canada from County Limerick fifteen years before the Buckleys. Mary Ann's father was also a Protestant who brought up his children as Catholics. The Langfords operated a pub in Oakville, Ontario. Seeking relief from John's asthma, John, Mary Ann, and their then two children migrated to Texas in 1874. They first made their home in Washington-on-the-Brazos, the state's first capital, where Will was born in 1881. Although his birthday was July 12, Will's mother celebrated it on July 11, because July 12 was Orangeman's Day.

When Will was a year old, the family relocated to San Diego, Texas, northeast of Corpus Christi, where they remained until Will's father died in 1904. Will was the third of six children born to John and Mary Ann. His older brother John was murdered at the age of nineteen. The five surviving siblings (Priscilla, Will, Claude, Eleanor, and Edmund) would remain close all their lives. All would play an active part in Will's professional and private life, and to some extent in his children's.

The John Buckley who set down roots in Texas was, in the words of one of his sons, "honest, fearless, unassuming, and uncommunicative."[8] His grandson Reid thought it indicative of John's independent nature that he chose to farm sheep in the heart of cattle country.[9] The San Diego where he and his family settled consisted of two hundred white Americans ("Anglos") and two thousand Mexicans or Mexican Americans. Most of the Anglos, transplants from other parts of the country, were well read and well versed in music, literature, and the visual arts. They made a stark contrast to the rest of the Texas population in the 1880s, which had more than its share of gunslingers, outlaws, and professional smugglers (primarily of tequila from Mexico).[10]

In 1890 John Buckley was elected Sheriff of Duval County on a "reform ticket." Like the machine-backed candidate he had opposed, John was a Democrat in what was still a one-party Democratic state.[11] His grandson (Will's son James) attributed Sheriff John's victory to his status as a practicing Catholic.[12] In a county where Mexican Americans outnumbered their mostly Protestant Anglo-Saxon neighbors by ten to one, Buckley had come to know many of his future constituents in church. Once in office, Sheriff John developed a reputation for standing up for the town's Mexican Americans when ranchers and other powerful interests sought to take advantage of them.

Sheriff John often found himself at odds with the county's corrupt political machine, which eventually came under the control of the powerful local boss Archie Parr. The machine made certain that its principal supporters (ranchers and businessmen) usually prevailed at the polls. To enforce their will, they frequently manipulated the votes of Mexican Americans through intimidation and fraud and, more than occasionally, relied on "politically tainted" elements within the Texas Rangers to do their bidding.[13] Sheriff Buckley found himself the target of several assassination attempts. The machine arranged for his indictment on trumped-up charges that he had abetted revolutionary activities on both sides of the border against Mexican President Porfirio Díaz. As evidence, his accusers pointed to John's close ties to the revolutionary leader Catarino Garza, who had campaigned for him.[14]

The charges were eventually dropped, and Buckley remained Sheriff until he was voted out in 1896. Family lore holds that on the day he lost, the machine turned out fifty people at gunpoint to vote against him. His son Claude recorded Sheriff's John's virulent rants against the "white trash of the town."[15] These were the uneducated, often poor, always racist whites Buckley and his descendants considered "morally leagues beneath black people."[16]

Sheriff John's death in 1904 threatened to put a financial strain on his family, but Will's facility in Spanish enabled him to complete his education. Mary Ann had taken charge of his early schooling, placing Will in the care of Basque-born Padre John Peter Bard, who exposed him to the intellectual underpinnings of the "true faith." By the time he reached high school, Will could speak and write Spanish well enough to teach the language at a local school, and he did so before he enrolled at the University of Texas. There, he placed out of several Spanish courses, enabling him to complete his undergraduate studies early. He helped make ends meet by tutoring other students as an assistant instructor in the Romance language department and acting as a guide to American businessmen touring Mexico.[17]

When his father died, Will moved his mother and siblings to Austin, where he took on an additional job as translator for the Texas General Land Office. The position came his way through the intervention of state Senator Marshall Hicks of San Antonio. When Hicks was serving as District Attorney of Duval

County, Sheriff John Buckley had foiled an assassination plot against him. After Will left the land office, his older sister Priscilla replaced him. She remained in the post for many years, helping finance the educations of her younger siblings. Will graduated from the University of Texas with a BS degree in 1904 and received his law degree a year later.[18]

He spent the next two years working in Austin for a local attorney. In 1908 Will opened a practice in Mexico City representing American clients. With the discovery of oil in the Tampico region, he transferred his operations there and, eventually, brought his brothers Claude and Edmund into the firm. He turned over most of his legal work to them as he ventured into real estate development and oil exploration. With the first of his fortunes, he developed his own island on a sandbar, which he named Buckley Island.[19]

Will and his clients grew prosperous in the latter years of Mexican dictator Porfirio Díaz's long reign. To entice foreign investment into his country, Díaz had granted foreign nationals generous land concessions. The policy aroused resentment within the country's middle class and among the peasantry, helping to usher in a decade of revolutionary and counterrevolutionary activity. The Mexican revolution began in 1910 after Díaz was declared the winner of a hard-fought campaign, characterized by widespread fraud, against middle-class reformer Francisco Madero. The ongoing struggle between supporters of the two began a cascade of alternating left- and right-leaning governments.

Madero overthrew Díaz in 1911. One of Díaz's generals, Victoriano Huerta, in turn, ousted Madero in a coup in 1913. Huerta was subsequently implicated in his predecessor's murder. Will, known and respected by the American government for his familiarity with Mexican politics and skills as a businessman, acted as informal adviser on Mexican affairs to Woodrow Wilson's Secretary of State, William Jennings Bryan. He was also on good terms with three Texans who served in Wilson's cabinet: Agriculture Secretary David Franklin Houston, former President of the University of Texas; Attorney General Thomas Watt Gregory; and Postmaster Albert Burleson, a former Congressman from Austin.[20] He also kept the Huerta regime up to date on political developments within the United States.

With leftist revolutionary leader Venustiano Carranza gaining control of much of Mexico and demanding fees from oil excavators, Will drew closer to Huerta. As Will sought to shore up Huerta's regime, Wilson was planning Huerta's demise. Persuaded that 85 percent of the Mexican people "remained submerged" under this dictator's grasp, Wilson withheld official U.S. recognition of Huerta's regime until Huerta agreed to hold free and open elections.

The arrest of eight American sailors in Tampico in April 1914 provided Wilson with a pretext to intervene. The sailors' swift release notwithstanding, he sent five U.S. battleships to the port of Veracruz and three thousand troops to reinforce them. Wilson told a reporter that his action was meant to usher in a "new order, which will have its foundations on human liberty and human rights."[21] Some time earlier, he had informed a British diplomat that his overriding objective in the Western Hemisphere was "to teach the South American republics to elect good men to office."[22]

To Wilson's surprise, both warring factions within Mexico opposed the American invasion. Two days of intense fighting left 17 Americans dead and 61 wounded, and 152 to 175 Mexicans dead and between 195 and 250 wounded.[23] Will had opposed Wilson's actions from the start. One of his friends, a minister in the Huerta government, decades later contemptuously quoted from Wilson's eulogy to the fallen Americans in which the American President said that Americans had gone to Mexico to "serve mankind." Wilson referred to the invasion as "a war of service" and proclaimed such a venture a "proud thing in which to die."[24] Whatever Wilson's intentions, to many Mexicans, this latest American meddling in their internal affairs differed little from previous episodes, whether undertaken in pursuit of William Howard Taft's "dollar diplomacy" or Theodore Roosevelt's "gunboat diplomacy." Wilson's intervention in Mexico, which produced strained relations between the two countries for decades, persuaded Will that it was folly to engage U.S. troops abroad to advance abstract objectives. He would deploy them only to protect discernable American interests, a view he passed along to his children. His son and namesake later voiced similar opposition to what Wilson's latter-day successors would refer to as "nation building."

During the invasion and its aftermath, Will acted as interpreter for the top command of U.S. naval and land forces stationed in Veracruz. He declined the administration's entreaties that he accept a top civilian post during the U.S. occupation that followed and further registered his opposition to Wilson's policy by acting as counsel to Huerta's delegation at a "peacekeeping" conference the governments of Argentina, Brazil, and Colombia convened. As Wilson had hoped and Will had feared, the American invasion hastened the fall of Huerta's regime.

After Carranza came to power, Will participated in coup attempts against the new left-leaning government. He also sheltered Catholic prelates and smuggled to safety artworks in the church's possession. During the Díaz and Huerta regimes, the Roman Catholic Church had allied itself with the plantation owners even to the point of sanctioning peonage among the peasantry. Huerta's leftist successor extracted vengeance upon the church for having supported such practices and for the fealty it had shown previous regimes.

In testimony before a subcommittee of the U.S. Senate Foreign Affairs Committee on December 9, 1919, Will likened Carranza and his partisans to the Bolsheviks who had seized control of Russia two years earlier. Will considered Wilson's policies not only misguided and impractical but also provincial, hypocritical, and self-righteous. In his congressional testimony, Will challenged Wilson's practice of placing the expansion of democratic practices abroad at the top of American foreign policy objectives. He also expressed the view that the majority opinion of the Mexican people did not matter because they did not have the ability to think clearly and lacked both the knowledge on which to base convictions and the public spirit to act on them.[25] Decades later, William F. Buckley Jr. would voice similar reservations about the wisdom of expanding voting rights to African Americans in the American South. He also voiced doubts about the capacity of newly independent former colonies in the third world for self-government and opposed the use of U.S. armed forces to further democracy in Bosnia, Kosovo, Afghanistan, and Iraq.

Angered at the willingness of major American oil companies to do business with the new revolutionary government, Will withdrew from an umbrella organization committed to protecting American rights in Mexico and formed his own lobbying group to oppose U.S. recognition of the Mexican government. He and his progeny would vigorously oppose U.S. corporations' engaging in commerce with leftist governments and using their political clout to obtain favors ("crony capitalism") from their own government at home. His efforts to bring down Carranza's successor, Alvaro Obregon, resulted in Will's expulsion from Mexico in 1921. The following year, Obregon's government seized Will's remaining assets in the country.

Back in the United States, Will relocated to Bronxville, New York, with his growing family. In December 1917, Will, thirty-six, had married a twenty-two-year-old "southern belle" from New Orleans, Aloise Steiner, daughter of Aloysius Steiner and the former Mary Louise Wassem. A decade and a half before the Civil War, Aloise's forebears had emigrated from the city of Bergt in the German-speaking canton of St. Gallen, Switzerland. Her mother traced her family's origins to Hesse, Germany. Aloise's maternal grandfather, Henry Wassem, served in the Confederate army and was wounded at the battle of Shiloh. A Lutheran, Henry Wassem was one of William F. Buckley Jr.'s three Protestant great-grandfathers.

All who came into contact with Aloise recalled her vivacious spirit, gentle nature, and ability to make people feel at home. She was said to be able to "smooth over" Will's "roughness" and to "soften" his "authoritarian" mien.[26] Though he could be warm, kind, and funny with his children, to most others

Will cut a proper Edwardian figure, attired in dark suits with a starched white shirt and stiff collar, his white hair parted near the center and pince-nez resting on his nose. Aloise imparted to her children a love of music of all kinds, especially Bach, whom her famous son would call the "greatest mathematical genius who ever existed."[27] As religious as her husband, Aloise expressed her faith openly and publicly, whereas Will came to his more through intellectual channels and conveyed his beliefs more privately.

Aloise Steiner carried with her into her marriage an affinity for the Old South and an adherence to its norms and social hierarchy, which neither she nor her husband ever questioned. Unlike Will, who was born poor but acquired status and wealth through his energy, his business acumen, his wits, and his marriage, Aloise was born into the station she occupied all her life. Through her, Will came to identify with the wealthy Bourbon class that ran most southern institutions in the decades following the Civil War. When segregation was the order of the day, the Bourbons practiced noblesse oblige toward African Americans.

Aloise and Will, as their son Reid noted, assumed that black people were intellectually inferior to whites. Nevertheless, they were appalled by the violence those Sheriff John Buckley would have considered "white trash" inflicted upon African Americans in an effort to express their own racial superiority and assert political control. Billy and his siblings grew up accepting the social mores and racial assumptions of their parents' native region. They resisted all outside interference, especially by the federal government, in the southern way of life, in which Jim Crow played an important part.

The Buckleys and others presumed that the old Bourbons would remain in charge of southern affairs in perpetuity. They took it for granted that this local elite knew best how to govern the South. Change would come only when the region's "betters" wished it. Within their own household, the Buckleys, like others of their station, considered African Americans in their employ almost part of their family. Billy would one day record that one of his great childhood disappointments was his discovery that, because he had not yet been confirmed, he could not serve as godfather to the child of an African American servant to whom he had grown especially close.[28]

Prior to the coming of the New Deal and the centralization of power it ushered in, Will and Aloise were, like their southern forebears, committed Democrats. While he could not say for certain whether or for whom his parents voted for President in 1928, James L. Buckley remembered sporting an "Al Smith" cap when he was five years old.[29] That year, Smith became the first Catholic to receive the presidential nomination of a major political party.

William F. Buckley Jr. remembered that his father disliked Jews, in part because he considered them "culturally un-integrated."[30] (His son Reid recalled Will occasionally voicing similar sentiments about his fellow Irish, especially recent immigrants, who he thought drank too much and could be manipulated by machine politicians.)[31] Will's namesake suggested that his father thought of Jews as "interlopers within a Christian nation."[32] Will's older children, perhaps in an attempt to support his opinions, once burned a cross on the lawn of a Jewish resort in Salisbury, Connecticut. Many years later, in an assertion of family solidarity, Billy remembered his disappointment in not being able to participate in the episode because, at the age of nine, he was too young.[33]

In 1924, a year before Billy was born, Will (having secured financing for his company, Pantepec) purchased a forty-seven-acre estate in Sharon, northwestern Connecticut, near the New York state border, ninety-five miles from New York City. Sharon, a rustic town in Litchfield County, incorporated in 1739, consisted of sixteen hundred inhabitants, a good many of them descended from early English settlers in the region. The overwhelming majority belonged to mainline Protestant denominations. The Buckleys named the property's main house, built in 1763, Great Elm for the giant elm tree that was planted in the early 1700s and stood on the property until it died in the late 1950s.

With his family situated in Sharon, Will cultivated his business interests, this time in Venezuela, where he founded the first of several oil-related enterprises. Will and Aloise had ten children: Aloise (born in 1918), John (1920), Priscilla (1921), James (1923), Jane (1924), William (1925), Patricia (1927), Reid (1930), Maureen (1933), and Carol (1938). Another child, Mary Ann, born in 1928, died two days after her birth. Until they reached their teenage years, the Buckley children were separated into two groups at mealtimes and during recreational activities. Billy was the oldest in the younger group.

With his father often away, Billy spent much of his time in female company, primarily that of his mother, his sisters, and his Mexican nanny Pupita, of whom he grew exceptionally fond.[34] At the age of five, Billy announced to his family that would henceforth be known as William Frank Buckley, like his father, and would drop his given middle name, Francis. He would use the suffix Jr. for the rest of his life.

Billy would recall that Spanish was his first language and French his second, and that he did not learn English until his family took up residence in Paris from 1929 to 1931.[35] Will had relocated his family to Europe in a search for investors for his companies abroad. In Paris, the Buckleys' four-story house functioned as a small elementary school, with teachers of Latin, French, and English installed on different floors, as were music instructors. Pupils rotated upstairs and down every hour. Other courses entered the curriculum, as did a number of recreational activities. At early ages, all the Buckleys learned tennis, swimming, and horseback riding. The family moved to London in the summer of 1931, remaining there for a short time. Will recalled on the eve of Billy's wedding that, as a six-year-old attending the St. Thomas More School in London, Billy wrote King George V to demand repayment to the United States of loans it had made to the United Kingdom during the Great War.[36]

On their return to Sharon, Billy and his siblings settled into what he would later describe as an "Arcadian" existence of private tutors, music, play, and companionship.[37] With Will's oil investments bearing fruit by the late 1930s, he enlarged his Sharon house, a new three-story Mexican patio being the most prominent addition. Will also acquired a winter home in Camden, South Carolina. Its builder had named it Kamschatka in the early 1800s. When in residence, Will actively participated in South Carolina's social and civic affairs. Strom Thurmond, the future Governor of the state, Dixiecrat candidate for President, and U.S. Senator, was a frequent guest at the Buckley home. The senior Buckley once wrote Thurmond that he knew of no other politician whose views he entirely approved of.[38]

In the summer of 1938, Will announced that the idyllic life to which Billy and his sisters Jane and Patricia had become accustomed would be interrupted. They would spend the next school year in England. Billy was to study at St. John's, Beaumont, an exclusive Catholic school for boys run by Jesuits, not far from Eton in Old Windsor. Will told the children that the reason for their change in venue was to improve their diction, which he said had steadily deteriorated since they had returned to Sharon from England six years earlier. In truth, Aloise was in what would be her last pregnancy, and her doctors anticipated a difficult and dangerous delivery. Will hoped to spare his middle children some of the anxieties that were sure to befall the household. The children voiced unhappiness at having to leave home to Will's sister Priscilla, who spent part of the year in Connecticut and the rest in Texas. Priscilla, who often acted as go-between for her brother and his children, refused to intercede on this rare occasion, being aware of the reason behind Will's decision.[39]

Billy was then thirteen years of age. He recalled that upon disembarking from the SS *Europa* in Southampton, he could sense in the air the international tensions that were besetting Europe. Before boarding the train to London, the Buckley party was fitted for gas masks. Conversations they overheard centered on whether Britain should yield to Hitler's demands for greater territory or resist. On September 30, 1938, as Billy and Will motored from London to St. John's, Beaumont, they spotted the plane carrying Prime Minister Neville

Chamberlain back from the Munich Conference as it descended nearby. Will ordered his driver to detour to the landing field so they could witness Chamberlain depart from the aircraft. From a distance, they saw him wave the agreement he had just signed transferring control of the Sudetenland from Czechoslovakia to Nazi Germany. Chamberlain assured his listeners that the agreement would assure "peace in our time."[40]

Once in his new school, Billy placed a five-foot American flag beside his bed. Presumably, he made no more effort to conceal his (and his father's) opinions about world affairs than he had the last time he had lived in England. (Both father and son were against American intervention in the war in Europe.) In his first novel, *Saving the Queen* (1976), Buckley cast as his protagonist an American boy in an English boarding school as Britain entered its darkest days. Buckley's lead character goads his classmates by sporting a button bearing the likeness of aviator Charles Lindbergh, perhaps the most well-known of American isolationists.

Billy came to enjoy St. John's, Beaumont. He liked his Jesuit instructors and grew especially close to Father James Sharkey, the school's headmaster, whom he found "affectionate, strict, but understanding, with a highly developed sense of humor."[41] He and Sharkey would remain in touch for the remainder of the headmaster's days. Buckley delighted in passing along a story Sharkey told him about one of the school's early headmasters, who challenged Eton to a soccer match and received back a note inquiring, "What *is* St. John's, Beaumont?" To this the Jesuit replied, "What Eton used to be, a school for Catholic gentlemen."[42] (That, of course, was before Henry VIII declared himself the head of the Church of England, persecuted those who retained their allegiance to the papacy, and dissolved the monasteries.)

Buckley's fondness for this story conveys his lifelong affinity for English Catholics and his admiration of the courage they displayed in adhering to their ancient faith, willingly becoming an unpopular and sometimes persecuted minority in the land of their ancestors. His identification with English Catholics may also have reinforced, or even kindled, a sense of pride and even of superiority in Billy as he became increasingly aware of their rich past. Here was, indeed, a parallel for American Catholics, who made their home in Yankee Protestant New England and the even more homogenous white Protestant (evangelical and otherwise) American South, where most people belonged to religious denominations that were considerably younger than the one to which his parents adhered.

As had his father, Buckley developed a taste for English Catholic writers such as Hilaire Belloc and G. K. Chesterton. He became a great admirer of

Evelyn Waugh. Years later, although Waugh declined Buckley's entreaties to write regularly for *National Review*, Waugh contributed a review of a biography of Chesterton and a critique of the Second Vatican Council to the magazine.[43] In 1982 Buckley introduced on camera each segment of the serialized adaptation of Waugh's *Brideshead Revisited* when it aired on PBS. He once told an interviewer that he declined an opportunity to meet Waugh because of the novelist's reputation for being "really sort of an ugly man."[44] By "ugly," he meant "nasty." He also had cause to believe the novelist was "two-faced," praising Buckley in letters he wrote him while belittling his writing style and politics to others.[45] Buckley also revered Malcolm Muggeridge, the British writer who converted to Catholicism at the age of seventy-nine.

While at St. John's, Beaumont, Buckley attended Mass every day with the other boys and spent considerable time at prayer alone, especially when he heard that his mother had gone into labor. His time spent in solitude had a profound impact on him. "When you're thirteen, certain things begin to become curious," he remembered. "One begins to sense there are depths in a position that one tended to accept rather two dimensionally. That happened to me at St. John's." He traced his love for the ritual and liturgy of the Latin Mass to the time he spent there.[46]

As his grades during this period attest, Billy paid less attention to the intellectual side of school than he did to his spiritual awakening. In March 1939 he was judged "fair" in English, "failed" in spelling, "bad" in writing, "weak" in Latin, "good" in French, "fair" in mathematics, "good" in history, "fair" in geography, and "good" in drawing.[47] Comments accompanying his grades from an earlier marking period suggest that he applied himself in the subjects he liked, but did not take well to pursuits that entailed "drudgery and discipline."[48] As would his future teachers and his parents, Billy's evaluators made note of his illegible penmanship, a failing for which he later compensated by acquiring superior typing skills. Having presented no disciplinary problems to the Jesuits, Billy avoided the indignity of being caned, a fate his older brother James twice endured two years earlier at a different English school. (Buckley would include a caning scene in *Saving the Queen*.)

In the spring of 1939, with war imminent, Will brought Billy, Jane, and Patricia back to Sharon. Billy spent the following year being tutored at home before enrolling at the Millbrook School, fifteen miles away across the New York state line, and the alma mater of his two older brothers. One reason Will selected Millbrook for his sons over more prestigious alternatives was because its headmaster, Edward Pulling, allowed students to spend most weekends at home. (He also disliked the headmaster at nearby Hotchkiss.) Pulling's weekend policy meant the Buckleys could attend Mass together and enjoy each other's company at meals and other activities. Born in England, Pulling had graduated from Princeton and taught at Groton and Avon Old Farms before founding Millbrook in 1931.

Pulling was an enthusiastic admirer of Endicott Peabody, founding headmaster of the Groton School, and he patterned Millbrook along the same lines. Like the elite English boarding schools, both Groton and Millbrook took as their mission the education of the country's future leaders. Peabody sat on the Millbrook board, and one of his former charges, New York Governor Franklin D. Roosevelt, offered a gift of land on his Hyde Park estate for Pulling's school. This Pulling declined in favor of a site on the Stephenson farm, five miles outside Millbrook.[49]

When Billy was at Millbrook, its student population numbered about sixty. At the time he enrolled, he was already displaying characteristics of the man he would soon become. He not only shared Will's views on politics and religion but had also learned to voice them in ways that drew his father's attention and admiration. "Exhibitionism, rather than intimacy," a family member recalled, "was the way you came to the attention of the father."[50] Billy's brother Reid thought his father had a special love for Billy and respected both his mental abilities and the moral control and self-discipline he exhibited.[51] Will's firstborn child, Aloise, dubbed Billy "the young mahster."[52] A friend of his older brother's described Billy as the "Little Lord Fauntleroy type."[53] Billy seemed not to mind. He had the unconditional support of the one person in the world whose opinion mattered most to him, William F. Buckley Sr.

Knowing that he had his father's support helped fortify Billy at Millbrook. Finding it difficult to relate to boys his own age, Billy had shied away from team sports in favor of activities in which he could measure his progress against his own previous performance: sailing, horse riding, skiing and, later in life, flying. As he began his stay at Millbrook, coming from a rather sheltered existence, Billy was judgmental about others and was anything but shy about voicing disapproval of people and views he disliked.

As Billy prepared to enter Millbrook, which he would do in the fall of 1940, the national debate between isolationists and interventionists over whether the United States should assist Britain as it struggled to withstand Nazi bombardments reached a peak. The controversy came to Sharon when the Committee to Defend America by Aiding the Allies, generally known as the White Committee after its founder, Kansas-based newspaper editor William Allen White, organized a rally in support of President Franklin D. Roosevelt's proposal to transfer to Britain fifty "retired" U.S. destroyers in exchange for

American occupancy of British military bases. FDR's critics opposed the measure on the grounds that it would lead to greater American participation in the war in Europe.

Will believed that the Western democracies had brought their problems on themselves—by their own corruption and laxity, the vindictive terms of the treaty they imposed on Germany at the 1919 Paris Peace Conference, and their failure to resist Nazi aggression early on. He considered the Soviet Union, because it was both collectivist and atheistic, a greater threat to the United States than Nazi Germany, and he would not have objected to a scenario of the Nazi and Soviet empires waging a long, mutually destructive war against one another with the United States on the sidelines. His children shared these views and, like Will, did not hesitate to make their feelings known.

Three of the older children, Aloise, James, and Priscilla, promulgated his opinions through a newspaper they assembled, the *Spectator*, which they circulated to neighbors. In an unsigned letter to the local newspaper, Will accused White's local representatives of trying to "pressure" the United States into war. The *Lakeview Journal* reprinted it over Will's signature along with comments from prominent neighbors, who took opposing views. Will's oldest son John submitted a letter praising his father for not responding to world events with panic or fear. Wife Aloise weighed in with a defense of Anne Morrow Lindbergh, the wife of the famous aviator and a leading isolationist. In her controversial best seller *The Wave of the Future*, Mrs. Lindbergh described totalitarianism as more suitable to the tenor of the times than democracy and urged that the West not resist its inevitable rise and spread.[54] (She argued that the world was dividing into two competing camps, fascism and bolshevism, and proclaimed the former the more attractive alternative.) *Foreign Affairs* called the book a "*vade mecum* for the defeatists."[55] Many critics considered it an apologia for fascism. Mrs. Buckley termed it an expression of the author's patriotism.[56]

With his parents and siblings fully engaged in the anti-interventionist debate, Billy found a symbolic, and not too subtle, way to advance their arguments. He named his first sailboat, a gift from his parents the summer before he set off for boarding school, *Sweet Isolation*. When he won the local yacht club's Community Service trophy, scoring thirteen racing wins, the boat's name shared the spotlight with its owner.[57] His sister Patricia thought she had found another way to convey her father's message. Upon winning a blue ribbon at the Dutchess County Horse Show in Rhinebeck, she rode past FDR's box and, as he applauded her feat, turned her head to one side rather than acknowledge his congratulations. When Will inquired her reason, she responded, "I thought you did not like him."[58]

Billy entered Millbrook with the air of a leader of the opposition to the prevailing interventionist opinion. He declared himself an "America Firster." (The title conveyed allegiance to the views of the anti-intervention organization founded by Charles Lindbergh, *Chicago Tribune* publisher Robert McCormick, and General Robert Wood, President of Sears and Roebuck.) He later recalled setting himself apart from the majority at the school in other respects. He confessed having deliberately been "obnoxiously Catholic" in a student body that was overwhelmingly Protestant. Within days of his arrival, Billy was the most conspicuous nonconformist at Millbrook. Will, with some embellishment, almost boastfully related how Billy stormed uninvited into a faculty meeting to complain that a teacher had deprived him of the right to express his political views in class. Will related that this son then proceeded to lecture his elders on "the virtues of isolationism, the dignity of the Catholic Church, and the political ignorance of the school staff."[59]

Not surprisingly given his tendency to form judgments of others based on their politics or religion, and his willingness to make his views widely known, Billy was, at first, not well liked or well received at Millbrook. Pulling thought him "haughty," a mild evaluation compared to those of his other teachers. Will advised Billy to rein himself in. "Your mother and I," he wrote, "like very much your attitude of having strong convictions and of not being too bashful to express them." But he counseled his son "to learn to be more moderate in the expression" of his views and to do so in a way that "would give as little offense as possible."[60] With pleasing his father still his highest priority, Billy adjusted his demeanor. Some weeks later, Will wrote again: "Mr. Gifford says that you have made a great improvement in English and that you're becoming less cocky in your opinions, which is all to the good."[61]

Nevertheless, Billy took advantage of whatever opportunities Millbrook afforded him to express his opinions. Pulling required that each student deliver a five-minute talk before the entire school body on a topic of his choosing. Billy titled his presentation "In Defense of Lindbergh." At the time he delivered it, Lindbergh had become the public face for the forces of opposition to American assistance to war-torn Britain. On January 23, 1941, the celebrated aviator testified for two hours before the House Foreign Affairs Committee against President Roosevelt's "lend-lease" proposals. The proposed legislation empowered the President to decide on his own which nations undergoing attack or invasion would receive American aid and what form that assistance would take.

Faculty who heard Billy defend his hero, much as they might have disagreed with his position, praised Billy's command of his material, the thoroughness of his research, and his strong and polished delivery. Three days after the President signed lend-lease into law, Will wrote Billy from South Carolina, "Don't forget to send me . . . your speech on Lindbergh." Mindful of Billy's penmanship, he asked for a typed copy.[62] On May 23, Billy was in attendance at an America First rally at Madison Square Garden to hear Lindbergh denounce FDR's efforts to assist war-torn Britain.

For the rest of his life, William F. Buckley Jr. retained vivid memories of the impassioned debate between interventionists and isolationists. Traces of both sides' arguments made their way into his future speeches and writings, carefully reworked during the Cold War, as he castigated those who opposed a strong U.S. response to Soviet aggression as the "new isolationists." Music teacher Nathan Abbott, who had once proclaimed Billy "impetuous, cocky, and obstinate," found him in this debate "more restrained in his obstinacy and more tolerant."[63]

In his second year at Millbrook, Buckley forged one of his longest-lasting friendships with someone outside his family. This was with Alistair Horne, an English student sent by his father to the United States to wait out the war (and a feared German invasion of Britain). At first, Buckley and Horne were more different than alike, especially in their politics. Horne considered the isolationists "the deadliest enemy of Britain, in league with the Devil and, compared with whom Hitler was only marginally worse."[64] Equally matched in their capacity to organize and present arguments, Buckley and Horne found themselves often pitted against each other in debate. Horne picked up early on Buckley's zest for combat and for public performance: "He inevitably won, on forensic skill, but lost the ensuing vote from the audience that had already made up its mind. Then as later, however, defeat and unpopularity only sharpened his appetite."[65]

Debate drew Horne and Buckley steadily into each other's company. "For several weeks we glared at each other, more intensely than usual," Horne said, as the lend-lease question continued to dominate headlines.[66] Tensions between them eased once the United States had entered the war, which Horne recalled put them finally on the "same side." Billy had heard the news of the Japanese attack upon Pearl Harbor over the car radio as he and Abbott motored back to Millbrook from Carnegie Hall, where they had seen Sergei Rachmaninoff perform.

With the United States now at war against Germany and allied with Britain, Buckley readily and fervently embraced positions he had not long ago opposed. Horne detected a rise in the respect the other students showed for Billy as he accommodated himself to new realities.[67] In January 1942, with his country now at war, Billy attended to some unfinished business. He sent Lindbergh a letter expressing his and his family's gratitude to the ex-aviator for the efforts he had made to keep America out of the war. After commending Lindbergh on the "brave fight" he had waged, Billy predicted that Lindbergh's words would continue to resonate the next time someone set out to "save the world for democracy" or "further the limits of the British Empire."[68] (These were arguments isolationists had made in opposition to intervention. The "make the world safe for democracy" line, of course, came directly from Woodrow Wilson's war message to Congress on April 2, 1917.)

Billy was voted the winner of a debate in which he had opposed censorship on the grounds that free dissemination of news was the best way to counter false rumors and disinformation instigated by enemy nations.[69] He took the negative, and losing, side in a debate entitled "Social Reforms for the Negro Now." Buckley asserted that the South's northern "aggressors" and their allies were using the war as a pretext to push the "Negro question" at a time when the nation had "so much else to do."[70] (Thus the Old Bourbon southern view found at northern Millbrook a voice in defense of Jim Crow.)

Their friendship deepening, Horne and Buckley found that they had much in common besides their fondness for debate. They both complained about what they considered the excessive emphasis American preparatory schools placed on athletics. In their personal associations, neither could "suffer fools gladly."[71] Horne pierced Buckley's veneer in ways few others had tried. Bill's most outstanding trait, Horne said, was his "unashamed ability to show affection and to *care* about his friends."[72] He described his friendship with Buckley as the longest and deepest of his lifetime and confessed, decades later, that while Buckley had been "wrong" on intervention in the 1930s, he proved a better prophet than Horne in gauging the Soviet Union's postwar intentions.[73]

The two roomed together in their final year at Millbrook. (Buckley crammed the four-year curriculum at the boarding school into three, taking an accelerated program, which included summer courses.) "Our attic suite swiftly became a haunt of undisturbed disorder," Horne said of the space they shared. He recalled installing for Billy a radio and a phonograph, both banned items at Millbrook. In return, Billy typed Alistair's handwritten essays. Horne recounted Billy's brief venture as a young entrepreneur, typing other students' papers for a fee.[74] Billy's own recollection was that he charged customers $1.25 per page, with additional charges for grammatical corrections. Pulling declared the capitalism in which Buckley was engaged "pernicious" and shut the enterprise down. The headmaster's choice of word sent the sixteen-year-old Billy to the dictionary, and *pernicious* soon found its way into his vocabulary. Thus began his lifetime quest to always use the perfect word to express his thoughts. In time, his voluminous vocabulary became one of his trademarks.[75]

For almost seventy years, Buckley and Horne remained close, as would their families. They reviewed and criticized drafts of each other's writings, vacationed together, helped each other expand their range of contacts within literary and political circles on two continents, and shared their most intimate thoughts. After Horne completed his two-volume biography of British Prime Minister Harold Macmillan, Buckley devoted two *Firing Line* programs to the former PM. In the first, he interviewed Macmillan. In the second, he moderated a discussion about Macmillan's relationship with John F. Kennedy in which panelists Horne, economist John Kenneth Galbraith, and historian Arthur M. Schlesinger Jr. shared their impressions and recollections. (Horne's friendship with Schlesinger helped melt the frost that had characterized Buckley's relationship with the liberal scholar and Democratic polemicist in their early years as public intellectuals.)

At Millbrook, Billy embraced, reluctantly at first, Pulling's major passion, community service. In keeping with the school's motto *Non sibi sed cunctis* (Not for oneself, but for all), Pulling insisted that the sons of privilege learn the needs of the greater community.[76] Billy and his peers made beds, served tables, cleaned halls, and provided other services to fellow students. Billy also oversaw the student bank. In the same report in which he commented on Billy's talk on Lindbergh, Abbott also mentioned Billy's increasing tolerance for drudgery.[77] In addition, Billy picked apples at a nearby orchard. (He reported years later that he selected this chore in lieu of alternatives because it afforded him the occasion to surreptitiously smoke cigarettes.)[78] In his book *Gratitude* (1990), which he dedicated to Pulling, Buckley endorsed the idea of community service for all high school graduates. He thought such a step would advance two worthy societal benefits: (1) provide assistance to the needy, and (2) inculcate in the young and privileged an appreciation of the gifts the United States had bestowed upon them. (On the flyleaf, he referred to having performed his own "national service" in the U.S. Army during World War II.)[79]

Billy excelled academically at Millbrook. He graduated first in his class and received citations for his community service and management of the student bank. In his three years at the school, he had served as assistant editor of the student newspaper (the *Silo*), editor in chief of the yearbook, and secretary of the debating team and music club. Pulling awarded him the first A the headmaster had ever given for an essay.[80] Billy distinguished himself in French, did well in history, and at one point received an A+ in math, previously his worst subject. Pulling also arranged for Billy, whose Spanish skills were more developed than those of most other students, to receive individual instruction, and he made certain that Billy had time to indulge his love for music and piano practice.[81]

Billy's father remained the dominant force in his intellectual development. In 1943, the year Billy graduated, Will Buckley introduced his children to an author and a book that would have a profound influence on his namesake. This man was Alfred Jay Nock and the book was *Memoirs of a Superfluous Man.*[82] Once a writer for the *Nation* and later, in the 1920s, an editor of the *Freeman*, both leading publications of the Progressive movement, Nock had become increasingly suspicious of state power and centralization, legacies of the Progressive Era. He had grown skeptical of democracy's capacity to further the general interest, maximize freedom, or improve the human condition. He feared that dynamic politicians, through their promises and personal charisma, could lead voters astray. The uneducated masses, he argued, could be persuaded to vote for politicians who promised them benefits financed through the taxes they paid. Over time, such an arrangement would erode ambition and industriousness among the populace, which would grow increasingly dependent upon officials, who would become less accountable. This would lead to the watering down of time-honored values in the pursuit of immediate gains and the convenience of rulers and ruled alike.

Nock thought that the only means by which civilization might be salvaged and liberty preserved would be through a small, educated minority, which would keep ancient truths alive and proselytize to acolytes the importance of restoring values and virtues long submerged by relentless appeals to the lowest common denominator within the electorate. He referred to this group of individuals who would come to work in concert as the "Remnant." In time, after they coalesced, they would supplant the existing order and give rise to a new, more virtuous status quo.

In his frequent visits to the Buckley household, Nock found a most receptive audience. Born in 1880, he acted somewhat as a surrogate father to Will and a grandfather to Billy. Both father and son were attracted to Nock by what the writer had to say, which echoed much of what Will had long recited at the dinner table, but also by the older man's erudition, aristocratic mien, colorful mannerisms, and biting wit. Billy read many if not all of Nock's writings and quoted them often. The similarity between the role that Nock assigned the Remnant and that which Buckley envisioned for the post-1945 modern conservative movement is unmistakable.

Surviving papers Billy wrote at Millbrook contain kernels of Nock's ideas and demonstrate a political sophistication rare among adolescents. In an essay on the weaknesses of democracy, he lamented that a ballot cast by an unintellectual, uneducated voter received the same weight as one cast by someone who had studied the issues and was able to distinguish among the candidates.[83]

He was appalled that the "ignorant idealist," William Jennings Bryan, received 5 million votes in 1896 and that, to defeat him, the Republican machine could "pull" out only 1 million more votes to elect McKinley.

Although he made no specific mention of Nock, Billy clearly had identified signs of the "watering down" of which Nock complained. He advocated reforms that allowed for only "informed" and "qualified" voters to exercise the franchise, hoping that this would weaken the hold political bosses exercised over less informed voters.[84] He was skeptical that a postwar "democratized" Germany would fulfill the Allies' expectations. In support of his skepticism, he provided the example of crowds he had observed in newsreels enthusiastically cheering for Hitler and other dictators. They appeared to do so, he pointed out, free of compulsion. He noted, too, that some of these dictators had been voted into office. Democracy, he argued, was not in and of itself a guarantor of the people's liberties, a theme to which he would return many times in the future.

Buckley remained friendly with his mentors at Millbrook throughout the decades, always addressing them as "Mr." A letter that Buckley's assistant Frances Bronson wrote to Pulling on Buckley's behalf when he was fifty-six years old reveals some of the closeness that existed between the two men and how frequently Buckley's staff was in touch with him at Buckley's behest: "Young Lockinvar is out of town lecturing, but asked that I write you to find out if dinner on January 8 would be convenient."[85] (By evoking the image of Walter Scott's gallant young knight, Bronson made a flattering reference to her boss's style and well-known image that Pulling would instantly recognize.) In her note, Bronson added that Buckley had arranged for Senator Daniel Patrick Moynihan to speak at a ceremony commemorating the fiftieth anniversary of Millbrook's founding. In advance of the school's celebration, Buckley wrote an article celebrating the school and its mission for the *New York Times Magazine*.[86]

Seven years later, Buckley, now sixty-three, chided Pulling for having remembered his charge in the (Martha's) *Vineyard Gazette* as an "able, interested, but extremely cantankerous student." Buckley countered: "I was a moderately cantankerous student. This is rooted in my mind because I think that was the last period in my lifetime during which I was moderate about anything!"[87] Pulling wrote back apologizing for having used the word *cantankerous*.[88]

In the same letter, Buckley noted that his wife had located a folder containing essays he had written for Pulling's class. (The packet included his essays on democracy and postwar Germany as well as a critique of Edith Wharton's novel *Ethan Fromm*.) He confessed that he marveled at the "meticulous" care Pulling invested in evaluating his students' work and the "adroitness" of his observations.[89] He included the essays with his letter, requesting that Pulling return them. Pulling responded that he was greatly impressed with the maturity of Buckley's thoughts at the age of seventeen and by his budding literary style.[90]

In the summer of 1943, having graduated from Millbrook and awaiting his induction into the U.S. Army, Billy journeyed with his parents and several siblings to Mexico City, where some of the young Buckleys would attend the summer session at the university. En route, they stopped in Austin, where his father's sisters continued to reside. At his first opportunity, Billy wrote one of his teachers, Henry Callard, about an experience he had at his aunts' home:

> We went to lunch one day and among the guests were two young (one 14, the other 12) boys. Both were very good looking, and were houseguests from Philadelphia. Before we knew anything about them, we started in on a friendly quarrel about the relative qualities of our respective home states. . . . After we had progressed a bit, we found ourselves confronted with the most amazing facts and figures! The older one seemed to know everything. He told us the amount of coal and oil that Pennsylvania produced; he told us the number of men Pennsylvania had sent to battle under Washington in the Revolutionary war. In short, we were completely flabbergasted at his seemingly inexhaustible store of knowledge. Anyway, we found out later that the older boy, named Paul Sigmund, was the quiz kid of quiz kids, and that he had won the nationwide contest for the quiz kids. They are both very normal, unspoiled boys, but just recently we found out, their mother, afraid that Paul's life would be ruined by too much publicity at his age . . . sent him down to the ranch of some of her friends in Texas. Anyway, we were thoroughly squelched; it was quite embarrassing. (Incidentally, you might find a write up on him in some issue of *Life*. He looks very much like Jim Hoyt when he smiles. He's a Catholic.)[91]

He signed off with a word of appreciation to Callard: "I have to tell you—perhaps you know—how much I have consistently appreciated the time you have taken with me at School. You were invaluable to me, and I shall always remember it."[92]

Buckley was inducted into the army in November 1943, as soon as he turned eighteen years of age. As he underwent basic training at Camp Wheeler, outside Macon, Georgia, he wrote home that he preferred the infantry to the navy because he thought his chances were better at landing a "desk job."[93] The freshly minted draftee from Sharon and Millbrook did not take well to military life. He found it awkward being in the company of people who were less well educated than he and resented having to take orders from people he considered his intellectual inferiors. He confessed to a colonel who shared many of his values that he found some of the noncommissioned officers "crude, coarse, vulgar, and highly objectionable."[94] When compelled to carry out their orders, he admitted, his "natural tendency was toward recalcitrance."[95]

While Bill was training for Officer Candidacy School (OCS), a lieutenant tried to impress upon him the importance of taking seriously tasks assigned him, even those he considered trivial. The officer tried to drive home the point that some young draftees at their base, a good number still in their teens, might be killed in action within weeks after completing their basic training.[96] Buckley's superiors and peers detected in him an air of superiority. Many resented the freeness with which he expressed his political views and his judgmental nature. Once, when his platoon leader advised subordinates to take condoms with them on leave, Bill "indignantly" (as one biographer recorded) blurted out that he would have no need of them.[97] His letters home betray the culture shock he experienced as he encountered on a day-to-day basis people whose backgrounds were so unlike his own: poor southern whites, Jews, Italian Americans, Polish Americans, and African Americans. Once again, he failed to fit in.

In a letter to Will, he spoke admiringly of the work ethic of Jews he encountered at Fort Macon, but made clear he did not care for their company: "There are about ten Jews in my company (240 men), and every one of them is a squad leader, and every one of them applied for OCS, and probably every one of them will be accepted. It is an amazing thing, but a Jew will do well no matter what he undertakes. There are four squad leaders per platoon, and the names of the four for the second platoon are Goldberg, Greenspan, Greenberg, and Schwartz! Anyway, it's a pleasure to see them in the Army, and I wouldn't object to a prompt shipment of Jews to the battlefronts!"[98]

In another letter home, he confessed his dislike for a captain named Rosenweig, whom he identified as a "flagrant" Jew (which apparently meant he exhibited the stereotypical behavior Buckley had anticipated). He also described a candidate for OCS, Gilbert Gildenberg, as "one of the more objectionable Jews" and a "repulsive creature" with a superior attitude. After his transfer to Fort Benning, Georgia, Buckley wrote of his surprise to encounter, in spite of legally sanctioned segregation, black and white soldiers in the same dining facilities and barracks. "There are some Negroes here," he reported. "This I don't particularly like, but there's nothing much I can do about it. I haven't had much to do with any of them yet, but I imagine they are the highest type of Negroes."[99]

In the fourth week of the eighteen-week program, Buckley discovered that his commanding officers had rated him fiftieth out of fifty on the weekly evaluation of his platoon. He was devastated. His commanding officer told him that those who evaluated him complained that he failed to take routine assignments seriously. As her father had done on an earlier occasion, his sister Patricia urged him to be more outwardly accommodating, or at least respectful, of the opinions of others. He must have succeeded because, after a lengthy and often arduous grilling, Buckley attained officer status. His superiors' decision, hardly unanimous, was not popular on the base.

In April 1945, President Roosevelt died suddenly of a cerebral hemorrhage while vacationing in Warm Springs, Georgia, just thirty miles from Fort Benning. Buckley was among the handful of young officers selected to serve as honor guard as the President's casket was taken to an awaiting train bound for Washington, DC.[100] Buckley re-created this scene, emphasizing the excessive amount of time it took the young soldiers to put on their finest formal attire, in his novel *Nuremberg* (2002). Buckley spent the next five months as an infantry-training officer at Fort Gordon, Georgia. He went on to conduct counterintelligence operations at Fort Sam Houston in Texas. Almost immediately he antagonized his new commanding officer there by writing a letter outlining how the War Department, with the war over, could speed up its demobilization process. His father told family and friends how an intermediary to whom Bill's letter had been routed intercepted it, thus sparing him from court-martial.[101]

San Antonio provided the young Buckley with distractions that made his final days in the military more bearable, if not actually pleasant. He spent much of his free time with his beloved uncle Claude and had a brief romance with Gloria Huddleston, a San Antonio co-ed.[102] When rumors that they were something of an "item" reached Sharon, Bill told his family that he and Gloria were not considering engagement or marriage. He added that he had derived great intellectual stimulation from writing a paper on Sam Houston and the Secession Crisis of 1861 for another young lady, a student at Incarnate Wood College in San Antonio.[103]

Bill and his family decided that he would attend Yale after his discharge. While awaiting his official release from military service, Buckley wrote his father that he was contemplating whether he might be better served by applying elsewhere, where he might enter as a junior, thus making up for lost time. He had hopes of a legal career. Will, citing his own experience at Texas and those of his older sons at Yale, answered that the friendships Bill would make in college would prove more valuable than almost any use he might make of the time saved by condensing his college career. Will also stressed the leadership opportunities a four-year stay at Yale would afford him.

Bill was honorably discharged in 1946 with the rank of second lieutenant. After two years in uniform, he had learned to form friendships more easily than before. He confided to Will that he regretted having so loudly voiced his disapproval of those who were not Catholic, isolationist, and anti-Roosevelt, and that he had learned that pummeling people in casual conversation was not the best way to befriend them. He said that he had come to appreciate the importance of tolerance and a sense of proportion.[104] It would be decades before he evolved into the charming, ingratiating personality later recognizable to millions on television. But in the army, as at Millbrook, he had taken the first steps toward becoming that person. Will, who had advised his son six years earlier "to learn to be more moderate" in expressing his views, so as to "give as little offense as possible," had to have been pleased.

2

God and Bill at Yale

Buckley's two older brothers, John and James, had graduated from Yale before Bill enrolled. Like Millbrook, Yale was close enough to Sharon for Bill to come home often and for his parents to follow his progress at school closely. In selecting Yale as the college for their male offspring, the Buckleys were, of course, aware of its role as a base camp for the sons of the elite on their climb to the pinnacles of power and influence in American society. They may have suspected that their outspoken third son, of whom one future critic would say, he "would rather argue than eat," might once again have trouble fitting in.[1]

At Yale, Buckley once again found himself a devout Catholic in a largely secular institution where the majority of students were nominally mainstream Protestants. And while the political tenor of the student body certainly was "conservative" in the context of the times, in contrast to what it would become years hence, it was a more moderate, establishmentarian conservatism than his. Most of Buckley's peers and their families had made their peace with the New Deal. If they were, in fact, "conservative" in outlook, they also sought to fit in with an establishment they would one day join.

Buckley's experiences at Millbrook and in the army had made him less judgmental of others and more tolerant of his peers' different religious and political views. By the time he entered Yale, he put greater effort into making friends than he had in his earlier days. "Charming and gregarious" was a classmate's first impression of Buckley. Not surprisingly, the same classmate also found Buckley a person of "very strong views."[2] At Yale, as at Millbrook, Buckley found ample outlets through which he could express those views (public speaking, debating, and writing) and for indulging his favorite avocation, music. Buckley kept a piano in his crowded suite and wrote an academic paper on Bach's

Brandenburg Concerto no. 2. Years later, he chose the piece's third movement as the theme for his television program, *Firing Line.*

The Yale that Buckley entered was undergoing considerable transition. The most visible was in the size of its incoming class. Buoyed by an influx of returning war veterans, the class of 1950 totaled eighteen hundred, the largest in Yale's history.[3] Buckley resided at Davenport College, where he shared quarters with three others in space that had been designed to accommodate two. A few months' shy of his twenty-second birthday on his first day at Yale in September 1946, Bill was older than his brother James had been on the day he graduated. The veterans on campus had little time or patience for the usual undergraduate frivolity. Buckley would later reflect on the challenges that confronted these "nontraditional students" and those who taught them. "How do you handle freshmen back from Omaha Beach?" he mused.[4] None was in a greater hurry to get on with his life than Bill. He arrived on campus in "full stride," recalled Thomas Guinzburg, whom he befriended early in his days at Yale and with whom he roomed as a sophomore.[5] Guinzburg considered Buckley the "most impressive" member of the class of 1950. He had come to Yale already having set two goals for himself: excelling in debate and serving as Chairman of the *Yale Daily News*, the key undergraduate leadership post on campus.

Buckley quickly bonded with fellow freshman debater Brent Bozell, and the two would exert a strong influence upon one another for decades. Bozell hailed from Omaha, served in the Merchant Marine, and won the American Legion Oratory Prize in secondary school. He had begun his college career a liberal Democrat, a Protestant, and an active participant in the World Federalist Movement. By the time he graduated, Bozell was a Roman Catholic, a conservative Republican, and the husband of Buckley's sister Patricia. With Buckley acting as campaign manager, Bozell would be elected President of the Yale Political Union. Debate coach and history professor Rollin G. Osterweis frequently assigned Bozell, who knew how to soften up audiences, the opening statement in debates against rival teams. Sensing Buckley's capacity to go after his opponent's jugular, Osterweis had him deliver rebuttals and closings.[6]

In debate, Buckley displayed a stage presence that millions would one come to know well. He would lift himself on his toes while speaking and make odd facial expressions and hand gestures, usually while his opponents were speaking. Osterweis proclaimed Bozell and Buckley the best freshman debating team he had ever coached. As upperclassmen, the two bested the previously undefeated Oxford team of Robin Day and Geoffrey Johnson-Smith.[7] "To debate before an overflow crowd was unheard of two years ago," Buckley's Class Book reported. "Not so in the fall of 1949, when Brent Bozell and Bill Buckley defeated Oxford 3–0."[8]

The topic, "Resolved: That Public Ownership of Basic Industries and Essential Services Is in the Best Interest of a Democratic Society," was tailor-made for the two Americans, who took the negative. Buckley and Bozell matched their visitors measure for measure in sarcasm, wit, and theatrics. In his summation, Buckley argued that socialism, which arose out of nineteenth-century excesses of capitalism, had been rendered obsolete by statutory and regulatory reforms. Francis Donahue, for years the professional manager of the *Yale Daily News*, recalled that Buckley delivered the coup de grâce when he took out his handkerchief and waved it during his opposite's summation, to the audience's delight.[9] Unknown to his visiting rivals, waving a handkerchief was a cue given fans in the stands at Yale sporting events to begin singing the school's anthem.

Buckley extended his debating prowess beyond the Yale campus. He and law professor Thomas Emerson became regular sparring partners on the radio program *Connecticut Forum of the Air*. Emerson described Buckley as cordial in private but "really vicious" onstage. The professor admitted that he could never hold his own against the undergraduate Buckley. This he attributed to Buckley's "hit and run" style, facility at spotting weaknesses in his opponent's positions, and capacity to unnerve competitors.[10] Another law professor, Fred Rodell, against whom Bill often squared off, said that, much as he detested Buckley's opinions, his younger opponent displayed a decency and a gentleness that prevented him from carrying an argument or sarcasm too far.[11] Rodell attributed these characteristics to the influence of Buckley's mother, who sometimes attended Bill's debates.[12]

Osterweis remembered that Buckley was always running some campaign or other while at Yale.[13] A year behind Buckley at Yale but five years younger, Ray Price, later a speechwriter for President Richard Nixon, remembered looking up in "awe" to Buckley, who as a sophomore was already a "big man on campus."[14] To assure the election of his choices to lead the Yale Political Union, Buckley tasked freshmen such as Price with turning out a certain number of votes. Price recalled that Buckley always seemed to know where additional votes could be found and held his young charges to account with the precision of "any good political boss."[15] Buckley and his allies successfully fended off efforts to establish a student government at Yale, believing that such an institution would become an outpost of liberal activism and its President a counterweight in influence to the *Yale Daily News* Chairman, a post on which he set his sights early.[16]

Although a good student, Buckley allowed the academic side of college to take a back seat to whatever political issue preoccupied him at any given moment. He settled into a pattern of going to class, reading whatever he could, and catching up as examinations neared.[17] He became what was known as a "divisional" major, concentrating in history, economics, and political science. By the time he chaired the *Yale Daily News* (*YDN*), Buckley, like his predecessors and successors, was spending nearly all his free time at the newspaper office. In the second semester of his freshman year, Buckley plunged into the competition that would culminate with his attaining the journalistic goal he had set himself.

In the eight-week "healing" or "trying-out" period, freshmen received points for the number of pieces filed, stories generated, and advertisements sold. They also had to run errands and tidy up the office. (Buckley would later describe the "healing process" in two novels, *The Redhunter* [1999], in which he shifted the setting to Columbia University, and *The Rake* [2007], where these scenes took place at the University of North Dakota.)

Buckley's tryout became a family affair, with his father pitching ads to colleagues and customers and two of his sisters doing likewise to merchants they patronized near Smith and Vassar, where they attended school. Buckley received the most points, which all but assured his selection as a member of the *YDN* board. The board members selected the Chairman from their number in the spring of candidates' sophomore year. The Chairman-designate would take office the spring semester of his junior year and retain it for the remainder of the calendar year. While considered a "natural" for the top spot because of his diligence, consistent outstanding performance, and presence, Buckley confided to his sister Patricia his fears that the electing body would hold his political views against him.[18] When the votes were counted, Buckley had won the secret election unanimously.[19]

In addition to the *Yale Daily News* and the debating team, Buckley joined the Elizabethan Society (a literary organization), the Torch Society (an honor society), and, in his junior year, the highly selective secret society Skull and Bones. His decision to learn how to fly a plane gave rise to some suspenseful moments, such as when he would, on the spur of the moment, decide to visit a sister or friends at another college and wind up landing in the dark. When the prestigious fraternity the Fence Club balked at admitting Guinzburg, who was Jewish, Buckley threatened to decline his own invitation unless the two could join together.[20] The ploy worked. Perhaps with his father's attitudes in mind, he told an interviewer years later that he had learned that anti-Semitism was not a "communicable disease."[21]

In his 1992 book *In Search of Anti-Semitism*, Buckley offered a glimpse into why his views toward Jews had changed in the short time between his days in the army and his matriculation at Yale. One reason he cited was "the immediate shadow" of what history would come to know as the Holocaust. Revelations of its horrors caused much of American society to reevaluate widely held views and behaviors that had been accepted as commonplace before the war. Another reason he referenced was the impact of movies, such as *Gentleman's Agreement*, which depicted the pervasive anti-Semitism that existed in the upper echelons of America society.[22] Buckley made note of restrictive quotas selective private universities placed on the numbers of Jews permitted to enroll and of the difficulties Jewish scholars encountered in obtaining tenure in many disciplines.[23] He was equally aware of similar discrimination against his fellow Catholics. Much of this prejudice began to give way in the postwar years.

Like his father, Buckley instructed other students in Spanish during his undergraduate years. He taught every semester while he attended Yale and for a time after he had graduated. When budget cuts threatened the elimination of one instructor position, Buckley offered to step aside in favor of fellow student Theodore Pichel who, he told department Chairman Thomas Bergin, spoke better Spanish. His real reason for offering to step down was that he knew Pichel was in greater financial need.[24] Bergin remained a Buckley confidant until the professor's death in 1987.

During his sophomore and junior years, presidential politics ranked high among Buckley's concerns. Having initially favored Ohio Senator Robert A. Taft for the 1948 Republican nomination, he spoke both on and off campus in favor of the eventual nominee, New York Governor Thomas E. Dewey. In his preference for President, Buckley was in conformity with most of his fellow students. (A poll of four hundred undergraduate and graduate students on election eve by the *Yale Daily News* put Dewey's support at 63 percent.)[25] He took an even greater interest in former Vice President Henry A. Wallace's third-party campaign on the Progressive Party ticket than he did the Dewey-Truman contest. In 1944, FDR, then seeking a fourth term, had dropped Wallace from his ticket in favor of Truman, then a U.S. Senator from Missouri. When Truman succeeded the deceased FDR, he dismissed Wallace as Commerce Secretary after he had publicly criticized U.S. efforts to contain the USSR. This set the stage for Wallace's renegade campaign.

With many members of the Communist Party USA openly supporting Wallace, suspicions were high that the Soviet Union, or its agents, was directing Wallace's campaign. In Buckley's view, and in many others', with Wallace as its mouthpiece, the Communist Party USA, which took its orders from Moscow, had come as close as it ever had to subverting the American political process. Wallace used his visibility to persuade opinion makers and parts of the public to accept positions that ran parallel to the Soviet line. He criticized Truman's defense policies (the Marshall Plan, NATO, the Berlin airlift, and military assistance to Greece and Turkey) as unnecessarily belligerent and confrontational and excused Soviet incursions into Eastern Europe as defensive in nature. Wallace's backers' major goal appeared to be to siphon sufficient numbers of votes away from Truman in order to defeat him. With that goal accomplished, they hoped that they could recast the Democratic Party along leftist ideological lines.

Many liberal intellectuals and Democratic officeholders shared Buckley and other conservatives' concerns about the threat the Wallace campaign posed to the American political system. In an opinion piece that he later expanded into a book, *The Vital Center,* Arthur Schlesinger Jr., a rising young historian and Pulitzer Prize winner, put forward a blueprint outlining how liberals might consolidate the achievements of the New Deal at home and contain Soviet aggression abroad. He envisioned a larger welfare state that would result in reduced class antagonisms, thereby weakening Communist appeals to the poor and to working people.[26] Along with Minneapolis Mayor Hubert Humphrey, Eleanor Roosevelt, economist John Kenneth Galbraith, labor leader Walter Reuther, theologian Reinhold Niebuhr, and others, Schlesinger founded Americans for Democratic Action (ADA) as a means of consolidating the anti-Communist American Left behind Truman, whose Cold War politics it supported. After the election the organization worked to advance other liberal policy goals. While Buckley would criticize the ADA's embrace of "mixed economies" as another form of socialism, albeit one more benign that that of the USSR, he respected its effort to discredit Wallace.

Buckley worked on several fronts to undermine Wallace's candidacy. Ridicule proved his preferred method. Buckley took to quoting Congresswoman Clare Boothe Luce's characterization of Wallace at the 1948 Republican National Convention as Stalin's "Mortimer Snerd" (a wooden dummy made famous by ventriloquist Edgar Bergen). When Wallace campaigned in New Haven, Buckley, his sisters, and a group of friends, posing as Wallace supporters, held up signs proclaiming, "Let's Prove We Want Peace—Give Russia the Atom Bomb." In other arenas, he sought out opportunities to confront Wallace supporters, many of them Yale luminaries, in debate.

He frequently took on Emerson, who ran for Governor of Connecticut on Wallace's ticket. In a radio debate, Buckley's partner, professor, and mentor, Yale political scientist Willmoore Kendall, accused Yale professor Nathaniel Colley of having "transferred his loyalty to the Soviet Union." When Colley threatened to sue Kendall, a man of lesser means than his student, Buckley proclaimed it "undeniable" that by supporting Wallace, Colley was "unwittingly furthering the ends of the Soviet Union."[27] Under Bozell's byline, the *Yale Daily News* published a list he and Buckley drew up of known Communists and members of known Communist front groups who were in the upper ranks of Wallace's campaign.

As Buckley noted decades later, while Wallace received only 1.3 million votes out of 48 million cast in 1948, intellectuals rallied to him in significant proportions.[28] Ascribing great weight to the ability of respected opinion leaders to build support for their ideas among the general public and especially the young and the idealistic, Buckley took the threat he believed Wallace's campaign posed to American society very seriously. His reading of history persuaded him that ideas advanced in the course of elections could outlast losing campaigns, capture the imagination of budding intellectuals and, under the right circumstances, gain acceptance over time. In subsequent years, he carefully studied how the Left, through myriads of organizations, publications, and communication outlets, had helped change social and political norms and policy outcomes. He would make it his goal to build a similar infrastructure through which a revitalized conservatism could similarly influence the national agenda.

In Kendall, Buckley had found a kindred spirit. The son of an itinerant preacher, Kendall, born in rural Oklahoma, educated at Oxford, and an ex-Trotskyite, was an excellent debater. Buckley was particularly drawn to this charismatic professor with a streak of the nonconformist. Kendall taught Buckley how to scrutinize political texts and to discipline his arguments. Kendall's chief contribution to political science was the doctrine of what he called "absolute majoritarianism." This concept, which he traced back to John Locke, held that a society's survival depended on its awarding higher priority to the views of the majority in the formulation of policy than to the rights of individuals.[29]

Buckley began his tenure as editor of the *Yale Daily News* in February 1949. His year in that post proved one of the most tumultuous in the newspaper's—and Yale's—history. Buckley's editorials, *The Yale Class Book of 1950* noted, "were read by everyone, and it was impossible to be neutral about them."[30] "There was never a time during the years I was at Yale when the paper was read so eagerly," philosophy professor Paul Weiss remembered.[31] Buckley's editorials occasionally ventured into national issues, taking on everything from the evils of Communism to the foibles of the Truman administration to corrupt labor unions. His *Class Book* noted that Buckley's reflections on national and international events, though few in number, "stuck in people's minds the longest."[32]

Most of his other editorials focused on campus issues. Among other things, he advocated that Yale give greater weight to teacher evaluations in determining faculty salaries and promotions; that it reduce the emphasis it placed on athletics; and that fraternities and "secret societies" coordinate their "rush" and "tap" schedules so that students would better know their options prior to deciding which organizations to join.

Four weeks into his tenure, Buckley ignited a political storm both throughout the campus and within his own editorial board when he criticized the teaching comportment of anthropology professor Raymond Kennedy. In an editorial entitled "For a Fair Approach," Buckley lambasted Kennedy for undermining religion "through bawdy and slapstick humor, circumspect allusions and emotive innuendoes."[33] He objected to Kennedy's awarding equal weight to pagan and tribal folklore and rituals as he did to miracles recorded in the Bible and to Christian liturgy. Christianity, in Buckley's view, was not just one among multiple religions but a religion *superior* to all others—and he wanted Yale to teach that it was.

Debates over his editorial continued for several days in the pages of the *YDN* and elsewhere. Kennedy was among the many who responded in writing. William Carlin, Vice Chairman of the *Yale Daily News*, spearheaded protests against Buckley both in print and within the *YDN* board of directors. At a hastily called meeting, editors debated whether Buckley should resign as Chairman or have to submit editorials in advance for collective approval. Buckley considered relinquishing his post or calling for a vote of confidence. After prolonged debate, he and his peers negotiated a compromise. Buckley would note in the *YDN* that its editorials represented the views of the Chairman alone.

Beginning with his campaign against Kennedy, Buckley commenced a lifelong crusade against what he would term "moral equivalency." He believed that when elite institutions ceased upholding certain time-honored truths, failed to distinguish in their official voice between truth and falsehood, and no longer proclaimed one economic or political system or religion superior to others, the nation's moral fiber would decay and the West would be less equipped to prevail in the major ideological challenge it faced from international Communism. Communists, he would point out, voiced certainty in their beliefs. The West should as well, he argued. He sensed that the political, educational, and social establishments had allowed "moral equivalence" to shape their agendas at the expense of clarity and conviction.

Later in life, he used the analogy of two passersby approaching a woman in a wheelchair at a busy intersection. He wrote that "a man who pushes an old lady out of the way of an oncoming bus should not be likened to a man who pushes an old lady into the way of an oncoming bus on the grounds that both men are pushing old ladies around."[34] Until the final days of the Cold War, Buckley reminded audiences that, while the United States and the Soviet Union both maintained nuclear stockpiles, operated an intricate network of spies, and, on occasion, sanctioned the breaking of laws, the two superpowers were not "morally equivalent" and that the United States was morally superior in its objectives.

In April 1949, Buckley drove to Cambridge, Massachusetts, to hear Winston Churchill address MIT's midcentury convocation. It was the former Prime Minister's first major address delivered in the United States since he declared at Westminster College in Fulton, Missouri, in 1946 that an "iron curtain had descended" over half of Europe. At MIT, Churchill proclaimed that, had the United States not maintained a monopoly over nuclear weapons at the end of World War II, all of Europe "would have been communized" and London would have been bombarded.[35] That monopoly ended five months after Churchill uttered those words, when the USSR tested its first nuclear weapon. For the rest of his life, Buckley maintained that only American superiority in nuclear weapons, both in technological capabilities and in quantity, would preserve the peace. He would oppose all negotiations that called for their reduction, including the Intermediate-Range Nuclear Force Treaty that Ronald Reagan negotiated with Mikhail Gorbachev and brought before Congress toward the end of his presidency.

In his *YDN* editorials, Buckley echoed Churchill's theme on defense issues. With regard to domestic politics, he editorialized against efforts by some Republican leaders to recast their party in a more "moderate" image, which he saw as moving the party more in the direction of the Democrats. "With all our heart," he wrote, "we wish them all the bad luck in the world."[36] He chided veterans' organizations for taking positions that had little to do with veterans' issues, such as the opposition some organizations raised to the Taft-Hartley bill, a measure intended to reverse some of the gains the union movement had made under federal protection during the New Deal and Fair Deal.[37]

President Truman became a favorite target of Buckley's. When Truman, not long after his surprise reelection victory, sought to raise taxes, Buckley argued that the President had been returned to office absent a mandate for this proposal. He suggested that if the American people really wanted socialism, they should be given the opportunity to vote for it, as had the people of Great Britain, who had recently done so by voting in a Labour government. Of Truman's overall performance on the economy, Buckley predicted that historians would record that "the greatest economic crisis the U.S. ever sustained was when Mr. Truman's haberdashery business failed."[38] (That event triggered Truman's entry into full-time electoral politics.) Of Truman's failings as an administrator and the public's acquiescence to them, Buckley observed:

> Once upon a time, the American people demanded integrity and a high and enlightened degree of dedication on the part of their public servants. Today the first Executive can name political hacks to the Supreme Court [a reference to Fred Vinson and Tom Clark, both personal friends of Truman's], brand "red-herring" any attempt to cope with the most extensive international threat to freedom history has ever known [a reference to Truman's characterization of the investigation into charges that State Department official Alger Hiss had spied for the USSR], anathematize any opponents to his program as "slavish tools" of vested interests [how Truman characterized private-sector lobbyists]; and command twenty-million votes in a national election.[39]

With the passage of time, Buckley would soften his stance toward Truman. He came to appreciate Truman's efforts to thwart further Communist advances in Europe and to admire the thirty-third President's combativeness. When the former President died in 1972, Buckley bemoaned attacks New Leftists had launched on Truman's reputation, which were reminiscent of those Henry Wallace had made while Truman was in office. Buckley referred to historians who maintained that Truman's policies had started the Cold War as "ideological egalitarians." Truman, he argued, was being taken to task not for his faults but for his triumphs.[40]

During his tenure as *YDN* Chairman, Buckley became embroiled in a national controversy. In June 1949, the *Harvard Crimson* reported that the Federal Bureau of Investigation had "moved in" on Communists and their sympathizers on the Yale faculty. According to the *Crimson*, one FBI agent had chastised physics professor Henry Margenau for speaking at a pro-Communist forum, while Yale provost Edgar Furniss, acting on information the FBI supplied him, had sought to block the promotion of philosophy professor Robert Cohen.[41] Buckley, the *Crimson* reported, had assigned a reporter to look into the matter but never ran an article about the FBI's alleged probe into the activities of the Yale faculty. Some speculated that Buckley withheld the story at the FBI's request.[42]

Amid the various charges and denials, Buckley had the *YDN* sponsor a forum at Yale Law School about the FBI's operations on campus. Before an audience of over five hundred, John J. Gleason, head of the FBI's New Haven office, and Assistant Director L. B. Nichols fielded questions from the university community. As he chaired the gathering, Buckley made clear where his allegiances lay. When a member of the audience asked why his old nemesis Thomas Emerson had been dropped from the panel, Buckley shot back that the *Yale Daily News*, not the FBI, had selected the participants.[43] Nichols wrote J. Edgar Hoover's assistant Clyde Tolson that Buckley was very pro-FBI and that he had a "definite feeling" that they would "hear from this young man" in years to come.[44]

In one of his last editorials before he stepped down as *YDN* Chairman, Buckley made the case for the nomination of Senator Robert A. Taft as the 1952 Republican presidential candidate. "Everyone knows Taft is brilliant, honest, dedicated and powerful, and most Americans, we are told, are vastly unimpressed. Primarily the politicians appraise him as a cold fish who hasn't the personality to carry the vote of the masses, who prefer, they insist . . . either the ingratiating voice and smile of a patent hypocrite or the All-American boyishness of a vastly ignorant political stumble-bum."[45] Five seniors, including the future historian Robert K. Massie, responded with a letter to the editor: "Many thanks for reminding us . . . of two uncounted blessings: 1) That Mr. Taft is not in the White House and, 2) That the days of the editorial writer in the News Building are numbered."[46] As Buckley stepped down, the Yale administration, which had borne the brunt of many a Buckley editorial, commended him on the standard of excellence he had set for the nation's oldest college newspaper. Dean William DeVane wrote Buckley that he had never seen a "more successful" college newspaper than the one Buckley had edited.[47]

In his farewell editorial, Buckley reflected that he had committed the "unpardonable sin" of taking on "stereotype liberalism" and the limits it placed upon tolerable opinion. Buckley believed that liberalism, then the predominant philosophy throughout the United States and at Yale, was intolerant of dissenting views and saw his role as providing a check on the monopoly it exercised on campus opinion. He acknowledged that the manner in which he had done so won him plenty of detractors and confessed that his major regret was that the alternative vision he advanced for both the university and the nation had not proved "more contagious."[48] He left the impression in his farewell, much to his detractors' chagrin, that he would find other forums in which to express his views.

Buckley turned the *YDN* annual banquet, traditionally a ceremonial and festive occasion, into a testimonial to retiring Yale President Charles Seymour—and, in turn, used that event as the opportunity to air his views before a national audience about how he believed major universities should be run. On hand to honor Seymour were the Presidents of Harvard, Princeton, the Massachusetts Institute of Technology, Columbia, and the University of Pennsylvania. With

Columbia's Eisenhower and Penn's Harold Stassen rumored to be weighing possible presidential runs, the gathering attracted considerable press attention.

Harvard President James Conant offered a wry musing about the gathering's convener: "In all my years in education, I had come to the conclusion that most bright young men were liberals at twenty or twenty-five and conservative at thirty-five or forty, but I wonder what will happen to William F. Buckley, who is more conservative at twenty or twenty-five than most Harvard graduates I have known at thirty-five or forty."[49] When it came his turn to speak, Buckley urged the heads of Yale's sister institutions to promote the free enterprise system and what he called an "active Christianity" on their campuses. Faculty who could not abide this new environment he wished "Godspeed" as they made their way to more liberal institutions.[50]

Not having learned their lesson from either his *YDN* editorials or his remarks at the banquet, Yale officials invited Buckley to speak on Alumni Day on February 22, 1950. By the lights of official Yale, Buckley was a quintessential "Eli" and the epitome of the kind of alumnus it sought to turn out. Articulate, athletic, a member of Skull and Bones, the past Chairman of the *YDN*, a star debater, and an excellent student, Buckley seemed to fit the bill perfectly. Perhaps the administration expected that Buckley would temper his remarks to suit the occasion, which called for solemnity rather than acrimony: the unveiling of a memorial to the university's 514 sons who had died in their country's service in the recent war. (In total, 18,678 Yale alumni served in the armed forces during that war.)[51]

In his prepared text, Buckley accused Yale of having abandoned its institutional mission to pass along time-tested truths to its students. Instead, he maintained, it promulgated "moral equivalency," which he saw as the new prevailing ideology—or at least allowed it to set the tone on campus. He questioned whether Yale, which claimed to present "every side with equal vigor," had indeed practiced what it preached and insisted that conservative opinions were less welcome on campus than those associated with the prevailing liberalism. Rather than take a stand on some of the moral issues of the day, Yale's administration, he insisted, limited itself to running the institution, raising money, and confirming appointments. As he had done at the *YDN* banquet, he called upon the university to impart to its students an "active Christianity" and to proclaim that "collectivism" was inimical to individual dignity and to the nation's strength and prosperity.[52]

After he submitted the text of his remarks to the Yale News Bureau, university officials advised Buckley to tone down the speech. They thought it might read as an indictment of Seymour's administration. Buckley agreed to omit references to specific individuals, but insisted on leaving the rest intact. His brother James told him that, given that "it was Yale's party," the university had a right to decide what presentations it would allow. He suggested that Bill offer to withdraw as speaker, a prospect neither brother thought the university would accept, given the limited time available to find a substitute.[53] To Buckley's astonishment, Seymour accepted Buckley's offer to stand aside. This decision would have ramifications on both Buckley and Yale that neither anticipated.

Selected by his classmates to deliver the class day oration prior to graduation, Buckley criticized Yale again. Traditionally, class day speeches at Yale are laden with humorous observations, venturing into frivolity. Buckley's dripped with sarcasm, bitterness, and anger. "Greetings from Colonel McCormick and from the archangel," he began. This was a response to critics on campus who joked that the *YDN* under Buckley's leadership read as if "it was owned by Robert McCormick [the isolationist publisher of the *Chicago Tribune*], edited by the ghost of Adam Smith [a reference to Buckley's advocacy of laissez-faire economics], and published by the Archangel Michael." He continued, "Here we find men who will tell us Jesus Christ was the greatest fraud that history has known." In some classrooms, he proclaimed, conventional morality was "presented as an anachronism, rendered obsolete by human thought." He characterized the overall intellectual climate at Yale as one of "debunking."[54]

When Buckley graduated from Yale, all conceded that he had made his mark. "There is no class but the class of 1950, and Bill Buckley is its prophet," the *Yale Class Book of 1950* broadcast.[55] It predicted that Buckley would attend his twenty-fifth reunion as a sitting Supreme Court Justice and aspiring presidential candidate.[56] Buckley's classmate and friend William Hitchcock MacLeish thought Buckley personified the ambition that burned brightly among the entire class. He described a typical evening with Buckley: at his piano in Davenport College, his left hand playing Bach, his right playing "Toot, Toot, Tootsie! Goodbye," and his feet typing the next day's *YDN* editorial.[57] One of his critics from a rival school captured the impact Buckley exerted during his undergraduate years: "Every so often, there appears on a college campus a personality so individual, so generously endowed with the ability to make himself heard, that a continuous storm beclouds the campus during his stay. . . . At Yale they had William F. Buckley, Jr., '50."[58]

Buckley had entered his senior year at Yale uncertain what he would do after graduation. He was accepted to Yale's law school and to its graduate school. Will recommended that he attend the graduate school, where he could continue to work with Kendall, but Bill did not fancy himself as an academic. His classmate Evan Galbraith saw Bill more as a man in the arena, using his visibility to influence public opinion. As Buckley explained to MacLeish's father, the poet and former Librarian of Congress, Archibald MacLeish, he did not see how graduate training would prepare him for what he really wanted to do, which was to build acceptance for the precepts he held.[59]

The outbreak of the Korean War in June 1950 added urgency to Buckley's decision. He did not welcome the idea of returning to military service and had already resigned from the Army Reserves. Kendall recommended that he consider joining the Central Intelligence Agency, then a popular destination for bright Ivy Leaguers. In his first novel, *Saving the Queen*, Buckley explained in some detail how the agency recruited such personnel through "old boy" networks on campus through former agents now serving as administrators and faculty. Kendall introduced Buckley to James Burnham, then a consultant to the Office of Policy Coordination, the CIA's covert-action wing. Also a former Trotskyite, Burnham had grown disillusioned with Communism after Trotsky supported the Soviet Union's militaristic attempts to bring Finland under its control in the late 1930s. During World War II, Burnham served in the Office of Strategic Services, the forerunner of the CIA. After the war, he played a leading role in formulating U.S. Cold War strategy. Burnham would exert a profound influence on Buckley as a colleague and mentor.

He introduced Buckley to E. Howard Hunt, a Brown alumnus who had tried his hand at both fiction and journalism. Hunt, later known for directing the enterprise in which Nixon campaign operatives were arrested for breaking into the Watergate office complex in 1972, was about to head up the CIA's operations in Mexico City. He was in need of people to work with Mexican students, with an eye toward turning as many as possible against pro-Soviet elements. Buckley's familiarity with campus politics, his fluency in Spanish, the contacts he had made in the country, and his hatred of Communism made him a natural for the job.

As he waited to hear back from the CIA, Buckley attended to two items of unfinished business. First, weeks after graduating from Yale, he married Patricia Alden Austin Taylor in Vancouver. The daughter of Austin Taylor, one of Canada's wealthiest men, Pat had attended Vassar for two years, where she roomed with Bill's sister Patricia, who introduced her to Bill. Pat proved Buckley's match in wit and style, and she shared his flair for the dramatic. She also had an imperious side that acquaintances quickly discerned. Buckley's sister wrote home that her roommate Pat "looked and acted like a queen." She pronounced her the "perfect match for Billy."[60] That Pat would emerge as a prominent New York socialite and philanthropist came as no surprise to those who knew her. *Women's Wear Daily* referred to her as "the chic and stunning

Mrs. Buckley," a designation bestowed upon her after she had repeatedly made the magazine's best-dressed list, gained entry into its Hall of Fame, and actively promoted the work of designers such as Bill Blass.[61]

In the summer before his senior year at Yale, Bill, while working for one of his father's companies in Canada, paid a visit to the Taylor home, summoned Pat away from a canasta game, and proposed marriage. Her response was in character. "Bill, I've been asked this question many times. To others I've said 'no.' To you I say 'yes.' Now may I please get back and finish my hand?"[62] She informed a previous biographer of her husband that her mother, a High Church Anglican of northern Irish descent, went into "total shock" at the thought of her daughter marrying an "unknown Catholic from the farthest reaches of Connecticut."[63] The couple exchanged vows on July 6, 1950, at St. Augustine's (Roman Catholic) Church in Vancouver, with the Reverend L. J. Sweeney officiating. At the reception, held at the Taylor estate, the Right Reverend Sir Francis Heathcoate, bishop of New Westminster, blessed the newlyweds before a thousand guests.[64]

During their nearly fifty-seven years of marriage, Bill and Pat Buckley threw themselves fully, if sometimes reluctantly, into each other's activities. They addressed each other as "Ducky." Pat joked about having to "drag" Bill to benefits she chaired on behalf of the Metropolitan Museum of Art, which made her an honorary Director and Chair of the annual dinner for its Costume Institute. Other favorite causes of hers included St. Vincent's Hospital and the Sloan Kettering Cancer Center. At dinner parties in the Buckleys' New York apartment, Pat would ask guests to identify their favorite author. When they failed to announce the name she most wanted to hear, she would inquire, raising her voice, "And what about *William F. Buckley, Jr.?*" Her son recalled that when "it came to protecting her men," Pat turned into Boadicea, the warrior queen.[65] A woman of multiple interests, she took as her life's work being "Mrs. William F. Buckley, Jr."[66]

Buckley drew close to his in-laws. He dedicated his third book, *The Unmaking of a Mayor* (1966), to Pat's recently widowed mother.[67] Whenever he was in Southern California, he would often stay with Pat's sister, Mrs. John Finucane, and her husband. Pat's brother became one of Bill's frequent sailing partners. After what Bill described as a "hedonistic" honeymoon in Hawaii, during which Pat worked on her tan and he read Burnham's *The Coming Defeat of Communism* on the beach, the Buckleys took up residence in Hamden, Connecticut, a suburb of New Haven.[68]

Once back in Connecticut, Buckley turned his attention to a second piece of unfinished business. Picking up the argument he had started with his alma mater, he began turning the speech he had intended to deliver on Alumni Day

1950 into a book, *God and Man at Yale: The Superstitions of "Academic Freedom."* The title came from the last line of Yale's unofficial anthem, "Bright College Years": "For God, for country, and for Yale." The title Buckley selected implied that, at Yale, "man" and materialism had replaced God and country as the center of the institution's concerns and that the university's purported adherence to the principle of "academic freedom" was a myth.

In Hamden, Buckley settled into an orderly routine. He resumed teaching Spanish at a salary of $125 per week. He taught most mornings and wrote in the afternoon. For inspiration, intellectual support, and guidance, he turned to Willmoore Kendall and Frank Chodorov, a disciple of Albert Jay Nock. Chodorov would become one of Buckley's most important mentors. Also a former leftist, Chodorov evolved into a prewar isolationist and an ardent anti-Communist. He held editorial positions at both *Human Events* and the *Freeman*, and published Buckley's earliest articles in both. Buckley confided to a mutual friend that, but for Chodorov's encouragement, he might not have made writing his career.[69] Buckley retained Ray Price, now a Yale senior, as his research assistant. By April 1951, Buckley had completed a manuscript.

Buckley's overall thesis was that Yale had deviated from its historic mission of transmitting to the next generation of American leaders essential truths upon which the United States had been founded. Central among those truths, he argued, were that Christianity was the "true religion" and, as such, superior to all alternatives and that free markets and limited government were the economic and political systems through which all human freedom, which humankind had been given by its creator and as described in the nation's founding documents, could be assured and preserved.[70] Buckley later credited Kendall for the sentence in *God and Man at Yale* that attracted the most attention and received the strongest criticism from reviewers: "I believe that the duel between Christianity and atheism is the most important in the world. I further believe that the struggle between individualism and collectivism is the same struggle on another level."[71]

With the West aligned with Christianity and capitalism and the Soviet Union committed to atheism and a command economy, Buckley wrote, the clash between the two ways of life was the most serious challenge that awaited Yale graduates. "The battle would be waged on ideological, diplomatic, and military fronts, and for the West to prevail," he insisted, "it must have help from the classroom."[72] He was convinced that, whether intentionally or otherwise, Yale and (by inference) its sister institutions were falling down on the job.

After surveying the texts assigned for courses on religion, economics, and other disciplines, Buckley concluded that most downplayed the importance of religion in general and Christianity in particular; and, after paying lip service to the free market system, made the case for "mixed economies" (greater centralization of the economy and increased government intrusion into economic affairs). Professors, Buckley concluded, rather than seeing themselves as inheritors of Western traditions that should be passed down through the ages, imparted to their students a sense of skepticism and cynicism toward Western and American values. He discerned through his research and experience that such attitudes, passed along in the classroom, had gained currency among "politically motivated" undergraduates.

He provided multiple examples of premises once accepted as absolutes being transformed by liberal professors into "value judgments," their veracity debated and their assertions disparaged and ridiculed. He saw eternal truths being crowded out of curricula and replaced with precepts that had taken hold in the Progressive and New Deal eras, which held that government power needed to be extended in order to meet the demands of an increasingly technological and complex world. In the interests of immediacy and urgency, long-standing barriers to centralization, such as constitutionally mandated checks and balances and separation of powers among branches of government, had become obstacles to "progress" and, as such, needed to be circumvented or eliminated.

As this stage of his intellectual development, Buckley referred to himself not as a "conservative" but as an "individualist." He later explained that he had selected the term as an antonym to "collectivist" which, in turn, was a synonym for "socialist." He explained that had he written the book a few years later, he would have used the word "conservative" when referring to his political beliefs and "monetarist" to describe his economic views."[73] He noted that, consistent with the nomenclature of the times, Frank Chodorov named the organization he founded to acquaint college students with conservative ideas the Intercollegiate Society of Individualists.[74]

In *God and Man at Yale*, Buckley anticipated how the university might rebut his criticisms. He expected it to claim that it embraced and disseminated no particular ideology as a matter of policy, but sought to maintain an atmosphere in which all sides of major questions were presented, leaving students free to select the values and beliefs with which they most agreed. Buckley found this argument specious in several respects.

First, he noted that no one who attempted to teach the superiority of the Aryan race or argue in favor of anti-Semitism or racism would be tolerated at Yale, a policy of which he approved.[75] This reality, he suggested, proved that the university did, in fact, deny a forum to those seeking to air *some* ideas. He pointed out, too, that Yale had denied known Communist and Communist front organizations access to its facilities on the grounds that such persons came to their views not through free inquiry but by their acceptance of party discipline, handed down to them by others. Buckley praised Yale's former President Charles Seymour for refusing to retain an admitted Communist on Yale's faculty precisely for these reasons.

Second, Yale's protestations that it did not sanction the dissemination of one particular set of beliefs at the expense of others notwithstanding, Buckley discerned that a certain unarticulated ideology had become ascendant in the university's hiring practices. He found it peculiar that the economics department, one of the largest on campus, contained only three "free marketers." He predicted that when they retired, Keynesians would replace them. Rather than assure diversity in a department's offerings, the university's administration, having delegated much of its power to the academic departments, merely rubber-stamped their recommendations. The university's abnegation of its power in this regard, while it retained the authority to close its doors to exponents of extreme views, made the idea of "academic freedom" a "hoax." In practice, the concept had become a shield behind which a self-perpetuating ideologically consistent group had rendered itself virtually unaccountable, whether to students, parents, trustees, or the general public. Under its aegis, students received a steady diet of secular humanism, situational ethics, atheism, and collectivism.

Buckley took issue with the very idea that a university of Yale's influence and prestige should even attempt to remain neutral in the clash of ideas. In an ironic twist, he termed such an approach "laissez-faire" education. Truth, he argued, was not something all individuals, armed with the same educational training, could select after shopping around. Truth, he insisted, "can *never* win unless it is promulgated."[76] Rather than ban certain texts, universities, he maintained, should see that students were exposed to the fallacies of pernicious ideas under the tutelage of a "watchful teacher."

Buckley's overall attack upon Yale was thus threefold: that it did not tolerate *all* opinions, that it had succumbed to a single organizing philosophy, and that it had deviated from the mission it had upheld from its founding to at least the end of the Second World War, to uphold the values upon which the nation was founded. He noted that Seymour, in his inaugural address as Yale's President in 1937, had exhorted his listeners to "recognize the tremendous validity and power of the teachings of Christ in our life and death struggle against the forces of selfish materialism." With fascism then on the rise in Europe, Seymour warned that if that struggle were lost, "scholarship, as well as religion, would disappear."[77] So, Buckley concluded, official Yale *had* in the lifetimes of most alumni declared Christianity the superior faith (if not ideology), a guarantor of religious and other freedoms, and had pronounced adherence to its truths a precondition of scholarship. Why, then, did Yale not assure that such principles were promulgated in its classes?

So that Yale might return to its roots, Buckley proposed two reforms in its governance. With the natural sciences as well as other disciplines committed to the discovery of new "truths," he proposed separating the faculty's "teaching" and "research" functions. He suggested that scholars whose ideas differed from the prevailing orthodoxy on campus (or who considered their teaching obligations of secondary importance to their research) be separately funded from the rest of the faculty, and perhaps conduct their activities off campus.

His other idea was so radical in concept that even his conservative allies such as Kendall refused to endorse it. Buckley called upon the trustees, who were elected by and said to represent the university's alumni, to assert their residual power to hire and fire faculty and approve curricula. Their power devolved from being the duly elected representatives of the majority of Yale's contributors (and the previous and future purchasers of its educational "product"), the alumni. And the alumni, Buckley said, constituted the true repository of knowledge that Yale would impart to future generations. He recommended that the majority of Yale's constituents (or stakeholders) assert their sovereignty over dissenting factions, especially the Yale faculty, whom he saw as out of step with the social values and expectations of the American public.

The university, Buckley argued, existed primarily to serve its true constituents ("customers")—meaning the students it admitted, their parents, and alumni, who supported the institution financially. Instead, he said, it catered to the interests and opinions of its paid employees, the faculty. Both his premises and proposed reforms anticipated what subsequently became known as the "school choice" movement (with regard to primary and secondary education). His ideas reflected Kendall's "majoritarian" view, which held that the concerns and interests of the broader base must receive greater priority than those of the unelected elite, even though this particular majority was rather atypical (exclusively consisting of Yale graduates).

Buckley showed a reluctance to extend this concept of majoritarianism to include the mass public, which he felt demagogues could easily manipulate. Again, he did not believe that truth was something that should be decided by public opinion. He disparaged the notion that political truths could be determined in a marketplace of ideas in the same way that the marketplace determined the price of goods and services.[78]

Buckley never completely reconciled in his own mind when reliance on majority rule can expand freedom and when it might constrict it. He would embrace extending decision making to a broader base as a means to curb the powers of elites who, in his view, were not acting in the interests of the broader society or upholding time-tested, ancient values. Yet, he did not consider the masses, who varied in educational attainment and outlook, capable of making informed choices or acting in the general interest. In his view, democracy, at its best, generated government by the lowest common denominator. Buckley told journalist Mike Wallace around the time he was working on *Up from Liberalism* that he was more concerned with whether a society was virtuous than whether it was democratic.[79]

He obviously thought that Yale-educated voters, more or less homogenous in educational attainment, economic status, and outlook, could be trusted as guardians of Yale's historic values and less swayed by demagoguery or the views of an insular elite than the mass public. He would always retain the reservations about democracy as a guarantor of liberty that he first expressed in papers he wrote at Millbrook. The image of Europeans in the 1930s willingly giving up their freedom to dictators remained an indelible memory in Buckley's mind. Yet, he was willing to appeal to that very public when he thought that certain elites had failed to safeguard the public interest or protect national security. He never resolved in his mind the tension between his elitist and populist strains.

Seen in this light, Buckley's famous observation that he would "sooner live in a society governed by the first two thousand names in the Boston telephone directory than in a society governed by the two thousand faculty members of Harvard University" takes on a different meaning than is commonly accepted.[80] Buckley's preference was not to be governed by the general public, as symbolized by the Boston telephone directory, but, if the choice was between it and the Harvard faculty, he would prefer to abide by the public's decrees than those of a liberal elite. His true ideal was governance by a new conservative elite in which he played a prominent role.

That conservative governing elite would act as "tablet keepers," defining, preserving, and transmitting time-honored truths, acting much as Nock's Remnant, until such time as it attained majority status. It would keep itself pure by expelling from its midst those who deviated from its tenets to the point that their continued presence jeopardized the standing and influence of the rest of the group. All his life, Buckley walked a tightrope between elitism and populism. At different times, he put himself in one camp or the other, depending on the issue at hand and the means he considered most expedient for achieving his goals.

As word of Buckley's forthcoming book began to leak out, Yale's officialdom began to ridicule the most controversial of his suggestions. The Reverend Henry Sloane Coffin, a former Yale trustee, asked Buckley why he wanted to turn the university's governance over to a "bunch of boobs." In response, Buckley inquired whether, if Yale's graduates were as inept and ignorant as Coffin maintained, Yale bore "procreative responsibility" for this.[81] (As if to prove Buckley's point, his long-time antagonist Yale law professor Fred Rodell suggested that the most damning indictment against Yale was its failure, over four years, to modify the dogma into which Buckley had been indoctrinated "before he ever got near the place.")[82]

In his search for a publisher, Buckley, aware that major New York publishing houses had large numbers of Ivy Leaguers on staff, approached none of them. At Chodorov's suggestion, he sent his manuscript to the Henry Regnery Company in Chicago. Its head, Henry Regnery, son of a textile magnate, was an MIT graduate and an erstwhile New Dealer who had moved rightward in opposition to Roosevelt's prewar intervention policies. In 1945, along with other former isolationists including Frank Hanighen, Felix Morley, and William Henry Chamberlain, Regnery had founded the conservative newspaper *Human Events*. Regnery favored rightward-leaning books and had published works by Nock, Wyndham Lewis, and T. S. Eliot. He was also known for his willingness to give new authors a hearing.

Eager to have the book appear as Yale celebrated the 250th anniversary of its founding, in October 1951, Buckley and his father advanced Regnery funds to speed up its publication and cover the costs of its promotion. Buckley asked journalist John Chamberlain, a former socialist and editor of the *Freeman*, to write an introduction. Chamberlain was already predisposed toward Buckley. On a visit to Yale in 1949, while working on a story for *Life* magazine about higher education in the United States, Chamberlain learned of the large shadow Buckley cast on campus.[83] Buckley would later say that Chamberlain's endorsement changed his life.[84] Decades later, Chamberlain explained why he had invested his reputation in the young Buckley: "To understand our feelings about nurturing Bill Buckley, one has to realize the pariah status of conservatism in the early '50's. We needed a young champion with the insouciance, the faith, the public presence, and above all, the wit, to carry on a fight that would ultimately redeem the conservative and libertarian movements from charges of antiquarian crack-potism."[85]

In April 1951, around the time Buckley mailed his manuscript to Regnery, the CIA accepted him into its service. From May through early September, Bill and Pat lived in Washington, DC, as Bill prepared for his new assignment. He also published three articles in *Human Events* under Chodorov's tutelage. While in Washington, Buckley renewed his association with FBI officials he had encountered at Yale. He and Pat visited the bureau and paid a call on its Director, J. Edgar Hoover. In the 1950s, Hoover, at the height of his power and popularity, had made rooting out alleged Communist infiltration and subversion of government agencies and private industries his highest priority.

As a result of his past contacts with its agents, the FBI opened a file on Buckley. Its early entries made note of the Buckleys' visit, Bill's past support for the bureau, and Bill and Pat's meeting with Hoover. Hoover added Buckley to his list of "special correspondents," those whose letters he personally read and to whom he sent materials he thought they might find useful. He also included Buckley on his list of "Ten Most Prominent Young Americans Who Love Their Country, their Flag, and the FBI."[86] The Director had his staff supply him with synopses of Buckley's articles, books, and television interviews. Hoover removed Buckley from his list of favorites in 1967, after *National Review* ran a lampoon issue that included a fictitious account of Hoover having been arrested in a YMCA men's room on a morals charge.[87] The story was a parody of an actual incident that involved Walter Jenkins, an aide to President Lyndon Johnson.

Although Buckley had defended Hoover when liberals accused him of being overzealous in his investigations, Hoover fell in his esteem when Buckley learned that Hoover had compiled files on the personal lives of celebrities and political figures who were not under investigation for suspected criminal activity. He was appalled when it was learned that Hoover shared that information with President Lyndon Johnson for the latter's entertainment.[88]

Once in Mexico, Bill, acting under the cover of "an entrepreneur in charge of an import-export business," translated, edited, and prepared for distribution the memoirs of Eudocio Ravines, a former Chilean Communist who had turned against Stalin. (Ravines would inspire a fictional character in Buckley's 1985 novel *See You Later, Alligator.* The actual Ravines later served as *National Review*'s correspondent in Latin America.) On the dust jacket of *God and Man at Yale,* Regnery identified Buckley as "operator of an import business in Central America."

Buckley and Hunt soon recognized that Bill was not cut out to be a CIA agent. His temperament was too much that of an activist and he had an uncanny ability to draw attention to himself. Intelligence work proved too covert a life for someone who had so enjoyed the spotlight at Yale. Buckley wanted to participate in the national debates on the major issues of his time. He was eager to promote his forthcoming book and keen to partake in the debate he knew it was likely to cause. Moreover, Pat was pregnant. She had already suffered an ectopic pregnancy and did not want to give birth in Mexico City. Not long before, Hunt's wife had nearly died in childbirth there.[89] Furthermore, although Buckley remained loyal to Hunt, he had his doubts about the overall competence of the CIA. Perhaps he saw no valid connection between the work he had been assigned and U.S. strategy to win the Cold War. In 1961, Hunt complained that every issue of

National Review contained "sly or not so sly digs" at the agency.[90] One quip that surely upset him was an item that appeared in the December 14, 1957, issue: "The attempted assassination of Sukarno has all the look of an 'operation' by the Central Intelligence Agency: everyone got killed except the appointed victim."[91]

As *God and Man at Yale* neared publication, Buckley telephoned Yale's new President, A. Whitney Griswold, to inform him of the book's pending appearance.[92] A week after their conversation, Buckley received a letter from Yale donor and railroad magnate William Rogers Coe, who tried to dissuade him from publishing his book. Buckley would later describe Coe as typical of "rich and vain" men easily "manipulated by skillful educators."[93]

Seeking to strike common ground with the young author, Coe wrote that he saw the "necessity of cleaning out the pinks and subversives from the faculty."[94] (Buckley had not referred to any Yale faculty member in the book as a Communist or security risk. Nor had he called for the dismissal of any particular professor.) Coe assured Buckley that Griswold and his team were aware of law professor Thomas Emerson's work with the National Lawyers Guild (a group widely believed to be a Communist front) and would "discipline" him.[95] This being the case, Coe suggested, there was no longer any need for Buckley's book. Outraged at this "blend of naiveté and effrontery," Buckley wrote Coe that his letter suggested that Yale officials would "betray their principles as they have upheld them." He proclaimed himself "loyal" to Yale and its traditions to an extent that very few people at Yale were.[96]

God and Man at Yale appeared on schedule in October 1951. Its initial printing consisted of five thousand copies. The book quickly sold out and went immediately into a second printing. A month after publication, Regnery had sold sixteen thousand copies, and by spring of 1952, thirty-five thousand. But Regnery paid a price for publishing Buckley's work. In retaliation, the University of Chicago cancelled its agreement with Regnery to publish its Great Books series.[97] As anticipated, mainstream and liberal-leaning periodicals ran unfavorable reviews. Conservative publications, including the *Daily News*, the *Freeman*, and *Barron's*, ran favorable ones.

Decades later, Buckley, reflecting back on Griswold's behavior at the time, commented that the new Yale President had yet to acquire "the savoir faire of high office."[98] Journalist Dwight Macdonald wrote that Yale reacted to Buckley's book with "all the grace and agility of an elephant cornered by a mouse."[99] Although Yale and its sister institutions had come under attack before, this time the assault came from one of its own. Moreover, the university had repeatedly bestowed honors and praise on the author, a factor that made it difficult for its officials to disparage him.

Before *God and Man at Yale* went to press, Lloyd G. Reynolds, Chairman of Yale's economics department, advised Griswold to "ignore the book" and thus deny its author the "martyrdom" he clearly sought.[100] Supreme Court Justice Felix Frankfurter recommended that Griswold take a "Swiftian" and "Shavian" response to Buckley's "wretched" book, and bury it in ridicule.[101] Yale took neither approach. "We intend to take the offensive in this matter and not sit by waiting for complaints to roll in when the book is published," Reuben Holden, Griswold's assistant, explained to U.S. Steel Chairman and Yale trustee Irving Olds.[102] In a preemptive attack, Griswold wrote an inquiring alumnus that the forthcoming book was the work of a "militant Catholic" who sought to restore the religious controls over education that "we had gotten rid of hundreds of years ago."[103]

University officials appear to have played a role in shaping, if not initiating, the most hostile review the book received. McGeorge Bundy, a rising academician at Harvard, wrote the piece, which appeared in the November 1951 issue of the *Atlantic Monthly*. Six years Buckley's senior, Bundy was also a graduate of Yale, a member of Skull and Bones, and a former student journalist. In preparing his review, Bundy spent a day with Griswold going over points he intended to make in print.[104] Bundy confessed to deriving a "kind of savage pleasure" from his mission.[105]

Entitled "The Attack on Yale," Bundy's review set the tone for much of the controversy that followed. At its outset, Bundy declared himself a "believer in God, a Republican, and a Yale graduate." Having demonstrated that he had the bona fides to assess Buckley's criticisms of Yale, Bundy declared the book "dishonest in its use of facts, false in its theory, and a discredit" to both its author and to Chamberlain.[106] He dismissed what Buckley said about how religion was taught at Yale on the grounds that, as a Catholic, Buckley came from a different tradition from that of Yale's Protestant founders. Buckley's religious background, he implied, disqualified him from being able to assess how true Yale remained to its religious tradition. One would not have known from the review that Buckley had not demanded that Yale impart an official religious dogma to its students, but that it profess that Christianity (or the Judeo-Christian tradition) was superior to all alternatives and to atheism.

Having admonished Buckley for not having the expertise necessary to judge how well Yale was living up to its Protestant traditions, Bundy then attacked him for ignoring the communitarian strains inherent in the teachings of the Catholic Church.[107] (Other critics of Buckley, some of them Catholic, suggested that his embrace of laissez-faire economics ventured on heresy. They reminded him that papal encyclicals issued by Popes Leo XII and Pius XI had condemned

editor of *Barron's*, in a letter to Griswold, said that he took "comfort" in the thought that "anyone one year out of Yale can write this kind of book."[118] He complained to George Van Santvoord, headmaster of the Hotchkiss School, that Yale had brought the controversy on itself through its strategy of "official silence and indirect innuendo."[119] John D. J. Moore of the W. R. Grace industrial company (and a Catholic) urged Griswold to disavow Bundy's comments about Buckley's Catholicism, which he said would "prove harmful to Yale."

In an editorial accompanying a story on Yale's 250th anniversary, *Life* likened Buckley to the "brat at a birthday party who tells the guests that the birthday boy is secretly a dope addict."[120] Its founder and publisher, Yale alumnus Henry Luce, was clearly toeing the Yale party line. In *Saturday Review*, Frank Ashburn, headmaster of the Brooks School, suggested that Buckley's arguments had "all the appeal of a fiery cross on a hillside at night." He added that the figures standing beside it would be wearing hoods, but not academic ones.[121] The magazine failed to note that Ashburn was a both a Yale trustee and head of its University Council. When Buckley appeared at Ashburn's institution years later, he declared that he had left his hood at home.[122]

Though few in number, conservative journals ran favorable pieces about the book. Max Eastman in the *American Mercury* praised the young author for having the "arrant intellectual courage" to take on his former teachers.[123] Positive reviews and editorials praising *God and Man at Yale* ran in the *Chicago Tribune*, the *Freeman*, and the *New York Daily News*. The last ran an editorial cartoon depicting a black sheep with the head of Karl Marx leading lambs away from the rest of the flock.

The *Yale Daily News* ran five different takes on the book, four of them negative. After Professor T. M. Greene suggested in the *Harvard Crimson* that Buckley was "even more of a Fascist than he was cracked up to be," Buckley and his father threatened legal action.[124] At their insistence, the *Crimson* published a retraction; each editor and the reviewer signed a statement, attesting that what the newspaper had printed about Buckley was "completely at odds" with Buckley's writings.[125] This would not be the last time Buckley threatened legal sanctions against critics who sought to discredit his arguments by likening him to fascists or Nazis.

Buckley emerged from his much-celebrated tiff with Yale fortified for future battles. He had learned that, despite the veneer of gentility, good breeding, and tolerance the establishment projected to the world, it, when challenged, would close ranks and go after renegades and fight as aggressively as any street fighter in a back alley. The controversy over his first book brought Buckley a wider platform from which to disseminate his anti-Communist, anti–secular humanist, and pro–free market message. Speaking invitations, interview requests, and fan letters began pouring in. At twenty-six, he was a husband, expectant father, author of a best-selling book, and army veteran with a Yale pedigree. Buckley was full of hope and ambition as he set out to move the fulcrum of political opinion closer in his direction.

3

Standing Athwart History

In March 1952, Bill and Pat Buckley relocated from Connecticut to New York City, where Bill took up his duties as associate editor of the *American Mercury*. Founded in 1920 by H. L. Mencken, the great contrarian, humorist, and libertarian-leaning journalist, the *American Mercury* enjoyed a circulation of ninety thousand by 1952. Soon, the Buckleys purchased a fifteen-room house on Wallack's Point in Stamford, Connecticut, that would be their home for the next half century. Its terraced gardens sloped down to Long Island Sound, where Buckley, often accompanied by visitors, would spend countless hours sailing. Bill lost no time in converting the four-car garage on the property into a cluttered study.

In accepting full-time employment, Bill had rejected advice from his father and his publisher, Henry Regnery, both of whom had urged him to continue his education. (Regnery encouraged him to study with the economist Friedrich von Hayek at the University of Chicago. Will pressed him to attend Oxford or Cambridge.) Bill, however, wanted to plunge into a more active position through which he could comment on the affairs of the day. He had made it his life's work to displace New Deal liberalism from its dominant position in postwar intellectual and social circles, and he did not want to waste time.

He chose the *American Mercury* over the *Freeman*, the other principal conservative magazine of the time, because its editor, William Bradford Huie, had promised Buckley complete autonomy over what he wrote for the magazine.[1] But Huie was away much of the time fund-raising, and in his absence Buckley's fellow associate editor Martin Greenberg exerted editorial control. He and Buckley soon fell out. Greenberg balked at Buckley's idea for an article about liberal hegemony, and Buckley departed mere weeks after he had joined the enterprise. He spent the rest of 1952 freelancing, contemplating ideas for a second book, and politicking. He and Pat also became parents. Their only child, Christopher, was born on September 28, 1952.

The upcoming presidential election was much on Buckley's mind. He published an article in *Commonweal* early in the year entitled "The Party and the Deep Blue Sea." Its subtitle, "Ideally, the Republican Party Platform Should Acknowledge a Domestic Enemy, the State," accurately summarized his arguments.[2] Buckley urged the GOP to present voters in the 1952 presidential election with a clear alternative to New and Fair Deal "collectivism." As he had while at the *YDN*, he rejected the conventional thinking of party leaders and commentators that the electorate would reject a party that repealed all the major programs enacted over the previous twenty years, which had greatly enhanced the role of the federal government and its relationship with the American people. Buckley maintained, as he and like-minded thinkers would insist during the next four presidential elections, that conservatives comprised a majority of American voters and that, if given a choice between two competing philosophies, conservatives in both parties would coalesce behind the more conservative of the two major party candidates. Were the GOP to nominate a conservative, Buckley believed, it would prevail by adding to its coalition conservative Democrats and conservatives who had not previously bothered to vote.

Buckley was unsparing in his criticism of past efforts the GOP had made to appeal to moderates and independents by casting itself more in the mold of Democrats—a strategy, he noted, that had repeatedly failed the party: "We have temporized with collectivism, and we have lost. And after the campaigns were over, we were left not with the exhilaration and pride of having done our best to restore freedom, but with the sickening humiliation of having failed to seduce the American people because we were pitted against a more glib, a more extravagant, a more experienced gigolo."[3]

By late spring, Robert A. Taft and Dwight D. Eisenhower were engaged in an epic struggle over which would lead the party and toward what ends. Taft, still Buckley's beau ideal, embraced the limited-government domestic agenda Buckley favored. Buckley was unsure, however, whether Taft's prewar isolationist views were sufficient to meet the challenges the USSR posed to the West in the postwar world. (In his *YDN* editorial praising Taft, Buckley expressed the hope that the Senator would drop his opposition to the North Atlantic Treaty Organization [NATO], a military alliance of Western democracies based on the doctrine of collective security.)

When it came to matters of national security, Buckley was of the view that as long as the USSR threatened Western interests, conservatives needed to abandon their historic isolationism and accept "Big Government" as a necessary means of resisting Soviet expansion for the duration of the Cold War, or for at least as long as the USSR adhered to its present course.[4] Eisenhower, NATO's first commander, not surprisingly shared this view, but was less prone than Taft to dismantling New Deal and Fair Deal programs in the domestic arena.

After Eisenhower, about whom Buckley remained unenthusiastic, had become the party's nominee, Buckley threw himself fully into what had become the greatest controversy in the land, Senator Joseph McCarthy's campaign to expose and remove security risks from the U.S. government. Here was a fellow Catholic, albeit of lesser social status than the Buckleys, who shared Buckley's hatred of Communism, his sense of urgency about Soviet espionage and the Communist infiltration into parts of the U.S. government, and his belief that the Democratic administration was too lackadaisical in its response to these internal security threats. Much of the liberal establishment sneered at McCarthy, who seemed intent on disrupting the status quo in political and diplomatic circles.

A series of rapid-fire events that occurred in the aftermath of World War II had left much of the public at least poised to believe McCarthy's allegations that Soviet spies had penetrated the highest levels of American government. After peace was declared in 1945, the Soviet Union, having retained troops in Eastern Europe, undermined duly elected governments and installed puppet regimes in their place. In 1949, it exploded its first atomic bomb, years before experts deemed this possible, thus bringing an end to the American monopoly on nuclear weaponry, which Churchill had credited with keeping his nation free of Soviet domination. Also in 1949, Communist forces under Mao Zedong defeated Chiang Kai-shek's government, with which the United States had been allied, in China's civil war. In 1950, Alger Hiss, a high-ranking State Department official who in 1948 was accused of having spied for the USSR, after repeatedly protesting his innocence was convicted of perjury and imprisoned. That same year, Klaus Fuchs confessed to spying for the Soviet Union while working on the Manhattan Project. The Fuchs case triggered the celebrated trial, conviction, and execution of Ethel and Julius Rosenberg for espionage. In June 1950, Soviet satellite North Korea invaded South Korea, launching a war that pitted a U.S.-led UN coalition against North Korean forces backed by Soviet arms and eventually reinforced by Chinese troops.

Elected to the U.S. Senate from Wisconsin as part of a Republican sweep in 1946, McCarthy burst onto the national stage when he declared in a speech in Wheeling, West Virginia, on February 9, 1950, that he had in his hand a list of persons—known to the Secretary of State as Communists—who were working to shape U.S. foreign policy. (Accounts vary as to whether he put the number at 205 or 57. His purported list never materialized.) The charges McCarthy made catapulted him to instant celebrity status and cast a shadow over the 1952 election. Campaigning in Wisconsin, Eisenhower omitted from his speech a defense of his wartime mentor General George C. Marshall's patriotism lest he offend McCarthy, who had branded Marshall a traitor.

In Connecticut, Buckley and Bozell formed the Independent Committee Against Communism, a group committed to the defeat of Democratic Senator William Benton, who had urged the Senate to expel McCarthy for reprehensible conduct in making his wild allegations. This excerpted script Buckley drafted for a radio spot against Benton is indicative of the style of the campaign Buckley and his cohorts waged: "Are you going to wear a blindfold when you vote next Tuesday? Senator Benton does not want voters to know that he has obstructed the fight against Communism in Washington. But, whether he likes it or not, the story is going to be told. Listen to this station Tuesday night at 8:00 and find out how Benton's actions have helped Communists to infiltrate into our government."[5]

Benton lost to William A. Purtell, 52.5 percent to 44.4 percent. In a letter to a fellow McCarthy critic, former Maryland Senator Millard Tydings, who had lost his seat after McCarthy targeted him for defeat, Benton referred to Buckley as a "smart, able, aggressive," and "potentially dangerous young man."[6] Running independent campaigns in Connecticut to defeat candidates he opposed or to help those he favored would become something of a hobby for Buckley.

After considering several topics for his next book, Buckley collaborated with Bozell on a defense of McCarthy. The Senator granted them access to his staff and files and Regnery agreed to publish it. In *McCarthy and His Enemies*, published in April 1954, the authors provided evidence that many of the allegations McCarthy had made against numerous persons had been justified. While sympathetic to McCarthy and his cause, Buckley and Bozell noted the Senator's faults, frailties, and errors. They cited instances in which the Senator exaggerated claims, levied charges in the absence of sufficient evidence, and misstated the contents of files. In the end, however, they concluded that McCarthy was more right than wrong in his suspicions in the majority of cases they investigated. In those instances in which their research showed the Senator to have been incorrect, Buckley and Bozell attributed blame not to faulty research on McCarthy's part but to the executive branch's refusal to supply him with documentary evidence. (The Truman and Eisenhower administrations withheld files from McCarthy and his investigators, citing "executive privilege.")

McCarthy and his wife, displeased with the book's criticisms of the Senator, declined to endorse it. Buckley's father, a supporter of McCarthy, worried that the authors conceded too much to McCarthy's detractors. Regnery assured him that in doing so, his son and son-in-law had assured themselves a wider readership. He also thought that the book might make McCarthy's case for him, in its exploration of the nature of his accusations.[7]

McCarthy's objections proved beneficial to Buckley in one respect. Seeking reassurance that Buckley and Bozell were correct in their overall conclusions, Regnery sent galleys to Whittaker Chambers, a former journalist and ex-Communist who, after he accused Hiss of spying for the Soviets, had become a hero to conservatives. Chambers thought Buckley and Bozell had done McCarthy a great service by revealing the obstacles he had faced in the course of his investigation, including a recalcitrant bureaucracy and a hostile media and intelligentsia. Still, Chambers was no fan of McCarthy, whom he likened to a "slugger who telegraphs his fouls in advance."[8]

Not taking this hint, Buckley pressed Regnery to ask Chambers to write a blurb for the book. Refusing, Chambers wrote to Buckley, explaining why he could not comply. He explained that he could ill afford to have McCarthy's investigations linked in the public mind with the Hiss case (which was still under litigation). Chambers drew distinctions between the methodical approach U.S. prosecutors and Congressman Richard Nixon (R-CA) had brought to bear in their investigation of Hiss and McCarthy's scattershot tactics.[9] Chambers questioned McCarthy's judgment and anticipated that the Senator's flair for the sensational, his distortions, his inaccuracies, and his tendency to sacrifice the greater objective for the momentary effect would get him into trouble.[10] McCarthy would "make an irreparable blunder," Chambers predicted, that would "discredit the entire anti-Communist effort for a long time to come."[11]

Although he disregarded Chambers's admonitions about McCarthy, Buckley seized upon the older man's suggestion that they meet. A fan of Chambers since the Hiss case, Buckley had grown even more in awe of him after he had read Chambers's 1952 memoir, *Witness*, in which Chambers described the struggle between capitalism and Communism as a contest between good and evil, much as Buckley had done in *God and Man at Yale*. Buckley and Willmoore Kendall, who had vigorously defended Chambers at Yale at the height of the Hiss controversy, paid Chambers a visit at his Maryland farm. Chambers and Buckley instantly bonded. Four times in his life, Chambers wrote afterward, he had sat down with a stranger and had the sense that he had resumed, rather than begun, a conversation that would continue for the rest of his life. He considered his encounter with Buckley one such occasion.[12]

In their book, Buckley and Bozell drew a distinction between McCarthy the person and the politician, whose limitations they acknowledged, and what would come to be known as "McCarthyism." They sought to separate the man from the "ism" because they believed McCarthy's detractors focused on his idiosyncrasies as a way of undermining his cause: removing security risks from government service. In essence, they agreed with Max Eastman, who maintained that McCarthy was "doing badly" a job that had to be done.[13] Chambers was more critical and less sanguine. He likened the Senator's approach to "setting fire to the foxes' tails and sending them helter-skelter against the enemy."[14]

Buckley and Bozell insisted that, but for McCarthy, the prospect (and even the reality) of Soviet agents penetrating the American government would not have received the attention that Truman and Eisenhower came to give it. Both administrations put into practice procedures that tightened the process through which government officials obtained security clearances. In Buckley's novel *The Redhunter* the fictional Harry Bontecou, an aide to McCarthy, proclaims that just over a year into Eisenhower's first term, fourteen hundred persons deemed security risks had been dismissed.[15]

As it was subsequently used by McCarthy's detractors, the term *McCarthyism* came to mean the leveling of accusations without evidence with the intent of impugning a person's character, reputation, or patriotism. However, in one respect, McCarthy gained credence when government spokesmen at the highest levels refused to acknowledge that Communist infiltration of U.S. agencies was a problem, let alone a security threat. Truman's first reaction to the allegations made against Alger Hiss, for example, was to proclaim the investigation of the State Department official a "red herring."[16] Some liberals, believing that the Right would use the Communist affiliations of some former government officials to discredit New Deal liberalism, rallied around the accused, without always differentiating among cases. Some "vital centrists," like Schlesinger, who thought Hiss guilty, sensed no reason to defend him. Buckley joked that, over the years, liberals changed their definition of *McCarthyism* from "calling a non-communist a communist to calling a communist a communist." He referred to this phenomenon as "anti-anti-communism." He also discerned a shift in their arguments from "They did not do it," to "They did it, but what they handed over did little if any damage."

In their book, Buckley and Bozell made clear that they considered internal subversion an immediate and extensive threat to the nation's security. "We are at war," they declared, and they characterized "McCarthyism" as a weapon in the nation's defense "arsenal." As they saw it, the nature of the threat McCarthy identified justified awarding a higher priority to removing security risks than to assuring to the accused the right to due process, or even the presumption of innocence. "Justice is not the major objective here," they insisted. The English common-law principle that it was better to let ten guilty persons go free than allow one innocent person to suffer, they argued, was insufficient to meet the threat at hand. In this dangerous nuclear age, ten persons whose guilt was not proven beyond a shadow of doubt could inflict irreparable damage on the nation. Investigators ferreting out such threats to the national security did not, in their view, need to satisfy the standards required of a prosecutor. One does not have a "right" to a government job, they insisted, and therefore one need not commit a crime in order to be discharged. An attitude or mindset could be sufficient, they argued. After the fact, appropriate restitutions could be made, they maintained, to compensate those wrongly accused.[17]

Going a step further than McCarthy, Buckley and Bozell sought to root out a class of persons they termed "policy misfits."[18] These were persons whose views rendered them incapable of furthering American Cold War objectives. In their ranks were not only the consciously disloyal but "incompetents" and persons of "bad judgment." In *Redhunter*, Buckley's fictional Joe McCarthy identifies two kinds of policy corrupters: those who oppose sending weapons to Chiang Kai-shek because they consider the Chinese Nationalists' cause lost, and those who delay sending weapons because they want the Communists to win. The fictional Senator wants to remove "both kinds" from government service.[19]

To assure that the nation's true interests be advanced, Buckley and Bozell favored reducing the role of civil and foreign service officers in the formulation of policy and in internal investigations of security breaches and awarding instead a greater role to Congress, which was elected by and accountable to the American people. They lamented that policies rejected at the polls might survive in the bureaucracy even after a change of administrations.[20] The two looked to the legislative branch to act as a check on unelected elites.

In his first two books, Buckley wrestled with how the number of decision makers might be increased to hold in check small, self-perpetuating elites that controlled institutions meant to serve large constituencies. He sought to reform first Yale and later the State Department by taking policy making out of the hands of the professionals and awarding it instead to those entrusted to act in the name of the general interest. In the case of Yale, power would reside with trustees, elected by alumni. In the case of the State Department and other government departments, power would rest with the people's elected representatives. Thus, in order to hold liberal elites to account, Buckley veered in the direction of the very populism he had come to distrust in other situations.

Buckley and Bozell foresaw a "new orthodoxy" emerging that would prevent subversives from penetrating the bureaucracy. Given that the American people had declared (in their repudiation of third-party and radical candidacies) the collectivist ideology an unacceptable alternative to their form of government, collectivists, they concluded, could secure their ends only through subversion. Several former Soviet agents, they noted, had testified that they had acted on orders from Moscow. Once again, Buckley articulated this idea through the voice of a fictional character in *The Redhunter:* "But what the people are saying is they don't want a society that tolerates people who might succeed in making society wobbly, or even want them in the American tent."[21] Again, majoritarianism, in his view, would trump the right of the individual to go his own way in exercising power on behalf of others.

McCarthy and His Enemies made its way into bookstores a month before the infamous Army-McCarthy hearings, which would do irreparable damage to McCarthy's reputation and hasten his downfall, got under way. At the time Buckley and Bozell's book made its debut, McCarthy's influence and public standing were at their height. At the beginning of 1954, Gallup reported the Senator's approval rating at 50 percent, with 29 percent disapproving. In a debate against two law professors at their alma mater, the authors praised McCarthy for alerting the nation to the danger of security risks "operating in sensitive positions." That service, they insisted, far outweighed any harm he may have done.[22]

In spite of the Senator's relatively high approval rating among the general public, his enemies held sway among opinion leaders, many in the mainstream media, within the academy, and even within the Republican Party. After Buckley accepted an invitation to address the Women's National Republican Club, his hosts decided to postpone his talk about McCarthy pending the conclusion of the hearings. A pro-McCarthy faction within the association moved the event to another site at which Buckley addressed more than two thousand persons, half of whom crowded into the hall and additional rooms, where his address was piped in by loudspeaker, with an equal number outside. Chartered buses transported a considerable number from surrounding locales. Buckley denied that McCarthy, contrary to what his critics said, had ushered in a reign of terror and that he engaged in witch hunts. He proclaimed that "only a society in an advanced state of rot" would tolerate the kind of things that were being said about McCarthy. He accused the press of having a "cynical attitude of malice" against the Senator, as evidenced by its failure to report "favorable facts about him."[23]

In a review of *McCarthy and His Enemies* for the *New York Times,* veteran journalist William S. White, while proclaiming it the "most extraordinary book" that had yet appeared about McCarthy, accused Buckley and Bozell of believing that a moral end justified amoral means. He considered their policy recommendations "authoritarian" and suggested that their true intent was not to preserve the existing social order, but to "uproot it."[24] Arthur M. Schlesinger Jr. drew parallels between Buckley and Bozell's book and Communist tracts of the 1930s, which also took into account their leaders' defects while declaring their goals deserving of support nonetheless. He termed the book "clever and sick."[25]

Max Eastman, weighing in from the right, thanked the authors for reminding readers of four basic facts: (1) treason (through internal subversion) posed a more immediate threat to the United States since the Soviet Union had become a nuclear power; (2) Communists knew their only chance to obtain power in the United States was through infiltration and subterfuge; (3) although the USSR had declared "war" against the United States in its official documents and pronouncements, the United States had not responded in kind; and (4) the State Department was lax in policing itself, having launched sixteen thousand investigations but finding cause to discipline only two persons.[26]

The Army-McCarthy hearings ran from April 22 to June 17, 1954. They resulted from an inquiry McCarthy, as Chairman of the Senate Government Affairs Committee, had previously conducted into possible Communist infiltration of the U.S. Army. After the army had complained of pressure it had received from McCarthy's committee counsel Roy Cohn to award preferential treatment to a former McCarthy staffer, David Schine, the Senate voted to look into those allegations. With McCarthy the subject of the investigation, Senator Karl Mundt (R-SD) presided over the hearings as the subcommittee on investigations convened. After a series of charges and countercharges, the tide turned against McCarthy on June 9 when, going back on an agreement, he disparaged the reputation of a young attorney who was to have joined the army's legal team. Joseph Welch, in his capacity as Counsel to the Army, in a crowded hearing room, turned to McCarthy and inquired, "Have you no sense of decency, sir?"

The hearings proved devastating to McCarthy's reputation. Television, then a new medium, had covered them extensively, some networks gavel to gavel. Some 80 million Americans were reported to have viewed all or part of them. By the hearings' end, Gallup reported that McCarthy's approval ratings stood at 34 percent, with 45 percent disapproving. Almost as soon as the hearings ended, McCarthy's colleagues considered censuring him. As attacks on McCarthy mounted, Buckley and Bozell threw themselves fully into McCarthy's defense. Buckley made numerous television, radio, and speaking appearances on McCarthy's behalf. He offered to refute Edward R. Morrow's denunciation of the Senator on the CBS television program *See It Now*, but the network refused to accept a surrogate. Bozell joined the legal team that defended McCarthy during his censorship trial. On December 2, 1954, the Senate voted, 67–22, to censure McCarthy for acting "contrary to senatorial traditions." He died less than three years later.

Even after McCarthy's disgrace, Buckley continued to assist and advise his wounded champion. In later years, Buckley never spoke ill of McCarthy or his allies. In *The Redhunter* and elsewhere, he presented McCarthy as patriotic, well meaning, and sincere, albeit impulsive. In his fictional account of the era, Buckley cast McCarthy as more victim than villain, a man who become more reckless as he came to rely almost exclusively on Roy Cohn. Buckley's ultimate judgment was that McCarthy acted out of nobler motives than did his enemies.

More than a decade after McCarthy's fall, in the midst of student disruptions on many campuses in the 1960s, Buckley looked back at the so-called witch hunts and other havoc McCarthy was said to have inflicted upon American intellectual life. McCarthy, he recalled, never interrupted a public meeting, encouraged the takeover of buildings, sanctioned bombings in the name of his cause, or destroyed the property of professors.[27]

Buckley's spirited defense of McCarthy enhanced his visibility considerably. The quotation about society's rot comes from a speech he delivered before the Women's National Republican Club in New York, with its spillover attendance.[28] Most of the city's newspapers covered his talk. Buckley's growing appeal extended well beyond conservative or Republican circles. Invitations for him to speak poured in from church groups, fraternal associations, and colleges. Barely five years out of college, he especially appealed to young audiences. Many of his new constituents were Irish Catholics and members of various ethnic groups who shared his anti-Communism. A good many of them considered themselves Democrats. They came to regard him, a familiar face on television, as a man they could count on to give voice to their views. A good many may well have voted for him for Mayor years later.

Buckley paid a price in other quarters for his outspokenness in McCarthy's defense. Some speaking invitations he had accepted prior to the McCarthy censure battle were withdrawn, and some lectures he was to have delivered were cancelled. Daniel Bell, an editor of *Fortune* and a member of the board of the American Committee for Cultural Freedom, ordered Executive Director Sol Stein "to steer clear" of Buckley, whom Bell termed a "McCarthy apologist."[29] All the while, Buckley appeared to relish being in the thick of the most pronounced political fight of the decade.

Henry Regnery, who had come to know Buckley well and often had him as a houseguest, left this depiction of what it was like to be around him as his public career began to unfold: "He was a great favorite with our four children, who were quite small then. He brought them presents, played games, and told them stories. Most memorable of all for them was his performance on our piano of 'Variations on the Theme *Three Blind Mice*.' It began quietly and demurely, became more and more flamboyant, and ended in a perfect torrent of pyrotechnics, at which point the children, whom we had carefully brought up on Bach and Mozart, having watched absolutely spellbound, would say in one voice, Do it again."[30]

While at work on *McCarthy and His Enemies*, Buckley discussed with Willi Schlamm, an editor of the *Freeman*, the possibility of founding a new conservative magazine. Regnery had retained Schlamm to cut seventy-five thousand words from the initial manuscript of *McCarthy and His Enemies* and asked him to write an introduction to the book. Like Chambers, Schlamm was an ex-Communist who had risen through the ranks at *Time* magazine and had briefly functioned as foreign policy adviser to its publisher, Henry Luce. With his second book now completed, Buckley's thoughts turned to founding a new conservative publication.

It was an especially propitious time to do so. The two respectable outlets for conservative writers, the *Freeman*, which traced its origins to a journal founded by Albert Jay Nock in the 1920s, and Mencken's old *American Mercury*, were on the verge of collapse. Leonard Read, head of the Foundation for Economics Education, had acquired the *Freeman*, brought on Chodorov as editor, and narrowed its focus exclusively to economics. The financially strapped *American Mercury* had come under the control of Robert Maguire, head of the company that produced the Thompson submachine gun. Maguire transformed the publication into a repository of anti-Semitic tracts. For years afterward, Buckley specified on his résumé that the *American Mercury* for which he had once worked was the one of an earlier incarnation. Once he had his own magazine going, Buckley forbade anyone whose name appeared on the *American Mercury*'s masthead to also so adorn *National Review*'s.[31] Buckley decided to found his own magazine after first trying and failing to acquire *Human Events*.

Early in their association, Schlamm gave the twenty-nine-year-old Buckley two critical pieces of advice. He suggested that Buckley serve as editor in chief (on the theory that established writers would be more open to taking instructions from a younger colleague, whom they might consider a protégé, than from a contemporary, whom they would consider a competitor). He also advised Buckley to retain ownership of all the magazine's stock. This reduced the chances of Buckley's losing control of his creation should it become beset with factional disputes. William Casey, an acquaintance of Regnery's who would later manage Ronald Reagan's successful campaign for President and become head of the Central Intelligence Agency, drew up the incorporating papers for Buckley's new enterprise. "We were always relaxed with each other," Buckley said of his relationship with Casey, "the way it is with people who are Catholic, anti-communist, and conservative."[32]

Buckley proved a most effective fund-raiser, bringing to this task the enthusiasm and sense of urgency of the most charismatic evangelist. Buckley and Schlamm calculated that they would need between $450,000 and $500,000 to fund the magazine. They had wanted to call their journal "National Weekly," but learned that another organization had copyright to that title so instead settled on "National Review." (This proved fortuitous, as they could not afford to turn out their product on a weekly basis.) With Will Buckley donating $100,000, Bill and Schlamm set out to raise the rest from wealthy donors who saw the world as they did.

In his letters to prospective donors, Buckley made the case for a conservative intellectual periodical. He began them by refuting an often-repeated leftist assertion that the business class determined national priorities. As Buckley saw it, opinion leaders drove the national agenda and a majority of them were decidedly liberal. This group, Buckley argued, determined public policy through the influence they exerted upon those in positions of public trust. Such persons were found in business, government, philanthropy, the clergy, universities, and elsewhere. In *National Review*'s first issue, he described in typically memorable terms how opinion makers on the left closed ranks behind commonly shared opinions: "Drop a little itching powder in Jimmy Wechsler's bath and before he has scratched himself for the third time, Arthur Schlesinger will have denounced you in a dozen books and speeches. Archibald MacLeish will have written ten heroic cantos . . . *Harper's* will have published them and everyone in sight will have been nominated for a Freedom Award."[33]

Those on the right, he went on, had made no sustained effort to counter liberal opinion makers. What little efforts they had made, he said, were merely sporadic endeavors to rally public opinion through intense and short blasts of "mass propaganda." By the time such attempts were made, Buckley declared, the matter would already have been decided, with liberals carrying the day. Conservatives, he proclaimed, needed a journal that would supply its readers with "live ammunition for every round of the battle." That journal would develop and disseminate a counter-narrative to the "liberal hegemony." Over time, an alternative network of commentators, academicians, and journalists would emerge. All would take their inspiration from *National Review*, which would function as "keeper of the tablets" for an emerging movement.[34] Buckley was nothing less than audacious in setting the mission for his magazine.

In his fund-raising rounds, Buckley made early inroads with wealthy fellow Yalies such as Roger Milliken, a South Carolina textile magnate, his brother Gerrish, and Lloyd Smith, a Houston oilman. Milliken became one of *National Review*'s most generous donors. In addition to his considerable contributions, he took out a full-page advertisement in every issue. Along with ex-President Herbert Hoover and several others, he underwrote thousands of student and other gift subscriptions to *National Review*.

Recipients of their gift subscriptions included the three thousand members of the Intercollegiate Society of Individualists (now the Intercollegiate Studies Institute [ISI]), which Chodorov had founded in 1953, with Buckley acting briefly as President. ("Am removing you as president, making myself president," Chodorov wrote him. "Easier to raise money if a Jew is president. You can be V-P.")[35] ISI was patterned after the Intercollegiate Society of Socialists, which Upton Sinclair founded in 1904. That entity, later renamed the League for Industrial Democracy, recruited young intellectuals to the socialist cause. Its early members included novelist Jack London and Russian Bolshevik American sympathizer John Reed.

Jeremiah Milbank, the scion of the founder of Borden (the company that introduced condensed milk into the American diet) and a Yale alumnus, added the magazine to his multiple philanthropic endeavors. General Electric executive Lemuel Boulware, Ronald Reagan's mentor after the Hollywood star became the company's corporate spokesman, who played a major role in Ronald Reagan's transformation from a liberal Democrat to a conservative Republican in the 1950s, supported *National Review* financially and suggested to Buckley topics he might wish to explore in the magazine.[36] Another giant in the textile industry, Alfred Kohnberg, a supporter of Chiang Kai-shek and a contributor to Senator Joseph McCarthy, backed Buckley generously and became a close confidant of Buckley's.

To Buckley's disappointment, H. L. Hunt, Texas oilman and financier of multiple conservative enterprises, shunned him, as did other wealthy Texans. Buckley proposed several areas in which he and Hunt might collaborate, but Hunt, who was involved in multiple media ventures, was not interested. Hunt's son pledged $10,000 to the enterprise, through an intermediary, but failed to honor it. One of Buckley's biographers wrote that many right-wing conservatives in Texas considered Buckley "too Catholic, too eastern, and too moderate." Buckley recalled that a person in the know confirmed to him that his religion worked against him in Texas.[37] Once again, he found himself an outsider, this time in a circle he sought to lead.

At the same time, Buckley found support where he had not expected it. While in California promoting *McCarthy and His Enemies*, he struck up a friendship with screenwriter Morrie Ryskind, who had worked on several Marx Brothers movies and collaborated with George S. Kaufman on *Of Thee I Sing*. A former socialist, Ryskind became an early benefactor of *National Review* and introduced Buckley to John Wayne, Bing Crosby, Adolphe Menjou, Ward Bond, and other celebrities. He also brought Buckley to the attention of future Reagan benefactor Henry Salvatori, who donated $50,000 to the enterprise, and to other California businessmen.[38] Producer Cecil B. DeMille, full of praise for Buckley's plans, but perhaps fearful of reprisals in his overwhelmingly liberal industry, contributed $150. DeMille, along with economist Ludwig Von Mises, ex-boxer Gene Tunney, Utah Governor J. Bracken Lee, and erstwhile FDR adviser Raymond Moley, provided supporting statements that appeared in the magazine's first issue.

Herbert Hoover, who found Buckley a "dedicated American boy," opened doors for him on both coasts.[39] In a progress report Buckley sent Hoover after he had concluded an intensive fund-raising swing through California, Buckley delicately quoted back to his sponsor words he had often heard the elder statesman use: "What we need is capital."[40] Picking up on a rumor that William Keck of the Superior Oil Company was concerned about the lack of intelligent conservatism on college campuses, Buckley asked whether Hoover knew anyone who might put him and Keck in touch.[41] He was particularly grateful that one of Hoover's friends offered to contact ten acquaintances on Buckley's behalf. At *National Review*'s fifth anniversary dinner in 1960, Hoover would appear on the dais along with two other Buckley admirers from an earlier generation, General Douglas MacArthur and Admiral Lewis Strauss, a former member of the Atomic Energy Commission.

Having come to value Buckley's judgment, Hoover asked him to provide him with suggestions for the next Director of the Hoover Institution, which he had founded in 1919 as a repository of materials pertaining to the rise of Communism and which evolved into a prestigious conservative-oriented think tank.[42] Buckley recommended four possibilities: Medford Evans, conservative intellectual, opponent of desegregation, and author of *The Secret War over the Hydrogen Bomb*; Georgetown history professor Charles C. Tansill, who had written critically of FDR's attempts to involve the United States in the war in Europe in the late 1930s; William T. Couch, editor of *Colliers Encyclopedia*; and Howard Penniman, a former instructor of Buckley's at Yale who had joined him in debates against Henry Wallace surrogates in 1948. (Penniman went on to become a prominent authority on U.S. and foreign elections.) Hoover eventually settled on economist W. Glenn Campbell. Hoover's neighbor at the Waldorf-Astoria Hotel, Charles Edison, son of the famous inventor and a former Governor of New Jersey, heavily supported Buckley's new enterprise. Industrialist W. Peter Grace provided a generous pledge, as did oilman J. Howard Pew and other corporate magnates.

Through interconnecting circles, Buckley came into contact with Senate Republican Minority Leader and presidential aspirant William F. Knowland of California, scion of the family that owned the *Oakland Tribune*. Knowland saw the younger man's magazine as a vehicle through which to telegraph his anti-Communist views to conservatives and introduced Buckley to potential donors. Knowland considered himself a possible replacement for Eisenhower as the GOP's presidential nominee in 1956 should the President, who had suffered a heart attack in 1955, decline to seek reelection. The California Senator authored the lead article in *National Review*'s first issue, a critique of international summitry, which both he and Buckley opposed on the grounds that in order for the international community to deem a summit a "success," both sides needed to make concessions. Both men wanted to offer none to the Soviets.

As he continued to raise funds, Buckley turned his attention to staffing. He assiduously courted two distinguished anti-Communist intellectuals he greatly admired, James Burnham and Whittaker Chambers. Burnham readily agreed. Once close to George F. Kennan, author of the policy of containment, Burnham now favored "rolling back" gains the Soviet Union had made in Eastern Europe. Having once commanded a place of respect among anti-Communist liberals, Burnham had been forced out of the *Partisan Review* after he refused to criticize McCarthy in public.

At *National Review*, Burnham became a strong voice for realpolitik in foreign affairs, and his influence on Buckley grew stronger with the passage of time. When businessman Robert Donner, a generous backer of *National Review*, objected to Burnham's hiring because of his Communist past, Buckley volunteered to "be blacklisted" along with Burnham, whom he described as the "dominant intellectual influence" at *National Review*.[43] Christopher Buckley recalled his father referring to Burnham as the "Rock."[44] Burnham would remain at *National Review* until his death in 1987.

Chambers did not officially join *National Review*'s masthead until 1957, and he resigned in 1959. As close as he had become to Buckley and as much as he admired what the younger man was attempting to do, Chambers objected to the magazine's stridency and to what he considered its excessive and unreasonable criticisms of President Eisenhower and Vice President Nixon. He continually urged *National Review*'s editors to make their brand of conservatism more appealing to a majority of Americans, who were not as hostile to New and Fair Deal policies as were Buckley and his colleagues. By the time Chambers resigned from the magazine in 1959, Buckley was showing signs of having taken Chambers's advice to heart.

Max Eastman, another former Communist, was among Buckley's first hires. Eastman, an avowed atheist, served as senior editor for several years until he resigned in a dispute over the religious tone he felt the magazine was taking on. In earlier days, Eastman had been active in leftist causes and had edited two socialist magazines, the *Masses* and the *Liberator.* He had been a friend of John Reed, whose accounts of the Bolshevik revolution he published, and was an ardent follower of Leon Trotsky. (Reed's recollections would later be published as the book *Ten Days That Shook the World.*) Impressed by the postwar writings of economists Friedrich Hayek, Ludwig Von Mises, and Wilhelm Ropke, Eastman became a defender of free markets. On foreign policy matters, he tended to align with Burhnam with regard to strategies the United States might employ against the USSR.

Suzanne La Follette, recently of the *Freeman,* served as managing editor during *National Review*'s first five years before she retired. Buckley's sister Priscilla, who had been with the magazine from its launching, succeeded her. Priscilla Buckley came to her brother's magazine after a distinguished journalistic career at United Press International in Paris. Willmoore Kendall served as book editor, a post Frank Meyer eventually filled. A former operative with the Communist Party USA, Meyer became *National Review*'s most prominent libertarian.

Bozell coined the term *fusionism* to describe how Buckley's enterprise brought together several strains of conservatives (traditionalists, libertarians, realists, and agrarians) all pulling together in opposition to a common enemy, world Communism. Russell Kirk, author of *The Conservative Mind: From Burke to Santayana,* was the foremost of the traditionalists. He and his followers emphasized the superiority of Western political thought, the Judeo-Christian tradition, and respect for institutions and the rule of law. Libertarians such as Meyer, Chodorov, Schlamm, and Chamberlain, among others, took as their principal focus free markets, individual freedom, and minimalist government. The realpolitik camp, which included Burnham, Eastman, and Chambers, believed in subordinating goals of lesser urgency to the group's most important objective: prevailing against Soviet aggression.

Richard Weaver, author of *Ideas Have Consequences,* added to this mix a small school that espoused *southern agrarianism.* Adherents deemed the social mores of the American South worthy of preservation and resisted pressures from outside that it change long-standing practices.[45] Weaver's influence can be seen in the stands *National Review* took during the 1950s and early 1960s in opposition to federal action to extend civil rights to African Americans. In the magazine's first decade in operation, internal dissenters from this view were few.

While Buckley alone decided *National Review*'s positions on issues of the day, he gave his editors their say before he took a stand in the name of the magazine. Sometimes he would soften an editorial's tone, showing respect and making allowance for the strengths of arguments he had rejected. On other occasions, he would allow editors with different points of view space in which to voice dissenting views. Most disagreements pitted libertarians against practitioners of realpolitik. Buckley once joked that he spent half of his time steering the magazine between these polar opposites.[46] During *National Review*'s first decade, Buckley most frequently sided with the libertarians. To Chambers's chagrin, Buckley's idealism also led him to advocate direct confrontation with the USSR. From 1965 onward, owing to Burnham's growing influence as well as his reflecting back on what Chambers had advised, Buckley more often sided with the realpolitik school. On domestic policy, he retained many of the libertarian impulses of his younger days.

As he prepared to launch *National Review*, Buckley anticipated the role he would play as spokesman for the conservative movement and as arbiter of different points of view within it. "I can give the Right the kind of decent image it needs instead of the image that some people are giving it now," he told Yale scholar and confidant Thomas Bergin.[47] When he died half a century later, virtually every story that ran about Buckley identified him as the founder of the modern conservative movement and credited him with rescuing it from that image and keeping it free of extremism, kookiness, and bigotry.

With nearly $290,000 raised or pledged from 125 donors—still shy of the goal they had set of just under $500,000—Buckley and Schlamm published the first issue of *National Review* on November 19, 1955. They forged ahead in the belief that Schlamm was correct when he said that once the magazine had attracted twenty thousand readers, its subscribers would not let it die.[48] It would take them three years to attract that number. And although subscriptions in the early years exceeded initial expectations, *National Review* ran an annual deficit of $200,000 to $300,000. To help close it, Buckley began writing annual letters of appeal for funds to donors and subscribers. One of the publication's "angels" was Will Buckley, who in his declining years made *National Review* his principal enthusiasm.[49] Will died in 1958.

In the first issue, Buckley listed himself as editor and publisher, with Burnham, Kendall, La Follette, Schlamm, and economic writer Jonathan Mitchell as editors and Bozell, Chodorov, Meyer, Kirk, Ryskind, and Weaver as associates and contributors. The presence of so many ex-Communists and writers who were either Jewish or of Jewish ancestry (including Ryskind, Chodorov, Meyer, Schlamm, and Eugene Lyons) was not lost on either supporters or critics. Of that entire assemblage, only Buckley had been both a conservative and a non-Communist since before he came of age politically.

Eager to see the magazine grow its circulation, Buckley's parents sent some of the early issues to their friend William Loeb, publisher of the *Manchester* (NH) *Union Leader*, then one of the most prominent conservative newspapers in the country, and asked his advice. Loeb wrote back that he agreed with Buckley's parents that the new magazine ought to be "more sensational at the expense of being less philosophical." He did like the phrase "the college underground," which Buckley used when he expressed the hope that *National Review* might benefit from the "natural rebellion of youth against the existing order," much as socialism had in previous eras (given that the then "existing order" was overwhelmingly liberal).[50] Loeb had no more success than Will and Aloise in persuading Buckley to seek a lower-brow audience. If he had to choose between the two, Buckley would always opt for influence over circulation.

The clarion call he published as the "Publisher's Statement" in the premier issue proved the most frequently cited lines ever to adorn its pages: "Let's face it: Unlike Vienna, it seems altogether possible that did *National Review* not exist, no one would have invented it. The launching of a conservative weekly in a country widely assumed to be a bastion of conservatism at first glance looks like a work of supererogation, rather like publishing a royalist weekly within the walls of Buckingham Palace. It is not that, of course: if *National Review* is superfluous, it is so for different reasons: It stands athwart history, yelling Stop, at a time when no one is inclined to do so, or to have much patience with those who so urge it."[51]

Stopping history implied reversing what the Left regarded as the world's steady and inevitable movement toward collectivism. In the Left's eyes, the story of the twentieth century, beginning with the advent of Progressivism in Western industrial democracies and the Bolshevik revolution in Russia and continuing through the coming of the New Deal, Britain's postwar election of a socialist government, and Communist penetrations into Eastern Europe and Asia, had been one of increased centralization of power.

With the two major political parties taking indistinguishable positions on the broad outlines of policy (with both accepting a welfare state at home and a containment stance abroad), Buckley dedicated his magazine to giving the public a choice of philosophies. For that to occur, the "liberal consensus" that characterized American politics in the postwar United States had to be first challenged and then, ultimately, dismantled. With his magazine now a reality, Buckley set out to use the weapon he had brought into being to attain his next objective, taking on the most powerful man in the world.

4

"Reading Dwight Eisenhower Out of the Conservative Movement"

Of all the presidents Buckley observed and assessed during his lifetime, he was most strident in his criticism of Dwight D. Eisenhower. He regarded the ex-General turned President as the opposite of the kind of conservative leader he wanted in the White House during the Cold War and in the aftermath of twenty years of Democratic activism on the domestic scene. Buckley hoped for a leader who would work to reverse inroads Communist forces had made in Europe and Asia in the aftermath of World War II and who would reduce the size and the reach of the federal government, whose powers had expanded exponentially since the 1930s. Throughout Eisenhower's time in office, Buckley gave the administration no quarter, whether the matter at hand was summitry with the USSR, economic policy, national defense, infrastructure, or civil rights. He considered Eisenhower's handling of patronage and intraparty affairs a Republican version of the clubhouse shenanigans that had characterized the Truman White House.

As Eisenhower's time in office wore on, Buckley continued in his role as activist, strategist, and tactician for a budding conservative movement. Causes that engulfed him in the 1950s included a spirited defense of Senator Joseph McCarthy's crusade against security risks in the U.S. government, protests against Nikita Khrushchev's visit to the United States in 1959, and founding the Young Americans for Freedom in 1960. Each of these actions placed Buckley in opposition to an administration that considered itself "conservative" and was thought of as such by much of the country, including American liberals. During the Eisenhower years, Buckley built up *National Review* and consolidated his hold over the nascent conservative movement.

Prior to Eisenhower's election as President, Buckley had two casual encounters with him, both friendly. In his letter thanking Ike, then President of Columbia University, for attending the *Yale Daily News* banquet in 1950, Buckley recalled his meeting with the General during his time in the U.S. Army: "I have long been a personal admirer of yours, from the day I met you as a young Second Lieutenant at Fort Sam Houston and you grabbed my hand before I had time to complete the traditional salute! I am, of course, deeply appreciative of your remarks to me after the dinner and shall always remember them in context of a person for whom I have such admiration."[1]

Three years after writing these words, Buckley had come to regard Eisenhower as the principal obstacle to the conservative cause. Eisenhower, with the help of multiple political operatives, had wrested the 1952 Republican presidential nomination away from Ohio Senator Robert A. Taft, Buckley's model of a conservative statesman. Buckley never forgave Eisenhower for that, even though Ike's support for NATO, which Taft had opposed, and other defense measures were more in tune with Buckley's views than were some of Taft's. Buckley disparaged the methods by which Eisenhower gained the nomination. "A good book needs to be done on the political assassination of Senator Robert A. Taft—by Republicans," Buckley declared four years into Ike's administration.[2] He declared the political machinations Ike's handlers had used to secure their man the presidential nomination worthy of Boss Hague or Harry Truman, two machine politicians he scorned.[3] Were this not enough, Eisenhower, once in office, worked to undermine another Buckley hero, Joseph McCarthy—a mortal sin in Buckley's book.

To Buckley's chagrin, as President, Eisenhower appeared in no hurry to reverse domestic policies he had criticized during his campaign. Commentators and GOP operatives saw the election of a Republican President a sufficient achievement in itself, considering that the party had been shut out of the White House for a generation. Eisenhower showed himself willing to continue New Deal and Fair Deal programs in exchange for a free hand from Congress in foreign affairs and defense policy. To intimates, Eisenhower confided that the record he established on domestic matters resulted neither from negligence, nor through inertia or lack of will, but from intent: "Should any political party attempt to abolish social security and eliminate labor laws and farm programs, you would not hear of that party again in our political history," he wrote his brother Edgar in 1954.[4]

The President suggested that those who argued otherwise were part of a "splinter group," which included H. L. Hunt and a few other Texas oil millionaires, politicians, and businessmen. He considered conservatives of their ilk numerically "negligible" and "politically stupid."[5] While Buckley hardly qualified as "politically stupid," he and his cohorts were certainly numerically "negligible." As commentator Michael Barone noted years later, what ran on the pages of *National Review* in the mid- to late 1950s carried little weight among policy makers and opinion leaders.[6] Conservative journalist Ralph de Toledano wrote Whittaker Chambers in January 1956 that conservative opinions carried about as far as Buckley's voice.[7] Nor did Buckley's movement command great intellectual respect. Liberal journalist Dwight Macdonald, who had lowered his opinion of Buckley in the years that had passed since the publication of *God and Man at Yale,* wrote that Buckley's new journal appealed to the "half-educated, half-successful provincials . . . who responded to Huey Long, Father Coughlin, and Senator McCarthy."[8]

Buckley and his fellow dissenters from the prevailing bipartisan liberal consensus took aim not only at Ike, but also at much of "big business," which considered itself both "conservative" and a natural ally of the administration. Buckley regarded the leadership and a good many members of the National Association of Manufacturers and the U.S. Chamber of Commerce stodgy and motivated primarily by self-interest. (As had his father, he opposed what later went by the name of "crony capitalism.") He and his fellow editors believed that during Eisenhower's first two years, when Republicans were in charge of both the executive and legislative branches of the federal government, Republicans had squandered an opportunity to reverse the centralization of power that had come to characterize domestic affairs. They were disappointed that Ike had settled for an armistice on the Korean peninsula rather than press ahead, as General Douglas MacArthur advised, for a united non-Communist Korea. To their dismay, Eisenhower and his Secretary of State John Foster Dulles appeared less eager to "roll back" Communist advances in Europe and Asia than Eisenhower indicated he would do in the course of his campaign.

In its premier issue, *National Review* noted the coincidence of its going to press on the very day Eisenhower left the hospital, where he had been recuperating from a major heart attack. Its very first editorial promised that, while the magazine would be "critical" of the administration, sometimes sharply so, no amount of disagreement would lessen its wish for the personal well-being and happiness of the man who was elected "head of our country and its government."[9]

In the same issue *National Review* also ran a piece by Senate Republican leader and presidential aspirant William F. Knowland, who voiced skepticism about summitry. His principal argument was that with pressures on both sides to make concessions at these meetings, the results would work to the West's disadvantage.[10] (Eisenhower hoped that summits with his Soviet counterparts would reduce world tensions.) When the Soviets rejected Eisenhower's proposal at a Geneva summit that the two nations agree to mutual inspections of their nuclear stockpiles ("open skies"), Buckley declared that American statesmen were "gluttons" for punishment. "One wink from a Soviet diplomat," he wrote, "and they are ready to rush halfway across the world to get kicked in the teeth."[11] With the mainstream press praising Ike for having tried to reach an agreement, *National Review* expressed the wish that Eisenhower had learned his lesson.

Buckley saw Eisenhower's attempt to portray himself as a "man above party" as ill-disguised "Caesarism."[12] He declared the Eisenhower program "undirected by principle, unchained to any coherent idea as to the nature of man and society, and uncommitted to any estimate of the nature or potential of the enemy."[13] He pronounced the President "a good man" who saw himself neither as an "adventurer," nor as a "redeemer cocksure of his afflatus."[14] By Buckley's lights, Ike's major fault was his "failure to treat the armed services as though they might some day come in handy."[15] He and his colleagues saw the administration's conciliatory rhetoric as evidence of appeasement.

Subsequent historical reevaluations of the Eisenhower presidency suggest that Buckley and his colleagues not only were wrong in their assessment of Eisenhower's strategy and intentions, but made the mistake of taking the thirty-fourth President at face value. Having invested heavily in nuclear deterrence (a policy Buckley firmly advocated after hearing Churchill expound on this topic in 1949) and having undertaken extensive surveillance of Soviet intelligence and military maneuvers, which conservatives also favored, Ike could well afford to don the robes of peacemaker.[16] He intervened in the internal affairs of other nations only when he felt U.S. interests were at stake, another approach Buckley favored. Eisenhower used this very rationale for justifying U.S.-sanctioned coups in Iran, Guatemala, and Congo, for sending U.S. forces to Lebanon to forestall a Soviet occupation, and for pledging to defend islands off the Chinese coast in the event of attacks by the People's Republic of China. (*National Review* supported all of these measures.) Unlike Will Buckley's nemesis Woodrow Wilson, Ike did not use American military power to further abstract goals.

In one respect, some of the criticisms Buckley levied against Eisenhower ran parallel to those some of his liberal counterparts raised at the time. Both camps regarded Eisenhower as a leader of limited intellect and vision. Both saw him as a "do-nothing" President, under whose watch the nation drifted into complacency. Liberals voiced disappointment that Ike proved less of an activist than Roosevelt and Truman. It took them decades to appreciate the positive impact, economic and otherwise, that the interstate highway system, the National

Defense Education Act, and the Defense Advanced Research Projects Agency (DARPA) had on the nation's future. *National Review* paid little attention to DARPA and considered the other two undertakings "boondoggles."

American liberals, while they came to champion Eisenhower's warning in his farewell address about the dangers of the "military-industrial complex" and would cite it in their opposition to U.S. intervention in Vietnam, Iraq, and elsewhere, largely ignored Ike's warning at the time he delivered it. Conservatives, while they castigated Eisenhower for not pressing to repeal programs he inherited, were slow to comprehend the President's conservative impulses on spending or the respect he showed federalism, providing "states' rights" were not evoked as pretexts to defy federal court orders mandating desegregation. The Hungarian uprising against Soviet domination in 1956 and the U.S. response to it occasioned *National Review*'s most bitter condemnation of the administration as well as an ideological split among some of its editors. In part, the internal debate over what policy the United States should adopt with regard to Eastern Europe was a continuation of an ongoing discussion in foreign policy circles over whether Khrushchev's 1956 denunciation of the "Stalinist terror" signaled an actual shift in Soviet intentions and behavior.[17] Burnham, the most "realpolitik" of the group, believed that it did. Buckley, Meyer, and Schlamm were skeptical.

With regard to Hungary, Buckley believed that the United States, through its propaganda broadcasts abroad, had given dissidents cause to think that the West would come to their assistance if they rose up against the USSR. He was embittered that once they had risen up, the United States stood idly by. *National Review* coupled its attacks upon the administration's passive response to the events in Hungary with its condemnation of two NATO allies (the United Kingdom and France) for taking military action together with Israel after Egyptian President Gamal Abdel Nasser seized control of the Suez Canal and closed it to world shipping. Buckley found the very prospect of an American President instructing the U.S. Ambassador to the United Nations to work with his Soviet counterpart in drafting a resolution that condemned the United Kingdom, France, and Israel appalling.

As he assessed how events had played out in Hungary, Burnham recommended that the United States support the neutralization of Soviet satellites in Eastern Europe in exchange for the USSR withdrawing its troops from the region. He envisioned an eventual breakup of the Soviet empire and thought that when this happened, the future former "satellites" would be able to sustain themselves after a period of time of having been allowed a greater say over their internal affairs. Burnham set forth his views in a piece for the magazine entitled

"Containment or Liberation."[18] His colleagues Buckley, Schlamm, La Follette, Meyer, and Bozell disagreed with this approach. All continued to favor liberation, presumably by military means.

Schlamm threatened to resign if Buckley published Burnham's piece. While Buckley disagreed with Burnham's principal recommendation (he would never completely embrace his colleague's realpolitik worldview), his respect for Burnham's way of thinking, which entailed the weighing of evidence, consideration of policy alternatives, and proportional responses to acts of aggression, was growing. Burnham was moving in a direction in which Buckley's intellectual mentor Whittaker Chambers was also traveling. In 1959, Chambers put to Buckley a simple proposition he urged him to take to heart: that if *National Review* favored the United States going to war against the USSR (whether as a preventive action or to liberate Eastern European nations), it should say so in print and allow the American people to consider its recommendation.[19]

Much as he disagreed with the administration's policies and questioned its competence, Buckley gave the President the benefit of one doubt. Eisenhower's team, he wrote, "may be drugged, immobilized, enchanted, but they would not willingly exchange freedom-and-war for subjugation and peace."[20] The danger, he said, lay in the administration's "invincible ignorance as to the intentions and resources of the enemy and a dangerous underestimation of the extrinsic value of the West for the freedom of other peoples."[21]

Buckley's decision to publish Burnham's recommendations with regard to the future of Eastern Europe intensified the ongoing conflict within *National Review*. After repeated quarrels with his colleagues, Schlamm took on a diminished role at the magazine and eventually departed. Although he had sided more with Schlamm than with Burnham in foreign policy matters at this juncture, Buckley concluded that Schlamm's open hostility toward Burnham exceeded the bounds of professionalism. He also came to trust Burnham personally and professionally more than he did Schlamm. Although Schlamm had initially suggested that Buckley take on the role of editor of the magazine the two had founded, Schlamm came to look upon the younger man more as a protégé than as his employer. Buckley's sisters Priscilla and Maureen, who functioned as their brother's eyes and ears when he was away—and often while he was present—may have helped persuade Buckley that Schlamm had become a disruptive force at the magazine.[22]

Schlamm's exit, combined with increased demands on Buckley's time, led Buckley to establish the new position of publisher. William Rusher, a former investigator with the Senate Internal Security Subcommittee and a seasoned New York State political operative, served in this role for the next two decades.

While not as libertarian as Schlamm, Rusher functioned as a philosophical counterweight to Burnham. He came to his post harboring an intense dislike of Vice President Richard Nixon, which stemmed from actions Nixon had taken, at Eisenhower's behest, to undermine Senator Joseph McCarthy among Republican conservatives.[23] Rusher would oppose a *National Review* endorsement of Nixon every time he ran for President.

As the election of 1956 approached, *National Review* was in no mood to endorse Eisenhower's reelection. In April of that year, Buckley lent his support to an attempt by former isolationist and Sears Chairman General Robert E. Wood and H. L. Hunt protégé Dan Smoot to mount a third-party challenge to Eisenhower's reelection. They hoped that, should the attempt gain traction, enough electoral votes might be drained away from Eisenhower to cost the President reelection.[24]

In October, Buckley published an exchange in *National Review* between Burnham and Schlamm (who would soon leave the magazine) under the heading "Should Conservatives Vote for Eisenhower-Nixon?" Burnham, arguing the affirmative, proclaimed Ike "marginally better" than the more liberal Democratic alternative, ex-Illinois Governor and 1952 Democratic presidential nominee Adlai Stevenson. Schlamm, taking the negative, declared that Eisenhower was the first Republican candidate to be elected a Democratic President.[25] In his own statement, entitled "Reflections on Election Eve," Buckley, like Burnham, conceded that Eisenhower, by conservative lights, was marginally better than his opponent, but not sufficiently so to merit the magazine's endorsement. His likened the situation facing voters to a choice between two masters: one would enslave the citizenry for ninety days, and the other for eighty-nine. He recommended that conservatives substitute "I *Prefer* Ike" for the slogan "I Like Ike."[26] *National Review* made no endorsement for President, and Buckley confided to friends that he had not voted for Eisenhower.[27]

On the domestic front, Buckley objected strenuously to the federal government's intruding into state and local affairs to protect the civil rights of African Americans. He and his colleagues opposed the Supreme Court's unanimous decision in *Brown v. Board of Education* on the grounds that it violated both states' rights and federalism. They failed to consider whether a state or local government, in denying millions of citizens, based on their race, the right to participate in the political process was itself a violation of the spirit of "home rule" or both the letter and the spirit of the U.S. Constitution. On top of their purported constitutional objections to the decision and subsequent efforts of presidents to enforce it, they rendered considerable harm to their own movement outside of the South and among opinion leaders of all persuasions when they opined that as the more "advanced" race, whites were entitled to govern.[28] (As will be shown in subsequent chapters, in time Buckley came to regret the stand he took in these editorials and changed his views, prompted in part by the increased violence unleashed by local citizens, often incited by race-baiting politicians he termed "welfare populists.")

At the outset of his second term, Eisenhower began to award civil rights a high priority. He instructed his Attorney General, Herbert Brownell Jr., to draw up legislation to safeguard them, placing an emphasis on voting rights. In opposition to the administration's proposals, Buckley family friend Senator Strom Thurmond (D-SC), a committed segregationist, mounted what became the longest filibuster in the history of the U.S. Senate. He spoke continuously for twenty-four hours and eighteen minutes in opposition to the 1957 civil rights bill.

Senate Majority Leader Lyndon B. Johnson, his eye cast toward the 1960 Democratic presidential nomination, in order to satisfy disparate factions within his party inserted an amendment allowing for jury trials for registrars charged with violating the act's provisions. (With jury rolls coming from lists of registered voters and with African Americans largely disenfranchised, the amendment all but assured that all-white juries would sit in judgment of those who violated federal law. Few expected such panels to convict offenders.)[29] The bill's passage, with Johnson's amendment affixed to it, enabled Johnson to assert to northern liberals that he had steered to passage the first civil rights bill in eighty years, while simultaneously reassuring southerners that the bill would have minimal impact. The measure passed the Senate 72–18 and the House 285–126.

Four days before Thurmond began his record-setting filibuster and a week before the Senate approved Johnson's jury amendment, *National Review* published an editorial Buckley wrote, entitled "Why the South Must Prevail." The piece put the magazine on record in favor of both legal segregation where it existed (in accordance with the "states' rights" principle) and the right of southern whites to discriminate against southern blacks, on the basis of their race. The editorial defended the right of whites to govern exclusively, even where they did not constitute a majority of the population in certain political jurisdictions. *National Review* justified its position on the grounds that whites were "the more advanced race," and as such were "entitled to rule."[30] Buckley, the author of the editorial, made no mention of the role southern whites had played, through the social and legal systems they had put into place, in keeping southern blacks from rising to the point where he—or their white neighbors—would consider them "advanced" and therefore eligible to participate in the region's governance. He went so far as to condone violence whites committed in order to perpetuate prevailing practices. "Sometimes the minority cannot prevail except by violence." Buckley wrote. Should a white community go this route, he urged that it first determine "whether the prevalence of its will is worth the terrible price."[31] (A decade later, after southern whites, often incited by political leaders, increasingly resorted to violence to repress African American aspirations, Buckley began to moderate his opinions and eventually changed them.)

In another editorial, Buckley concluded that as long as African Americans remained "backward" in education and in economic progress, southern whites had a right to "impose superior mores for whatever period it takes to affect a genuine cultural equality between the races." In defense of his position that whites, for the time being, remained the "more advanced race," Buckley pointed to the name a major civil rights organization, the National Association for the Advancement of Colored People, had adopted for itself as evidence that its founders considered its constituents "less advanced." Buckley advised southerners against using the "fact of Negro backwardness" as a pretext "to preserve the Negro as a servile class."[32] He offered no guidance as to how blacks might attain what he called "cultural equality," save for by the sufferance of the white population.

National Review's opposition to federal civil rights legislation put it at odds not only with self-proclaimed "modern Republicans" such as Eisenhower and Nixon (who termed Johnson's jury amendment "a vote against the right to vote"), but also with conservative Republicans whom the magazine supported editorially, such as Senate Minority Leader William Knowland, the bill's primary sponsor.[33] Barry Goldwater, who would replace Knowland (who lost his bid for reelection in 1958) as the conservatives' favorite in future Republican presidential nominations, also supported the 1957 bill, as he would another measure Eisenhower proposed in 1960. So did Everett Dirksen, who succeeded Knowland as Senate Republican Leader in 1959. In the Senate, forty-three of the forty-seven Republicans supported the final version of what became the Civil Rights Act of 1957. No Republican voted against it. In the House, Republicans supported it 167–19. (*National Review* remained opposed to it with and without Johnson's jury amendment, but voiced relief when the Texan's compromise won approval.)

The stand *National Review* took on the bill was an odd one for the leading journal of a movement that professed to believe in individual rights and personal liberty. Buckley and his colleagues did not question the appropriateness of government (in this case, state governments) depriving citizens of rights the U.S. Constitution afforded them (especially in the First, Fourteenth and Fifteenth Amendments). The magazine's editors awarded a higher priority to the prerogatives of state governments selected by only some of a state's eligible voters than they did to the civil liberties of people whose rights these local authorities had violated. Nor were they concerned that these bodies had excluded people from the political process on the basis of race. They also put their opposition to extending the powers of the federal government ahead of whatever concerns they had for individuals whose rights other layers of government were denying them.

Bozell recognized some of the contradictions in the magazine's expressed views. He thought it unwise for a conservative "journal of fact and opinion," which so often made the case for respect for institutions (including the courts) and respect for law, to give the impression that it sanctioned law breaking. He wrote in a dissenting essay that his colleagues had presumed that African Americans, if granted the vote, would necessarily use it to accelerate desegregation. (He was not persuaded that all African Americans opposed the prevailing social structures or would necessarily vote in a bloc to change them.) Bozell also thought it odd that conservatives, who advocated a "strict constructionist" interpretation of the Constitution, would sanction the willful disregard of the Fifteenth Amendment.[34]

Bozell also maintained that if a governing body decided to disenfranchise a large number of voters, it had to write the law in such a way that it applied to whites as well as blacks. In an editorial in the same issue as that in which Bozell's dissent appeared, Buckley, taking the southern point of view, asserted that many in the region considered the Fourteenth and Fifteenth Amendments "inorganic accretions" to the original Constitution in that citizens of states that had seceded had agreed to them under coercion in exchange for the restoration of their rights to citizenship and their states attaining readmission to the Union.[35]

While he allowed his brother-in-law to press his case up to a point, Buckley's views continued to run parallel to those of his father. Months before Buckley's editorial "Why the South Must Prevail" ran in the magazine, Will Buckley wrote Thurmond that Bill "is for segregation and backs it in every issue."[36] In his editorial of "clarification," Buckley revealed that the suspicions he already harbored about the merits of democracy in general played a role in his decision to oppose the expansion of voting rights. He proposed as an alternative to disenfranchising all African Americans on account of their race that all the states disenfranchise the uneducated of all races. He saw no reason to confine such practices to the South. In Buckley's view, too many ignorant people were being allowed to vote elsewhere.[37]

As he contemplated whether and how to extend or restrict voting rights and to whom, Buckley restated views he had advanced while a student at Millbrook.

He had then lamented that "the ballot of an unintelligent, uneducated, thoughtless voter" was allowed to counteract the vote of an intelligent, educated person who could carefully distinguish among the different candidates. "The red-neck vote, dominated by primitive and earthy passions; and the big city vote, dominated by special interest manipulations, are hardly contributions to faith in the democratic system," he now argued. Buckley feared that the exponential expansion of African American voters in the South would lead to a situation in which an embittered and long-suppressed population would use the ballot "as an instrument of vengeance" and that whites would react to the transformation of southern life with violence.[38] (He would later rejoice in print and in speeches that his fears had not come to pass.)

In the fall of 1957, Governor Orval Faubus, in defiance of a court order to integrate Little Rock Central High School, ordered the Arkansas National Guard to block nine African American students from entering the school. In response, Eisenhower nationalized the state's guard and sent one thousand paratroopers with the 101st Airborne Division to assure the students' admission in the face of an angry mob. *National Review* was more critical of Eisenhower's actions than it was of the Governor's. While it conceded the President's right to enforce the law and did not question the courts' right to compel compliance with court orders, it accused the President of adopting a course calculated to inflame passions to the maximum so as to create the very "mob rule" that necessitated the "imposition of bayonets." Eisenhower, "the darling of the moderates," it concluded, had "delivered himself into the hands of the extremists."[39]

While it opposed federal intervention to dismantle segregation, *National Review* supported the right of local residents to withhold their patronage from public or private concerns that discriminated against them. During the Montgomery bus boycott, it urged the city to accommodate African American riders either by integrating its transit system or by allowing African Americans to operate a separate bus line. "It is one thing to take the position that the government has not the power to compel integration; it is another to take the position that Negroes be compelled to support a legally constructed monopoly," Buckley wrote.[40]

As the year 1957 progressed, Buckley upped his criticisms of Eisenhower, who, he maintained, lacked the most basic of communications skills and vision that were inherent requirements of the position he held. He took Ike at his word when the President said he would be "hard pressed" to refute a Soviet official's assertion that Communism was an economic system rooted in idealism whereas capitalism thrived on greed.[41] He did not allow for the possibility that Ike intended through this remark to encourage his countrymen and women to be less conspicuous in their consumption and to challenge his own administration to do a better job in making America's case to the rest of the world.

Buckley surmised that behind the image of amateurism and affability Ike presented to the world resided an insatiable ambition. He shared his friend Murray Kempton's view that Eisenhower's "indifference to practical matters was one of the most successful dissimulations in political history."[42] This realization caused Buckley to resent Eisenhower all the more because, as President, Ike had not employed his political skills to advance even the most elementary conservative principles or invest any of his personal popularity to persuade the public of their value. "There never was," he wrote after Ike had left office, "in all American history, a more successfully self-serving politician." He added, "Eisenhower did nothing whatever for the Republican Party; nothing to develop a Republican philosophy of government; nothing to catalyze a meaty American conservatism. But he was unswervingly successful himself. He never went after anything involving himself that he did not get."[43]

Had Eisenhower been willing to make the conservatives' case, Buckley would still have found him wanting because of the President's (intentional or otherwise) rhetorical deficiencies. Buckley wrote that Eisenhower had the capacity to turn virtually any subject into a "syntactical jungle in which every ray of light, every breath of air" was "choked out."[44] Looking across the political divide, Buckley took stylistic inspiration from Adlai Stevenson, Eisenhower's Democratic opponent in 1952 and 1956. He admired Stevenson's ability to "verbalize an innate intelligence, idealism, and wit" in ways that brought credit to him and his country. Stevenson, Buckley declared, was "the genuine article."[45]

Buckley was particularly taken with Stevenson's capacity to draw to his side the best talent available in the rising generation of American liberals. "They all ghosted for him at one time or another," he observed.[46] In contrast, Buckley reflected that Eisenhower surrounded himself with a "battery of sycophantic (and opportunistic) big businessmen with whom he loved to while away the hours."[47] Buckley envisioned a time when a leading conservative statesman could reach out to a network of articulate and idealistic conservatives every bit as bright as Stevenson's liberals. He spent two decades building a fraternity of such individuals, upon whom Ronald Reagan would eventually draw.

In 1964, Buckley used the passing of General Douglas MacArthur, whom he called "the last of the great Americans," as the occasion to lament his country's forsaking a leader as colorful, eloquent, and bold as MacArthur in favor of a "mediocrity" such as Eisenhower. This he attributed to the unimaginative and "conservative nature" of the American people. In this sense, Buckley used the word *conservative* to convey excessive prudence, caution, and commitment to the status quo. "Temperamentally, I am not of that breed," he told *Time* magazine, referring to the "conservatism" so often associated not only with Eisenhower but also with the traditional heads of big business.[48]

Buckley saw Tammany-style politics at play in the manner in which the Eisenhower Justice Department handled its investigation of Harlem Congressman Adam Clayton Powell (D-NY) on corruption charges. After investigating Powell for months, the government terminated its probe five days before Powell crossed party lines and endorsed Eisenhower for reelection. Acting on a tip from an assistant U.S Attorney, who had been ordered off the case, that the Justice Department was not going to prosecute Powell, Buckley ran an exposé of Powell's misdeeds and of the administration's reluctance to take action against him.[49]

A grand juror read the piece, requested a meeting with Buckley, and asked that the article be shared with his fellow jurists. The juror informed Buckley that he and his colleagues intended to instruct U.S. Attorney Paul W. Williams that, if he did not prosecute Powell based on evidence his office had compiled, they would pursue the matter on their own. After subpoenaing Buckley to ascertain why he had contacted jurors, Williams declined to charge Buckley with jury tampering. Powell was indicted on May 8, 1958. (The Powell case would drag on for years.)

As he simultaneously took on both the liberal intellectuals and a Republican administration, Buckley paid close attention to changing currents within the conservative movement. In the 1950s, militant "individualist" Ayn Rand was emerging as a competitor to Buckley in the affection of young conservative activists and intellectuals. Buckley's match in intellect and wit, Rand advanced a vision of the conservative movement that was substantially different from his. Born in Russia in 1905, Rand left her native land for the United States in 1926. She gravitated to Hollywood and performed a variety of jobs at its studios, ranging from playing as an extra to screenwriting to directing and working the costume departments.

A committed anti-Communist, Rand dabbled in Republican and conservative politics. Her third novel, *The Fountainhead,* published in 1943, sold more than four hundred thousand copies in its first year in print. She wrote the screenplay for the 1948 movie of *The Fountainhead,* which starred Gary Cooper and Patricia Neal. Not long afterward, Rand moved to New York and gathered about her a committed band of acolytes who called themselves "the Collective." Rand and Buckley met in 1954. He developed an instant aversion to her when—in what Buckley's friend Wilfred Sheed called "the perfect icebreaker"—Rand told Buckley that he was too intelligent to believe in God.[50] Taking umbrage at the remark, Buckley took to sending her postcards bearing Latin inscriptions, many with religious messages.

The permanent rupture between them occurred three years later after Buckley ran a review of Rand's 1957 novel *Atlas Shrugged.* He had commissioned Whittaker Chambers to write the piece, entitled "Big Sister Is Watching." Chambers tore into Rand's philosophy: its unabashed atheism, its espousal of naked self-interest as the highest possible virtue, and its embrace of the acquisition of wealth for its own sake. "Randian man like Marxian man is made the center of a godless world," Chambers wrote. If the Communists sought to replace constitutional checks and balances and other institutional checks in order to ram through their materialistic, collectivist program, followers of Rand, he suggested, would do the same, while allowing nothing but self-interest to determine societal actions.[51]

Chambers saw the struggle Rand presented between the Children of Light (the rich and successful) and the Children of Darkness ("looters") and the subordination of the latter to the former as the reinstitution of the very fascism the Allies had defeated in 1945. Having disposed of Rand's ideology as narcissistic, materialist, and hedonistic, Chambers turned to her writing style: "Over a lifetime of reading, I can recall no other book in which a tone of overriding arrogance was so implacably sustained. Its shrillness is without reprieve. Its dogmatism is without appeal."[52]

Rand's response was succinct and personal. "What would you expect from an ex-communist writing in Buckley's Catholic magazine?" she inquired.[53] She never talked to Buckley again and made it a point to absent herself from receptions and events she suspected he might attend. Upon Rand's death in 1981, Buckley paid tribute to her eloquence and anti-statist views. "If only she had left it at that," he added, but "no. . . . She had to declare that God did not exist, that altruism was despicable, that only self-interest is good and noble. She risked, in fact, giving to capitalism that bad name its enemies have done so well in giving it; and that is a pity."[54] After he received more than one hundred letters in response, most of them hostile, Buckley recorded that Rand's followers "cannot stand it that some people should be as stern with Miss Rand as Miss Rand was stern with them."[55] In Buckley's novel *Getting It Right* (2003), a memoir of the conservative movement in its youth, when its youthful followers flocked to competing organizations, Rand appears as a character.

Also in the 1950s, Buckley, perhaps unintentionally, fired the opening salvo in what would become a major battle between him and Robert Welch, founder of the John Birch Society. Buckley had been considerably moved by Boris

Pasternak's novel *Doctor Zhivago*—especially at the vivid and depressing glimpse it provided into Communist society in the aftermath of the 1917 Bolshevik revolution. He was also impressed by how CIA operatives, after the book had been published in the West, with help from a member of the Italian Communist Party, managed to print the novel in its original language, smuggle it back into the USSR, and disseminate it throughout the country.[56] Buckley considered this action among the CIA's major ideological victories during the Cold War.

The Soviet government all but assured Pasternak a wide following when it exerted strong pressure on him not to accept the Nobel Prize in Literature in 1958 he had been awarded. None of this impressed Welch, who considered the book a fraud. In the February 1959 edition of *American Opinion*, the primary publication of the John Birch Society, Welch argued in an unsigned piece that the Soviets wanted the West to think the novel the work of a dissident, whereas it was really an anti-capitalist book the Soviets wanted to foist upon the West.[57] Buckley, having already run a review of the book by John Chamberlain the previous September, subsequently published a review essay of it by Eugene Lyons, a former Communist who had spent years studying the Soviet system.[58] Buckley advised Welch in advance that he would be running Lyons's piece and suggested that "a little friendly controversy" among conservatives would not be a bad thing.[59] Welch professed not to mind.

However, after Lyons's piece ran, Welch let Buckley know, through others, that the head of the JBS did not view kindly *National Review*'s taking issue with his opinion of the book. Writer and editor Medford Evans, who appeared on *National Review*'s masthead and belonged to the John Birch Society, advised Buckley not to criticize what ran in other conservative periodicals except when its authors made grievous errors.[60] In the May 1959 issue of *American Opinion*, Welch, in a signed letter to his readers, complained of the ingratitude a conservative to whom he had extended generosity had shown him.[61] (Welch was clearly referring to Buckley. The JBS founder had made two $1,000 contributions to *National Review*, one in 1955 and one in 1957.) Welch wrote Buckley, criticizing him for having recommended that Harvard academician Henry A. Kissinger be named to a panel to assess the effectiveness of Radio Free Europe. He informed Buckley that he considered Kissinger a committed Communist and part of an establishment that had "sold the United States out."[62]

When Eisenhower announced that Soviet Premier Nikita Khrushchev would pay an official visit to the United States in September 1959, Buckley organized a national protest. Khrushchev, he noted, would be arriving on

American shores less than three years after the Kremlin had suppressed the Hungarian uprising. Eisenhower's hospitality to the man to whom Buckley referred as the "Butcher of Budapest," he argued, would bestow undeserved "legitimacy" on the Soviet regime. Bumper stickers proclaiming "Khrushchev not welcome here," offered for sale by *National Review*, began appearing all across the country.[63] At a press conference, Buckley pledged to dye the Hudson River red the day Khrushchev arrived in commemoration of the blood shed by Communism's victims. He announced the formation of the Committee Against Summit Entanglements to coordinate nationwide demonstrations. Under the direction of Rusher and public relations guru Marvin Liebman, the group held a protest rally at New York City's Carnegie Hall.

Before an audience of twenty-five hundred, Buckley said that American public support for the visit, if it existed, signaled the nation's declining morale. He lambasted New York City's Mayor Robert F. Wagner Jr. for welcoming Khrushchev to the city, an honor he had denied King Ibn Saud of Saudi Arabia when he had visited New York. On that prior occasion, Wagner had cited the Saudi government's discrimination against Jews as his reason for the snub. Khrushchev, Buckley said, "not only discriminates against Jews, he kills them."[64] (This was a reference to Soviet mistreatment of Jews who sought to practice their religion openly or emigrate.) He noted that the Soviet leader, who headed an atheistic state, also persecuted Catholics and Protestants, as he did all dissidents irrespective of religion. Turning his attention to Eisenhower, Buckley voiced outrage that the very administration that had banned Senator McCarthy from official functions would hold a state dinner for the Soviet leader.

Whittaker Chambers, who joined the masthead of *National Review* in 1957, disapproved of how Buckley was responding to Khrushchev's visit. He warned that through their bellicose rhetoric, Buckley and his colleagues had lowered their prospects of being taken seriously by both the public and opinion leaders. "Russia go home," he complained, did not constitute a coherent policy.[65] In late September 1959, Chambers resigned from *National Review*.

His differences of opinion with Buckley and his deteriorating health were certainly factors that contributed to this decision. He was also taking into account something else. Chambers surmised that Buckley and his cohorts would seek to frustrate Richard Nixon's hopes of succeeding Eisenhower as President in 1960. While a freshman Congressman on the House Un-American Activities Committee, Nixon had stood by Chambers after he had accused State Department official Alger Hiss of having been a Communist spy. Most of the political establishment of both parties had rallied behind Hiss. But for Nixon's support, Chambers concluded, he would have been ruined. He would not be part of any enterprise that sought to frustrate the political advancement of his primary defender.[66]

Throughout the 1950s, as Buckley's friendship with Chambers blossomed, Chambers remained in frequent touch with Nixon, often acting as a mentor to the Vice President. John Chamberlain wrote that Nixon referred to Chambers as "Uncle Whit."[67] Hopeful that Buckley might at least keep an open mind about Nixon, Chambers and Ralph de Toledano, a journalist on good terms with Nixon and a friend of Buckley's, arranged for a meeting between Nixon and Buckley in 1957. Nixon was certainly aware of *National Review*'s criticisms of the administration. His files contain a marked-up copy of a scathing piece Buckley wrote entitled "The Tranquil World of Dwight D. Eisenhower," in which he accused the President of not understanding the nature of the Communist threat and called on Republicans and conservatives to repudiate Eisenhower and his legacy.[68]

In their hour together, Nixon and Buckley discussed Cold War strategy, national politics, and the controversy surrounding the lifting of security clearances to Los Alamos scientist J. Robert Oppenheimer, purportedly because of his leftist political affiliations and leanings. "Before seeing you," Buckley wrote Nixon afterward, "I told Whittaker Chambers it was not likely that I would fail to be impressed by someone who had impressed him; and the unlikely did not happen."[69] He made reference to Nixon's remark at the end of their meeting that those in the center and those on the right needed to band together. Buckley said that, while he agreed, he thought that a "little tension between the tablet-keepers and the governors is good for both."[70] Buckley was never one to gloss over differences with acquaintances, least of all with a prospective President of the United States.

As he had already advised Nixon, Chambers counseled Buckley to adopt what he called the "Beaconsfield position" in domestic and international affairs. The doctrine took its name from British Prime Minister Benjamin Disraeli (later the Earl of Beaconsfield), who had repositioned the Conservative Party from the champion of the aristocracy to a voice for the aspirations of British workers. (Historians refer to this phenomenon as "Tory Democracy.") Disraeli, after extending the franchise (traditionally a Liberal Party position), persuaded newly enfranchised voters to back the Conservatives and their imperialist ventures. Chambers urged Buckley and his colleagues to make their peace with the New Deal (as Eisenhower had done) so that they might forge a majority coalition behind policies to check Soviet ambitions. "To live is to maneuver," Chambers instructed Buckley.[71]

Buckley took Chambers's resignation especially hard. Chambers, he later observed, had been the only person to quit the editorial board of *National Review* because he could no longer live within its ideological compass.[72] Unprepared to follow Chambers's strategic advice when he first received it, Buckley showed signs of having embraced much of what Chambers had pressed upon him by the time he published his next book.

In *Up from Liberalism* (1959), Buckley followed up on an idea he had wanted to pursue since his days at the *American Mercury*. He took as his theme how liberal intellectuals established and maintained a monopoly over so much of intellectual opinion and political commentary in the United States. Buckley's choice of title had been inspired by Booker T. Washington's autobiography, *Up from Slavery*. Buckley began by identifying leading "pillars" of the liberal establishment: Eleanor Roosevelt, Arthur M. Schlesinger Jr., United Auto Workers President Walter Reuther, journalists James Wechsler, Richard Rovere, and Edward R. Murrow, current and past elected officials such as Chester Bowles, Hubert Humphrey, Adlai Stevenson, and W. Averell Harriman, and the communication arteries through which they and their supporters disseminated their message—the *New Republic*, the *Washington Post*, the *Saint Louis Post-Dispatch*, the *Minneapolis Tribune*, and "most of the *New York Times* and all of the *New York Post*."[73]

Those in this establishment, Buckley said, shared common premises and attitudes, displayed common reactions, enthusiasms, and aversions, and demonstrated an "empirical solidarity." They tended to believe that human beings were perfectible, social progress predictable, truths transitory and empirically determined; that governments could be put at the service of scientific principles; and that equality in condition was both desirable and attainable through state power. In pursuing their ends, Buckley wrote, they were prone to justify their positions through emotion rather than reason. Following Eleanor Roosevelt "in search of irrationality," he observed, was like "following a burning fuse in search of an explosive; one never has to wait long." Liberals, Buckley wrote, were "obsessed" with procedure and placed unwarranted faith in the power of democracy to determine "truths" around which societies should be organized. Buckley made clear that he did not regard democracy as either an absolute or an end in itself. "Democracy of universal suffrage," he declared, "is not a bad form of government; it simply is not a good form of government."[74]

Late in the book, Buckley offered reasons why conservatives had had little success at persuading a majority of the public to go along with their ideas. He offered two possible explanations: (1) that repeated conservative prophesies that economic catastrophes would follow the enactment of liberal agendas had not come to pass, and (2) that conservatives had failed to accommodate themselves to the expectations and values of the masses.[75] While he continued to criticize New Deal programs, for the first time Buckley seemed prepared to accept them until the public showed itself ready to consider alternatives. In defense of this position, which Chambers had urged upon him, Buckley referenced British commentator Peregrine Worsthorne's observation that the welfare state had advanced at least one conservative value: reducing by some degree grievances and class warfare that Communists had traditionally exploited. (Buckley had come to concede part of an argument that "vital centrists" such as Schlesinger and Viereck had been making for some time and for which he had previously shown little use.)

Buckley's willingness to distinguish between immediate objectives and long-range ones signified a major change in his thinking and approach. In their campaigns, neither Buckley nor his brother James argued for an immediate repeal of New Deal entitlements. Had they done so, they would have blunted their appeal to working-class New Yorkers (uniformed personnel, socially conservative union members) and others who supported their broader message with regard to anti-Communism and social and tax policy. Ronald Reagan followed this same approach. Eleven months into Reagan's governorship, Buckley proclaimed him the very sort of conservative statesman Chambers had envisioned.[76]

Buckley's liberal critics discerned a change in his tactics. Arthur M. Schlesinger Jr., in his review of *Up from Liberalism*, suggested that Buckley cease reading liberal writings lest they rub off.[77] Although Buckley came around to Chambers's way of thinking with regard to suborning his anti–New Deal impulses to his more immediate goal of curbing the spread of Communism, he failed to warm to Chambers's other pupil, Richard Nixon, who was doing likewise. Other factors were at work that precluded such a coalescing, at least during the 1960 election.

In the run-up to the 1960 Republican National Convention, Chambers confided to Buckley that he had met with Nixon and come away pessimistic about his prospects. Chambers did not sense he had been in the company of "a vital man" bursting with energy and ideas. He revealed that he and Nixon had little to say to each other. Chambers confessed feeling "dismay," even "pity," as he watched Nixon contemplate the "awful burden" he sought to take on. He prophetically speculated about the impact defeat might have on the Vice President.[78] Buckley, for his part, was not about to make Nixon's path to the presidency any easier.

As he worked to shore up his nomination, Nixon met with little opposition from his right flank. He had, however, grown increasingly concerned about a possible challenge to his nomination from his left, in the person of Nelson Rockefeller. On the eve of the Republican National Convention, Nixon flew to New York to resolve differences he and Rockefeller had over the party platform. Rockefeller demanded a stronger civil rights plank and increased defense and other spending. Rockefeller had been using his alleged disappointment with the platform as a pretext for a possible quest for the nomination. Finding language on defense that both sides could live with proved especially challenging for Nixon, given that the Democratic Party's presidential nominee, John F. Kennedy, had already charged that, under Eisenhower, a "missile gap" had developed between the United States and the Soviet Union, and in the latter's favor. Nevertheless, Nixon, Rockefeller, and Eisenhower came to terms.

Angered that Nixon had taken them for granted, conservatives failed to note, or even notice, that on defense, Rockefeller was pushing Nixon in the same direction they had been, and well to the right of Eisenhower. In his best-selling book, *The Conscience of a Conservative* (1960), which Bozell ghosted, Barry Goldwater called for keeping the nation's "defensive and offensive military forces superior to the attacking power of any potential aggressor or aggressors, regardless of the costs in dollars and manpower."[79] Yet when Goldwater learned of the Nixon-Rockefeller accord, he denounced it as the "American Munich."[80] In the statement Rockefeller released to the press after his meeting with Nixon, he said that the platform now called for massive arms buildups, technological upgrades of weapon systems, and a powerful "second-strike capacity" (a nuclear retaliatory power capable of surviving surprise attack and inflicting devastating punishment on an aggressor).[81] (Years later, Buckley would point to these recommendations in support of his recommendation of Rockefeller for a high national security or defense post.)

Nixon antagonized party conservatives a second time when he chose as his vice presidential running mate United Nations Ambassador Henry Cabot Lodge—a key architect of the strategy Eisenhower used to defeat Taft for the presidential nomination, a critic of Joseph McCarthy, and, most recently, Khrushchev's official escort as he toured the United States. In 1952, McGeorge Bundy, mindful of Lodge's acceptability in liberal circles, discouraged Congressman John F. Kennedy from opposing the incumbent Senator in the 1952 Massachusetts senatorial election.[82] In the course of that campaign Buckley witnessed the formation of a tacit alliance between McCarthy and the Kennedy forces at Lodge's expense.

In Buckley's presence, McCarthy, while a houseguest of Buckley's, received a telephone call from national Republican operatives beseeching him to campaign for Lodge in Boston. McCarthy said he would comply if Lodge personally and publicly made the request. He confided to Buckley that Lodge, fearful of losing the "Harvard vote," would not do as McCarthy asked.[83] He proved correct. McCarthy wanted to stay away. Joseph P. Kennedy was a personal friend and generous donor of his, as was Will Buckley. McCarthy had befriended JFK when both men served in the Solomon Islands during World War II, and the two resumed their friendship after both began serving in Congress. McCarthy had dated two of Kennedy's sisters. As McCarthy launched his investigations, he retained Kennedy's brother Robert as Assistant Counsel to the U.S. Senate Permanent Subcommittee on Investigations.

Both McCarthy and Buckley believed that a McCarthy appearance on Lodge's behalf might improve the incumbent Senator's showing among staunchly anti-Communist Irish Catholic voters, most of whom were Democrats. In his reelection campaign, Lodge met resistance from some conservative Republicans angry over the role he had played months earlier in ending Taft's presidential prospects. To assure that those wounds would not heal, Joseph P. Kennedy recruited a former Taft campaign staffer to direct the Independents for Kennedy Committee. The *New Bedford Standard Times*, whose publisher had been a strident Taft supporter, endorsed Kennedy.[84] As the Kennedy-Nixon contest unfolded, Buckley kept in the back of his mind the appeal Kennedy had had to some McCarthy and Taft enthusiasts and the hostility some of them held toward Nixon, who, as part of Eisenhower's camp, had worked against both of these conservative icons.

In the final tally, JFK defeated Lodge in 1952 by 70,000 votes, while Eisenhower defeated Stevenson in Massachusetts by 109,800 votes. Once in the Senate, Kennedy took care to distance himself from the more liberal elements of his party. In the hospital when the Senate voted to censure McCarthy, Kennedy never declared how he would have voted had he been present. That he selected Robert A. Taft as one of the eight Senators profiled in his 1956 Pulitzer Prize–winning book did not escape the conservatives' notice.[85] With Nixon having antagonized some conservatives and Kennedy presenting himself as less ideologically offensive to them than other Democrats, conservatives like Buckley, a consistent critic of the outgoing Eisenhower administration, reasoned that they had nothing to lose by keeping their distance from Nixon in 1960.

Unenthusiastic about the Nixon-Lodge ticket, Buckley found an outlet for his political talents in 1960 outside the presidential campaign. On September

11, 1960, weeks after the Republican National Convention had adjourned, Buckley hosted at his family homestead in Sharon a gathering of ninety conservative college students and recent graduates. Most were unenthusiastic about Nixon because of the accommodations he had made to party moderates and liberals and unimpressed at the tone of his campaign, in which he seemed to blur rather than accentuate his policy differences with Kennedy. Douglas Caddy of Georgetown University and David Francke of George Washington University helped organize the event, with a heavy assist from publicist Marvin Liebman.

The group that gathered at Sharon became the Young Americans for Freedom (YAF). Attendees signed and released a declaration of principles that became known as the Sharon Statement. Written by the twenty-six-year-old journalist M. Stanton Evans and edited by Buckley, the statement echoed ideas Buckley had been proclaiming for almost a decade, first in *God and Man at Yale* and again in *McCarthy and His Enemies* and *Up from Liberalism*, in the pages of *National Review*, and in multiple public forums. Its signers acknowledged the salience of the Judeo-Christian tradition and its impact upon the American founding and pledged to work actively against Communism. Buckley nostalgically recaptured the Sharon assemblage in his novel *Getting It Right* (2003).

In its first year of operation, YAF boasted a membership of nearly three thousand, spread across one hundred campuses.[86] Liebman attributed its influence not to its numbers but to public and media perceptions of its strength.[87] Buckley enthusiastically announced YAF's founding in *National Review*: "A new organization was born last week and just possibly it will influence the political future of this country, as why should it not, considering that its membership is young, intelligent, articulate and determined, its principles enduring, its aim to translate these principles into political action in a world which has lost its moorings, and is looking about for them desperately?"[88] He predicted a steady rise in conservative sentiment on college campuses.

National Review declined to endorse a presidential candidate in 1960. Conservatives, Buckley wrote, had a "higher political mission than merely electing Republican candidates."[89] He and Meyer believed that the principal function conservatives had come to play in national elections was to determine which of two liberals prevailed at the polls.[90] "Illusions of liberalism" Buckley advised readers, "dominate Mr. Kennedy and influence Mr. Nixon."[91] He saw Nixon as less the leader of the GOP than as the "amalgamator" of all the forces that composed it. A Nixon defeat, he suggested, would provide conservatives with the hope of developing "in the next four years a true and effective opposition to the Left-Democratic President."[92]

He saw an inspiring precedent in the manner in which Taft had positioned himself as opposition leader to Truman after the Republicans took control of Congress in 1946. For a time, Taft rallied conservatives in both parties to block some of Truman's more liberal proposals and, on occasion, was able to pass Republican initiatives over Truman's veto. Such a coalescing of conservatives, Buckley insisted, could occur only once Eisenhower, whom many still regarded as "conservative," had left office. "We actually increase our leverage," Buckley told a friend, "by refusing to join the parade."[93]

Not all of Buckley's colleagues at *National Review* agreed with this assessment. Burnham, who had argued for endorsing Nixon, was less worried about a possible Nixon loss than he was about the kind of administration Kennedy would assemble. Supporting Kennedy, Burnham wrote Buckley, "are virtually all the forces, groups, tendencies and individuals that *National Review* is not merely against, but recognizes as its primary targets."[94] (He was, of course, thinking of the Americans for Democratic Action, organized labor, and intellectuals like Bundy, Schlesinger, and Galbraith.)

Burnham considered the difference in the composition of the entourages that surrounded the two candidates ample reason for conservatives to rally behind Nixon. In 1956, he pointed out, conservatives had had the luxury of not having to state a preference, because all knew that Eisenhower would win. With the 1960 election expected to be exceedingly close, he thought that conservatives would be able to exercise leverage on a freshly elected Nixon administration. They might even have sway over the new administration, pulling it in a more rightward direction than it might have followed had they withheld their support. Their sitting out the election could indeed determine the result, he warned, but not in a way that would ultimately work in their favor.

Buckley continued his attacks on the retiring President. Ike, he said, was a "good man, but in the wrong job." He could not resist adding, "And yet it must be said, what a miserable President he was."[95] He suggested that if St. Francis of Assisi had been made President of the Chase Manhattan Bank, he too would have done a terrible job. A decade later, after Lyndon Johnson had massively increased the federal government's footprint through a multitude of new federal programs and left the nation divided over a costly, ill-defined, and poorly executed war in Vietnam, Buckley was anything but nostalgic for the President of a decade earlier, who had held the line on federal spending, relied on overwhelming military superiority to preserve the peace, and prided himself, as he said in his farewell address, that on his watch, not a single American soldier had fallen in combat anywhere in the world. All of these factors led historians and others to show an increased appreciation for how Eisenhower had comported himself as President.[96]

Buckley was not among them. To these revisionists, Buckley wrote, Ike appeared the "Raggedy Ann of yesteryear, the warm puppy of the cuddly past when the White House was occupied by competent bridge-playing businessmen, rather than ideological scriveners," who stayed up late "writing new laws for us to obey."[97] Days before Kennedy took office, *National Review* contemptuously dismissed Nixon as "the mechanical reincarnation of Mr. Eisenhower's Progressive Moderation."[98]

5

The Editor, the Colossus, and the "Anti-Communist at Harvard"

If Buckley had found himself an outsider in the past—as an American in Britain, an isolationist at Millbrook, a Yankee in South Carolina, a southerner and a Catholic in Yankee Protestant Connecticut, a conservative at Yale, and an activist in the buttoned-down CIA—he could not have found a more inhospitable place to base a conservative journal and build a conservative movement than New York City. Manhattan was both the capital of New Deal liberalism and the epicenter of the Republican Party's liberal wing, which had chosen each of the GOP's presidential nominees between 1940 and 1960.

To the eastern establishment Republicans who secured Eisenhower's nomination, the ex-General's presidency seemed the culmination of all they sought to achieve: an internationalist and interventionist foreign policy, pro-business economic policies, and a coming to terms with the changes the New Deal had wrought in American political, social, and economic life. Prior to Eisenhower's ascendency, the main division within the party had been between the eastern, internationalist, big-business Wall Street wing and its isolationist, small-business Main Street counterpart, centered primarily in the Midwest and rural areas elsewhere. In Congress, on economic issues, the "Main Streeters" forged an alliance with southern Democrats in what became known after 1938 as the "Republican-Dixiecrat" coalition. On foreign policy, the southerners tended to side with the eastern interventionists, and on civil rights, the GOP tended to unite in support of modest proposals, while Democrats divided on regional lines.

From his election to the Senate in 1938 until his death in 1953, Ohio Senator Robert A. Taft was the undisputed leader of the Main Streeters and the isolationists and was their choice for the Republican presidential nomination in

1940, 1944, 1948, and 1952. As Buckley liked to point out, moderates who bested Taft, thereby frustrating conservative hopes, in his first three tries (Wendell Willkie once and Thomas E. Dewey twice) went down to defeat in general elections.[1] He cited these losses, plus Nixon's defeat in 1960, as evidence that conservative-leaning voters had either sat out the election, given the relative lack of difference between Republican and Democratic national platforms or, especially in the South, habitually voted for the party of their Democratic forebears. Eisenhower, of course, with his two landslide victories, proved the exception to this rule. The patronage his administration had at its disposal had temporarily driven internecine divisions within the GOP beneath the surface and helped paper over ideological differences. As Buckley anticipated, ideological and factional strife reemerged with a vengeance after Eisenhower left office.

During the twenty years in which the GOP was shut out of the presidency (1933–1953) and the eight years of Eisenhower's reign (1953–1961), the eastern establishment ran party affairs through the institutions it controlled: the great financial houses; the *New York Herald Tribune*, which functioned as its official mouthpiece; Henry Luce's *Time-Life* media empire; boards of trustees of the great universities; and the upper echelons of advertising, publishing, public relations, and industry. In New York, these entities exercised a particular lock on state politics. At the top of its pyramid there sat for two decades Thomas E. Dewey, legendary crime fighter turned Governor and presidential aspirant. The political machine Dewey built perpetuated itself through the powerful and patronage-rich New York governorship, which it controlled from 1942 through 1974 with only a four-year interruption.

Dewey accepted most of the New Deal reforms and in some ways went beyond them, as he did in aggressively championing civil rights. He doubled state spending on education, created the thruway that bears his name, reduced state debt, and established a reputation for sound management and integrity in government.[2] He controlled the state Republican Party with a firm hand. Its candidates were selected not by voters in primaries but in state party conventions whose delegates often came from Dewey's machine. Conservatives seeking a future in politics either made their peace with the organization or were crushed by it. Two who would distinguish themselves in the conservative movement, Goldwater's pre-nomination political strategist F. Clifton White and *National Review* publisher Bill Rusher, cut their political teeth in Dewey's clubhouse.[3]

In 1956, some conservatives thought they saw an opportunity to wrest control of the party away from Dewey operatives. After Dewey declined to seek reelection in 1954, his designated successor, Irving Ives, lost the gubernatorial election to W. Averell Harriman by a narrow margin. (Harriman polled 49.6 percent to Ives's 49.4 percent.) Two years later, succumbing to pressure from the Liberal Party, without whose cross-endorsement Democrats feared they could not win a general election, the Democratic Party at its convention passed over former Postmaster General and ex-Democratic National Committee Chairman James A. Farley for its senatorial nomination in favor of New York City Mayor Robert F. Wagner Jr. When the Republicans selected as their senatorial nominee the equally liberal New York State Attorney General Jacob K. Javits, talk erupted about the need for a new Conservative Party that might exert over the GOP the kind of leverage the Liberal Party had used to discipline Democrats they considered out of touch with a significant part of the party's base. It would function as that other's party's mirror image, pulling the Republicans rightward, as the Liberals pushed the Democrats leftward.

The Liberal Party applied pressure mostly through its power to cross-endorse Democratic Party nominees. When it failed to bless a Democratic nominee in this way—or opted to run a separate candidate instead or even endorsed a Republican—the Liberal Party assured that Democrat's defeat. Conservative activists, frustrated with Dewey's brand of Republicanism, hoped to assemble a coalition of right-of-center Republicans and Farley Democrats in a third party that could act as a check on the existing GOP power structure. (Farley remained popular among his fellow Catholics and had endeared himself to conservatives by refusing to support FDR when he sought a third term.)

Javits catapulted to the head of the Republican pack for the senatorial nomination in 1956 after he defeated Franklin D. Roosevelt Jr. for Attorney General in 1954, the year Harriman won the governorship. After carrying heavily Democratic New York City by 143,000 votes and doing well in traditional GOP enclaves, Javits emerged from the election as the sole Republican to hold statewide office. Riding on Eisenhower's coattails in 1956, Javits defeated Wagner by more than half a million votes.

An early follower of Fiorello La Guardia, once a Republican Congressman who had won election as New York City Mayor on a "fusion" ticket and served for twelve years, Javits attributed his attraction to the GOP more to his aversion to Tammany-style corruption than to ideology. In the House of Representatives, where he served from 1947 to 1955, Javits had been that body's most liberal Republican. He supported most Democratic spending initiatives and opposed such conservative staples as the Taft-Hartley Act, funding for the House Un-American Activities Committee, and legislation requiring Communists to register with the U.S. Attorney General.[4] Buckley took to repeating with great delight George Sokolsky's comment that Javits had as much business in the Republican Party as Leon Trotsky.[5]

Conservative activist Eli Zrake, a young public relations executive and veteran of Robert Taft's presidential campaigns, had tried to persuade the state GOP convention to select Douglas MacArthur in Javits's stead. He later mounted a write-in campaign for his favorite, which MacArthur disavowed. Months after Javits was elected to the Senate, Zrake began conversations with Buckley about founding a Conservative Party. They stressed, in their releases, that they were recommending this course of action only in New York and not in other parts of the country.

On the day after Eisenhower's second inauguration, Buckley circulated a "To All Concerned" memorandum to key conservatives in which he outlined the new party's mission. At the very least, he argued, it would register the size of the hard conservative vote. That, he reasoned, would give conservatives standing at future state GOP conventions. He anticipated that the new party, functioning as a pressure group, would endorse all GOP nominees save those liberal enough to obtain the Liberal Party's endorsement.[6] Buckley recommended that the Conservative Party follow the Liberals' example and designate as its official head a widely respected intellectual. Buckley set his eyes on former FDR adviser Raymond Moley, who had drifted rightward over the years, with Zrake presiding over the nuts and bolts of the new operation.[7] Buckley's efforts stalled in 1958 when Zrake died suddenly of a heart attack at the age of thirty-nine. But the initiative the two men discussed sprang back to life when it received a powerful jolt from a not altogether unexpected corner.

Nelson A. Rockefeller, grandson of the founder of Standard Oil, announced that he would be leaving the Eisenhower administration to play a greater role in the civic life of New York State. Under Ike, Rockefeller had served as Undersecretary of the newly established Department of Health, Education and Welfare, and later as Special Adviser to the President for Foreign Affairs. He had previously held the post of Chairman of the International Development Advisory Board under Truman, and during World War II as Assistant Secretary of State, he acted to thwart Nazi penetration into Latin America. At the time he left the administration, Rockefeller was pressing for significant increases in defense spending. His agitation in this direction put him at odds with Treasury Secretary George M. Humphrey, who had Eisenhower's ear and, ultimately, his support.

With Rockefeller back in New York, Buckley wrote him requesting an interview for a piece *National Review* planned to run on Eisenhower's foreign and defense policies. He pointed out that *National Review* had shared some of the views Rockefeller had been pressing upon the administration in Washington.[8]

Rockefeller adviser Francis A. Jamieson recommended that Rockefeller grant Buckley's request. Seeing the meeting as an opportunity for Rockefeller to explain himself "to party conservatives," Jamieson urged Rockefeller to "be friendly and cooperative" and respectful of his guests' right to hold their own point of view.[9] Buckley was called out of town on the day the meeting had been scheduled and Jonathan Mitchell interviewed Rockefeller in his stead.

Rockefeller's efforts to enhance his visibility in New York State received an unexpected boost when Governor Harriman, in an effort to build bipartisan support for changes in the state constitution, named him Chairman of a commission that would call for a constitutional convention. He later headed a legislatively designated group that pressed for the adoption of the recommended changes. Some Republicans, aware of Rockefeller's presidential ambitions, tried to persuade him to run for Senator rather than Governor. He declined, having already concluded that his best route to the White House passed through Albany.

As the 1958 election neared, Rockefeller and Westchester Assemblyman Malcolm Wilson embarked on what a student of the New York Conservative Party later termed "the first listening tour," visiting forty-nine of New York's sixty-one counties.[10] Conservatives had regarded Wilson as one of their own and had been urging him run for Governor. The early support he gave Rockefeller, on whose ticket he would be elected Lieutenant Governor four times, dampened their hopes. With Wilson unavailable as an alternative to Rockefeller for Governor in 1958, Buckley and his cohorts showed interest in Walter Mahoney, a state Senator from Long Island. Mahoney also declined to enter the race.

With Rockefeller's nascent campaign steamrolling onward, Buckley put readers on notice through editorials and articles in *National Review* that the multimillionaire turned "citizen politician" posed a serious threat to conservative and their ideas gaining ascendancy within the Republican Party. Of the pressures being placed on New York Republicans to nominate Rockefeller, Buckley wrote and ran on the third page of *National Review*'s February 15, 1958, issue these telling lines: "Calling all students of public relations. Study carefully the job being done for Nelson Rockefeller as Governor of New York. You may live a hundred years and not see its equal."[11]

In other pieces that year, the magazine spelled out how Rockefeller extended his influence through foundations he controlled, commissions he launched, or at least in which he participated, and a multitude of press and policy operatives scattered throughout these entities and others whom he kept on retainer. One sees in these exposés annoyance that Rockefeller's approach was working, as well as a grudging respect for his methods. If there was a lesson in all this for conservatives, Buckley, who was already operating on multiple levels to advance his own goals, was paying close attention.

The possibility of Rockefeller being elected Governor and, as a result, immediately catapulting to the front ranks of presidential contenders, catalyzed Buckley to pick up where he and Zrake had left off. Again, he made the case for a new Conservative Party in New York, which, if it did nothing else, would have the effect of causing Rockefeller, should he be elected, problems at home. If the Right could not block Rockefeller's ascendancy, it could at least establish a mechanism to register its opposition to his proposals and attract attention to its criticisms. Buckley foresaw that as the Conservative Party grew in strength, it would eventually force the state GOP to reach an accommodation with it.[12] He had no way of knowing that, twelve years later, such a coalescing would occur or that its first beneficiary would be his own brother, who won election to the U.S. Senate from New York in 1970.

Theodore H. White, the chronicler of U.S. presidential elections, described how Rockefeller and his family conducted business and shaped public policy. One can glean from his account much of what caused conservatives to oppose him so ardently. The theme running through it was concentration of power:

> To a Rockefeller, all things are possible. This is a family that examines New York City, decides to clear a midtown slum and then erects the greatest executive building complex in the world; it examines a rotting tenement area and decides it must be abolished and begins there to realize such a dream as the Lincoln Center for the Performing Arts, designed to be the most fantastic monument of man's spirit since Athens. . . . Whether in missiles, electronics, real estate, oil, or Latin-American investments, when the Rockefellers decree, that which they decree comes to pass. This sense of public power, moreover, has always been accompanied by a strange, pietistic sense of responsibility. . . . Universities, museums, foundations, all have flourished when the Rockefeller taste or conscience has been touched. . . . Their attitude to America as a whole is not a patronizing one; rather, America is their patrimony. Their stupendous fortune . . . is so vast that it is affected by every rustling and turning of America's mood and destiny. They are so big they cannot help being concerned by all America's problems. Whatever happens, it must touch on a Rockefeller interest, either financial or philanthropic somewhere on the national scene.[13]

With Rockefeller poised to capture the Republican nomination for Governor in the summer of 1958, *National Review* warned conservatives across the country that Rockefeller would not govern as a conservative. In a hard-hitting article signed by Buckley intimate J. P. (James) McFadden, the magazine went after Rockefeller from every possible angle. Years later, Buckley revealed to an interviewer that (future CIA Director) Bill Casey, who had political ambitions of his own in New York, was the true author of the piece.[14]

The article presented Rockefeller as one of the "tame millionaires" whom FDR intimate Harry Hopkins brought in to the Democratic administration to give a bipartisan cast to Roosevelt's policies.[15] It homed in on ex–New Dealers who were supporting Rockefeller's campaign and highlighted several Rockefeller associates, who moved back and forth between public, philanthropic, and private-sector entities. It related how Rockefeller brought these disparate worlds together in reports the Rockefeller Brothers Fund (RBF) released at his direction in early 1958. In the international arena, Rockefeller intended those reports as blueprints for foreign policy and defense initiatives he would undertake as President. On domestic matters, the reports' recommendations provided the public justification for Rockefeller's campaign for Governor.

To oversee the production and release of those reports, Rockefeller retained Harvard Professor Henry A. Kissinger, for whom Buckley had already developed a liking. While still a member of the Eisenhower administration, Rockefeller had observed Kissinger brief a select group of officials in advance of the 1955 summit in Geneva at which Eisenhower made his "open skies" proposal (which would have allowed the two superpowers the right to inspect each other's missile sites). *National Review*'s profile of Rockefeller and his associates made no mention of Kissinger or the role he played in various Rockefeller operations.

With Rockefeller not yet the official Republican nominee for Governor, his staff prepared talking points designed to blunt *National Review*'s criticisms of him and his advisers. One talking point they developed stressed that he had played no role whatsoever in formulating domestic policy while serving in the Roosevelt and Truman administrations. Rockefeller's team also noted that among Rockefeller's advisers were prominent conservatives such as Justin Dart, President of the Rexall Drug Company. (Dart would play a similar role in Ronald Reagan's 1966 campaign for Governor of California.)[16] On the eve of Rockefeller's formal nomination, Buckley summarized *National Review*'s major reservations about the gubernatorial hopeful in an editorial: "We should like to make it very clear that we have nothing, nothing in the world against Nelson Rockefeller. . . . We have maintained, very simply, that he is not a Republican. Or, if it is better put another way, if he is a Republican, 'Republicanism' is a farce."[17]

Rockefeller defeated Harriman by 573,000 votes in a year in which the GOP fared poorly nationally, losing forty-eight seats in the House and thirteen in the

Senate. As Buckley foresaw, most of the stories about Rockefeller's election cited him as a possible presidential contender. Commentators proclaimed his inaugural address, heavily peppered with references to the Cold War, the equivalent of a presidential State of the Union Address.[18]

As Governor, Rockefeller fully lived up to *National Review*'s expectations. He awarded civil defense a major priority and significantly upped spending on education, roads, housing, and power development. Rockefeller raised taxes multiple times and introduced both a state sales tax and a payroll withholding system. He restructured and expanded the state university system and created 230 new agencies and independent authorities (all of the latter with the power to issue their own bonds). By persuading the legislature to guarantee those bonds, Rockefeller had found a way to initiate programs without having to seek legislative approval or raise taxes.[19] Rockefeller's spending practices made him even more of an anathema to conservatives than Dewey had been. So preoccupied were they with this part of his record that they all but overlooked, in spite of James Burnham's constant reminders, Rockefeller's credentials as a committed anti-Communist and Cold War hawk.[20]

On occasion, Buckley used ridicule to call into question the reputation Rockefeller had established as a competent executive, able to attract the best talent available. He related that on one occasion, a Rockefeller aide, in replying to a request for a copy of a recent speech by the Governor, mistakenly enclosed with the text of Rockefeller's remarks the writer's original letter. On the back of it, an aide had written in pencil along with his initials, D.F.B., that the Governor's correspondent was "currently engaged in running a segregationist and anti-Semitic newspaper down south."

The man in question was Robert Morris, a personal friend of Buckley's, who had once worked as an investigator under McCarthy. After vouching for Morris's character, a *National Review* editorial stated: "It is frequently said of Mr. Rockefeller that . . . [he] surrounds himself with first-class men. Maybe he has so many people working for him he has lost personal control over the quality of the men from whom he takes his opinions and draws his conclusions. If that is so, how is he going to handle the problem if he becomes President of the United States?"[21] Rockefeller would feel Buckley's sting many times.

On November 14, 1960, a group of young Republican lawyers, in a discussion over lunch, resolved to continue Eli Zrake's efforts. They would start a New York Conservative Party and assign it the mission Buckley had articulated years earlier. J. Daniel Mahoney and his brother-in-law Kieran O'Doherty were its principal organizers. Buckley considered Mahoney "relaxed, humorous, wise and a peerless conciliator."[22] He and Buckley had first met in 1954, when

Mahoney, then a student at Columbia Law School, invited Buckley, already a hero to young conservatives, to speak at an event on campus. Buckley described O'Doherty as "intense . . . prodigiously informed, with an infinite capacity for righteous indignation."[23] O'Doherty became embittered after having witnessed eight delegates from Queens to the 1952 Republican National Convention go back on their pledge to vote for Robert A. Taft and defect to Eisenhower in the face of relentless pressure from Dewey operatives. He and Mahoney resolved not to allow themselves to be intimidated in a similar fashion by Rockefeller minions in the future.[24]

Buckley lent his support to the fledgling Conservative Party in multiple ways. He awarded it ample coverage in *National Review*, provided it with lists of *National Review* donors and subscribers, acted as its conduit to conservatives across the country, and used his own increasing visibility to help publicize its activities. He also reassured GOP regulars nationwide, many of them conservative, that the party would not serve as a catalyst to similar undertakings outside New York State, where conservatives were less able to work for reform within the established party structure. The Dewey-Rockefeller machine, Buckley would point out, had rendered such changes impossible through its "undemocratic" procedures and refusal to allow primaries.

He encouraged the young renegades on. "The older generation hardly qualifies, on the basis of their performance, as preceptors," he wrote Mahoney.[25] Buckley helped the new party raise funds so that it could assist its candidates to obtain ballot access, a process the machine had deliberately made cumbersome. The state GOP also used its power over local and state nominations to discourage its candidates from accepting cross-endorsements from the Conservatives and its officials from assisting the Conservatives in any way.[26]

When Rockefeller sought reelection in 1962, his operation went into overdrive to discourage Conservative Party organizers. James Desmond, whom Buckley described as a Rockefeller "publicist by avocation," reported in the *New York Daily News* that "some far out conservatives," many drawn from the extreme Republican Right, were surveying the feasibility of fielding a candidate against Rockefeller when he sought reelection.[27] He noted that the group, which included Buckley, Rusher, Frederick Reinecke (whom he described as a "John Birch Society bigwig"), and others, had used *National Review* as their unofficial headquarters. (Desmond would produce a campaign biography of Rockefeller in the run-up to the 1964 presidential primaries.)[28]

Under Buckley's tutelage, the Conservative Party waged guerilla warfare against Rockefeller's tightly run organization through the media. Mahoney charged that the Governor's campaign was deploying state employees on its behalf and that party officials were threatening economic retaliation against Conservative Party candidates and their supporters. The Conservative candidate for Comptroller publicly charged that Rockefeller had used his banking connections to assure that the mortgages of people who signed Conservative Party petitions were foreclosed. The *Daily News* ran an editorial entitled "Call off Your Dogs, Rock," while the *Buffalo Courier Express* demanded that the "right of petition must not be abridged."[29] Not anticipating that the Conservatives would poll well and eager to avoid further adverse publicity, Rockefeller's forces relented.[30]

At a pre-election Conservative Party rally at Madison Square Garden held immediately after President Kennedy went on television to announce that Soviet-installed missiles had been detected in Cuba, Buckley parodied what he thought to be Kennedy's preferred policy. "The Cubans will not . . . be permitted to accumulate more than their fair share of nuclear missiles," he declared. David Jaquith, the Conservatives' gubernatorial candidate, followed Buckley to the podium and attacked Rockefeller for "playing Santa Claus with our [the taxpayers'] money."[31] Jaquith pulled 141,877 votes—well over the 50,000 his party needed to qualify for official status on future ballots, but shy of the 250,000-vote goal his managers had set.[32] Although Rockefeller handily defeated Democrat Robert Morgenthau by more than 500,000 votes, his winning margin was 80,000 fewer than he had drawn against Harriman four years earlier.[33]

Senator Javits, running for reelection on the Liberal line as well as the Republican, defeated his Democratic rival, Richard B. Donovan, by more than a million votes. To explain this phenomenon, Buckley cited Jaquith's explanation ("just stupidity on the part of voters") as evidence of the political genius for which the Conservative Party was becoming renowned.[34] The Conservatives' showing, *National Review* contended, had put a damper on Rockefeller's running as an "out-and-out liberal" for the Republican presidential nomination two years hence.[35] With Buckley's help, the renegade party forced Rockefeller to look over his shoulder at home while he traveled the country in his quest for the 1964 presidential nomination.

All the while he was fomenting dissention within and open rebellion against Rockefeller's base of operation within New York State, Buckley was cementing ties to a man he would later call an "important arm of Nelson A. Rockefeller, Inc.," Henry A. Kissinger.[36] Born in the German town of Fürth in 1923, Kissinger had fled Nazi persecution with his family in 1938, settling in the Washington Heights section in upper Manhattan. A private in the U.S. Army during the war, Kissinger worked in military intelligence and participated in the U.S.-led de-Nazification of his native land. Kissinger got to know Buckley in 1954, the year the rising scholar obtained his PhD at Harvard. At the time, Kissinger was editing the journal *Confluence*. He had invited Buckley to contribute an article that would be, in essence, an intellectual defense of Senator Joseph McCarthy. Fearful that his colleagues would take offense at such a display of ideological pluralism, Kissinger declined to run Buckley's submission.

To make amends, Kissinger invited Buckley to address the Harvard International Seminar, composed of visiting students from abroad, who had been identified by their sponsors as future leaders of their respective countries. In their discussions about Buckley's availability, the two found that they had many common interests. Buckley recalled his first meeting with Kissinger, over lunch at the New York Yacht Club in 1956: "He was captivatingly bright and engaging, and from that moment on we were in regular touch."[37] They had much to discuss.

Both were well educated, well read, fluent in several languages, possessors of a self-effacing wit, highly ambitious and, as Kissinger would one day joke, spoke with accents unfamiliar to their audiences. Each, in his way, was also an outsider. Buckley was a devout Catholic usually operating in Protestant and secular environments, a renegade within the Ivy League, and a conservative intellectual in liberal New York. Kissinger was a Jewish refugee of modest means who rose to become a principal adviser to a pillar of the very establishment Buckley sought to displace. Having also founded a journal, Kissinger understood the challenges of raising funds, placating donors, and meeting deadlines, all major Buckley preoccupations.[38]

Kissinger was also somewhat of a conservative in liberal academe—he of the European, Burkean tradition, who saw the state as a necessary mechanism, rather than of the American "laissez-faire" and libertarian variety, who regarded the state as a necessary evil and wanted its size and scope limited. Many liberals looked askance at Kissinger's first book, *Nuclear Weapons and Foreign Policy*, in which he argued that in certain situations, limited use of nuclear weapons might prove more effective than reliance on conventional weapons.[39] Buckley remained a fan of it even after Kissinger had distanced himself from recommendations he had made early in his career.

Unexpectedly, from the voice and pen of Nelson Rockefeller's principal foreign policy adviser, Buckley was receiving ideas and strategic advice similar to that which Whittaker Chambers and James Burnham were pressing upon him: the importance of prioritizing goals, the need to cultivate public opinion for what one was proposing, the need to respond to aggression in concert with allies and through means that were more than exclusively military. Kissinger and Buckley were equally suspicious of Soviet motivations and intentions. By

1968, Buckley had taken to referring to Kissinger as "the anti-Communist at Harvard."[40] His point was not that the others were Communists or pro-Communist, but that many, it not most, had come to regard the United States and the USSR as morally equivalent. As such, they took a more laid-back approach in confronting both Communist ideology and Soviet actions.

Buckley and Kissinger both took care not to allow their professional and political activities and their occasional disagreements to strain their friendship. They took particular pains to remain on good terms during Rockefeller's three attempts to obtain the Republican Party's presidential nomination, an objective Kissinger worked to advance and Buckley labored to retard. However strident their respective candidates grew in their criticisms of each other, the two men kept their lines of communication open. As their careers unfolded, Rockefeller, Buckley, and Kissinger unwittingly formed a triangular orbit in which they functioned sometimes as adversaries (Buckley and Rockefeller), sometimes as go-betweens (with Kissinger usually, but not always, in that role), and, on occasion, as allies.

6

SAILING AGAINST THE NEW FRONTIER

Having ruled out a Nixon endorsement in the 1960 election on the grounds that the Republican presidential contender had not campaigned as a conservative and would probably not govern as one, and that Kennedy, as President, might prove less of a liberal than some of the Democrats against whom he competed for his party's presidential nomination, Buckley could comfortably claim that the differences between the candidates were not sufficient to warrant *National Review*'s taking sides. With Nixon having moved leftward in the hope of improving his prospects among independents and Democrats, Kennedy rendered himself less objectionable to the Right through the hawkish stance he adopted toward the Soviet Union. His past praise of Robert Taft and his having gone easy on Joe McCarthy also worked to his benefit with some elements on the Right.

As a Congressman, Kennedy often deviated from the conventional Democratic and liberal lines on foreign policy. He criticized Truman for pulling back from Chiang Kai-shek in the final stages of the Chinese Civil War. "What our young men had saved, our diplomats and our President frittered away," Kennedy said, in an obvious reference to Secretary of State George C. Marshall and China specialists in the State Department who advised policy makers that Chiang would not prevail and had siphoned off sufficient funds intended for his troops for himself and officials in his government.[1] When Kennedy ran for the Senate in 1952, the conservative *Chicago Tribune* described him as a "fighting conservative."[2] After he had succeeded Lodge, Kennedy, in a remark that could have been tailor-made to annoy leftist elements within his party and catch the eyes of conservatives in both parties, told the *Saturday Evening Post* that he did not consider himself a liberal and had not joined the Americans for Democratic Action (ADA) because he was "not comfortable with those people."[3]

As he prepared to run for President, Kennedy, as a means of rendering himself at least acceptable to Democratic liberals, brought a good many of "those people," including Harvard Professors Arthur M. Schlesinger Jr. and John Kenneth Galbraith, both former advisers to Adlai Stevenson, into his entourage and relied upon them to make himself palatable to the dominant liberal wing of the Democratic Party. Schlesinger grew concerned that because Kennedy had not denounced McCarthy during the Senator's censure trial and because Nixon had succeeded to some extent in modifying his image from that of right-wing firebrand to Republican moderate, party liberals might not turn out for Kennedy in sufficient numbers. To persuade them to do so, he published a short book, *Kennedy or Nixon: Does It Make a Difference?* His central argument was that Kennedy, as a Democrat, would prove a more worthy heir to the New Deal tradition than Nixon, whose party never enthusiastically embraced it, a point Kennedy would make repeatedly when he debated Nixon.[4] In essence, Schlesinger was making the same argument on behalf of his candidate as Burnham had for his when he sought to persuade conservatives to support Nixon, but in reverse. Both intellectuals were betting that the candidates' party affiliation would cause them to select advisers who would push the next President in the direction of his respective political base

Late in the campaign, with Burnham pressing him to state that Nixon might make a better President than Kennedy, Buckley conceded that as President, Kennedy might be less steadfast in facing down the Soviet Union than he had been as a candidate. He voiced this misgiving in an editorial in the form of a response to the Reverend Norman Vincent Peale, author of the best seller *The Power of Positive Thinking*, who had publicly warned that Kennedy, as President, would take guidance from the Vatican in deciding policy. Wrote Buckley: "Mr. Kennedy is a disappointment and a serious threat, but not as Dr. Peale recklessly suggests, because he is a Catholic." He accused Kennedy of speaking in "faltering accents about the Soviet menace" and declared that he was more concerned about Kennedy "not showing independence from economist John Kenneth Galbraith and United Auto Workers Union President Walter Reuther" than he was about his not taking an independent line from the pope.[5] Yet, Buckley's reservations about Kennedy were still not sufficient to cause him to endorse Nixon.

With a Democrat in the White House, he reasoned the prospects of *National Review* becoming the place where all conservatives and a good many Republicans would go for policy guidance were brighter than they might be under a second purportedly "modern Republican" administration, which the publication would oppose much of the time. After Kennedy took office, Buckley found that whenever *National Review* attacked the administration's economic and foreign policies, it was often firing from the same direction as most of the Right and much of the center. Still, given the liberal tenor of the times, Buckley's influence over the direction of national policy remained minimal. He was able to draw increased attention to himself and his ideas, however, through his quick wit, magnetic personality, and well-developed media savvy. He proved a natural before college audiences and as a guest on late-night television. In 1962, he launched his syndicated column, On the Right, and became an anomaly on the editorial pages of mainstream newspapers. By the time the Kennedy administration came to its tragic end, Buckley's column was appearing in 150 newspapers thrice weekly.

With a President in office who presented himself as open to new and unconventional ideas, Buckley seemed a perfect fit for television bookers looking for someone who came across as the intellectual equal of Kennedy's "best and brightest," but who as a conservative could hold his own in debate with them. Buckley was handsome, athletic, Ivy League, well traveled, and spoke with an accent not all that dissimilar from Kennedy's. Buckley gave the impression that, but for his political ideas, he might have felt right at home in Kennedy's circle, many of whose members he knew socially. Kennedy's administration was very much aware of Buckley's presence. Several of his erstwhile and future adversaries in debate held high posts within it. Although they did not give his ideas much credence, some of them grasped the political threat conservatism might one day pose to continued Democratic and liberal hegemony.

Buckley grew disillusioned with Kennedy early during his presidency. He sensed that the new President acted more out of opportunism than conviction in making decisions and formulating policy. Until the very recent past, the Kennedy and Buckley families had been on the same side of many controversies. Joseph P. Kennedy, William F. Buckley Sr., and their children had been outspoken isolationists during the 1930s. John F. Kennedy, while a student at Harvard, joined the America First Committee around the time Billy Buckley was defending Lindbergh's anti-interventionist views at Millbrook.[6] Both families supported Senator Joseph McCarthy and his investigation into possible Communist infiltration of the U.S. government.

The Kennedys, however, adjusted their sails to prevailing political winds. The Buckleys did not. As U.S. Ambassador to the United Kingdom, Joseph P. Kennedy paid a steep political price when he publicly opposed Franklin Roosevelt's declared policy of assisting Britain to resist Hitler in every way short of the United States going to war. While his sons, especially the one who became President, would praise historic figures who had taken unpopular stands, they took care, perhaps with their father's example in mind, not to deviate too far from public opinion. By the time JFK entered politics, winning had become the primary Kennedy goal. That was an important part of the Kennedy mantra Joe Kennedy bequeathed to them. Will Buckley preferred that his children uphold the principles he had imparted to them.[7] To them, campaigns were opportunities to air their views, make their case, and ascertain what public support there was for them. Bill, for instance, described his candidacy for Mayor of New York City as a "paradigmatic" campaign. When, however, the Buckleys saw a chance to win and govern on their own terms, they proved as apt political tacticians and strategists as the Kennedys, especially as a Kennedy presidency became more within the realm of possibilities.

On the surface, the Kennedys and the Buckleys had many similarities, which did not go unnoticed, especially by the media. Both were large Irish Catholic families headed by strong-willed fathers who had, through intelligence and business acumen, joined the ranks of the wealthiest men of their time. John F. Kennedy and William F. Buckley Jr. were both accomplished sailors and made the sport one of their primary recreational activities. They were also great political wits, with a talent for making their points through poignant one-liners.

After James L. Buckley's election to the Senate in 1970, *Life* magazine ran photos of the Buckleys playing touch football on Aloise's lawn in Sharon, just as it had shown the Kennedys doing the same at Hyannis port a decade earlier.[8] *Harper's Bazaar*, in its 1969 centennial issue, featured Aloise Steiner Buckley and Rose Fitzgerald Kennedy in a photo spread entitled "Great Matriachs." In a television interview in 1962, Gore Vidal, then an outspoken ally of the Kennedys, referred to the Buckleys as "sort of like sick Kennedys."[9] (This insult, one of many Vidal hurled at Buckley, preceded the famous altercation they would have on network television by six years.)

Kennedy, an acquaintance of McGeorge Bundy's from their days together at the Dexter School in Brookline, was serving in Congress when Bundy's review of *God and Man at Yale* ran in the *Atlantic Monthly*. Kennedy's friendship with Bundy deepened after the Massachusetts Senator joined the Harvard Board of Overseers in 1957, an appointment that demonstrated the degree to which Joseph P. Kennedy's son had gained entry into the upper echelons of an American establishment that had once snubbed Irish Catholics. Kennedy's father considered his son's selection a particularly good omen. If an Irish Catholic could get elected as an overseer at Harvard, he reasoned, he could get elected to anything.[10] Attaining this distinction, however, required the kind of accommodation to the prevailing opinion among the university's governors that would have been totally out of character for any son of Will Buckley. (When Bill sought to join Yale's governing board, he was nominated by petition and defeated by the Yale administration's designated slate.)

Buckley took issue with the extent to which JFK tried to deflect attention from his Catholicism and failure to state whether or how his Catholic rearing or Catholic teachings had influenced his political development. To Buckley, Kennedy represented the very kind of Catholic that Bundy lamented Buckley had not been at Yale. Kennedy made his position clear in a presentation before an assembly of Protestant ministers in Houston late in his presidential campaign, when he said that his religious beliefs would have no direct bearing on how he would comport himself as President: "Whatever issue may come before me as president I will make my decision in accordance with . . . what my conscience tells me to be the national interest, and without regard to outside religious pressures or dictates."[11]

While he thought this statement appropriate, Buckley had hoped Kennedy would go further. "What would have happened," he later inquired in a review of a book about Kennedy and American Catholicism, "if Mr. Kennedy said . . . that although he would not permit his Catholicism to stand in the way of his constitutional duties, neither would he . . . suggest that his own conscience and attitudes were uninfluenced by Catholicism?"[12] As Buckley saw it, Kennedy left his listeners with the impression that the Democratic candidate saw his religion as having played as much a role in the development of his political views as had his eye or hair color. At the same time, Buckley recognized and appreciated what the election of a Catholic President meant to Kennedy's fellow practitioners (acceptance by the larger non-Catholic majority) and the precedent it might set for members of other minority groups for one of their own to attain the nation's highest office.[13]

On policy matters on which the Catholic Church and mainstream Protestant denominations differed, Kennedy usually took positions that aligned with those of the latter. He opposed government assistance to parochial schools, saying that he believed it unconstitutional. In the distribution of foreign aid, Kennedy allowed the dissemination of information on birth control as well as of devices intended to control population growth. Some of his Catholic critics, including Buckley and New York's Francis Cardinal Spellman, thought that Kennedy had gone farther than necessary to avoid appearing to favor a group to which he belonged. (The Cardinal used his influence to hold up Kennedy's education agenda in Congress because it exempted parochial schools from receiving federal assistance.)

Not long after Kennedy's election, Burnham's prediction that, once President, the Democrat would populate his administration with the very kind of liberals *National Review* most disparaged began to come true. Bundy was named National Security Advisor, Schlesinger joined the White House staff as Special Assistant to the President, Galbraith became U.S. Ambassador to India, and multiple others of their ilk filled posts high and low throughout the administration. Buckley's initial reaction was one of grudging respect. Having praised Stevenson for bringing prominent intellectuals into his midst, he could not quarrel with Kennedy's following this example. Buckley looked forward to a time when a conservative-leaning President would act similarly.

In the decade that had elapsed since Bundy and Buckley battled over the analysis and recommendations Buckley had made in *God and Man at Yale*, neither man had raised the esteem in which he regarded the other. Early in Kennedy's administration, Buckley told *Newsweek* that, by 1965, he expected to be "using Mr. Bundy's stationery, perhaps as the occupant of a post comparable to Bundy's, in a Goldwater administration." Bundy responded that he read *National Review* to stimulate his "bile."[14]

Shortly after Kennedy had taken office, Buckley found himself back in what had become a familiar role for him: Arthur M. Schlesinger Jr.'s opponent in a highly publicized debate. Before a thousand onlookers at Newton College of the Sacred Heart in Massachusetts, the two squabbled over the merits of the welfare state. Informed in advance that the audience would be evenly divided, Buckley observed that Schlesinger was more accustomed to speaking in settings "where they preach academic freedom and practice liberal indoctrination."[15] Schlesinger, whose behavior Buckley would later describe as "oleaginous," opened with a sarcastic declaration. Buckley, he said, had "a facility for rhetoric, which I envy, as well as a wit which I seek clumsily to emulate."[16]

Afterward, Buckley reprinted those comments at Schlesinger's expense when, without the historian's permission, he used Schlesinger's intended put-down of him as a blurb for his first published collection of commentary, *Rumbles Left and Right: A Book about Troublesome People and Ideas.*[17] When Schlesinger threatened to sue, Buckley replied that the quote was in the public record. After Schlesinger complained to Buckley's publisher, Buckley wired back, "Tell Arthur . . . not to take it so hard: No one believes a thing he says anyway." He copied Schlesinger on the letter and referred to himself in the return address as "Wm. 'Envy His Rhetoric' Buckley." To Schlesinger's attorneys, Buckley wrote, "Now, there is a very good case to be made for everyone's apologizing who has ever quoted Arthur Schlesinger; but isn't it droll to be asked to apologize to Schlesinger for quoting *from* Schlesinger."[18]

Nearly a decade later, after Schlesinger boasted that liberalism had become so enshrined that "no one listens to Buckley anymore," Buckley said on CBS's

60 Minutes: "Schlesinger is an ideologue. My influence is much greater than his as it happens which is a surprising thing for me to say. Child prodigy [Schlesinger], landed at the right hand of Camelot in the [Kennedy] White House, who has trained a whole generation of historians, should be almost universally discarded as irrelevant. I really feel sorry for him under the circumstances."[19] (History has shown that Buckley had the better of the argument. Weeks after the program aired, James L. Buckley won election to the U.S. Senate from New York on the Conservative Party ticket and Ronald Reagan won reelection as Governor of California. Two years later, Nixon would be reelected President, carrying forty-nine states. But for Watergate, the conservative ascendancy Ronald Reagan began in 1980 might have happened earlier.)

In their later years, relations between Buckley and Schlesinger warmed somewhat. Schlesinger attributed this to the influence of their wives and their mutual friend Alistair Horne, Buckley's former roommate and a friend of Schlesinger's. Buckley, Schlesinger noted, had by then put aside the "wrathful conservatism of his youth."[20] (He noted that Buckley had ceased defending Joe McCarthy at every opportunity.) "I have always regretted that we didn't become friends," Buckley wrote after Schlesinger predeceased him by a year. No liberal, he observed, had served the movement more diligently in modern history.[21]

Galbraith became the most celebrated member of Kennedy's orbit to transcend political differences and forge a genuine and lasting friendship with Buckley. The two grew close while spending long stretches of their winters in near proximity to one another in Gstaad, Switzerland. Their mutual friend and neighbor, the actor David Niven, introduced them. Buckley and Galbraith sensed they were kindred spirits in one of their early encounters. After watching Galbraith, an avid skier, take a tumble on the slopes, Buckley telephoned for an ambulance and then rushed to Galbraith's side. To help pass the time, he inquired how long Galbraith had been skiing. "About thirty years," Galbraith answered. "About as long as you have been studying economics," Buckley replied.[22]

As Kennedy unfurled his agenda for his administration, Buckley took him to task for favoring increased regulations on business, filling key economic posts exclusively with Keynesians, and seeking to centralize government-funded research (a decision he believed would shortchange the hard sciences).[23] He soured on the President permanently after JFK, by his own admission, botched a planned invasion of Cuba in which fourteen hundred Cuban exiles attempted to topple the Castro regime. The anti-Castro forces expected to be joined in their operation by Cubans on the island. Instead, they found Castro loyalists awaiting them. Kennedy called off the expedition as it was still in motion.

Kennedy, who had wanted the American role to be minimal, declined to provide the rebels with air cover after having demolished only one half of the Cuban air force. One thousand of the invaders were taken prisoner. "From Kennedy . . . we have expected more," Buckley declared, continuing: "Perhaps Harvard will even add to the graduate curriculum a course or two on 'Invasions, Amphibious,' to fill in the little lacunae in the expertise of future Harvard administrations."[24]

Buckley grew even more caustic as Kennedy veered toward negotiation and accommodation with the Soviet Union. He opposed the administration's acceptance of the neutralization of Laos, and was unimpressed at its attempts to find common ground between leftist forces and the right-wing dictatorship in Congo. He repeated doubts he had voiced in *Up from Liberalism* about the capability of newly independent nations in the third world to govern themselves effectively after their European overseers had departed. When an interviewer asked him when he thought they would be ready to do so, Buckley responded, "When they stop eating each other."[25] Years later, he would challenge guests on *Firing Line* to name a single third world nation that was better governed and better off economically than it had been under colonial rule.

Buckley voiced approval when Kennedy consented to an interview with the head of *Izvestia*, the official propaganda machine of the Soviet government. Unable to resist another dig at Eisenhower, he said that it was a "relief to have a President who can discuss complicated problems in literate prose."[26] Yet Buckley's skepticism about the utility of summits continued, and he joined ranks with those who proclaimed Kennedy's June 4, 1961, meeting with Khrushchev in Vienna a failure. There, Khrushchev demanded that Western forces abandon West Berlin, which he insisted belonged to East Germany. He threatened to recognize the independence of East Germany, which would then assert its sovereignty over all of Berlin. Instead, two months after he met with Kennedy, the Soviet leader ordered the construction of the Berlin Wall.

"If Kennedy was 'standing firm' on Berlin, we shudder to think what he will concede when he wobbles," Buckley wrote.[27] Not surprisingly, the administration took a different view. "Better a wall than a war," Kennedy said in private.[28] Berlin would become a major theme in Buckley's writings. He set many of his novels in that city and reviewed its significance as a central theater of the Cold War in *The Fall of the Berlin Wall* (2004).

As Kennedy's presidency advanced, Buckley wrote, both admiringly and with trepidation, about how the President used his personal glamour as a means of persuading the public to support his agenda. He lamented that the President's charm appeared to be having desired effect. "His photogenic stewardship . . . is a formidable thing for any dissent to cope with," Buckley observed.[29] Having initially feared that the President's popularity would enable him to circumvent constitutional checks on presidential power, Buckley rejoiced when many of Kennedy's initiatives stalled in Congress. Buckley saw these setbacks to the administration as evidence of the country's essential conservatism: "JFK is king, the ADA tells the Pentagon what to do, the witch crafters of Liberalism dominate our social science departments in the colleges, the nation tilts left: but even so, *something* . . . keeps the nation from a totally rampageous leftism."[30]

His skepticism about how Kennedy used his charisma to affect policy outcomes notwithstanding, Buckley showed signs that he considered at least some elements in the President's strategy worthy of emulation. With Kennedy as his role model, whether consciously or otherwise, Buckley too used his distinctive personal characteristics—especially his sense of humor, erudition, good looks, and capacity to coin a phrase—to command attention, which he used, in turn, to build support for his conservative ideas. Photographs of Buckley that appeared on the dust jackets of his books suggest that he was aware of his physical attraction and that he took care to project a certain image. Most of those photos were "action" shots, depicting Buckley in shirtsleeves at a typewriter, working in the back of his limousine with his dogs wandering to and fro, navigating through Manhattan traffic on a motor scooter, or sailing. In photographs of Buckley standing with a group of young people, the expressions on his admirers' faces leave the impression that they were in the company of a rock star.

On June 11, 1962, to Buckley's surprise and to the consternation of some Kennedy advisers, the President referred to Buckley by name in a speech JFK delivered at the Yale University commencement. Upon receiving an honorary degree, Kennedy declared that he now had the "best of both worlds—a Harvard education and a Yale degree." The freshly minted Yalie then noted that many other Yale men featured prominently among his critics: "Among businessmen I have had a minor disagreement with Roger Blough, of the law school class of 1931, and I have had some complaints from my friend Henry Ford, of the class of 1940. In journalism I seem to have a difference with John Hay Whitney, of the class of 1926—and sometimes I also displease Henry Luce of the class of 1920, not to mention also William F. Buckley, Jr., of the class of 1950."[31]

The President had put Buckley in some powerful company, many of whom he had criticized almost as much as he had Kennedy. Most came from the world of big business and played prominent roles in the wing of the Republican Party Buckley sought to displace (the Eisenhower moderates). Blough, the Chairman of U.S. Steel, had recently engaged in a public spat with Kennedy over steel pricing. Ford, the scion of the automobile company's founder, had supported Nixon in the last election. Whitney, a society sportsman and Eisenhower's Ambassador to the United Kingdom, was publisher of the *New York Herald Tribune*, the voice of liberal Republicanism. Luce, publisher and founder of *Time, Life, Fortune,* and *Sports Illustrated,* headed a sizable media empire. All were pillars of the Republican eastern establishment.

Schlesinger, who was responsible for the speech, had circulated various drafts of it to others in the administration for comment. No mention of Buckley appeared in early versions. In later ones, Buckley's name had been inserted and deleted. The final text, which Kennedy had personally approved, included the reference to Buckley. Schlesinger expressed his disappointment to Bundy: "The President told me before he left for Mexico that he wanted to restore some, but not all, of the introductory jokes . . . You may want to take a hard look at the second paragraph. I wish we didn't have to dignify Buckley by Presidential allusion."[32]

An avid reader of the press who had once dabbled in journalism and mused about operating a small newspaper after he retired from the presidency, Kennedy may well have read Buckley's criticisms of the administration, perhaps even in Buckley's syndicated column, which began running weeks before Kennedy spoke at Yale.[33] Buckley's column grew out of an exchange in print Buckley had had with Gore Vidal. At the request of the North American Newspaper Alliance, both had submitted essays about the future of American conservatism. The pieces ran in the Alliance's affiliated newspapers in December 1961. Buckley detected that conservatism was on the rise—especially on college campuses—and lauded this development.[34] Vidal maintained that Kennedy was the true "conservative," as the term was usually understood, and was under attack, not from conservatives, but from "reactionaries" and "radicals."[35]

At the time he wrote the piece, Vidal enjoyed frequent access to JFK and his family. Vidal's mother, Nina Gore, and Jacqueline Kennedy's mother, Janet Bouvier, had, at different times, been married to Hugh Auchincloss, a socially prominent stockbroker and lawyer. While growing up, Mrs. Kennedy and Vidal had seen each other frequently on family occasions. On one of his visits with the Kennedys, Vidal informed JFK of what he had written about him. "Just talk to Eisenhower if you want to meet a real conservative," Kennedy replied.[36] Kennedy's characterization of his predecessor ran parallel to how most liberals and intellectuals regarded Eisenhower at the time.

Kennedy and those who populated his administration thought of themselves less as "liberals" than as "problem solvers" who used the marvels of technology to transcend ideology. Kennedy had made this a major theme of his commencement speech at Yale. The quintessential New Frontiersman who most personified this outlook was Kennedy's Secretary of Defense Robert McNamara, who brought systems analysis to the Pentagon. Buckley, like most conservatives, was skeptical about technology's capacity to render debates over values obsolete.

Not long after Buckley's North American Newspaper Alliance piece ran, Harry Elmark of the George Matthew Adams Syndicate, acting on a young assistant's hunch that Buckley's unconventional opinions and acerbic style would attract a wide audience, proposed that Buckley write a regular column.[37] The column premiered in April 1962 under the title A Conservative Voice and ran once a week. Four months later, the title changed to On the Right. By 1964, it was appearing three times a week.

Between the time Buckley published his year-end essay for the North American Newspaper Alliance and launched his column, he appeared on NBC's *Tonight Show*. Its host, Jack Paar, invited him to respond to criticisms Vidal had made of Buckley on an earlier program. On January 31, 1962, for nearly thirty minutes, Buckley fielded Paar's questions. Buckley described himself as a "radical conservative," which he defined as "someone whose ideas are rooted in unchanging principles, but whose respect is great for organic growth and the body of settled opinion." After Buckley had departed, Paar declared his recent guest devoid of "all feeling for people." Two other guests, Canadian editor Pierre Burton and author and humorist Harry Golden, whom Buckley later described as the "high priest of left-wing yahooism," declared that Buckley was an "extremist," if not a "fanatic." Paar said he did not consider Buckley "dangerous" because he lacked the communications skills necessary to move audiences. He then mimicked Buckley's mannerisms.[38]

The night after he had interviewed Buckley, Paar reported on the air that the station had received hundreds of telegrams, most of them favorable to Buckley, and a telephone call from a "very important person from Washington." He related that the VIP had told him that the "greatest service" Paar could do for the country was to "show these people and let them all speak." Presumably the term "these people" included not only Buckley but others Paar's caller thought "extremists." Paar implied, and Buckley later confirmed, through information he had received via other contacts, that Paar's caller had been President Kennedy.[39]

Vidal returned again to Paar's set the following evening and made a series of unflattering comments about Buckley, including his comment that the Buckley family were "sort of like sick Kennedys." Buckley, about to depart for his winter skiing sojourn to Switzerland, wrote, but did not send, the following telegram to Paar: "Please inform Gore Vidal that neither I, nor my family, is disposed to receive lessons in morality from a pink queer. If he wishes to challenge that designation, inform him that I shall fight by the laws of the Marquess of

Queensberry. He will know what I mean."[40] Buckley's mention of the Marquess of Queensberry referred not only to the rules the Ninth Marquess of Queensberry wrote for the sport of boxing, but also to the libel suit Oscar Wilde brought against the Marquess, who had alleged that the playwright had indulged in homosexual behavior. Upon the defendant's presentation of evidence, Wilde withdrew his suit and was instead prosecuted for what was then illegal activity.

Buckley's column provided him with an additional platform, along with his editorials, articles, and speeches, to rally against the administration's proposals for government-funded health insurance for the aged, sales of arms to Soviet satellites and of wheat to the USSR, and increased foreign aid. He took umbrage when Kennedy acquiesced to the Supreme Court's decision that banned prayer in public schools. The President had advised those opposed to the ruling to "pray at home." Buckley had another idea. He founded an organization to press for a constitutional amendment to overturn the decision. On its letterhead, he listed the three living former Presidents—Eisenhower, Truman, and Hoover—as honorary chairs.[41] Buckley did not join in the national euphoria when Kennedy pledged to land a man on the moon and return him safely to earth by the decade's end. He decried the costs and characterized the mission as an attempt by the "most public-relations conscious" administration in history to score a PR victory.[42]

When Kennedy proposed marginal tax cuts to stimulate the economy, Buckley took a position that at the time was considered an unusual one for a conservative. Keynesians had divided into two camps over how best to jump-start the economy. (Having run for President when the nation was experiencing a recession, Kennedy had pledged to "get America moving again.") Some, like Galbraith in his book *The Affluent Society*, argued for increased public-sector spending.[43] James Tobin, who chaired Kennedy's Council of Economic Advisers, argued that cuts in marginal tax rates cuts would channel private-sector investment into new industries. He and his followers were willing to tolerate a modest increase in the deficit over a short period of time until the effects of the tax cuts could be felt.[44] Fiscal conservatives, including most prominent conservatives and most Republicans of the era, fearful of increasing the deficit, opposed such tax cuts, absent commensurate cuts in spending.

Buckley made the case for across-the-board marginal tax cuts. Although *National Review*'s editorial did not explicitly say so, the stand the magazine took put it on the same side of the issue as the administration.[45] Meanwhile, the U.S. Chamber of Commerce, leading financial institutions, Eisenhower, Nixon, and others voiced opposition to Kennedy's plan.[46] Goldwater voted against it when it came to a vote early in Johnson's presidency. In taking the stand he did on tax cuts in 1962, Buckley showed himself to be a "supply-sider" on economics a generation before the term was coined and years before either Jack Kemp or Ronald Reagan, both advocates of these kinds of tax cuts, entered electoral politics.

Throughout Kennedy's time in office, Buckley continued in public to oppose federal intervention to extend civil rights and voting rights to African Americans. He thought it unwise and unjust for the North to ask the South to abandon its traditional way of life and continued to insist that the region's white population should decide the region's destiny. In the fall of 1962, the Kennedy administration acted to implement a federal court order that the University of Mississippi enroll the African American military veteran James Meredith. Angry white mobs rioted in protest, many of them incited by the inflammatory rhetoric of General Edwin Walker, whom Kennedy had relieved of command in Germany for pressing John Birch Society literature on his troops. Two people were killed and six U.S. Marshals were injured. Five hundred Marshals, backed up by the Seventieth Army Engineer Combat Battalion, relocated from Fort Campbell, Kentucky, to accompany Meredith when he eventually registered for classes. Buckley later described these events in detail in his novel *Getting It Right* (2003). While Buckley proclaimed Meredith a "courageous human being," he still took a dim view of the federal government interfering with state practices of long standing.[47]

Such was his public position. Privately, Buckley was beginning to harbor doubts about legal segregation, a practice he had accepted without question his entire life. Early in 1963, he wrote his mother, inquiring how she could "reconcile Christian fraternity" with "the separation of the races."[48] Aloise responded that she had gone to church and prayed for humility and wisdom from the Holy Spirit and that she would answer his question as the inspiration came to her.[49]

As tensions mounted in Birmingham, Alabama, that May, with civil rights protesters turning up the size and intensity of demonstrations and the Commissioner of Public Safety, Bull Connor, ordering that hoses, nightsticks, and dogs be turned on young demonstrators, Kennedy, moved by what he had seen on television, for the first time made civil rights a high priority of his administration.[50] Before then, the administration had accepted that protests in favor of civil rights might be the order of the day and regarded them as a problem to be managed, while expressing limited support for the cause for which so many had rallied. Up to this point, Kennedy had not shown much concern for civil rights. Yet, forty years after Kennedy's assassination, Buckley noted, with regret, that when it came to protecting the civil rights of all Americans, Kennedy had gotten there "sooner" than he had.[51]

As racial tensions mounted, Buckley remained on an intellectual and emotional seesaw that still tilted southward. He wrote that the police had no alternative but to impose order and that the South could do without "massive infusions of northern moralism." Yet he juxtaposed these statements with calls upon southerners to respect the right of people to demonstrate, lest they ease over into the "hands of the federal government . . . a greater and greater role in the revolution of Southern affairs."[52]

In June 1963, Alabama Governor George Wallace announced that he would "stand in the schoolhouse door" to prevent two African American students from enrolling at the University of Alabama. After nationalizing the Alabama National Guard and backing it up with U.S. Marshals and federal troops, the Kennedy administration persuaded the Governor to stand down after having allowed him to play the role of hero to his supporters. Buckley, who considered Wallace nothing more than a "welfare populist" and a demagogue, criticized the Governor's behavior—but not the principle he claimed to uphold. (He defined "welfare populist" as a southern politician who had no problem with increased centralization of federal power so long as it was not used on behalf of African Americans.) He remained unimpressed either by Kennedy's speech in which he called civil rights a "moral issue" or by the August 28, 1963, March on Washington for Jobs and Freedom, which he regarded as a venture into "mobocracy."[53]

Buckley was outraged when, days after the march, white supremacists set off a bomb in a Birmingham church on September 15, 1963, killing four young African American girls. The event seems to have been a major turning point for him. An early biographer reported that Buckley privately wept when he heard about the incident. He blamed Wallace for the tragedy. The Governor's "noisy opposition" to integration, Buckley wrote, "galvanized the demon" who committed the murders in the name of "racial integrity."[54] Wallace, he said, sought to perpetuate himself in power by appealing to the racial resentments of those who had elected him.

In an awkward choice of words, Buckley predicted that the church bombing would "set back the cause of the white people" in the region. His tone suggested that he still regarded southern whites as injured parties subjected to injustices through federal decrees and court orders, even though he was coming to regard African Americans being denied their rights as victims of abusive state and local governments. Buckley wrote that he would not be surprised if the bombings turned out to be the work of a Communist, some other extremist, or a "deranged Negro" intent on eliciting a violent response to the bombing, presumably launched against southern whites.[55] He had been partially correct in his first supposition.

The "demons"—whether aroused by the Governor or self-motivated—were members of the Ku Klux Klan.

On Kennedy's handling of the major international crisis that confronted him as President, the Cuban Missile Crisis, Buckley dissented from the contemporaneous consensus, which most historians later endorsed, that Kennedy demonstrated superior statecraft in reducing international tensions and averting a nuclear war.[56] While he did not dispute that obvious outcome, Buckley traced the origins of that crisis to Kennedy's failure to topple the Castro regime during the Bay of Pigs episode and faulted him for allowing a Soviet-styled dictatorship to remain in power ninety miles from the United States. What Khrushchev most cared about, Buckley noted, was the survival of the Castro regime, "not the lousy missiles."[57]

When he wrote those words, Buckley did not yet know that Kennedy had also agreed to withdraw American missiles in Turkey after the Soviets had packed up the missiles they had placed in Cuba. Buckley would certainly have disapproved. He, like the rest of the public, also learned years later that Kennedy, in spite of his pledge not to invade Cuba if the missiles were removed, undertook extensive clandestine efforts to eliminate Castro by other means. Buckley took these failed attempts as evidence of incompetence on the part of the administration. He wrote two well-researched and well-received novels about Kennedy's handling of what was at the time an ongoing Cuba situation: *See You Later, Alligator* (1985), in which the hero, sent by JFK to negotiate with Che Guevera, discovers hidden Soviet missiles, and *Mongoose, R.I.P.* (1987), in which the possibility that Castro played a role in assassinating President Kennedy is explored.

As Kennedy entered his third year in office, Buckley voiced skepticism that members of the President's "brains trust" were up to the job of confronting the USSR. He attributed the American failure to reverse inroads the Soviets had made in Eastern Europe and elsewhere since the end of World War II in part to the political climate that prevailed at the universities those who made policy had attended. "I happen to believe," Buckley wrote, "that if there were not a single Communist spy in America, we would still be losing the Cold War—because the classrooms of Harvard are simply no substitute for the playing fields of Eton. And where our statesmen go to school, they drink deeply in Liberalism; and Liberalism makes for the worst and most ineffective foreign policy in the history of diplomacy."[58] (Lord Wellington purportedly said that the battle of Waterloo had been won on the playing fields of Eton.)

The author of *God and Man at Yale* attributed this failure to the institutionalization of curricula based not on values but on moral equivalency and liberals' tendency to award a higher priority to process over substance and to managing problems rather than solving them.[59] Buckley considered Kennedy the quintessential representative of this new breed of manager such institutions were churning out. He proclaimed Kennedy the "ultimate man in the gray flannel suit: the great accommodator, the weather vane on the perfect ball bearings—soul-free, immune from any of the frictions of reality."[60] Buckley opposed the treaty Kennedy negotiated that would effectively ban atmospheric nuclear testing, as he would oppose subsequent arms reduction treaties, always with Churchill's warning about the importance of U.S. superiority in the quantity and quality of nuclear weapons in the back of his mind.[61]

At first, Buckley was unimpressed by the stirring "Ich bin ein Berliner" speech Kennedy delivered before the Berlin Wall on June 26, 1963. "Crowds don't mean much," Buckley declared. "They have more to do with glamour than with anything and Kennedy after all has lots of glamour." Kennedy, he suggested, came across as "Gregory Peck with an atomic bomb in his holster." The only good Buckley saw emerging from Kennedy's trip to Germany and his memorable speech, he said, was the opportunity it afforded the American leader to "utter some truths about the Soviet Union." For that and that alone, Buckley suggested, Kennedy's visit was worthwhile.[62]

In the final months of Kennedy's presidency, Buckley reported that he had come into possession of a letter that UAW President Walter Reuther and his brother Victor had written to Attorney General Robert Kennedy in preparation for the President's reelection campaign. The Reuthers urged that certain right-wing groups be listed as "subversive organizations," that the IRS revoke the tax-exempt status of right-leaning nonprofit and educational entities, and that the Federal Communications Commission "harass" radio stations that gave time to conservative commentators.[63] Buckley saw these recommendations as part of a strategy Kennedy embarked on in a speech he delivered in Seattle on November 16, 1961, in which he warned of the "dangers of the radical right." In that address, Kennedy cast his administration as steering a steady course between ideologues of the left and right, who sought "simple solutions to complex problems." One side, he said, sought peace through appeasement, while the other saw all negotiations as appeasement. He rejected what he called a false choice between "suicide and surrender."[64]

In Los Angeles two days later, Kennedy spoke of "discordant voices of extremism." He said the real danger to the nation came from extremist elements within rather than from foreign powers without.[65] The President was referring to the John Birch Society, which had begun to attract considerable press attention. When asked whether he thought it dangerous to the electoral process that large financial contributions were going to "right wing extremist" entities, Kennedy responded, "The only thing we should be concerned about is that it does not represent a diversion of funds which might be taxable for non-taxable purposes."[66] Days after this press conference, IRS Commissioner Mortimer H. Caplin launched a "test audit" of twenty-two organizations the administration considered "extremist."[67] The agency termed this the Ideological Organizations Audit Project.[68]

Buckley believed that Kennedy intended through his speeches and follow-up remarks to disparage all the administration's conservative critics, the responsible as well as the extreme. He may even have surmised, given Paar's public denigration of him and Kennedy's praise of Paar's actions, that he had become one of the administration's targets. He anticipated that the administration would seek to vilify, if not silence, its conservative opposition: "Because [John Birch Society founder] Robert Welch has written that Eisenhower is a communist, it is insinuated by the political opportunists that all who dare raise their voice in protest against the foreign policies of the President are the kind of people who think that poor old Ike is a commie."[69] By the time Buckley wrote those words, the charges Welch had levied against Eisenhower had become a staple in the media's coverage of American conservatism. Welch, a believer in and propagator of conspiracy theories, suggested that the attention the media paid to his allegations was "communist inspired."[70]

Buckley was not alone in suspecting that liberals and Democrats would seek to paint all of Kennedy's conservative critics as "Birchers." *New York Times* columnist James Reston saw Kennedy's speech and follow-up comments as part a reelection strategy John Bailey, Kennedy's recently designated pick as Chairman of the Democratic National Committee, had put in place. After having barely defeated Nixon in 1960, Kennedy had lost considerable support in the South because of the stand he had taken on civil rights. As Reston noted, JFK needed to offset these issues by maximizing his support from other segments of the electorate. That entailed increasing his share of the vote among independents; improving his margins among African Americans, who had given Nixon one-third of votes they cast in the previous election; and pulling moderate Republicans to his side. All could be targets of opportunity for the Democrats if they could cast the GOP as having been taken over by fanatics. Reston considered it significant that Bailey charged Republicans with taking their ideas from "extreme agitators."[71] Buckley termed such assertions "the hoariest in political polemics."[72]

Weeks before Buckley revealed the existence of the Reuthers' memorandum, the IRS sent a detailed report of its investigation into right-wing organizations to Myer Feldman, Deputy Counsel to the President, who furnished Kennedy with a five-page report detailing the operations of certain organizations and media enterprises.[73] Feldman cited a paper the Anti-Defamation League (ADL) of the B'nai Brith had written in which it divided right-wing groups into two categories: "the radical right" and "extreme conservatives." (The main difference between the two was the degree to which they subscribed to conspiracy theories.) Both types of organizations opposed the postwar bipartisan consensus that arose after World War II that accepted the welfare state at home and viewed containment as the best strategy on which to base an approach to the USSR. Feldman supplied Kennedy with recommendations as to how the federal government might move against these organizations.

The IRS, Feldman wrote, could investigate political organizations that claimed tax exemptions and businesses that took tax deductions for what were really political contributions. The Federal Communications Commission could invoke the Fairness Doctrine in parts of the country where there were few alternatives to right-leaning radio stations. The post office could deny bulk mail rates to certain entities. A week after Feldman wrote to Kennedy, Mitchell Rogovin, Special Assistant to IRS Commissioner Caplin, advised his superior that he had informed Robert Kennedy and Feldman about the special attention the agency was paying to right-wing organizations, and that the Attorney General supported the program and would defend the IRS against any lawsuits that resulted.[74]

Kennedy took a personal interest in the project and discussed it by telephone with Caplin. Among the groups that received special government attention were the Christian Anti-Communist Crusade, the American Enterprise Institute, and the Foundation for Economic Education.[75] Feldman attached to his memo to Kennedy a nearly one-hundred-page report on the activities, funding sources, and operations of twenty-six "major right wing organizations." Although *National Review* did not make it onto Feldman's list, organizations in which Buckley had a played a major role and helped found, such as the Intercollegiate Society of Individualists and Young Americans for Freedom, did, and Buckley's name appeared in the report more than once.[76] (A subsequent White House document mentioned the Conservative Party of New York.) Also on the list were the National Right to Work Committee and *Human Events*. As Reston had surmised, a plan was clearly under way to paint all conservatives with the same brush. As the administration was contemplating its next moves, Wyoming Democratic Senator Gale McGee suggested to Feldman that Kennedy deliver a series of "fireside chats" in which he pushed back against ideas and arguments being advanced by the Right.[77]

In 1964, months after Kennedy's assassination, two ADL staffers, Arnold Foster and Benjamin R. Epstein, reworked the organization's report and published it as the book *Danger on the Right.*[78] Having taken their title from Kennedy's Seattle speech, the authors retained the typology they had used in the previous study but added a new category, "Extreme Conservatives." In this section, they included chapters on Buckley, the Young Americans for Freedom, the Intercollegiate Society of Individualists, *Human Events,* and Americans for Constitutional Action. In a backhanded exoneration, they said that Buckley was "no anti-Semite" and "will have no truck with anti-Jewish bigotry."[79] Nonetheless, they considered his views "extreme" and therefore appealing to those who did engage in such bigotry.

The ADL's characterization of him caused Buckley considerable consternation. The study both damaged his reputation with the general public and brought him praise from allies he would have preferred not to have. Gerald L. K. Smith, one of the nation's most notorious anti-Semites, wrote Buckley that "organized Jewry" (as represented by the book's sponsor) sought to tar "constructive and effective" enemies of Communism with the label "anti-Semite" in order to reduce their effectiveness.[80] "I wish your generosity to me would extend to others, even though they be Jewish," Buckley replied.[81] For years he had been urging Smith to "repent" the "sin" of anti-Semitism, and he chastised him for resisting "the road to Damascus."[82]

Playwright Dore Schary, the ADL's national Chairman, speaking in New Jersey, stated that since his organization published *Danger on the Right,* membership in organizations like the John Birch Society (JBS) had declined considerably. In support of his claim he listed Buckley as one of several prominent persons who had resigned from the JBS.[83] An admirer of Buckley's, after reading *Red Bank Register*'s account of Schary's presentation, wrote a letter to the newspaper's editor in which he pointed out that Buckley had never belonged to the JBS and had been a consistent critic of it.[84] He copied Buckley on his communication. This precipitated a lengthy back-and-forth between Buckley and Schary.

"I have not heard you or any of your associates apologize for your efforts over the years to suggest that the kind of conservatism that I approve of and is approved of by millions of Americans is other than diseased, fanatical, and subversive," Buckley wrote Schary. He informed the ADL Chairman that the book had harmed Buckley's reputation and, in support of his argument, recounted that when renowned clarinetist Artie Shaw was asked in an interview how he knew that William F. Buckley Jr. was a "purveyor of hate," an accusation the musician had made, Shaw cited *Danger on the Right* as his source.

(Shaw subsequently apologized and Buckley withdrew a lawsuit he had filed.) Buckley informed Schary of the work he had done to "expunge anti-Semitism" from the conservative movement and to keep the pages of his magazine free from any hint of racism.[85]

In 1966, Buckley had Schary as his guest on his recently launched public affairs program, *Firing Line*. In their exchange, Buckley said that the ADL tended to think that the antonym to "liberal" was not "conservative" but "radical" or "extreme." He also faulted the organization for failing to address extremism on the left and far left.[86] Buckley came to describe the ADL as two organizations: "one half committed to fighting anti-Semitism; and the other a liberal lobby."[87] Even after Buckley had fired writer Joe Sobran from *National Review* for writings Buckley considered anti-Semitic and publicly criticized presidential candidate and fellow conservative Patrick J. Buchanan for committing what he believed to be similar infractions, some within the ADL's upper echelon remained wary of him. In his book *Never Again*, Director Abraham H. Foxman lumped Buckley together with Pat Buchanan and the Reverends Jesse Jackson and Al Sharpton among public figures of whom the ADL official remained suspicious.[88] He offered no evidence of anti-Semitism on Buckley's part in support of his view.

When the news broke that President Kennedy had been assassinated, Buckley rushed a special column to his syndicator in which he attributed the universal outpouring of grief to Kennedy's personal qualities. He cited Kennedy's charm, personal energy, and robust enjoyment of life as factors that "invigorated almost all who beheld him." He also paid tribute to the "fairy land quality" of the First Family: "After all, no divine type caster could have done better than to get JFK to play JFK, Jackie to play the First Lady, and the children to play themselves."[89]

As commentaries and narratives began to flow out of Dallas, Buckley grew concerned that the Left would portray Kennedy's assassination as part of a right-wing conspiracy. He found such talk absurd, given that the suspect the police had arrested, Lee Harvey Oswald, was a confessed Communist who had formerly lived in the Soviet Union, and upon his return to the United States joined the Fair Play for Cuba Committee and agitated on its behalf for a softer American stance toward Castro.[90] Buckley considered the relentless talk of an "atmosphere of hate" that existed in Dallas a preview of a "pogrom" the Left was preparing to launch against the American Right.[91] He believed that such talk and coverage could turn public opinion against legitimate and responsible conservative figures. As evidence that the city had become a "hotbed" of intensive activity by the Far Right, the media pointed to a Birch-placed ad the *Dallas*

Morning News had run the day Kennedy arrived in the city in which the President's photograph appeared above the words "Wanted for Treason." The President and First Lady had seen the advertisement in the newspaper before leaving their hotel. Other parts of the narrative that underscored the prevalence of right-wing extremism in the city included an assault on UN Ambassador Adlai Stevenson by the wife of an insurance executive and a follower of Bircher enthusiast General Edwin Walker. It was later learned that Oswald had attempted to assassinate Walker.[92]

Buckley wrote that the greatest tribute readers could pay to Kennedy's memory was to continue to engage in vigorous debate over best policy options for the United States: "Jack Kennedy wouldn't want a caterwauling public besotted by its own tears for its own self, or accepting his program for sentimentality's sake," Buckley wrote.[93] (That, however, was precisely what Kennedy's successor would soon demand.)[94] The greatest tribute the public could pay Kennedy's memory would be that "each of us according to his own lights . . . keep this country at least as strong, and as free, stronger we hope and freer, by acting on his own idealism, than it was when John Kennedy last knew it," he continued.[95]

Buckley did not extend to Kennedy's brother Robert the benefit of the doubt he had once shown JFK. He saw raw ambition as the underlying motive for every political action Robert Kennedy took and criticized the speed with which the fallen President's brother changed his ideological spots to suit shifting climates of opinion. In slightly more than a decade, RFK had gone from Joseph McCarthy enthusiast to Vietnam War hawk to peace candidate. Nor was he pleased that the media bestowed celebrity status on Kennedy. "Bobby, Bobby everywhere. It drives a man to drink," he complained.[96]

After Buckley waged his losing but attention-getting campaign for Mayor of New York City, many speculated that Buckley might oppose Kennedy when the Senator sought reelection in 1970. Kennedy's mother, whose political acumen was as well honed as that of her sons, thought this a distinct possibility. In 1966, while in attendance at Truman Capote's Black and White Ball at the Plaza Hotel, Buckley found himself seated beside her. Sensing an opportunity to forge a new friendship, he wrote Rose Fitzgerald Kennedy afterward and told her how much he had enjoyed their conversation.

Mrs. Kennedy wrote in response that Buckley had been endowed with "rare talents," and she expected he would "discharge" them with "wisdom, imagination, and enthusiasm and fortitude." The Kennedy matriarch added: "Naturally, I do not expect that, in so doing, your ideas will run counter to those of a certain Kennedy who is almost your twin."[97] Buckley thanked her for her "sweet and tantalizing" letter, which he pronounced "full of kindness and moxie."[98] A year later, after Robert Kennedy declined Buckley's invitation to appear on *Firing Line*, Buckley mischievously inquired, "Why does the baloney reject the grinder?"[99]

Primarily through his wife Pat's work with the Metropolitan Museum of Art, Buckley met and came to like Jacqueline Kennedy Onassis, a viewer of *Firing Line*.[100] He later said he and Jackie were "moderate friends."[101] For a time Buckley also had cordial relations with the late President's youngest brother, Senator Edward (Ted) Kennedy. After Ted drove off the Chappaquiddick Bridge and a female passenger in his car drowned, Buckley wrote him a letter of condolence. He added that, given his role as a commentator, he had to speak his mind on the impact the tragedy might have on the nation's politics and enclosed a column he had written on the subject. Buckley concluded that, whatever happened at Chappaquiddick that night, "the personal humiliation" Kennedy endured was "enough punishment . . . in this world at least."[102] When Buckley received a letter from a person wishing that physical harm would befall Kennedy, Buckley sent the letter on to the Senator, informing him that he "did not want to take any chances, at the risk of being ridiculous" and suggesting that Kennedy forward it to the FBI.[103] Kennedy did, and thanked Buckley for his concern.[104]

In February 1972, John Kenneth Galbraith brought Kennedy, his wife, Joan, sister Jean Kennedy Smith, Senator John Tunney, and another Kennedy friend to Buckley's chateau in Gstaad.[105] The group took turns painting canvases in the Buckleys' basement. At the end of the evening, Kennedy asked to borrow a car to drive his party back to their lodgings. Pat Buckley nixed the idea—on the grounds that there were two bridges between the Buckleys' residence and the Kennedys'.[106]

As the decades passed, Buckley often revisited John F. Kennedy's presidency. He devoted the December 31, 1994, cover story of *National Review* to Richard Reeves's book on Kennedy's time in office, which Buckley considered the best account that had yet appeared.[107] In his annotations there and elsewhere, he lamented that Kennedy had been struck down before he could achieve his true potential, voiced disappointment at Kennedy's limited achievements, and recorded his disgust, contempt, and repulsion at Kennedy's character flaws, especially his serial adultery.

Looking back on Kennedy more than forty years later, Buckley attributed the thirty-fifth President's enduring hold on the public to his incomparable style and charisma. He termed Kennedy "all American, splendid to look at, his expression of confident joy in life and work transfiguring. Add to this that he was slaughtered, almost always a mythogenic act, and what we came to know about the awful physical afflictions he suffered, making his appearances as a whole, vigorous man the equivalent of seeing FDR rise from his wheelchair and play touch football."[108] All of this taken together, in his view, constituted Kennedy's true legacy.

7

BILL, BARRY, AND THE BIRCHERS

The 1958 elections proved disastrous to Republicans. Nationwide, the GOP lost thirteen seats in the Senate and forty-eight in the House of Representatives. A national recession, the Soviets' surprise launch of Sputnik, and a bribery scandal surrounding Eisenhower's Chief of Staff, Sherman Adams, all contributed to the outcome. *National Review* saw the returns as evidence that voters had repudiated Eisenhower's brand of Republicanism, which included an acceptance of FDR's New Deal, while the administration attributed the result to the electorate's traditional turning away from whichever party held the White House after a certain amount of years.[1] Among the casualties of the election was William F. Knowland, once considered the conservatives' best hope for the 1960 Republican presidential nomination. In a calculated risk to further his presidential prospects, Knowland had persuaded the incumbent California Governor, Goodwin Knight, to run for Senator in his stead, with Knowland running for Governor. Both he and Knight went down to defeat.

With Knowland out of the picture, Buckley and his cohorts began to shop around for another contender to carry the conservative banner. For years conservatives had maintained that if given a choice between two competing governing philosophies, voters would choose the conservative alternative. They maintained that a bipartisan conservative majority existed within the electorate, but that the prevailing hold liberals exerted on the presidential nominating process in both parties prevented its emergence. They were not alone in advocating a realignment of the two parties. In 1950, the *American Political Science Review* published a report calling precisely for a new political alignment with all liberals in one party and all conservatives in the other.[2] In 1963, political scientist James MacGregor Burns argued in *The Deadlock of Democracy: Four Party Politics in America* that the prevalence of two broad-based parties impeded rather than promoted government accountability.[3] His book went to press a year before Barry Goldwater won the 1964 Republican presidential nomination. Goldwater's nomination would prove a critical step in producing the very realignment Burns, a liberal Democrat, and Buckley and his fellow conservatives had long advocated.

Goldwater, elected to the U.S. Senate in Arizona in 1952, by his own admission on Eisenhower's coattails (having won by 6,725 votes while Ike had swept the state by 43,144), handily won reelection in 1958, when so many other Republicans were faring poorly nationwide. Through his reelection by 35,563 votes Goldwater had added to the star status he had steadily begun to build. He emerged from that campaign a possible presidential contender and with a national following among conservatives. On the same day that Goldwater won reelection in 1958, Nelson A. Rockefeller defeated incumbent New York Governor W. Averell Harriman by 573,000 votes. Their dual victories set into motion an ideological power struggle within the GOP that proved even more significant to the party's future than the Eisenhower-Taft contest of 1952.

Early in his senatorial career, Goldwater attracted attention through his work on the Select Senate Committee to Investigate Improper Activities in Labor Management Relations. He formed a friendship with another freshman Senator and rising star on that committee, Massachusetts Democratic Senator John F. Kennedy.[4] Both were veterans, sons of successful businessmen, intellectually curious, and known for their quick wit. Not surprisingly, they became friends as well as sparring partners. They made a friendly wager that whichever of them became President first would invite the other to sit in the presidential chair in the Oval Office. When Goldwater, an amateur photographer, showed up at the White House to collect on the bargain, he took Kennedy's picture and sent it on to his former colleague to autograph. Kennedy's inscription read, "For Barry Goldwater—whom I urge to follow the career for which he has shown talent—photography—from his friend—John Kennedy."[5]

Buckley was not the first to see Goldwater as a natural conservative champion. Clarence Manion, former dean of Notre Dame Law School and host of the popular radio program *The Manion Forum*, and Frank Cullen Brophy, an Arizona-based businessman and Goldwater benefactor, were both ahead of him. Buckley, however, would be drawn into the emerging Goldwater movement through his associations. Sharing Buckley's concern that Nixon, the presumed GOP nominee in 1960, would continue along Eisenhower's moderate path, Manion and Brophy formed the Committee of One Hundred in 1959. Its mission was to nominate Goldwater for either President or Vice President the following year. *National Review* donor Roger Milliken, who had revitalized the

Republican Party in South Carolina, was certain that his state's delegation would stand with Goldwater at the national convention, as would one hundred other delegates from across the South.[6] Others rallying behind Goldwater included Wisconsin industrialist Herbert Kohler, another friend of Buckley's and backer of *National Review;* Fred C. Koch, founder of Koch Industries, whose sons would also play significant roles in the conservative movement; and Robert Welch, founder of a new organization the media would soon make famous, the John Birch Society.[7]

Manion and Brophy thought it would be helpful to their cause if Goldwater published a manifesto that would serve as a rallying cry for conservatives. At Brophy's urging, Brent Bozell, Buckley's brother-in-law, now a member of Goldwater's staff, assembled a short book based on Goldwater's speeches. *The Conscience of a Conservative* became one of the most popular and influential political tracts in history. It sold eighty-five thousand copies in its first month, becoming an instant best seller. In the next four years it would go through twenty printings, selling 3.5 million copies.[8] Buckley proclaimed the book a guide on "how to defeat the threat of the Soviet Union, and how to remain free."[9]

Domestically, Goldwater wanted to restrict the federal government's role to those areas over which the Constitution expressly granted it jurisdiction. He set forth a vision of a smaller and more limited government: "I have little interest in streamlining government or in making it more efficient, for I mean to reduce its size. I do not undertake to promote welfare, for I propose to extend freedom. My aim is not to pass laws, but to repeal them. It is not to inaugurate new programs but to cancel old ones that do violence to the Constitution, or that have failed in their purpose, or that impose on the people an unwarranted financial burden. I will not attempt to discover whether legislation is 'needed' before I have first determined whether it is constitutionally permissible."[10] In foreign policy, he urged the defeat of Communism rather than its containment.

The book's publication in the spring of 1960 transformed Goldwater from an attractive and charismatic politician into a cult figure, especially among young conservatives, and made him the spokesman for the national conservative movement. Youth for Goldwater clubs sprang up on sixty-four college campuses in thirty-two states.[11] Americans for Goldwater, another group Manion and others assembled, boasted four hundred chapters nationwide. The John Birch Society sent postcards to convention delegates reading, "Nominate anybody you please, I am voting for Goldwater."[12]

With Nixon having secured enough IOUs to assure his nomination, Goldwater concluded that 1960 was not the year for him to wage a presidential campaign. Yet, fearful that Nixon would veer leftward, he hoped that conservatives might act as a countervailing force to party moderates to keep the presumed nominee "on track."[13] In his best-selling book, Goldwater had dismissed Eisenhower's "modern Republicanism" as "dime store New Deal." He had little use for Republicans who took what he called a "me-too approach" to public policy in the hope of making themselves more attractive to liberals and moderates and thought the GOP should offer voters a "choice not an echo."[14] He believed that southern Democrats would respond especially favorably to his pro–states' rights and strong defense messages.

Goldwater did not at first think that conservative ideologues were sufficiently dedicated to doing the "dirty, hard work" necessary to take control of a political party.[15] The Young Americans for Freedom and other conservative entities set out to prove him wrong. Stephen Shadegg, Goldwater's chief strategist, set down the basics of a plan through which Goldwater operatives would take control of the party's infrastructure. "It may take us four years; it may take us eight years, but to that objective we are committed," Shadegg declared.[16] With that as their goal, they set their sites on the Young Republicans, the Federation of Republican Women, state committees, and party caucuses. *National Review* dutifully reported on their progress.

With these undertakings in progress, the casual acquaintanceship that Buckley had forged with Goldwater blossomed into an important political alliance as well as a personal friendship. Such might not have been the case had either allowed early minor misunderstandings to stand in their way. In January 1961, Buckley voiced disappointment to Goldwater that the Senator had twice failed to mention *National Review* when he listed news sources he considered reliable and regularly read.[17] He reminded Goldwater that when Buckley complained about such an omission Goldwater had made on an earlier occasion, Goldwater had responded that he distinguished between newspapers and journals of opinion. On that occasion, Buckley reminded Goldwater, the Senator had offered a poor memory as his excuse. Buckley joked that if Goldwater had "a third memory loss," Buckley would throw himself out the window.[18] Goldwater yielded. "Telling audiences to read *National Review*," he replied, "was tantamount to telling them to read the Bible."[19]

A month later, Goldwater took umbrage when *National Review*, as part of a promotional campaign for the magazine, sent prospective subscribers postcards bearing Goldwater's photograph above the words "Barry Goldwater tells you how to survive Jack Kennedy." While Goldwater did not object to the use of his likeness or to the rest of the copy, he protested the headline's reference to Kennedy. "I have never told anyone how to survive Jack Kennedy," he complained to

Buckley. He said that the cards were a personal "embarrassment" to him and "degrading" to his position as a Senator. He demanded that the magazine stop using them and insisted that it consult him before using his name again.[20] Goldwater was clearly concerned that the incident might adversely impact his relationship with the President.

Anxious not to alienate the nation's most celebrated conservative but unwilling to incur the costs of a new advertising campaign, Buckley, in what he offered as a letter of apology, presumed to lecture the Senator on semantics. The word *survival,* he wrote, need not be interpreted in its "literal sense." Goldwater held his ground. After two more attempts to turn him around, Buckley capitulated.[21] He and *National Review* publisher William Rusher concluded that Goldwater's goodwill was worth more than the price of commissioning a new promotional effort. It proved a wise decision. As Goldwater's popularity and name recognition rose and his presidential campaign went into high gear, *National Review*'s circulation jumped from fifty-four thousand in 1961 to ninety thousand in 1964.[22]

In May 1961, Goldwater sought Buckley's advice before he debated Norman Thomas, the six-time Socialist Party candidate for President. Buckley replied that he found it effective to depict Thomas and his philosophy as "out of touch with modern times."[23] Having grown weary of seeing liberals portray conservatives as "reactionaries," Buckley advised conservatives to turn the tables on their accusers by casting them as the true reactionaries, resistant to new ideas and change. Buckley believed that the young, who had a dimmer memory of FDR than their elders, might be more open to alternatives to the New Deal than would older voters.

Impressed with Buckley both as a tactician and a strategist, Goldwater suggested that his younger friend run for Congress from Connecticut in 1962. "Don't laugh this off," he advised. "There is going to be a great conservative resurgence this year and we need our cleanup hitters in place."[24] Buckley responded that he would hold out until Goldwater was President and could name him Assistant Postmaster General, so that he might find out why it took three days to get a copy of *National Review* to make its way to New York from New Haven.[25] By this time, Goldwater had taken to praising *National Review* in his speeches and quoting from it in his syndicated newspaper column. He also approved subsequent requests to use his name in *National Review* advertising campaigns. In a letter to the head of the Idaho Republican Party, Goldwater described Buckley as "the 'Egg Head' of the conservatives in that he can take on any college professor in this country who professes to be a liberal and make the individual sorry that he ever got on the same stage with him."[26]

As Goldwater and Buckley were seeking to expand their influence, Robert H. W. Welch, whom history recalls as the founder of the John Birch Society, was doing the same. Although Buckley and Welch agreed on many issues and favored advancing their cause through both intellectual debate and grassroots activism, Buckley was growing concerned about behavior patterns Welch was exhibiting. He would eventually characterize certain actions Welch took as evidence of "nuttiness." On his retirement as editor of *National Review* in 1990, Buckley cited among his own greatest achievements "the absolute exclusion of anything anti-Semitic or kooky from the conservative movement."[27]

Of all the crusades Buckley took on in his half century on the national political stage, none did more to cement his reputation as a gatekeeper of the conservative movement—or consumed more of his time—than that which he launched against the John Birch Society, an organization Welch founded in 1958 and used as his personal vehicle to influence public policy. In 1961, Buckley complained to a supporter of both *National Review* and the JBS, "I have had more discussions about the John Birch Society in the past year than I have about the existence of God or the financial difficulties of *National Review*."[28]

Born in 1899 in North Carolina, Welch was admitted to the University of North Carolina at the age of twelve, graduated at sixteen, and attended both the U.S. Naval Academy and Harvard Law School, but graduated from neither. He became a chocolate salesman and introduced such items as Sugar Daddies (caramel lollipops), Junior Mints, and Pom Poms. Later, he served as Vice President of his brother's candy manufacturing company. He ran unsuccessfully for Lieutenant Governor of Massachusetts in 1950 and, like Buckley, supported Robert Taft's campaign for President and Joseph McCarthy's investigation of Communist infiltration of the government. In the mid-1950s, Welch served as a Director and regional Vice President of the National Association of Manufacturers until he retired in 1956 to concentrate exclusively on politics.

Buckley and Welch met in 1952. Their mutual publisher, Henry Regnery, introduced them and they maintained cordial relations throughout the 1950s.[29] Despite their difference in age, they appeared, at first, to have much in common. Both were men of means. Each demonstrated strong organizational and communication skills. Each edited a political journal. Welch titled his *One Man's Opinion* when he launched it in 1956. He changed its name to *American Opinion* after he founded the John Birch Society two years later. Buckley and Welch made it a point to support each other's enterprises. In a note accompanying his second $1,000 contribution to *National Review*, Welch made a passing reference to President Eisenhower not being on the "same side" of the ideological divide as were he and Buckley.[30] Buckley let the comment pass. Welch voiced doubts about Eisenhower's loyalties again a year later. In a letter to Buckley, he spoke of "conscious treason in propelling our ship of state down its present dangerous course."[31] Welch informed Buckley of a new organization he had started. This was the John Birch Society. Buckley offered to provide a "little publicity" for it, presumably in *National Review*.[32]

While both Buckley and Welch lamented the military and diplomatic setbacks that befell the United States in the early years of the Cold War, they disagreed as to the causes. Buckley attributed policy outcomes such as the stalemate in Korea, Soviet occupation of Eastern Europe, Soviet acquisition of nuclear weapons, the Communists' victory in China's civil war, and the success of Fidel Castro's Communist revolution in Cuba to misguided policies and lack of resolve among Western leaders. Welch considered them the result of Soviet penetration into the highest echelons of the U.S. government. In 1961, he estimated that 50 to 70 percent of the United States was "communist controlled."[33] Increasingly, Welch advised Buckley that he neither liked nor appreciated Buckley occasionally disagreeing with him on certain matters.

They had different takes on the impact Boris Pasternak's novel *Doctor Zhivago* would have. Buckley thought it would set back the Communist cause. Welch thought it to be a piece of Soviet propaganda. Welch took it upon himself to advise Buckley that Henry Kissinger, a young Harvard academician whom Buckley had proposed be named to the board that would assess the effectiveness of Radio Free Europe, was a Communist. He also passed along what he said was the opinion of "a growing number of people on the right" that *National Review* had succumbed to "modulation." For emphasis, Welch added that such criticism had not emanated exclusively from the "lunatic fringe."[34]

Late in 1958, Welch called a two-day meeting of prominent business leaders in Indianapolis during which he outlined the extent of Communist penetration in the United States. Three former heads of the National Association of Manufacturers attended. This was the first meeting of what became the John Birch Society. Welch named the group in honor of a young missionary who was killed by Chinese Communist forces in the waning days of World War II. He set as its mission countering Communist influence throughout the United States. In November 1958, Welch sent Buckley and several others a typed copy of "The Politician," a manuscript he had written. He had numbered each copy and asked that recipients return it to him after they had read it. The work's most startling conclusion was that Soviet penetration of the United States extended deep into the White House and that one of the USSR's principal agents was none other than the President of the United States. Dwight Eisenhower, he concluded, was a "dedicated, conscious agent of the Communist conspiracy."

He also identified as Communists who took their orders from Moscow Eisenhower's brother Milton, then President of Johns Hopkins University; his Secretary of State, John Foster Dulles; Dulles's brother, Allen, then Director of Central Intelligence; and former Secretary of State George Marshall, among others. In a note Buckley sent Welch along with the returned manuscript, he said that he found the charges against Eisenhower "curiously—almost pathetically optimistic." If Communist infiltration of the American government was as extensive as Welch claimed, Buckley argued, changing presidents would not relieve the situation. Nor would political organizing. "Reaching for rifles" might be a better approach, Buckley argued.[35]

In time, Buckley would say that Welch inferred "subjective intention from objective consequences"—because things went badly for the United States, policy makers must have intended those results and worked to achieve them; because China fell to the Communists, by Welch's lights, those heading the U.S. government must have planned that outcome.[36] Buckley's comments about the manuscript upset Welch. The JBS founder protested he had sent the manuscript to many people and that only Buckley "completely disagreed" with its hypotheses.[37] However, Goldwater voiced identical objections. "If you were smart," he wrote Welch, "you would burn every copy you have."[38] Years later, Buckley wrote that the "mischievous unreality" of Welch's charges "placed a great weight on the back of responsible conservatives."

Welch decreed that the John Birch Society would be autocratic in its governance. Any other organizational method, he insisted, would leave the society open to "infiltration, distortion and disruption." He proclaimed the very word *democracy* a "deceptive phrase, a weapon of demagoguery, and a perennial fraud."[39] The JBS would consist of clusters of chapters, each with about twenty carefully screened members. He set a goal of building a million-member force. Estimates of how many people actually became Birchers range from twenty thousand to one hundred thousand.[40]

Welch had JBS run "stealth" campaigns to win seats on local government bodies, where it would work to counter "communist domination." Its members paid close attention to book acquisitions by local libraries and pressed for the banning of certain titles. They organized boycotts of stores that carried goods imported from Communist countries. A merchant who stocked such items could find that Birchers had placed cards on counters and shelves bearing the words "Always buy your communist goods at ——," with the name of the store written in the blank space.[41] Birchers pressed local governments to impose heavy taxes, fees, or regulations on such merchants.[42]

Of the various projects the JBS took on, its campaign to impeach Chief Justice Earl Warren drew the most attention from the mainstream media. Welch pointed to a litany of actions the Supreme Court had taken under Warren's leadership that facilitated a Communist takeover of the United States: its striking down loyalty oaths; its extension of First Amendment protections to Communists; its ban of school prayer in public schools; its imposition of the "one man, one vote" principle in legislative apportionment; and, above all, its overturning of the "separate but equal" doctrine, which put the nation on a path to desegregation. Welch turned his disagreement with the Warren Court and its decisions into a national crusade.

National Review had editorialized against all the Supreme Court decisions to which Welch objected. It favored reversing them through congressional action, appointment of rightward-leaning Justices, and, where necessary, constitutional amendment. As a result of Buckley's opposition to the "impeach Earl Warren" campaign, *National Review* received numerous complaints by mail, many of them Birch generated. His sister Jane Buckley Smith, who had joined *National Review*'s staff, patiently explained to those writing in that a jurist's written opinions, however inflammatory, did not constitute "treason, bribery, or other high crimes and misdemeanors," the constitutional standard for impeachment.[43] Buckley argued in print that Warren rose in public esteem in direct relation to the intensity of Welch's efforts against the Chief Justice.[44] In a tongue-in-cheek parody of Welch's logic, Buckley suggested that the effort to remove Warren had failed because a Communist plot to discredit those opposed to Warren had succeeded.[45]

As the John Birch Society increased its influence, especially within conservative circles, Buckley tried to remain in Welch's good graces. His reasons were simple: *National Review* and JBS had many common subscribers, donors, and writers. At first, Buckley tried to differentiate between Welch and those who had joined his organization, attempting to make common cause with the latter while ignoring their leader.[46] That strategy worked for a time, until Welch's characterizations of Eisenhower became widely known. Once they began to appear regularly in the mainstream media, Buckley and others found it difficult to draw distinctions in the public mind between the JBS founder and his organization. In the fall of 1960, Buckley wrote Welch to inform him of a telephone conversation Buckley had had with Cap Breezley, a donor to *National Review* and a member of the JBS. Breezley had complained that Buckley was speaking ill of the JBS. Buckley related to Welch that he had informed Breezley that he had not spoken ill of the JBS, but he had criticized Welch. He had also taken that occasion to let Breezley know that he approved of actor Adolphe Menjou's decision to resign from the JBS once Menjou learned that Welch had proclaimed Eisenhower a Communist.

When Breezley made mention of the financial support he had given *National Review*, Buckley replied that *National Review* was "not for sale."[47] He refused Breezley's demand that he forge a "common front" with the JBS and refrain from criticizing people in the conservative movement he considered irresponsible. In response to Buckley's summary of the exchange he had had with Breezley, Welch wrote Buckley that he considered the differences between them minuscule.[48] By now, Buckley had learned to be wary of such reassurances.

Increasingly, it was becoming apparent to Buckley and his intimates that he could neither publicly maintain that he and Welch were comrades in arms nor successfully distinguish between Welch and the JBS in the public mind. In a memorandum to Buckley, a *National Review* staffer suggested that Eisenhower and several of his friends were determined to make Welch pay a price for slandering the former President. The employee told Buckley that Eisenhower was contacting friends of his in the media (people like William S. Paley, President of CBS News; and Henry Luce, publisher of *Time*) and voiced concern that *National Review* might become a casualty in the upcoming crossfire.[49] As the staffer had anticipated, once Welch's assertions about Eisenhower began to circulate, reporters began to take an interest in the JBS's more prominent supporters and members. It would only be a matter of time, Buckley's associate warned him, until they learned that several persons associated and affiliated with *National Review* also maintained ties to the JBS.

Among those who did were E. Merrill Root, J. B. Matthews, and Medford Evans (all of whom were on the magazine's masthead), Clarence Manion, Spruille Braden, and Mrs. Seth Milliken. Buckley's aide urged him to speak out against the JBS, lest he and *National Review* be harmed in an "atmosphere of smear."[50] In a heated meeting, Buckley and his editors debated how they might handle what promised to be a major problem. Neil McCaffrey and Bill Rusher urged that the magazine stay silent, fearful that a strong stand against Welch and his organization would put *National Review* in jeopardy. McCaffrey recanted but remained anxious. "Permit me to retreat on Birch—lest the magazine perish. . . . We can't afford to jeopardize the grudging status we've earned in the Liberal community, nor renounce our role of tablet-keeper, but the Liberals aren't going to bail us out of debtor's prison."[51] Rusher, worried about losses in readers and revenues, recommended founding a grassroots conservative organization that would act as a counterweight to what Welch was attempting through the JBS.

As rumors began to spread that *National Review* might issue a statement about Welch or the JBS, donors began to remind Buckley of their past contributions to his enterprise.[52] Mail poured into his office—again, much of it Bircher induced—advising Buckley to refrain from criticizing Welch. Fellow columnist James J. Kilpatrick, who had criticized the organization, warned Buckley of what lay in store for him: "As you know, these idiots set off on a harebrained campaign to impeach Earl Warren. The word got back to Welch that I thought the idea preposterous, whereupon he commanded all his faithful members to write Mr. Kilpatrick a letter. By God, they all did. The first 20 or 30 I answered with individual letters. The next 100 we answered with a mimeographed reply. The next 400, we filed. I am not even sure my Girl Friday is opening the damned things now. This has been the most incredibly disciplined pressure group ever to come my way, and we are frankly a little stunned by it."[53]

A sequence of unraveling events persuaded Buckley that he needed to act. The Kennedy administration was upping its attacks upon right-wing "extremism" in general and the JBS in particular. California Governor Pat Brown instructed his Attorney General to investigate John Birch Society activities in the state. The *Los Angeles Times* published a two-page letter from Richard Nixon decrying Welch's opinions and tactics. The California state Senate scheduled hearings. Senator Jacob Javits (R-NY) and Representative Henry Reuss (D-WI) pressed for congressional investigations. Senators Tom Kuchel (R-CA) and Thomas Dodd (D-CT), the latter a friend of Buckley's, denounced the JBS on the Senate floor. Attorney General Robert Kennedy called the JBS's activities a "matter of concern" to the Justice Department.[54]

While he disapproved of Welch and his antics, Goldwater was hesitant to denounce the JBS. He did his presidential prospects no favors when he called its members the "type of people we need in politics" and proclaimed the Birchers were some of the "finest people" in his community.[55] Sensing a liberal campaign to present all conservatives as indistinguishable from Birchers, Buckley swung into action. He wrote Goldwater in March 1961 that "Bob Welch" was "nuts on the Eisenhower-Dulles business" and said that Welch would do their common cause "much damage."[56]

A month later, Buckley ran the first of what would be several editorials on this subject. Entitled "The Uproar," it appeared at a time when Buckley still thought it possible to differentiate between Welch's observations and those issued in the name of the JBS. With the intention of unifying most conservatives behind the stand he was about to take, Buckley began with a strong attack upon the Left.

The John Birch Society was in the news, he said, because "liberals" and "the Communists" felt "threatened by revived [conservative] opposition" to their agenda. Given the widespread publicity the JBS was receiving, he noted with sarcasm that it could hardly operate in "secret," as was commonly reported.

He then speculated on the intentions of the organization's critics: "Certain elements of the press are opportunizing on the mistaken conclusions of Robert Welch to anathematize the entire American right wing. In professing themselves to be scandalized at the false imputation of pro-Communism to a few people, the critics do not hesitate to impute pro-fascism to a lot of people. In point of fact, the only thing many of these critics would like more than a conservative organization with vulnerabilities is a conservative organization without vulnerabilities."[57]

Having set the stage, Buckley repeated in public what he had privately said about the main failing in Welch's logic: that he inferred "subjective intention" from "objective consequences." He closed with the hope that the JBS would reject Welch's trajectory and thrive. Buckley was aware that once he had criticized Welch in this way, his target might suggest that Buckley had gone over to the Left or that he, like Eisenhower, had secretly been a Communist all along. He also knew that some would take advantage of the split within conservative ranks to discredit the entire conservative movement. "I wish the hell I could attack them [the JBS] without pleasing people I cannot stand to please," he mused in private.[58]

Reaction to Buckley's editorial was immediate and heated. To a Texan who wrote to cancel his subscription, Buckley answered: "Your letter deploring the stand of *NR* on the John Birch Society was written four days before *NR* took a stand on the John Birch Society, raising the question of whether you are a psychic, or merely credulous. Or maybe there is a Communist in our office who gives you bad information. We don't want any communist dupes as readers of *NR*, thank you very much."[59] To another he wrote, "You are a very unreliable reporter. I did not call the John Birch Society 'a bunch of fanatics,' though from the tone of your letter I rather gather that you yourself are one."[60] He would make more broadsides against Welch in the months to come and, four years later, would drop the pretense that Welch and the JBS membership could truly be differentiated either in the public mind or in reality.

As these internecine battles ensued within the conservative camp, Goldwater's much-anticipated presidential campaign began to take shape. On October 18, 1961, twenty-one men, including *National Review*'s leading benefactor, Roger Milliken, and its publisher, William Rusher, convened in Chicago to lay plans. They became the nucleus of what became the Draft Goldwater movement.

Goldwater, though he encouraged their efforts, had not yet committed to run. More than a year later, Rusher reported to Buckley that Goldwater believed Kennedy would defeat any Republican in 1964 and that the Senator was worried that if he was nominated and defeated, his failed candidacy would set the conservative cause back.[61] Nevertheless, he inched closer to running, fueled by a sense of loyalty to his supporters. Goldwater also relished the idea of debating Kennedy. He recalled in his memoirs that he had discussed with Kennedy the possibility of their touring the country together and exchanging views in a Lincoln-Douglas–style format.[62]

F. Clifton White, Rusher's former comrade in arms in the New York Young Republicans, began implementing the strategy Shadegg had devised the previous year. One of the challenges he faced was keeping John Birchers from infiltrating Goldwater's campaign. "We've got super-patriots running through the woods like a collection of firebugs, and I keep running after them, like Smokey Bear, putting out fires. We just don't need any more enemies," one Goldwater campaign official complained.[63] The candidate proved an unreliable ally to his managers who sought to keep the Birchers at bay. "Every other person in Phoenix" belonged to the John Birch Society, Goldwater wrote Buckley. They were hardly "cactus drunks," he said, "but highly respected people."[64] Goldwater singled out as a case in point Phoenix businessman Frank Brophy, who helped finance *The Conscience of a Conservative.* Goldwater's campaign manager, Denison Kitchel, like Menjou, had resigned from the JBS, but only after Welch's comments about Eisenhower began to generate headlines.[65]

Early in 1962, Goldwater convened a "summit" of key conservatives at the Breakers Hotel in Miami Beach to discuss how his campaign might handle the John Birch Society. In attendance were Buckley, Goldwater friend and General Motors publicist Jay Gordon Hall, Shadegg, William Baroody Sr. of the American Enterprise Institute, and author Russell Kirk. Buckley and Kirk suggested that conservatives simply "excommunicate" Welch from their movement. Buckley never tired of quoting Kirk's response when the subject turned to Welch's attack upon Eisenhower: "Eisenhower is not a communist; he is a golfer."[66] Buckley offered to write an even tougher editorial about Welch, advising conservatives to shun the JBS until Welch came to his senses. After Kirk joked that Welch might be "put away," Buckley suggested that Alaska was an appropriate venue, given that Welch had offered to send there anyone who doubted that the Communists were behind ongoing efforts to add fluoride to drinking water.[67]

As Buckley prepared to take on Welch for the second time in print, Burnham and Buckley's sister Priscilla were the only editors at *National Review* who favored such a move. "It is essential that we effect a clean break this time," Buckley wrote Goldwater in a not-too-subtle note. He added that the *John Birch Bulletin* reported that Goldwater's friend Frank Brophy had joined the JBS Council. "How's that for a sense of timing!"[68] Buckley also informed Welch of what he intended to do. "You will no doubt be hearing from around the country that I have been criticizing you and the John Birch Society. I want you to know that that is incorrect: I have been criticizing you, but not the Society. I am forced to criticize you because of your continued line (which as you know I believe defies reason) on the reaches of the Communist conspiracy within our own government. . . . We shall continue, then, to do much disagreeing about this and no doubt in vigorous language; but I hope we can maintain a pleasant personal relationship. I am prepared to, if you are."[69]

In a February 13, 1962, editorial headlined "The Question of Robert Welch," Buckley noted that many prominent conservatives had begun to doubt Welch's utility in the struggle against Communist domination. He questioned how the JBS could be effective when its leader held views so disparate from those of its members and "so far removed from common sense."[70] Buckley reported that Goldwater thought Welch should resign as leader of the JBS and that if he refused, the organization should dissolve and regroup under different leadership.[71] Again, Buckley criticized Welch for failing to distinguish between an "active pro-Communist" and an "ineffectual anti-Communist Liberal."[72] Of Welch's refusal to allow dissent within his organization, Buckley wrote, "He anathematizes all who disagree with him."[73] Buckley urged all who shared those goals to "reject, out of a love of truth and country," Welch's "false counsels."[74]

Before the issue went to press, Buckley tried to line up support from key conservatives, including a relatively new acquaintance he had made. "Dear Mr. Reagan," Buckley began, "Well, we have battened down our hatches and it's going to be hell. But as somebody said, the right thing remains the right thing to do. Would you let us have a short comment for publication in [*National Review*'s] next issue? I'd greatly appreciate it."[75] Reagan complied in the form of a letter to the editor in a subsequent issue.[76]

Buckley's second broadside against Welch had major consequences, both for him and for his magazine. James Lewis Kirby declined to seek reelection to the *National Review*'s board of directors and stopped his contributions.[77] Buckley described a "wrenching conversation" with longtime benefactor and Birch member Roger Milliken, who nonetheless continued to support the magazine.[78] Rusher reported that a "substantial fraction" of the magazine's readership "bled away" over the rest of 1962 and into 1963. He attributed the disappointing results of *National Review*'s direct mail campaign to the preponderance of

Welch loyalists on its mailing lists.[79] Mail protesting the editorial was so voluminous that Buckley responded by form letter. "I have letters from some . . . which are the quintessence of intolerance, of a crudeness of spirit, of misanthropy," he wrote in his column.[80] To Burnham, he complained that there was "no stopping these bastards."[81]

On the upside, as he had anticipated, mainstream and liberal commentators praised Buckley for taking on Welch. James Reston termed Buckley's editorial "brilliant."[82] The *Washington Post*, in its editorial praise of his stand, referred to Buckley as "a conservative Catholic who recently scolded the Pope for showing socialistic tendencies."[83] *Time* pronounced *National Review* a "surprising" new recruit to the ranks of the JBS's critics and proclaimed it an "increasingly lively, literate journal."[84] Clearly, Buckley was having an impact beyond the confines of the conservative movement.

Still, Buckley tried to retain a façade of cordial relations with the man he had denounced. One can only imagine Welch's reaction when he received this note from Buckley ten months later: "Three months have gone by since I read your bulletin. . . . I am very anxious to keep current on your thinking and the society's activities, and would be grateful if you would look into this. If our subscription has expired, I should be only too happy to look to renew it."[85]

As Buckley strove to cast Welch outside the parameters of responsible conservative opinion, Goldwater's handlers cut Buckley out of the inner circle of Goldwater's campaign. As White was overseeing delegate recruitment and mapping out convention strategy, Kitchel became campaign manager and William Baroody Sr. of the American Enterprise Institute took over the campaign's issues desk. Buckley had been trying to persuade the campaign to tap into the expertise of conservatives to provide Goldwater with intellectual support for his positions. He also wanted to brief the campaign about a potential donor who wanted to make a sizable contribution. He and Bozell arranged to have dinner in Washington with Dr. Charles Wiggamore Kelley, a friend of Goldwater's, to discuss both matters. When they arrived they found, in addition to Kelley, Kitchel and Baroody waiting for them. Buckley pursued the idea of the professors' committee, but refrained from bringing up the subject of the still anonymous donor.[86]

The next day, the *New York Times* reported on its front page that the Goldwater team had "just repelled a boarding party" from the Far Right.[87] In an odd twist of fate, the man who had worked to shield Goldwater from the taint of the John Birch Society was now being described by Goldwater operatives as "too far right" to be part of Goldwater's operation. By all accounts, including Goldwater's, Baroody was the source of this story.[88] In all probability, Baroody regarded Buckley and Bozell as competitors to his operation. Journalist Ralph de Toledano, a friend of Buckley's, thought that Baroody, the son of immigrants who had come up the hard way, considered Buckley a dilettante and did not take him seriously.[89]

Years later, Goldwater would write that had he known that Buckley and Bozell were willing to help him, he would have welcomed them into his campaign with "open arms."[90] He protested that at the time there was little he could have done. One of Goldwater's biographers, who had also worked as his campaign's Communications Director, disagreed: "There were several things he could have done to involve 1) the man who wrote the book that helped make him [Goldwater] a national political leader [Bozell]; 2) the editor of the most important conservative journal in America [Buckley]; and 3) the man who had been instrumental in creating the Draft Goldwater Committee without which the senator would not have been nominated for president [Rusher]. He could have asked Bozell to research and write speeches; he could have melded Buckley's contacts with Baroody's to produce an outstanding academic committee; he could have directed Kitchel . . . to include Rusher in their strategy sessions."[91]

Shunted to the sidelines, Buckley continued to advise the campaign through his column and in *National Review.* He decided that *National Review* would go all out for Goldwater in the run-up to the convention.[92] Burnham, who preferred Rockefeller to Goldwater as the 1964 GOP presidential nominee because of the Governor's hawkishness on defense and access to multiple resources—especially financial and well-networked staff—thought that the copy his colleagues turned in on Goldwater's behalf read like handouts from Goldwater's campaign.[93] Buckley grew increasingly frustrated at the amateurishness that both the candidate and his campaign were exhibiting. Although he privately complained that he devoted "roughly 75 percent" of his columns to "running interference" for Goldwater and "cleaning up after him," in public Buckley remained Goldwater's loudest cheerleader.[94] He informed his readers that what he most admired about Goldwater was that he appeared not to crave power for its own sake. Buckley praised Goldwater's "high purpose, intelligence, decency, humility, fear of the Lord, and . . . passion for freedom."[95]

To make Goldwater more palatable to party moderates who disparaged his candidacy, Buckley publicly recommended that Goldwater offer the vice presidential nomination to Dwight Eisenhower. (He was of the view that this would be constitutional provided that the Vice President did not succeed to the presidency, which would be in violation of limits the Twenty-Second Amendment set on the number of terms and years any person could serve as President) He wrote to the former President to ascertain his thoughts on the matter and enclosed a draft of a letter he intended to send to the *New York Times* in support of the idea.[96] As precedent for an ex-President returning to public service, Buckley cited the example of John Quincy Adams serving in the House years after leaving the White House.[97]

Buckley tried out his idea on Walter N. Thayer, President of the *Herald Tribune* and a prominent voice of liberal Republicanism.[98] That he had sought support for this concept from one of the pillars of the very establishment the conservatives sought to undermine through Goldwater's candidacy indicates the lengths to which Buckley was prepared to go to make Goldwater more palatable to the party's elite. Thayer wrote back that Goldwater would not be nominated and Eisenhower was finished with electoral politics. He offered Buckley a counter-proposal: a GOP ticket headed by Pennsylvania Governor William Scranton with Eisenhower's brother Milton, President of Johns Hopkins University, as Scranton's running mate.[99] Eisenhower kept his silence, and Buckley's "Draft Ike for vice president" became one of the shortest-lived publicity stunts in American history.[100]

In 1964, the vast majority of convention delegates were selected not in primaries but in party caucuses and conventions. Rockefeller, Goldwater's main rival, who was unpopular among party conservatives because of his high taxing and spending practices, detested in the South for his advocacy of civil rights for African Americans, and disliked by many because of his divorce and controversial remarriage, sought to demonstrate to party leaders and the media that he would be a more competitive candidate than Goldwater in the general election. He decided his best vehicle to show his electability was by doing well in a limited number of primaries. He resolved to go all out in New Hampshire, Oregon, and California. New Hampshire provided Buckley with one of his many opportunities to "clean up" for Goldwater. Before an audience in Florida, Goldwater recommended that Social Security be made a voluntary program. In a nationally televised interview, in response to a hypothetical question, he suggested that U.S. forces could employ tactical nuclear weapons to clear away the underbrush concealing the movement of the Viet Cong along the Ho Chi Minh trail en route to South Vietnam. Both comments proved highly controversial.

To the surprise of most pundits, Henry Cabot Lodge, then serving as U.S. Ambassador to South Vietnam and the beneficiary of well-managed write-in campaign, won the New Hampshire primary. With Lodge now considered a likely challenger to Goldwater's ambitions, Buckley wasted little time tearing into this new potential threat to Goldwater's nomination. After Lodge said "emergency conditions" in South Vietnam prevented his returning to the United States to campaign for the nomination, Buckley suggested that there were Vietnamese who felt that if Lodge left, "so might the emergency."[101] (He was referring to the recent American-approved coup that toppled South Vietnam's President Ngo Dinh Diem, to which Lodge had consented.)

Before publishing his tirade against Lodge, Buckley apprised the Ambassador's brother, John Davis Lodge, former Governor of Connecticut and a Buckley friend, of his intentions. He expressed the hope that his criticism would not affect their friendship. "I hope you will understand," Buckley wrote, "that the forthcoming assault on your brother is not meant in the least personally. . . . We are as convinced that . . . we would be better off with Senator Goldwater, as your brother was convinced in 1952 that . . . we'd be better off with Eisenhower. I hope that our publication of this piece in the next issue will not in any way damage our relationship. Even if it did, I should continue to have the greatest respect for you personally and professionally."[102] The friendship continued, as did Buckley's criticisms of Henry Cabot Lodge, who never entered the race.

After Rockefeller won easily in Oregon, he and Goldwater prepared for a dramatic showdown in delegate-rich California, which awarded all of its delegates to the victor of its June primary. Buckley launched a major print assault against the New York Governor. Weeks before voters went to the polls in California, he rhetorically inquired why, given Rockefeller's poor showing in primaries to date, as well as in polls, the New Yorker had not quit the race.[103] "Rockefeller will never quit," Goldwater wrote Buckley, "until he is sure he has destroyed me politically and, at the present rate, he has a little doing ahead of him."[104] Buckley next ventured into territory that was on many people's minds, but which few brought up publicly and especially in print: Rockefeller's marital situation. "Every serious political figure," Buckley wrote, believed that the Governor's decision to "take another man's wife, irrespective of the ravages of that decision on that man's children," foreclosed any chance of his nomination. He cited Connecticut Senator Prescott Bush, a well-respected party moderate, who had repudiated his early endorsement of Rockefeller on account of the Governor's complicated domestic situation.[105]

After Goldwater won the California primary, 52 percent to 48 percent, Buckley attributed the win to the Arizonan's conservative message rather than to his opponent's defects—which Buckley had been trumpeting, perhaps more than had most other commentators, for more than a year.[106] From Buckley's perspective, Goldwater's triumph was nothing less than spectacular: he had fulfilled the conservatives' decades-old dream of shifting the base of gravity within the GOP away from the eastern establishment and toward the more rightward-leaning South and West, regions from which most of Goldwater's delegates came. Buckley forecast that southern white voters would desert the Democratic Party and, together with conservative Republicans and other ex-Democrats elsewhere, would form the basis of a new governing coalition that would rule for a generation.

In his exuberance, Buckley all but lost his sense of perspective and proportion. He equated what he termed the ex-Confederacy's "sectional emancipation" from national liberal Democrats, who set policy for their party as well as for the country, with the struggle African Americans were waging against the very southern whites, many of them segregationists, whom Buckley praised Goldwater for "liberating." Buckley even evoked Dr. Martin Luther King Jr.'s words "free at last," which had so stirred his listeners at the 1963 March on Washington for Jobs and Freedom, in celebrating Goldwater's purported freeing of southern whites from liberal and Yankee rule.[107] That African Americans had yet to exercise the right to vote in much of the region Goldwater, in Buckley's words, had "set free" escaped his commentary, if not his notice.

Weeks later, Buckley appropriated another phrase associated with another liberal icon, this time John F. Kennedy, when Goldwater became one of six Republican Senators (out of thirty-two) to vote against the 1964 Civil Rights Act. Buckley declared Goldwater a "profile in courage."[108] The phrase came from the title of John F. Kennedy's Pulitzer Prize–winning book, in which he discussed eight U.S. Senators who had gone against the prevailing opinion (usually in their states and among their constituents).[109] One month after the bill became law, the Harris poll reported that national support for the bill stood at 54 percent and opposition at 18 percent, with the rest undecided. (At the same time, Goldwater's position was exceedingly popular in the South, a region he was courting.) Years later, Buckley would regard the stand he, Goldwater, and other conservatives had taken on this issue that year as a major mistake (see chapters 6, 8, and 10).

With Goldwater prepared to accept the nomination, Buckley cautioned conservatives against overconfidence. Though they had already made history, he said, an arduous task remained ahead of them. He put the odds of Goldwater defeating Johnson at five to one against. Proclaiming the task difficult, but not insurmountable, he sought to inject a dose of realism into conservative veins: "It is not helpful to Goldwater or to the conservatives to assert apodictically . . . that he will win. Goldwater's supporters have a less theatrical, but ultimately more alluring standard: that he should win."[110]

All the while Buckley continued to make Goldwater's case as persuasively as he knew how, Goldwater's official campaign continued to snub him. At a Young

Americans for Freedom rally at the Republican National Convention in San Francisco, Ronald Reagan, the master of ceremonies, received instructions to end the event before Buckley was scheduled to speak.[111] This had to have been a major humiliation to Buckley. He was proud of his association with YAF, a group he helped found, and its members all but idolized him. At a previous YAF reception at the same convention, groups of them threw streamers Buckley's way and serenaded him in song.[112] (A favorite was "Won't You Come Home, Bill Buckley?") Buckley wrote Reagan afterward suggesting that Goldwater's operatives had pulled Buckley from the program in order not to antagonize Eisenhower who, Buckley said, went "nuts" at the mere mention of his name.[113]

In a joint appearance with Buckley on David Susskind's television program *Open End,* broadcast from the convention, Gore Vidal chided Buckley about his exclusion from Goldwater's campaign. Sensing a chance to needle his adversary, Vidal suggested that without Buckley playing a major role in the campaign, Goldwater's chances might actually improve.[114] One reviewer of their exchange said that Susskind played the role of "zookeeper" between warring beasts. The *San Francisco Chronicle*'s Terrence O'Flaherty described Buckley's comportment as "bile with a smile." He suggested that the network was wise to retain two liberals, Susskind and Vidal, to contain Buckley, whom he described as "their guest from the radical right."[115] Buckley's bout with Vidal proved but a dress rehearsal for the personal confrontation the two would have at another national party convention four years hence. Buckley would also engage in future, if less heated, debates with Susskind, of whom he said, "If there were a contest for the title of 'Mr. Eleanor Roosevelt,' he would win it."[116] (In Buckley's view, the former First Lady was the quintessential mid-century liberal, who exuded compassion devoid of logic.)

On July 15, 1964, the night Goldwater officially became his party's presidential standard-bearer, Buckley received word that his sister Maureen, age thirty-one, had suffered a cerebral hemorrhage. Her illness resulted in his leaving the convention earlier than anticipated. Her death two days later marked the first serious tragedy in Buckley's life. "It didn't occur to me before that someone thirty-one years old could die," he said.[117] (The sad scene was replayed three years later when his oldest sister, Aloise, died of the same cause.)

Buckley's absence from San Francisco kept him from witnessing Goldwater deliver his combative and defiant acceptance speech, which included the memorable lines: "I would remind you that extremism in defense of liberty is no vice. And let me remind you that moderation in pursuit of justice is no virtue."[118] With Goldwater's opponents in both parties having made his campaign's purported tolerance of "extremism" a major issue throughout the primary season, the nominee's open embrace of the term ignited a new controversy. Soon Buckley was back in his familiar "cleaning-up" role. The Senator, he said, was as extreme in his advocacy of his cause (anti-Communism and limited government) as Martin Luther King Jr. had been in his (civil rights). By "extremism," Buckley said, Goldwater implied his total dedication to his cause.[119]

Observers picked up that Buckley and his cohorts at *National Review* had been shunted aside by Goldwater's operation. One well-placed Republican told presidential chronicler Theodore H. White, "You had got to say this for a liberal S.O.B. like [Arthur M.] Schlesinger [Jr.]: when his candidates got into action, he's there writing speeches." "Where . . . was Buckley and the *National Review* crowd?" White wanted to know. He reported that Goldwater's group considered Buckley, Burnham, Bozell, and others "too arrogant, too cold, too intolerant" and believed they "couldn't talk to people." White concluded that the campaign suffered from their absence, in that such intellectual heavyweights would have peppered it with concrete proposals and exciting ideas.[120]

Despite being sidelined, Buckley turned *National Review* into a think tank that he gladly put at the candidate's disposal, whether welcome or otherwise. He devoted an entire issue to what might be expected of a Goldwater administration. Ever audacious, he expressed the hope that future scholars would regard the issue's contents much as liberals looked back at seminal journalism that presaged the "Roosevelt revolution" of the 1930s.[121]

In addition to keeping Buckley outside their operation, Kitchel and Baroody shunted aside F. Clifton White the instant Goldwater had won the nomination. They also tried to prevent the airing of a major event that proved the one bright spot in an otherwise bleak campaign. Reagan had developed a speech, "A Time for Choosing," that humanized Goldwater and defended the principles he advanced. The campaign had rejected its use, but after Goldwater viewed it at Reagan's request, the candidate overruled his advisers and the speech was broadcast on October 27, 1964.[122]

In September, Buckley wrote Kitchel suggesting that Goldwater develop and release a coherent position on the ever-expanding welfare state. Liberals took this phenomenon as a given, he pointed out. He suggested that Goldwater advance a different view, and reassert his commitment to federalism as an alternative to an ever-increasing concentration of power in Washington. He also recommended that Goldwater pledge his administration to adopt the principle that no state whose median income was above the national average would receive federal assistance.[123] Buckley told Kitchel that he had once raised the idea with Goldwater and the Senator had expressed enthusiasm. He enclosed a memorandum he had prepared on the subject and volunteered to draft a speech for the nominee. He also offered to pitch it to friendly columnists, editorial writers, and intellectuals in advance of Goldwater's announcement, so that his proposal would receive ample coverage.

Kitchel wrote back that he doubted that the nation was "in a deliberative mood" and that the time was not right to make any suggestion that might entail a constitutional amendment.[124] A few days later he wrote Buckley again, promising to review his suggestions.[125] Kitchel wrote him a third time in late October to say that he found Buckley's ideas insufficiently conservative: "Frankly, Bill, I can't get over the idea that the fallacies of 'welfarism' would be begged by saying that it is all right to help States whose median income is below the national average. . . . I also have the feeling that such a proposal would present the Senator in the light of one trying to water-down his principles for the sake of public imagery and additional votes. This, I believe, could hurt more than it might help."[126] In other words, Buckley's ideas were too bold and not daring enough at the same time.

In the final weeks of the campaign, Buckley began preparing conservatives for a likely Goldwater defeat. He told a gathering of Young Americans for Freedom that, while victory was too much to expect, given the tenor of the times and the sympathy voters extended to John F. Kennedy's party after the President's assassination less than a year earlier, Goldwater's very nomination by a major political party, given his conservative beliefs, was a "glorious development" for conservatives. "Now is precisely the moment to labor incessantly to educate our fellow citizens," he said. "The point is to win recruits whose attention we might never have attracted but for Barry Goldwater; to win them not only for November 3 but for future Novembers: to infuse the conservative spirit in enough people to entitle us to look about on November 4, not at the ashes of defeat but at the well-planted seeds of hope, which will flower on a great November day in the future, if there is a future."[127]

In the campaign's closing weeks, Buckley denounced what he considered unfair and demagogic attacks against the Republican nominee. He reported that in a forty-eight-hour period, Southern Christian Leadership Conference Chairman Martin Luther King Jr., AFL-CIO President George Meany, and House Judiciary Committee Chairman Emanuel Celler all issued statements comparing the Goldwater movement to Hitler's.[128] Buckley was so disturbed at *Ramparts* magazine's special issue, entitled "The Compleat Goldwater," that he circulated it around his office with a note inquiring whether any of his colleagues had ever seen a candidate more maligned in such a way by a magazine that claimed to appeal to intellectuals. On the cover was a cartoon of Goldwater's head on a cobra about to inflict venom on its victims. Inside were the perspectives of half a dozen writers likening Goldwater and his movement to Hitler and his followers.[129] *National Review* took *Fact* magazine to task when it published an article in which 1,189 psychiatrists declared Goldwater "unfit" for the presidency.[130] (After the election, Goldwater won a libel suit against its publisher, Ralph Ginzburg.)[131]

After the election, Buckley lambasted certain scholars for evoking their professional credentials as a cloak behind which they issued unabashed partisan pronouncements. As a case in point, he cited Columbia historian Richard Hofstadter, author of an essay and a book on the Goldwater movement, both of which he titled "The Paranoid Style in American Politics."[132] Buckley considered Hofstadter representative of how liberal academicians assessed those who challenged their underlying premises: "Moderate liberalism is analyzed, but radical conservatism is diagnosed."[133]

Goldwater lost to Johnson by the largest margin in American history up to that time: 61.1 percent to 38.5 percent. He drew 27 million votes to Johnson's 43 million and carried just six states: his native Arizona and South Carolina, Georgia, Alabama, Mississippi, and Louisiana. In *National Review's* postelection editorial, Buckley picked up on the theme of his YAF address. The editorial presaged what would become a popular refrain among conservatives, "27 million Americans couldn't be wrong." Buckley proclaimed that number a significant base on which to build.

Working in Johnson's favor, Buckley argued, were a strong economy and a world that appeared to be at peace. (LBJ's decision to send hundreds of thousands of troops to South Vietnam was several months away.) Johnson also benefited, in Buckley's view, from Goldwater's failure to advance concrete policy recommendations. Buckley found it disappointing that, having won the Republican presidential nomination, Goldwater rarely returned to arguments he had made in *The Conscience of a Conservative.* (He did not rehearse all the suggestions the Senator's campaign had rejected.)

Buckley concluded, as did Theodore H. White, that Johnson had waged his campaign on fear: fear of nuclear war, fear of the end of the social safety net, fear of the loss of farm and other subsidies. He noted that after losing the 1924 presidential election in a landslide, Democrats had "seized American history by the mane eight years later and ruled supreme for twenty years."[134] He suggested that if conservatives were to duplicate FDR's success in redirecting the course of American politics, they needed to develop a massive public education campaign that demonstrated how their agenda would leave the country in a better place. Unless conservatives did so, he warned, "they will never have a president they can call their own."[135]

In a letter to Buckley two days after the election, Ronald Reagan, whose destiny was to be that President, offered his own views as to why Goldwater had not prevailed as well as ideas of how conservatives might more forward. "I think at the national level there were some errors in strategy," he wrote.[136] Yet, he saw the 27 million voters, not all of them Republicans, who had stood with Goldwater as part of an emerging conservative coalition. Reagan, like Buckley, voiced disdain for Republicans who had not enthusiastically supported Goldwater and who rejoiced in his defeat.[137] In a postelection submission to *National Review,* Reagan made two additional points: (1) the electorate had rejected not conservatism but the false image of it that Goldwater's detractors presented, and (2) conservatives needed to present their ideas in a more positive way that addressed the concerns of ordinary, hard-working Americans.[138]

Goldwater's campaign proved pivotal to the conservative movement and to Buckley's career. It demonstrated that an effective nuts-and-bolts operation mobilized by a dynamic candidate could emerge as the dominant element within a major political party, transform that party's basic philosophy, and produce a new electoral coalition. It underscored to him how a candidate's opponents would undermine that entire effort by defining it to the public and the media by the actions and words of its most extreme supporters. It afforded him the opportunity to forge bonds with a kindred spirit, Ronald Reagan, who was able and willing to learn from Goldwater's mistakes and open to what Buckley and others had to teach him. It also demonstrated to him that a candidate's failure to run an issues-oriented campaign in general elections, as well as in primaries, could discourage supporters and embolden opponents.

Confident in his political instincts and his skills as a strategist, Buckley began to wonder how he himself might fare as a political candidate. Were he to run for office, he would have the power to decide on tactics and strategy that would guide his effort and would be free to run on issues of his own choosing. Late in 1964, Buckley the columnist peppered F. Clifton White with intricate questions about how Buckley might transition himself into the role of a candidate. On December 7, 1964, Buckley, Reagan, and their wives sat down to dinner in Los Angeles. Within months, both would be contemplating campaigns of their own. With Goldwater's star fading and Reagan's yet to rise, Buckley had become the de facto leader of the conservative movement.

8

PART OF THE WAY WITH LBJ

In December 1963, *National Review* offered an early appraisal of Lyndon Johnson's transition into the presidency: "The editors of *National Review* regretfully announce that their patience with President Lyndon B. Johnson is exhausted."[1] Johnson had been in office less than a month. The line was vintage Buckley. It reflected his concern that Johnson, the consummate politician, would use any means available, including emotional appeals, to move through Congress proposals Kennedy could not. In a televised address to a Joint Session of Congress two days after Kennedy's funeral, Johnson urged swift passage of four of Kennedy's priorities: tax cuts, federal aid to education, the War on Poverty, and what would become the Civil Rights Act of 1964.[2]

Buckley opposed all of these measures save the tax cuts. All would pass by the summer of 1964. By the time Johnson was elected President in his own right, carrying forty-four states and piling up two-thirds Democratic majorities in both houses of Congress, he seemed poised to achieve the primary objective of his political career, picking up where Franklin D. Roosevelt had left off when it came to marshaling the resources of government to solve the nation's domestic problems and improve the quality of life of all Americans. That would mean greater centralization of power in Washington at the expense of the states and localities, more federal intervention in the economy, higher taxes, increased regulations, more social engineering, and at least two new entitlements. Kennedy, a Democrat by convenience and historical circumstance, was fundamentally interested in foreign affairs. Johnson was a committed New Dealer who owed his political career to government connections and largesse. As President, he saw himself primarily as a domestic reformer.

With liberalism approaching its high-water mark by the mid-1960s, conventional wisdom held that conservatism faced a bleak future. At *National Review*'s tenth anniversary dinner in the fall of 1965, Buckley cautioned his audience to pay close attention to what was transpiring in Washington. "It is all very well to ignore the Great Society, but will the Great Society ignore us?" he inquired.[3] The nascent conservative movement could and would criticize the "Great Society" as it was unfolding but remained too weak a force to slow it down, let alone stop it.

With regard to the most immediate foreign policy challenge the nation faced, whether and how to prevent a Communist takeover of South Vietnam, an American ally, conservatives vacillated over how much support to give an administration that seemed not to know its own mind. When Johnson appeared to rule out using all the means at his disposal to assure a military victory over the Viet Cong (Communist forces in the South) and its patron, North Vietnam, they found it increasingly difficult to defend a policy whose major objective was stalemate.

By and large, through much of Johnson's tenure, Democrats all but exclusively set the nation's policy agenda, with the major exception of California, where Ronald Reagan, elected as Governor in 1966, proceeded in a direction different from both the national administration as well as governors of both parties. That would begin to change in 1968, when a series of rapidly unfolding events brought down Johnson's presidency and helped unravel the New Deal coalition of northern political machines, labor unions, intellectuals, Catholics, white ethnic groups, African Americans (who could vote in states outside the South), and white southerners that had made the Democrats the predominant political party since at least 1936.

Early in Johnson's tenure, Buckley praised the President for projecting "an air of competence."[4] He even appeared relieved that Johnson lacked Kennedy's charisma. Because Johnson's personality was "not of the kind that demands lionization," Buckley said the country would be spared the necessity of a "fresh emotional commitment" after the grief it had endured following Kennedy's assassination.[5] Sensing a lack of enthusiasm for Johnson among liberal intellectuals and Kennedy enthusiasts, Buckley referred to the new President as the Democrats' "institutional" choice in 1964 and credited his nomination to Democrats' perception of an absence of a better alternative. Observing the candidate on the stump, Buckley, like Johnson's Democratic detractors—many of them ex-Kennedy aides—referred to LBJ as "Dr. Cornpone."[6]

Still, Buckley marveled at the vigor and ambition Johnson displayed in his first days in office. "There is an energy about the man," he wrote, "which mortifies those of us in our thirties, who would not have the energy to give away more than a few million dollars a day, if we were president."[7] The "liberal mode" was so much more appealing to so many more people than the conservative one, he continued, because of its capacity to give the impression of instant gratification. Johnson was the "perfect embodiment of that kind of national exuberance and he is giving us a wonderful ride."[8]

When a month after Johnson's election the press reported that the IRS would be "cracking down" on the tax-exempt status of some right-leaning organizations, Buckley seemed less concerned than he had been when the previous administration had attempted the same. He advocated moving to a tax structure that eliminated most exemptions and reduced "polarities" in the tax rate as the only failsafe way to keep the tax code free of such abuses.[9] His relative nonchalance could perhaps be attributed to Robert Kennedy having left the Justice Department, which meant that he personally would have no direct role in such audits.

With Johnson having "colonized everyone from the militant left to the easygoing right" in his recent campaign, Buckley predicted that LBJ's main opposition would come not from Republicans but from Kennedy, now the newly elected Senator from New York. (Comparing RFK's hold on the public to Johnson's, Buckley remarked, "It is always easier to be seduced by Don Giovanni than by Leporello.") Kennedy, he predicted, would move either to Johnson's left or to his right, depending on wherever Johnson happened to be.[10]

As Johnson's presidency unfolded, African Americans upped their efforts to secure the right to vote in the South and southern whites grew increasingly resistant, with the Ku Klux Klan and other white vigilantes resorting to violence and terrorism. In his writings and speeches, Buckley showed increased sympathy for the goals of the civil rights movement and for the rights of citizens to demonstrate. While he continued to oppose an increased federal role in guaranteeing voting rights, he shifted his emphasis, criticizing more frequently those who resisted change in the South than he did those seeking federal assistance in bringing it about.

Buckley ridiculed practices designed to keep African Americans off the voter registration rolls, such as making would-be registrants state the number of bubbles in a bar of soap. He condemned proprietors of commercial establishments who declined service to African Americans in violation of the recently enacted Civil Rights Act. When future Georgia Governor Lester Maddox protested against the open public accommodation section of that law by chasing African Americans out of his restaurant, wielding the handle of an ax, Buckley found it "theoretically and morally inexplicable" that anyone would voice opposition to a law by retaliating against its "innocent beneficiaries."[11]

Increasingly, Buckley's columns sounded like lectures to southern conservatives to obey laws and court orders rather than reiterations of the doctrine of states' rights, the traditional argument southern politicians evoked against federal intervention. He appealed to the best instincts of southern society to eschew violence and other acts of cruelty. "And the best elements of the South will bear in mind that no hardship visited upon it by Northern egalitarians or judicial ideologues warrants retaliation against Negro school children," he cautioned.[12] Gone were references to the southern "cause" and the perpetuation of existing practices through extreme measures that had peppered his editorials a decade earlier. Increasingly, Buckley made appeals to southerners to change their ways, evoking idioms they would recognize.

By now, Buckley was no longer describing African Americans as less "advanced" than their white counterparts in the South. He showed no patience for whites he considered "primitives" (southern politicians who incited racial violence and race-baited in their campaigns) and evidenced increased sympathy for their victims. And he demonstrated nothing but contempt for southern officials who evoked what he considered sound constitutional principles (such as federalism and states' rights) solely to perpetuate a system that oppressed African Americans. Mississippi, he concluded, could not "have it both ways": it could not preserve its right to set voting requirements while using race as the single criterion of (voter) eligibility.[13]

Still, Buckley remained skeptical of democracy's capacity to improve social conditions. He worried that once enfranchised, African Americans in the South would prove just as easily manipulated by demagogues as had other voters: "Too many countries in the democratic world have gone down into totalitarianism because some demagogue or other has persuaded everyone who can stagger to the polls to go there, and vote: usually to give power to himself—that was the route the Argentinians took when they voted to surrender their freedom to Peron. The challenge . . . is to lure to the polls those who will cast responsible votes."[14] He recounted how urban machines had sustained themselves in power by manipulating turnout and committing voter fraud, and wrote that he had seen how "welfare populists" had wrested control of southern state governments from the more genteel Bourbons by stirring up racial resentments among poor southern whites. (Once elected, they, to his dismay, had no qualms about accepting federal aid and intervention for programs of all kinds, but put up obstacles to African Americans enjoying any of the benefits.)

On March 7, 1965, the Alabama State Police violently assaulted civil rights demonstrators on the Edmund Pettus Bridge as they marched from Selma to Montgomery in pursuit of voting rights. In a televised address to the nation before a Joint Session of Congress days later (March 15), President Johnson put the federal government on the side of the marchers. As he proposed what became the Voting Rights Act of 1965, he evoked the phrase "We Shall Overcome" (the title of what had become the unofficial anthem of the civil rights movement). Buckley found Johnson's speech "moving" but called the President's proposed remedy to the problem "a monument of inexactitude." Yet he left no doubt in readers' minds that he considered the denial of the vote to African Americans on equal terms with whites a denial of "true equality": "On the single issue of whether a Negro in Alabama should be deprived of the vote simply because of the color of his skin, it seems to me there cannot be any argument: none moral, and certainly none constitutional."[15]

By coincidence, on March 7, 1965, the very day of the assaults on the Pettus Bridge, the *New York Times Magazine* published the transcript of a debate Buckley had had with novelist James Baldwin weeks earlier at Cambridge University on the topic "Has the American Dream Been Achieved at the Expense of the Negro?"[16] More than seven hundred had crowded into the hall, with another five hundred watching on closed-circuit television. Taking the affirmative, Baldwin maintained that much of the nation's economic success came through the exploitation of African Americans over the centuries. In rebuttal, Buckley cited the very heights Baldwin had attained in the literary world as evidence that African Americans could and did succeed in the very society Baldwin condemned. This being the case, he denied the necessity of government action to enable people to overcome past hardships and espoused self-help movements within African American communities as both morally preferable and more effective. The audience voted Baldwin the winner, 544 to 164.[17]

In August 1965, after the Voting Rights Act became law, *National Review* praised the "seriousness and hope and quiet pride" it detected on the faces of African Americans lining up to register to vote. It also acknowledged the role religion played in the civil rights movement: strengthening the resolve of the early marchers and embellishing the rhetoric they used to make their case. Buckley's editorial spoke of the tremendous transformation this extension of the franchise would bring to the South. The editorial cautioned against policy makers using voting rights as a precedent for further federal encroachments upon the powers of state and local governments.[18] But, consistent with Buckley's prior statements, *National Review* had not opposed the act per se. The editorial's tone suggested that its author had come to accept this instance of federal intrusion as a necessary step to bring an end to what had been a decade of strife in the region.

Looking back on this period thirty years later, Buckley voiced regret that *National Review* had not looked more favorably on the cause of civil rights earlier. "I rather wish we had taken a more transcendent position, which might have been done by advocating civil rights legislation with appropriate safeguards," he wrote a historian in 1995.[19] In 2001, he told the journalist Jeff Greenfield, an early *Firing Line* regular, that he lamented that conservatives had not been more forceful in their advocacy of civil rights in the 1960s.[20] In 2004, Buckley was even more emphatic when he told *Time* magazine, "I once believed we could evolve our way up from Jim Crow. I was wrong. Federal intervention was necessary."[21]

Buckley objected when civil rights leaders shifted their attention to other matters, such as increased spending on public works, higher minimum wages, and federal housing legislation, all of which were then part of the liberal agenda. "There are millions of Americans," he insisted, "who wish actively to fight prejudice but who do not wish, in the course of doing so, to commit themselves to the socialization of American life."[22] He criticized the Reverend Martin Luther King Jr. when the civil rights leader used the moral authority he had attained through the civil rights movement to condemn the war in Vietnam. Buckley was incensed when King called the United States the "principal purveyor of violence in the world" and likened U.S. behavior in Vietnam to atrocities committed by Hitler. He noted that prominent African Americans, including Senator Edward Brooke, diplomat Ralph Bunche, NAACP Executive Director Roy Wilkins, and former Johnson aide Carl T. Rowan, had also criticized King's remarks and shared his view that, in making them, King had set back the cause of civil rights.[23] Buckley attributed King's veering into the antiwar movement to a desire to appease younger, more radical elements within the civil rights movement who had grown impatient with his leadership.[24]

In 1966, in the aftermath of riots in northern cities and the accompanying "white backlash," Buckley called for a five-year moratorium on new civil rights legislation. He urged that people of goodwill use that hiatus to enforce existing laws, secure order, and provide educational and employment opportunities for African American students and workers. He also called upon civil rights leaders to condemn civil disturbances and exclude from their movement those who committed or encouraged violence and to be more vigilant in denouncing crime.[25]

Buckley's comments on the civil disturbances of 1966 occasioned both an exchange and a warming of relations between him and Johnson's Vice President, Hubert Humphrey. After Humphrey was reported to have said that, if he had to live in a slum, he himself might revolt and would "lead a mighty good" uprising, Buckley, in his column, accused Humphrey of having condoned violence.[26] Humphrey wrote Buckley that the media had misrepresented the Vice President's remarks, having compressed them into a single "clip" that was shown on television. Humphrey invited Buckley and others of his "brilliance" to lend his voice to efforts to "clean up our cities."[27]

Buckley, in response, suggested that the two of them meet in person. "You are one of the few public men of liberal bias with whom I always fancied that a dialogue would be possible," Buckley wrote Humphrey. He reminded his new correspondent that he and Humphrey had a mutual friend in Buckley's erstwhile professor and colleague Willmoore Kendall, who had known Humphrey when the two were on the faculty at Louisiana State University early in their careers.[28] Later in his term as Vice President, Humphrey wrote Buckley complimenting him on something he had written: "I'm beginning to believe you are a nice man."[29] Buckley replied that he found that possibility "disconcerting."[30]

Buckley dissented when the Kerner Commission, a group LBJ appointed to study the causes of the 1967 riots in Newark and Detroit and to recommend policies that might prevent further violence, identified white racism as the root cause of the racial disturbances. Buckley embraced the commission's call for increased efforts to improve education, job training, and employment in minority communities and said that such efforts would have been necessary had the riots not occurred. To Buckley, the riots originated in the psychological disposition of their perpetrators, who experienced boredom, suffered from self-hatred, and believed that society as a whole had caused their poverty and its accompanying maladies. He noted that not all who suffered the effects of poverty and discrimination resorted to violence.[31]

After the Reverend Martin Luther King Jr. was assassinated in April 1968 in Memphis, Buckley praised the fallen leader's "extraordinary capacity to inspire." He also criticized King, as he had in the past, for not having condemned tyrannical one-party African regimes that denied freedom to their citizens as vigorously as he had denounced white segregationist state governments in the United States. Although he praised King for having made nonviolence a hallmark of his movement, Buckley never accepted civil disobedience as a legitimate form of protest. He even suggested that King, through his advocacy of breaking the law in obedience to a "higher law," might have unleashed the forces that led to his own death.[32] "Dr. King's discovery of the transcendent rights of the individual conscience is the kind of thing that killed Jim Crow all right," Buckley wrote. "It is also the kind of thing that killed Bobby Kennedy."[33] To Buckley, law breaking was law breaking, whatever the motives of the offender. Most criminals, he would maintain, in some way thought they had been in the right when they took it upon themselves to commit an offense against society. If others could consider "just" a law King determined "unjust," surely, while most would condemn "murder," an assassin might justify it as a means of serving a higher cause. So Buckley argued.

Buckley thought it appropriate to construct a physical memorial in the nation's capital to the slain civil rights leader for his "courage, moral strength, and great eloquence." Initially, though, he found the expenditure of public funds to honor someone who sanctioned the breaking of laws—for whatever reason—at odds with the maintenance of civil society.[34] In time, Buckley came to favor designating King's birthday a federal holiday, notwithstanding the irony he noted that such a measure would bestow upon King an honor the nation had yet to extend to Abraham Lincoln, who had ended slavery in North America and whose work King had continued. Still, Buckley argued, a King holiday was a fitting tribute to a race of people greatly oppressed during much of U.S. history.[35]

Buckley proved particularly astute in his analysis of Lyndon Johnson's handling of American involvement in Vietnam. Four months after having defeated the seemingly more hawkish Barry Goldwater, in part by casting himself in the role of the "peace candidate," Johnson substantially increased American participation in the ongoing conflict months after the election. In response to an attack by the Viet Cong upon the American military base at Pleiku, Johnson sent thirty-three hundred additional U.S. troops to South Vietnam. (These were in addition to the sixteen thousand noncombat forces already there when he took office.) By the end of 1965, Johnson had increased the number of U.S. ground troops to two hundred thousand.

At this juncture, Buckley proclaimed Johnson a worthy heir to the Democratic Party's liberal anti-Communist wing. When Johnson later drew fire from liberals, many of whom had advised his predecessor, such as Arthur M. Schlesinger Jr. and Robert Kennedy, Buckley accused Johnson's now left of center critics of hypocrisy and wrong-headedness. From the first, Buckley anticipated that liberals within and outside Johnson's coalition would press for an American withdrawal from South Vietnam once Johnson had steered the Voting Rights Act to passage.[36] Up until that time, the liberal coalition, including hawks and doves, that had been in place since at least 1948 had held together.

From the time he had worked to discredit Henry Wallace's presidential campaign in 1948, Buckley proved a shrewd observer of left-wing opinion leaders, organizations, publications, and networking patterns. He sensed in the months following Johnson's reelection that many, not only the Left but also much of the establishment, liberal and otherwise, that had swelled the size of his landslide, were not that all keen on committing a large influx of American military forces and other treasure to assure an independent South Vietnam. "Virtually every conservative and Republican was endorsing Johnson's hardening policy," Buckley noted. He then inquired, "Where are those liberal businessmen, who pilgrimage every few months to kiss the emperor's ring?"[37] Big business remained a special target of Buckley's over the years. Like his father before him, he thought it too willing to trade with Communist powers, too accommodating to increased federal intervention in the economy, and too eager to use its influence to obtain government subsidies, contracts, and other favors.

As far as Johnson's inner circle was concerned, Buckley had little confidence in Johnson's three top advisers on national security, National Security Adviser McGeorge Bundy, Secretary of State Dean Rusk, and Defense Secretary Robert McNamara, all Kennedy holdovers. The three had played a role in shaping Kennedy's policies toward Cuba (which began with a botched insurgency against Castro and ended with the Cuban leader remaining in power, free to support revolutionary activities elsewhere in the Western Hemisphere). Buckley correctly credited Bundy with recommending the policy of "gradualism," which entailed meeting every aggression the enemy committed in kind, as opposed to overwhelming it with sufficient and sustained force. He noted that Rusk had been part of the faction at the State Department that pressed the Truman administration to cut off aid to Chiang Kai-shek during China's civil war and doubted that Rusk would show greater tenacity in the face of a strong Communist adversary than he did then. Buckley belittled McNamara for thinking he could measure American progress through systems analysis, flow charts, and body counts. He dubbed this trio the three points of Mars's trident.[38] He sensed that this team regarded Vietnam as a problem to be managed, rather than a war to be won.

By the summer of 1965, Buckley was voicing concern about mounting casualties in Vietnam and the absence of a coherent American strategy to reverse this trend. "An American boy who turns 18 on the first day of July," he wrote, "may well be dead by Easter, having meanwhile been drafted, trained, and sent to Southeast Asia." (These words were practically identical to those Lieutenant John Lawrence had uttered to impress upon Buckley, then in training for OCS in 1945, to take seriously tasks assigned him. Clearly, they had made a lasting impression upon him.) Buckley wondered out loud why Johnson did not ask U.S. allies in the region, such as the Philippines, Thailand, Malaysia, and Taiwan, to help resist a Communist takeover of South Vietnam.[39] (He would make this very argument a generation later when George W. Bush ordered the invasion of Iraq.)

Buckley urged Johnson to bomb the North Vietnamese oil tanks that fueled the trucks that carried ammunition south to be used against American soldiers. Drawing a distinction between "liberating" Hanoi from Communist rule and weakening its capacity to wage war against the South, he made clear that he was not arguing for the former.[40] (This represented a change from the position he had once held with regard to North Korea after General Douglas MacArthur advocated unifying the peninsula by force.) He also urged Johnson to order a blockade of North Vietnam.[41] (LBJ would do most of what critics to his right, Buckley included, had urged, but at a slower pace than they had advocated and after opposition to the war had hardened.)

Buckley noted that Republicans and conservatives, normally expected to constitute the responsible opposition to the liberal Democratic President, were of two minds with regard to Vietnam. They deplored the administration's handling of the war and the relatively low priority the President appeared to be awarding it, compared to that which he gave his activist domestic agenda.[42] But they largely left it to liberal Democrats and moderate Republicans to question the war's purpose.

By the end of 1965, Buckley, breaking ranks with some of his fellow hawks, demanded that if Johnson was not prepared to win the war, he should withdraw U.S. forces—and quickly. Buckley's colleague James Burnham maintained that by repeatedly stressing that he was not seeking a military solution to the conflict and insisting that he was using U.S. military power to entice Hanoi to negotiate with the United States and South Vietnam, Johnson had limited his options, therefore making eventual withdrawal more likely. Prolonging the existing situation, Buckley and Burnham agreed, would only delay the inevitable and add to the sacrifice of American troops and treasure.[43] They had little use for Johnson's argument that the United States, through the sacrifices it was making, sought no more than a chance for the South Vietnamese to determine their own destiny. (Again, he awarded greater salience to the substance of freedom than he did to the forms of democracy. He certainly was unwilling to wage war in support of the right of Vietnamese to elect a Marxist government.)

Buckley was openly contemptuous when Johnson asserted that if South Vietnam elected a Communist government, the United States would pull out its troops. "If we accepted such relativist standards 25 years ago," Buckley wrote, "we would never have liberated France, which settled down in 1941 quite comfortably to rule by the Nazis."[44] Again, echoing a position his father had taken decades earlier, Buckley argued that the U.S. military should be used only to further discernible American interests, not be deployed in the service of an abstract principle, in this case, the right of self-determination. Buckley would voice similar objections when Nixon echoed Johnson's justification for a continued U.S. presence in South Vietnam. He would also oppose deploying U.S. military forces in "nation-building" efforts in the Balkans and Iraq.

In an editorial published in *National Review* early in 1966, Buckley laid out the dilemma Johnson confronted within his domestic liberal coalition: whether to shrug off the militant Left or capitulate to its demands.[45] Resolving it in a way that pointed toward a military victory, Buckley suggested, would prove difficult for a man with Johnson's "ravenous appetite for power" who desired the affection of a group as powerful and influential as the Left.[46] As the year wore on, Buckley reflected on the irony of the GOP, the purported more "hawkish" party, supporting Johnson on Vietnam, while "pacifists," "collaborators," and "isolationists," all to the President's left, opposed him.[47]

He dubbed the antiwar movement the "new isolationists" and satirized some of its most prominent leaders. He derisively referred to famous pediatrician Benjamin Spock, co-Chairman of the Committee for a Sane Nuclear Policy, as a prominent "babyologist" and proclaimed that Yale chaplain Reverend William Sloane Coffin would rather bomb Alabama than North Vietnam.[48] Likening opponents of the war in Vietnam to the isolationists of the 1930s and 1940s (in whose ranks he once belonged) would become a familiar Buckley refrain. He would recycle the phrase, using it to characterize those who opposed Reagan's military buildup in the 1980s.

Buckley voiced exasperation when, on those few occasions when Johnson did take bold military action against Hanoi, he did so without accompanying fanfare. He believed that Johnson had wasted an opportunity to build support for his policies after he ordered the bombing of Haiphong harbor in the spring of 1967.[49] Buckley detected a disturbing pattern in Johnson's behavior: taking strong military action, then following it with delays in the hope that the enemy would negotiate, if only to avert a greater U.S. military offensive—only to find that the enemy had used the interval to fortify, regroup, and advance. This cycle repeated many times.

Early in 1968, after Communist forces mounted coordinated attacks upon U.S. installations throughout South Vietnam during the Tet Offensive, Buckley urged Johnson, in another break with many hawks, to refuse General William Westmoreland's request for an additional two hundred thousand troops.[50] Instead, he favored renewed attempts to reduce the enemy's capacity to prosecute the war through blockades, economic embargoes, attacking the overland supply routes, freezing financial assets, and other tactics that did not depend on military action on the ground.

In response to arguments some within the administration voiced that such actions would bring North Vietnam's patrons (the USSR and the PRC) into the war, Buckley retorted, "Isn't it curious that [Johnson] . . . should fear the Kremlin more than he fears Arthur Schlesinger, Kenneth Galbraith, and Robert Kennedy?"[51] Buckley reserved his harshest criticism for former Kennedy advisers who, once out of office, turned on JFK's successor; he taunted them by suggesting that Johnson had proved a more effective President than had their hero: "And the spirit of John Kennedy will be evoked by the doves, who have always been anxious to disapprove of the man who occupies their idol's chair, whose style is so different from that of their fallen hero, and who, to their considerable vexation, manages to get more done in Congress than ever their man was able to do."[52]

As frustrated as he was by the President's indecisiveness, Buckley showed compassion for the Johnson the man. "The left," he wrote, "was not content merely to abominate the policies of Lyndon Johnson. Now they are going one step further—the final step, which is to justify their hatred intellectually."[53] He held up as an example cartoonist Jules Feiffer's confession, made in the introduction to the book *LBJ Lampooned*, that the "secret ingredient" of truly successful lampooning was "professional hate." Feiffer explained that as long as Johnson was passing programs that those on the left supported, they had endured his "bad moral style."[54] They grew less tolerant of it and showed increasing incivility toward him once Johnson took actions they opposed in Vietnam.

After Johnson announced on March 31, 1968, that he would not seek another term as President, Buckley interpreted Johnson's action as nothing less than a complete capitulation to Robert Kennedy. The New York Senator had declared his own candidacy for President on March 17, five days after Minnesota Senator Eugene McCarthy captured 42 percent of the Democratic vote in the New Hampshire primary, nearly matching the write-in vote for Johnson. People "built like Lyndon Johnson," Buckley declared, "do not voluntarily give up their power."[55] He hoped that once Johnson was no longer a presidential candidate, he would use his remaining time in office to do all within his power militarily to bequeath to his successor an independent and secure South Vietnam.[56] Instead, to Buckley's dismay, Johnson opted for more bombing halts and negotiations, absent suspension of hostilities.

Skeptical of plebiscitary democracy, which he saw as having driven Johnson from office, Buckley doubted that even half of those who had voted for McCarthy could identify the Senator's position on Vietnam.[57] Conservatives, he wrote, had learned to be fearful of electoral stampedes; history taught that "instant guidance by the people" was often followed by instability, and instability was "subversive to freedom."[58] By appearing to welcome his "pop-star" status, RFK, Buckley said was practicing "cult of personality" politics, which was almost always "dangerous."[59]

While Buckley had little personal contact with Johnson, the President and his staff were aware of his influence, and not only with conservatives. Johnson's files contained clippings of columns Buckley had written in support of bipartisan efforts to pay the legal expenses of a Johnson ally, the hawkish Democratic Senator Thomas Dodd of Connecticut, who would ultimately be censured for corruption. White House aides sent Buckley's columns to prospective donors. Late in her husband's presidency, Lady Bird Johnson wrote a letter to Buckley thanking him for having praised her for speaking out against the anti-American bias that had been part of an international exhibition in San Antonio. Mrs. Johnson told Buckley that his comments about the show were a "delight to read" and said that she was a "great admirer" of his syndicated column.[60]

As Johnson prepared to leave office, Buckley begged his readers' indulgence as he listed, by category, all that Johnson had wrought in the name of improving the quality of American life—a list he found exhausting to assemble:

> Anti-poverty programs, mass transportation bills, model cities help, rent supplements, crime control, anti-segregation acts, voting acts, housing acts, communications relations act, acts on water and air pollution, on waste, roads, recreation and parks, on meat and poultry and fabrics and farm prices, on truth in lending, on fair packaging, on electronic radiation, on traffic; aid to elementary schools, for higher education, for teacher corps, aid to the poor, adult education, job opportunity training, the job corps, business aid, aid for Appalachia, an increase in the minimum wage, Medicare for the elderly, Medicaid for the non elderly, doctors training, nurses training, mental health, immunization, health centers, and child health.[61]

He noted the paradox that in spite of such a legacy, Johnson left office "lonely, unloved, and discredited"—including by those who purportedly benefited from his initiatives.[62]

On learning of Johnson's death, he wrote, "The Great Society did not lead us into eudemonia."[63] He was even more damning when it came to Johnson's handling of the issue that destroyed his presidency. "Even if history justifies Lyndon Johnson's determination to stand by South Vietnam, it is very difficult to believe that history will applaud his conduct of the war. We set out in Vietnam to make a resonant point. We did not make it resonantly. In international affairs as in domestic affairs, crime is deterred by the predictability of decisive and conclusive retaliation."[64]

Having spent his entire life as a politician and almost exclusively interested in domestic concerns, Johnson was used to negotiating with pragmatists. Buckley believed that LBJ had never encountered an adversary as implacably committed to his cause as Ho Chi Minh. The stance he adopted toward his adversary suggests that Johnson regarded his rival not as the determined ideologue and nationalist that he was but as a fellow politician interested in striking a deal. He therefore adopted an approach not unlike that which he might show in negotiations with a recalcitrant congressional committee Chairman. In a speech delivered at Johns Hopkins University, after he had decided to increase the number of U.S. forces in South Vietnam, Johnson offered no less than a New Deal and Great Society for the people of Southeast Asia. He proposed damming the Mekong River to provide food, water, and power on a scale that would "dwarf even our TVA" (Tennessee Valley Authority) and a host of other investments in education, health care, and agriculture—all in exchange for a cessation of hostilities.[65]

Johnson, Buckley noted, "paid a high price for the office he discharged" and probably endured up to that time "the greatest sustained vituperation in American political history." Through it all, Johnson, he thought, acquired a certain dignity, which lifted him up from "buffoonery into tragedy."[66]

9

"Demand a Recount"

Buckley's decision to run for Mayor of New York City in 1965 as the candidate of the three-year-old Conservative Party proved a turning point in his career and in the life of the conservative movement. By challenging a charismatic liberal Republican in a place where this brand of Republicanism was strong and at a time when Lyndon Johnson, buoyed by his landslide victory in the 1964 election, was pressing ahead on his Great Society initiatives, Buckley invigorated conservatives, still devastated by Barry Goldwater's defeat just months earlier, all across the country.

Having nothing to lose by conducting what he termed a "paradigmatic campaign," Buckley sensed an opportunity to showcase conservative alternatives to liberal policies at a time when such programs were becoming the norm in big cities.[1] Much of what he proposed would later become conventional dogma, and not only for conservatives. Buckley challenged the very idea of "group interest liberalism," a system in which power brokers maintained control by drawing support from voting blocs anticipating future favors. Such a system, he argued, perpetuated the status quo and blocked real reform, as most voters belonged to more than one such bloc. Buckley appealed to voters as individuals concerned with the "general interest" of the entire city. With his relative youth (just under forty), wit, erudition, colorful personality, and penchant for the theatrical, Buckley easily attracted attention. In time he would use the attention he received for broader purposes than outlined in 1965.

Buckley's mayoral run originated in a speech he delivered at the New York City Police Department's Holy Name Society Communion Breakfast on April 4, 1965. Before an audience of fifty-six hundred police officers, he spoke about increased allegations of police brutality. These remarks came a month after law enforcement personnel had attacked civil rights marchers on the Edmund

Pettus Bridge in Selma, Alabama, creating nationwide sympathy for the marchers and their cause. Outside the South, allegations of brutality against local police departments and individual officers were also on the rise. The summer before Buckley addressed the Holy Name Society, a New York police officer had shot and killed an African American teenager. Calls for the establishment of civilian review boards to investigate charges against police officers had become a steady refrain among liberals.

Buckley opposed the idea. He believed that charges against the police had been overstated and that rising crime posed a greater threat to New Yorkers than occasional overreactions by the police. (As he had done in his defense of Joseph McCarthy, Buckley put what he considered the welfare of the majority ahead of the rights of the perceived and alleged victims.) He acknowledged that abuses of authority by police did occur and maintained that such incidents were best addressed through procedures already in place. He also argued that recent Supreme Court decisions had made it more difficult to apprehend and convict criminals and predicted that law-abiding citizens would suffer the consequences.

In his talk, Buckley referred to the events in Selma, which he said had "aroused" the "conscience of the world."[2] The controversy that followed his presentation flowed from what he said next. Relying on information from an unnamed source (he later confessed he had been misinformed), Buckley said that coverage of the Selma events on television had not included footage of police showing considerable restraint while demonstrators provoked them "beyond endurance."[3] Even if he believed what he was reporting at the time to be true, his decision to reference the events in Selma to argue against a civilian review board in New York seemed ill advised. If he was looking for an example of a false accusation against a police officer to bolster his case against a civilian review board, he might have found an example closer to home.

Also in his talk, Buckley said that he failed to comprehend why the murder of civil rights activist Viola Liuzzo, a white woman from Detroit who had journeyed south to participate in the civil rights protests, received the press attention it did. Given the warnings southern officials had issued about local resentment of "outsiders" coming into communities and interfering with customary social arrangements, Buckley said the attacks could have been anticipated. Liuzzo, he pointed out, had made the decision to drive on a "lonely road in the dead of night" in the company of a young African American man. Critics later charged that Buckley had implied that Liuzzo was responsible for her fate.[4] Any neutral observer might have found his comments, combined with what he said about the Alabama State Police, insensitive at the very least. Still, the misreporting of his audience's reaction to his speech and the disinclination of public figures to correct that faulty reporting taught Buckley a lesson about both municipal politics and the press.

The next day's *New York Herald Tribune* reported that the audience had applauded Buckley's praise of the Alabama police and laughed at his comments about Liuzzo. Buckley remembered that his listeners remained silent in both instances. The *New York Times*, having made no mention of applause or of laughter in its "bulldog" edition (the first issue that went to press and hit the streets, usually around midnight), published an expanded story the next day under the headline "Buckley Praises Police of Selma: Hailed by 5,600 Police Here as He Cites 'Restraint.'" Legendary baseball great and civil rights activist Jackie Robinson, who had not been present, criticized what he took to be Buckley's remarks and chided Mayor Robert F. Wagner, who was in attendance, for remaining silent as Buckley had spoken ill of civil rights marchers. Robinson also demanded to know how many police officers belonged to the John Birch Society.[5]

Unable to persuade the *Herald Tribune* to retract or modify its story, Buckley sued for libel. Fortunately for his case, his hosts had recorded his remarks and Buckley played the tape to the press. The recording captured neither the applause nor the laughter that the two newspapers had mentioned. Clearly audible were Buckley's references to the "injustices" African Americans suffered. After hearing the tape, John Leo, an associate editor of *Commonweal*, reported in the *National Catholic Reporter* that nineteen of the twenty-six quotations the *Herald Tribune* story attributed to Buckley were misquotes.[6] The *Herald Tribune* agreed to correct the record and Buckley withdrew his suit.

Buckley had seen up close how politicians, in this case Wagner, can become evasive—even misleading—in answering direct questions from the press. Rather than address the false reportage, Wagner told reporters that he disagreed "fundamentally with Buckley's views" (as if the controversy that erupted had been about Buckley's position on taxes). Wagner also said that he could not control the "off-duty reaction" of city employees (giving credence to allegations about laughter). Buckley had also seen up close how, in an era of "pack journalism," a single newspaper (however wrong in its facts) could determine the official narrative of its competitors and how reporters could be oblivious to the damage their coverage inflicted on those wrongly charged. "Corrections," he observed, "very seldom catch up with distortions."[7]

Buckley told a biographer that he decided to run for Mayor forty-five minutes after he addressed the Holy Name Society.[8] This glimpse of how politics was practiced in New York and his rising disdain for the city's political class encouraged him. That liberal Republican Congressman John V. Lindsay was also contemplating a mayoral run provided Buckley with an additional incentive. Should Lindsay win the top electoral post in a city where registered Democrats outnumbered Republicans three to one, Buckley surmised, commentators and national power brokers would declare him a contender for the 1968 Republican presidential nomination. Lindsay's nomination—or that of someone with a similar ideology—might reverse inroads conservatives had made into the party's infrastructure and philosophical orientation the previous year with the nomination of Barry Goldwater for President.

In 1964, Lindsay had won reelection to a fourth term in Congress with 71.5 percent of the vote in what had been a banner Democratic year. His campaign telegraphed his national ambitions with the reelection slogan "The District's Pride, the Nation's Hope." In 1965, the mayoralty seemed the only available way station for him that lay between the House of Representatives and the White House. The state's Republican Senator, Jacob Javits, had considered a mayoral run but chose to remain in the Senate, and Nelson Rockefeller, still a presidential prospect, was planning to seek a third term as the state's Governor in 1966.

With Wagner retiring after twelve years at City Hall and the Liberal Party poised to endorse Lindsay over any likely Democratic nominee, the Congressman's prospects appeared reasonable. In exchange for their support, the Liberals demanded that Lindsay name one of their operatives to his ticket and award the Liberal Party one-third of mayoral patronage. Buckley referred to this arrangement whenever Lindsay donned the robes of a reformer and attacked his Democratic opponent as "boss backed." He delighted in asking the Congressman if he considered Liberal Party Chairman Alex Rose and his deputy David Dubinsky, President of the International Ladies Garment Workers Union, political "bosses."

Born in 1921, the son of a well-to-do investment banker and lawyer, Lindsay attended the prestigious Buckley School (no relation) in Manhattan, St. Paul's School in New Hampshire, and Yale, from which he graduated in 1943. He advanced the date of his graduation in order to enlist in the navy, served in both theaters of World War II, and won five battle stars. Discharged with the rank of Second Lieutenant, Lindsay entered Yale Law School, graduated in 1948, began practicing law in New York, and gravitated into politics. He helped found the Youth for Eisenhower club in 1951 and a year later became President of the New York Young Republican Club.

After Eisenhower became President, Lindsay became Special Assistant to U.S. Attorney General Herbert Brownell, who had managed Thomas E. Dewey's campaigns and kept a hand in New York politics. In 1958, with Brownell's backing, Lindsay obtained his district's GOP congressional nod and

Left: Buckley's paternal grandfather, John Buckley, served as Sheriff of Duval County, Texas, in the late nineteenth century. He acquired a reputation for integrity, honesty, and empathy for Mexican Americans. (Courtesy of Cameron O. Smith.)

Right: Aloise Steiner Buckley as a young bride. Buckley's mother, the daughter of a socially prominent New Orleans family, was twenty-two at the time of her marriage in 1917. (Courtesy of Cameron O. Smith.)

Below: The Buckley family in Gstaad, Switzerland, 1930. Five-year-old Billy is to the right on the front sled (wearing the black and white hat). (Courtesy of Cameron O. Smith.)

Above: Billy Buckley with sisters Patricia and Priscilla, 1936. (Courtesy of Cameron O. Smith.)

Below: The ten children of Aloise Steiner Buckley and William F. Buckley Sr. in 1941. *Back row, left to right:* John, James, Bill, and Patricia; *front row:* Reid, Aloise, Priscilla, Carol, Maureen, and Jane. (Courtesy of Cameron O. Smith.)

Second Lieutenant William F. Buckley Jr. Drafted into the U.S. Army at eighteen, he could not easily relate to people who differed from him in background, interests, and political and religious views. (Courtesy of Cameron O. Smith.)

Buckley as a Yale undergraduate. Fresh from military service at the age of twenty-one, he enrolled at Yale University and immediately cast a long shadow on campus. (Courtesy of Cameron O. Smith.)

Left: The William F. Buckleys, Sr. and Jr., at Bill's wedding, 1950. (Courtesy of Cameron O. Smith.)

Right: Mr. and Mrs. William F. Buckley Jr., 1950. (Courtesy of Cameron O. Smith.)

Below: Buckley siblings and spouses, early or mid-1950s. *Back row, left to right:* sister Jane and husband, Bill Smith; brother Reid's wife, Betsy; brother Reid; and sister Aloise's husband, Ben Heath. *Middle row:* sister Patricia's husband, Brent Bozell (Buckley's debating partner at Yale and later coauthor); sister Patricia; brother John's wife, Ann; Bill's wife, Pat; sister Priscilla; brother Jim's wife, Ann; and sister Aloise. *Front row:* John, Bill, and James. (Courtesy of Cameron O. Smith.)

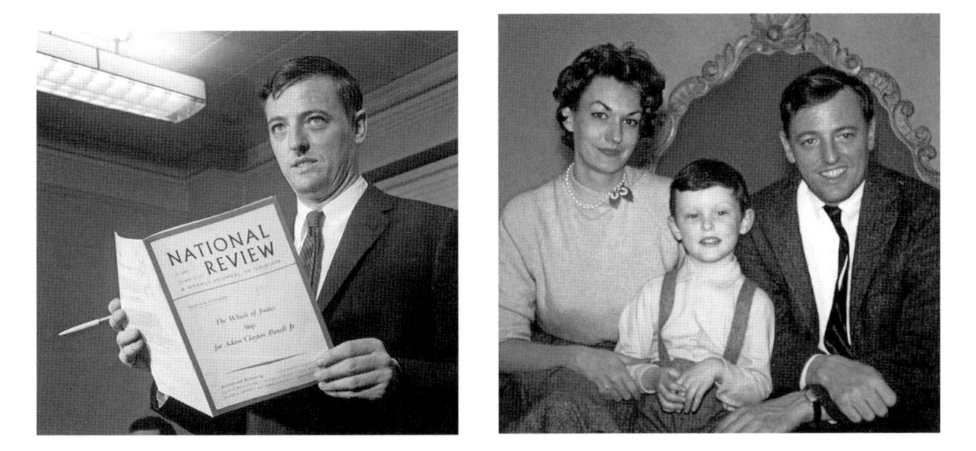

Left: Thirty-year-old Buckley examines the first copy of *National Review*, a "journal of fact and opinion," in 1955. (Bettmann Collection/Getty Images.)

Right: Bill, Pat, and Christopher Buckley, circa 1956. (Courtesy of Cameron O. Smith.)

Buckley and Barry Goldwater, the candid and charismatic Senator from Arizona, in 1969. After Goldwater won the Republican presidential nomination in 1964, Buckley turned *National Review* into the candidate's unofficial headquarters. (From *Firing Line*, episode #166, Firing Line Broadcast Records, Hoover Institution Archives.)

Above: The New York City mayoral hopeful with reporters and advisers in 1965. Buckley became a favorite of the city's press corps when, in response to a question, he declared that he would "demand a recount" in the event he was elected. Leaning against the wall is Buckley's brother James, the official manager of the campaign. (Photograph by Cornell Capa © International Center of Photography / Magnum Photos.)

Below: Buckley and Congressman John V. Lindsay, the Republican-Liberal candidate for Mayor of New York in 1965, listening to their Democratic opponent, Abraham D. Beame. An experienced debater, Buckley knew how to capture an audience's attention even when he was not speaking. (Photograph by Cornell Capa © International Center of Photography / Magnum Photos.)

Buckley holds up a one-word letter of protest ("Judas!") he received in 1965 from a member of the John Birch Society in response to his sustained criticism of the organization and its founder, Robert Welch. (Truman Moore/The Life Images Collection/Getty Images.)

Buckley, man about town. During a subway strike in 1966, he navigated through Manhattan traffic on a motor scooter. Often his destination was a television studio. (Philippe Halsman/Magnum Photos.)

On November 3, 1967, *Time* put Buckley on its cover. (From *Time Magazine*, November 3, 1967, © 1967 Time Inc. Used under license. *Time* and Time Inc. are not affiliated with, and do not endorse products or services of, Licensee. Drawing by David Levine.)

Favorite sparring partners. Buckley and Harvard economist John Kenneth Galbraith enjoyed a decades-long friendship and shared a reverence for language, style, and wit. (From *Firing Line*, episode #465, Firing Line Broadcast Records, Hoover Institution Archives.)

June 29, 1962

MEMORANDUM FOR

MR. McGEORGE BUNDY

I attach herewith the approved text of the Yale speech. The President told me before he left for Mexico that he wanted to restore some, but not all, of the introductory jokes. You may want to take a hard look at the second paragraph. I wish we didn't have to dignify Buckley by Presidential allusion.

Arthur Schlesinger, jr.

as:gs

John F. Kennedy was the first President to refer to Buckley in public. In an address at Yale University in 1962, JFK cited Buckley among other Yale alumni who had caused problems for the administration. (Memo, Schlesinger to Bundy, 6/29/1962. Arthur Schlesinger, Jr. Personal Papers. Series 2.6.2. Remarks for the President, 1961–1963, Box WH-67, Folder: "Address at Yale University, 6/11/1962 (1 of 3)." John F. Kennedy Presidential Library and Museum.)

Buckley and Robert Kennedy at a chance encounter at New York City's El Morocco restaurant in 1967. After Kennedy declined his invitation to appear on *Firing Line*, Buckley inquired, "Why does the baloney reject the grinder?" (*New York World Telegram and Sun* Archives. Photograph by Al Levine.)

Informed that Senator Edward M. Kennedy was spending a skiing holiday at the Galbraith residence in Switzerland, Buckley invited Kennedy and his party to dinner at the Buckleys' chalet. As was his custom, Buckley suggested that his guests join him in a favorite pastime, painting. Here, circa 1970, the two hold up their work. (Courtesy of Cameron O. Smith.)

Buckley with presidential aspirant Richard Nixon on *Firing Line*, 1967. (From *Firing Line*, episode #69, Firing Line Broadcast Records, Hoover Institution Archives.)

Buckley helped Nixon's 1968 election campaign significantly by undermining third-party candidate George Wallace's claims to be the true "conservative" in the race. In this exchange on *Firing Line*, Buckley charged that Wallace was just another big-government Democrat who supported increased federal spending and intervention in most areas except those intended to uphold the civil rights of African Americans. (From *Firing Line*, episode #88, Firing Line Broadcast Records, Hoover Institution Archives.)

Below: ABC retained Buckley and novelist Gore Vidal as commentators during the 1968 national conventions. Their nightly appearances produced some of the most memorable and vitriolic exchanges in the history of television. (Image courtesy of Magnolia Pictures and Participant Media and the Estate of Stanley Tretick from the documentary film *Best of Enemies*.)

Above: Buckley and colleagues at work at the *National Review* office, early 1970s. *Clockwise from left:* Chris Simonds, assistant managing editor; Pat Carr Simonds, copy editor; Priscilla Buckley, managing editor; Buckley, editor in chief; James Burnham, whom Buckley considered the "leading intellectual force" at the magazine; and Linda Bridges, Buckley's close collaborator and one of the few he trusted to edit his writing. (Alfred Eisenstaedt/The Life Picture Collection/Getty Images.)

Below: Buckley with South Dakota Senator George McGovern. Although they agreed on little, the conservative commentator and the 1972 Democratic presidential nominee respected each other's intellect, independence, and integrity. (Photograph by Jan Lukas. © Helena Lukas. Reproduced courtesy of Helena Lukas.)

Above: The brothers Buckley celebrate James L. Buckley's election to the United States Senate in 1970. Throughout Senator Buckley's years in office, *National Review* consistently referred to him as the "Sainted Junior Senator from New York." (Bettmann Collection/Getty Images.)

Below: Buckley and former protégé George F. Will share a relaxing moment in 1978 while taking part in a debate against Ronald Reagan and two compatriots over the future of U.S. control of the Panama Canal. (From *Firing Line*, episode #306, Firing Line Broadcast Records, Hoover Institution Archives.)

Above: President Ronald Reagan and Buckley in 1986. Reagan attributed his transformation from liberal Democrat to conservative Republican to Buckley's tutelage. (Courtesy of Ronald Reagan Presidential Library and Museum and Ronald Reagan Presidential Foundation.)

Below: First Lady Nancy Reagan and Buckley at the Waldorf Astoria Hotel in 1984. Buckley defended Nancy Reagan against critics' barbs as strenuously as he did her husband. (Courtesy of Ronald Reagan Presidential Library and Museum and Ronald Reagan Presidential Foundation.)

Although Buckley knew George H. W. Bush longer than he did Reagan, their friendship was rooted more in personal chemistry and common associations than in a shared philosophy. Here, Bush awards Buckley the Presidential Medal of Freedom in 1991 as the First Lady looks on. (Courtesy of the George Bush Presidential Library and Museum.)

President George W. Bush congratulates Buckley in the fall of 2005 upon his eightieth birthday and the fiftieth anniversary of *National Review*. (Photograph by Paul Morse. Courtesy of the George W. Bush Presidential Library & Museum/NARA.)

The ever-effervescent William F. Buckley Jr. in 1985. (Courtesy of Christopher Little.)

won election to Congress from the Upper East Side. Buckley liked to say that Lindsay's district, the so-called Silk Stocking District, "sheltered not only all the resident financial, social, and artistic elite in New York, but the national concentration of vegetarians, pacifists, Communists, Randites, clam-juice-and-betel-nut eaters" alongside a "sprinkling of quite normal people."[9]

Lindsay became known as the most liberal Republican in the House of Representatives. The liberal Americans for Democratic Action gave him an 85 percent approval rating. He was among the House Republicans who voted to enlarge the Rules Committee, then seen as a move to ease consideration of President Kennedy's civil rights agenda. Conservatives chafed at Lindsay's support for foreign aid and opposition to the House Un-American Activities Committee, loyalty oaths, and confiscation of obscene materials sent through the U.S. mail. (In justifying these positions, Lindsay joked that Communism and pornography were major industries in his district.)[10] Most significantly, conservatives resented Lindsay for having refused to support Barry Goldwater for President in 1964.

On May 13, 1965, the forty-three-year-old Lindsay announced his candidacy for Mayor. Labeling his campaign a "moral crusade," he claimed ideological kinship with three Republican historical figures: Presidents Abraham Lincoln and Theodore Roosevelt, and Fiorello La Guardia, New York's fusion Mayor of the 1930s and 1940s. Days later, Buckley published a column titled "Mayor, Anyone?" in which he put forth a ten-point program to lead New York City out of what he termed its "perpetual crisis."[11] His blend of social conservatism and economic libertarianism would later find echoes in proposals made in the campaigns of Jack Kemp, Ronald Reagan, House Speaker Newt Gingrich, and future New York Mayors Ed Koch, Rudy Giuliani, and Michael Bloomberg.

To reduce crime, Buckley would either imprison juvenile offenders or release them in the custody of parents or guardians, who would be responsible for future offenses their charges committed. He would provide property tax relief to communities that undertook voluntary community policing. He favored the repeal of narcotics laws that pertained to adults and would allow addicts to purchase drugs at pharmacies with prescriptions, with the possible proviso that they undergo treatment. He favored legalizing gambling in all its forms. He wanted to exempt teenage workers from minimum wage laws, thereby reducing youth unemployment, and end union monopolies over city contracts. Businesses that located in depressed areas and hired local residents would, under Buckley's plan, receive tax benefits.

To keep traffic moving, Buckley wanted to ban commercial vehicles from loading and unloading between the hours of 8:00 a.m. and 4:00 p.m. and relieve taxi shortages by allowing anyone without a police record and with a valid driver's license to operate any vehicle as a taxi.[12] He favored residency requirements for welfare and wanted to require that recipients without children under fourteen years of age perform some kind of work. He would ban sending children to any school outside the "plausible geographical limits of their residence" for whatever reason (a long way of saying he opposed "busing" to achieve racial balance).[13]

When *National Review* reprinted the column in the back section of the magazine, as it did with three of Buckley's columns in each issue, Priscilla Buckley, the magazine's managing editor, placed a teaser on the upper left corner of the cover: "Buckley for Mayor?" That, along with the column's recommendations, fed speculation about her brother's intentions. Though registered to vote in Connecticut, Buckley maintained an apartment in the city. After ascertaining that he had sufficient time in which to change his legal residence, Buckley informed Conservative Party Chairman Daniel Mahoney on June 7 that he would accept the party's nomination for Mayor.[14] Whenever Lindsay or others referred to Buckley as a Connecticut resident, Buckley would point out that he had lived in the city longer than Robert Kennedy had when he won election to the U.S. Senate from New York the previous year.[15] "I don't know why Mr. Lindsay is so hostile to Connecticut," Buckley would say. "Perhaps because he went there to be educated and, for manifest reasons, is displeased with the results."[16]

Buckley made rising crime his signature issue. Insisting that crime was exclusively the fault of lawbreakers and not in what he termed the "genealogy of their aberration," he demanded tougher sentences.[17] He never tired of pointing out that the vast majority of the city's poor were not criminals; indeed, they were often the victims of criminals. In contrast, Lindsay spoke of the social origins of crime: The "better off," he declared, "must finally learn that there are no islands anymore; that their security can be protected and preserved only if those less fortunate are rescued from the long night of misery and deprivation. . . . As long as inequity remains a dominant fact of life for millions, New York will remain a powder keg of unrest."[18]

Buckley argued strenuously against relaxing accepted rules of conduct to the point that antisocial behavior was accommodated in the name of social protest. He noted that novelist James Baldwin had declared tenants' throwing garbage out of windows a form of protest and mischievously inquired whether conservatives might be allowed to toss refuse out of their windows as an act of protest whenever John Lindsay passed below.[19]

On June 24, 1965, Buckley officially announced his candidacy at the Overseas Press Club. His opening line—that he often wished all of the press was overseas—received sustained laughter. Buckley said that he was running on the Conservative Party line because the Republican one was not available to anyone in the mainstream of Republican opinion.[20] (Those he opposed maintained that Buckley's views were outside the "mainstream" of New York or national opinion.) Buckley was running, he declared, to advance core conservative beliefs. He said that while he intended to get as many votes as possible, he would not modify his positions to gain them. He appeared caught off guard when someone asked if he wanted to be Mayor. "I have never considered it," he said. When asked how many votes he expected to win, he replied, "Conservatively speaking, one."[21]

Even though most of the press expressed reservations about Buckley's politics, a good many reporters who covered him found his nonchalant approach to campaigning and his tendency to say what he thought refreshing. They also gravitated to his unconventional political style. "He talked with his eyebrows," columnist Dick Schaap observed in the *Herald Tribune*. "My fingers are killing me," a stenographer complained to a reporter as she struggled to keep up with the polysyllabic waterfall. Murray Kempton, a liberal columnist, supporter of Lindsay's, and friend of Buckley's, observed that the candidate enunciated his political principles in the manner of an Edwardian colonial Governor reading aloud the thirty-nine articles of the Anglican establishment to a conscript assemblage of Zulus.[22]

In the press conference after his declaration, Buckley said that he did not expect to do much campaigning, given his other responsibilities. Kempton found it reassuring that a candidate would absent himself from campaign duties during the day to attend to the demands of his occupation when elected incumbents seeking election to other offices campaigned on taxpayers' time and subsidies. Buckley professed not to like campaigning, which he described as "streetwalking."[23] The inference was that he considered it both vulgar and beneath him. "I will not go to Irish centers and go dancing," he said. "I will not go to Jewish centers and eat blintzes, nor will I go to Italian centers and pretend to speak Italian."[24] He much preferred releasing well-crafted and well-reasoned position papers and debating their merits with reporters. Of the many he put out, his proposal to build a bikeway from 125th Street to 1st Street generated considerable interest.[25] As the campaign progressed, and with his competitive instincts aroused, Buckley did engage in the more traditional aspects of electoral politics.

In his second press conference, this one called to introduce his running mates for City Council President and Comptroller, Buckley made news in two respects. First, he broke with the conventional practice of ethnic ticket balancing by selecting two other Irish Catholics. (He said afterward that he did not know their ethnic origins but even if he had his decisions would have been the same.) Second, when a reporter asked what he would do if he won the election, Buckley shot back, "Demand a recount."[26] The line became the most memorable of the entire campaign.

Though his witticisms delighted reporters and listeners, intimates feared that Buckley gave the impression he did not take his campaign seriously. Two months after Buckley jumped into the race, Barry Goldwater wrote him: "The last thing in the world you need is advice from me; however, I have a distinct feeling that if you get more serious about your campaigning, you could generate a lot of interest and a lot of life."[27] Many other friends advised him likewise.

Although Buckley's campaign would never have the organizational or financial resources of the major party candidates, as it advanced it took on a more professional look. His brother James, in the official role of campaign manager, ran interference for the candidate. Neal Freeman, a young alumnus of Yale, handled day-to-day operations. Marvin Liebman, who had organized the anti-Khrushchev rally at Carnegie Hall, was in charge of major events. Richard Viguerie, who would later make direct mail efforts staples of political campaigns, sent mail solicitations to conservatives across the country. Youthful volunteers flocked regularly into Buckley's headquarters. Their number, energy, and enthusiasm led one observer to describe the operation as "a 'New Frontier' elite of the political right."[28] Such a description of the kind of people he was attracting to his banner delighted the candidate.

Buckley took issue with Lindsay's contention that, if elected, the Congressman would actually change the way the city was governed. "The most sensitive seismograph in the country," Buckley wrote, "would not detect the slightest interruption in the city's disintegration should . . . Lindsay become mayor."[29] He noted that both of Lindsay's running mates had deep ties to the Wagner administration. He relentlessly pointed out that much of what ailed the city resulted from the policies of Wagner and his predecessors rather than from corruption, as Lindsay's anti-Tammany tirades suggested.[30] In a backhanded compliment to the retiring Mayor, Buckley allowed that by New York standards, Wagner's administration had been relatively corruption free.

Buckley tore away at Lindsay's central argument that his very "newness" on the scene would enable him to cure the city's ills. Lindsay's staffers were so taken with a line from one of Kempton's columns—"He is fresh, when everyone else is tired"—that they printed it on the candidate's campaign posters.[31] Cartoonists often presented Lindsay as a knight in shining armor slaying various dragons, each representing a city problem. Buckley complained that Lindsay's platform was long on symbolism and short on specifics. He called Lindsay's ten-point plan to revive the city's economy "an affront to the intelligence of teen-agers."[32] After the election, Lindsay's advisers conceded that Buckley had had a point.[33]

In mid-September, Abraham D. Beame, the City Comptroller, won a hotly contested Democratic primary for Mayor with a heavy assist from Representative Charles Buckley (no relation) and his Bronx Democratic organization and Brooklyn Democratic leader Stanley Steingut, both considered "bosses" of the old school. When asked the differences between his two opponents, Buckley pronounced them more "biological than ideological."[34] From their respective heights, Buckley discerned that he would be running against a tall liberal as well as against a short one. (Lindsay stood six feet four; Beame was barely over five feet tall. Buckley was nearly as tall as Lindsay.) While he maintained that he did not care from which man he drew votes, in debates, in interviews, and on the stump, Buckley was more vocal and persistent in his criticisms of Lindsay.

Buckley said many times that he had not entered the race out of personal dislike for Lindsay, whom *National Review* described as "destiny's tot." He insisted that his only objection to the Congressman was that Lindsay belonged in the Democratic Party.[35] This was the same criticism he had made against Rockefeller in 1958 and Javits in 1962. New York Conservative Party cofounder Kieran O'Doherty, however, thought Buckley harbored "a special animus against Lindsay."[36] If it existed, that animus may have originated in the two men's similar backgrounds and the different paths they chose to follow once they became politically active.

After graduating from Yale Law School, Lindsay gained easy access to the upper echelons of the Republican Party's eastern establishment wing, whose most exalted members included some of the same Yale officials, trustees, and alumni with whom Buckley had tangled. Yale nominated Lindsay as one of its preferred candidates for election to its sixteen-member governing board, the Yale Corporation. (He was one of six alumni fellows elected annually by the alumni.) Lindsay brought to the Yale board much of what Senator John F. Kennedy had carried with him to the Harvard Board of Overseers, the prestige of his name and office along with support for the university administration and its policies.

When Buckley sought the same post four years later, he was nominated by petition. Yale, from its past experiences with him, knew that Buckley would be a very different kind of trustee, if not a gadfly. Sam Chauncey, assistant to Yale President Kingman Brewster, recalled that Yale aggressively worked to defeat him.[37] (After it recruited Deputy Defense Secretary Cyrus Vance to oppose him, Buckley declared that he hoped Vance would prove more successful against him than he had been against the Viet Cong.[38] He did, and purportedly defeated Buckley by a wide margin in the secret mail ballot.)

With two relatively young, charismatic, intelligent, and idealistic Yale graduates taking divergent political views and with each claiming to represent the "true" Republican Party, the mainstream press took more interest in them than it did in the more traditional candidate for municipal office, Beame. *New York Times* columnist James Reston parodied the two Yale men's respective campaigns:

> Once upon a time two Yale men set out to rescue the Great city of New York from a plague of pygmies. Handsome John and Witty Bill, they were called, and both were members of the Grand Old Party. . . .
>
> "We must kick the midgets out," said Handsome John.
>
> "But first," said Witty Bill, "we must purify the people and cleanse the Grand Old Party. . . ."
>
> "If you go on like this, you'll wreck the party," said Handsome John.
>
> "But we'll own the wreckage," said Witty Bill.[39]

When a reporter asked Buckley whether he had known Lindsay at Yale, the Conservative Party candidate replied that he had. (His brother James and Lindsay's twin brother David had become close friends in law school.) "As a matter of fact," Buckley added, "we did a little witch-hunting together."[40] He explained that they, along with two friends, had heckled "fellow travelers" who spoke at Yale. This may have been a reference to Buckley's efforts to undermine Henry Wallace's 1948 presidential campaign. At the time, both Lindsay and Buckley were supporting Dewey. Buckley may have intended his reference to "witch hunting" to erode Lindsay's support among liberal Democrats and civil libertarians.

Lindsay denied having known Buckley at Yale and charged his rival with "delusions of grandeur." Buckley replied that, when he was at Yale, "grandeur" had not been defined as knowing John Lindsay.[41] "It's too bad to have someone deny the single glory in his past," Buckley lamented.[42] He supplied the names of two people, both of them supporters of Lindsay, who attested that Buckley and Lindsay had known each other at Yale.

On another occasion, Lindsay said that the first he heard of Buckley was when he read *God and Man at Yale*. He added that he thought the book "badly written."[43] Buckley replied, "I ask Mr. Lindsay, 'How can you tell?' "[44] He recommended that Lindsay read more of his writings. Columnist Joseph Kraft remarked in the *New York Post* that Buckley, through his "devil may care style," brought out two of Lindsay's less attractive traits: his lack of humor and his nasty temper. Lindsay' demeanor, Kraft wrote, was more reminiscent of the Sheriff of Nottingham than of Robin Hood.[45]

Perhaps feeling slighted by all the attention paid to Yale in the campaign, Democratic candidate Beame complained in an early debate about "these pleasant men from Yale who are so rarely seen around City Hall."[46] Beame's comment reminded his listeners of his clubhouse roots. In the world in which the three mayoral hopefuls were reared, one did indeed encounter few Yale graduates hanging around City Hall. After Beame stressed that he had received his entire education in New York City public schools and colleges, Buckley, in a remark he later confessed he was "ashamed" to have made, chimed in, "which fact should be obvious."[47]

At the campaign progressed, Lindsay touted his independence of both political parties and promised to govern in a nonpartisan manner. His leaflets made no mention of his Republican affiliation, and he made a point of requesting that national Republican leaders keep their distance from his campaign. Eisenhower, taking insult at this, made his feelings known to friends he knew to be supporting Lindsay. When Lindsay telephoned the former President to say that he intended no slight to him, Ike voiced opposition to Lindsay's advocacy of a civilian review board to hear complaints against the police.[48] When this leaked to the press, Buckley was delighted to have found an issue on which he and Ike were in agreement. To remind Republican voters of Lindsay's heresy to the GOP, former Congresswoman and Ambassador Clare Boothe Luce signed on as Chair of Republicans for Buckley.

Lindsay's ban on assistance from national party leaders did not include Nelson Rockefeller who, Lindsay pointed out, was "a fellow New Yorker." That convenient loophole allowed Lindsay to accept $500,000 from the Governor for his campaign. Lindsay's insistence that the money was a "loan" and his failure to invite Rockefeller to campaign with him put a strain on their relationship. Javits emerged as the campaign's most prominent Lindsay surrogate, a move intended to render Lindsay attractive to Jewish voters in his race against Beame, who, like Javits, was Jewish.

While Lindsay eschewed his party's label, Beame went to considerable lengths to stress his Democratic credentials and cast himself in the tradition of FDR, JFK, and LBJ. He relied heavily on Senator Robert Kennedy to rally Democratic—and especially Catholic—voters behind him. President Johnson, concerned that a poor showing by Beame would reflect poorly on himself a year after his landslide election, released a statement late in the campaign endorsing Beame, but did not personally campaign for him.

Buckley seemed no more eager to have prominent conservatives campaign for him than Lindsay was to welcome national Republicans. As a matter of courtesy, he said, he had informed Goldwater of his upcoming candidacy. He added that, while he would be "delighted" if the Arizonan appeared on his behalf, he did not intend to ask him to.[49] Goldwater supplied a handwritten endorsement, but Buckley never used it. Buckley did not want too much attention paid to his almost certain inability to attract as many votes as Goldwater had the previous year (eight hundred thousand) while running on the Republican line for President.

Richard Nixon, who qualified as both a national GOP leader and a New York City resident and voter, played no role in the campaign. In an aside to columnists Rowland Evans and Robert Novak, he expressed the Republican establishment's view that Buckley was running as a spoiler. Nixon told them that the "Buckleyites" presented a greater threat to the GOP than did the "Birchers."[50] (Nixon, through an aide, would later qualify that statement, explaining that Buckley's attack on the John Birch Society made it harder for his liberal opponents to tie him to extremist organizations.)

Picking up where he had left off in 1961 and 1962, and before the campaign was in full swing, in August 1965 Buckley extended his criticisms of Welch to include the John Birch Society as a whole. He wrote three columns denouncing the organization, which he republished in *National Review* prior to the election with supportive comments by other prominent conservatives, including Goldwater, Texas Senator John Tower, and retired Admiral William Radford.[51] In the first of these columns, Buckley listed the society's take on ten policy matters, all culled from a single issue of *American Opinion*. Each of the magazine's positions took as its premise Communist control of a federal agency or branch of government. He inquired how the society's membership could tolerate "such paranoid and unpatriotic drivel."[52]

Until the organization's members rose up and demanded a leadership that did not attribute all to which it objected to the work of Communist agents, he insisted, they ought not go about the country complaining that their views were being misrepresented.[53] An avalanche of protest followed. One writer advised him to "comply or else" with Birch demands lest his magazine not be distributed by "accepted" vendors. Another urged him to ask Congress to take testimony from one Colonel Goliewski, who would prove that Eisenhower was a Communist. One of his favorites of the mail he received was a piece of paper with a single word written on it in magic marker: "Judas."[54] *Life* magazine ran of photograph of Buckley delightedly holding it up.[55]

Buckley reported that of the two hundred letters he received about the JBS, only two agreed that assertions Welch had made in the JBS's house organ,

American Opinion, were excessive.[56] His friend James Kilpatrick, who had warned Buckley what to expect when he first criticized Welch, grew concerned enough this time to request in his own column that readers rally behind Buckley and *National Review.* "The skipper of 'Suzie Wong' [the name of Buckley's yacht] is catching a terrible lot of flak these days," Kirkpatrick noted. "It would be ironical if, indeed, Skipper Buckley's brash and audacious vessel [*National Review*] were sunk by those humorless torpedo men who steam from Belmont, Mass. If only a small fraction of the wealth that flows into JBS headquarters could be diverted instead to the support of the thoughtful and high-spirited conservatism of *National Review,* perhaps more men of independent mind might be wooed to the genial cause."[57]

On September 16, Buckley's campaign received an unexpected boost when a strike shut down six of the city's daily newspapers for twenty-three days. The *New York Post,* then a liberal newspaper, continued to publish, while the *Herald Tribune,* having settled with the union, reappeared eleven days later. The shutdown left television, radio, and out-of-town newspapers to fill the void. As a result, voters received almost all their information about the mayoral candidates through the electronic media, which upped the number of individual interviews and debates. Buckley's skills as a debater and his telegenic looks, ready wit, and elegant manner all worked to his advantage.

In the campaign's early weeks, Beame's campaign manager Ed Costikyan effected a tacit understanding with Buckley's campaign whereby Buckley and Beame would go after Lindsay more than they attacked each other. This agreement was much in evidence during the candidates' first radio exchange on September 23 on WMCA. After touting his Democratic and liberal credentials, Beame harped on Lindsay's failure to mention his Republican affiliation. He said that his principal opponent was acting as if he were "ashamed" of being a Republican. "I'll buy that," Buckley blurted out in an obvious reference to Lindsay's refusal to endorse Goldwater in the previous election. The studio erupted in laughter when, in response to Lindsay's comment that he was running alone against the Democratic organization, Buckley said, "I wish I could run alone with a million bucks and with the press engraving my every word on Mt. Rushmore."[58]

In the candidates' first televised debate three days later, Buckley put into play techniques he had perfected at Yale. He made facial expressions and gestures, often while his opponents were speaking. These diverted audience attention away from his opponents and conveyed Buckley's disapproval of what they were saying or registered his more than occasional boredom. Mary McGrory of the *Washington Star* wrote that when Buckley was seated between his opponents, he wore "an expression of haughty amusement, doodling as Lindsay and Beame glared at each other."[59]

In one exchange, Buckley denounced Lindsay an "imposter," a Democrat with presidential ambitions masquerading as a Republican. "Mr. Beame," he went on, "does not pretend to be anything but what he is, a very ordinary politician."[60] One of Buckley's best moments came when he was asked if he cared to say anything more in the unused time he had remaining. "No," he answered. "I think I'll just contemplate the great eloquence of my previous remarks."[61] Of Buckley's overall public persona, Norman Mailer remarked, "No other actor on earth can project simultaneous hints that he is in the act of playing Commodore of the Yacht Club, Joseph Goebbels, Robert Mitchum, Maverick, Savonarola, the nice prep-school kid next door, and the snows of yesteryear."[62]

In early October, the *Herald Tribune*'s straw poll showed Beame running ten points ahead of Lindsay (45 percent to 35 percent, with Buckley pulling 10 percent). Lindsay's campaign, for all its favorable press attention, had yet to make much of a dent. Several days later, the straw poll showed that Buckley had jumped to 13 percent. On October 21, the *Daily News*, back on the streets, put Buckley's support at 20 percent, Beame's at 37 percent, and Lindsay's at 42 percent. Three days later, the same poll had Buckley at 18 percent, Lindsay at 43 percent, and Beame at 40 percent.[63] Clearly the electorate had yet to settle on a favorite, and Buckley had become a factor in the race. Unknown was from which candidate he was drawing the most votes, or whether he was hurting both equally.

Lindsay, who had heretofore largely ignored Buckley, changed course. The Republican-Liberal nominee characterized Buckley's proposal to relocate unemployed women with children and on welfare to areas where the city would provide them with housing and job training, and their children with schools and recreation, as the advocacy of "relocation" or "deportation centers."[64] Buckley shot back that Lindsay had "entered the *feline* phase of his campaign," causing him to scratch around and make personal observations.[65] Javits, upping the ante, asserted that Buckley wanted to set up "concentration camps."[66] Coming just twenty years after the end of World War II, in a city whose large Jewish population included many who had survived Nazi atrocities, the accusation appeared calculated to play on people's emotions, if not to instill fear. In his next joint appearance with his rivals, Buckley went on the attack. Casting his gaze at Lindsay, he said, "You are trying to do to Jewish voters what the Ku Klux Klan has been trying to do to the white people in the South—keep them scared. You are in there saying, in effect to Jewish voters: 'Vote for me, vote for me, because over here is an ultra-rightist who is trying to bring bloodshed to the city.'"[67]

Buckley's description of how the Klan had operated was in part correct. It certainly played upon fears southern whites had of African Americans, assisted by outside forces, including the federal government, exercising dominance over them, and it incited them to inflict violence upon African Americans. The KKK also, through intimidation, threats of violence, violence, and terrorism, instilled fear in southern blacks as a means of keeping them in subservient roles. Javits and Lindsay, while not seeking to instigate violence, were, as Buckley suggested, playing upon people's emotions in ways to make certain New Yorkers fearful of the Conservative Party candidate and his agenda. Most of the press reported Lindsay's and Javits's attacks on Buckley without commenting on the validity of the comparison they drew between Buckley's proposals and practices Nazis had inflicted in Europe. Editorials denounced Buckley's proposals as if they were as his attackers characterized them.

Beame, worried that Lindsay's attacks were working in the Republican's favor with Jewish voters, also began to characterize Buckley as a bigot or worse. Acting as a go-between, Roy Cohn, the erstwhile counsel to Joe McCarthy, advised Buckley that Beame would be attacking him and recommended that Buckley hold his fire.[68] Buckley went into the next debate expecting Beame to proceed in this way, but not knowing what exactly lay in store. Beame charged that Buckley, to whom he referred as the "Clown Prince" of the campaign, with appealing to people's "base instincts." Behind Buckley's "warped humor and twisted wit," the Democrat said, were at work "sinister and evil philosophies." New Yorkers who believed that "it cannot happen here" (a reference to past Nazi atrocities), he said, were not taking Buckley's suggestions seriously enough.[69] He asked which groups Buckley intended to send to "concentration camps" next after he had removed all the welfare recipients and drug addicts.[70] Thus ended the truce between Buckley and Beame.

This was the fourth time in a dozen years that Buckley had either been called a fascist or likened to Nazis. Feeling that a line of civility had been crossed, he lamented the absence of public arbiters with the power to declare such accusations out of bounds: "The question is whether an attempt should be made to jam the dialogue between the demagogue and the masses: by society's *ex officio* censors, the columnists, the editorial writers, the ministers, the professors—again, the lords spiritual."[71] In a speech, Buckley suggested that his opponents were in competition to determine which could do a better job of smearing him: "I can see it now: 'Abe,' someone says. 'Lindsay is getting a lot of publicity on the concentration camp bit. Why don't you upstage him, and suggest that the Conservative party plans concentration camps for everyone in New York?' "[72]

As the campaign progressed, experts noted that Buckley was picking up support from white ethnic voters, many of them Democrats, primarily in the "outer boroughs." Pollster Samuel Lubell attributed Buckley's rise in the polls to his "giving emotional voice to many racial discontents among white voters."[73] Lindsay's assistant campaign press secretary recalled that a British reporter covering the campaign referred to these people as the "lumpenproletariat."[74] Decades later, a writer looking back on Buckley's campaign referred to him as the "voice of the angry white working class."[75]

Buckley's candidacy certainly had become a vehicle for some voters to register their objections to the direction the civil rights movement had taken in the North, with its emphasis on school busing and open housing, as well as to voice support for tougher measures to reduce crime and incarcerate offenders. Beame and Lindsay, while attuned to the aspirations of the city's growing minority population, seemed oblivious to anxieties other New Yorkers were experiencing as the city was undergoing major demographic transformations. In preparation for his mayoral campaign, Buckley became a devotee of the book *Beyond the Melting Pot* by Nathan Glazer and Daniel Patrick Moynihan.[76] Glazer was a prominent Harvard sociologist, Moynihan a young academic who had served as an aide to Governor Averell Harriman in Albany and as a junior official in the Kennedy and Johnson administrations. He lost a primary election for City Council President the year Lindsay, Beame, and Buckley ran for Mayor.

As Assistant Secretary of Labor, Moynihan had written a memorandum to President Johnson on the crisis besetting the black family: the rise in out-of-wedlock births, the absence of fathers from homes, and growing unemployment among black men compared to their white counterparts. He attributed these phenomena to the legacy of slavery and segregation and said all he described was being made worse by a welfare system that discouraged work.[77] In the book that emerged from their research, Glazer and Moynihan discussed challenges besetting not only African Americans but also other urban ethnic groups in the city. During his campaign, Buckley quoted from *Beyond the Melting Pot* so often that Moynihan joked that the mayoral candidate was committing plagiarism.[78] Buckley may have been the first political figure to grasp how phenomena the book detailed would impact upon future voting patterns.

The book's chapter on Irish Americans, which Moynihan wrote alone, told of how these and other Catholic voters, especially in the outer boroughs, who had once been the bedrock of Democratic machines and the prime beneficiaries of Tammany largesse, had lost influence to "reform" Democrats. These

Democrats, whom James Q. Wilson referred to as "amateur Democrats," were largely upper-middle-class professionals and almost exclusively Protestant or Jewish. In New York, they had entered into an alliance with the needle trade unions whose members filled the ranks of the Liberal Party. The amateur Democrats placed a higher premium on programmatic issues and programs, often devised and administered in Washington, than they did on neighborhood problems and political patronage, preoccupations of the "regulars."[79]

This transfer of power from the clubhouse to the reformers coincided with a heavy inflow of African Americans and Spanish-speaking residents and an accompanying outflow of whites to the suburbs. Among the immediate effects of "white flight" was a growing sense of isolation from City Hall among the white ethnics who remained. Increasingly, regulars and reformers battled over school busing, public funding for private and parochial schools, crime control and prevention, taxation, abortion, civilian review of police, and accommodation to alternative lifestyles. Court decisions on school prayer, busing, abortion, and other matters accelerated the sense of powerlessness among the white working class.

Between 1945 and 1965, the percentage of white children among the city's public school population dropped from 62 percent to 34 percent as the number of minority students increased substantially. This put new pressures upon families who remained in working-class enclaves and parochial schools, which experienced rising enrollments. Parents in these neighborhoods whose only option was to send their children to public schools worried about the effects overcrowding, crime, drugs, and the increasing numbers of underprepared students might have on the quality of overall education. Compulsory busing, mandated by courts as a means of achieving racial balance, added to their concerns.

Buckley spoke out early against busing. "Either schools are places where education is the primary consideration," he declared, "or they are places where social policies of politicians are the primary consideration."[80] He urged decentralization of schools, sequestering disruptive students, and financial inducements to encourage first-rate teachers to "take on the rigors of teaching undisciplined and uncooperative students."[81] Later, Buckley endorsed vouchers (often referred to as school "choice"), charter schools, state takeovers of failing schools, and other means of giving parents a greater say in the education their children received and of improving educational quality through enhanced competition.

Buckley predicted that "if the public schools became little more than social laboratories for the promotion of integration, parents most ambitious for the educational advantages of their children will, if they can afford to do so, send their children to private schools; those who cannot afford to do so will continue to send their children to the public schools but will become bitter, and even hostile, toward the minority groups whose pressures they hold accountable for unnatural arrangements."[82]

A good many liberals dismissed Buckley's comments on education and other issues as "racist"—or race based. Joseph Kraft of the *New York Post* dismissed much of what Buckley said about crime, drugs, and protesters as "code words" and race baiting.[83] Jimmy Breslin of the *Herald Tribune* described the Conservative Party candidate as an "elegant cracker."[84] Writing of Buckley's campaign four decades later, Sam Tanenhaus said that he brought two personas to his campaign: "the ideological firebrand who made direct appeals to the mob" and the "comic patrician who charmed sophisticated audiences."[85] Such comments missed, or at least underreported, an important undercurrent in city politics at the time Buckley ran for Mayor and in the time since. Timothy Sullivan, looking back on the 1965 mayoral campaign decades hence, concluded that voters in the outer boroughs responded positively to Buckley because he understood their frustrations and treated them and their concerns with respect.[86]

The reaction to Buckley and his candidacy among lower-middle- and working-class voters contained multiple ironies. An elitist by temperament, skeptical about democracy's ability to remedy to social ills, Buckley became the voice that brought into the public square grievances of a constituency that had not been predisposed to favor conservative economics and was less hostile than he to government intervention in other areas. Having eschewed appeals to voting blocs per se, Buckley made his greatest gains among a group that had become one of the city's largest blocs. Buckley appealed to primarily white, working-class Democrats of the outer boroughs, the same constituency that would reemerge in subsequent years as Nixon's "silent majority" and as "Reagan Democrats." They gravitated to James L. Buckley's 1970 New York senatorial campaign, whose slogan was "Isn't It Time We Had a Senator?" To them, the "We" needed no defining.

The cultural distance between Buckley and his most loyal followers could not have been more pronounced. "Every time he went to Queens," a campaign aide remarked, "he thought he was taking off for Istanbul or something."[87] Perhaps. But, in another sense, Buckley had come to understand the concerns of these supporters of his and knew much about how they thought. In the 1950s and early 1960s, Buckley had often spoken before Catholic fraternal, educational, and church-related groups in the outer boroughs, where support for his anti-Communist views and sympathy for Joseph McCarthy were very strong.

When Buckley began his campaign, few even within his own camp imagined that a Yale-educated patrician with a British-sounding accent, a laissez-faire economic orientation, and a penchant for quoting obscure texts and authors could pull working-class voters away from their Democratic roots. Buckley and his advisers expected his appeal to be greatest among Republicans concerned with rising taxes, deficit spending, and a declining city economy. His aide-de-camp Neal Freeman recalled his surprise when he saw the response Buckley received from "people who made the city go—corner-store owners, cops, schoolteachers, first-home owners, firemen, coping parents."[88] Through much of the campaign, Buckley and his Conservative Party supporters, preoccupied with the ideological divide within the GOP, failed to notice the inroads Buckley was making among Democrats, who could not have cared less whether he or Lindsay represented the GOP's future.

Buckley did not ignore African Americans in his uphill battle for Mayor. In his declaration of candidacy, he made clear, however, that he would not relate to them in ways to which they were accustomed. "The ill feeling that exists between the races in New York is due in part to a legacy of discrimination and injustice committed by the dominant ethnic groups. The white people owe a debt to the Negro people against whom we have discriminated for generations. The debt we rightly struggle to discharge in various ways, some of them wiser than others, and we should continue to seek out ways to advance the Negro, and other victims of oppression explicit and implicit, by sounder means than undifferentiated infusions of politically deployed cash."[89]

As he had with other groups, Buckley appealed to African Americans as individuals. He saw no need to rely on community "leaders" to "deliver" him their votes. But as he made his points, he exhibited an awkwardness that detracted from his message. He also gave unintended offense through ill-chosen comparisons and rhetoric. Speaking off the cuff before the 100 Men Committee, a group of prominent African Americans, Buckley said:

> You suffer disadvantages that the white men did not suffer.
>
> It is incorrect that the American Conservative is animated by hostility to the legitimate aspirations of the Negro race. The Jew with his crooked nose, the Italian with his accent, they were nothing like the disadvantages you suffered. But socializing the country is not the answer.[90]

He went on to proclaim educational attainment, bootstrapping, and capital formation more effective ways for people to rise out of poverty than government programs, and proposed ways to help minority communities do so. But his introductory comments, dutifully reported in the press, drew most of the attention.

"What's this crap in the *Post* about the 'Jew' with his crooked nose, etc. etc.?" Harry Elmark, who managed Buckley's syndicated column, demanded to know.[91]

When speaking to African American audiences, Buckley sometimes allowed himself to be sidetracked, often spending more time decrying the ethical misdeeds and legal problems of Harlem Congressman Adam Clayton Powell, whom he urged be replaced, than he did discussing why his listeners should vote for him for Mayor. In remarks before the Overseas Press Club, Buckley said that he welcomed "any white backlash" as a result of his having resisted the "special pleading" of certain leaders within the African American community. At the time, the phrase *white backlash* was used to describe voters who objected to recently enacted legislation mandating desegregation and extending voting and other rights to African Americans.

Few candidates, least of all those running for office in urban areas, would admit to welcoming such votes. Not surprisingly, Buckley's use of the term in a way that suggested he awarded it a positive connotation received more notice than did his denunciation of the other connotation of "white backlash" and how it was used or his call for "the kind of special treatment [of African Americans] that might make up for centuries of oppression."[92] Buckley may have been the first conservative in the country to take this stand. He also promised to crack down on labor unions that discriminated against minorities.[93]

In Buckley's response to a list of concerns Harlem community leaders had requested that the candidates for Mayor address, his denunciation of Powell again deflected from his other points: "I guarantee you justice. I guarantee you order. I guarantee you moral cooperation in replacing your bad leadership. Beyond that, I don't guarantee you a single thing. If elected Mayor, I will help you by ostracizing Adam Clayton Powell, Jr."[94]

Late in the campaign, John Birch Society member Kent Courtney, based in New Orleans, sent a mailer to one thousand New Yorkers accusing Lindsay of being "pro-Communist" and urging his defeat. Lindsay proclaimed the letter part of an effort by Barry Goldwater to extract revenge on him for not having supported Goldwater's 1964 presidential campaign.[95] Buckley's by now famous denunciations of the John Birch Society worked to his benefit. After dismissing Courtney as a "kook," Buckley suggested that by advancing such conspiracy theories about Goldwater and others, Lindsay sounded more like Robert Welch than a candidate of the New York Liberal Party.[96]

Irked by teen hecklers, some cheering for Buckley, as he tried to deliver a speech, Lindsay declared their manners and tactics "reminiscent of some of the worst moments of history."[97] One youth hit Lindsay with the sharp end of a

Buckley placard. Stories circulated about others stabbing him with campaign buttons as he moved through crowds. Lindsay aides complained to reporters that Buckley volunteers had vandalized Lindsay storefront headquarters but did not specify the storefronts' addresses.[98] When what appeared to be organized disrupters drowned out Lindsay as he tried to deliver a speech in Queens, the Congressman charged that Buckley was "doing his best" to "light a fuse to a city that had become a powder keg."[99]

Buckley fired back in a prepared statement: "John Lindsay has nothing at all to fear from crackpots. He has a great deal to fear from rational and intelligent men." He invited Conservative Party volunteers to distribute Lindsay literature along with his own, and predicted that anyone who read them side by side would be persuaded to vote Conservative.[100]

Lindsay's campaign proved adept at undertaking some questionable practices of its own. One Democratic operative leaked to the press a tape on which a Lindsay supporter is overheard seeking to persuade a Democratic leader to promote Buckley's candidacy among ethnic voters in Queens, presumably for a fee, in order to drive down Beame's vote in certain precincts. In that conversation the Lindsay supporter also made disparaging comments about certain ethnic groups. In response, former Democratic National Chairman James A. Farley, a Beame supporter, declared that he did not see how anyone "of Irish or Italian extraction" could vote for Lindsay.[101]

Four days before the election, Buckley had lunch with the editorial board of the *New York Times*. He recalled receiving an enthusiastic welcome from secretaries, janitors, and noneditorial staff, but coolness from his hosts.[102] He later wrote that they appeared to resent his seeking to deprive the city of the benefits of a Lindsay administration. He tried to put them at ease by volunteering that he had asked a seasoned observer of city politics which of his two rivals would make a better Mayor and that the person, without hesitation, replied, "Beame." (Years later, Buckley revealed that the person he consulted had been none other than master builder Robert Moses, who had over decades shaped much of the city's built environment of roads, tunnels, bridges, public housing, and cultural centers.[103] Moses famously said of Lindsay after he had won, "If you elect a matinee idol as mayor, you get a musical-comedy administration.")[104] After the lunch, Buckley told waiting reporters outside of the building that he felt as though he had passed through the Berlin Wall.[105]

Asked what he would do if he woke up the morning after the election as the next Mayor, Buckley replied, "Hang a net outside the window of the [*Times*] editor."[106] The net proved unnecessary. Lindsay won the mayoralty with 45.3 percent of the vote to Beame's 41.3 percent and Buckley's 13.4 percent. Buckley's strong showing meant that in the following election, the Conservatives replaced the Liberals in the third ballot line.

On Election Night and afterward, conventional wisdom had it that because he had failed in his chief objective of defeating Lindsay, Buckley had had no significant effect on the outcome, except perhaps to enhance Lindsay's winning margin by pulling votes away from Beame. Conservative Party leader Kieran O'Doherty, still fixated on internecine Republican politics, initially felt that because Lindsay had won, Buckley's campaign had been a failure. "I felt like I had ashes in my mouth," he recalled.[107] As Buckley had foreseen, most of the mainstream media were predicting that the Republican Lindsay's proven vote-getting ability in an overwhelmingly Democratic city had made him a force in national politics who could become a presidential possibility as early as 1968.[108]

In a bitter concession statement, Beame went so far as to suggest that Buckley had cost him the election.[109] Still smarting from Beame's eleventh-hour attacks on him, Buckley responded: "It was not I who wrote Mr. Beame's speeches: not I who posed beaming, alongside Adam Clayton Powell, Jr., not I who attempted to demonstrate to voters that John Lindsay was a conservative Republican; not I who accused conservative-minded New Yorkers of desiring to construct concentration camps. It was taxing enough to run my own campaign, without having to run Mr. Beame's."[110]

Buckley polled worst in Manhattan, where he received 7.2 percent of the vote to Lindsay's 55.8 percent and Beame's 37 percent. He did his best on Staten Island, receiving 25.2 percent of the vote to Lindsay's 45.8 percent and Beame's 28.9 percent. He polled 21.9 percent among Irish American voters and 17.8 percent among Italian Americans. Had Buckley not run, it is impossible to say where these votes would have gone. Tempting though it was at the time to conclude that many of these traditionally Democratic voters would have gone to Beame, it was also likely that many had decided to pass on the Democratic nominee that year. That Lindsay and Buckley between them won 58.7 percent of the vote could be cited as evidence of this. Late in the campaign, polls showed voters who had defected from Buckley going to Lindsay 2.5:1. This Buckley attributed to voters' reacting positively to Lindsay's theme of change. (In the Bronx and Brooklyn, Buckley defectors went to Beame 6:1 and 3.5:1, respectively.) Lindsay was a runaway favorite among WASPs, who gave him 60.9 percent of their vote. For a Republican, he polled exceedingly well with two traditional Democratic constituencies, drawing 42.4 percent of African American votes cast and 34.8 percent of Jewish votes. In Manhattan, Lindsay's tally among Jewish voters was 49.3 percent. Clearly those votes came at Beame's expense, and Buckley was not a factor. Beame ran strongest among Puerto Rican voters, with 72.4 percent.[111]

Buckley emerged from that campaign second to Goldwater as the nation's best-known American conservative. His influence was clearly on the rise. Hundreds of letters poured into his office each week. Most he answered personally. People stopped him at airports to have their pictures taken with him and to ask for autographs. Subscriptions to *National Review* jumped to 117,000. The number of newspapers carrying his column doubled from 150 to 300. He was awarded "Best Columnist of the Year" in 1967. Buckley's byline began appearing with greater regularity in popular magazines like *Esquire, Playboy*, and the *New York Times Magazine*. He became a favorite and frequent guest on late-night television programs, including *The Dick Cavett Show* and *The Tonight Show* with Johnny Carson, and he appeared on popular satirical programs hosted by Woody Allen. Buckley began publishing books at the rate of at least one per year. Most became instant best sellers. Presidential contenders began cultivating him.

Significantly, less than three months after his campaign, Buckley launched his public affairs television program *Firing Line*. The program premiered in early 1966 on WOR-TV, a stationed owned by RKO General, and its inaugural guest was Norman Thomas, six-time Socialist Party candidate for President. Most weeks, Buckley matched wits with a liberal intellectual or activist. After introducing his guest, Buckley would pose to his visitor a question in the genre of "Are you still beating your wife?" The person's response, often defensive, would set the tone for the hour that followed. The program was quickly syndicated and won an Emmy Award in 1969. *Firing Line* moved to the Public Broadcasting Service in 1971. *Firing Line* ran for thirty-three years, setting a record as the longest-running public affairs program featuring the same host.

The program made Buckley a familiar face not only to conservatives but also to liberals and centrists. Within a few shows, Buckley's magnetic personality, television presence, and inimitable style created an indelible presence in the public mind. Trademark clipboard on his lap, pen in his hand, and Ivy League wardrobe (with its omnipresent rep tie), Buckley entertained guests and audiences alike with his inexhaustible wit, voluminous vocabulary, and unforgettable mannerisms, which he used to great effect. Among them were his radiant smile and the exuberant glow in his eyes whenever he thought he had lured his guest into a trap. One reporter likened the look Buckley cast to that of a mischievous child who had just discovered a horrid use for the microwave oven and the family cat. The same writer referred to the special use Buckley made of his tongue, which the interviewer likened to an anteater's darting out in pursuit of prey.[112] One of Buckley's producers noted how Buckley elegantly arranged his long frame to strike the pose of "cocktail-lounge cool."[113] Whether the Buckley persona emerged naturally or through affectation, the character of "William F. Buckley Jr.," recognizable to millions, became a staple of both public television and conservatism.

Buckley was keenly aware of his drawing power and how he might use it to build a wider constituency for conservatism. Reflecting on the impact of G. K. Chesterton, one of his literary favorites, Buckley said that until Chesterton came along, "all the laughs were on the other side." Chesterton, he said, "lightened Toryism. And arguments that were not heard before were heard."[114] Buckley would do the same for his own brand of conservatism. The extent to which he had succeeded, within two years of his mayoral run, can be seen in the caption *Time* magazine printed under his name on the cover story it ran on him on November 3, 1967: "Conservatism Can Be Fun."

After he had terminated the program, Buckley commented: "I think that *Firing Line* had enormous influence in suggesting to people . . . that liberals weren't simply dispositively correct on all issues, because they all appeared on *Firing Line*, and were contested. Now it had, of course, a much, much larger audience, television does, than a magazine." At the same time, he noted that what he said in a magazine, a column, or in another form of print (such as a book), had more "staying power" and "greater resonance."[115] The program, like his mayoral campaign, enabled him to multiply opportunities available to him in those other forums.

Buckley, in all likelihood, would never have attained the prominence he did or achieved the influence that flowed from his sustained public exposure had he not run for Mayor. Though he received only a small percentage of the vote, Buckley had a greater impact on the course of American politics than either of his opponents—both of whom went on to serve as New York City's Mayor, Lindsay from 1966 to 1974 and Beame from 1974 to 1978. Lindsay is most remembered for a series of interminable strikes by city workers and fiscal crises. In 1971, Lindsay joined the Democratic Party, where Buckley said he had always belonged, and in 1972, he mounted an unsuccessful campaign for the Democratic presidential nomination. He placed third in a four-person New York Democratic senatorial primary in 1980. During Beame's single term, the city went to the brink of bankruptcy, which it averted through state and federal influxes of assistance and mandated administrative reforms.

Centrist Democrat Ed Koch, whom Buckley frequently praised for his outspoken manner, succeeded Beame and embraced some of Buckley's 1965 proposals, especially his advocacy of bicycle lanes. By that time, Buckley was paying less attention to municipal affairs. Among the many new roles he took on was that of "tutor" (his word as well as his pupil's) to a future President who, one year after Buckley concluded his "paradigmatic" campaign, was elected Governor of California.

National Review celebrated its tenth anniversary days after the 1965 election. Barry Goldwater was on hand to pay tribute to the magazine and its editor. What Goldwater said that night proved more prescient over the coming decades than either man realized at the time. Bill Buckley, Goldwater declared, had "lost the election but won the campaign."[116]

10

Buckley and Nixon: Mutual Suspicions

William F. Buckley Jr.'s relationship with Richard Nixon, while anything but close, proved significant to both men's careers. His early support for Nixon enabled the former Vice President to make himself palatable to Republican conservatives in the run-up to the 1968 Republican National Convention. After Nixon received his party's nomination, Buckley repeatedly made the case that Nixon, rather than third-party contender former Alabama Governor George Wallace, was the true "conservative" in a three-man race.[1] After Nixon won the election by a narrow margin (carrying 43 percent of the vote in a three-man race), Buckley passed along names of people he thought could contribute to the success of the new administration. One he recommended proved to be Nixon's most significant appointee. Nixon, in turn, granted Buckley access to both himself and his administration. This further enhanced Buckley's influence within party and government circles and beyond.

By the time Nixon reached his third year in office, his having lurched leftward on both foreign and domestic policy (rapprochement with Communist China and the USSR, imposition of wage and price controls, creation of new agencies) had made conservatives suspicious of him once again, as they had been during his years as Vice President. For a time, he kept them at his side as he enacted his "anti-crime" agenda, pressed for the appointment of "strict constructionists" to the Supreme Court, and appealed for support for his Vietnam policies to those he called the "silent majority." When Nixon's culpability in the Watergate cover-up became apparent, Buckley became one of the first conservatives to call for the President's resignation. His public break with Nixon may well have hastened the thirty-seventh President's departure from public life.

As he made his way back into public life after losing the 1960 presidential election and his 1962 campaign for Governor of California, Nixon resolved to make himself more acceptable to the Republican Right, which had given him, at best, tepid support in those elections. His opportunity came during Barry Goldwater's presidential campaign. Moderates who had failed to defeat Goldwater in the primaries kept their distance from him after he became the Republicans' 1964 presidential nominee. Nixon presented Goldwater to the convention and campaigned for him in dozens of states, while his two most likely rivals for the 1968 GOP nomination, Michigan Governor George Romney and New York Governor Nelson Rockefeller, sat on the sidelines.

When he appeared on *Firing Line* in the fall of 1967, Nixon told Buckley he had learned that Republicans could not win elections with only conservatives behind them (as Goldwater had demonstrated), but also that they could not win without them.[2] After President Kennedy, as Burnham had anticipated, appointed liberal establishmentarians to key policy posts, most of whom Buckley considered "accommodationist" both toward the USSR and the welfare state, Buckley began to see the former Vice President in a new light. "How is Mr. Nixon doing?" he wrote a friend who was working on Nixon's 1962 gubernatorial campaign. "You may not believe it, but I am all for him."[3] (One can rest assured that the candidate was all too well aware that *National Review* did not endorse him when he ran for President in 1960.)

During the run-up to the 1968 Republican convention, what became known as the "Buckley rule" first entered the American political lexicon. In an interview with the *Miami News* in the spring of 1967, Buckley, looking ahead to the 1968 presidential race, said that he would be for "the most right, viable candidate who could win."[4] He added that he saw Nixon as that candidate. Buckley did not think that the GOP would nominate Nelson Rockefeller or Michigan Governor George Romney, after each had publicly snubbed Goldwater in 1964. The most obvious conservative possibility and Goldwater enthusiast, California Governor Ronald Reagan, would, by the time of the convention, have been in his first electoral post for only eighteen months. Buckley believed that Reagan was not ready to be President, that he would lose if nominated, and that the defeat of two consecutive movement conservatives in two consecutive elections would be devastating to the conservative cause.

Buckley's initial favorite for President in 1968 was Charles Percy. Though considered a moderate, Percy had endorsed Goldwater and campaigned with him while running for Governor of Illinois. Two years after he lost that election, Percy defeated liberal incumbent U.S. Senator Paul Douglas. Buckley's willingness to support a man who was perceived to be a moderate but who had stuck with Goldwater suggested that he had begun to follow the Lord Beaconsfield path, as Whittaker Chambers had urged on him more than a decade earlier. He was willing to work with nonconservative elements within the GOP as long as they were willing to work with and support conservatives. In a new burst of ecumenicalism, six months after his interview with the *Miami News*, Buckley joked to *Time* magazine that his ideal ticket would be Reagan in the top spot with Javits as his running mate. As if to protect his standing with his fellow conservatives, Buckley added one condition: that Javits promise that he would throw himself on the presidential funeral pyre if Reagan were to die in office.[5]

Weeks after Percy won election to the U.S. Senate, Buckley's friend Evan Galbraith wrote him to ask whether conservatives might find Percy an acceptable compromise. "I think you might be in the position of a king-maker," Galbraith suggested. "It is curious," Buckley responded, "but you are the only person I have heard utter what goes on in my mind, namely the desirability of conservatizing Percy . . . Ronald just isn't plausible at the moment."[6] Over the next several weeks Buckley and Percy maintained a cordial correspondence. But after Percy aligned with Senate doves on Vietnam, Buckley veered in Nixon's direction.

If conservatives had been wary of Nixon, the former Vice President was equally leery of them. Nixon confided to Pat Buchanan, who functioned as his liaison to the right, that he found conservative activists a constant irritation. They were always trying to get him to take positions that would cost him support in other quarters.[7] Kissinger later confirmed that while Nixon liked Buckley, he felt "uneasy" in his presence.[8] As Buckley was warming to Nixon, his colleagues at *National Review* reasoned that if they could not constrain Buckley in his newly demonstrated enthusiasm for the former Vice President, they could make Nixon work for their magazine's support. Its publisher, William Rusher, wrote Nixon several times, demanding to know what precisely Nixon had meant when he told columnists Evans and Novak when Buckley ran for Mayor in 1965 that the "Buckleyites" were a "threat to the Republican Party even more menacing than the Birchers."[9] In an editorial, *National Review* demanded an explanation, noting that it had thrice written to Nixon for clarification.[10]

Patrick Buchanan, a former editorial writer for the *Saint Louis Globe-Democrat* who had joined Nixon's nascent presidential campaign, was tasked by Nixon to restate Nixon's position. In what Buchanan later termed a "tortured" letter, he said that it was Nixon's view that, by having repudiated the John Birch Society in his column and in *National Review*, Buckley had made it difficult for liberals to characterize him as an extremist and that Buckley had, therefore, strengthened his candidacy. ("Certainly as a rule, a conservative who repudiates the Birch Society becomes a much stronger candidate than one who refuses to do so," Buchanan wrote.") Therefore, Buckley, as a third-party candidate, Buchanan continued, posed a greater threat to the official Republican nominee than might otherwise have been the case. Nixon, Buchanan went on, hoped that in the future Republicans would settle their disputes within the GOP rather than through third-party candidacies.[11]

Having thus turned Nixon's remark, which some considered disparaging, into a compliment, Buchanan's ghosted letter set in motion a détente that developed between the former Vice President and *National Review*'s editor. "So, all's well that ends well," the magazine declared in an editorial, continuing, "and if Richard Nixon is willing to give personal leadership to Republican conservatives, he will find them ready to follow him."[12] Through this back-and-forth, contact had been made between the two camps and signals had been sent that the two sides might reach an accommodation. Nixon began making favorable mention of points Buckley had made in his columns. He wrote Buckley periodically to praise his columns, thank him for speaking kindly of Nixon's prospects, and wish him well in his race for the Yale Corporation.[13] (Buckley's 1967 campaign for the Yale post attracted considerable media attention, with the *New York Times* awarding front-page coverage to it. In his highly publicized campaign, Buckley pledged to work for greater ideological balance on the Yale faculty and to reverse university policies that awarded diminished weight to alumni legacies in its admission process.[14])

In January 1967, Nixon invited Buckley, Rusher, and other Buckley intimates to his apartment to discuss presidential politics. (This was Buckley's first meeting with Nixon since their conversation nearly a decade earlier, their only subsequent exchange in the intervening years being a letter Nixon wrote Buckley in 1961 praising the tribute to the recently deceased Whittaker Chambers *National Review* had run.[15] Buckley replied that he was aware of the high regard in which Chambers held Nixon and suggested that two meet one day to discuss their mutual friend.)[16] When they met in early 1967, Nixon asked Buckley to assess Reagan's prospects for the 1968 nomination. Buckley replied that he thought a Reagan nomination "implausible" given that Reagan was a former actor who had been in office for barely a month.[17] Nixon responded that a Governor of California who had won the office by more than a million votes was an ex officio presidential contender.[18]

After their meeting, Buckley wrote Buchanan that he had found Nixon "wonderfully candid and ingratiating."[19] In August 1967, Buchanan sent Buckley a copy of Nixon's interview with the *Christian Science Monitor,* in which Nixon and his camp thought the opinions Nixon offered reflected Buckley's thinking. Donning his tutorial robes, Buckley, a tough grader, wrote back that while Nixon had come the "closest" to "saying the right things," "confusions" remained.[20] Reconciling the statements of a politician in search of as many votes as possible with the writings of a conservative intellectual interested in consistency, clarity, and purity in principle proved no easy matter.

On September 14, 1967, Buckley had Nixon as his guest on *Firing Line.* This was Nixon's opportunity to make his case to an audience that was bound to include large numbers of conservatives. Buckley pitched a series of soft questions, each posed in such a way as to render it impossible for Nixon to reject suppositions inherent in Buckley's questions. One example was whether Nixon thought that the last Republican administration had been open to energetic young conservatives and intellectuals. Nixon, unwilling to offend either Eisenhower, whom Buckley had criticized for not having done so, or Buckley, whose views on the subject Nixon already knew, responded tersely, "Not enough."[21] After the broadcast, the two had an animated conversation as they drove through Central Park en route to Nixon's apartment, where James Kilpatrick was waiting to interview Nixon for *National Review.* Buckley wrote Nixon afterward suggesting that he would like the forthcoming piece.[22]

By the fall of 1967, going even further than he had in his interview with the *Miami News,* Buckley endorsed Nixon by inference. "If you say to someone, 'I don't think Reagan is a serious candidate.' And he knows that you loathe Rockefeller, you don't have to say, 'I am for you'" (meaning Nixon), he wrote.[23] Buckley's endorsing Nixon without explicitly saying so was a weak attempt to placate some of his colleagues who did not share his enthusiasm for the former Vice President. His personal support of Nixon, however indirect and independent of *National Review* he made it seem, became a point of contention between Buckley and virtually all of his fellow editors. With the exception of Burnham, who favored Rockefeller, most of the others were pulling for Reagan. Even after Nixon had won the election, Buckley found himself reassuring intimates that he had made the right decision. "Remember, a phony would not have got by Whittaker Chambers," he wrote Hugh Kenner after Nixon had taken office.[24]

After Romney, Nixon's only primary rival, withdrew from the race, Buckley mused on how Nixon might assemble a winning center-right coalition: "If you add to those attracted to Nixon as a reasonable conservative with a granitic determination to contain the Communists abroad, those who are attracted to George Wallace for reasons good and for reasons bad; throw in those whose first preference is Ronald Reagan, the paradigm of conservatism in national politics, you get, well, a great many people."[25]

When Lyndon Johnson announced in March 1968 that he would not seek another term as President, and with Romney not running, Nelson Rockefeller declared his candidacy for President. Buckley wasted little time going after his favorite target. He detected in Rockefeller's choice of advisers signs that the Governor was moving away from his previous hawkish views on Vietnam. In a column intended both to weaken Rockefeller's campaign and shore up a friend within it, Buckley reported that Rockefeller had brought in as an adviser journalist Emmet John Hughes, who, he said, had been a "dove before Picasso." He surmised that Hughes had been brought on board as a counterweight to Henry Kissinger, whom Buckley identified as "the anti-Communist at Harvard." Buckley's take on this situation: "*That* will be a happy office."[26]

Buckley struck again in the days preceding the Republican National Convention. His suspicions had been aroused by an ad that ran in the *Miami Herald*, purporting to be the work of an independent committee and signed by seventy-six prominent African Americans. In it, the group proclaimed that neither Nixon nor Reagan was "acceptable" to African Americans.[27] Buckley declared the ad the work of a "a Rockefeller operation." Asked for comment, Rockefeller suggested that people needed to understand that "Mr. Buckley fell off a boat a couple of days ago." (Buckley had injured his collarbone in a sailing accident.) "You'll be sorry, Governor," Buckley recalled thinking as he watched Rockefeller's press conference on television. In a column he titled "Sherlock Buckley Rides Again," he reported that his staff had ascertained that a Rockefeller associate had placed the ad and paid for it in cash, and that at least thirty of the signatories denied giving permission for their names to be used.[28]

Throughout the 1968 political season, Buckley and Kissinger remained in close contact. With Rockefeller considering another presidential run, Kissinger arranged a meeting between the Governor and Buckley. Rockefeller wanted to know whether Buckley was willing to persuade conservatives to back him.[29] The Governor joked that he considered himself a conservative, given that he had a lot to conserve. Buckley, while cordial, explained that the strains between the two wings of the party were so severe that only a Goldwater endorsement of him might turn Rockefeller's dream into reality. He added that he thought this highly unlikely and did not offer to intercede on Rockefeller's behalf. Buckley wrote Kissinger afterward that he found Rockefeller "an interesting man" and was exceptionally pleased to have met "*her.*"[30] (This reference to the second Mrs. Rockefeller was telling, given the columns Buckley had written four years earlier about both Rockefellers' divorces and their marriage.)[31] At their meeting, Rockefeller, like Nixon before him, said to Buckley that the size of Reagan's win in California made him a contender for the nomination.

During the Republican convention, Kissinger and Buckley saw each other daily. Buckley surmised that Kissinger's assigned role, in the event Rockefeller was nominated, was to prevail upon Buckley to minister to conservative wounds.[32] Nixon won the nomination on the first and only ballot, with 692 votes to Rockefeller's 277 and Reagan's 182. Afterward, Kissinger wrote Buckley that Rockefeller would have acquitted himself better in the eyes of conservatives than would the man the party had nominated. He suggested that New York Mayor John Lindsay and Oregon Senator Mark Hatfield, not Rockefeller, were the party's true liberals.[33] "You are a good loser," Buckley wrote back.[34] His second sentence, "Come see me," proved fortuitous.[35]

With Buchanan as intermediary, Nixon sought Buckley's suggestions on vice presidential possibilities. Buckley recommended John W. Gardner, Johnson's Secretary of Health, Education, and Welfare, an architect of Medicare, founder of Common Cause, and a nominal Republican. Nixon found the suggestion so surprising that he asked Buchanan to verify that the idea had actually been Buckley's. Buckley explained that Gardner would help Nixon's electoral prospects. (In a quip reminiscent of what he had said about a Javits vice presidential nomination months earlier, Buckley told Nixon's camp that he had predicated his endorsement of Gardner on the expectation that Nixon, as President, would have reduced crime to the point at which there would be no chance that he would not survive his term.) When Nixon's eventual running mate, Spiro Agnew, came under attack, Buckley rose to Agnew's defense. Agnew, he said, possessed a toughness, sincerity, and decisiveness, qualities that made Harry Truman a "happy memory."[36]

Pleased with Nixon's nomination and having enjoyed his daily exchanges with Kissinger, Buckley took care to maintain lines of communication with two other friends, Ronald and Nancy Reagan. He did not, however, enjoy his nightly appearances with Gore Vidal on ABC News. The network had retained the two to provide running commentary on the conventions in fifteen-minute intervals each evening. Running third in the ratings behind the better financed CBS and NBC, ABC decided that it could attract more viewers by hosting segmented lively nightly debates between a well-known liberal and a well-known conservative.[37]

When ABC first approached Buckley, it inquired whether he had any objections to appearing opposite anyone in particular. He volunteered that he had had unpleasant encounters with Vidal and did not trust him.[38] He was referring to comments Vidal had made about him on *The Tonight Show* in 1962 and to Vidal's attempts to discredit him as a Goldwater adviser two years later on David Susskind's *Open End*. He may also have felt uncomfortable sharing the stage with a celebrity author who so openly and often discussed homosexuality and bisexuality.[39] Writer Louis Auchincloss, a friend of both men, remarked that Buckley considered Vidal "not the devil's emissary, but the devil himself."[40]

In their nightly exchange during the 1968 Republican convention, Buckley and Vidal made no effort to conceal their dislike of each other. Buckley, fresh from a sailing vacation, went into these exchanges less prepared than his rival, but confident that he could easily handle the moderator's questions and fend off anticipated Vidal barbs. Vidal, on the other hand, came armed with carefully selected Buckley quotations, which he used to discredit and embarrass his adversary. It was not long before the two began to exchange insults and give way to personal invective.

Nancy Reagan was among the viewers who sensed that there was more to their exchange than a difference in opinion. "Do you have to go to Chicago [the site of the upcoming Democratic National Convention] with Mr. Vidal? If so, I hope you take your bullet-proof vest," she wrote Buckley.[41] In response to her mentioning that her daughter Patti had also watched the two square off, Buckley referred to Vidal in the identical language he had employed in his unsent telegram to Paar years earlier—and which he would repeat on network television several weeks later. "Tell Patti," he wrote, "that I was buoyed by the news that she watched me contending with the pink queer."[42]

Between the conventions, Buckley read Vidal's recently published novel *Myra Breckinridge,* which focused on bisexuality and transgenderism. In an exchange during the Democratic convention, Buckley pronounced Vidal's book an "assault on traditional, human sexual morality; on the family as the matrix of society; on the survival of heroism, on the very idea of heroism." Vidal fired back, "If I may say so, Bill . . . if there were a contest for Mr. Myra Breckinridge, you would unquestionably win it." He sarcastically volunteered that he had "based the entire style polemically upon" Buckley. This was not the first time Vidal had suggested that Buckley was homosexual. He had previously referred to the conservative writer as the "Marie Antoinette of the American right." (The reference implied that Buckley was insensitive to the needs of the poor as well as effeminate.) On camera, Buckley let Vidal's Mr. Myra Breckinridge remark pass. Off camera, Pat Buckley did not. "Two hundred million Americans think William F. Buckley is a screaming homosexual and I've got to do something about it," she told columnist Murray Kempton.[43]

August 28, 1968, was to have been a triumphant moment for Hubert Humphrey. He was about to fulfill his long-standing ambition and become his party's nominee for President. But his selection, exclusively the product of party bosses, left antiwar Democrats who had been elected on slates committed to antiwar candidates Eugene McCarthy and the recently slain Robert Kennedy particularly bitter. Outside the convention hall, where demonstrators had gathered from across the country to protest the Vietnam War, police charged at the crowd swinging billy clubs. With media attention shifting from the convention floor to the streets of Chicago, Buckley and Vidal weighed in on allegations of police brutality. On air, Vidal compared the police beatings of demonstrators to the actions of a "Soviet-style police state."[44] Buckley praised the Chicago police for showing restraint and said that demonstrators had provoked them. (Instinctively, he advanced the same view of the Chicago police that he had offered about the Alabama State Police in Selma three years earlier. As in that earlier instance, facts ultimately proved him incorrect.)

Buckley's stance put him in the awkward position of defending Chicago Mayor Richard Daley, whom he had frequently criticized for corruption and election fraud, telling friends that Daley ran the city like a "fascist" dictator. Asked whether he considered Daley a fascist, Buckley replied that if Daley were, he wondered why the Kennedys had not sought the indictment of their "favorite mayor."[45] This was a reference to Daley's purportedly having delivered the state of Illinois to John F. Kennedy in the 1960 presidential election through voting irregularities and fraud.

ABC News moderator Howard K. Smith asked his guests whether the actions of antiwar demonstrators, such as raising the Viet Cong flag, had been inflammatory and whether the raising of a Nazi flag by protesters during World War II would have produced a similar assault upon demonstrators. Vidal defended the right of anyone to voice any views they wished at any time or place. Buckley, talking simultaneously, tried to make the point that in both instances demonstrators would have been in favor of an American military defeat. He considered such actions treasonous. Twice he said the words "and some people were pro-Nazi" with Vidal talking over him. Buckley said he was "for ostracizing people who egg on other people to shoot American Marines and American soldiers." Repeatedly, Vidal told him to be quiet, with Buckley responding, "No, I won't." After some additional back-and-forth, Vidal blurted out, "As far as I am concerned . . . the only sort of pro or crypto Nazi I can think of is yourself."[46]

Visibly angry, Buckley, shot back, "Now listen . . . you queer, stop calling me a crypto Nazi . . . or I'll sock you in the goddam face and you'll stay plastered." He went on, "Let the author of *Myra Breckinridge* go back to his pornography and stop making any allusions of Nazism to somebody who was in the infantry in the last war and fought Nazis." Vidal interjected, incorrectly and over Buckley's protests, that Buckley had not served in the infantry. He was literally correct when he said that Buckley had not "fought in the war," but wrong to imply that Buckley had sought to avoid doing so. (Buckley served in the army and in the infantry, but the war had ended before the unit he was in could be sent overseas.)[47]

"I guess we gave them their money's worth tonight," Vidal said as the two removed their earphones.[48] Ignoring him, Buckley departed the set, angry at what Vidal had called him and upset with himself for having lost his temper. Buckley found Vidal's characterization of him as a secret Nazi particularly stinging. Actor Paul Newman, a longtime friend of Vidal's, a Eugene McCarthy supporter, and a war critic, admonished Buckley for his on-air remarks. When Buckley inquired whether Newman had ever been called a Nazi, the actor responded that what Vidal said about Buckley was "purely *political,*" whereas Buckley's characterization of Vidal was "*personal.*" Media condemnation of Buckley was all but universal. One holdout was the *Arizona Republic,* which asked how the *New York Times* would have reacted if Buckley had called Vidal a pro- or crypto-Communist.[49]

More than a year later, in back-to-back issues of *Esquire,* Buckley and Vidal published dueling justifications for the charges they had levied against one another on television. Buckley pondered whether or when it was an insult to refer to someone as homosexual when that individual had so candidly discussed his personal behavior. He also asked why left-leaning critics of conservatives so frequently referred to their adversaries as homosexual in their efforts to discredit them (as Vidal had done to him on television). As an example of this process at work, Buckley cited a gay-oriented liberal publication's characterization of his syndicated column as an exercise in "faggot dialectic." Borrowing the language of the publication, he asked, "Why is faggotry okay, but the imputation of it discreditable?"[50]

Elsewhere in the piece, Buckley related that he had received a letter from a former admirer who denounced him for alluding to Vidal's sexuality. Buckley's erstwhile fan recalled a scene from Somerset Maugham's novel *Of Human Bondage* in which one character calls another, who suffers a disability, a "cripple."[51] Regarding homosexuality as a malady, if not a burden, to be endured, if not overcome, Buckley's correspondent instructed him that homosexuality, like other afflictions, should not be introduced to demean the afflicted or to score debating points.

Buckley rejected the parallel on the grounds that Vidal did not consider himself "afflicted." Vidal, he continued, proclaimed "the normalcy of his affliction" and in his art celebrated "the desirability of it." He contrasted this comportment to that of "the man who bears his sorrow quietly." (Vidal, however, had not declared himself homosexual. The words *homosexual* and *heterosexual,* he said, were adjectives rather than nouns. As such, there were only homosexual or heterosexual "acts," not people.)[52] Buckley ended his piece by admitting that he had used the word *queer* in anger (and in retaliation for what

Vidal had called him) and offered Vidal what he confessed was a not all that sincere apology.[53]

In his rejoinder, Vidal justified his characterization of Buckley as a "crypto-Nazi" and set out to prove that Buckley harbored "fascist" sentiments and was both racist and anti-Semitic. He wrote of an incident that occurred in Sharon on May 13, 1944, in which some of the Buckley progeny entered Christ Church Episcopal, poured honey on the rector's chair, and inserted bawdy illustrations in prayer books. Vidal claimed that they had acted in retaliation against the wife of the church's minister, James Francis Meadows Cotter, who had sold a house to a Jewish family in violation of a local "gentlemen's agreement." Vidal implied that young Bill Buckley had been among the perpetrators. (In their televised exchange, Vidal had goaded Buckley with the question, "What happened in Sharon?" with Buckley ignoring him.) Vidal concluded that his only error on air was his use of the prefix "crypto" in front of "Nazi" as there was nothing "hidden" in Buckley's prejudices. He therefore offered an apology to Buckley that was as anemic and insincere as the one Buckley had made to him.[54]

Vidal's detective work had been shoddy. Buckley's sisters Priscilla, Jane, and Patricia, along with two friends, had broken into the church on the night in question. They were fined $100 each and further disciplined by their parents. On the day the incident took place, young Bill Buckley was at a southern army base, awaiting his physical examination prior to his induction into the U.S. Army.[55] Vidal's primary source for the Sharon story had been actress Jayne Meadows, daughter of the minister whose church had been ransacked. Meadows had related to him what she had heard from others.[56]

After *Esquire* published Vidal's article, Buckley sued the publication for $1 million and Vidal for $500,000. He filed an affidavit from the surviving member of the Jewish couple who purchased the Sharon property, attesting to his lack of racial and religious prejudice. As evidence that Vidal's depiction of him had harmed his reputation, Buckley related that in December 1970, student protesters unfurled a Third Reich banner from the balcony of the auditorium where he was speaking at the University of Pennsylvania.[57]

Buckley withdrew his suit against the magazine in exchange for its agreeing to pay him $115,000 to cover his legal expenses, take out $100,000 in advertising in *National Review,* and issue a statement disassociating itself from Vidal's charges. He also dropped his suit against Vidal, declaring victory and suggesting that Vidal's unreimbursed legal fees would "teach him to observe the laws of libel."[58] Striking back through a less costly weapon than a lawsuit, poetic license, Vidal based one of his characters in his novel *Burr* (1973) on Buckley. William de la Touche Clancey is described in the text as "an Irish Catholic sodomite who puts on airs and is despised by everyone."[59]

Back in New York after the conventions, Buckley and Kissinger met over lunch. Kissinger had foreign policy concerns he wanted to share with Nixon. Buckley made Kissinger's interest known to Frank Shakespeare, head of Nixon's media operations, who had himself come to Nixon's attention through Buckley's intervention. Shakespeare arranged for Kissinger to meet with John Mitchell, then Nixon's campaign manager.[60] Kissinger told Mitchell that he thought the Johnson administration would announce a halt to the bombing of North Vietnam as the election neared.[61] Buckley's bringing Kissinger into Nixon's orbit proved a critical turning point in the careers of all three men.

Another service Buckley rendered Nixon was helping to undermine third-party contender George Wallace's credibility among conservative voters. Through his firmly established record as a segregationist, Wallace had the potential to hurt Nixon in the South, where Republicans were hoping to build on inroads Goldwater had made in the region four years earlier. Through his tough talk on crime and populist attacks on liberal elites and "pointy headed bureaucrats," Wallace also had support among white working-class voters in the Northeast and Midwest, who were disillusioned with the Democratic Party for what they regarded as its preoccupation with the concerns of racial minorities and its "softness" on crime. In 1964, Wallace, having entered several Democratic primaries, carried 34 percent of the vote in Wisconsin, 30 percent in Indiana, and 43 percent in Maryland.

As the political season was getting under way in 1968, Buckley vigorously argued that Wallace was a phony conservative who preached the doctrine of "states' rights" not so much because he shared conservatives' opposition to federal intervention in principle, but as a means of denying African Americans civil rights and government services, whether initiated at the state or federal level. Buckley characterized Wallace as one of several "welfare populists" who had ridden to power, displacing the old Bourbons, by appealing to southern white (Sheriff John's "white trash") prejudice against African Americans. He repeatedly pointed out that Wallace and his ilk had been as much in favor of increased federal spending and redistribution of funds from more well-off to less well-off states as any liberal Democrat.

On January 24, 1968, hosting Wallace on *Firing Line*, Buckley asked his guest why if he was in fact a "conservative," as he claimed to be, none of the two hundred prominent conservatives surveyed by *Human Events* supported him for President. Wallace, striking his populist pose, replied that he did not need the blessing of intellectuals, newspaper editors, or columnists to run for

President or to be a conservative and said that voters held him in high regard and would reward him with their votes just as they had in Alabama. (So much for Buckley's declarations about the need for "tablet keepers.")

Repeatedly, Buckley's made the case that Wallace had not governed as a conservative and did not believe in basic conservative beliefs, such as a reduced federal presence in state and local affairs, except when the issue at hand was civil rights. Buckley's major point was that on matters other than race, Wallace was as much a big-spending, welfare liberal as any other liberal Democrat and that he had seized upon conservative ("states' rights") rhetoric as a means of denying African Americans benefits he was happy to pass along to his white constituents. "For the first time, I feel like a liberal," Buckley said as he hammered away at Wallace's record.

Wallace replied that he would not apologize for favoring programs to assist the aged and improve the quality of schools in Alabama, which he said had been held down by a legacy of northern occupation, the Great Depression, underfunding, and neglect. Alabama schools, he said, were among the poorest in the nation and deserved federal aid as a form of reparations.[62] When Wallace tried to refute Buckley's charge that Wallace had discriminated against his African American constituents, boasting that both he and his wife, who had succeeded him as Governor, had polled well among African American voters, Buckley cited this truism as evidence that Wallace had been correct when he proclaimed the quality of the schools in Alabama substandard.[63]

Buckley related to Nelson Rockefeller that he had found Wallace's behavior "boorish."[64] He wrote Nancy Reagan that he was "rather weary from an encounter with George Wallace," whom he considered a "dangerous man." He told her further that he especially resented Wallace's asserting his fealty to conservative principles and citing them in support of ends that were "wholly individual" in nature and based entirely on opportunism rather than on a coherent set of beliefs.[65] Days before the 1968 election, in *Look* magazine, he urged conservatives to reject Wallace in favor of Nixon. No one who favored federal welfare programs and tripled his state's bonded indebtedness, as had Wallace, he wrote, merited the label "conservative."[66] Buckley advised his brother James, then running against Jacob Javits on the Conservative Party ticket for Senator, to stress Wallace's conservative "disqualifications." Nearly all of Wallace's support in New York State, he reminded his brother, came from members of building trade unions who opposed apprenticeships and promotions for African Americans.[67]

Nixon won the election with 43.9 percent of the vote to Humphrey's 42.7 percent and Wallace's 13.5 percent. In the South, Wallace won four states that Goldwater had carried four years earlier—Alabama, Mississippi, Louisiana, and Georgia—as well as Arkansas.

With the election of a President to whom he was favorably disposed, Buckley turned his attention to the transition. He passed along to John Mitchell information on persons interested in serving the new administration and volunteered to write a draft of Nixon's upcoming inaugural address. He advised Mitchell that he expected the press to draw comparisons between that speech and the fiery address Kennedy had delivered eight years earlier.[68] Mitchell did not take him up on his offer.

Two weeks after the election, Buckley recommended in his syndicated column that Nixon name William Scranton Secretary of State and Nelson Rockefeller Secretary of Defense. Rockefeller, Buckley suggested, echoing both Burnham and Kissinger, "would be the last man in America" to be fooled by phony disarmament drives or taken in by the sentimental pretensions of nonproliferation treaties.[69] Some White House aides reacted to these recommendations in the same manner in which Nixon had greeted Buckley's prior musings about John W. Gardner for Vice President: with disbelief.

Kissinger had grown concerned that before Nixon took office, the Johnson administration would undermine the government of South Vietnam, which was resisting making concessions to Hanoi at the Paris peace talks. He confided to Buckley his suspicions that the Johnson administration might sponsor a coup against the Thieu regime. When, days after the election, Defense Secretary Clark Clifford issued a public warning to South Vietnam's President Nguyen Van Thieu that, if he boycotted the Paris peace talks, the United States would negotiate with North Vietnam and the Viet Cong without him, Kissinger grew more suspicious.

To make certain that Kissinger's concerns received the attention within Nixon's camp that he felt they deserved, Buckley raised them in his column, without mentioning Kissinger by name. He urged that Nixon threaten to veto any agreement that compromised South Vietnam's independence. He passed along a warning of an expert he did not identify that, if the United States abandoned its ally, the international community would conclude that "it might be dangerous to be America's enemy, but fatal to be its friend."[70]

Kissinger had his first sit-down meeting with Nixon on November 25, 1968. Two days later, he accepted the post as National Security Adviser. "You will never be able to say again that you have no contact inside the White House," he wrote Buckley.[71] In his memoirs, Nixon made no mention of Buckley's role in shepherding Kissinger's appointment. Perhaps neither Mitchell nor Shakespeare had mentioned to the President-elect that Buckley had first brought Kissinger to their attention. Nor was Buckley the only one making Kissinger's case. Nixon wrote that Henry Cabot Lodge, who as Ambassador to South Vietnam received advice from Kissinger, had recommended him. Nixon also recalled meeting Kissinger at a party Clare Boothe Luce had hosted in 1967 and remembered her having spoken well of him.[72] He also recorded that Mitchell had arranged his November 25 meeting with Kissinger.[73]

After Kissinger's appointment became public, a *National Review* editorial described him as a "realist" and a "patriot" who saw a "problem whole." Buckley took the occasion to chide his old friend about what he considered Kissinger's major failing, being "sometimes a little dreamy on disarmament matters."[74] Some within Nixon's White House voiced doubts about the National Security Adviser's ideological consistency. They were especially wary of Kissinger because of his Harvard affiliations and his Rockefeller connections. Buckley took advantage of opportunities to bolster his friend's spirits. After the *Philadelphia Bulletin* reported that Frank Shakespeare had expressed doubt that Kissinger was at heart a conservative, Buckley fired off a terse note to the National Security Adviser: "Said Shakespeare to me a month ago, 'if you never do another thing for your country, your introducing Henry Kissinger to the Nixon people will still qualify you as a hero.'"[75]

Kissinger's appointment produced blowback from conservatives both inside and outside the administration. Rusher reported to Buckley that he had learned through Jeffrey Bell, a young Nixon staffer, that other Nixon aides resented the role both Mitchell and Buckley had played in bringing Kissinger into Nixon's orbit. With Kissinger a month into his new post, Bell complained to Buckley that under Kissinger, the National Security Council was turning into a hotbed of dovish activity. Young conservatives in the administration, he continued, were asking themselves "what rug Buckley would next pull out from under them."[76] Buckley reminded Bell that in 1960, when Rockefeller argued for raising levels of defense spending by considerably more than Eisenhower had recommended, Kissinger was the New York Governor's principal adviser on defense. "I have every reason to believe in his toughness and constancy on the anti-communist question, and still do," Buckley wrote Bell.[77]

As the Nixon administration took form, Buckley walked a narrow line between voicing skepticism about the President's détente policy toward the Soviet Union and support for its principal implementer, Nixon's National Security Adviser. When *National Review* benefactor Roger Milliken took Buckley to task for his support of Kissinger, Buckley responded that Milliken would be "surprised by the extent to which Kissinger's thinking parallels our own."[78] Kissinger, he wrote, had "no interest" in being "dominated" by the Soviet Union.[79]

David Keene, a former head of YAF and now an aide to Agnew, thought that Buckley allowed himself to be conned by Kissinger because he "did want to be in."[80] "In" Buckley certainly was for most of Nixon's first term. He had regular contact not only with Kissinger, Shakespeare, Buchanan, and others but also with Nixon, who periodically invited him in for chats. In an interview with *Playboy* magazine in May 1970, Buckley said that he had discovered a new "sensual treat": "to have the President of the United States take notes while you are speaking to him, even though you run the risk that he is scribbling, 'Get this bore out of here.'"[81]

Buckley occasionally used his access to the Nixon White House to weigh in on behalf of other conservatives. Shortly after the inauguration, he wrote Kissinger that former Congressman Walter Judd was feeling "blue and neglected." Judd, who had delivered a fiery keynote address at the 1960 Republican convention, had remained a steadfast Nixon supporter. "The trouble with conservatives," Buckley told Kissinger, is that "they do not retrieve their wounded." Kissinger promised to look into the matter.[82] On another occasion Buckley sought Kissinger's assistance in identifying the person at the White House who had sent him a congratulatory note about one of his recent columns. "The President of the United States," Kissinger tersely responded.[83] (Buckley had been unable to decipher Nixon's initials.)

In the spring of 1969, at the behest of Whitney Young, President of the National Urban League, Buckley joined several other journalists on a tour of inner cities. Afterward, the delegation gathered at the White House for a debriefing with Nixon's principal domestic adviser, Daniel Patrick Moynihan. Buckley returned from the experience with a deepened understanding of the estrangement African American youths felt from mainstream American society and the almost universal distrust so many inner-city residents had of the police. Several activists and local residents with whom Buckley met provided him with evidence of corruption in several departments and of selective harassment of African Americans.[84] Buckley found many of the community leaders he met open to ideas conservatives had advanced on education, self-help, self-discipline, hard work, and the importance of capital formation.

Buckley wrote admiringly of the charm, street smarts, and idealism he detected among the young African American leaders he encountered: "Anyone expecting to hear better speech, better-organized ideas, greater enthusiasm, in the graduate schools of the Ivy League, has a pleasant surprise coming." He said that many of the people he had met, be they graduates of ghetto schools or of no schools, "through wit and grace, singing their song in a strange land, have made a triumphant entry upon the scene."[85]

It was almost as if, notwithstanding political disagreements and differences in background and temperament, Buckley had come to identify with some of the young, proud, and committed radicals he had encountered. As was he, they were skeptical that distant and insensitive bureaucracies and uniform federal programs could remedy what was ailing their communities. Columns he filed during and after his tour leave the impression that Buckley felt as though he had stumbled upon dozens of young would-be Bill Buckleys, albeit a generation or more younger and shaped by different intellectual and social currents. He singled out for special praise "community organizers" who "work in straightforward social work in the ghettos, in economic cooperatives, who are arguing that progress is possible within the System."[86] In an article in *Look* months after the tour, Buckley anticipated that the United States could well elect an African American President within a decade, and that this milestone would confer the same reassurance and social distinction upon African Americans that Roman Catholics had felt upon the election of John F. Kennedy. That, he said, would be "welcome tonic" for the white soul.[87]

In his *Look* essay, Buckley recalled that decades earlier, Whittaker Chambers had written of African Americans that "they have been the most man-despised and God-obsessed people in the history of the world, that on coming to this strange land they had struck their tuning fork, and the sorrow songs, the spirituals, were born."[88] Buckley was quoting from a *Time* cover story Chambers had written on singer Marian Anderson that had appeared on December 30, 1946.[89] Buckley was a freshman at Yale at the time it ran. As he had on previous occasions, when he moved away from positions he had once stridently held (such as immediate abolition of the welfare state in 1953 and the rolling back, by force if necessary, of Soviet occupation of Eastern Europe), Buckley took inspiration from Chambers's words. The man who wrote this essay in *Look* bore little resemblance to the person who penned the editorial "The South Must Prevail" a dozen years earlier.

On a visit to Mississippi during Nixon's early years in office, Buckley voiced both surprise and delight at the transformations that federal legislation, court orders, and presidential decrees (many of which he had opposed), in conjunction with the work of local residents, had brought to the American South, and how little these changes had disrupted the rhythms of ordinary life. He likened the results to what had occurred in Germany during the "de-Nazification" period. He expressed the hope that responsible and established African American leaders would distance themselves from extremists within their movement, much as he and other conservatives had purged from their ranks "kooks and bigots." He praised Whitney Young and Bayard Rustin for attempting precisely that.[90]

As it pursued its agenda, the Nixon's administration solicited Buckley's support for its nominees and policy proposals. Often Buchanan sent Buckley background materials he might use in columns in which he made the administration's case.[91] After the Senate rejected Nixon's first Supreme Court nominee, Clement Haynsworth, Nixon personally thanked Buckley and *National Review* for the editorial support they had given the failed nominee.[92] Buckley drummed up support for Nixon's "Vietnamization" policies (gradual replacement of U.S. troops in combat roles in Vietnam with freshly trained South Vietnamese ones).[93] *National Review* had called upon its readers to flood the White House with congratulatory telegrams after Nixon delivered his "Silent Majority" speech on November 3, 1969, in which he urged listeners to support his Vietnam policies. Nixon again expressed his gratitude.[94]

Buckley used the resources at his command to buttress the administration's case that network news was biased in its coverage of the Nixon White House. In fall 1969, Vice President Agnew embarked on a speaking tour in which he denounced newscasters and commentators as "nattering nabobs of negativism." As head of the Historical Research Foundation, a group that helped fund conservative research efforts, Buckley commissioned a study of the media's coverage of the 1968 presidential campaign that subsequently appeared as the book *The News Twisters*. Its author, Edith Efron, a former assistant to Mike Wallace at CBS News, applied content analysis to the televised coverage of the 1968 election and concluded that the three networks had consistently aired more positive stories about Humphrey than about Nixon and more negative stories about Nixon than about Humphrey over the same period.

Buckley sent copies of the book to Nixon, Buchanan, and others.[95] In her acknowledgments, Efron thanked the board of directors of the Historical Research Foundation for making her undertaking "possible," but made no specific mention of Buckley. On the flyleaf, Buckley referred to Efron as "the Ralph Nader" of journalism. (His meaning was that Efron had taken on the role as public watchdog over the media in the same way Nader stood guard over large corporations in the interests of consumers.) On the back cover of her book appeared a blurb in which Buckley proclaimed Efron's study a "prodigious achievement."[96] Buckley moderated a lively debate between Efron and journalist Andy Rooney on *Firing Line*.

After Kissinger shared his frustrations with Buckley that the State Department was subverting Nixon's Vietnam policies, Buckley proposed that Rockefeller spearhead a study on how the department might best be reformed. Upon its release, Nixon, he suggested, might name Rockefeller Secretary of State with a directive to implement the report's recommendations. To clear Rockefeller's path, Nixon would appoint William Rogers, then the Secretary of State, to the Supreme Court. Kissinger responded that Buckley's plan could not be implemented quickly enough.[97] (Much of what Buckley envisioned did come to pass, however. Six months into his second term, Nixon replaced Rogers with Kissinger and Rockefeller resigned as Governor to chair a commission he created to develop policy proposals as he prepared for another presidential run in 1976.)

At the urging of Frank Shakespeare, now head of the United States Information Agency, in May 1969 Nixon named Buckley to the agency's three-person Advisory Commission, where he joined CBS President Frank Stanton and novelist James Michener. While he found the monthly meetings tedious, Buckley very much enjoyed the company and the social connections that came his way by virtue of his new role, especially among the mainstream media, which came less and less to look upon him as an anomaly. One indirect benefit Buckley may have derived from his perceived closeness to the Republican administration was PBS's decision to air *Firing Line.* Henry Cauthen, a conservative Democrat and head of South Carolina Educational Television, believed Buckley's program would enable PBS, widely perceived to be liberal in its programming, to broaden its viewer base and attract conservative donors. The program moved to PBS in 1971.[98]

One of the few conservatives to make his way into popular culture, Buckley was a frequent guest on network television. On December 27, 1970, he appeared on NBC's satirical *Rowan & Martin's Laugh-In.* In a skit devoted to his habits and interests, Buckley was asked why he usually remained seated when addressing audiences, to which he replied that he could not stand up under the weight of the wisdom he was carrying.[99] When *Playboy* magazine inquired why he granted it a lengthy interview when he so publicly disdained the magazine's philosophy, Buckley answered, "In order to communicate with my sixteen year old son."[100]

As his celebrity increased, Republican leaders speculated about a possible second William F. Buckley Jr. campaign for public office. Conservative Party officials had wanted him to run for Senator on their ticket in 1968. In what would have been a rerun of his mayoral race but over a wider geographic terrain, they calculated that he might attract enough votes to deny Javits a third term. Buckley was not enthusiastic. His syndicated column was now running twice a week in more than three hundred newspapers. *Firing Line* was growing in popularity. Buckley remained a favorite speaker on college campuses and at other venues, chalking up as many as seventy public appearances a year. And he was turning out at least one book per year. Buckley was not prepared to give up all that for another "educational" or "paradigmatic" campaign.

He suggested that his brother James, then a lawyer at the family-owned Catawba Company, run instead. He likened making at least one run for public office to "jury duty." He suggested that his brother might enjoy the "exhilaration" of making his points and feeling the crowd's response.[101] James's advocacy of federal intervention to curb water and air pollution during his 1968 campaign, even as he favored a reduced federal role elsewhere, led the *New York Times* to recommend that Nixon appoint him Secretary of the Interior. James L. Buckley captured 17 percent of the vote. In Long Island's two counties, he ran ahead of the Democratic candidate, Paul O'Dwyer.[102] Conservative Party leaders estimated that 40 percent to 50 percent of his vote came from Democrats.[103]

One race in which Bill Buckley had shown interest (as Rose Kennedy had surmised) was a possible Senate matchup in 1970 against Robert Kennedy. Buckley expected few Republicans would want to enter this race because Kennedy would be regarded as unbeatable. He speculated that he might be able to run on both Republican and Conservative Party lines. With Kennedy, like Lindsay, expected to run for President, such a race would attract national attention, and if Buckley made the race a closer contest than many anticipated, he might succeed in dimming some of the Democrat's luster. Buckley lost interest in running for the seat after Kennedy was assassinated and Rockefeller appointed Charles Goodell, a centrist to conservative Republican Congressman from Jamestown, New York, to complete Kennedy's term.

Within days of taking office, Goodell introduced a resolution calling for the withdrawal of all U.S. forces from South Vietnam by the end of 1970, a position that earned him the instant enmity of the Nixon administration. With the electorate now facing a choice between a liberal Republican incumbent and a certain liberal Democratic challenger, a path was open for a well-funded Conservative to make a competitive run in a three-way contest. Buckley briefly reconsidered his decision not to run. He asked Goldwater strategist F. Clifton White what his chances might be, if elected, of becoming President one day. White thought them reasonable, but by no means certain. "If someone had said that I could be President," Buckley recollected, "I would have said, 'yes,' which is different from saying, 'I can give you a twenty percent chance of being President, if you desert your career and try to climb this particular ladder.'"[104] Already better known than were most Senators in visibility and able to exert wider influence on public policy than a good many of them, Buckley decided not to run. Again, he urged James L. Buckley to make the race.

Politics in New York, always tumultuous, exhibited unusual dynamics in 1970. Rockefeller, planning to seek a historic fourth term as Governor in preparation for another stab at the presidency in 1976, had taken note of the state's changed political climate and of the Conservative Party's rising strength.[105] He had begun moving rightward, reversing some long-held positions, including his opposition to a residency requirement for welfare. Nixon, hopeful that he could carry New York in 1972, deputized Kissinger to draw upon his friendships with both Rockefeller and Buckley in the hope that the Republican and Conservative parties might form a common front.

In early 1970, at a meeting at Rockefeller's New York City apartment that Kissinger helped arrange, Buckley and Rockefeller discussed the possibility of cross-party endorsements, with the Conservatives designating Rockefeller as their official candidate and Republicans and Conservatives fielding identical candidates for down-ballot positions. Buckley may well have been the first magazine editor and newspaper columnist to dangle a party nomination before a sitting Governor seeking reelection. Buckley wrote Kissinger afterward, "The time has come for a major New York Republican to baptize the Conservative Party."[106] Although a public embrace of Rockefeller proved too much of a stretch for both sides after so many years of internecine bickering, the Buckley-Rockefeller entente paved the way for informal understandings the Republican and Conservative parties reached. Kissinger wrote Buckley, "I am pleased to learn that my servant [Rockefeller] did as suggested and that you had a useful chat with the Governor.[107]

The Rockefeller who sought reelection in 1970 bore little resemblance to the one Buckley had so strenuously opposed in the past. He was tough on crime, advocated stiffer penalties for drug offenders, and favored mandatory sentences for those who committed certain kinds of crimes. Former Supreme Court Justice and United Nations Ambassador Arthur Goldberg received the Democratic and Liberal parties' endorsements and selected as his running mate Basil Paterson, an African American state Senator. Although Rockefeller had previously run well among Jewish and African American voters, his campaign concluded that, with the Democrats making a concerted effort among these groups of voters, he might offset defections from these constituencies by improving his standing among Catholics and suburbanites.[108]

James L. Buckley encountered little difficulty in mounting an effective campaign. Given the number of Nixon donors inside and outside New York State, many of them upset with Goodell's maverick stance, he had a relatively easy time attracting funds. F. Clifton White became his campaign manager and he, in turn, brought on board Arthur Finkelstein, a rising political consultant and pollster. Finkelstein coined the campaign's slogan "Isn't It Time We Had a Senator?" an overt appeal to Nixon's "silent majority." Buckley's campaign took as its logo an American flag placed to the right of the word *Buckley* in capital letters. A version of it began to appear on hard hats worn by construction workers.

The unstated Buckley-Rockefeller entente began bearing fruit all over the state. Several Republican legislative candidates endorsed Buckley.[109] Five incumbent New York Republican Congressmen attended a reception for the Conservative Party candidate.[110] Unlike in past years, Rockefeller and the state GOP were slow to enforce party discipline, so long as those who defected from Goodell endorsed Rockefeller for reelection.[111] Though officially sanctioned by neither camp, "Rockefeller-Buckley" bumper stickers and signs appeared at some local GOP headquarters. For the first time in history, the Patrolmen's Benevolent Association and the Uniformed Firefighters Association declined to back the Democratic ticket and endorsed Rockefeller and Buckley.[112] Several independent union committees also endorsed them.[113]

Although James L. Buckley declared that he would be casting his vote for the Conservative candidate for Governor, Paul Adams, White said that he would be voting for Rockefeller.[114] For the benefit of conservatives who had not picked up on these signals, *National Review* ran a few lines of verse by W. H. Dreele under the heading "The Alternative Is Goldberg": "And so, despite the trauma and the shock, / November, I'll be voting for the Rock."[115] By running Dreele's ditty, the magazine's editor made clear where he stood on the gubernatorial race.[116]

By the campaign's end, James L. Buckley had spent almost as much as his two opponents combined—$1,129,654, compared to Democrat Richard Ottinger's $728,795 and Goodell's $516,187. He ended his campaign free of debt.[117] In another break with tradition, Rockefeller did not contribute as generously to Goodell as he had to previous Republican candidates. He did make a personal donation of $45,000 and arranged for the state GOP to kick in $250,000 to its official nominee's effort.[118] (Rockefeller's personal contribution was considerably smaller than the $500,000 he had made available to Lindsay's 1965 mayoral campaign.) Some speculated that Rockefeller funds seeped into other efforts that were assisting Buckley.[119]

To help Buckley and drive some liberal voters from Ottinger to Goodell, Nixon aides had Vice President Agnew, an anathema to New York liberals, savage Goodell. He denounced the Republican candidate as a "radical liberal" and proclaimed him "the Christine Jorgensen of the Republican Party."[120] (The reference was to one of the first Americans to undergo a sex-change operation.) Agnew posed for photographs with Buckley at a Conservative Party fund-raiser. Nixon, on a campaign swing through Connecticut, by prearrangement crossed into Westchester County, where he posed for photographs with many of the one thousand volunteers, waving "Nixon and Buckley" placards.[121] The impression that Nixon preferred Buckley to Goodell had been made in no uncertain terms. Asked whether he was supporting Buckley, Nixon replied that he appreciated Buckley's support for him.[122] Buckley said his win would be a victory for the "silent majority."[123]

The candidate's brother Bill, who had remained largely behind the scenes for most of the campaign, reappeared in the national spotlight in the campaign's closing weeks. In a September 29, 1970, profile of him on CBS's *60 Minutes*, its correspondents made mention of James's senatorial campaign and showed footage of it. Asked by interviewer Mike Wallace to account for conservatism's growing acceptance, Buckley cited liberal disappointment with the results their policies had produced: "Now what has happened in the last few years is that the myths which became a political religion during the '30's and '40's have finally revealed themselves as myths, causing an awful lot of frustration, an awful lot of despair, and an awful lot of puzzlement. Some people are searching for radical solutions on the left. And some people are looking back on what the conservatives have been saying for a number of years."[124] Buckley took some credit for having accelerated this process. Shifting gears from the ideological to the personal, the candidate's brother forecast in an opinion piece for the *Daily News* that James L. Buckley's strength of character was such that it could earn voters' confidence even among those who disapproved of his positions.[125]

James L. Buckley scored a historic upset, winning the election with 39 percent of the vote to Ottinger's 37 percent and Goodell's 24 percent. Rockefeller won reelection with 52 percent of the vote to Goldberg's 41 percent. Conservative Paul Adams, who had all but disappeared from sight as the campaign progressed, polled 7 percent. Rockefeller's hold on Albany remained secure, as did the Conservative Party's third-place position on the ballot. Bill Buckley described his brother's victory to a *New York Times* reporter as "the crystallization of counter-revolutionary impulses."[126] "With the election of Jim Buckley," he told the same reporter a day later, "people will no longer think, as they have been trained to think, of Conservatives as a batch of Birchers and a congeries of crackpots." Whenever *National Review* reported about James L. Buckley over the next six years, it consistently referred to him as "the Sainted Junior Senator from New York."

After the election, Nixon hosted the Senator-elect's brother Bill, Conservative Party founders Kiernan O'Doherty and J. Daniel Mahoney, and their wives at his friend Robert Abplanalp's retreat in the Bahamas. The group discussed the effectiveness of the GOP's electoral strategy with an eye toward Nixon's upcoming 1972 reelection campaign.[127] Nixon agreed to speak at *National Review*'s fifteenth annual dinner, a promise he would be unable to keep due to the death of French President Charles de Gaulle, whose funeral Nixon attended on the day the dinner had been scheduled. The group discussed Efron's forthcoming book, Agnew's suitability as a possible conservative alternative to Reagan in the run-up to the 1976 presidential primaries, and federal patronage for New York Conservatives.[128]

James L. Buckley's candidacy and election put the entire Buckley family in the national spotlight. *Newsweek*'s postelection story on the congressional elections featured a sidebar entitled "The Buckleys: An Extraordinary Family." *Life* put Aloise and her surviving children on its cover.[129] Inside, photographs of the Buckleys playing touch football at the family estate seemed intended to evoke in readers' minds memories of the Kennedys, who had appeared in the same magazine in similar poses a decade earlier. Javits sounded the only sour note when he sought, unsuccessfully, to bar James L. Buckley from the Republican Senate Conference on the grounds that he had not been elected on the Republican ticket. James's election to the Senate in 1970 marked the high-water mark in William F. Buckley Jr.'s relationship with the first President who had granted him access both to him and to his administration. In less than a year it would begin to unravel.

11

"Let the Man Go Decently"

The rapport Nixon had worked so hard to establish and maintain with the responsible American Right began to rupture in January 1971, when, after an interview with the three networks, he declared himself a "Keynesian" on economic matters. In subsequent commentary, Buckley listed a series of Nixonian deviations from conservative orthodoxy. The President had taken the United States off the gold standard, committed himself to a policy of "full employment," increased federal spending on entitlements and other programs, and brought into being a series of new policy initiatives, agencies, and regulations. Nixon was an early backer of the newly established Environmental Protection Agency (EPA), the Occupational Safety and Health Administration (OSHA), Title 9, and the "Philadelphia Plan" (a measure to assure hiring and promotion of African Americans in the building trades), which was a forerunner of "affirmative action" in other hiring. In mid-1971, Nixon committed the greatest heresy of all in the eyes of the Right when he imposed wage and price controls.[1]

Nixon did not limit his offenses to domestic matters. On July 15, he surprised and antagonized much of the Right when he announced that he would visit the People's Republic of China the following winter. Buckley was so angered at the news that he found something nice to say about his family's nemesis, Franklin D. Roosevelt, at Nixon's expense. FDR never offered to visit Nazi Germany, Buckley said in a column. He went on to call the People's Republic China the "home of terror, slaughter, sadism, xenophobia, and guile."[2] He was just warming up. Buckley would return to this theme with a vengeance once Nixon embarked on his historic journey.

While he objected to all of these policies, Buckley supported the administration in other areas. Outraged that Daniel J. Ellsberg, a government official with access to classified information, had "leaked" documents detailing the history of U.S. involvement in South Vietnam to the press ("the Pentagon Papers") and that the *New York Times* and the *Washington Post* would publish them, Buckley worked his way into the story in the summer of 1971. He published in *National Review* what he said were memos that had been part of the original document dump. Several newspapers reported on *National Review*'s alleged scoop. Within days, Buckley admitted that the exercise had been a hoax intended to satirize the media and its fixation on making Ellsberg a hero. Not amused, several newspapers dropped his syndicated column. "Well, I am down to 348 papers," Buckley sighed.[3]

Meanwhile, the breach between Nixon and the Right continued to widen. In July 1971, Buckley convened a meeting of conservative leaders at his Manhattan residence to discuss their unhappiness with the administration.[4] Calling themselves "the Manhattan Twelve," the participants released a statement in which they "suspended" support for the Nixon administration. While they said they were not at this time encouraging formal political opposition to Nixon, they would keep their options open. Buckley used his special standing within the conservative movement to tone down the militant rhetoric of his colleagues. "The only thing that gave us credibility was Buckley," Stan Evans said afterward.[5] Buckley's influence can be seen in the statement's closing lines, in which the writers "reaffirmed" their personal admiration for the President and stated that they considered their defection an act of loyalty to the Nixon they had supported in 1968.[6] This was a subtle reminder of why they had backed Nixon then against the alternatives.

Buckley had kept Kissinger apprised of the group's thinking and read him excerpts from the statement prior to its release. Kissinger said he hoped the conservatives would confine their criticisms to the administration's handling of Vietnam. Opposition from the Right to the pace of troop withdrawal (they thought it too rapid), he suggested, would help the administration counter criticism from the Left that it was moving too slowly. At the same time, Kissinger thought, conservative criticism of Nixon's policy shift on China would help the administration's negotiating posture with Beijing, enabling Nixon to claim that the degree to which he could make concessions was limited by domestic pressures from an important part of his governing coalition. "I am speaking to you as a friend," Kissinger told Buckley, but added, "I will have to start attacking this thing as a Presidential assistant." Buckley told Kissinger to be on the watch for a forthcoming article by Buckley in the *New York Times Magazine* about Nixon and the conservative movement.[7]

The title of Buckley's piece, "Is Nixon One of Us?" originated in a comment Nixon had made to Buckley at a state dinner honoring Australian Prime

Minister John G. Gorton. In an aside to Buckley, Nixon had assured him that Gorton was "one of us." This, Buckley informed his readers, prompted him to ask himself what Nixon meant to convey through the words "one of us." Clearly, Buckley surmised, "Mr. Nixon was not revealing himself to me as a *National Review* conservative. Nor was he suggesting that Mr. Gorton was one." He concluded that Nixon meant that he, Buckley, and Gorton were all committed anti-Communists.[8]

Buckley then inquired whether the term *anti-Communist* retained any meaning, given that most mainstream commentators had taken to presenting the United States and the Soviet Union as morally equivalent. He cited three developments, all occurring on Nixon's watch, that gave conservatives cause to worry: overtures made to China absent significant concessions from the other side (but with anxieties raised about the future of Taiwan); deep cuts in defense; and the possible acquiescence to *Ostpolitik*—a term West German Prime Minister Willy Brandt had used to convey "normalization of relations between the two Germanys," leading to the possible demilitarization and neutrality of West Germany.[9]

Having deemed Nixon the most rightward viable candidate in 1968, Buckley suggested that conservatives should not have expected him to take aim at the very idea of a welfare state, which had been part of the American policy fabric since at least 1936. (Chambers's admonitions against tampering with what FDR had put in place were much in evidence in the thinking of both Nixon and Buckley.) Still, Buckley noted, the burden was on Nixon to demonstrate that he had not taken up the "other side's reveries." (This was clearly a reference to Nixon's increased domestic activism.) Turning to his principal reservation about the President, Buckley concluded that if Nixon continued to act as though he believed the USSR had given up its hope of world conquest or had become more peace loving as a result of arms limitations, conservatives would conclude that the President was not "one of us."[10]

Having thus put Nixon on notice, Buckley joined the ranks of the administration's critics, especially with regard to its policies toward the People's Republic of China and the USSR. On November 1, 1971, the Manhattan Twelve released a six-page list of demands to which Nixon had to agree in order to regain their support. They debated among themselves whether to endorse Representative John Ashbrook (R-OH), who was expected to challenge Nixon in the upcoming New Hampshire primary. Buckley initially opposed the idea, arguing both that Nixon would easily prevail, drawing considerable conservative support, and that Representative Pete McCloskey (R-CA), who was opposing Nixon from the left, would outpoll Ashbrook. He nevertheless put his reservations aside and wrote in an editorial in *National Review* that, if Ashbrook entered the race, the magazine would endorse him. The editorial suggested that a "lightning rod" was needed to attract dissent among Republicans, so that Nixon could "feel the shock."[11] He later recorded a radio spot for Ashbrook's use.

In response to all of these actions, the administration went into overdrive. Agnew, Buchanan, Kissinger, and others tried to charm Buckley back into the fold. Peter Flanigan, a former investment banker—a descendant of the founder of the Anheuser-Busch beer company—who had joined Nixon's staff as an adviser on business matters, telephoned Buckley and berated him for his defection to Ashcroft. Flanigan considered this an act of "disloyalty" after all Nixon's team had done to help elect James L. Buckley to the Senate. The White House aide said that he found it strange that Buckley, who had recommended a certain person for an ambassadorship, should expect the administration to proceed with the appointment when Buckley and his magazine were opposing Nixon.

"I know that politics does strange things to people," Buckley wrote back to Flanigan, "but men of your breeding ought really—if politics has so seized you—to try to leave certain things implicit."[12] He said that he had recommended the person in question (for the ambassadorial post) not as a favor to the individual, but because he thought the country could benefit from the individual's service. Buckley continued that he would not act contrary to his conscience in return for perceived favors the administration had done a relative and explained that he had an obligation to other conservatives who looked to him for leadership.[13] Buckley copied Mitchell, Kissinger, Shakespeare, James L. Buckley, and Nixon Chief of Staff H. R. Haldeman on his letter.

"One of these days," Buckley wrote his antagonist, "you will have to remind yourself that there are really quite a lot of people in the United States who are not running for office, and for whom patronage from the White House is not the supreme ambition."[14] After word of their altercation appeared in a column by Rowland Evans and Robert Novak, Buckley published parts of his correspondence with Flanigan in *National Review*.

Perhaps with hopes of luring Buckley back into the fold, the White House offered him one of the scarce seats on the press plane that accompanied Nixon to China on February 15, 1972. Any hope Nixon and his advisers had that Buckley might toe the line vanished when he filed his first story from China. He compared Nixon obsequiously cozying up to the Chinese ruling elite to a Nuremberg prosecutor descending from his stand to "embrace Goebbels and Doenitz and Hess" and beseeching them to "join with him in the making of a better world."[15] Having observed Nixon praise "Chairman Mao,

Chou En-lai, and the whole lot of them," Buckley declared afterward that he would have not been surprised if the President "had lurched into a toast of Alger Hiss."[16] When Nixon compared the Chinese Revolution of 1949 to the American Revolution of 1776, Buckley passed along to his readers a comment from an American reporter covering the event: "That should dispel the last suspicion that there is a trace of ideological conviction left in Richard Nixon."[17]

Buckley interpreted the absence in Nixon's remarks in China as well as at home to U.S. treaty obligations to Taiwan as evidence that the administration intended to abandon an ally. If Buckley had intended through his reporting to anger Nixon and his entourage, he succeeded. "We made a mistake in taking him," Kissinger told Nixon. "There would have been a lot of columns he couldn't have written if he hadn't been along."[18] This prompted Nixon to reply, "Just never take your enemies; I've told Haldeman that a thousand times."[19] Nixon's comments make clear that the President had come to regard the conservative spokesman not as a critic, but as a personal enemy. He seemed not to comprehend that Buckley objected not so much to the reversal of long-standing policy under changed geopolitical circumstances as he did to the exuberance Nixon displayed on the trip, his hyperbolic rhetoric, and his proceeding as if the two nations had no disagreements, past or present, which he intended through this visit to begin to bridge.

As Buckley saw the world, an act of strategic necessity was not a moral good and should not be presented as such. He was appalled that an American President would proclaim the American and Chinese revolutions "morally equivalent." He was also incensed that the trip took place while China was still in the throes of a brutal "cultural revolution" in which millions died at the hands of their own government—about which Nixon said not a word, either while in China or after his return to the United States. Needless to say, Buckley was no more supportive of Nixon's subsequent journey to Moscow, months after the China visit, or of his signing the Strategic Arms Limitations Treaty, in which the two sides limited themselves to no more than two hundred antiballistic missiles each.

In March, Buckley announced that he would not accept reappointment to the United States Information Agency (USIA) advisory commission. He declared that it was inappropriate to continue on as a Nixon appointee at the same time he was writing "scathing attacks" on the administration for what he perceived to be its leftward tilt.

With Nixon's renomination virtually assured and the President running against the dovish George McGovern, Buckley and his cohorts reached an uneasy accommodation with the administration. Throughout the 1972 campaign,

Buckley's commentary focused more on McGovern's liberal economic and foreign policy views than on Nixon's virtues or achievements. After Nixon was returned to office in a record landslide, in which he carried all jurisdictions except Massachusetts and the District of Columbia, Buckley paid him a congratulatory visit. He remembered finding the reelected President in a foul mood, fixated on exacting retribution on his enemies. "There really isn't a feeling of satisfaction in the air," Buckley said to a friend.[20] Nixon, he predicted, could "suffer the fate of Harold Macmillan, who in 1959 won the most triumphant re-election in modern English political history, and eighteen months later everything lay in ruins about him."[21]

As 1972 drew to a close, Buckley became privy to details about a much-undercovered incident that occurred during the campaign, which would erupt into a major scandal that would cut short Nixon's presidency. In the preface to his 1975 collection of writings, *Execution Eve and Other Contemporary Ballads*, he explained that he had not written much about the Watergate scandal between December 1972 and April 1973 because he felt "greatly encumbered." He wrote that he could not reveal details a friend had confided to him about his participation in several misdeeds on Nixon's behalf.[22] During those four months, Buckley also absented himself from editorial meetings at *National Review* whenever Watergate was discussed.[23] Buckley's friend and informant was none other than E. Howard Hunt, his onetime superior at the CIA. Hunt had overseen the Watergate burglary and had been involved in other illegal undertakings.

On December 8, 1972, Hunt's wife died in a plane crash. She had been carrying with her $10,000 in cash. Speculation immediately arose that the money had been given to her husband by Nixon operatives in exchange for his silence about the break-in. Ten days after her death, Hunt telephoned Buckley to relate that Mrs. Hunt had earlier named Buckley alternate executor of her estate in the event that her husband could not fulfill his duties as such should he be found guilty of conspiring to burglarize the Democratic National Committee's headquarters at the Watergate (an eventuality that came to pass a month later).[24] Buckley was godfather to Hunt's three oldest children. The previous June, after learning that Hunt had been arrested, Buckley had telephoned the Hunt residence to express his concerns and offer to help defray some of Hunt's legal expenses.[25]

The day after he had telephoned Buckley, Hunt paid him a visit. Fearful that he might be assassinated, Hunt, for the next two hours, shared with Buckley what he knew of the Watergate operation. According to Buckley's account of their conversation, Hunt denied knowledge of any complicity by Nixon in the

Watergate affair, but said he believed John Mitchell had authorized the break-in.[26] Buckley noted in his recollection that Hunt offered this opinion of Nixon's role before it became known that the President had engaged in conversations regarding payments to the Watergate defendants and for what purpose. Hunt subsequently made several telephone calls to Buckley at prearranged intervals.[27] At one point, Hunt admitted that he had taken part in the burglary of Ellsberg's psychiatrist's office, an action that led to the dismissal of the Justice Department's case against Ellsberg and would serve as the basis for one of the two articles of impeachment against Nixon that the House of Representatives subsequently approved. Hunt also told Buckley that he and G. Gordon Liddy, another of the Watergate burglars, had, upon White House instructions, contemplated how they might murder the columnist Jack Anderson, one of Nixon's fiercest critics.[28]

According to Buckley's son, Christopher, Hunt informed Buckley that, were he to die, Buckley would be contacted by a person he did not know who had a key to a safe deposit box, which the two of them would open together. When Christopher asked his father what the box might have contained, Buckley replied, "I don't know exactly, but it could theoretically involve information that could lead to the impeachment of the president of the United States."[29] He felt bound to keep confidential what he knew.[30]

He did not record whether he unburdened himself to a priest or to anyone else, or under what circumstances his conscience would have prompted him to share what he knew with authorities in order to prevent future crimes, possibly including a murder. "Only after it was all over did we learn that Hunt had burdened Buckley with the story as far as he knew it," two of Buckley's colleagues recalled. "His knowledge was only partial, but still difficult enough for a working journalist to live with."[31] Christopher remembered his father's demeanor during his self-imposed silence about Watergate as "pure Gethsemane: "*Let this cup pass from me.*"[32]

Months after Nixon resigned, a White House tape from January 8, 1973, surfaced in which Nixon is heard suggesting that Buckley be approached to write a column supporting clemency for Hunt. Nixon proposed that Buckley could cite Hunt's dire financial situation, his grief over the death of his wife, and his having to raise six children on his own. Asked to comment on the tape, Buckley said, "I don't need to be reminded to write a column urging clemency even for sons of bitches, as Mr. Nixon should know from personal experience."[33]

When Buckley began to write about Watergate in April 1973, he voiced increasing skepticism about whether Nixon could survive the unraveling scandal. He faulted Nixon for not having named a special prosecutor immediately after Watergate burglar James McCord suggested in a March 20, 1973, letter to Judge John Sirica that the White House had been pressuring the burglars to remain silent.[34] In an effort to explain the President's apparent sense of certainty that none of his close aides participated in the scandal that became known as "Watergate," Buckley offered this theory: "Poor Mr. Nixon suffers not only from the excessive desire of his friends to please but also from the ravenous appetite of his enemies to harm. This appetite Mr. Nixon has . . . fueled by that curdling sanctimony that is his trademark; and by that articulate impatience with the imperfect performance of others on which he built his early career."[35]

Buckley wrote that Nixon, in a speech he delivered on April 30, 1973, which he intended to calm the nation's anxieties about Watergate, had aroused the "Puritan Conscience of America." In his televised presentation, Nixon "accepted responsibility" for the scandal, offered no means through which he might be held accountable, announced the resignations of White House aides H. R. Haldeman and John Ehrlichman, whom he proclaimed "two fine public servants," and pledged to bring the perpetrators of the break-in to justice, all the while denying to investigators access to information that might establish his innocence. Buckley noted that before Nixon went on the air, the Gallup Poll reported that 40 percent of the public thought he had foreknowledge of the break-in. Buckley predicted that after hearing what Nixon had to say, many more would come to doubt him.[36]

Buckley did not advocate Nixon's impeachment. That, he said, was a power the Constitution bestowed on Congress not as a means of punishing presidents but to "get rid of them."[37] Impeachment, Buckley argued, was a "technical resource" the framers inserted into the Constitution to rid the nation of a would-be "Caligula" (a despot or a madman). Nothing Nixon might have done with regard to Watergate constituted in his view a "national threat to individual freedom by virtue of his exercises in managerial tyranny."[38] He lamented that history had proven it more difficult to remove a head of government elected by the people than one selected by a parliamentary majority: "It is one thing to replace the government of Anthony Eden with a government of Harold Macmillan, or the government of Harold Macmillan with that of Alec Douglas-Home—the kind of thing the English can do without the piano player missing a note. Another, to elevate the Vice President by removing the President."[39] He did not think at this juncture that any of Nixon's misdeeds, which were yet to be established, warranted putting the nation through such a trauma.

Still, he found Nixon's behavior contemptible. He thought "contumacious" Nixon's refusal to cooperate with the Senate Select Watergate Committee and his invocation of executive privilege to bar aides from relating White House conversations.[40] Buckley believed that Nixon had lost an opportunity in his April speech to put the scandal behind him. He thought that after he had gone through the motion of having accepted responsibility, Nixon should have offered to accept Senate censure as punishment for his negligence.[41] Such an act of self-flagellation, he suggested, would have been the twentieth-century equivalent of Henry II's submitting to flogging to atone for his culpability in the murder of St. Thomas à Becket.[42]

Buckley's ire was most aroused after a memorandum White House Counsel John Dean had written to Deputy Chief of Staff John Ehrlichman became public. Entitled "Maximizing the Incumbency," Dean's memo recommended that the administration make full use of its incumbent powers to "screw" its political "enemies." Buckley termed the document "*an act of proto-fascism.*"[43] Proclaiming it "altogether ruthless in its dismissal of human rights," he continued: "It is fascist in its reliance on the state as the instrument of harassment. It is fascist in its automatic assumption that the state in all matters comes before the individual. And it is fascist in tone: the stealth, the brutality, the self-righteousness."[44]

In a telling aside, Buckley reminded his readers that he had not used the word *fascist* lightly: it was a term he believed liberals often applied to their ideological adversaries without foundation.[45] He did not rehearse all the times his critics had applied that label to him as a means of discrediting his arguments. In this instance, he wanted to make clear, he believed that the term so often associated with authoritarian and totalitarian regimes of the 1930s applied. While Buckley had no way of knowing whether Nixon had seen the Dean memorandum prior to its release or whether he agreed with what Dean recommended, he questioned why, after its contents became known, the President had not denounced it.[46]

When it was learned that Nixon had been taping his Oval Office conversations, Buckley cautioned the President against making blanket assertions that everything on the tapes was "privileged" information, protected by the Constitution's separation of powers doctrine. He recommended that Nixon turn the tapes over to a distinguished group of two or three persons, perhaps retired judges, to determine whether the President had participated in a cover-up. Nixon should not assume, he warned, that even the 18 percent who still supported him would remain in his corner as more damning facts dripped out.[47]

In September 1973, at Kissinger's behest, Buckley agreed to serve for three months as delegate to the United Nations General Assembly. Some saw in this move an effort by the administration to bolster its right flank during the first phase of the Watergate affair (the Senate Select Committee's investigation).[48] In a memoir of his experiences at the UN, Buckley wrote that he had accepted the appointment because it afforded him the opportunity to observe how that body approached human rights and because he harbored Walter Mitty–like illusions that he might be able to read excerpts from Solzhenitsyn and other Soviet dissidents to his fellow delegates. Although that was not to be, the experience gave him ample opportunity to collect anecdotes he would later share about the hypocrisy, cynicism, and protocol he had witnessed in abundance.

In his UN memoir, Buckley related that a foreign dignitary had asked him at a luncheon how he intended to vote on a question that appeared on the New York ballot. Buckley explained that he would be voting in Connecticut, where he resided. After his hostess explained to Buckley's questioner that, in the United States, people voted not where they worked but where they slept, Buckley interjected, "If I voted where I slept, I would vote in the United Nations."[49] He made it a point not to repeat his one venture into international diplomacy. All the while, he kept an eye on the Watergate matter as it continued to unfold.

In January 1974, Buckley for the first time publicly raised the possibility of Nixon resigning. He devoted an entire column to how this might occur, as several competing Nixon personalities reached an internal accord. First there was the obstinate Nixon, who insisted he was not a "quitter." Then there was Nixon the "realist," who could aptly gauge any political situation. The third Nixon was withdrawn, moody, introspective, and reveled in pain, often self-inflicted. For such a man, Buckley concluded, resignation constituted the ultimate suffering. "If, for a man on the make, power is an 'aphrodisiac,' for the man facing the end, martyrdom is 'orgasmic.'" Finally, there was a fourth Nixon, anxious to demonstrate to the world both his victimization and his humanity. That Nixon, Buckley predicted, allied with the third Nixon, the sufferer, would lead the President eventually to resign "not only with honor, but with pleasure."[50]

On March 19, Senator James L. Buckley called upon the President to resign so that the country, long distracted by Watergate, might focus on other pressing matters before it.[51] Such a move, he said, would be an extraordinary act of statesmanship and would not necessarily be an admission of wrongdoing. Days before Nixon did announce his resignation, William F. Buckley Jr. declared the President's situation irreparable. He lamented that Nixon had not destroyed the White House tapes and doubted that Congress would have impeached him for this, given that it had no way of knowing what portions of them pertained to national security. "Now," he observed, Nixon "will be thrown out with the chicken thieves."[52] Sending Nixon to prison, he said would be an act of "sadism" that would "contaminate" the body politic. "Let the man go decently," he wrote.[53]

Buckley and Nixon had intermittent contact during Nixon's retirement. Once Buckley arranged for Nixon to host a meeting with senior editors of *National Review* at the former President's New Jersey home. Early in the Reagan presidency, Buckley encountered Nixon in Paris and passed along a message from the former President to the incumbent President (Reagan). Buckley asked Nixon to consent to an interview with a biographer of Whittaker Chambers. Nixon declined.

"It can happen only to a man who takes very large strides in history," Buckley wrote upon Nixon's death, "that he could win re-election with a runaway majority, and in less than two years leave the White House in greater ignominy than was ever before suffered by a departing American president." Reviewing the ups and downs in Nixon's career and his relationship with American conservatives, Buckley termed it a remarkable fact that the Right rallied to Nixon's side whenever he came under attack from liberal adversaries, considering that he had done so little to advance the conservative cause.[54]

He traced whatever affection they retained for him to Nixon's having wagered that Whittaker Chambers and not Alger Hiss had told the truth in one of the most famous confrontations in American history. That decision, which Nixon made as a junior House member in 1948, had earned him a supply of allies and enemies that he retained for the rest of his life. The Hiss case, Nixon wrote in 1962, "brought me national fame. But it also left a residue of hatred and hostility toward me . . . among substantial segments of the press and the intellectual community—a hostility, which remains even today."[55] Buckley's final verdict on the man on whose behalf he had rallied conservatives in 1968, when their hearts were with Reagan, was that Nixon was both the "weakest of men and the strongest: a master of self-abuse and of self-recovery."[56] Whittaker Chambers would have agreed. Nixon might have as well.

12

Bill and Ronnie: Preparing a President

William F. Buckley Jr. first encountered Ronald Reagan in January 1961, the same month John F. Kennedy became President. Reagan, the host of the popular television program *General Electric Theater*, had completed his political transformation from liberal to conservative and would officially change his party registration from Democrat to Republican the following year, after having backed the GOP presidential nominee in the past three elections. (He had most recently served as head of Democrats for Nixon in the 1960 election.) As Reagan was making his political journey rightward, while Buckley may have had some passing familiarity with the former Hollywood star's political opinions, Reagan was very much aware of Buckley's. A subscriber to *National Review* since it began publication, Reagan joked that in its early days, the magazine would arrive in a plain brown wrapper and that, by the time he had become President, it came with the wrapper off.[1]

Reagan came to follow Buckley and *National Review* through the influence of his mentor at General Electric, Lemuel Ricketts Boulware, its Vice President for Labor and Community Relations. Boulware was an admirer of Buckley's and an early donor to *National Review*. It was he who brought the young magazine to Reagan's attention.[2] Years later, Reagan recalled reading each issue from cover to cover, often as soon as it arrived. In addition to his role as host of and occasional actor in *GE Theater*, which aired from 1954 to 1961, Reagan traveled the country as a GE spokesman, giving hundreds of talks each year to employees and community leaders about the virtues of the free enterprise system.

The role Buckley played in advancing Reagan's career, both through his writings and through his personal intercession on Reagan's behalf, cannot be overstated. By making *National Review* the principal voice for modern conservatism and himself what the Associated Press termed "the leading proponent of conservatism after Goldwater," Buckley made the very idea of a Reagan presidency possible.[3] Through the people he steered into influential posts, his vigorous defense of Reagan as a candidate and as an officeholder, and the policy recommendations and back-channel assistance he regularly provided, Buckley became Reagan's most trusted adviser outside his official family and, after Nancy Reagan, Ronald Reagan's primary enabler and protector. When the two men first encountered one another, Buckley's visibility and influence were on the rise just as Reagan's public persona was shifting from that of actor to conviction politician.

Buckley's lecture agency had booked him in early 1961 to deliver a speech in Beverly Hills to the Citizens for Better Education, a group highly critical of President Kennedy's proposal to provide government-funded health care to senior citizens. Reagan was to introduce him. Before the program, the two men and their respective parties (Reagan accompanied by his wife, Nancy, Buckley by his sister-in-law) happened to dine at the same restaurant across the street from where Buckley was to speak. As they were leaving, Reagan approached Buckley and introduced himself and Nancy to him. He made a favorable impression upon his new acquaintances when he mentioned that he had enjoyed the way Buckley had depicted Eleanor Roosevelt in his book *Up from Liberalism*.[4]

Buckley's talk got off to an unconventional start. The microphone had not been turned on, and the control room, which was at balcony level, was locked. Reagan exited the room through the window, walked a foot-wide ledge to reach the control room several feet way, and entered through a window he broke with his elbow. Minutes later, to the delight of the audience, the microphone was on and the program proceeded. Reagan had impressed Buckley a second time, now with Reagan's savoir faire, athleticism, and take-charge demeanor.[5]

It did not take the two men long to become allies and friends. Their increasing familiarity can be seen in the salutations with which Buckley began his letters to Reagan, which progressed from "Dear Mr. Reagan" to "Dear Ron" to "Dear Ronnie" to "Dear Mr. President." Reagan always began his written communications to Buckley with "Dear Bill" and always signed off as "Ron." Buckley's son Christopher believed his father "got as close" to Reagan as any friend could. "It certainly *was* a friendship," he recalled.[6] Reagan bonded with Buckley, although, famously, he let few people besides his wife draw close to him.[7] Reagan's director of correspondence during his presidency referred to Buckley as one of Reagan's "real pen pals."[8]

Buckley was a frequent guest in the Reagan home and Ronald and Nancy visited and occasionally stayed with the Buckleys when they came east. The couples sometimes spent holidays and vacations together. Reagan's children went to Buckley for advice on academic plans, career possibilities, things they had written, and television presentations.

From their initial meeting, Buckley stayed in frequent contact with the Reagans. He wrote Reagan to thank him for publicly acknowledging Buckley's presence at a youth rally at the 1964 Republican National Convention after Goldwater operatives had pulled Buckley from the program.[9] Buckley told Reagan that his "A Time for Choosing" speech, which he delivered on Goldwater's behalf on October 27, 1964, was a "joyous moment" and "high point" of Goldwater's presidential campaign.[10] When the two men and their wives sat down to dinner in Los Angeles a month after Goldwater's defeat, Reagan volunteered that influential conservatives were pressing him to run for Governor of California, and that before he made his decision he would travel the state, testing out his message and gauging public sentiment.

While he took to addressing his friend in jest as "Guv," Buckley doubted that Reagan would be able to make the transition to electoral politics. A year later, Reagan's "listening tour" completed, Buckley changed his mind. Reagan, he wrote, was "developing a political know-how" that astounded professionals. Buckley expressed doubt that Democrats, given Reagan's genial demeanor, would succeed in persuading voters that his opposition to Lyndon Johnson's antipoverty programs resulted from a "mean streak." He also thought that Reagan's criticisms of Governor Pat Brown's spending practices and his "get tough" stance toward criminals and student protesters would resonate with voters.[11]

In his writings and lectures, Buckley continually reassured his fellow conservatives that Reagan's conservative bona fides remained intact while he broadened his appeal to moderates. He also began a friendship with Nancy Reagan, who emerged as her husband's principal confidante, and worked with her behind the scenes to advance her husband's prospects. Buckley became as close to Nancy Reagan as he did to Ronald. Often, he advised her on how to deal with her critics in the media and with her children. When she drew criticism or came under attack, he rushed to her defense—in print and in other ways. Buckley's chivalry endeared him all the more to her husband. By the time Reagan was elected President, Buckley and Mrs. Reagan were fantasizing in letters to each other about secret assignations in places like Casablanca. They cheerfully let their spouses in on these fictional romantic encounters.[12]

"Well, we're in it with both feet—and we'll see what happens," Nancy wrote Buckley after her husband declared his candidacy for Governor. She regularly provided Buckley with updates on the California political landscape during the primary campaign. She complained that a Birch-backed candidate, who had opposed Nixon in the gubernatorial primary four years earlier, had spread the word that Reagan was an admitted Communist. She worried that a certain would-be primary entrant might run merely to drain votes away from Reagan, and voiced annoyance when his principal primary opponent, San Francisco Mayor George Christopher, criticized Reagan for having once been a Democrat.[13]

Buckley used his influence to persuade *Esquire* magazine not to proceed with a piece it had commissioned on Reagan from the left-leaning journalist Jessica Mitford. The offending journalist subsequently published the article in *Ramparts*, which was a far more liberal magazine with fewer subscribers than *Esquire* and which had less of a cachet with the mainstream media. Buckley took special pleasure in having "defanged" the Mitford piece.[14]

Three months into Reagan's campaign, Buckley reported that Reagan had been "doing disconcertingly well . . . to the distress of those who would clearly like to see him foam at the mouth and come out for the repeal of the internal combustion engine."[15] When a group of renegade conservatives threatened to withhold support from Reagan unless he endorsed their entire policy agenda, Buckley declared their demands out of bounds, given that they pertained to foreign policy, an area in which the Governor of California could exert little influence.[16] What distinguished Reagan in Buckley's eyes was his capacity to project his conservative ideas as a positive agenda, stating what he was *for* rather than delivering a litany of what he opposed. Reagan, Buckley declared, offered an attractive alternative to the Democrats' "dreary statism" and "gave Californians a sense of pride and manhood" that belied the "spirit of the age."[17]

As Reagan sailed toward the 1966 California Republican gubernatorial nomination, Buckley put the Californian's photograph on the cover of *National Review*'s June 28 issue and ran two favorable stories about him inside. He speculated that a Reagan win against incumbent Governor Edmund G. ("Pat") Brown would spark talk of a presidential run in 1968, but predicted that Reagan would disavow it "convincingly enough to discourage the professionals from launching a campaign." Still, Buckley noted, talk of a Reagan national run could act as a check upon Nixon, should he veer too far in Rockefeller's direction.[18]

Late in the campaign, Buckley had some fun at the Democrats' expense. *National Review* had misreported in its October 18 issue that Helen Gahagan Douglas, former actress and three-term Congresswoman, who lost the California 1950 senate election to Richard Nixon, had endorsed Reagan. After Reagan privately voiced his disbelief, Buckley had a *National Review* staffer check with Douglas. She said that she found Reagan "a very agreeable man" but was not supporting him because of his party affiliation. Douglas added that she did not believe anyone was "ipso facto incompetent" to serve in public office "because he or she has been an actor." Buckley sent Nancy Reagan a "Night Letter" the day after the first story ran, which contained the correction he would make to the Douglas story in *National Review*'s next issue.[19] In a story purporting to retract the magazine's initial error, Buckley broke some news. Here was a liberal Democrat on record refuting the Brown campaign's principal argument against Reagan's candidacy.

On the eve of the election, an ebullient Buckley wrote that Reagan all but disproved the conventional wisdom that to win in California, a Republican candidate had to become "super-specially liberal" in the manner of U.S. Senator Tom Kuchel (California's ideological equivalent of New York Republicans Nelson Rockefeller and Jacob Javits). Buckley discerned, too, that moderate and liberal Republicans were rallying behind Reagan, while centrist Democrats were drifting away from Brown. In Reagan's manner of campaigning (unabashedly conservative, but upbeat and far from angry), Buckley saw a path to electoral success he hoped other conservatives might follow. Reagan pulled 58 percent of the vote to Brown's 42 percent.

After Reagan took office, Buckley furnished the new Governor with suggestions on policy and personnel, defended his proposals, and worked to gain Reagan entry into enclaves where conservatives seldom ventured. ("The rumor here is that Ronnie is looking for help," Buckley wrote Nancy early in her husband's administration. Always, he was ready to provide it.) On July 6, 1967, Reagan made his first appearance on *Firing Line*.[20] He and Buckley discussed the topic "Is it possible to be a good Governor?" Reagan used the opportunity to advance an argument Buckley had once pressed upon the Goldwater campaign, with little success: that states be allowed to retain more of the funds their residents sent to Washington in taxes rather than have the federal government redistribute monies from richer states to poorer ones while imposing restrictions on how states spent what they received from Washington.

The system in place, Reagan and Buckley both maintained, made it difficult for a Governor to be innovative when Washington played a large role in setting the states' priorities. Reagan likened Washington's retaining part of the funds the states sent it to a theatrical agent taking a commission. He proposed allowing each state to keep a minimal percentage of what it sent to Washington and was open to subsidizing the poorer states. The idea was meant to reverse the flow of funds from the states to Washington that had been in place since the 1930s.

Buckley encouraged Reagan to grant access to his critics, particularly opinion leaders and persons of note, who disagreed with him politically. Such an approach, he reasoned, would make them less likely to dismiss the California

Governor as an "ignoramus," "ill-informed," or a "warmonger," all terms his detractors had used to describe him. At Buckley's urging, Reagan met with writer Truman Capote and arranged for him to tour San Quentin State Prison as part of his research for a documentary on capital punishment. In a letter to Nancy Reagan, Buckley described Capote, known for his eccentricities, as "an influential guy and worth giving a little time to."[21]

In September 1967, the Buckleys hosted a dinner for the Reagans in New York. Among the guests were Capote, Republican Rhode Island Governor John Chafee and his wife, and Richard Clurman of *Time* magazine and his wife. Before the event Buckley described the Clurmans to Nancy Reagan as "good fun" and influential. He mentioned that Mrs. Clurman had suggested that the Buckleys also invite Governor Rockefeller and his wife, an idea, Buckley wrote, that he hadn't had time to assimilate. He also told Nancy that he wanted to take the opportunity at the dinner to dampen Chafee's enthusiasm for presumed presidential contender Michigan Governor George Romney: "Perhaps we might brainwash him."[22] (This was a reference to a phrase Romney had used in explaining why he had shifted his position from dove to hawk and back again on Vietnam.)

A few months later Reagan, with Buckley much in evidence, spent three days in residence at Yale as a Chubb Fellow. His visit sparked controversy on campus. Classics professor Adam Parry declared that the invitation and the $500 honorarium Reagan would receive implicated the university in "third-world wars, atomic holocausts, and anti-intellectualism."[23] *Yale Daily News* editor Donald MacGillis, while sympathetic to Parry's views, wrote that were Yale to rescind the invitation, a "national scandal" might ensue, which could possibly work to Reagan's advantage.[24] When Reagan arrived on campus, his detractors presented him with a petition one thousand students had signed that criticized him for vetoing seven antipoverty programs. The organizer of the event, sophomore Robert Hanson, declared the episode "proof that Reagan was not warmly received at Yale."[25]

After Reagan's visit, the *Yale Alumni Magazine* commented on the lack of "heat" Reagan's actual presentations had generated among his audiences, considering the negative publicity the invitation to him had received. The authors of the article made note of an aspect of Reagan's style that would become familiar to millions: his projecting the image of himself not as the star attraction but as a member of the audience who had mounted the stage to voice the concerns of those who remained in their seats. Reagan, they prophesized, could emerge as a leading presidential contender, a prospect to which they did not look forward.[26] Buckley, interviewed for the piece, said that to the "disappointment of the tricoteuses . . . Reagan had persuaded a number of 'oh-so sophisticated Easterners' to take him seriously."[27]

With Reagan one year into his term, Buckley, grading his performance, declared Reagan the "next Goldwater" and a "pragmatist." In pressing his conservative agenda, Reagan was moving more with the grain of public opinion than against it, he said. He praised Reagan's approach to education, mental health, and taxes. Reagan, he suggested, had cast himself as the defender of a besieged public that relied on public services, in opposition to remote and intrusive bureaucracies.[28] As Buckley saw it, Reagan had taken on the role of populist, giving voice to the views of the majority of Californians against the dictates of an unaccountable elite.

As several of Reagan's prior critics began to cede some of his success, Buckley lamented that so many, perhaps to protect their standing among fellow liberals, felt the need to qualify their praise of Reagan by noting where they disagreed with him. As a case in point, he cited James Q. Wilson's article in *Commentary*, "A Guide to Reagan Country: The Political Culture of Southern California."[29] Wilson suggested that Reagan's philosophy, which put a premium on self-reliance, personal responsibility, and individualism, was more in sync with the prevailing California political culture than were liberal embraces of higher taxes and increased regulation as well as the liberal assumption that government action in and of itself would produce wise, equitable, and positive outcomes. Buckley interpreted Wilson's piece as a warning to liberals about the threat Reagan posed to the monopoly they retained over setting the nation's priorities rather than as an endorsement of Reagan's ideas and policies.[30]

As pleased as he was with Reagan's performance as Governor, Buckley privately urged his friend in Sacramento to counter impressions that he was anti-intellectual, deficient of curiosity, or "unread." He urged Reagan to take stock of how the "Academic Establishment" functioned and identify a few scholars with whom he might make common cause. Those who had initially voiced skepticism about Reagan found confirmation of their suspicions in some ill-chosen rhetoric Reagan had used. As a case in point, Buckley cited Reagan's stated opposition to subsidizing "intellectual curiosity." In their written exchanges, the two voiced different understandings of the meaning of those two words.

Reagan explained to Buckley that he had used the term to decry what he considered waste and frivolity, not to disparage genuine academic pursuits. He specifically mentioned such practices as universities flying guest lecturers to campuses to instruct students in bowling and fly-casting. He also criticized professors who delivered the same lectures year after year. Such academics, he suggested, could be replaced by professional note-taking services, which could sell previous years' notes to students—at a considerable saving to the state. Reagan's administration, he reminded Buckley, had increased the University of California's budget by 11.3 percent (four times the average increase he had proposed for other state agencies) and that of the state colleges by 21 percent.[31]

He did not think this a poor record and said that he had come to accept that he would never receive the credit he deserved from academicians for reforms he had undertaken. "When the intellectuals are concerned, I can be the kiss of death without half trying," Reagan wrote Buckley.[32] Yet he accepted Buckley's point that intellectuals could mar his public image and increasingly relied upon Buckley as a bridge to at least some of them.

Buckley cautioned Reagan to couch his calls for cutbacks in university budgets, the imposition of tuition, and increases in student fees in language that did not make him appear anti-intellectual. Should that impression take hold, Buckley warned, it could create a "class solidarity" among educators that "Karl Marx, Eugene Debs, and James Hoffa together might never have been able to achieve within the proletarian classes."[33] Reagan eventually argued that by financing higher education through tuition, student fees, and generous financial aid to students from families with modest means, as opposed to having all taxpayers pay the costs of all students regardless of their families' income and net worth, he was advocating a system that was both more fair and financially stable.[34]

Between the lines in his letters, Buckley was urging Reagan to forge alliances with whatever conservative elements existed at California institutions. Building enduring ties between conservative politicians and conservative intellectuals had long been a Buckley goal. Buckley saw Reagan as the kind of public figure who, because of his demonstrated appeal to young voters and activists and his respect for ideas, might replicate on the right a network that could do for conservative administrations what liberal think tanks had for Democratic ones.

Perhaps with his own experience in mind, Buckley complained to Reagan that Goldwater had been "scandalously late" in organizing academic support.[35] On one occasion, when he recommended that Reagan set up a conservative think tank to pepper him with policy proposals, Buckley invited Reagan to "imagine a mini–Ford Foundation at the service of conservative minded scholars." Had such a vehicle existed on the other side of the political spectrum, he added, Robert Kennedy would have staffed it with former aides and commissioned studies from it.[36]

Having admonished Reagan to tread lightly in areas where national opinion leaders would be paying close attention, Buckley cautioned those on the right who were skeptical of Reagan's propensity for pragmatism and compromise to give him room to maneuver. "They say that his accomplishments are few, that it is only the rhetoric that is conservative," Buckley wrote. "But the rhetoric is the principal thing. It precedes all action." He predicted that by changing the nature of the political conversation, Reagan might "become a part of the American story."[37] Buckley grasped intuitively that Reagan used speeches to change the political agenda in his state and to prepare the public for policies he intended to pursue. He praised Reagan for casting his proposals as means through which the people of California could be empowered as bureaucratic control from Sacramento was diminished.

The run-up to the 1968 presidential nomination placed Buckley in a difficult political situation. The heart of the movement of which he was a leader yearned for Reagan, while party pragmatists, primarily interested in winning and chastened by the overwhelming defeat the GOP had suffered in 1964, were for Nixon. At first, Reagan seemed at least open to exploring his presidential prospects. He authorized a member of his staff, Thomas C. Reed, to assess his prospects and coordinate his efforts with F. Clifton White, Goldwater's prenomination strategist in 1964. During Reagan's early months as Governor, Buckley informed Nancy Reagan that he had made one "concrete suggestion" to Reed.[38] The tone of Buckley's letter, which reads more like a report, suggests that his meeting with Reed took place at her request. By the summer of 1967, however, Reagan had put Reed's work on hold.

A scandal had erupted within Reagan's state administration in which two male Reagan staffers were reported to have had sexual assignations with other males, often on state time and occasionally at state expense. Other Reagan aides, including Press Secretary Lyn Nofziger, Counsel Bill Clark, adviser on appointments Ed Meese, and Reed investigated the matter and, in a meeting with Reagan, then on vacation at the Hotel del Coronado near San Diego, presented him with their report. Reagan quietly eased out of his employ the two staffers in question, his Executive Secretary (or Chief of Staff) Philip M. Battaglia, and a scheduler, Richard M. Quinn.[39] In the fall of 1967, the matter became national news when, in his syndicated column of October 31, 1967, Drew Pearson, a Democratic partisan, reported some of the details. "The most interesting speculation in this key state of California is whether the magic charm of Governor Ronald Reagan can survive the discovery that a homosexual ring has been operating in his office," Pearson began.[40]

Pearson likened episodes he reported having taken place to an incident that had occurred three years earlier in which Walter Jenkins, a longtime aide to President Johnson, was arrested in a Washington, DC, YMCA lavatory for engaging in sexual activity with another man. The columnist praised LBJ for immediately having discharged Jenkins and criticized Reagan for waiting six months to take action.[41] He failed to note that, unlike Jenkins, the Reagan aides had not been arrested and were not charged with a crime. Reagan had acted quietly out of concern for the individuals involved and their families. He even had Battaglia and his replacement, William Clark, who would follow Reagan to the White House as National Security Adviser, explain at a news conference that his first Executive Secretary had intended to return to private life.

At a press conference, Reagan denied all Pearson's charges, saying that the columnist had been "on his back" long before Reagan had entered politics. He charged that Pearson specialized in destroying "human beings" and innocent people and suggested that most newspapers would not run Pearson's salacious accusations. It subsequently surfaced that Nofziger had leaked to reporters at a Governors conference that the aides had been removed because they were homosexual.[42] (It was presumed at the time that such persons were automatically security risks, given their potential susceptibility to blackmail.)

Reagan held his ground. He declared Pearson a "liar," suggesting that the columnist, if he came to California, had better "not spit on a sidewalk," a statement for which he later apologized. At a November 14 press conference, he said that Pearson had "no evidence to warrant an accusation" and that none had been made. He refused to get into a debate with the press as to what his press secretary had revealed.[43] It was apparent all along that Pearson objected more to Reagan's retention on his staff of people believed to be homosexual than to any possible wrongdoing on their part. "He has been posing as Mr. Clean and yet tolerated homosexuals for approximately six months and did not act . . . until he was pressured," Pearson wrote. He attributed the actions of Reagan's aides less to their eagerness to root out homosexuals than their interest in removing from their conservative clique an executive secretary whom they deemed too much of a moderate.[44]

Buckley saw the episode as revelatory of Reagan's character. If it turned out that the two men were indeed security risks, he argued, Reagan's duty was to remove them from their posts, not to ruin their lives, which public disclosure of why they were dismissed or of their sexual preference would have surely done. He commended the Governor for resisting the "momentary satisfaction of being complimented by the prurient." He castigated Pearson for implying that conservatives were less attentive than liberals to security risks at the very time Pearson's fellow liberals were arguing that the dismissal of homosexuals from government service was indicative of the "primitivism of our politics."[45]

The entire episode revealed Reagan's inattentiveness to his immediate surroundings and his deficiencies as an administrator, for which he would compensate with strong chiefs of staff. The reorganization of his office that followed Battaglia's departure anticipated a similar one that would occur during the Iran-Contra scandal that erupted in Reagan's second term as President.

Reagan biographer Lou Cannon is one of many who argue that even before this disruption in his internal operation, Reagan was ambivalent about a presidential run.[46] He was in his second year in office, in the midst his first round of budget negotiations with the state legislature, and beginning to shape the state's agenda. Seasoned political observers thought that had Reagan gone after the nomination early, he would have assembled enough delegates in southern and Rocky Mountain states, along with the California delegation, to deny Richard Nixon a first-ballot nomination. According to this thinking, Reagan then would have picked up steam on subsequent ballots. In his book on the 1968 election, Theodore H. White recorded that Reagan, at this point in his career, cast the image of a graceful, witty leader who was a thorough conservative, but at the same time not racist.[47]

In late spring, Reagan agreed to go to the convention as a "favorite son" from California. This afforded him the opportunity to head his state's large delegation and use that position as leverage in the event that no candidate entered the convention with an assured majority. As a courtesy to Reagan, other candidates ceded him all of California's delegates and stayed out of the primary, thereby avoiding a repetition of the fratricidal Goldwater-Rockefeller primary battle that had taken place in the state four years earlier. As the convention neared, Reagan began to act more like a presidential hopeful. He addressed various state delegations and made his pitch before the national media.

While Reagan's late entry into the race diminished Nixon's drawing power somewhat, the former Vice President had picked up a sufficient number of IOUs over the years through his efforts to elect GOP candidates to local, state, and congressional office to have all but shored up the nomination. Reagan's best prospects of denying Nixon the necessary votes to be nominated on the first ballot lay in the Californian's popularity in the South. His hopes evaporated when several power brokers in the region—South Carolina Senator Strom Thurmond, Texas Senator John Tower, and Mississippi leader Clarke Reed and his counterparts in Louisiana, Georgia, and Alabama—all came out for Nixon. Barry Goldwater, who had carried five southern states in 1964, joined them.

Buckley's characterization of Nixon as "the most right, viable candidate, who could win" played no small role in helping Nixon solidify his hold upon some delegations. Through his endorsement of Nixon, Buckley had buttressed support Nixon had among conservatives nationally. Buckley maintained that Reagan's chances of winning the presidency in 1968 were negligible, given that he had only recently won his first political office. He remained disappointed at Reagan's inability to build an intellectual infrastructure necessary to put together a successful conservative administration. Nixon, much to his credit in Buckley's eyes, had gathered to his side not only writer and strategist Pat Buchanan but also economist Martin Anderson and foreign policy adviser Richard Allen. "Where are the assistant professors?" he asked a protégé who was supporting Reagan.[48] By the time Reagan captured the nomination twelve years later, Buckley had helped him assemble a considerable "brains trust."

All the while he was making Nixon's case to his fellow conservatives, Buckley retained close ties with both Ronald and Nancy Reagan. After Nixon won the nomination, Buckley wrote a tender letter of condolence to Nancy in which he praised her stoicism. He said that he could tell from her expression during their brief encounter at the convention that she understood "that in 36 hours it would all be over." In an effort to lift her spirits, he enclosed his latest column, in which he commended Reagan's comportment in defeat: "It is seldom recognized in politics, in particular where presidential candidates are involved, that gentle and obliging and self-effacing men are capable of asserting themselves into presidential races. Ronald Reagan was one such." Prior to this tribute, Buckley offered this explanation for Reagan's candidacy: "What then happened is what so often happens in politics. Contingent operatives become vested interests. The royalist passions of the entourage take over and before long the principal is carried into the vortex, without the rationale he had been promised to hang on to."[49] He said that Reagan would return to California, where he was conducting the "most interesting experiment in state administration in the country."[50]

As Buckley and his entourage prepared to set sail from Miami on his yacht *Cyrano*, the Coast Guard summoned him to the telephone: it was Reagan, calling to thank him for the piece.[51] In the following days, Buckley twice wrote Nancy to commend her husband for his gracefulness in defeat and to express his hope that the column he had written about Reagan was of some consolation. He told her that he would soon attempt to "persuade the relevant figure" (Rockefeller) to allow the Conservative and Republican parties to file common electors so that Nixon might run on both the Republican and Conservative Party lines in New York that fall.[52] (Rockefeller nixed the idea and Nixon ran solely as a Republican.)

The following spring, Buckley defended Reagan after the Governor, in response to pleas from the local Sheriff and university officials, sent state police to restore order in the city of Berkeley, where protesters had illegally occupied university property. Reagan's critics accused him of overreacting. Buckley praised Reagan for being "resolute." He later wrote Reagan a note advising him that "some brutes" are present in all police forces and that "traces of sadism" existed among some law enforcement personnel that merited watching.[53] (These admonitions suggest that Buckley, after his hasty judgments in response to incidents in Selma and Chicago, had become more sympathetic to allegations of police misconduct.)

When Reagan sought reelection in 1970, the same year that James L. Buckley, in his second try, would win a seat in the U.S. Senate, Bill Buckley kept one eye on each coast. In a personal letter to Bill Buckley, which Reagan said James was free to use, Reagan referred to the candidate as the "the only Republican running for the Senate in New York." James L. Buckley's campaign made use of Reagan's endorsement, and Bill Buckley in his columns made the case for Reagan's reelection. Reagan won, defeating California Assembly Speaker Jesse Unruh 53 percent to 45 percent.

On welfare reform, as on continued U.S. defense of Taiwan, on which conservatives regarded Nixon as an unreliable ally, Reagan and Buckley forged a tactical alliance to prod the administration to move in their direction. In late 1971, Buckley wrote that Reagan was pressing back against the view of some liberals (including some Nixon appointees) that welfare was an absolute "right," and that the administration was frustrating the Governor's attempt to impose conditions recipients must meet in order to qualify for assistance.[54] Reagan had steered through the California legislature a measure requiring that able-bodied persons who applied for welfare benefits first present themselves for work at a county-managed enterprise.

Buckley reported that after this change had gone into effect, the number of new welfare recipients fell from fifty thousand a month to thirty thousand. Although Nixon had expressed sympathy for this approach in his presidential campaign, Buckley noted that the President had not communicated his position "lucidly" to the rest of his administration.[55] Reagan had repeatedly, and to no avail, applied for a waiver (permission for California to be exempted from federal guidelines) so that the changes he initiated would be made permanent.

Three months later, Buckley noted that 140,000 fewer persons were receiving welfare in California than before the state changed its law—this despite the best efforts of Washington bureaucrats to undermine it.[56] In language the White House could hardly misunderstand, Buckley volunteered that when Nixon sought reelection in 1972, he would need Reagan more than Reagan needed Nixon.[57] (He was clearly hinting that in a tight race, Reagan might be less than fully available to assist Nixon's campaign, especially when it came to mobilizing conservative support.)

In the early months of 1972, a presidential election year, Buckley grew more blunt. With conservative Congressman John Ashbrook planning to challenge Nixon for the 1972 Republican nomination, Buckley wrote that the last thing Nixon needed was dissension within GOP ranks in California. While Reagan was firmly committed to Nixon, Buckley suggested, the Governor might have trouble holding his constituency behind the President if Nixon were challenged from the right. Again, he praised Reagan's work on welfare reform and complained that Washington was resisting him.[58] Reagan received the waiver he had requested and the program remained in operation.

Buckley and his brother, the recently elected Senator from New York, happened to be dining with Reagan at his official residence in Sacramento on July 15, 1971, when Nixon announced that he would visit the People's Republic of China the following year. "In a matter of hours," Buckley remembered, "the political emotions of the country had been permanently rearranged."[59] Minutes after Nixon concluded his televised remarks, Kissinger telephoned Reagan to assure him that the President's strategic intentions were in "total harmony" with the concerns of the conservative community. Nixon soon sent Reagan to Taiwan to reassure its leaders that the American President's visit would not significantly affect their relations with the United States. Buckley and Reagan separately tried to persuade the administration—to no avail—to abstain when the United Nations voted on whether to give the PRC the seat Taiwan had occupied since 1945.[60]

Foreshadowing how he would comport himself as President, Reagan complained to Buckley that conservatives had failed to develop a positive message on tax cuts and had proved inarticulate trying to explain how lower marginal tax rates could spur economic growth. In a letter to Buckley, he raised the paradox of some union leaders, themselves in upper income brackets, touting the virtues of progressive income taxes while taking advantage of loopholes their Democratic political allies had inserted into the tax code.[61]

When Spiro Agnew resigned the vice presidency in October 1973 after pleading *nolo contendere* to charges of having accepted bribes while Governor of Maryland and as Vice President, Reagan became the only Republican officeholder with a national following among conservatives who could, with credibility, contest for the 1976 presidential nomination. That, of course, assumed that the reelected Nixon, then embroiled in the Watergate scandal, completed his term. By telephone and in other confidential communications, Buckley advised Reagan to distance himself both from Nixon's détente policies (which Reagan was already known to oppose) and from Nixon personally. "As I suggested," Buckley wrote Reagan, "the information that reaches me privately is that Our Leader is in deep trouble, and that it is altogether possible that he will not succeed, finally, in extricating himself."[62] He recommended Reagan adopt "a patient, cautious disassociation" from the administration."[63]

He also passed along that someone he identified as a "highly regarded figure" had told him that the 1976 nominee "would have to be Rockefeller," because Reagan "refuses to wrap his mind" around foreign policy.[64] Buckley's informer was undoubtedly Kissinger, and Buckley's intent was clearly to prod Reagan into building a powerful intellectual apparatus, which he had been urging upon his friend for years. (In preparation for another presidential run, Rockefeller had resigned as Governor to head a commission to study issues he expected would be on the national agenda in 1976.) Buckley advised Reagan that the "best talent available" was on the staff of Senator Henry Jackson (D-WA), Chairman of the Senate Armed Services Committee, who, in Buckley's view, had made the best case against détente. Buckley then related that he and Nancy Reagan had discussed authors who might be approached to do a piece on Reagan for a popular magazine.[65]

By January 1974, Buckley was telling Reagan that he doubted Nixon would remain in office. "My own feeling is that the wheel is turning decisively against our leader. And, of course, the question is: should one help to accelerate that turn?"[66] While he thought each of the "members of the [conservative] fraternity" would have to answer that question for himself or herself, Buckley suggested to Reagan that they keep one another apprised of what they planned to say.[67] Reagan, not sharing Buckley's pessimism, replied that he had a "a sneaking instinct that there may have, with regard to our leader, been overkill."[68]

On July 29, 1974, Buckley reported to Reagan that he had discussed Nixon's situation at the Bohemian Grove Club with George H. W. Bush, then Chairman of the Republican National Committee, and presidential advisers Bryce Harlow and Peter Flanigan. All thought the tide had turned against Nixon. "Don't make the mistake of hanging in there too long," he beseeched Reagan.[69] On August 9, Nixon resigned the presidency.

Buckley favored George H. W. Bush as Ford's successor as Vice President. He wrote Ford urging him to select Bush and sent Bush a copy of the letter. When Ford chose Nelson Rockefeller, Buckley acquiesced. His column on the subject, perhaps encouraged by Kissinger, read like a brief in favor of Rockefeller's confirmation by both houses of Congress, as the Constitution required. In making Rockefeller's case, he acknowledged the reservations conservatives had about the former New York Governor, including Rockefeller's spending practices, which had boosted New York State's budget by 300 percent over a dozen years and its bonded indebtedness by 600 percent in the same time, and the hostility Rockefeller had shown Goldwater during and after their bitter contest for the 1964 GOP presidential nomination.[70]

Buckley also noted where Rockefeller had atoned for past misdeeds, such as in his agreeing to a residency requirement for welfare after years of having opposed it, and his conceding that Reagan's welfare policies had proved more effective than his own in weaning people off public assistance. Buckley also brought to bear arguments he had made in 1968 when he urged Nixon to name Rockefeller Secretary of Defense, citing his hawkish advocacy of increased defense spending. Mindful of Rockefeller's hard-charging ways, Buckley wondered in print whether the ex-Governor would eclipse Ford.[71]

At first, Buckley did not know what to make of the new President, Gerald R. Ford. He used an early occasion to assess Ford as an opportunity to rehearse all the ways in which Nixon had proved a disappointment to conservatism; his imposition of wage and price controls, his lack of concern about deficit spending, his accommodationist foreign policy, and so on. The time, he said, had come for conservatives to press Ford on the relevance of the conservative vision. Buckley called the damage Nixon had done to conservative principles "the major cover-up of the age."[72]

Buckley decidedly cooled toward Ford after the Democrats gained forty-nine House seats and three in the Senate in the 1974 congressional elections. With Ford now facing a "veto-proof" Congress and possessing "the temperamental ambiguities of a lifelong compromiser," Buckley questioned whether Nixon's successor was the right person to lead the party into battle in 1976.[73] Months later, he proclaimed Ford "a genial man of conservative disposition," but chided the President for accepting the "coils of détente."[74] (Somehow Buckley always managed to omit specific mention of Kissinger when criticizing the policies his friend had recommended to both Nixon and Ford.)

Some of Buckley's conservative allies, namely *National Review* publisher Bill Rusher, direct mail pioneer Richard Viguerie, and former YAF official Howard Phillips, proposed abandoning the GOP in favor of a new Conservative Party. Under its banner, they hoped to assemble voters who had supported Goldwater, Nixon, and Wallace in the previous three presidential elections. The new party would focus on crime prevention and punishment, "judicial tyranny" (especially with regard to court-ordered busing to achieve racial balance in the schools), and military preparedness. Many of those who advocated this approach enthused about a Reagan-Wallace ticket. Buckley vigorously dissented, insisting that any formal association with the Alabaman would set back the conservative cause.

He still considered Wallace a "dangerous man and a demagogue," and he doubted that Wallace's "welfare populism" could ever be made compatible with the free market economic views of most conservatives. Populists, Buckley noted, usually searched for a villain to blame for whatever grieved them.[75] Among Wallace's villains, by the mid-1970s, were large American oil companies. The Alabaman proposed higher taxes for individuals and especially corporations (particularly oil companies) and advocated using the proceeds to lower gas prices at the pump. That, Buckley argued, would not address the problems of scarcity or overdependence on imported oil. Buckley favored higher gasoline taxes to encourage domestic exploration, whereas the purported "populists" sought to redistribute the industry's profits.

Buckley's distaste for this brand of populism earned him the enmity of some former allies. Kevin Phillips, whose book *The Emerging Republican Majority* had forecast the ideological realignment of the two parties, denounced Buckley as an "elitist" and accused him of abandoning Middle America "to load up his yacht with vintage wines and sail across the Atlantic." The professors and philosophers who adorned the pages of *National Review,* he suggested, had little to say to Kansas City or Scranton.[76] His colleague Jeffrey Hart, rising to Buckley's defense, countered Phillips's anti-intellectual attack upon *National Review,* contending that it was never intended to be a "mass circulation" magazine, while Buckley maintained that he would have nothing to say to someone who was "proud of his ignorance" of philosophers and economists whose ideas provided the theoretical foundations of modern conservatism.[77]

In their censure of him for emphasizing foreign policy over domestic matters, Buckley's critics on "the New Right" (a term Kevin Phillips had coined to differentiate populist conservatism from the older, *National Review* elitist version) seem to have ignored a book he published in 1973 that dealt exclusively with domestic concerns as well as scores of his columns. "Do read my book, *Four Reforms,*" he advised Reagan, "as I value your opinion of several chapters in it. In one of them you figure largely."[78] The book, subtitled "A Program for the Seventies," dealt with welfare reform (in which he discussed Reagan's success) taxes, education (with an emphasis on vouchers), and criminal justice.[79]

Ultimately, it was Reagan who put the damper on efforts to draft him as the first presidential candidate of Rusher's new party. He also opposed any formal alliance with Wallace, although he, as was Buckley, was open to reaching out to Wallace's supporters. Speaking before the Young Americans for Freedom in the summer of 1974, Reagan proposed as an alternative to a third political party a "new first party" that would raise a "banner of bold colors, not pale pastels." Having disparaged calls by some that the GOP broaden its base by blurring differences between the two parties (the very criticism Buckley had made of the GOP in the late 1940s and throughout the 1950s), he urged that the party accentuate its differences with Democrats and bring into the GOP tent like-minded conservatives in both parties and independents.[80]

Reagan's decision not to seek a third term as Governor in 1974 and his not having served in Nixon's administration shielded him from any backlash voters unleashed against Republicans in the aftermath of Watergate. After that election, Buckley began touting Reagan as the Republicans' standard-bearer in 1976. Some of his columns during this period seemed calculated to goad Reagan into running. (At one point, Buckley chided the ex-Governor for his "slow-gaited-ness.")[81] Buckley countered arguments that Reagan should defer to the incumbent President because Ford, having never been elected President or Vice President, was anything but a traditional incumbent. He also pointed out that Ford had become the Republican leader in the House after successfully challenging the then incumbent in a leadership contest after the 1964 election.[82]

Buckley argued that Reagan's personal qualities, especially his skills as a communicator and his self-deprecating wit, would serve him well as the party's presidential nominee. He saw these characteristics at work in Reagan's response to Democrats' demands that they be awarded equal time whenever Reagan's movies were aired on television. Reagan responded that whenever he watched his old movies on television, he also wanted to demand equal time.[83] Buckley saw in a Reagan challenge to Ford the opportunity for the party to debate the merits of détente with the Soviet Union.[84]

"Finally there is someone running for President who has opened up the question of détente," Buckley wrote after Reagan declared his candidacy in February 1976.[85] Reagan, he said, had raised the question of whether the Soviets profited more from the Anti-Ballistic Missile (ABM) Treaty than had the United States. He noted that "deeply informed people within the Pentagon" agreed with Reagan that the arms control agreements the United States was negotiating with the USSR were paving the way toward Soviet hegemony in nuclear arms.[86] (His source may have been James Schlesinger, whom Ford had removed as Defense Secretary, purportedly because of his hawkish views.)

The policies Reagan attacked were commonly understood as the handiwork of Kissinger. As a result, Buckley walked a fine line as he maintained his friendship with both the Secretary of State and Kissinger's most vocal Republican critic. When Congress refused Ford's request to provide additional assistance to South Vietnam after Hanoi violated the terms of the peace accords it had agreed to two years earlier, Buckley suggested in print that Reagan might be better able than Ford to sell the President's proposal. Reagan, he said, had the capacity to get across the sincerity of his convictions. "The reason the Republican Party has become nothing much more than an administrative convenience for a few politicians is that it is lacking in any capacity to galvanize." That Reagan could do, he insisted.[87]

Ford handily defeated Reagan in the New Hampshire primary and others that followed, but Reagan picked up steam when North Carolina Senator Jesse Helms put his organization at the challenger's disposal. Helms sprang into action once Reagan voiced opposition to Ford's apparent willingness to relinquish U.S. sovereignty over the Panama Canal to Panama. With Reagan winning easy victories in North Carolina, Texas, and elsewhere, and Ford capturing his native state of Michigan, the race for the nomination suddenly narrowed, with the nomination being decided at the convention.

Buckley threw himself completely behind Reagan's attempts to persuade uncommitted delegates to support him. His advice to Reagan became more frequent and more specific, and Reagan was clearly paying attention. "Pages twelve to fourteen May thirty-first issue of *Aviation Week and Space Technology* confirm absolutely Soviet violation of Salt 1 accord. Strongly urge you to have researcher see these pages," he wired Reagan in June.[88] Days later, Buckley wrote Nancy Reagan that the police had stopped his schooner, even though he was fifty miles out at sea. "I could only assume that they thought I had on hand the same stash of marijuana I tried out in 1966 . . . I was merely instructed to call Governor Reagan."[89]

In the midst of an intense and suspenseful battle for the party's presidential nomination, Buckley did not hesitate to impose upon Reagan to assist Buckley's favorite cause, *National Review.* In May 1976, he wrote Reagan asking for a list of campaign contributors.[90] Reagan also signed fund-raising letters for the magazine. When Reagan, in an attempt to appeal to party moderates, declared on the eve of the convention that he had settled on Pennsylvania Senator Richard Schweiker as his running mate, Buckley, at the behest of Reagan's campaign staff, wrote three separate columns in support of the idea.[91]

After Ford defeated Reagan for the nomination on the first ballot by 118 votes, the President made the unconventional move of inviting Reagan up to the podium after Ford had concluded his acceptance speech. After some hesitancy, which Buckley attributed to the "sportsman's instinct" dictating that the "loser absent himself from the winner's circle," Reagan ascended the podium and delivered one of the most stirring orations of his career.[92] In his address—surely intended as an acceptance speech, replete with echoes of his 1964 "A Time for Choosing" speech—Reagan said that the voters would decide between two different futures: one in which freedom would be preserved and another in which their descendants would be sentenced to a thousand years of darkness.[93]

Declaring Reagan the "dominating presence of the 1976 campaign," Buckley offered a telling prophecy: "Some time in the future, the Presidential candidate of the Republican Party will have to arrive as though to the Finland Station, grim with historical purpose. The challenge, for which providence provides few precedents, lies in his coming to town not for the purpose of taking power, but of redistributing it to the people. That challenger will arrive preaching the furtive excitement of a republic of law, and he will address a Convention, which declines to relegate its Jeffersons and Madisons and Hamiltons to the rear of the hall. . . . Until then, it's Gerald Ford and, thanks to the spirit of Ronald Reagan, he is off to a very good start."[94]

Buckley's "Finland Station" reference was to Lenin's return to Russia from exile in order to foment revolution. His piece conveys the sense of urgency conservatives felt about the need to change the direction in which the nation was heading and to replace a GOP leadership they considered moribund. Clearly, Buckley considered Reagan the leader who would eventually bring all this about. The mention of three of the nation's founders was an attempt to cast Reagan as their ideological heir. Buckley's embrace of populism in this instance as the means to accomplish his goals is obvious.

With Reagan temporarily on the sidelines, Buckley sought to rally conservatives behind Ford by focusing on the dangers he thought inherent in a Jimmy Carter presidency. Despite Carter's southern roots and claims to be a moderate or even a conservative, by the time he became the Democratic presidential nominee, Buckley declared Carter very much in the tradition of previous liberal Democratic nominees. He recounted the former Georgia Governor's shifts in position as he made himself more palatable to the Democratic base and even detected some fading in the Georgian's southern accent as he carried his campaign beyond his native region.[95]

As Carter waged a spirited campaign against Ford, James L. Buckley sought reelection to the Senate against a tough Democratic challenger. For a time, it appeared that the Senator's opponent would be ultra-liberal icon Congresswoman Bella Abzug. Such a contest would have enabled him, running on both the Republican and Conservative lines, to broaden his appeal to centrists in both parties and to conservative-leaning Democrats. This strategy came to naught, however, after Daniel Patrick Moynihan narrowly defeated Abzug in the Democratic primary. Moynihan had endeared himself to *National Review* and its editor when, as Ford's Ambassador to the United Nations, he denounced the hypocrisy of leftist dictatorships on human rights and delivered a fiery speech in opposition to a General Assembly resolution that declared Zionism a form of racism.[96]

As the Democratic nominee, Moynihan repeatedly attacked James L. Buckley for opposing federal loan guarantees to New York City when it was on the verge of bankruptcy. The incumbent had taken the position that citizens of other states should not have to pay the costs of New York City's mismanagement and that such a bailout would encourage poor administration in New York and elsewhere. On August 30, Bill Buckley wrote Reagan, as he had six years earlier, requesting a letter of support for his brother. "It would mean a great deal, and of course, as always, we're in a hurry."[97] Reagan complied. Moynihan defeated Buckley, 54.1 percent to 44.1 percent.

Bill Buckley played a less prominent role in his brother's 1976 campaign than he had six years earlier. His comments on another race, however, angered many of his conservative admirers and bewildered more than a few liberals. In a display of personal independence and political myopia, Buckley endorsed liberal activist Allard Lowenstein, then running for Congress as a Democratic challenger against Republican incumbent John Wydler in a Long Island district. Lowenstein had attained national fame in 1968 as the organizer of the "Dump Johnson Movement," which helped entice Senator Eugene McCarthy (D-MN) to mount an insurgency campaign against LBJ. *Human Events* declared Buckley's endorsement of Lowenstein an example of "conservative chic."[98] Conservative Party officials strained to conceal their embarrassment at their 1965 mayoral nominee's heresy. (Wydler, like James L. Buckley, was running on the Conservative and Republican Party lines.)

Buckley endorsed Lowenstein again when he ran, again unsuccessfully, for Congress two years later in a different district, and again against a Republican incumbent with Conservative backing. With so many liberals expected to be in the next Congress, Buckley suggested, Lowenstein would make a worthy addition to a liberal movement that had grown "hoary, and bureaucratic."[99] He did not suggest how reducing Republican ranks would advance the conservative cause. After Lowenstein was shot and killed by a deranged former associate in 1980, Buckley and Senator Ted Kennedy were among his eulogizers.

With Carter now in the White House and making ceding U.S. sovereignty over the Panama Canal an early priority, Buckley found himself on the same side of the issue as Carter, Ford, Kissinger, and even George McGovern—and, for the first time in their long association, in opposition to Reagan. Buckley attributed his change of heart on the matter to a visit he had made to Panama in October 1976. Local sentiment, he reported, had been strongly in support of the United States relinquishing control of the Canal Zone. He urged that the

United States continue to defend the canal, establish a fund through which tolls on shipping financed the resettlement of the American community in the area, and grant Panama control of the canal's day-to-day operations. "That," he wrote, "is the way great nations should act."[100] The Carter White House and Senate Minority Leader Howard Baker found Buckley's stand particularly helpful in persuading wavering Republican Senators to approve the canal treaties.

Buckley and Reagan assured one another that their disagreement about the canal's future would not adversely affect their relationship.[101] Buckley instructed his staff to send Reagan everything Buckley wrote about the issue and promised to read everything Reagan put out on the subject.[102] For months the two privately debated the various options available to the United States with regard to the canal. Reagan, echoing Buckley's prior opinion, said he did not see how the United States could consider ceding control after Panama's President, General Omar Torrijos, had given the United States an ultimatum. Buckley responded that it was "part of the responsibility of big nations to transcend provocative jibes from silly little dictators."[103] When Reagan speculated that certain banks with overextended loans to Panama were pressing for the treaties as a way of forestalling a default, Buckley called this notion the "right wing's Grassy Knoll."[104]

Buckley proposed that he and Reagan debate the issue in a special two-hour broadcast of *Firing Line*. Each would have two additional speakers join him. Buckley selected George F. Will and James Burnham, and Reagan chose Pat Buchanan and Roger Fontaine, the latter a professor of Latin American studies at Georgetown. Former U.S. Senator Sam Ervin, famous for his recent service as head of the Senate Select Committee that investigated Watergate, moderated. Reagan argued that the United States should not negotiate with foreign governments in the face of threats and insisted that any agreement should allow the United States to intervene if its access to the canal were ever blocked. Buckley, for the first time on *Firing Line* since he clashed with George Wallace, found himself cast to the left of his opponent. Again he appeared to relish the role.

In their opening statements, both men were at their rhetorical best. Buckley said that were Lloyds of London asked to give odds that he would disagree with Reagan, it would have declared the prospect either inconceivable or a mistake. He called Reagan the public figure he admired more than any other. Picking up on this, Reagan asked Buckley why, given what he had just said, Buckley hadn't rushed across the room to tell Reagan that he had seen the light. "I'm afraid that if I came any closer to you," Buckley replied, "the force of my illumination would blind you."[105]

Buckley always maintained that Reagan's opposition to the Panama Canal Treaties helped him clinch the Republican presidential nomination in 1980 and that the treaties' passage spared Reagan from having to confront the issue as President. Had they been defeated in the Senate and violent anti-American uprisings resulted, Buckley suggested, many would have held Reagan responsible. On a visit to the Reagans' home months after the *Firing Line* debate, Buckley encountered signs posted along Reagan's driveway: "We Built It," "We Paid for It," "It's Ours" (all quotations from Reagan's previous speeches).[106] The friendship remained intact.

In the run-up to the 1980 primaries, Buckley raised Reagan's standard early. He confessed to one reservation: the candidate's age. (Reagan was sixty-nine when he accepted the 1980 presidential nomination.) Reagan dispelled Buckley's doubts during a Thanksgiving get-together at the Buckley estate in Sharon in 1978. When Buckley asked Reagan to act as referee during a family touch football game, Reagan insisted on playing. Buckley recalled that Reagan displayed as much energy as his eighteen-year old son.[107] "It is a biologically observable fact of American history," Buckley concluded, "that Ronald Reagan is simply not out of breath."[108]

Buckley also pushed back against another argument he expected Democrats to make against a Reagan presidency: that he was too "extreme." In refutation, he referred to Reagan's record as Governor and his proven ability to attract votes from Democrats and independents. He also argued that the decline of American prestige in the world and the failures of the welfare state had moved public opinion in Reagan's direction.[109] On *Firing Line* on January 14, 1980, Reagan laid out the parameters he had set for his presidency: a bolder response to Soviet aggression, a defense buildup, across-the-board tax cuts to stimulate economic growth, and a greater respect for the principle of federalism.[110]

Buckley continued to pass policy recommendations and political intelligence along to Reagan and tried to bring his attention to people he thought could be of help to his campaign. In the spring of 1979, Buckley suggested that Reagan retain as a press aide Tony Dolan, a young journalist whose work Buckley had been following since Dolan's days at Yale. He urged Reagan not to let Dolan "slip through" his fingers.[111] Reagan passed Buckley's suggestion along to his aide Michael Deaver. After no follow-up had taken place, Buckley arranged for Dolan to fly to Minneapolis to meet with Reagan's campaign manager, John Sears. Again nothing came of it.

Dissatisfied with how John Sears had been running the campaign, Reagan, on the day of the New Hampshire primary, but before the results were known, replaced Sears with Buckley's old friend Bill Casey. In advance, Reagan telephoned Buckley, who was vacationing in Switzerland, to advise him of the change and request his help in rallying the faithful behind Casey. Complying, Buckley paid Casey what he considered the highest possible compliment when he wrote that Reagan's new manager personified Whittaker Chambers's observation that "to live is to maneuver."[112] Reassuring the conservative base that Reagan and his campaign were competent was one of countless tasks Buckley performed over and over again to ease his friend's path to the presidency and to help him succeed in office.

Writing about the 1980 election, Theodore H. White, who sixteen years earlier had noted and lamented Buckley's absence from Goldwater's campaign, credited three men with providing intellectual firepower to Reagan's campaign: Casey, Richard Allen, who advised on foreign policy, and Buckley, whom White described as the most important to Reagan personally and the one to whom Reagan would turn for comfort.[113] While Buckley gave editorial and other public support to Reagan, his primary role in Reagan's 1980 campaign was that of personal adviser, protector, go-between, and validator. He had a direct line to the Reagans, Casey, and others, and Reagan and his team often sought Buckley out for advice and assistance. Six months after Casey took command, Buckley's protégé Dolan was on board. He would draft some of Reagan's most memorable lines, including his reference to the Soviet Union as an "Evil Empire." "The best thing Buckley did," Casey later said, "was bugging me into hiring a guy named Tony Dolan."[114]

In April 1980, Buckley wrote Reagan advising him that he had heard through a friend that Max Kampelman, former principal adviser to Hubert Humphrey, intended to vote Republican in 1980 for the very first time. Buckley advised Reagan that Kampelman exercised considerable influence on American political opinion, especially among centrists, and recommended that Reagan have someone reach out to the disenchanted Democrat.[115] He also urged Reagan to add to his team Richard Perle, then a member of Senator Henry Jackson's staff. (Kampelman would go on to serve as President Reagan's principal arms negotiator with the Soviet Union. Perle became Assistant Secretary of Defense for International Security Policy.)

After losing the Iowa caucuses to George H. W. Bush, Reagan won the New Hampshire primary and sailed to an easy nomination. Once Reagan had secured the number of delegates that assured his nomination, Buckley for the second time recommended Bush for the nation's second-highest office. Buckley, as a friend of both Reagan and Bush, was perfectly poised to play the role of go-between. Nicholas Brady, a friend of Bush's and Buckley's and a fellow Yale alumnus, urged Buckley to make a direct pitch to Casey on Bush's behalf.[116]

Buckley not only did so, he also wrote a column suggesting that Reagan's selecting Bush would be an appropriate conciliatory gesture. All along, Bush had been Buckley's second choice for the Republican presidential nomination. Speaking before the Young Republican National Federation in June 1979, Buckley said he would support Bush for the 1980 nomination if and when an "antecedent commitment of a dozen years' standing [to Reagan] should lapse."[117]

As the convention neared, a short-lived obstacle arose to the arrangement Buckley thought he had helped broker. Reagan and Ford operatives bogged down in negotiations over a possible Reagan-Ford ticket. Some conservatives saw in this move an attempt by Kissinger to facilitate his return as Secretary of State. Through his column, Buckley sent a pointed message to both sides. First, perhaps to assuage Kissinger's conservative detractors, he knocked down reports that Kissinger had acted as Ford's principal negotiator. Then, in a pointed reminder to Kissinger, Buckley wrote that the former Secretary of State "knew from Nixon's treatment of Secretary [of State William P.] Rogers [and his preference for working through Kissinger, his NSC Director, in Rogers's stead] that the office of Secretary of State was absolutely worthless unless the president himself desires a particular man as his special counselor on foreign policy."[118] His point was that, unless Reagan and Kissinger were comfortable with one another, Kissinger could, like Rogers, find himself sidelined.

Buckley proclaimed Reagan's acceptance speech "lucid," galvanizing," "transparently genuine," and an "awesome performance by a man born to unite and to govern." To bolster his case, he quoted liberal commentator Jeff Greenfield, who declared Reagan "the principal rhetorician in American politics.[119] In his acceptance speech, Reagan pledged to confront and reduce, if not reverse, three grave threats to the nation: a disintegrating economy, a weakened defense structure, and an energy policy based on scarcity. To make the point that his administration would be bold and would put the nation on a new course, Reagan quoted Thomas Paine, the most radical of the nation's founders: "We have it in our power to begin the world all over again."[120]

During the remainder of the campaign, Buckley took as his mission winning Reagan wider acceptance within the American mainstream. This he repeatedly did by presenting his candidate as the opposite of the extremist his liberal critics sought to cast him as. Buckley made it a point to cite liberal intellectuals who found Reagan a serious man with a sense of purpose however much they disagreed with him over policy. Buckley employed that tactic in March 1980 when he made note of a comment left-learning journalist and antiwar activist Robert Scheer made to Reagan while interviewing him: "It seems to me that you're a lot more reasonable, humanistic, than your press makes you appear. . . .

I think you've been unfairly criticized in a lot of ways."[121] With the general election in full swing, Buckley quoted New York University Professor Melvyn Krauss's comment that Reagan possessed "an intellectual sophistication that many professional historians would envy."[122]

In the weeks after the convention, Buckley tried his hand at the kind of shuttle diplomacy he had observed his friend Henry Kissinger practice on many a stage. Acting as go-between, Buckley passed along to Reagan and his team Kissinger's report of the meeting he had had with families of the more than fifty Americans being held hostage by the revolutionary government in Iran. He also told the GOP presidential nominee that Kissinger was willing to issue a statement declaring his "non-availability" for future full-time public service.[123] This would make it easier for Reagan both to benefit from Kissinger's thinking and to derive support from a public association with Kissinger, without appearing to parts of his political base that disliked Kissinger as being beholden to him. The strategy was vintage Buckley.

In early September, Buckley informed Reagan that Deaver had arranged for a meeting between Reagan and Kissinger. Mindful of how Deaver had handled his request months earlier that Reagan's campaign retain Dolan, Buckley kept Reagan apprised of his behind-the-scenes efforts to facilitate the Reagan-Kissinger meeting in order to assure that it actually took place and that Reagan was fully briefed. Before the meeting actually occurred, Buckley informed Reagan that Kissinger had been reluctant to declare outright that he would not serve again as Secretary of State. He added that he had sought to "soften the blow" to Kissinger's ego by suggesting that he, Buckley, would likewise "offer to withdraw his own name for consideration as King of England."[124]

Buckley and Reagan agreed that Kissinger would make it known that he was not available for "steady" work in Reagan's administration.[125] With that task accomplished, Buckley instructed Reagan that Kissinger had a "jeweler's eye for geopolitical interrelationships" from which the Californian would be able to profit.[126] Weeks later, Reagan wrote back that he and Kissinger had had a "very fine meeting" and that Kissinger was "most helpful."[127] A month later, Buckley proposed that Reagan's campaign air a television commercial in New York in which Kissinger asserted that Reagan's policy of peace through strength offered the "best chance" of avoiding war between the United States and the Soviet Union. Lest Reagan conclude that Buckley was meddling too much in his campaign, Buckley added, "Any time you wish me to abdicate my career as ventriloquist you need only say so . . . reagan tells buckley / shut up."[128]

Confident that Reagan would win the election, Buckley sent him one of his favorite lines from the Scriptures (James 3) with the suggestion that Reagan consider using it, perhaps in his inaugural address: "Behold, we put bits in the horses' mouths, that they may obey us; and we turn their whole body. Behold also the ships, which though they be so great, and are driven of fierce winds, yet are turned about with a very small helm, whithersoever the governor listeth. Even so the tongue is a little member, and boasteth great things. Behold, how great a matter a little fire kindleth!"[129]

Reagan did not tell Buckley to shut up, and Buckley continued to pass along suggestions. The question of whether Carter would participate in a debate that included not only Reagan but also independent candidate John Anderson, a Republican Congressman, dominated the early weeks of the general election campaign. Confident that he could best Reagan in a debate, Carter, insisting he would not share a stage with "two Republicans," held out for a head-to-head debate with his major opponent. Reagan debated Anderson on September 21 and Carter on October 28. (In between the two debates, Anderson had plummeted considerably in the polls.)

In the run-up to Reagan's only debate with Carter, Buckley noted, perhaps for Reagan's benefit, that a challenger's mere appearance on the same stage with an incumbent President elevated him to "psychological parity" with his opponent.[130] It would be a mistake, he warned, if Carter tried to overwhelm Reagan with excessive details about policy. Referencing his own debate against Reagan four years earlier, Buckley declared Reagan a "cool customer" who knew that at a certain point, "particularization becomes exhibitionism."[131] Buckley's forecast proved prescient.

While unimpressed with the overall content of the debate, Buckley declared that Reagan won the exchange in his closing statement, when he asked listeners whether they were better off than they had been four years earlier. As for Carter's recounting, in an effort to present Reagan as a warmonger, a conversation he had had with his young daughter about nuclear weapons, Buckley remarked, "Can you imagine Abraham Lincoln saying, 'I talked this morning to my son Tad, and he told me he thought the issue of human slavery was the most important issue of our age.'"[132] Of the ongoing crisis regarding the American hostages being held in Iran, Buckley lamented that Reagan had not referenced Kissinger's observation that it was telling that were no Soviet hostages anywhere in the world.[133]

Knowing that he would be in Rio de Janeiro on Election Day, Buckley drafted a congratulatory letter to Reagan before he departed and instructed his staff to send it if Reagan won. "Dear Ron," he began. "This is the last time I will address you by your first name. I take some satisfaction in recalling that, sixteen years ago, I teased you by addressing you as 'governor,' anticipating an event, which came to pass. Obviously you didn't know when to stop."[134] He passed along one piece of advice with regard to the peopling of Reagan's administration that the new President's transition staff followed. What Reagan needed most, Buckley wrote him, were not people interested in filling various posts but people who "might be persuaded to take them."[135]

He urged that Reagan consult with three individuals in whom Buckley had the greatest confidence: Tony Dolan, already on Reagan's staff; Irving Kristol, editor of the *Public Interest* and the father of the "neoconservative" movement; and Buckley's Yale classmate Evan Galbraith, whom Reagan, at Buckley's urging, would make U.S. Ambassador to France.[136] Later that month, at a reception David Rockefeller hosted in Argentina, Buckley received a call from Alfred Bloomingdale, a longtime Reagan friend, asking whether Buckley would serve as Ambassador to the United Nations. Buckley declined. He would also turn away suggestions that he head the United States Information Agency.[137]

As Reagan prepared to take office, a misunderstanding inserted a temporary strain into his friendship with Buckley. Buckley had written Reagan the previous April to say that if Reagan were elected President, Buckley would neither seek nor accept any post for himself and would not press for government positions for any of his relatives. (The two had a running joke about Buckley serving as Reagan's informal ambassador to Afghanistan.) He asked in return that Reagan be the guest of honor at the twenty-fifth anniversary of the founding of *National Review* at the Plaza Hotel in New York City on December 5.[138] "Think of it," he wrote Reagan, "twenty-five years it took us to put you in the White House! Ah, but it was worth it."[139]

Reagan wrote back that he would pencil in the date on his schedule, but warned that events might disrupt those plans: "I want you to know that I will give full consideration to your kind invitation. After all, I've been reading *National Review*, for twenty-five years. Now, you know, and I know, that December 5th is a long way to go. It could be that I will have attained a certain job by then and might find myself with some serious problems concerning scheduling. On the other hand—I might be looking for employment at that time, and I'm sure I would make a great many useful contacts at your dinner—so only mark it down that I have marked the date and hope with all my heart I can be there."[140]

Weeks before the election, Buckley reminded Reagan again of the dinner.[141] But as December 5 approached, he learned that Reagan would not be in attendance. In public, he pretended not to mind, telling reporters that "the best [*National Review*] could hope for was to be the principal journal that instructs the President of the United States."[142] Privately, his disappointment erupted into anger. He told intimates that he was considering staying away from Reagan's inauguration.[143] Some close to him suggested that either Deaver or another Reagan insider had scratched the event off Reagan's schedule so that he not appear too close to the conservative movement.[144]

At the dinner, in recognition of the part he and his publication had played in making Reagan's election possible—and perhaps also out of personal pique—Buckley publicly embraced the role he had offered to play in private communications with the President-elect: he said he had told Reagan that when *Who's Who* asked him whether he would like to make any corrections to his biography, he suggested that under "profession" the words "editor and writer" be replaced with "ventriloquist." He volunteered that Reagan laughed longer upon hearing this suggestion than Buckley would have, thereby proving Buckley a failure in his new role.[145]

Reagan worked hard to make amends. He wrote Buckley to say that he had not seen mail sent to him in Middleburg, Virginia, where he had taken up temporary residence during the transition. He took full responsibility for the mix-up and begged Buckley's forgiveness.[146] Decades later, Buckley attributed the incident to the "sweeping away" of Reagan's civilian calendar the instant he was elected.[147] Reagan appeared at two subsequent *National Review* events during his presidency, a reception at the magazine's Washington office in 1983 and *National Review*'s thirtieth anniversary celebration two years later. On December 16, Buckley assured Reagan that all was forgotten. He passed along a few jokes and ended with an entreaty:

> Now: Ron: In the months and years ahead, I shall probably feel the impulse to communicate a piece of information or analysis to you maybe once or twice a year. Such communications will be motivated exclusively by a desire to pass along information I think you would want to have. Over the years, you have always answered my letters. I appreciate this greatly, but appreciate also that the magnitude of your correspondence in the days ahead will make this impractical. Would you, then, consent to an arrangement? Unless I know that a letter I write you will be read by you, constipation would seize me. Now, we don't want this, do we? So: if you would make an arrangement with your staff as follows, I'd be entirely satisfied.[148]

He then supplied the draft of a letter Reagan should have a staffer write back:

> quote: Dear Mr. Buckley: The president gratefully acknowledges your recent letter about the Zeitgeist. end quote. This will mean to me one simple thing: that you have read my letter, on which no comment is expected, let alone required. If at the White House end it would help for me to scribble some

> code or other on the face of the envelope (e.g. Attn: Miss Whatnot), then Miss Whatnot has merely to advise me of this. If this arrangement is satisfactory, mark it down on your calendar.[149]

Reagan wrote back offering a less elaborate way to reach him. Buckley should send his letters directly to Helene von Damm, whom Reagan described as his "Gal Friday."[150]

13

Bill and Ronnie: Advising a President

Throughout Reagan's presidency Buckley remained in close touch with both Ronald and Nancy Reagan. He recommended scores of people for important posts, suggested top talent to perform at state dinners, and schemed to get packages, books, and even wines past official gatekeepers. Buckley had few qualms, either in public or in private, about making his feelings on policy known. Time after time he rode to Reagan's defense, whether to extricate the President from an embarrassing situation or to fend off attacks. While they could not overcome their one principled disagreement (Reagan's pursuit of an arms reduction treaty with the Soviet Union), they continued to engage each other in ways that strengthened their mutual bond. That neither gave up attempting to persuade the other of the rightness of his position attests to the strength of their friendship.

In the interval between the 1980 presidential election and the commencement of what promised to be the most ideologically conservative administration in American history, Buckley advised Reagan to be both bold and cautious. He saw no contradiction between these two approaches so long as Reagan came across as reasonable and pragmatic. Buckley recommended that the President-elect make strategic use of the transition, a time when his opposition would be at once "weak" and "curious."[1] He suggested that Reagan make three audacious proposals at the outset of his presidency: cap the federal income tax at 25 percent of income, a Milton Friedman recommendation; propose a constitutional amendment restricting the courts' jurisdiction in determining racial composition of schools, with an accompanying ban on compulsory school busing and all racial discrimination in education; and endorse another constitutional amendment limiting federal spending to a fixed percentage of the gross domestic product.[2]

Reagan did not go along with all Buckley had proposed. He did push ahead on tax cuts, but did not propose implementing them with the speed Buckley had advocated. Consistent with his campaign promise, Reagan proposed a 30 percent cut in marginal tax rates, phased in at a 10 percent cut over three years. Buckley felt that the slow phase-in would delay the plan's anticipated benefits from taking effect, thereby allowing the administration's critics to argue that Reagan's tax cuts had not produced the promised accompanying growth in the economy, and therefore should be scrapped.[3]

The high inflation rate, which reached nearly 20 percent under Jimmy Carter, had worked in Reagan's favor during the campaign. It now proved the new administration's major domestic challenge. Ever since Nixon's time in office, commentators spoke regularly of the phenomenon of "stagflation," meaning simultaneous high inflation and high unemployment. Presidential challengers Carter (in 1976) and Reagan (in 1980) spoke of the "misery index"—the sum of the inflation and unemployment rates—as they denounced the economic performance of the incumbent presidents they sought to replace. To bring inflation down, the Federal Reserve had, during Carter's tenure, tightened the money supply, causing a brief but sharp recession.

Buckley worried that with unemployment standing at 7.5 percent when Reagan took office, and with the recession hitting low-income groups the hardest, the new President's critics would accuse him of being cold and uncaring in proposing tax cuts that returned the largest proportion of money to people in high tax brackets. He urged Reagan to make clear that he intended the tax cuts as a means of growing the economy so that businesses, buoyed by increased capital, would produce new jobs, thereby facilitating an accompanying drop in unemployment. Buckley had feared that Reagan's advisers, concerned that Democrats and the media would attack the President for cutting the taxes of the rich, voiced relief that Reagan had remained true to his campaign promise and introduced the Kemp-Roth bill, which cut taxes across the board. Still, Buckley lamented what he saw as Reagan's failure to make the case aggressively enough for his own proposal. "The pity is," Buckley wrote, "that the greatest living political communicator did not take the opportunity" to remind Democrats that high tax bills on the investor class reduced economic opportunities for the nonrich and reduced overall revenues available to the government, as the wealthy availed themselves of loopholes.[4]

He also criticized Reagan's failure to point out that Democratic Congresses had approved all the loopholes—which liberals habitually denounced—that worked to the benefit of the wealthy. (Reagan was keenly aware of this and had, dating back to his days as Governor, complained about Democratic hypocrisy in letters to Buckley.) Buckley voiced dismay that Reagan's critics denounced tax cuts as benefits for the rich but never conceded that there was a philosophical case to be made for them: "The superstition is that to restore to somebody something that is his is to take something from somebody else. . . . It appears to be impossible to get anyone to acknowledge that if someone is paying 70 percent of his . . . income to the government, and you propose to reduce taxation from 70 percent to 63 percent, you are not 'giving' that man something."[5] He urged Reagan to encourage savings and investment and faulted the President for leaving the impression that spending could be brought under control without touching entitlement programs.[6]

As Reagan fought for his life after an assassination attempt barely two months after taking office, Buckley praised the President's stoic, reassuring comportment in the aftermath of the shooting. Reagan buoyed the public's spirits when he complained that his best suit had been ruined, inquired who was "running the store" in his absence, and expressed the hope that the members of the medical team about to operate on him were all Republicans.[7] Buckley saw in the wounded President's remarks the strength of his character. (Buckley voiced identical sentiments in a telegram to Nancy Reagan.) During Reagan's convalescence Buckley was one of the few non-family members to visit the First Couple at the White House residence. He found Reagan in good spirits but relying on his wife to steady him as he walked. Over lunch, conversation focused on the Reagan children: Ron's career with the Joffrey Ballet, daughter Patti's increasingly outspoken liberalism—and rumors of her possible appearance as a *Playboy* centerfold. (She posed for the magazine years later, and a photo spread of her ran in its July 1994 issue.)[8]

As Reagan's presidency progressed, Buckley provided the same kind of assistance to his friend as he had for the previous two decades. Often he passed along political intelligence that came his way. Aware that Reagan did not like to receive unpleasant news, Buckley communicated any forebodings he had to presidential aides or the First Lady. "Apparently the choice for Science Advisor is disastrous," Buckley wrote a White House staffer, passing along confidential comments he had received from a well-regarded scientist, whose name, he said, he would divulge only over the telephone.[9]

Early in his presidency, Reagan requested Buckley's assistance on some delicate matters that pertained to his relations with his daughter. Patti had asked her father to look into the death of Karen Silkwood, a pro-union activist who had accused her employer of disregarding the health and safety of employees at the nuclear fuel plant where she worked. After Silkwood died in a car crash on her way to an interview with a *New York Times* reporter, her supporters charged that the fatal accident had been a deliberate attempt to silence her. Buckley sent Reagan a packet of articles that disputed this claim. Reagan thanked him.[10] Obviously uncomfortable at the prospect of delegating such chores to his White House staff or government agencies, Reagan preferred to handle them through back channels. Buckley frequently made himself useful to the Reagans in this way.

Reagan confided to Buckley his displeasure that Patti had befriended antiwar activists Jane Fonda and Tom Hayden, who, he felt, had influenced her political opinions. He volunteered that he had told Patti he considered the two "traitors to their country" but had not pressed the point.[11] (Reagan was obviously referring to Jane Fonda's much-publicized visit to North Vietnam, where she was photographed cheering as its armed forces fired upon U.S. bomber planes.) Buckley was sympathetic. He told Reagan that "having done his best," there was little more that he as Patti's father could do. "If one permits Jane Fonda to serve as mentor," he wrote, "unpleasant analytical habits are acquired."[12]

Patti supported the "nuclear freeze" movement that had arisen in Western nations in opposition to Reagan's decision to place ICBMs in West Germany. At his daughter's request, Reagan agreed to meet with Australian physician Helen Caldicott, the President of Physicians for Social Responsibility and a leading figure in the movement. He asked Buckley to supply him with reading material about Caldicott and how her views were regarded within the scientific community. Buckley had *National Review*'s librarian prepare a one-page summary of what he had uncovered and attached it to the bulky file he sent the President. In an accompanying note, Buckley urged Reagan to be sure to read four pages in particular "to get the full flavor of the lady's fanaticism."[13]

Again, Reagan thanked Buckley for his efforts. He wrote him that the package Buckley had sent left him with only one question: "Why the h——l did I ever say I would see her?"[14] Reagan met with Caldicott in December 1982. The following May, Caldicott told United Press International that Reagan told her that the United States could win a nuclear war with the Soviet Union. Reagan insisted he never uttered those words and that he believed no such thing. He accused Caldicott of violating an agreement they had made not to discuss what had been a private conversation.[15]

Buckley occasionally provided professional and personal advice to the Reagans' son Ron, sometimes passing along what he had imparted to Ron's parents. Ron's decision to withdraw from Yale in his freshman year to join the Joffrey Ballet had been a major topic of conversation when the Reagans spent the 1976 Thanksgiving weekend with the Buckleys.[16] Buckley tried to persuade Ron to remain in school but, having failed, encouraged Ron's parents to see that he received the best possible professional training.[17] When Ron's interests later shifted to journalism, Buckley commended him on an article he published in *Playboy* in 1986.[18] After watching the younger Reagan interviewed on CBS, Buckley wrote the Reagans that their son "handled himself with the most superb of finesse."[19]

Not surprisingly, given his criticisms of past Supreme Court decisions, Buckley pressed Reagan to appoint reliable conservatives to the nation's highest judicial tribunal. He urged Reagan several times to nominate Yale Law School Professor and former Nixon Solicitor General Robert Bork to the Supreme Court. Reagan expressed high regard for Bork but said that, consistent with a campaign promise, he wanted to name a woman to the court at his first opportunity. He assured Buckley that Bork would be "highest on the list for the next appointment."[20] After Reagan settled on Sandra Day O'Connor, Buckley wrote in his column that he was prepared to give her the benefit of the doubt on abortion, an area on which her Arizona State Senate record was ambiguous.[21]

Given the popular support for O'Connor's nomination, Buckley urged his fellow conservatives, who were skeptical of her, to exercise caution in opposing her. Should they go all out to deny her confirmation and lose, he argued, they would have created the impression that the right-to-life movement was smaller than it actually was.[22] As the Senate debated O'Connor's appointment, Buckley briefed Reagan on what retiring Justice Potter Stewart, whom O'Connor would succeed on the Supreme Court, had related to him at Bohemian Grove about his own confirmation a generation earlier. Prior to his confirmation, the Court rendered its unanimous decision in *Brown v. Board of Education, Topeka* that declared segregation of the public schools inherently unconstitutional. Stewart had declined to state during his confirmation hearing how he would have decided that case. O'Connor did the same when questioned on the previously decided *Roe v. Wade*. (The Senate confirmed O'Connor in a vote of 99 to 0. Stewart had won confirmation in 1959 by 70 to 17.)

In the fall of 1981, the administration suffered its first major embarrassment when the *Atlantic* published an interview with David Stockman, Reagan's Director of the Office of Management and Budget, in which he stated that Reagan would find it impossible to balance the budget by 1984, as he had promised, without raising taxes and cutting federal spending from 23 percent of GDP to 19 percent. Stockman implied that Reagan's entire economic message had been devised as a means of selling his tax cuts.[23] Democrats cited Stockman's words as evidence that Reagan's economic program projections had been based on deceit. A good many Republicans demanded that Reagan fire Stockman for his disloyalty. Buckley took the Stockman controversy as an occasion to lecture Reagan again on what he thought the President should do to grow the economy.

He denied Democratic assertions that Reagan had cut taxes by too much. He found Stockman's assertion at a press conference that 70 percent of the tax cuts Reagan had signed into law had gone to persons in the middle and lower tax brackets, if true, a "salient disability of the Reagan program." He considered such measures attempts to fend off inevitable suggestions that the administration was favoring the rich. In reality, Buckley believed such measures were a drag on economic growth. He argued that had Reagan's initial recommendations, advanced in his campaign, been left intact, the economy would have recovered at a faster pace. Even more of a "supply-sider" than the administration, Buckley insisted that the way to grow the economy was to cut the taxes of those in the highest brackets. He again urged Reagan to cap the highest marginal rate at 25 percent.[24]

Reagan, donning the robes of the politician and not of the economist or conservative intellectual, replied that he did not see how he could prevail in a debate over the "fairness" of his tax cut proposals, given that the press awarded so much more attention to his critics' assertions than his responses. Apparently he had found no better way to make the conservative case against progressivity as President than he had as Governor. He reminded Buckley that he had promised additional tax legislation that would remove loopholes and subsidies that favored the wealthy to the disadvantage of those in lower brackets.[25]

Weeks later, Buckley was back in his now familiar role as go-between, this time between a President and a former President. Buckley had his first sit-down meeting with Richard Nixon in a decade at the American Ambassador's official residence in Paris. He wrote to Reagan afterward that Nixon was the same man he had known since the late 1950s and described the former President's grasp of the political cosmos as "masterful."[26] As he related to Reagan what Nixon had told him verbatim, Buckley, suspecting that Reagan would share the letter with his wife, apologized in advance to Nancy for its colorful language.

Nixon thought Reagan was spending too much time responding to critics and urged that he delegate those tasks to surrogates. Reagan, he said, needed to retain a person to act as "nut cutter" who would attack the opposition with abandon, as Agnew had done for Nixon and Nixon had done for Eisenhower. Given that Vice President Bush was "too nice in manner" to play the part, Nixon suggested that former Treasury Secretary and Texas Governor John Connally, who Nixon had once hoped would succeed him as President, serve in this capacity. Nixon and Buckley also discussed the possibility of Connally replacing Stockman at the Office of Management and Budget.[27] Nixon also advised that Reagan persist in his efforts to reduce inflation, however his critics pilloried him. He predicted that the Republicans would lose twenty-five to thirty House seats in the 1982 congressional elections, but could pick up as many as three seats in the Senate. (They lost twenty-six House seats and held steady in the Senate.)

Six months into Reagan's presidency, Buckley joked that if Reagan achieved "nothing more" in office, he would still go down in history as "having catalyzed a fear of inflation in liberals such as John Kenneth Galbraith, Senator Ted Kennedy, and House Speaker Tip O'Neill."[28] He noted that they and their allies showed little concern about the national debt, the deficit, or inflation so long as domestic programs were generously funded, and that the only spending increases they opposed were in defense. After Reagan left office, Buckley attributed the rise in the federal deficit during Reagan's presidency (from $79 billion to $153 billion) to two factors: the 30 percent increase in defense spending and the increasing cost of entitlement programs.[29]

On Washington's birthday in 1983, Reagan officiated as *National Review* opened an office in the nation's capital. In words that may have originated with Buckley, the President said: "There's a problem, though, Bill, that I think you should know about. It's all the talk about your being aloof and insensitive and an out-of-touch editor. People are saying that you spend too much time away from New York. They're also saying you're being pushed around by your staff. And I understand there's a new button on the market, 'Let Buckley be Buckley.' Some people question whether you're going to seek another term."[30] This, of course, parodied what the media were saying about Reagan's own management style as well as conservative complaints that Chief of Staff James Baker, Deputy Chief of Staff Michael Deaver, and the First Lady, among others, were preventing Reagan from following his natural conservative instincts.

On foreign policy, Buckley generally supported Reagan's tough stance toward the USSR and attributed whatever setbacks the West suffered on the world stage to a decline in American resolve. After the USSR downed a Korean Airlines jet that had veered over Soviet territory, killing 269 persons including Congressman Larry McDonald, Reagan called the act an attack "against the world and the moral precepts which guide human relations among people everywhere."[31] Yet, Buckley pointed out, the Soviets paid no significant price for their action.[32]

Under such circumstances, Buckley suggested that the West's response to this act of aggression was analogous to Churchill having followed up his "blood, sweat, and tears" address with a call for parliamentary censure of Hitler. War between great powers, he continued, "is excluded these days, and everything short of war runs into a vested interest: the wheat farmer, the Pepsi Cola people, the gas pipeline manufacturers, the truck people, the bankers." Had Reagan not paid attention to these groups, Buckley noted, he might not have been elected President. Still, he insisted, "Sometimes leaders can bring an entire people around, and sometimes Abraham Lincoln is President."[33] This was the closest he would come to chastising Reagan until very late in the President's first term.

When the United States invaded Grenada in 1983, aborting a Marxist-inspired coup, Buckley was ecstatic. Had the United States succeeded in its attempts to bring down the Castro regime in Cuba during the Kennedy presidency, he declared, a Soviet enclave would not have been able to assist revolutionary movements in the Western Hemisphere a generation later. Of those who criticized Reagan's intervention, Buckley wrote, "Why are they appalled when the United States makes an intelligent move on the world scene?"[34] He defended the military's decision to ban press coverage of the invasion. The media's presence, he insisted, would only divert the military from its mission as reporters intruded on its terrain and military personnel were assigned to protect them both on and off military bases. When Reagan telephoned him to thank him for his supportive columns, Buckley shared with him Nixon's comment: during World War II, the press wanted the United States to prevail, but in contemporary times, the press regarded itself as a "neutral" observer of the events it covered.[35]

Buckley, however, did not approve of all military deployments abroad. He favored sending U.S. troops to foreign lands solely to protect or advance a discernible U.S. interest. Buckley dissented strongly when Reagan sent American troops to Lebanon in 1983 as part of a multinational peacekeeping force during that country's civil war. In pressing his views upon the President, Buckley was aware that he was inserting himself into an ongoing and intense policy debate within the administration. In a reversal of expectations of how occupants of their respective offices might come down on matters such as these, Defense Secretary Caspar Weinberger, often thought a "hard-liner," seeing no American interests at stake, opposed the introduction of U.S. forces. Secretary of State George Shultz, often described as a "realist" or "pragmatist," favored it as a means of cultivating goodwill for the United States in the region.

Reagan had sent U.S. troops to Lebanon to help oversee the withdrawal of Israeli, Palestinian, and Syrian forces that had come to the aid of factions with which they had been allied in the Lebanese civil war. He ordered them removed after other foreign powers had withdrawn their forces. Four days after the Americans left, radical forces aligned with the Palestine Liberation Organization assassinated Lebanon's President-elect, Bashir Gemayel. Fighting resumed and Israeli troops reoccupied a portion of the country. As the Israelis held back, forces loyal to the Lebanese government slaughtered seven hundred Palestinians living in refugee camps in retribution for Gemayel's murder. In response, Reagan sent U.S. forces back to Lebanon to protect the refugees. A month before the warring factions were expected to reach an accord, a car bomb exploded at the American embassy, killing sixteen U.S. citizens.

On May 17, 1983, Special Envoy Philip Habib, with Shultz's support, arranged for all Israeli and Syrian forces to exit Lebanon, to be replaced by international peacekeepers. Syria, going back on its "hands-off" pledge, provided safe passage for Hezbollah, a terrorist group closely allied with the Iranian revolutionary government, to enter the country. On October 23, a bomb-laden truck drove through the gates of an American barracks at the Beirut airport and detonated, killing 241 soldiers and wounding 60 others.

With Reagan vowing to avenge the fallen, Buckley urged him to withdraw all remaining U.S. forces from the country. Their correspondence suggests that they also discussed the matter over the telephone. Shultz and others argued that the world would interpret an American withdrawal as a "cut and run." Weinberger wanted to "redeploy" the troops to a waiting U.S. carrier, reasoning that the Lebanese, whatever their internal divisions, would close ranks to oppose a sustained American presence. He identified twenty-six different groups operating in Lebanon, none of which approved of the presence of U.S. forces.[36]

Weeks before the first attacks on U.S. forces, Reagan had replaced National Security Adviser William Clark, who shared Weinberger's views on the Lebanon situation, with Robert C. McFarlane, who agreed with Shultz.[37] This change left the National Security Council without an internal advocate for Weinberger's position. Trying to avert this very situation, CIA Director Casey had pressed Reagan, unsuccessfully, to replace Clark with UN Ambassador Jeane Kirkpatrick, but Reagan, mindful of Shultz's misgivings about her, looked elsewhere.[38] Odds are strong, especially given Buckley's close friendship with Casey and the cordial relations he had developed with Clark, that someone in Reagan's camp aligned with Weinberger asked Buckley to weigh in with the President in favor of scaling back the U.S. presence in Lebanon.

When he did so, Buckley made clear that he was speaking not only for himself but also for an important part of Reagan's constituency: "The sharp worsening of the situation in Lebanon requires American conservatives who presumptively (as distinguished from categorically) back the Reagan administration to emphasize considerations that are now pre-eminent. The first of these, of course, is the consideration of necessity, as distinguished from secondary—even tertiary—American interests." Buckley then listed what he considered the three most important American interests in the Middle East: the survival of Israel, the containment of "that part of the Syrian offensive that can be described as a Soviet salient," and the unimpeded flow of oil to Western Europe and Japan. Lebanon, he insisted, bore little relevance to any of these.[39] His tone suggested that his column was intended as much for one particular reader, the President, as for his others.

If a permanent presence of outsiders was needed to end the violence there, Buckley added, U.S. allies, particularly those in the region, should perform that mission. (A generation earlier, he had made a similar argument with regard to the U.S. defense of South Vietnam and would do so again a generation hence after the United States invaded Iraq.) Buckley then alerted Reagan to the dangers inherent in a continued U.S. presence in Lebanon, as no American President would commit troops to a certain place and not defend them. In an obvious attempt to catch the President's attention, Buckley declared, "In my experience, the friends of Ronald Reagan have never been more united than on the belief that our troops should be withdrawn from Lebanon." Troops, he insisted, should be employed to advance national interests, not in pursuit of intellectual abstractions.[40]

Buckley's arrow reached its target. After reading Buckley's second column urging withdrawal, Reagan wrote him: "Bill, I know Lebanon looks like a lost cause but there are things going on that don't make the front page. As long as there is some room for maneuver we must stay. If the running room closes down, I'll be the first to say, 'home and mother.'"[41] Buckley was troubled by Reagan's dismissal of dissenting views from his ill-defined policy. He saw parallels between the President's stance and Lyndon Johnson's during the early stages of the American buildup in South Vietnam. He cautioned his friend against falling victim to "misplaced pride." (He would write the same when he urged George W. Bush to withdraw from Iraq.)

Weeks after their exchange Reagan wrote Buckley again. He said he would respond to Buckley's criticisms—"glass in hand"—at some future get-together. Sounding even more Johnsonian, especially when he suggested that presidents inherently were privileged to more information than were their critics, Reagan wrote: "Bill, the Middle East is a complicated place—well not really a place—it's more a state of mind—disordered mind. But, of course, you know that without me telling you. I'm not being stubborn or too proud to admit to error. There has been progress precisely because the M.N.F. [Multi-National Force] is there. There could be instant chaos if a wrong or precipitate move is made. Withdrawal would be such a move. . . . Let me just say, there is a reason why they are there."[42] (Buckley, convinced that the United States was overextended in the multilateral operation, could not derive comfort from the President's reassurances.)

On February 7, 1984, a month after he wrote those words, Reagan ordered all American forces withdrawn from Lebanon. He based his decision on several factors: the deteriorating situation in that country, the difficulty in identifying and retaliating against those responsible for the American deaths, growing dissent within his administration, increasing congressional opposition, and, not to be understated, his upcoming reelection campaign.

As Reagan's presidency advanced, Buckley continued to perform favors large and small for the First Couple and asked their intervention on behalf of mutual friends and allies. He confided to them that the actor David Niven, a skiing buddy of Buckley's and his "second favorite Hollywood alumnus," had contracted Lou Gehrig's disease, and he asked permission to contact the First Lady "if the time came" when a note from Reagan to Niven might be appropriate.[43] He requested that Clare Boothe Luce—who, he said, was feeling neglected—be invited to a state dinner and that harpsichordist Rosalyn Tureck, a favorite of his, be asked to perform at the White House. He also requested that the President consent to a sit-down interview with British writer and lay theologian Malcolm Muggeridge.[44] The Reagans granted all of these requests.

On occasion, Buckley also tried his hand at "casework." He wrote Reagan on behalf of a former Yale professor, Vladimir Sokolov-Samatinm, who faced deportation to the Soviet Union for allegedly having lied about his pro-Nazi activities in German-occupied Russia during the Second World War. To provide Reagan with political cover, Buckley noted that Hannah Gray, acting President of Yale, and Strobe Talbott, then senior diplomatic correspondent at *Time*, had weighed in on the professor's behalf.[45] He passed along to Reagan aide Lyn Nofziger a suggestion from Clare Boothe Luce that Jack Lord, star of the *Hawaii Five-O* television series, be approached about a possible candidacy on the Republican ticket.[46]

Throughout Reagan's time in office, Buckley used his influence with the administration to draw attention to people he believed might be able to help Reagan advance his goals. He recommended that Reagan nominate Buckley's friend and Yale classmate Evan Galbraith, a Francophile and a conservative, as Ambassador to France. Reagan was agreeable, but after France's socialist government objected, the State Department showed little enthusiasm for the appointment. Buckley, frustrated, raised the issue directly with Reagan, who sent the nomination to the Senate and pressed for speedy confirmation.[47] With regard to lower-level appointees, Buckley relied on those he had already steered into important posts to clear paths for others he recommended. "I hope you don't mind me using you as a transmission belt, but I trust you and you have an eye for talent" Buckley wrote Tony Dolan, now a Reagan speechwriter. Dolan advised Buckley that he was trying to help Peter Robinson (presumably at Buckley's request), another young protégé of Buckley's, obtain a position within the administration.[48] Robinson also became one of Reagan's writers and would pen one of Reagan's most memorable lines: "Mr. Gorbachev, tear down this wall."

When Bork resigned from the Circuit Court of Appeals in Washington, DC, Reagan replaced him with Buckley's candidate, Steven Williams, son of Buckley's lawyer, C. Dickinson Williams.[49] Buckley rejoiced in a letter to Reagan that Williams would be joining other Buckley favorites in the federal judiciary, including his brother James (who had served as Undersecretary of State until Reagan named him in 1985 to the U.S. Court of Appeals for the District of Columbia) and J. Dan Mahoney, founder of the New York Conservative Party, whom Reagan named to the U.S. Court of Appeals, Second Circuit. "By God," he wrote the President, "before you're through, you might even reinstate the Constitution of the United States."[50] Reagan also named Buckley's friend Dan Oliver to chair the Federal Trade Commission.[51]

Troubled by what he considered an inflammatory article that had run in what he presumed to be a Catholic magazine, Reagan sought Buckley's advice. The offending article, "Reagan Echoes Hitler's Strident Anti-Communism," which appeared in the *National Catholic Reporter* in 1984, predicted that a Reagan presidency would usher in a wave of fascism in the United States.[52] Its author, Alden Whitman, an obituary writer for the *New York Times,* had for thirteen years been a member of the American Communist Party and had once belonged to a communist cell. "You are being picked on by the right people," Buckley wrote Reagan. He related that the bishop of Kansas City had tried repeatedly and unsuccessfully to have the word "Catholic" struck from the magazine's title.[53] Years later, after Buckley sent Reagan a copy of Whitman's obituary, the ex-President answered that he had not shed a single tear.[54]

When Reagan sought reelection, Buckley again passed along suggestions and political intelligence. He urged that Reagan propose a "Digital Peace Corps" as a means of drawing upon the talents of "inventive, bright, and idealistic young people."[55] (His admiration for Kennedy's capacity to inspire young people to take an interest in public service endured.) Buckley voiced surprise when the President asked to read a copy of remarks Buckley delivered at a gathering at Bohemian Grove, a prestigious men's association Buckley had joined in the late 1960s at the invitation of California Senator George Murphy, a former actor and Reagan's friend. As his topic, Buckley's had selected Blackford Oakes, the fictional hero of several Buckley novels.[56] After Reagan had delivered his second acceptance speech at the Republican National Convention, weeks later in Dallas, Buckley wrote the President: "You appeared to be enjoying the zest of it all and that itself was good to see."[57]

Buckley made no mention in his letter that he had helped draft UN Ambassador Jeane Kirkpatrick's keynote address to that same convention. A Democrat for most of her life, Kirkpatrick had come to Reagan's attention through an article she published in *Commentary* in November 1979, "Dictatorships and Double Standards." In the piece, she had distinguished between totalitarian and authoritarian regimes and argued that the United States should occasionally work with authoritarian states to achieve limited strategic purposes.[58] In advance of her convention speech, Kirkpatrick reached out to Buckley for suggestions. His influence can be seen in her choice of words and phrases as well as in her overall theme.

In her remarks, Kirkpatrick charged that critics of Reagan's tough stance toward the Soviet Union made it their practice to "blame America first" for all that was not right with the world. The phrase became the refrain of her speech, with her audience echoing those three words. She spoke of "San Francisco Democrats" (delegates who convened in that city and nominated Walter Mondale, Carter's Vice President, to oppose Reagan) as the "new isolationists," who, she said, were as blind to Soviet aggression in the postwar era as the isolationists of the 1930s had been to Nazi Germany's global ambitions. On both occasions, she said, those opposed to an assertive role for the United States in the world had, wittingly or otherwise, played into the hands of would-be aggressors.[59]

Buckley was all too familiar with the isolationists of the 1930s, to whom she compared nuclear "freeze" advocates in the 1980s. In his teenage years Buckley had vigorously supported the isolationists' cause and belonged to the America First organization. He had carefully studied the rhetoric and arguments FDR had used to undermine their case and injected much of what he had learned into Kirkpatrick's speech. In her thank-you letter to Buckley, Kirkpatrick called his phrase "San Francisco Democrats" "an inspired concept."[60]

Many Reagan loyalists, including Buckley, grew concerned after Reagan performed poorly in the first of two debates against Mondale. Reagan's apparent loss of his train of thought at one point fueled speculation that, at the age of seventy-three, he was not up to the job he sought to retain.[61] In his column, Buckley focused less on this aspect of Reagan's performance and more on what he perceived to be the President's deviation from the conservative line to which he had so strongly adhered four years earlier. Buckley found it odd that Reagan would boast that on his watch, the federal government was doing as much or nearly as much as it had done under Carter.[62] He had hoped that the President would discuss how he planned to reduce the size and scope of government.

He also thought it a mistake for Reagan to pledge never to cut back on entitlement spending, when all knew that fewer workers were subsidizing more retirees than at any time since Congress first passed the Social Security Act. Buckley's preferred remedy to address what he saw as a coming crisis in entitlement growth and spending was means-testing recipients. He believed Reagan had erred in not preparing the country for inevitable changes in the Social Security program that lay ahead. He was also disappointed that Reagan, running on the slogan "Morning in America," failed to advance an agenda for his second term. If given a choice, Buckley would have preferred that Reagan win a close election and return to office with a mandate, rather than win in a landslide assembled entirely around Reagan's personal popularity and engaging personality.[63]

Whatever his misgivings about the campaign's strategy, Buckley collaborated with the First Lady to deflect attention from Reagan's poor debate performance. A week after the debate, he apprised Nancy Reagan of press reports that Mondale was taking three "high blood pressure pills" a day.[64] If true, the two hoped that questions about Mondale's health might counter doubts about Reagan's age. The age issue vanished after Reagan, in response to a direct question about it during his second debate with Mondale, responded, "I want you to know that . . . I will not make age an issue of this campaign. I am not going to exploit, for political purposes, my opponent's youth and inexperience."[65] Even Mondale laughed at Reagan's comeback line.

Severe weather conditions caused Reagan's inaugural planners to move the traditional outdoor swearing-in to the Capitol Rotunda, resulting in a reduction of the number of invitees and the postponement of the inaugural parade. Buckley was among the handful of non-government and non-family members on hand to witness Reagan take the oath of office for the second time. He wrote Nancy Reagan afterward: "When El Presidente was sworn in, and after he spoke, I was standing five feet behind him—and you. And I saw your fingers caressing his. You thought the gesture entirely private, but I have Eyes That See All, and I was not, in living memory, so moved by so tender a liaison between a great leader and his incomparable wife."[66] Months later, Buckley gave his readers his take on the Reagans' mutual bond. "Theirs was the real thing." The First Lady, he wrote, should not be thought of as a "silent female appendage" who limited her role to gazing adoringly at her husband. "She has positions stated and unstated" on people, issues, and other matters.[67] This became evident in abundance four months later.

Reagan was scheduled to visit West Germany in May 1985 to participate in a summit of leaders of industrial states. As this visit would coincide with the fortieth anniversary of the defeat of Nazi Germany, West German Chancellor Helmut Kohl suggested that he and Reagan use the occasion to commemorate the alliance between the United States and West Germany that began with the destruction of Nazism. Kohl recommended that the two leaders visit a former concentration camp, a cathedral, and a military cemetery. In suggesting that they stop at a military cemetery, Kohl sought to draw a distinction between German soldiers who died in defense of their country and those who had subscribed to Hitler's genocidal policies. The military cemetery at Bitburg was added to Reagan's schedule.

Shortly before the trip was to take place, the press reported that among the two thousand German soldiers buried at Bitburg were forty-nine members of the Waffen SS, the very kind of combatants neither country wished to honor. One of the forty-nine had killed ten U.S. prisoners of war. Jewish leaders, Holocaust survivors, veterans' organizations, fifty-three U.S. Senators, and hundreds of House members demanded that Reagan scratch the Bitburg visit.[68] Not wishing to embarrass Kohl, who had stared down fierce domestic opposition when he accepted American ICBMs on West German soil, Reagan wanted to stick with the original plan.

At a White House ceremony on April 19, days before Reagan was to depart Washington, human rights activist and Holocaust survivor Elie Wiesel beseeched the President to forego the stop at Bitburg. "That place, Mr. President, is not your place. Your place is with the victims of the SS," Wiesel said, with a visibly uncomfortable Reagan seated beside the podium.[69] Charles Z. Wick, a longtime personal friend of Reagan whom the President had named head of the United States Information Agency (USIA), publicly rebuked Reagan for not striking the Bitburg visit from his itinerary.[70] Given the closeness between the men and their wives, it is unlikely that Wick would have retained his post had he acted without the First Lady's approval, or even encouragement. In her memoir, Nancy Reagan all but said this had been the case.

The White House inserted into Reagan's schedule a visit to the Bergen-Belsen concentration camp after a much-abbreviated stop at Bitburg. This last-minute adjustment was not without a touch of irony. Mrs. Reagan had previously vetoed a planned visit to a former death camp on the grounds that her husband became emotionally overwrought whenever he reflected on the Holocaust.[71] After he toured Bergen-Belsen, Reagan delivered one of his most eloquent speeches as President.[72]

Buckley wrote three successive columns about the "Bitburg matter," each of them supportive of whatever official position the White House was taking at the time. Buckley maintained that as they condemned Reagan for his clumsiness in his handling of the entire episode, the President's critics had overlooked the "greatest menace to Jews in the post-Hitler era," the Soviet Union. The "genocide is muted, though the anti-Semitism is rife," he argued. In the end, he said, on balance, the Bitburg visit had not been "worth it."[73]

Reagan telephoned Buckley to thank him for being so supportive of him throughout the controversy. Buckley wrote Reagan afterward that he knew no better way to honor those who perished in the Holocaust than through Reagan's eloquence in his speech at the former death camp. He informed Reagan that several influential persons, many of them Jewish, considered the Soviet Union the most active perpetrator of anti-Semitism in modern times. He made specific mention of three he had consulted: Kissinger, Irving Kristol, editor of the *Public Interest,* and Norman Podhoretz, editor of *Commentary.*[74]

The Bitburg brouhaha occasioned a controversy involving Buckley and Joseph Sobran, his colleague and protégé at *National Review,* who he believed had crossed a delicate line in his commentary that would reflect badly on the conservative movement, if allowed to pass. Commenting in his syndicated column on objections that had been raised to Reagan's Bitburg visit, Sobran suggested that the *New York Times* rename itself the *Holocaust Update.*[75] More than a year later, when Reagan ordered bombing attacks on Libya in retribution for its government-sanctioned terrorist assault against U.S. servicemen stationed in West Germany, Sobran attributed the *New York Times'* support for the American military action to its Jewish ownership. In yet another piece, Sobran criticized Pope John Paul II for visiting a Jewish synagogue in Rome, arguing that it would divert attention from the historical Jewish persecution of Christians.[76]

Midge Decter, co-Chair of the Committee for the Free World and wife of Norman Podhoretz, complained to Buckley that Sobran was a "little more than a crude and naked anti-Semite."[77] After reviewing several of Sobran's columns, Buckley declared six of them "contextually anti-Semitic."[78] He forbade Sobran to write about Israel in *National Review* and disassociated himself and the magazine from Sobran's extracurricular writings, which he said showed an "obstinate tendentiousness."[79] (This being the case, some questioned why Buckley allowed Sobran to continue writing for the magazine.) In 1993, Buckley fired Sobran outright, purportedly for making public the conditions Buckley had set in order for their professional association to continue. Sobran charged that Buckley had dismissed him to gain acceptance among New York's intellectual elite, much of which was Jewish.[80]

Late in 1985, a group of White House conservatives, anxious that in his negotiations with the Soviet Union, Reagan might succumb to pressures from the media and the foreign policy establishment to soften not only his rhetoric but also his policy demands, voiced their concerns to Buckley at a private dinner in Washington. They worried that the President might abandon the Strategic Defense Initiative (SDI), which he had proposed as the cornerstone of his defense strategy, in exchange for Soviet concessions on arms reductions.

Bentley T. Elliott, the leader of this group, was directing Reagan's speechwriting operation. He requested that Buckley urge Reagan to continue to support "freedom fighters" across the world; assert the moral distinctions between the West and an "evil empire"; and accelerate the arms buildup, which the Soviets could match only at the expense of an already faltering economy.[81] Elliott also complained that certain Reagan loyalists, whom he identified, were being forced out of the President's inner circle.

Buckley found the report of Elliott and his colleagues disconcerting. They agreed upon a strategy for Reaganites—within and without the administration—to follow for the remainder of Reagan's presidency. Buckley resolved to use the platforms available to him to make the conservatives' case and pledged to try to keep Reagan grounded in the movement from which he had come. He would continue to speak his mind to the President and let him know when his supporters in the movement felt let down by his actions or those of his administration. At the same time, he would also vigorously defend Reagan whenever he believed that the President was in personal or political danger. Buckley would use his public remarks at *National Review*'s thirtieth anniversary dinner, which Reagan was scheduled to attend, to signal that he was aware of ideological tensions within the Reagan camp, to declare which side he was on, and to express the hope that Reagan was in agreement with his audience.

In advance of the dinner, Nancy Reagan asked Buckley for suggestions about what Reagan might say and reviewed comments her husband had made at *National Review*'s 1983 reception in Washington. She also kept in close touch with White House speechwriters as the event approached. Unlike five years previously, "this time, there was no slip up," Buckley recalled, and Reagan did indeed make it to the dinner.[82]

Buckley preceded Reagan to the podium. In introducing the President, he declared that Reagan had kept the peace and preserved freedom not by accommodation but through his willingness to resist even the "ultimate" Soviet aggression. The USSR knew that under Reagan, "the ambiguists with whom it so dearly loves to deal are not in power this time." Buckley said that he had lived his sixty years in a country that remained free and sovereign primarily because the United States maintained a nuclear deterrent and "made clear its disposition to use it, if necessary."[83] He had pitched his remarks to an audience of one, Reagan, whom he urged not to allow the "ambiguists" to lead him away from the path he had followed in the course of his presidency. The stage had been set for a major policy disagreement these two friends would have the following year.

When it came his time to speak, Reagan lavishly praised Buckley and his magazine. He recounted how closely the world had come into alignment with the principles *National Review* had enunciated at its founding. He called Buckley "the most influential journalist and intellectual in our era" and credited him with changing the United States and the world. He proclaimed Buckley "our clipboard-bearing Galahad" who "came upon the scene in a forest primeval when nightmare and danger reigned and only the knights of darkness prevailed; when conservatives seemed without a champion in the critical battle of style and content."[84]

As 1985 gave way to 1986, the Buckleys and Reagans shared many light moments. Buckley presented the President with a Cavalier King Charles spaniel that had come from the same litter as his own. The President immediately gave it to the First Lady as a Christmas present. In February 1986, in a rare departure from their decades-old routine, Bill and Pat Buckley interrupted their winter sojourn in Switzerland to attend Reagan's seventy-fifth birthday celebration at the White House, to which only intimates of the First Couple had been invited.

As the year wore on, Buckley became increasingly concerned that the Soviet Union had outmaneuvered the United States on several fronts. He objected in print to the sale of American wheat to the USSR at a price that both undercut the domestic market price and was lower than the United States charged its allies.[85] After reading the article, Reagan immediately telephoned *National Review* and explained to Rusher (Buckley was out of the office) that his administration had acted in order to preempt an even worse measure that Congress was about to pass. Buckley was unrelenting. "I wish I could report better news," he wrote Reagan afterward, "but there is from the anti-communist community . . . deep dismay . . . over that measure." He said in a note to Reagan that the symbolism of giving a "special break" to the USSR upset many who looked upon the President as "keeper of the anti-communist flame."[86]

Buckley took the occasion to warn Reagan that many within the foreign policy establishment who had never taken kindly to Reagan's tough stance toward the USSR were "stigmatizing" the SDI as an obstacle to peace and trying to gut it by insisting that the Anti-Ballistic Missile (ABM) Treaty, which the United States and the USSR had signed during the Nixon era, forbade development of a new weapon system. Although a "strict constructionist" in his interpretation of the U.S. Constitution and statutes, Buckley took a more expansive interpretation of the ABM Treaty, arguing that its text had not specifically forbidden such weaponry. He was eager to see the ABM Treaty lapse in any case and voiced frustration at Reagan's willingness to extend it for up to seven years. If he could be assured that Reagan's hands would remain on the controls during all that time, Buckley wrote the President, he would feel better about Reagan's compromises.[87] His letter generated another presidential phone call in which Reagan tried to convince his friend that he was relying on more than the good intentions of his Soviet opposite and that agreements reached would survive his administration.

Veering back into domestic policy, Buckley warned Reagan that he detected slippage in the administration's willingness to stand guard against the gradual reestablishment of programs Reagan's budget cutters had either eliminated or curbed. He cited federally financed legal aid to the poor as a case in point. Unless Reagan stood firm, Buckley warned, Senator Warren Rudman (R-NH) would "sneak" back into the budget federal funding for legal services—which, he reminded Reagan, the administration had "knocked" out of previous appropriation bills. "Unless there is a General Alert, we will be back to subsidizing class-action suits against everything we hold dear, including our hero," Buckley added.[88] Days later, Buckley gave his column's readers, who surely included Reagan, a history lesson. Lyndon Johnson had initiated the program as a means of allowing the less affluent access to legal representation. Over time, he wrote, ideologues had commandeered those funds to litigate the enactment of radical policy agendas.[89]

On April 21, 1986, Buckley tried to prevent a falling-out between two of his closest friends, Reagan and Kissinger. In an interview on ABC News, Kissinger had remarked that those encountering Reagan for the first time would have a hard time believing that he had been elected Governor of California, let alone President of the United States. Buckley wrote Reagan that Kissinger had intended to suggest that Reagan had learned how to mask his "intuitive grasp of policy." He added that historian Gertrude Himmelfarb and her husband, the neoconservative intellectual Irving Kristol, shared this interpretation of Kissinger's comments. "Henry is anxious not to offend," Buckley wrote the President. He asked that Reagan share his opinion on the matter with the First Lady.[90] (Buckley's invocation of Himmelfarb and Kristol, whom Reagan respected, suggests that the First Lady had already expressed disapproval of Kissinger's remarks.)

Buckley also briefed Reagan on a new controversy Buckley himself had ignited when he suggested in a *New York Times* op-ed piece that to curb the spread of AIDS, people afflicted with the disease should be tattooed to forewarn potential sex partners. His position, which awarded higher priority to the overall public health than to individual privacy rights, paralleled views he had expressed during the McCarthy era, when he argued that policy makers and law enforcement authorities should place national security concerns ahead of the rights of those accused of disloyalty. "Got a certain amount of flak on that one," he wrote Reagan.[91] That was an understatement.

Civil libertarians and AIDS activists picketed the *National Review* offices, chanting, among other things, "Homophobes ain't got no class; Buckley wants to brand your ass." Impressed with the humor of critics who satirized him, Buckley posted one of the protesters' leaflets on a wall in his home office.[92] The *New York Native*, a gay publication, termed his proposal "Buckley's Buchenwald."[93] Buckley held his ground. "There ought to be a Gay Right not to be infected by someone already infected," he wrote Reagan.[94] He relayed to the President a quip Joseph Sobran (whom Buckley would soon fire from *National Review*) had made: that the tattoos should carry words from Dante's *Divine Comedy*: "Abandon hope, all ye who enter here."[95] As was his custom, Buckley awarded space in his magazine to people who disagreed with public stands he or *National Review* had taken. He devoted a cover story to the objections of an anonymous gay conservative to Buckley's views.[96] Two decades later, Buckley told an interviewer that had his recommendation been followed, perhaps a million lives would have been saved.[97]

With the AIDS epidemic cresting during Reagan's second term, Buckley voiced doubts that Surgeon General C. Everett Koop's public education campaign, which placed much of its emphasis on "safe sex," would curb the spread of the disease. He noted that similar "sex education" undertakings had failed to halt the rise of teen pregnancy and argued that greater emphasis needed to be placed on abstinence.[98] Buckley's criticisms of Koop ran parallel to those of Reagan advisers, including Gary Bauer, White House adviser on domestic policy; Patrick Buchanan, Director of Communications; and William Bennett, Education Secretary, had made.[99]

There were signs that Nancy Reagan, and possibly her husband as well, may not have shared these views. As in the case of Charles Wick at USIA, it is doubtful that Koop's public awareness campaign would have been allowed to proceed as it did or that the budget for AIDS research would have been increased to the extent that it was, given the number of prominent Reaganites opposed, without a powerful advocate at the highest level. While Koop had grown accustomed to opposition, criticism from the right was something new for him. Liberals had opposed his confirmation because of his known opposition to abortion. Many of these former critics rallied to his side with regard to his efforts to combat AIDS.[100]

Under such circumstances, Buckley argued, it was understandable that Reagan might not want to telegraph his true intentions. Buckley was overjoyed when the Reykjavik summit collapsed over Reagan's refusal to scale back on SDI in exchange for Gorbachev's proposal that both sides eliminate nuclear weapons within a decade. "Ronald Reagan's faith in his own insights is a continuing inspiration," Buckley declared in his column.[112] "By God, you lived up to our faith in you," he wrote Reagan.[113] The President responded, "I'll wait till we can have a talk to relay all the details but it was quite a ten or eleven hour set-to—no plenary meetings, just the two of us plus Shevardnadze, Shultz, and interpreters."[114] Although many experts as well as commentators declared the Reykjavik summit a failure, the face-to-face meeting with his opposite afforded Reagan an opportunity to press the Soviet leadership on human rights. The pause in the negotiations and the time it gave both sides to regroup may well have helped pave the way for the Intermediate-Range Nuclear Force (INF) Treaty, which both sides approved the following year.

Days later, Buckley weighed in on the disaster he believed Reagan had averted. Had the United States abandoned SDI in exchange for arms reductions, he wrote, its European allies would have become more vulnerable to Warsaw Pact conventional forces.[115] Much as he and Reagan agreed on SDI, Buckley never came around to Reagan's view that the very existence of nuclear weapons endangered peace or that their elimination or reduction would further American interests or enhance American security. Never far from Buckley's mind was Churchill's observation, made back in 1949, that the American monopoly over nuclear weapons had prevented the enslavement of Western Europe. Pleased with Buckley's review of his performance in Iceland, Reagan wrote him, "Why don't you devote yourself to writing? You are very good, might become a columnist and someday write a book."[116]

By year's end, Reagan was embroiled in a scandal that threatened his presidency. Contrary to the President's claims that he had not negotiated with Iranian terrorists to help secure the release of U.S. hostages being held in Lebanon, evidence mounted suggesting that his administration had done precisely that and more. It was established that officials at the National Security Council and Oliver North, a colonel on assignment at the White House, had sold arms to Iran in violation of an arms embargo, and that U.S. agents used the proceeds of the sales to fund the Nicaraguan Contras, armed groups seeking to overthrow the Marxist Nicaraguan government. This transfer of funds violated the spirit, if not the letter, of the Boland Amendment, which prohibited the United States from providing military assistance to the Contras without the direct approval of Congress.

Buckley went into overdrive to exonerate Reagan of wrongdoing and to defend the policy National Security Council officials sought to advance. Taking Reagan at his word that he had not approved the transfer of funds to the Contras, Buckley argued that even if Reagan had done so, his action would have been "extra-constitutional" (as opposed to "unconstitutional") and on a par with measures other presidents had undertaken to advance the national interest. He cited as precedents Jefferson's Louisiana Purchase, Lincoln's suspension of habeas corpus, and FDR's pushing the limits of, and perhaps violating, the Neutrality Acts, which forbade the United States to arm foreign nations at war. Given that Congress subsequently approved the Contra aid Reagan had requested—after the transfer had occurred—Buckley argued that the President's differences with Congress were not great, and the administration's transfer of funds to the Contras had been appropriate. When it came to defending Reagan, Buckley was willing to abandon his long-standing preference for congressional supremacy in setting national policy and the need for presidents to consult with Congress on a regular basis as safeguards against an "imperial presidency."

In his columns, Buckley urged North and National Security Adviser John Poindexter to waive their Fifth Amendment protections against self-incrimination and spell out before Congress what role they had played in the "arms for hostages" transfers. The American people, he said, were beginning to conclude from the two officials' silence that Reagan, whose credibility was at the heart of the case, had lied about how much he had known about the affair. Unlike Nixon, Buckley said, Reagan had never looked the American people in the eye and lied.[117]

Reagan also, unlike Nixon, gave congressional investigators complete access to documents pertaining to the inner workings of his administration, in essence waiving his constitutional right to assert "executive privilege." In response to the recommendations of an independent commission charged with investigating the causes and effects of Iran-Contra, Reagan reorganized his White House operation. Late in Reagan's presidency, Buckley urged the President to pardon both North and Poindexter. Such a move, he wrote, would spare the next President from having to deal with the repercussions of the scandal and Reagan from having to testify at a trial.[118] Reagan did not follow this advice.

In early 1987, Buckley urged Reagan to appoint noted Washington attorney and power broker Edward Bennett Williams head of the Central Intelligence Agency.[119] His raising the idea was part a quiet campaign Nancy Reagan was waging to ease out the ailing William Casey and replace him with someone who enjoyed credibility with the press and the public.[120] Over the years, Buckley had had his ups and downs with Williams. They were allies when Williams managed

Joseph McCarthy's defense against censure by the U.S. Senate. Buckley lowered his opinion of the lawyer when Williams helped Representative Adam Clayton Powell fend off a corruption conviction on legal and procedural technicalities, rather than on the substance of the case. In a review of Williams's autobiography, *One Man's Freedom*, Buckley declared Williams the prototype of the amoral attorney who made a lavish living by helping the guilty escape justice on technicalities.[121] When asked about Buckley's criticisms of him at a public forum at Yale Law School, Williams called Buckley "a kind of Ivy League George Lincoln Rockwell" (Rockwell at the time headed the American Nazi Party).[122] In response, Buckley speculated that Williams must have been drunk when he made that remark. "If he wasn't, it will obviously be necessary, on behalf of free speech, and on behalf of my own reputation and that of my colleagues, to wash his mouth with a little legal soap and water."[123] Williams apologized, and Buckley took no legal action.

The two men's relationship took yet another turn in the 1970s when Buckley retained Williams to handle the appeal of Edgar Smith, a convicted murderer on death row in New Jersey who had persuaded Buckley of his innocence.[124] Williams also represented Buckley in 1979 before the Securities and Exchange Commission after he encountered difficulties with regulators who questioned investments he and associates had made in a group of radio stations. Buckley's complicated relationship with Williams attests to three aspects of Buckley's character: his disinclination (most of the time) to hold grudges, his capacity to recognize and avail himself of the best talent available, and the lengths to which he would go to help a friend (in this case, Reagan).

Buckley assured Reagan that Williams had always been "adamantly anti-Communist" and possessed a "finely developed nose for bums and bummery."[125] That Williams was a Democrat, he argued, could work to Reagan's benefit politically, just as FDR's bringing Republicans Henry L. Stimson and Frank Knox into his administration, respectively as the Secretary of War and Secretary of the Navy, on the eve of World War II had given a bipartisan cast to his national security apparatus. At Nancy Reagan's request, Chief of Staff Donald Regan approached Williams, who declined the appointment because of failing health.[126]

The INF Treaty, negotiated during Reagan's seventh year in office, occasioned Buckley's most strident private and public disagreement with the man he had worked so hard to make President. The treaty provided for the withdrawal of all Soviet and American intermediate-range and short-range nuclear missiles from Europe. Its implementation, over three years, would entail the destruction of 1,836 Soviet nuclear missiles with a range of between three hundred and thirty-four hundred miles, and 859 American missiles. For the first time, the Soviet Union agreed to on-site inspections of its nuclear arsenal.[127]

Most conservatives, Buckley advised Reagan, believed that the treaty would jeopardize the security of Western Europe.[128] The Soviets, they pointed out, had superior conventional forces that could be mobilized rapidly. The concerns of Reagan's critics on the right were not assuaged by the administration's argument that the Soviets were destroying more nuclear missiles than the Americans were. "For the first time," Buckley reported to Reagan, "I and my colleagues need to take very serious issue with you."[129] On May 22, 1987, *National Review* published a cover story entitled "Reagan's Suicide Pact" in which the author, John P. Roche, a former adviser to Lyndon Johnson, recounted what he regarded as the INF Treaty's shortcomings.[130] Buckley sent Reagan the first copy that came off the presses. This precipitated a conversation between them in which Buckley promised that, in expressing future disagreements, the magazine would not speculate about the administration's motives.

Buckley feared that the USSR would find a way around the agreement, whether through direct violation or by technically complying with it, while secretly breaching it. Buckley contended that future presidents and Congresses would steadily chip away at SDI, which remained at the heart of Reagan's plan to safeguard the United States against a nuclear attack. He feared that Reagan, eager to recover from the political fallout of the Iran-Contra affair and concerned over his place in history, might agree to a deal that could in the future work to the disadvantage of the United States. His suspicions grew when Gorbachev announced his willingness to "unlink" SDI from an interim agreement on missile reductions in Europe.

Reagan's schedule for much of that year suggests that his administration was at least seeking to change the political narrative. As the various investigations into Iran-Contra were getting under way, Reagan embarked on a ten-day swing through Western Europe. It was on this trip that Reagan delivered his famous line, "Mr. Gorbachev, tear down this wall," at Berlin's Brandenburg Gate on June 12, 1987. As the treaty meandered its way through the Senate, Buckley remained opposed. He grew alarmed when he heard Reagan remark that nuclear weapons had become obsolete and fired off a blunt letter to his friend in the White House.[131] Reagan replied that he had not said nuclear weapons were obsolete, just that he hoped to make them so.[132]

Twice Reagan telephoned Buckley to explain his reasons for wanting the treaty. Both times, he insisted that Buckley and his cohorts at *National Review* had either misunderstood or misrepresented his position on SDI, arms reductions, and the INF itself. He invited Buckley to a private meeting at the White House, where he and advisers briefed him on the treaty. The two exchanged many more telephone calls, and on one occasion, Buckley asked the President to hold a conference call with *National Review*'s editors while Buckley played scribe. After the conversation, Buckley assured Reagan that *National Review* would abstain from questioning Reagan's motives or attacking him personally.

Still, Buckley insisted that in exchange for reductions in intermediate-range nuclear weapons, Reagan was abandoning significant gains he had achieved when he placed Pershing missiles in Western Europe. The Soviets, Buckley insisted, feared those weapons more than any other, which was why they so urgently pressed for their removal. He reminded Reagan that the Left had fought Reagan when he had placed ICBMs in West Germany as fervently as American isolationists had fought against Roosevelt's assisting Britain in 1940 and 1941. Buckley concluded that Reagan had been outmaneuvered.[133]

Buckley voiced annoyance after Reagan suggested that those who opposed the INF Treaty did so because they believed that war with the Soviet Union was inevitable. He wrote the President that he knew of no conservative who thought that. Most, he insisted, agreed that the best way to maintain peace was through American superiority in the quality and quantity of its nuclear stockpile. What conservatives feared, he added, was a steady erosion of Western resolve. This, they worried, could enable the USSR to attain its goals without war. Conservatives, he said, also wondered how strenuously the United States would resist Soviet violations.[134]

Such concerns had caused many erstwhile Reagan allies, such as former United Nations Ambassador Jeane Kirkpatrick, former Secretaries of State Henry Kissinger and Alexander Haig, and former NATO Commander Bernard Rogers, to voice reservations about the treaty. Buckley, outlining his own objections to the President, argued that once land-based missiles had been removed from Europe, the Soviets could speedily subdue the continent. He inquired what the President would do should Soviet forces appear with SS-29 missiles at the Brandenburg Gate."[135]

Buckley found it both ironic and galling that, with the Democrats back in charge of the U.S. Senate after the 1986 elections, Alan Cranston of California, the new Chairman of the Senate Foreign Affairs Committee, long a critic of Reagan's defense policies, was the treaty's principal sponsor.[136] He was troubled that Reagan would close ranks with those who had been the most resistant to the very defense buildup that had brought Gorbachev to the conference table. He feared that once the treaty was approved and the Pershing missiles withdrawn, negotiators would interpret the ABM Treaty in a way that blocked the

United States from developing the SDI. All the while he voiced his policy disagreements with the administration, Buckley reassured the Reagans of his personal devotion to them. Reagan, he wrote the President, would be "dismayed" to discover how much Buckley had suffered because of his fealty to the chief executive. "Perhaps in the days ahead," he wrote, "I shall be canonized, having now been martyred."[137]

In January 1988, reports circulated that Reagan's former aide Michael Deaver was about to reveal in a soon-to-be-published book confidences of the First Couple. Buckley wrote Reagan that, while other conservatives had castigated Deaver for his revelations, *National Review* had remained silent. "If you and/or Nancy has a nifty way of handling it, ask her kindly to give me a buzz." While he hated to hit Deaver when he was "down" (Deaver was being investigated for ethical violations and suffering from advanced alcoholism), Buckley confessed that he did not understand friends who "turn around and divulge confidences."[138] Reagan asked Buckley to hold his fire. He said that he had information suggesting that Deaver's comments had been taken out of context. ("We'll have to wait until we see his book.")[139]

When he eventually weighed in, Buckley wrote, "Michael Deaver was treated by the Reagans as an adopted son, and soon after leaving the White House repaid their loyalty by a) breaking the law; and b) writing a book suggesting that the president is a creature of a left-minded virago." (The suggestion confirmed to some conservatives, but not necessarily to Buckley, their long suspicion that the President was dominated by his liberal-leaning wife.) He noted that Reagan's former Chief of Staff Donald Regan, in his own memoirs, had informed the world that Nancy Reagan consulted an astrologer when planning her husband's schedule. Trying to blunt the impact of this revelation, Buckley suggested that relying on astrologers was no different from indulging superstitions, as people regularly did. Having come again to the Reagans' defense, Buckley could not refrain from one more dig against the INF Treaty. "Could it be," he inquired, "that the INF Treaty the President had submitted to the Senate is numbered Senate Treaty Resolution No. 666?" (That was the original number of the Reagans' new street address in Los Angeles. They had changed it to 668, Buckley wrote, purportedly because 666 "signified the devil's code number.")[140]

Striking a more serious pose, Buckley eloquently reminded Reagan that there were worse things than the ever-present fear of a nuclear exchange: "I know what you mean about the nuclear age, but in fact we owe the liberty of most of those who are free to the existence of nuclear power. And almost certainly I owe my own life to it, having been a nubile 2nd lieutenant in the infantry at the time of Hiroshima. Seventy-five million people were killed on earth, violently, during this century, before the bomb was discovered that has thus far killed one hundred thousand."[141] "Damn I wish I could be on your side on that one," Buckley wrote Reagan toward the turn of the year. "Haven't had a significant difference with you since Panama Canal."[142] Holding his ground, Reagan wrote back that "Gorby knows what our response to cheating would be—it's spelled Pershing."[143] (This was a reference to conventional weapons at the disposal of NATO.)

Nancy Reagan, concerned about Buckley's criticisms, sent him a packet of materials in the hope its contents might persuade him to back the treaty. Buckley diplomatically replied that he wished he had had the information before he had written his columns.[144] Yet he remained opposed to the treaty. "I simply couldn't understand his enthusiasm for a treaty that minimized the number of weapons but wasn't tied into the larger question of whether Europe was more or less safe than before," he told a Reagan biographer.[145] The Senate approved the treaty by a vote of 93 to 5 on May 27, 1988.

As the Reagans prepared to leave the White House, Buckley wrote a tribute to them in his column. Rather than recapitulate the highlights of Reagan's administration (those would be covered in a special issue of *National Review*), he focused on what the Reagans had said and, more important, not said in an interview with Mike Wallace on CBS's *60 Minutes*. Focusing on Reagan's lack of pretense, Buckley wrote, "Ronald Reagan would not engage in affectation to storm the gates of heaven." He described the "hard, attentive look" of disbelief Reagan gave his interviewer when he was asked whether the report was true that Reagan read the comics and sports pages of the newspaper each day before he turned to the news sections. "That's true about the funny pages," Reagan replied, adding that he no longer had time for the sports section. Buckley saw in this answer Reagan's understanding of the country he had led. "It's there [on the funny pages] that the day-to-day character of American thought is most vividly transcribed," he wrote. Reagan, he said, tried to get this across "without being didactic about it."[146]

Buckley's last personal encounter with Reagan occurred when he interviewed the former President on *Firing Line* about his memoir, *An American Life*. On their way to lunch afterward at the former President's home, Reagan confessed that one of his greatest disappointments was his failure to convince certain African American leaders that the views he espoused as President (such as welfare reform and cuts in spending increases) were not rooted in racism and that he had never harbored any such prejudices.[147]

Telephone conversations between the two grew infrequent as Reagan's already poor hearing grew worse, but they continued to correspond. "I was astonished that you saw fit to come out in favor of the Brady Bill [a gun-control bill named after Reagan's former press secretary, who was seriously wounded when Reagan was shot] without even consulting me," Buckley wrote his friend, before he himself capitulated on the issue. "But, as they say, seriously folks, what on earth is wrong with asking people to wait seven days before they buy a pistol. After all, some people have to wait seven days before *National Review* arrives."[148]

Buckley continued to protect both Reagans' historical legacy. While pleased that Nancy Reagan had followed his advice, opting not to make her memoirs bland, he warned the Reagans to expect people she had criticized in *My Turn* to fire back at her vigorously.[149] He agreed to speak with Reagan biographer Lou Cannon, but only after Nancy assured him that Cannon was "an ok guy."[150] He declined to grant an interview to author Kitty Kelly as she was preparing a tabloid-style biography of Nancy. After the book appeared in print, Buckley assured the Reagans that a quotation attributed to him in the book emanated from something he had written, and not from an interview with Kelly.[151] (Among the salacious assertions Kelly made in her book was that Nancy Reagan maintained a decades-long affair with singer Frank Sinatra.)

As Kelly made the rounds on television talk shows, Reagan unburdened himself to his friend on the East Coast. "Nancy is sadly bruised and feeling very low right now," he wrote Buckley. He was concerned that gossip in the book, which he labeled untrue, was finding echoes in the media.[152] Buckley sprang into action. He published a scathing column about Kelly's account of Mrs. Reagan's secret life, which he labeled fictitious, and advised readers interested in the salacious to turn instead to reportage about alleged antics that had taken place at Ted Kennedy's home in Palm Beach.[153]

In a letter to Nancy, Buckley wrote: "I talked yesterday with our favorite president and he told me you were feeling a little blue. And why not? It hurts that anyone, even a certified viper, should have written such stuff. . . . I have published 32 books, and I'd have bet everything, after the first twenty, that there remained no unspoken calumny about me. Well, it isn't true. They keep coming. I guess it's fair to say that I get over it much quicker than I did when I was 24 . . . but it still stings, and so I know what pain you were going through."[154] Months later, Buckley wrote Reagan, "I do desperately hope she accepts history as your greatest vindicator and ceases to be tormented by the little scorpions who will never forgive you your success in office."[155]

A month later, Reagan, unable to attend *National Review*'s thirty-fifth anniversary gala, acknowledged his debt to the magazine's founder. "Looking back," he wrote Buckley, "I now see you played a part in my becoming a Republican. Again, thank you."[156] That gala bore special significance to Buckley as it marked his formal retirement from the magazine. His correspondence with Reagan continued until the former President's Alzheimer's disease rendered such communication impossible. He stayed in close contact with Nancy Reagan for the rest of his days.

The public letter Reagan wrote to the American people on November 5, 1994, in which he announced that he was suffering from Alzheimer's disease and about to "begin a journey" that would lead him into "the sunset of his life," together with biographer Edmund Morris's observation that he often forgot the names of people he saw regularly, caused Buckley to recall incidents in which Reagan had exhibited signs of suffering from the disease in earlier stages of his life.[157] He remembered the distant glaze he had seen fall over Reagan's eyes as he was shaking hands in a receiving line. In such instances, Reagan would appear unaware of the person to whom he was talking. He would reengage only if the person persisted and was someone he knew well. Buckley saw this happen at Yale in 1967. The man shaking Reagan's hand blurted out, "Ronnie, this is me. George Bush."[158] Thirteen years later, Buckley's fellow Bonesman would become Reagan's Vice President. Eight years after that, George Herbert Walker Bush was elected President of the United States.

14

Disappointed with G. H. W. Bush; Unsold on Clinton

Buckley knew George Herbert Walker Bush longer than any other man who became President. He liked the first President Bush and supported him as he ascended the political ladder. Yet their friendship was grounded more in social bonds and common associations and experiences than in a shared political philosophy. Buckley never acted as informal policy adviser and confidant to Bush as he had to Reagan. Nor was Bush as concerned as Reagan had been about maintaining his standing within the conservative movement. This inattention proved a political miscalculation that may have helped cost George H. W. Bush his presidency.

Bush was in his junior year when Buckley arrived at Yale. Both affiliated with Skull and Bones and distinguished themselves academically and in extracurricular activities. Bush made Phi Beta Kappa, an honor Buckley narrowly missed. Outside the classroom, Buckley made his mark as a champion debater and Chairman of the *Yale Daily News;* Bush was captain of the baseball team. After they graduated, they frequently came into contact through mutual friends and common political pursuits. The Buckley family had given political support to Senator Prescott Bush, George's father, and was on good terms with the Senator's family.

Like Reagan, George Bush was an early subscriber to *National Review.* Unlike Reagan, who had yet to meet Buckley when the magazine was first launched, Bush's primary motivation in subscribing was to support a friend's new business venture. Although he regarded himself as a "conservative," Bush was never an ideologue. While Buckley was writing editorials denouncing Eisenhower's leadership and agitating to push the Republican Party rightward, Bush, like his father, remained an Eisenhower stalwart. Like his associates in the oil business in his adoptive state of Texas, Bush deemed Ike sufficiently "conservative" and liked his administration's pro-business stance.

Once in his new environs of the Lone Star State, Bush, the Connecticut Yankee, threw himself deeply into local politics and adjusted his philosophical stands to make himself more palatable to the Texas GOP. These moves put him on the same side of the ideological divide within the GOP as Buckley. Bush became Chairman of Harris County's Republican organization and enlisted in Barry Goldwater's presidential campaign. With Kennedy's popularity sagging in the South, largely because of his support for a greater federal role in protecting the civil rights of African Americans, Republicans began to think they might win Texas in 1964. In 1960, even with the state's powerful favorite son and Senate Majority Leader Lyndon Johnson running for Vice President on Kennedy's ticket, Kennedy only narrowly carried the state. He won it with 51 percent of the vote, compared to Nixon's 49 percent. As part of his efforts to shore up his support in the state, Kennedy made what would be a fatal trip to Texas in November 1963. As Kennedy was planning his reelection campaign, Bush had begun his own campaign to oppose Texas's liberal Democratic Senator Ralph Yarborough in the upcoming election. On the very day on which Kennedy would be assassinated, the *Houston Chronicle* ran on its front page that a poll it had conducted showed Kennedy losing Texas to Goldwater 52 percent to 48 percent.[1]

With Lyndon Johnson rather than Kennedy heading the Democratic slate in 1964, the political climate in the state had changed considerably from what it had been a year earlier. Bush secured the Republican senatorial nomination but became a casualty of the Democratic landslide that ensued that year. Johnson defeated Goldwater in Texas 63 percent to 36 percent and Yarborough, riding Johnson's coattails, defeated Bush 56 percent to 44 percent. Buckley had donated to Bush's campaign, supplied his friend with tactical advice, and helped rally conservatives to his side. In a postelection piece in *National Review*, Bush attributed the GOP's poor performance nationally to Johnson's presenting himself as a conservative, the strength of the economy, and the media's depiction of Goldwater's campaign as captive to an extremist fringe.[2] He had privately voiced support for Buckley's criticisms of those extremist elements that had affixed themselves to the GOP and would, after the election, weigh in in support of Buckley's attacks upon the John Birch Society.[3]

When Buckley ran for Mayor, Bush stayed publicly silent. Given his political ambitions, it would have been politically unwise for Bush to have openly backed a third-party insurgency campaign against the designated Republican candidate. At the same time, John V. Lindsay's call upon Republicans based outside New York to keep their distance from his campaign foreclosed his endorsing Lindsay, whom Bush had known socially.[4] But Bush did support Buckley when he sought election as Alumni Fellow on the Yale Corporation in 1968. Buckley related to a friend that before the Yale administration settled on Defense Department official Cyrus Vance as its designated candidate, it had first approached Bush, who declined the honor because he intended to vote for Buckley.[5]

Buckley actively supported Bush in his successful races for the House of Representatives in 1966 and 1968. He was back in Bush's corner in 1970 when Bush ran a second time for the Senate in 1970. Hoping for a rematch against Yarborough in a more receptive political climate, Bush wound up instead facing a more conservative Democrat, Lloyd Bentsen, who polled 54 percent to Bush's 46 percent. Bill and Pat Buckley sent Bush a three-word telegram: "We are heartbroken."[6] Bush replied that one of his few consolations that year was James L. Buckley's election to the Senate.[7]

After Nixon named Bush Ambassador to the United Nations in late 1970, the Buckleys and Bushes saw each other often. Buckley interviewed Bush on *Firing Line,* and Bush hosted the staff of *National Review* at a dinner at his official residence at the Waldorf Astoria. In his thank-you letter to Bush for his hospitality, Buckley said that he was grateful for the opportunity to get to know Bush's "extraordinary wife" better.[8] Thus began a lively correspondence between Buckley and Barbara Bush. Their letters are chattier than those Buckley exchanged with Nancy Reagan, but less flirtatious and less policy oriented. When Bush left the UN in 1973 to become Chairman of the Republican National Committee, Buckley told Bush that he had "brought more distinction" to the position he was vacating than any of his predecessors. At the Republican National Committee, Bush often consulted with Buckley on political strategy.

Shortly after Nixon's resignation, Buckley wrote the new President, Gerald Ford, urged him to select Bush as the next Vice President, and informed Bush of what he had done. "I am sorry it happened as it did," Buckley wrote Bush after Ford chose Nelson Rockefeller, "but I am pleased, as you should be, that your name figured so prominently."[9] The two maintained lengthy exchanges on the evolution of Sino-American relations during Bush's tenure as U.S. liaison to the People's Republic of China and sent each other books annotated in various spots with their own thoughts. In the time Bush served as Director of Central Intelligence, he and Buckley saw each other frequently at the Bohemian Grove Club, where they bunked together in the "Hillbillies" cabin and competed at horseshoes and dominoes.

In the run-up to the 1980 presidential primaries, Buckley reminded Bush of the "antecedent commitment" he had made to Bush's major rival, Reagan, a dozen years earlier. He added that he very much looked forward to helping Bush become President one day, just not in 1980. Buckley voiced annoyance when Bush, having been criticized for his membership in the Council on Foreign Relations, resigned from the organization. Wrote Buckley in his column:

> In recent days, presidential candidate George Bush resigned his membership in the Council on Foreign Relations, the New York–based organization viewed as subversive by those American right-wingers who specialize in ignorance. I have been a lackadaisical member of the CFR for a half-dozen years (other commitments absorb me), but my mere membership in it is responsible for three-quarters of the kook-mail that comes into the office. Poor George Bush, at one point a director of CFR, . . . feels that resigning his membership is the expedient thing to do, if only to save postage required to answer patiently the number of people who would be denouncing him as a pro-communist or a "One World-er" or as an Instrument of the Rockefeller Interests (the three most frequently leveled charges against the CFR).[10]

After Reagan had secured the 1980 GOP presidential nomination, Buckley actively promoted Bush for the second spot on the ticket both in his column and behind the scenes. Acknowledging Buckley's congratulatory message after the Reagan-Bush ticket triumphed in the fall election, Bush, mindful of conservative suspicions of him, assured Buckley of his fealty to Reagan. He also expressed his disappointment that James L. Buckley, this time running in Connecticut, had failed in his attempt to return to the Senate.[11] (He lost to Christopher Dodd, 56 percent to 43 percent.)

Buckley was delighted when the Vice President, after reading an article Buckley's son, Christopher, had published in *Esquire*, retained the younger Buckley as his speechwriter.[12] Christopher remained in the post for eighteen months. In a letter to Bush, Buckley wrote of the mutual affection between the two clans and of the importance he and Bush placed on family: "I remember your telling me one day at the Grove, shortly after Our Leader [Reagan] disappointed you by coming out against George, Jr., that by God family is everything. By God, you're right. Your treatment of Christopher has meant a great deal to me. I have already attempted in some small way to reciprocate this by trying to help brother Pres. [Prescott]."[13] Buckley considered it another personal kindness when Bush suggested that Reagan bestow the Presidential Medal of Freedom posthumously upon Whittaker Chambers.[14] As President, Bush bestowed the same honor on Buckley in 1991.

During Reagan's presidency, George and Barbara Bush periodically congratulated Buckley on his television performances. A typical letter from Barbara read: "Talking to my only and favorite daughter the other morning and she almost said, 'Hang up, Ma, I'm watching Bill Buckley crush Phil Donahue' & I . . . watched. He's a dreadful man and you masterfully made all his hate show."[15]

A year later, Barbara informed Buckley that he had misstated her husband's position on gun control. It was not George, she explained, who advocated greater gun control, but she. Mrs. Bush also took issue with Buckley's reference to activist Richard Viguerie as a "distinguished conservative" and asked who considered him such. "Not me," she added. Mindful that she was writing to a journalist, the First Lady instructed Buckley that her comments were not for attribution.[16] Buckley was much impressed by Barbara Bush's feistiness. "Had a marvelously funny letter from your inimitable wife," he wrote Bush. He delighted in how she lamented her inability "to bring" George around on gun control.[17]

As he had done with Nixon, Ford, and Reagan, Buckley did not hesitate to criticize Bush in print. In a column entitled "Bush Has Got It Wrong," he chastised the Vice President for allegedly requesting that Saudi sheiks restrict oil production to "regularize" prices.[18] Buckley had long favored breaking the power of OPEC through increased domestic production, which he hoped a tax on imported oil might spur. Bush, concerned that Buckley's readers would think the Vice President favored higher prices at the pump, faulted Buckley for relying on press accounts of what he had told the Saudis. Perhaps in an attempt to rein Buckley in, Bush added that Reagan had read what the Vice President had actually said to the Saudis and stated that he was in total agreement.

Buckley replied that Bush had read a truncated version of what he had written. He joked that one should not "take such liberties with great writers!"[19] He also let Bush know that he objected to the Vice President's attempt to pull rank on him by invoking Reagan's opinions and for implying that, had Buckley been aware of Reagan's position, he would have trimmed his sails. "I make it a point," he wrote, "never to argue with el Presidente when we write or converse—I just state my position, and will merely re-state it here."[20]

In the run-up to the 1988 presidential primaries, Bush courted Buckley assiduously in the hope that Buckley would proclaim him the "rightward most viable" contender for the GOP presidential nomination.[21] Days after he appeared on *Firing Line* with his likely Republican rivals, he wrote Buckley, in what may have been a pitch for his support, that "those who were a little cautious about accepting his [Reagan's] words [that he had not known about the diversion of funds to the Contras] are not going to look very strong" after all the facts have been revealed.[22]

Yet, to Bush's disappointment, Buckley insisted that neither he nor *National Review* would endorse any candidate before the 1988 primaries had gotten under way.[23] This was somewhat of a departure from the approach he had taken with regard to Goldwater in 1964, Nixon in 1968, and Reagan in 1980. Buckley's caution undoubtedly reflected—and perhaps perpetuated—lingering conservative suspicions of Bush. *Newsweek* had run a cover story on the "wimp factor," questioning whether Bush had sufficient fortitude to follow in Reagan's footsteps. Conservative columnist George F. Will likened Bush as Vice President to a lapdog.[24] Another reason for Buckley's hesitancy to endorse Bush early was his growing respect for Congressman Jack Kemp, who had been a guiding force behind Reagan's tax cuts.

Buckley suggested that Bush might develop a public persona distinctive from Reagan's without criticizing the retiring President. "Bush should not be understood as seeking to slay his father," he wrote, "but as preparing to leave his father's house, prepared to inhabit his own."[25] He was far from impressed with the acceptance speech Bush delivered upon receiving his much-sought nomination. Bush, he said, had made a mistake by not asking anything of his followers. In his view, the nominee came across as believing that all that was needed was for voters to put Bush in the cockpit, where he would depress a few levers like "no new taxes," ending pollution, and improving schools.[26] In his reaction to Bush's acceptance speech, Buckley may have been influenced to some degree by Nancy Reagan's reported disdain for Bush's comment that he wanted to lead a "kinder and gentler" America. She was reported to have said, "Than who?"[27]

As the campaign progressed, Buckley showed disappointment that Bush did not echo Reagan's tough line regarding Soviet ambitions, seemed less committed than Reagan to SDI, and could not "crank himself up into criticizing any of the wastrel programs in which Washington is permanently engaged."[28] Still, Buckley insisted, Bush was "conservative by instinct" and thus preferable to his opponent, Massachusetts Governor Michael Dukakis, to whom Buckley referred as "the little technocrat from Brookline."[29]

As summer turned to fall, Buckley diverted his attention from presidential politics to indulge a favorite pastime, undermining Connecticut's liberal Republican Senator, Lowell Weicker. With no Republican having challenged Weicker in the primary that year and with pundits giving Republicans no chance of regaining control of the Senate in 1988, Buckley deemed it safe to commit another act of political heresy, one that would prove more popular with conservatives than had his previous endorsement of Allard Lowenstein. He declared his outright support for Weicker's Democratic opponent, Connecticut Attorney General Joseph Lieberman. Lieberman, Buckley noted, "applauded Reagan's use of military force in Grenada, his bombing of Libya, and his deployment of naval forces to keep open the sea channel in the Persian Gulf." Weicker had been critical of all these actions, Buckley noted.[30]

Buckley had known Lieberman from the time the Democratic candidate chaired the *Yale Daily News* in the 1960s. At a time when the Yale campus had become a hotbed of left-leaning activity, Lieberman, although he had opposed the war in Vietnam, had never disparaged U.S. troops. Buckley had followed Lieberman's writings and subsequent career. He relished the opportunity to defeat a longtime irritant while also helping to elect a friend who would be in agreement with his positions at least some of the time. Buckley made sure to keep Reagan apprised of the state of the senatorial contest in Connecticut. He sent the President a pro-Lieberman column he would be publishing and promised not to let anyone know he had shown the piece to Reagan. "But I could not withhold the sheer pleasure of it from you and Nancy," he added to his note.[31]

The column, in the form of a self-interview, announced the formation of "Buckleys for Lieberman," or "BuckPac." "The future of self-government," Buckley proclaimed, "depends on retiring Weicker from the Senate." He made clear that his PAC would use the words "Weicker" and "Horse's Ass" interchangeably. At the piece's end, he supplied a mailing address to which readers could send donations.[32] Two similar columns followed. *National Review* set up a regular campaign feature, "Weicker Watch," which featured anti-Weicker comments from readers. It also pitched anti-Weicker bumper stickers at $2. After Lieberman won, Buckley proudly shared in the credit. A *National Review* headline shouted, "buck-pac kills!"[33] By his own admission, Buckley threw himself more energetically into defeating Weicker than he did to electing Bush, whose success he considered a virtual certainty from start to finish.

As Bush reached his first hundred days in office, Buckley reported that while the new chief executive had faced no dramatic crisis in that time, neither had he conveyed a clear sense of mission. He termed Bush's budget proposals "a coterie of concessions, abstractions, and hallucinations that an inventive polemicist might describe as 'voodoo.'"[34] (This was a reference to a criticism Bush had made of Reagan's economic proposals before the 1980 New Hampshire primary. Reagan had promised reduced taxes, a balanced budget, and a major defense buildup.) On the positive side, Buckley proclaimed the new President's inherent good nature a national asset. Yet he bemoaned Bush's reluctance to acknowledge the aspirations for independence of former Soviet satellites in Eastern

Europe and what Buckley considered Bush's insufficient, even timid, response to the Chinese government's suppression of student protests in Beijing's Tiananmen Square.[35]

Taking a cue from Reagan, Bush paid a visit to *National Review*'s Washington, DC, office. Unlike Reagan's much-anticipated and carefully orchestrated appearance, Bush's was more spontaneous, with the President speaking off the cuff. While friendly, Bush articulated no agenda toward which he and his hosts might work in pursuit of common goals. "I was unprepared for your coming and apologize for not having come up with something brighter and more scintillating," Buckley wrote the President afterward.[36]

Nine months into Bush's term, Buckley expressed concern that the passage of the INF Treaty in 1988 combined with the positive media Gorbachev was receiving in the West had lulled Americans and their government into a false sense of security. Despite its economic difficulties, the USSR was still in command of twelve thousand nuclear warheads, he noted. He was dismayed that Bush had trimmed the administration's annual appropriation request for the SDI from Reagan's proposed $5.9 billion to $4.9 billion, and that the Senate had further reduced it to $4 billion and the House to $3.1 billion. Considered in the context of China's selling missiles to Middle Eastern countries—and the possibility of a "madman" appearing on the scene—Buckley warned that history might remember Bush as a President who "forfeited historical opportunities."[37]

By year's end, Buckley had grown concerned enough to write several columns and to commission numerous articles on how Bush should handle what remained of the Soviet threat. He sent them to Bush, joking that if he followed their advice, Bush would win the Nobel Peace Prize. He requested that the President acknowledge receipt of the enclosures with the words, "I got your interesting letter."[38] "I hope this acknowledgement passes muster," Bush replied. In his own hand he penned at the bottom, "Yes, I got your interesting letter."[39] Reagan's successor rarely engaged in the kind of intensive back-and-forth on policy Buckley had conducted with Reagan.

As Bush and the Democratic Congress quarreled over the size of domestic spending and deficit reduction, Buckley conceded that new revenues were needed, given that the deficit in 1990, exacerbated by the collapse of the savings and loan industry, stood at $200 billion, three times what it had been a decade earlier. With the Democrats pressing to raise marginal tax rates, Buckley publicly warned, "The moment one begins to steepen the progressive rate the slippery slope becomes icy."[40] He called Bush's acquiescence to raising the top marginal tax from 28 percent to 31 percent the most prominent political-moral event of 1990. Bush's going back on a pledge his supporters expected him to keep ("no new taxes") reminded Buckley of the disappointment he felt in his teens when Wendell Willkie, having denounced policies FDR pursued in 1939 and 1940 on the grounds that they would bring the country closer to war, not only embraced them after the 1940 election but proclaimed his prior criticisms mere "campaign oratory."[41] In Buckley's eyes, Bush's surrender to his critics—without so much as offering a reasoned explanation as to why he was changing course—was nothing less than an "arrant act of hypocrisy" and a breach of faith with his most loyal supporters.[42]

In the fall of 1990, Buckley announced at *National Review*'s thirty-fifth anniversary celebration that he would step down as editor. "We did as much as anybody, with the exception of himself, to shepherd into the White House Ronald Reagan," Buckley said of his magazine.[43] He passed the post and its accompanying responsibilities to John O'Sullivan and assumed for himself the title of "Editor at Large." He would continue to be a visible presence and a source of influence through his column, television show, lectures, and novels.

In the run-up to Operation Desert Storm, Buckley paused to consider whether the President as Commander in Chief had the constitutional authority to send U.S. forces into combat and under what circumstances. The Cold War and the sense of urgency it interjected into presidential decision making having ended, Buckley was restating the traditional conservative view that Congress possessed the ultimate authority to take the nation into war. He noted that the United Nations Participation Act of 1945 required that Congress approve the number and types of armed forces to be placed at the Security Council's disposal. Still, the act provided that the President "shall not be deemed to require the authorization" of Congress for the use of military force per se. Truman's conclusion that he did not need congressional authorization to commit U.S. troops to enforce a UN "police action" in Korea, Buckley said, had tilted the scales in the traditional struggle between the two branches in the executive's favor.[44] Still, he called for Congress to provide the President with guidance in the form of a vote.[45]

Although he conceded that, given the Truman precedent, the President had the authority to act on his own, he was appalled that Bush, like Truman before him, would seek an international body's permission to send U.S. forces into battle but seemed unwilling to make his case before the U.S. Congress. He cited in agreement an observation of his fellow commentator Charles Krauthammer: "There is something crazy about a secretary of state going around the world begging and bribing a half-dozen countries (China, the Soviet Union, France and others) to allow—allow!—American boys to go fight and die in the sands of Arabia. Yet such is the current American fascination with multilateralism that this absurd activity is considered normal."[46] When Bush decided to request a congressional resolution in support of Operation Desert Storm, Buckley praised this decision and urged Congress to give its assent. Turning down the request, he warned, would signal the end of the United States as a superpower.[47]

After U.S. forces quickly restored Kuwaiti independence, Buckley was effusive in his praise:

> Whatever byways on the road to this final third act George Bush may have missed, this is the time to adjourn any complaints about them and to concentrate on an ennobling performance. Bush gave the reasons for the stand he took in August; he persuaded all but the un-persuadable . . . that the challenge posed by the aggression of Saddam Hussein threatened nothing less than the stability of the entire world. His success in marshaling the vote of the Security Council . . . is a feat that will live in diplomatic history. His understanding with his generals, with whom he has with exact correctness shared responsibilities—his political, theirs military—is exemplary.[48]

In the run-up to Operation Desert Storm, Buckley became embroiled in a second controversy that would have a more significant impact upon the state of the conservative movement than the stand he had taken on the first U.S. war against Iraq. On the television program *The McLaughlin Group*, Pat Buchanan, former communications adviser to Nixon and Reagan with whom Buckley had once collaborated, said, "There are only two groups that are beating the drums for war in the Middle East—the Israeli Defense Ministry and its amen corner in the United States."[49] The language Buchanan used to clothe his opposition to using force to repel Saddam Hussein's invasion of Kuwait was not all that different from that which Charles Lindbergh had used on September 11, 1941, when he told a gathering of America First in Des Moines, "The three most important groups who have been pressing this country toward war are the British, the Jewish, and the Roosevelt administration."[50] Weeks earlier, on the same television program, Buchanan had referred to the U.S. Congress as "Israeli occupied territory."[51]

In a column in which he criticized several commentators who argued in favor of an American invasion, all of them Jewish, Buchanan wrote: "'The civilized world must win this fight,' the editors thunder. But, if it comes to war, it will not be the 'civilized world' humping up that bloody road to Baghdad; it will be American kids with names like McAllister, Murphy, Gonzales, and Leroy Brown."[52] While stopping short of pronouncing Buchanan "anti-Semitic," Buckley said that Buchanan was "saying anti-Semitic things."[53] In response to those, like A. M. Rosenthal of the *New York Times,* who faulted him for not declaring Buchanan an anti-Semite, Buckley suggested that it was possible for someone to utter anti-Semitic statements without being anti-Semitic, just as it is possible someone to say stupid things without necessarily being stupid.[54]

Buckley said he agreed with Buchanan that supporters of Israel, many of them Jewish, asserted a disproportionate influence on U.S. foreign policy. But he declared this a good thing, given that America and Israeli interests so often coincided. Buckley found Buchanan's suggestion that Jews avoided military service, leaving others to fight in their stead, and his assumption that all Jews were similar in their political and national security views likely to provoke "hostility against those deemed to exert inordinate influence on US public policy."[55] He concluded that Buchanan's remarks in these instances were not only anti-Semitic but, possibly, incendiary. While he detected a decline in the "country club" anti-Semitism his father and many of his generation displayed, Buckley discerned a rise in the more virulent kind and was troubled by it.

Buckley's criticisms of Buchanan made headlines comparable to those that followed his denunciations of Robert Welch a quarter century earlier. And, as his comments had then, his criticisms of Buchanan drew praise from many who disagreed with him a good deal of the time. Much of the mainstream media praised Buckley for his willingness and ability to exert discipline within his movement by pronouncing certain views and use of language as unacceptable. Writing in the *New Yorker,* Paul Berman lamented that liberals lacked anyone within their camp who could exert an influence that was in any way comparable to that which Buckley commanded among conservatives.[56] Buckley's criticisms of Buchanan, liberal columnist Richard Cohen concluded, had stripped Buchanan of any pretense of being a responsible spokesman for the conservative movement.[57]

New York Times columnist William Safire, a conservative and, like Buchanan, a former Nixon speechwriter, speculated that Buchanan had visions of forging a coalition between the nativist Right and the isolationist Left with the possible intention of bringing the two together in a new political party. He praised Buckley for taking Buchanan on.[58] "You should pay special attention to the issue [of *National Review*] you will receive about the time you get this letter," Buckley wrote Reagan.[59] At his behest, *National Review* devoted its year-end issue in 1991 to Buckley's article "In Search of Anti-Semitism," which he later expanded into a book by the same title.[60]

As the afterglow of Bush's successful management of Operation Desert Storm receded, Buckley returned his focus to Bush's handling of the economy. In September 1991, he called for the removal or resignation of Richard Darman, the Director of the Office of Management and Budget and the perceived architect of Bush's capitulation to the Democrats on tax hikes. He held the OMB Director primarily responsible for reversing economic progress the country had made under Reagan. Turning his fire upon Bush's erstwhile liberal critics, Buckley found it no surprise that those who had railed so hard against the "Reagan deficits" fell largely silent once Bush and Darman ceded to them much of what they wanted: higher top marginal rates, increased regulation, and increased government spending.[61] He passed along a comment by a Democratic Congressman he thought prophetic: "The ways things are going, a year from now, it could be Saddam Hussein still in power and George Bush out."[62]

Buckley spent much of 1992 reminding Bush and his team that Republicans had won the last three presidential elections largely because of their economic agenda. He was troubled that Bush, now under fire from Buchanan, who was now opposing the President for the 1992 presidential nomination on a populist platform, rather than defend his free trade agenda and make a strong case for cutting the capital gains tax, tried to cast himself in the role of an "ordinary" man. Rather than feign a personality that was not his own, Buckley suggested that Bush remind voters of the reasons they had elected him and make the necessary policy corrections.[63] Bush's now-abandoned "no new taxes pledge," Buckley said, had been the "hard anchor that protected" him from leftist inroads. By going back on his promise, he continued, the President had detached himself from the conservative base whose confidence he had worked so hard to bring into his corner.[64]

As he chided Bush for trying to present himself as a "regular guy," Buckley took on presidential critics who insisted that because of Bush's upper-class background and lifestyle he could not empathize with regular Americans. Attempting to shift the onus from the President onto himself, Buckley wrote, "I have never seen a professional baseball game," nor had he viewed "an episode of 'Dallas,' or of 'Roseanne,' or 'Geraldo,' or the black lady, who is alternately fat and thin, I forget her name."[65] None of this, he argued, rendered him indifferent to human anxieties, problems, or vexations.

As New Hampshire primary voters prepared to go to the polls, Buckley, still trying to move Bush rightward, surprised and confused both his allies and his critics when he urged conservatives to vote for Pat Buchanan as a "protest" against Bush's handling of the economy and for his going back on his "no new taxes" pledge. Conservatives, he maintained, always had the option of supporting Bush at a later time, should he return to the fold. Buckley's counsel was identical to that he had given conservatives twenty years earlier, when he endorsed John Ashbrook in the New Hampshire primary over President Richard

Nixon. Then, however, he had not preceded his endorsement of the protest candidate with stinging criticism of the kind he had levied against Buchanan.

After Buchanan received over 40 percent of the vote in New Hampshire, Buckley argued that the maverick had made his point, that an important message had been sent to the President, and that unless Buchanan believed that Bush's "convictionless conservatism" was so dangerous that only his replacement by a Democrat could bring conservatives to return to first principles, it was time for conservatives to rally behind Bush. He recalled that exactly twenty years earlier, while Buckley had been traveling with Nixon's party through China, Buchanan made the identical argument to him with regard to the possible damage a continued Ashbrook campaign could do to Nixon's reelection. Buckley concluded that Bush's support for a cut in the capital gains tax, his judicial appointments, and his foreign policy achievements, to say nothing of the possible loss of Republican seats in Congress should he be defeated, were sufficient reason to reelect him.[66]

Buckley certainly did not consider Bush's eventual Democratic opponent, Arkansas Governor Bill Clinton, a self-proclaimed "new Democrat," a suitable replacement for the President. He speculated as to how Clinton might govern: "Balance the budget by paying for abortions, expanding child care, increasing taxes on the wealthy (and therefore diminishing revenues from them), speeding up civil rights protection for homosexuals, promulgating universal medical insurance, requiring unpaid leave for workers during family emergencies, indexing the minimum wage, renewing the infrastructure, and demobilizing all those military units that aren't absolutely needed to protect the spotted owl."[67]

With regard to foreign policy, Buckley joked that the Democrats' return to power might not endanger American security—because with the Soviet Union gone, they would have no one to surrender to. He faulted Bush for not touting his foreign policy credentials more than he had and suggested that his administration had "grown intellectually lazy."[68] With Bush unwilling to fight and Clinton, the purported "new" (fiscally conservative) Democrat, working overtime to ingratiate himself with the "old" (high-taxing and big-spending) Democrats who still dominated his party, Buckley was not surprised that the independent candidate Ross Perot led in the public opinion polls when the Democrats convened in New York to nominate Clinton. With rumors circulating that Bush might drop Vice President Dan Quayle as his running mate, Buckley suggested Department of Housing and Urban Development Secretary Jack Kemp as Quayle's replacement. Kemp, he wrote, had "a kind of communicable optimism George Bush simply lacks." Aware of Bush's purported dislike of Kemp, Buckley noted that Bush well knew from experience that "vice presidents can be sequestered."[69]

Buckley castigated Bush's team for making Clinton's character, rather than Bush's agenda for a second term, the major theme of the Republican National Convention and of his general election campaign. Ex-President Reagan's address at the convention, which also proved to be his farewell address to public life, was the only memorable or uplifting aspect of the convention. Reagan, Buckley wrote, retained the "aptitude to amuse while deriding." He especially liked Reagan's humorous retort to assertions Democrats made at their own convention: "They kept telling us with straight faces that they're for family values, they're for a strong America, they're for less intrusive government—And they call *me* an *actor*."[70]

As the election neared, the best argument Buckley could make for Bush was that, in contrast to his opponents, he was a "reluctant statist."[71] In making this anemic endorsement, Buckley expressed regret that Bush had neglected opportunities to alert the public to the harm Clinton's promises to expand entitlements and increase spending would do to the economy. In a clear indictment of Bush for failing to advance the conservative cause, Buckley, evoking his magazine's founding statement, commented, "George Bush has not looked the zeitgeist in the face, and said to it that, in his second term, he will stand athwart it, yelling stop."[72] Reading these words written by a friend of over forty years must have been painful for Bush. In the end, Buckley gave Bush a tepid endorsement, declaring him the least objectionable of three candidates.

After the election, Buckley chastised Bush for having authorized his surrogates to imply that there was something suspicious about Clinton's applying for a visa to visit the Soviet Union while he was studying at Oxford. To have done so without evidence, Buckley pronounced, was "just plain stupid," bordering on the "grotesque."[73] Buckley was less willing than others on the right or the Bush administration to disparage Clinton's patriotism. While he declined to speculate on the ethics of the machinations Clinton went through to avoid military service (using political contacts to obtain entry into the ROTC as a means to join the National Guard as opposed to a branch of the military, and later resigning and exposing himself to the draft, reasonably certain he would not be called due to his having drawn a high number in a national draft lottery), Buckley pronounced Clinton's actions typical of those many young men in similar circumstances had faced in the latter years of the Vietnam War. Several of his protégés and young admirers had sought his counsel on their own dilemmas regarding the draft. At the time, Buckley had tempered his own support for the war once he concluded that the United States would not press on to military victory. He also sensed real "torment" in the language the youthful Clinton had used in his letter to military personnel who had assisted him in gaining entry into the ROTC and to whom he explained his opposition to the war and his desire to avoid service in a way that allowed him to remain politically "viable."[74] Buckley was certain that, if given a choice between living his life in Canada or serving in the military, Clinton would have opted for the latter.

Although he initially praised Clinton's decision not to answer questions about his private life, Buckley looked askance at the candidate's tendency to respond to questions with nondenials. After the *National Enquirer* ran a story in which a woman named Gennifer Flowers claimed that she had maintained a longtime affair with him, Clinton said that she had been paid for the interview. Informed by an interviewer on CBS's *60 Minutes* that a poll reported 14 percent of Americans would not vote for a known adulterer, Clinton was quick to point out that 86 percent would.

After listening to this particular exchange, Buckley suggested that the media set standards outlining what questions were appropriate to ask presidential candidates. Direct questions about whether they had committed adultery, he argued, should be off limits.[75] (In response to such questions in the interview, Clinton confessed to having had "troubles" in his marriage and demanded that he receive credit for being more candid about his personal life than had previous presidential contenders.) On the degree to which voters should consider a candidate's "character" in deciding upon that contender's suitability for high office, Buckley, citing William Bennett, author of *The Book of Virtues*, drew a distinction between private and public character: "The 'private' character has to do with whether or not he has lived scrupulously by his wedding vows; the public character has to do with whether he has deceived the American people."[76] Clinton's behavior as President would lead Buckley to conclude that there were instances in which the public and the private definitions of "character" intersected, such as when a public official lies under oath to conceal a private action.

With regard to questions other than about Clinton's patriotism or his marital fidelity, Buckley extended the Democratic contender few benefits of many doubts that arose during and after the 1992 presidential campaign. Clinton, he felt, obfuscated more than was necessary, even for a politician. Buckley voiced exasperation at how Clinton responded when asked whether he had ever smoked marijuana. The Governor said that he had tried it while a graduate student at Oxford, that he did not inhale, that he disliked it, and that he had not broken the laws of his country. Buckley found Clinton's answer both peculiar and beset with too many qualifications. He was most troubled by Clinton's defense that he had not broken the laws of his country, noting that at the time, marijuana use was illegal in the United Kingdom.

Buckley contrasted Clinton's answer with how he himself had responded to an identical question on *The Tonight Show* in the late 1960s, around the time Clinton was studying in England. Buckley had told host Johnny Carson that he had smoked marijuana at sea, beyond the reach of any nation's drug laws. When Carson inquired how the marijuana had made it onto his boat, Buckley replied, to the delight of the audience, "parthenogenesis."[77] Buckley could not comprehend what Clinton intended to convey by saying he had not "inhaled." Had Clinton simply said that he smoked marijuana once and did not like it, Buckley suggested, he would not have lost a single vote—save those of gag writers.[78]

Buckley saw Clinton's refusal to say whether he supported Operation Desert Storm ("I guess I would have voted with the majority if it was a close vote. But I agree with the argument the minority made") as an attempt to be all things to all people. He also detected a tendency on Clinton's part to play the demagogue when it suited his purpose. As evidence, he cited what he believed to be Clinton's deliberate distortion of California Governor Jerry Brown's position on abortion. Clinton had run an ad in which Brown was quoted as saying he was opposed to abortion. It did not mention that Brown wished neither to outlaw abortion nor to bar the use of federal funds for the procedure. Buckley called Clinton's action "the filthiest single act of political theater in a dirty campaign season." By its logic, a person opposed to smoking cigarettes could be presumed to be against the sale of cigarettes.[79]

Buckley found Clinton as a candidate and as President deficient in at least three respects. First, he believed that, at his core, Clinton was hardly the "New Democrat" he claimed to be. Buckley saw Clinton's support for welfare reform, balanced budgets, and free trade as positions carefully calculated to attract votes he needed to win. Second, he disliked Clinton's reliance on what Theodore Roosevelt had termed "weasel words," phrases intended to give disparate elements of his audience the impression that he agreed with them, while always allowing himself an escape hatch. Clinton's rhetoric proved a cornucopia of such words and phrases: "I will reform welfare *as we know it*"; "I won't raise taxes on the middle class to *pay for my programs*"; and the infamous "It depends on what the meaning of the word *is* is."[80] Finally, Buckley found Clinton's moral compass and grounding more than wanting.

Buckley criticized Clinton when he proposed raising the top marginal tax rate to 36 percent, and, again when Clinton sought a series of spending increases. All of this, in Buckley's eyes, represented wrongly applied idealism, which he thought constituted so much of contemporary liberalism. "It is increasingly apparent," he wrote, "that President Clinton and his economic advisers are either much dumber than is really believable, or else they are engaged in disingenuous analysis done one part by tendentious arithmetic, one part by a refusal to face realities." He also criticized Clinton's use of "Orwellian" language to justify domestic spending increases as "investments" and "incentives."[81]

Buckley thought Clinton's spending increases would move money out of the private sector, the source of jobs and the true generator of economic growth, and into the hands of government, which he considered less efficient in the allocation of goods and services. Since Buckley conceded that Clinton was by every assessment extraordinarily intelligent, he found no plausible explanation for the President's actions other than sheer opportunism. Clinton's budgetary proposals, he said, were nothing other than "payback" to voting blocs and special interests that had helped make Clinton President. "For all Bill Clinton likes to think of himself as the reincarnation of American idealism," Buckley wrote, "he has the capacity to vulgarize much that he touches."[82]

Buckley objected to what he considered Clinton's deliberate distortion of Reagan's economic record in order to make his own agenda appear palatable to political commentators. Clinton, as Buckley saw it, sought to rewrite history by mischaracterizing the Reagan tax cuts and what they produced. According to the new President, only wealthy individuals benefited by what Reagan had wrought. Clinton, Buckley argued, conveniently ignored private sector investment that worked its way through the entire economy, resulting in the creation of 18 million new jobs in the course of Reagan's presidency. He saw Clinton's declaration that he would not "balance the budget on the backs of older Americans while protecting the wealthy" as rhetorically setting up a straw man. "Who asked him to?" Buckley inquired.[83]

Like most other conservatives, Buckley supported the North American Free Trade Agreement (NAFTA). In taking this stand, he parted company with some long-standing supporters, especially South Carolina textile magnate and *National Review* patron Roger Milliken. Perhaps to assure Milliken that the magazine's editors had taken his views into account, Buckley wrote a four-page essay in *National Review* in which he argued that free trade furthered conservative ideals by expanding consumer choice. "We looked at it very hard," he wrote, "examined it critically, and urged fellow conservatives to stand steady, joyful in our faith in the basic propositions of a free society."[84]

Buckley opposed Clinton's efforts to enact government-mandated health-care insurance (which the media dubbed "Hillarycare" in honor of the First Lady, whose aides designed it). Anticipating arguments others would make a generation later against "Obamacare," Buckley asked whether there were better ways to insure the then 37 million uninsured Americans without disturbing the coverage of all other Americans. A fifty-five-year-old schoolteacher who did not need coverage for pregnancy or, in all likelihood, alcohol abuse programs would pay as much as a "30-year old alcoholic libertine." He dismissed Clinton's proposal with the line: "It's spinach, and the hell with it."[85]

Much as he disagreed with Clinton's policies, Buckley readily conceded the President's skills as a public performer. He wrote of Clinton's "capacity to reflect awe and delight, as though every five minutes he was rushing down the stairs to look under the Christmas tree."[86] A month into his presidency, Buckley stated: "It is my feeling that Bill Clinton has the most salable political personality since John F. Kennedy. He gives the impression of total immersion in the problems of everybody . . . as though he has risen from a Baptist initiation with water coming out of every one of his pores, designed to wash away the problems of industrial workers, farmers, merchants, shipbuilders, gays, deficit watchers, the sick, the halt, and the lame."[87] On another occasion, he said, "Laurence Olivier plays many roles. If you stipulate somebody as a good actor, why should it surprise you when they act well? Is someone who's always sincere ever sincere?"[88]

Buckley detected in Clinton "the encroaching sense of the con man."[89] Clinton gave him the impression of having cultivated for public consumption the capacity to "smile a little" as he talked, which made him appear "genial." Buckley found the slight "crack" he heard in Clinton's voice ingratiating; he would not be surprised if both the smile and the slightly strained voice were the products of careful practice. The President's upswept hair conveyed "perpetual youth and energy."[90] Clinton was the inspiration for Reuben Castle, the lead character in Buckley's novel *The Rake* (2007).

When talk of impeachment surfaced early in Clinton's tenure, triggered by the Whitewater scandal (a purportedly fraudulent real estate venture for which one of the Clintons' partners, James McDougal, was eventually imprisoned), Buckley urged caution. Even if the worst suspicions proved true, he argued, impeachment was a "convulsive political act." He hoped that Clinton could be held to account by means short of it.[91] After Arkansas state employee Paula Jones sued the President for sexually harassing her while he was Governor, Buckley, while proclaiming Clinton a "moral swinger" and an "unregulated lecher," advised Republicans to go easy on him. He presumed that Clinton would find a way to settle with his accuser, offering an apology without admitting guilt.[92] (Clinton would later regret not having followed such advice.)

Buckley was delighted when the 1994 elections left Republicans in control of both the House of Representatives and the Senate for the first time in forty years. (They gained fifty-four seats in the House and nine in the Senate.) He was effusive in his praise of House Speaker–elect Newt Gingrich who, he said, promised much of what Buckley had been advocating for decades. He was particularly supportive of Gingrich's brainchild "The Contract with America," which placed a premium on congressional reform and accountability. He prophesized too that, Gingrich, "an assertive human being," would make enemies.[93]

Gingrich received the brunt of criticism from Democrats and the media after Congress and Clinton failed to agree on the size of the federal budget and the government shut down as a result of this impasse. Buckley conceded that in the short run, Clinton had gotten the better of his adversaries. He complained that he could not turn on his television without hearing Clinton "lecture . . . in a moralizing tone of voice that had become creepy."[94] Clinton's strategy had been to present himself as a fiscal conservative while accusing his adversaries of advocating irresponsible cuts in Social Security, Medicare, education, and the environment. Still, Buckley was not surprised when Clinton, whom he accused of putting convenience over conviction, moved away from his party's liberal base to find common ground with Republicans on welfare reform, deficits, trade, and taxes as he approached reelection. He also attributed Clinton's shift on such issues to Gingrich's tenacity.[95]

Buckley tore into Clinton with a vengeance after the country learned that the forty-nine-year-old chief executive had had a series of trysts with a twenty-one-year old White House intern.[96] Presidents, Buckley wrote, should control their appetites and act as appropriate role models. He wondered in print whether Clinton should be forced from office.[97] With Clinton not disposed to resign even as evidence mounted against him, Buckley increasingly looked to impeachment as the most appropriate way to hold the President to account. He doubted that Clinton would be able to talk his way out of this scandal, as he had so many others. "Given that Mr. Clinton has over and over again not told the truth," Buckley wrote, "he is speaking to a skeptical congregation."[98] After it was revealed that White House intern Monica Lewinsky paid the President thirty-seven private visits over sixteen months, Buckley wrote of Clinton's "inexhaustible hospitality."[99]

After Clinton acknowledged in an address to the American people on August 17, 1998, that he had not told the truth about his relationship with Lewinsky, Buckley admitted that the entire episode left him in a quandary. While he found nothing in what the President had done that met the constitutional standard for impeachment, he did not see how the country could simply put the matter aside.[100] In an imaginary interview with the biblical King Solomon, Buckley had the King work his way slowly and deliberately to the appropriate remedy Congress and the nation needed to apply: Clinton had to go, not because of the sex but because of his lapse in judgment. "To expose oneself to such a risk as Clinton had" (exposure, blackmail, security lapses, gossip) was sufficient cause for the imaginary Solomon to come down against the President. "To go on to deny everything only to be uncovered eight months later as a liar and a perjurer, was a critical misjudgment."[101]

Buckley's Solomon rejected "censure" as an alternative to impeachment on the grounds that this "compromise" allowed Clinton to retain the "usufructs of office," which were, for people who seek the presidency, one of its primary attractions. Clinton needed to be punished, Buckley's Solomon maintained, as his offenses warranted and, given the extent to which his repeated lack of judgment had led him, nothing less than removal from office would suffice. The fictional Solomon noted that Clinton had been alone with Lewinsky on thirty-seven occasions and that she discussed their trysts with eleven people. Here Buckley's reasoning ran in a direction contrary to that which he advised Congress to take with regard to Richard Nixon a generation earlier.[102] Then Buckley had argued that impeachment should not be used to punish a President, but to get rid of him. Now he was advocating impeachment as the appropriate punishment for actions he considered compromising to the security of the nation.

Buckley commented on the differences Nixon and Clinton had shown in their demeanor during their travails: "Good old Tricky Dick . . . always looked guilty, never so more than when he was facing the public and averring his innocence. His face was a polygraph. Clinton's face is that of the freshly minted altar boy. . . . We have looked at that face through Gennifer Flowers, draft resistance, marijuana non-smoking; through Vincent Foster, [Webb] Hubbell, the Lincoln Bedroom, Huangs, and what we see is something in the nature of incorrigibility."[103]

As the House Judiciary Committee prepared to hold public hearings on the Lewinsky matter, Buckley grew outraged at the "nomenklatura's" refrain that Clinton's transgressions should be overlooked so that his accomplishments as President, of which the public approved, would not be reversed.[104] He voiced impatience and annoyance at having to remind Clinton defenders that, were their champion to be removed from office, his successor would not be a Republican but Clinton's handpicked successor, Vice President Al Gore. Buckley sought to rally all conservatives to vote to remove Clinton from office, if only to uphold standards of personal and professional conduct on the part of public officials.[105] Congress, he said, should do its duty as a matter of "constitutional hygiene."[106]

Buckley did not consider that the Republicans' loss of five House seats in the aftermath of those hearings in the congressional elections of 1998 or Clinton's high approval ratings as reasons that Congress should not impeach the President.

"The sense of it all is that the elections made Clinton a folk hero," he wrote. "If he had screwed two interns, maybe he'd have carried Texas."[107] By his lights, the opportunity for the nation to uphold appropriate moral standards, especially in its public officials, trumped all arguments advanced in Clinton's defense: "A society is surely healthier when whoring is common but commonly disapproved than when it is common and commonly accepted."[108]

After the House approved two articles of impeachment, one for perjury and one for obstruction of justice, Buckley accepted that Clinton would escape conviction in the Senate, where Republicans held fifty-five seats and Democrats forty-five, and that the Constitution required a two-thirds majority to remove a President from office. Still, he considered a numerical majority vote in both houses against Clinton a "moral victory." History, Buckley wrote, would record that Clinton was "saved only by a non-democratic feature of the Constitution."[109] This was a paradoxical view for someone who had been skeptical about the wisdom of majoritarianism. It also ignored another reality: that given the malapportioned nature of the U.S. Senate, a majority of its members did not necessarily speak for a majority of the American people, a possible reason for the required two-thirds vote for conviction.

Buckley found in Joe Eszterhas's *American Rhapsody* an answer to a question he and many Americans pondered throughout Clinton's career: why would a man as politically gifted and as ambitious as he choose to live so much of his life on the edge and serially take risks that could prove his undoing? Eszterhas attributed these traits Clinton repeatedly exhibited to his having grown up amid the red neon of corrupt and oversexed Hot Springs, Arkansas, where everyone learned to lie routinely in order to protect someone else's feelings or reputation. Buckley concluded that Clinton perfected his "silver tongue" in the same manner as Jerry Lee Lewis had cultivated his piano style or Elvis Presley his singing voice.[110]

During the campaign to elect Clinton's successor, Republican candidate George W. Bush pledged to "elevate the office of the presidency." Buckley found that a low bar for any new President to meet. "Al Gore would do that," he observed, and "so would Ralph Nader."[111] Clinton's controversial eleventh-hour use of his presidential pardoning powers, in Buckley's view, shed additional light on the President's character. "Suppose that Denise Rich had never given money to the Clinton complex—would Marc Rich [the beneficiary of Clinton's most scandalous pardon] have been given five minutes time on pardon day? It is generally understood that it is only because Clinton is the kind of person who has a Mafia-type sense of favors given, favors returned, that he was approached in the first instance."[112]

Five years later, Buckley still found Clinton a baffling mix of optimism and self-confidence, a man with a flawed persona and a lack of conviction: "Well, I think Bill Clinton is the most gifted politician of, certainly of my time. There's nobody who can match him. He generates a kind of a vibrant goodwill with a capacity for mischief, which is very, very American, and a sense of survivability, which is dismaying. He gives the impression that nothing in the world can ultimately really hurt him. I don't think anybody could begin to write a textbook that explicates his political philosophy because he doesn't really have one."[113]

15

W: "Counting the Silver"

Buckley enjoyed less access to and exerted less influence on the administration of George W. Bush, the last President to serve during his lifetime, than with any Republican President since Nixon. Some of this was intentional. By the time Bush took office, Buckley was winding down.

A year before Bush was elected Buckley terminated his long-running television program, *Firing Line*, after a thirty-three-year run. (He purportedly told a friend that he had done so because he did not wish to "die on the set.") By the time Bush left office, Buckley had gone off the lecture circuit, surrendered a controlling interest over *National Review* to a board he had selected (although commentators, whether left, right, or center, would continue to refer to it as "Bill Buckley's magazine"), and cut back on his column from three times a week to twice. He exercised what influence remained to him through this column and his capacity to attract media coverage whenever he wished.

At the same time, partly because of Buckley's success in bringing conservatism from the fringes of American politics onto its main stage, multiple other conservative voices, with increasingly diverse opinions, made their way into the public square. Technological changes within the communications industry and legislative and regulatory accommodations transformed the ways ideas were transmitted. The repeal of the Fairness Doctrine (which had required radio programs to air opposing points of view) in 1987 and the Telecommunications Act of 1996, which allowed companies to own more stations and facilitated the syndication of radio programs, led to a proliferation of conservative talk radio. Conservative hosts and audiences gravitated to this medium because they perceived that people with their point of view were underrepresented and unwelcome on network and cable television.

The launching of the Fox News Channel in 1996 provided an additional outlet for conservative opinions and celebrities. It found its niche and grew its audience with the outbreak of numerous controversies and scandals during the Clinton era. After Bill Kristol, Fred Barnes, and John Podhoretz launched the *Weekly Standard* in late 1994, *National Review* was no longer the sole respectable venue for conservative intellectuals. Nor was Buckley the sole syndicated conservative columnist to whom right of center readers looked for guidance. George F. Will had launched his syndicated column through the *Washington Post* Writers Group in 1974, twelve years after Buckley began his. Others followed. And the Internet, of course, opened the public square to many other voices, whether affiliated with the traditional media or as independent bloggers.

While most conservatives who took to the airwaves, print, and the Internet in the last decades of his life showed deference to Buckley and honored him as the progenitor of their movement, the mere proliferation of right of center voices assured a rise of diversity of conservative opinion. President George W. Bush said at a White House ceremony honoring Buckley in 2005: "And today, we've got, of course, an abundance of conservative columnists and radio hosts and television shows and think tanks and all kinds of organizations. I guess in an intellectual sense, you could say these are all Bill's children. And like children, they grow up and go their own way."[1] No longer would there be a single voice speaking for the conservative movement. By the time Bush took office, even Buckley was no longer that voice.

Buckley took Bush to task during his presidency for compromises he made with Democrats on tax cuts and education policy, and for what he regarded as Bush's lack of fiscal discipline. While he praised Bush's resolve after the terrorist attacks of September 11, 2001, and initially supported the military actions Bush launched in Afghanistan and Iraq, Buckley came to oppose the President's efforts at "nation building" after the United States had toppled Saddam Hussein and U.S. forces failed to find the weapons of mass destruction Saddam was supposedly developing. Buckley's criticisms of Bush brought to the surface divisions within the conservative movement that had remained submerged during the Cold War. Even though most self-identified conservative opinion leaders did not voice objections similar to Buckley's, the administration, cognizant of his enduring influence with the conservative movement, the media, and the general public, pushed back against his criticisms. The situation also launched a debate over who spoke for the movement, and who had earned the right to do so.

Buckley was skeptical about Bush from the start of the 2000 presidential campaign. He considered Bush too tentative and insufficiently conservative when, for instance, he did not include school choice in his proposed educational reforms, and when he supported "free" prescription drugs for senior citizens. Buckley worried that too many conservative spokespeople and elected officials flocked to Bush in the hope that he would govern as a conservative without sufficiently vetting him.[2]

Yet he ultimately found Bush preferable to other contenders for the Republican nomination, though he cautioned his fellow conservatives to expect numerous disagreements with the Texas Governor should Bush become President. After twenty conservative opinion leaders had convened to discuss Bush's candidacy, Buckley described their collective mood as favorable to Bush's election, but fully expecting to have to "count the silver."[3]

Buckley did not take kindly to Bush's insertion of the adjective "compassionate" in front of "conservative" in characterizing his governmental philosophy. He considered the term "compassionate conservative" defensive, apologetic, and superfluous. Compassion should be discernible from a candidate's campaign, record in office, and life story, he asserted, and conservatism was a more positive philosophy than Bush and his handlers seemed to think.[4] His objection was reminiscent of Nancy Reagan's reaction to George H. W. Bush's call for a "kinder and gentler" nation when he accepted the 1988 Republican presidential nomination. (The First Lady was reported to have wondered out loud, "Than who?" when he uttered those words.)[5] In Bush, Buckley also saw echoes of Clinton's tendency to evade specifics and qualify his pledges, such as Bush's statement that he would continue to fund bilingual education "where it works."

He was also wary of Bush's personal qualities and political style and skeptical of his electability. Buckley acknowledged Bush's attraction to Hispanic voters and other nontraditional Republican constituencies, but he added that the Texan also appealed to "non-thinkers" and he saw in the candidate "a trace of indifference to the intellectual and artistic life" as well as a "rudimentary cultural intelligence" that led him to defer to those who were more knowledgeable than he.[6] "He may be indifferent to ballet, but he is not a Philistine," Buckley said.[7] Bush's choice of the "quiet operator" Richard "Dick" Cheney as his running mate drew his enthusiastic approval, as did Democratic nominee Al Gore's selection of Senator Joseph Lieberman, a longtime Buckley friend.

Buckley responded warmly to Bush's gracious side, which he witnessed when the candidate addressed the Alfred E. Smith dinner in New York City on the eve of the election. He praised Bush for his self-effacing humor and was especially taken with the generous tribute he paid his opponent, Vice President Al Gore, but did not comment on Bush's tongue-in-cheek comparison of himself with Buckley.[8] In addition to their alma mater, said Bush, the two had much in common: "Bill wrote a book at Yale; I read one. He founded the

Conservative Party. I started a few parties myself. Bill was certain he won every debate he had. Well, I know how he feels."[9]

Buckley discerned in Gore a "hunger for power" bordering on "mania."[10] He grew uneasy watching how Gore comported himself during the candidates' debates: audibly sighing while Bush was talking during their first joint appearance, crossing over onto Bush's side of the stage during another. Hours after the polls closed, with neither candidate able to claim a majority in the Electoral College, Buckley directed his humor at Florida's archaic voting mechanisms. He suggested that Democrats wanted to award most of the disputed ballots to Gore because Republican voters were more likely to obey voting instructions and therefore less likely to leave "dancing chads" on their ballots.[11] Taking note of Bush's popularity among senior citizens, Buckley urged more of them to move to Florida.[12] After the Supreme Court ended the Florida recount, effectively declaring Bush the winner of both the state and the Electoral College, Buckley anticipated that Democrats would seek to undermine Bush's legitimacy as President.[13]

Mindful of the voters' split decision, Buckley thought Bush should act in ways that reassured his base while not antagonizing those who had voted against him. He recommended that the new President work with Congress to abolish the inheritance tax and enact a ban on late-term abortions. He also pushed an idea that had intrigued him since his days at boarding school: requiring six months of voluntary service as a prerequisite for college admission. When Bush moved to cut taxes, Buckley played the dutiful soldier. He continued to believe, buoyed by Reagan's example, that cuts in marginal income tax rates would do more to stimulate economic growth than the "targeted" deductions and credits that Bush included in his tax-relief plan for middle-class households. Buckley urged the President's advisers to concentrate on the overall increase in revenues the plan would produce and on the economic growth that would follow.[14]

In the end, he deemed Bush's tax cuts (or any tax cuts) preferable to the status quo. Anything that chipped away at the progressivity in the tax code, which he thought the least fair method of raising revenues, Buckley favored: "If a government engages in redistributionist policies without any sense of the subordinate right to property, there are no theoretical limits to the progressivity of taxation."[15] He interpreted the palliatives and concessions Bush inserted into his tax proposals as attempts to blunt criticisms that the administration "favored the rich."

As he assessed Bush's other signature domestic issue, "No Child Left Behind," Buckley discerned a disturbing pattern in the President's whole approach to domestic policy: "Mr. Bush's tendency in the tax bill and the education bill has been to yield principle in order to effect legislation. Politicians need to do that, up to a point. But to assert principle gives perspective. That is useful to those congressmen who will listen, and to voters who seek to inform themselves about the character of their representatives."[16]

Years later, Buckley pronounced Bush "conservative" but "not a conservative," and certainly not "an active conservative."[17] He criticized Bush's failure to hold the line on spending, his refusal to take a definitive and forthright stand on certain social issues, and his proposal to establish a new entitlement (Medicare, Part D)—the last on grounds that it was unjust (taxing young workers to pay for prescription drugs for wealthy retirees). Early in Bush's presidency, Buckley noted that the budget surplus Bush inherited from Clinton was rapidly evaporating and the budget was veering into deficits. (Clinton had left a surplus in excess of $86 billion. At the end of FY 2001, the deficit was in excess of $32 billion. It rose to over $317 billion in FY 2002, $538 billion in 2003, and $567 billion in 2004. It then slowly declined until 2008, when it jumped to more than $641 billion.)

On federal spending overall, Buckley urged Bush to make greater use of his veto in standing up to lobbies and interest groups that used their clout to insert loopholes into the tax code.[18] "Never mind that George W. promised to reduce federal spending," he wrote near the end of 2003. "The fact of the matter is that he has not done so."[19] (Later in Bush's tenure, Buckley put the jump in nondefense discretionary spending under Bush at 35.7 percent.)[20] Other conservatives shared his dismay. Columnist Peggy Noonan wrote that had she known Bush was a "big spending Republican," or that he could not comprehend the "damage big spending does," she would not have voted for him.[21]

Bush also came up short on several social issues, in Buckley's view. He noted that the President had declared himself "pleased" that the Supreme Court found "diversity" a legitimate objective in hiring and in university admissions. As he had done with Nixon, Ford, Bush Sr., and even Reagan on occasion, Buckley admonished Bush "to concern himself with the care and feeding of American conservatives." These people of the Right, he wrote, were "men and women who believe that there are institutional matters that governments rightly concern themselves with that past generations have taken for granted."[22] Two issues he specifically mentioned were the display of the Ten Commandments on public property and the traditional view of marriage as between parties of opposite sexes.

After the terrorist attacks on the United States on September 11, 2001, Buckley envisioned a two-pronged American response: bringing Osama bin Laden to justice and launching an ideological war against bin Laden's brand of Muslim fundamentalism in a manner reminiscent of the "war of ideas" the West had waged against Soviet-style Communism after the Second World War. He took issue with Bush's comment, in a statement released from an Air Force base in Louisiana, that those who carried out the attacks were "cowards." That term, he said, did not apply to people who were willing to give up their lives to advance their fanatical aims.[23]

Buckley praised Bush for promising that the United States would act as harshly against governments and individuals who harbored terrorists as it did against the terrorists themselves. He urged that war against the Taliban be waged quickly, be massive in scope, and end with the death of bin Laden, and he suggested that the best way to honor the memory of victims of the 9/11 attacks was to abide by the principles that made the United States the object of the Islamists' special odium (respect for the rule of law, tolerance, freedom of speech and expression, equality before the law).[24] He also supported the administration's plan to try accused terrorists in military tribunals: "We should always give solicitous attention to liberty. . . . What we are struggling to do right now is to discover how 15 steel-willed enemies of the United States succeeded in destroying the two largest buildings in New York and one part of the Pentagon." Finding the hidden enemy would require both "Yankee ingenuity" and "a couple of days off for the American Civil Liberties Union."[25]

In the weeks that followed, Buckley, like the Bush administration, turned his sights on Saddam Hussein. Saddam, he noted, had acted in ways suggesting that he was developing weapons of mass destruction, had committed genocidal acts against the Kurds, used torture and poison gas against internal dissidents, and funded terrorist activity throughout the Middle East. Citing Laurie Mylroie's 2000 book, *Study of Revenge: Saddam Hussein's Unfinished War Against America*, a work that had found favor among those advocating an American invasion of Iraq, Buckley related that Saddam had sheltered Abdul Rahman Yasin, mastermind of the 1993 al Qaeda attack on the World Trade Center. The United States did not "need conclusive evidence of Iraq's participation in anti-US terrorism," he concluded, to issue Saddam an ultimatum to open his borders to uninhibited inspection, cease funding and encouraging terrorism, and surrender Yasin to U.S. authorities.[26]

Buckley vigorously defended Bush, as he had Reagan, when European elites dismissed the American President as "simplistic" or "bombastic" and questioned his intellectual acumen.[27] Buckley found the President's "elaboration of the truth" indicative of the character he brought to the presidency.[28] He liked that Bush made his points directly and showed an aversion to nuance. That Europeans referred to both presidents as "cowboys" was, in Buckley's book, a mark in their favor.

In response to Vice President Cheney's declaration that "the risks of inaction" toward Iraq outweighed the "risks of action" and his insistence that the United States had evidence that Saddam was pursuing nuclear weapons, Buckley demanded that the American people be told that they were already at war. It was "inconceivable," he wrote, that Cheney would have made that statement without sufficient evidence.[29] He found the case the U.S. government laid out against Saddam Hussein for violations of UN edicts and resolutions "unsparing in detail."[30] After Bush detailed in his 2003 State of the Union address the nature of the threat the administration believed Saddam posed to the United States and its allies, Buckley proclaimed the President a "fit leader" who had risen to the occasion.[31]

But he raised cautionary notes in the form of two questions as Bush prepared for war. First, if Saddam constituted a grave threat to U.S. security, why did it take the attacks of September 11 to arouse the American government to action? Second, how did Bush propose to defend American troops in the event that Saddam used weapons of mass destruction against invading forces?[32] After watching Bush's speech before the United Nations, in which he urged that body to enforce its own resolution calling for Saddam to suspend his weapons development program and approve a multinational invasion, Buckley passed along the thoughts of a student of rhetoric. Bush, Buckley's correspondent wrote, displayed a "plainspoken integrity that unites emotions and intellect."[33] In subsequent days, Buckley urged Bush to take action even without the support of the United Nations.[34]

In March 2003, Buckley voiced an area of disagreement with Bush that would grow in significance in the ensuing years. Once Saddam was removed from power, he said, it was unlikely the people of Iraq would opt for democracy, given the country's internal division between Sunni and Shia Muslims, and he questioned whether imposing democracy in the region was a worthy American objective. "Mr. Bush," he wrote, "would have done better to speak more modestly about expectations." Bush could accomplish the removal of a regime and its infrastructure, but "the Iraqi people will have to take it from there."[35]

After Bush stood on the USS *Abraham Lincoln* under a banner proclaiming "Mission Accomplished" and declared victory (in what proved to be only the first phase of a prolonged struggle), Buckley saluted the President on what he had achieved: the toppling of a barbarous regime without committing violence against civilians or destroying entire cities.[36] A month later, however, Buckley turned his attention to the other side of the ledger: the United States had failed to locate the weapons of mass destruction Saddam was said to have had and hidden. "Where is all this stuff?" he inquired. He posed a series of questions for the administration: "How was intelligence information, presented as conclusive, so apparently illusory? Who was it, on the assembly line between the first man who spotted what he took to be WMD activity in Iraq, and the Defense Intelligence Agency and the president . . . who beamed out to the world, not suspicions of WMD activity but affirmations of it, who screwed up? Who deceived, or was carried away? And what vaccines have our leaders taken to guard against other deceptions of like character?"[37]

A month later, citing developments on the ground in Iraq, Buckley called upon the U.S. government to abandon its policy of "nation building." He warned of a long insurgency: "The nation-changing program in Iraq is going muddily, and it is good news that the Iraqi guerillas don't have weapons of mass destruction at hand, but rifle fire and an occasional hand grenade serve their political purposes. There aren't enough to drive the coalition forces out of the country, but they are enough to give off a Chechnyan smell of perpetual armed resistance."[38]

In the run-up to the 2004 election, while confident that the President would win reelection, Buckley saw Bush going into the campaign with three vulnerabilities: a "style" some found "grating," easy spending practices, and continuing losses of American lives in Iraq.[39] In mid-March he added a fourth burden Bush would bear, having to reconcile the deteriorating situation in Iraq with the administration's reassurances that the war was under control and democracy was taking hold in a nation where it lacked roots. He found Bush's repeated assertions that progress was being made reminiscent of Lyndon Johnson's insistence, a generation earlier, that the United States "will not be defeated," "will not grow tired," and "will not withdraw" from Vietnam.[40]

When fighting turned particularly intense and costly in Fallujah, Buckley called upon Bush to explain in the clearest possible terms what was at stake for the United States in Iraq and why the President believed that an American withdrawal would undermine the United States' ability to assert its influence and leadership elsewhere in the world. The administration owed this explanation, Buckley insisted, to soldiers in the field, Iraqis who stood with the United States, other nations in the region, and above all the American people, who had seen six hundred of their own die trying to curtail the insurgency, to say nothing of the wounded. (U.S. fatalities in Iraq would reach four thousand before the American occupation ended.)

"Inspired leadership does not necessarily bring a democratic nation around," Buckley wrote about growing internal opposition to a continued U.S. presence in Iraq. He noted that voters had turned Churchill out of office after the Allies prevailed in World War II. An explanation was "critically needed."[41] "Even those who do not question the sincerity of [Bush's] conviction are not necessarily moved by it," Buckley wrote. "On the contrary, some of his critics are indignant and even inflamed by it." He was not hopeful that the administration would indulge in self-inspection or serious reflection, especially in public. "The cow will jump over the moon" before Bush answered two other questions: how the United States was deceived about weapons of mass destruction, and how it misjudged the nature of the resistance.[42]

On April 16, 2004, the same day Buckley called upon Bush to explain his policies in Iraq, *National Review* published an editorial questioning the rationale the administration had given for the American occupation of Iraq: democratization. Buckley's influence can be seen in the sections of the piece decrying this adventure as a modern-day application of "Wilsonianism": the use of U.S. armed personnel in pursuit of abstract ideals not necessarily shared by the local population they were intended to help. The editorial asserted that the occupation's underlying mission flowed from the fundamental mistake of underestimating the "difficulty of implanting democracy in alien soil, and an overestimation . . . of the sophistication of what is fundamentally still a tribal society and one devastated by decades of tyranny." Foreshadowing arguments Buckley would later advance in favor of an American withdrawal, the editorial proclaimed, "The world isn't as malleable as some Wilsonians would have it."[43] It reminded readers that the United States went into Iraq to protect its security interests, not in pursuit of idealistic goals. The United States should install a government that served American interests primarily and Iraqi ones secondarily.

Buckley was not the sole voice on the right to urge Bush to change his strategy. The libertarian Cato Institute called for a swift American exit from Iraq. Pat Buchanan, who had opposed both Iraq wars when Buckley was supporting them, opposed the occupation.[44] George F. Will took the President to task for characterizing those who questioned his nation-building attempts as racists who considered Arabs or Muslims incapable of self-governance. The administration, Will said, had difficulty distinguishing between "cherished hopes and disappointing facts."[45] Other dissenters included senior Republican Congressman Henry Hyde and economist Stephen Moore.[46] Nobel Laureate Milton Friedman opposed the occupation as he had opposed the invasion.[47] Other voices on the right, primarily those of neoconservatives, talk radio, and commentators on Fox News, weighed in in support of Bush's approach.

In response to revelations that American troops had abused prisoners at Abu Ghraib prison, Buckley decried what he termed the "sheer sadism" of what had transpired. He likened Defense Secretary Donald Rumsfeld's "apology" to that which a Mayor of San Francisco might make after an earthquake: it occurred on his watch, but he was not responsible.[48] Yet he contemptuously dismissed calls for the accused American offenders to face trial before an international war crimes tribunal, arguing that those who advocated such a course were more interested in prosecuting Americans than in punishing war criminals.[49]

Buckley's overall view of the initial invasion remained unchanged: if Bush had acted on compelling evidence that Saddam was stockpiling weapons of mass destruction and intended to use them, it was better that the United States invade and suffer embarrassment afterward than not invade and put millions of civilian lives in jeopardy. But, in retrospect, with the dearth of facts coming to light that bolstered the administration's case, he began to feel differently. In June 2004, with Bush running for reelection, Buckley raised more than a few eyebrows when he told the *New York Times*, "If I knew then what I now know about what kind of situation we would be in, I would have opposed the war."[50] While he conceded Bush's argument that, but for the U.S. invasion of Iraq, Libya might not have voluntarily divested itself of its own supply of dangerous weapons, he did not consider this a sufficient justification for the continued American occupation of Iraq or for an attempt at nation building. To the list of reasons he had previously given in favor of an American withdrawal, he added a new one: the mounting financial costs of staying.[51]

As he had in the previous election, Buckley presented his decision for whom to vote as a process of elimination. He characterized the Democratic alternative to Bush, Senator John Kerry, as "an ambiguist" who would weaken America's purpose "while enlivening the combative resources of a radical Islamic community that never rose up against the savagery of a great despot, and that now celebrates not those who put him away, but those who seek to emulate him."[52] In advance of Bush's debates with Kerry, Buckley informed his readers that Rollin Osterweis, who had coached both Buckley and Kerry in debate at Yale, described Kerry as the "second best" debater he ever handled. He counseled Kerry to accept his status as perpetual runner-up.[53] Having endorsed Bush as the least bad choice, Buckley continued to criticize him.

He took Bush to task for offering "no clue" as to how he would handle the situation in Iraq in a second term and argued that there was nothing the United States could do to stop factional nationalists from using terrorism to roll back modernization.[54] Drawing upon Alistair Horne's *A Savage War of Peace*, in which his former Millbrook roommate brought back to life France's experience with the insurgency in Algeria decades earlier, Buckley warned, "Not even an atom bomb would turn insurrectionists away from their daily delights in slashing throats and car-bombing schoolchildren."[55]

In a letter to a young admirer, which he quoted in his column, Buckley wrote that by 1961, "Charles De Gaulle had mentally worked his country's way out of Algeria." He doubted Bush had begun to do the same with regard to Iraq. "If one acknowledges that, in human action, prudence can sometimes trump honor, and go even further to say that it should do so, then the question before the house is when?"[56] Bush should use his 2005 State of the Union Address, Buckley suggested, as the occasion to tell the American people that the United States went to Iraq for "the right reasons," but that it had been ill prepared to meet the challenges that lay ahead after Saddam was toppled, and that the United States had achieved all it could do.[57] Such a speech, he advised, could pave the way to an orderly withdrawal.

Buckley's impatience with U.S. policy in Iraq gave way to exasperation and even anger after Bush, in his second inaugural address, declared it U.S. policy "to seek and support the growth of democratic movements and institutions in every nation and culture."[58] Invoking the aphorism that "hard cases make bad law," Buckley asked whether the President seriously wanted to "importune Chinese dissidents," engage every one-party state in Africa, or stop importing oil from Saudi Arabia.[59] "A certain point is reached," Buckley observed, six months into Bush's second term, "when tenacity conveys not steadfastness of purpose but misapplication of pride." (Here he was echoing the very argument Robert Kennedy had voiced in 1968 when he urged Lyndon Johnson to change course in Vietnam.)[60]

Unless U.S. policy changed, Buckley warned, conservatives' skepticism about it would turn into contempt.[61] As he said to the *Wall Street Journal* later that year: "Conservatism, except when it is expressed as pure idealism, takes into account reality, and the reality of the situation is that missions abroad to effect regime change in countries without a bill of rights or democratic tradition are terribly arduous. This isn't to say that the war is wrong, or that history will judge it to be wrong. But it is absolutely to say that conservatism implies a certain submission to reality; and this war has an unrealistic frank and is being conscripted by events."[62]

The undercurrent of conservative unhappiness over Bush's neglect of issues of importance to them erupted into a full-scale revolt when Bush announced his intention to nominate White House Counsel Harriet Miers to the Supreme Court. Up until this point, conservatives of all stripes, however much they may have disagreed with Bush or with each other, had found Bush's record on judicial appointments exemplary. They had been all but unanimous in praising John Roberts, whom Bush had first designated to replace the retiring Sandra Day O'Connor but subsequently appointed to succeed the deceased Chief

Justice William Rehnquist. Roberts had come up through conservative legal circles, belonged to the conservative Federalist Society, served in the Reagan administration, clerked for Rehnquist, and, as a federal judge, had hinted that he preferred to see policy set by elected legislative bodies rather than by an unelected judiciary. Miers was neither a distinguished jurist nor a constitutional scholar. Nor had she articulated a particular judicial philosophy. Many conservatives saw her appointment as both an act of political patronage and a sign that Bush, now safely reelected, took his conservative base for granted.

The Miers kerfuffle crested just hours before Bush was to host a White House ceremony honoring Buckley on his eightieth birthday and *National Review* on on its fiftieth anniversary. In his syndicated column, George F. Will had just declared the Miers nomination "not a defensible exercise of presidential discretion to which senatorial deference is due."[63] The audience Bush was to address, most of whose members had some tie to Buckley or the conservative movement, was aware of what Will had written and agreed with him. Many had publicly voiced objections to the nomination.

Bush's speech avoided controversy, consisting only of a few self-deprecating comments. Paraphrasing a remark JFK made about his wife, he described himself as the man who would be escorting Buckley to lunch. He added that his approach to classes at Yale was similar to *National Review*'s view of history, in that both had shouted, "Stop."[64] Bush earned his listeners' respect for the stoicism and graciousness he exhibited in a tense atmosphere. In the face of unanimous conservative opposition to the Miers nomination, Bush ultimately appointed Samuel Alito, whom conservatives considered better qualified than Miers and with whom many of them were familiar. But the fragile peace between Bush and some on the right, including Buckley, soon fractured.

As President, Bush took a different view of what "conservatism" meant and who should define it than did many of the conservative spokespeople, intellectuals, writers, and activists in his audience. Like his Republican predecessors, who had also courted conservatives, he regarded the conservative movement's leaders as a group to keep at arm's length and saw them more as a potential problem to be managed than as a source of advice. Like Nixon and, perhaps, George H. W. Bush, George W. Bush grew to be wary of some conservatives, who he suspected were trying to lock him into positions that could foreclose his capacity to maneuver later on. By the time of his election, Bush had come to believe that as President, he had the right to declare what "conservatism" was and to reshape the GOP in his own image.

Of the six postwar Republican presidents, only Reagan had come from the conservative movement, and only he had forged a bond with it based on more than mutual advantage. As Reagan's persistent (and futile) efforts to persuade conservatives to support the INF Treaty demonstrate, he desperately wanted the support of Buckley and his movement and tried to obtain it, even though he knew he could prevail without it. Bush's attitude was the direct opposite. A Bush speechwriter recalled Bush requesting that references to the conservative movement, its leaders, its history, and debts policy makers owed it be omitted from a speech the President was to deliver before the Conservative Political Action Committee in 2008. Bush explained that he had bested other self-proclaimed "conservatives" in his quest for the GOP presidential nomination and that, by virtue of being elected President twice, he had become the conservatives' leader.[65]

While he generally tried to remain on good terms with conservative intellectuals and others who disagreed with him, Bush sought to bolster his own standing among centrist and right of center parts of the electorate who had consistently supported his policies since the 9/11 attacks. He did so in speeches, interviews, and public appearances and through the media. The tensions between Buckley and those who agreed with him on Iraq and the administration revived an old dilemma that Buckley had never resolved for himself: should policy, for both the movement and the nation, be set by elites (Buckley's "tablet keepers") or, in the case of Bush, by an elected leader who enjoyed the support of a broader (and populist) base? (After Bush left office, parts of that base rose up in manifestation of what they regarded as both elite and remote elements within the GOP, especially its congressional leaders.) All his life, Buckley had alternated from one side to the other, depending upon the issue before him.

In February 2006, Buckley declared that the U.S. mission in Iraq was a "failure." "Iraqi animosities," he wrote, "have proved uncontainable by an invading army of 130,000 Americans." Bush's challenge, he argued, was to recognize the necessity of reversing policies "he has several times affirmed in high-flown pronouncements."[66] Continuing this line of argument in a column days later, Buckley asserted that Bush's reputation would ultimately rest on his making the case that the United States had succeeded in its aims of toppling Saddam's regime and demonstrating that Iraq was not a repository of weapons of mass destruction, but that achieving the goals he had set forth afterward required more deployable resources than were available.[67]

Buckley's comments attracted considerable attention. In an exchange with Bloomberg News, Buckley termed Bush's post-Saddam policies "bad executive action insufficiently thought through and terribly, terribly disadvantageous." The United States, he said, had presumed that it would quickly meet its goals in Iraq and was now paying a price for that overconfidence. Moreover, the administration had so stretched public patience that its policies appeared unreasonable.[68] Buckley also faulted neoconservatives, many of whom he had helped bring into the conservative movement and had once beseeched Reagan to employ, for failing to consider the limitations of American resources as they continued to argue for a heavy American presence in Iraq. "A conservative," he said, "always measures capabilities and resources, and these are simply incapable—now, even as they were in 1919—of bringing on democracy."[69] (His harking back to the Wilson era in the example he selected shows the continuing influence of his father's warning to Congress about the deployment of troops in defense of abstractions.)

Other conservative voices joined Buckley in his dissent, as they had done two years earlier when he first raised doubts about the continuing American mission in Iraq. George F. Will urged the administration to concentrate the public mind on the difficulties that lay ahead for the United States in Iraq and to acknowledge that its theory that democracy can be imposed from without had been proven a failure.[70] In a *New York Times* op-ed, Francis Fukuyama reminded the administration that supporters of the President had backed the war because they wanted to deter terrorism, not because they wanted to bring democracy to Iraq. Citing polls showing declining support for U.S. policy in Iraq, he warned of an upswing in isolationist sentiment.[71]

Stung by these defections on the right coming at a time when overall public support for his policies was falling, Bush declared, "We will not lose our nerve."[72] In a twenty-four-hundred-word piece in the *Wall Street Journal* under the headline "The Wrong Time to Lose Our Nerve," White House aide Peter Wehner accused a "small group of current and former conservatives—including William F. Buckley, Jr., George Will, and Francis Fukuyama"—of doing precisely that.[73] By inference, he suggested that the White House had the right to determine who belonged in the movement Buckley had begun and who had forfeited the right to be considered a "conservative."

After citing evidence that democracy was, as Bush maintained, taking hold in Iraq, Wehner charged, as Bush had previously done, that the administration's critics were asserting a Western sense of superiority over Middle Eastern cultures in their certainty that democracy could not take hold in the region. In his 2003 speech before the American Enterprise Institute, Bush had said that it was "presumptuous and insulting to suggest that a whole region of the world that was Muslim—or one-fifth of humanity that is Muslim—is somehow untouched by the most basic aspirations of human life."[74]

"A mark of serious conservatism," Wehner argued in the *Wall Street Journal*, "is a regard for the concreteness of human experience." As parts of that experience,

Wehner cited Japan's embrace of democracy after World War II and, in recent decades, the spread of democracy elsewhere in the world where it had not always existed. He also submitted as evidence the rocky road the United States had traveled on its way to building its own strong and viable democracy, which included fighting a civil war. Accusing Bush's critics of both pessimism and impatience, he argued that Bush's "freedom agenda" encompassed a more realistic view of the future. It was Bush's detractors, not the President, Wehner maintained, who had broken faith with the nation's founders, who had proclaimed that the fundamental truths they advanced in the Declaration of Independence were universally applicable.[75] Neither he nor Bush argued that the framers intended for the universal, God-given rights to "life, liberty, and happiness" to be spread to other parts of the world through the force of American arms.

To be sure, the administration retained the support of many other self-identified conservatives. Fox News anchors and commentators as well as talk radio hosts Rush Limbaugh, Laura Ingraham, Sean Hannity, and others rallied to the administration's side. Bush's press secretary Tony Snow went on conservative and other radio and television programs to arouse conservative support for the administration's policies.[76] Bush also enjoyed continued support from the *Weekly Standard*, the Heritage Foundation, and analysts at the American Enterprise Institute, the Hudson Institute, the Manhattan Institute, and other conservative-leaning think tanks. In his defense of Bush, Limbaugh noted Buckley's criticisms but did not comment on them. Other Bush defenders, unwilling to take issue directly with the founder of the modern conservative movement, were likewise silent.

Yet Buckley was hardly a "party of one."[77] Weeks after Buckley's Bloomberg News interview aired, former House Speaker Newt Gingrich told students at the University of South Dakota that "it was an enormous mistake for us to try to occupy that country after June 2003" and called for a scaling back.[78] Writing in the *New York Daily News*, General William Odom called for an immediate pullout.[79] Former Republican Congressman Joe Scarborough, his focus fixed on Iraq, began his television program with a ten-minute discussion in which he asked guests whether Bush had the intellectual capacity to decide major public questions. As they talked, a caption flashed across the screen essentially asking: "Is Bush an Idiot?"[80]

In the summer of 2006, Buckley stated that the United States was not in Iraq to "choke off nuclear arms development" but to "save the locals from the kind of government they would have if left to their own resources." He suggested the time was at hand to "lower the flag on American universalism not to half-mast, but not as toplofty as it has been flying since the end of the Second World War."

The next order of business, he said, was for U.S. intelligence agencies and intellectuals to figure out why the followers of a certain form of Islam fought so resolutely for their values, and whether their intended Western victims would be as resolute in fighting for theirs.[81]

A final controversy Buckley aroused regarding the administration and Iraq began with a statement he made on CBS News prior to the 2006 congressional elections. "If you had a European prime minister who experienced what we've experienced it would be expected that he would retire or resign."[82] He thought Bush would not survive a parliamentary "vote of confidence" if such a practice were part of the American political system and suggested that the congressional elections of 2006 were the American equivalent to this parliamentary practice. Had the Democrats not retaken both houses of Congress that year, he wrote after the 2006 election, "democratic governance would have been guilty of being asleep at the wheel."[83] (Democrats won control of both congressional chambers, picking up six seats in the Senate and thirty-one in the House.)

Buckley initially opposed Bush's call for a "surge" of 21,500 additional U.S. troops to reverse inroads insurgents had made against the Iraqi government. "Why not 200,000?" he asked, recalling General William Westmoreland's recommendation to Johnson after the Tet Offensive, an increase he had also opposed.[84] The insurgents' strength, he pointed out, lay not in the size of their military organization but in the techniques they employed against occupying forces. Most American combat losses were not coming from battles in the field but from an "apparently inexhaustible supply of IEDs [improvised explosive devices] and a steady stream of insurgents able and eager to use them."[85]

Gingrich took a similar tack. Columnist and commentator Charles Krauthammer, who distrusted the existing Iraqi government, did as well. Again, the administration's allies in talk radio and elsewhere rallied to its side. Fearful of Buckley's influence on American opinion—and not only with the Right—the White House lobbied the networks not to invite him on the air as often.[86]

Over time, the support of self-identified conservatives among the general public, whose support Bush worked so hard to maintain, began to move in Buckley's direction. When the war commenced in 2003, 90 percent of self-identified Republicans supported it, according to the Pew Research Council. By 2005, that number had dropped to 82 percent, dwindling to 73 percent by the time Bush left office. (By 2013, 58 percent of Republicans thought the invasion had been a mistake.)[87] With Democrats heavily against the venture from the outset, this drop in conservative support constituted the largest decline among any ideological group.

As he took measure of the latest entry into the presidential sweepstakes in 2008, Senator Barack Obama, Buckley summarized what he saw as the state of the American political landscape with regard to the willingness of leaders to send American forces into combat abroad: "Nobody . . . is going to favor aggressive military action. The politicians therefore make it clear that such appropriations as they support for the military are for beefing up our self-defense. Kindly do not muddy this proposition by interjecting that, sometimes self-defense is best done through pre-emptive military initiatives."[88] Buckley was doing more than taking a final swipe at Bush. He was advocating a more constrained presidency in which incumbents acted less on their own authority and their own vision, in closer collaboration with Congress, and in ways that preserved and advanced discernible and definable American interests.

Whittaker Chambers would have marveled at how far his protégé had traveled, over six decades, in the direction of the Beaconsfield position. When the two first met, Buckley and his nascent movement sought to reverse the New Deal, "roll back" Soviet expansion, and perhaps wage preventive war against the USSR, all at the same time. Over his career, Buckley had learned to prioritize, had trimmed his sails, and, along the way, had helped change the world.

16

The Ancient Truths

William F. Buckley's death came on February 27, 2008, less than a year after that of his wife, Pat, his best friend and most ardent and loyal fan for more than fifty-six years. President George W. Bush succinctly and aptly summarized Buckley's place in history: Buckley "brought conservative thought into the political mainstream, and helped lay the intellectual foundation for America's victory in the Cold War."[1]

Interestingly, the President did not refer to Buckley's writings, eloquent and significant to his legacy though they were. That omission was altogether fitting. Buckley never claimed to be an original political philosopher, nor did his admirers and detractors consider him one. He saw his role not as a discoverer of new truths, but as a retriever of ancient ones. He believed those truths to be the best means to preserve human freedom, enhance civilization, create wealth, enable people to attain their full capabilities, and glorify God, in whose image humankind was created. Those truths, he believed, had been nearly forgotten by the time he came of age—relegated to the background of intellectual thought, daily life, and popular culture by the steady rise of communitarianism, moral equivalency, and secular humanism in Western liberal democracies.

It was not only through the written word that Buckley made his mark. Through the multiple platforms he occupied—writer and editor, debater, publicist, organizer, political candidate, activist, and networker extraordinaire—and through an inimitable style marked by elegance, humor, wit, and grace, Buckley worked vigorously to bring the beliefs he held back into public consciousness and make them a priority of policy makers. Often, and especially during the Reagan era, views Buckley had disseminated for all of his adult life inspired public policy at the highest level of government. In his eighty-two years of life, Buckley achieved much, if not all, of what he set out to do—and did so vigorously, joyfully, often noisily. Whatever his critics thought of him, especially in his younger days, when he burst onto the public stage as an acerbic *enfant terrible*, they could not ignore him. He was one of the few people engaged in the public discourse of his time who could lay a legitimate claim to having changed history.[2]

Buckley's fealty to principle did not blind him to his own imperfections and inconsistencies. And by no means did his devotion to truths that had been passed down to him through the generations make him a prisoner of dogma. He had also learned to free himself of views that had come to him by the circumstances of his background that he concluded ran counter to values he cherished. By the time he had enrolled at Yale, he had cast aside the anti-Semitism of his father. His experiences in the military, where he was exposed to people of backgrounds far different from his own, led him to judge people not according to their social, religious, or political views, but by what Martin Luther King Jr. termed the "content of their character." To have done anything less would have been in his eyes a violation of the spirit of individualism he both cherished and practiced. Similarly, at the height of the civil rights revolution, Buckley sensed a tension between the institutional segregation that had been part of his southern-reared parents' world and his deep Catholic faith. Doubts he had developed over the rightness of positions he had held for years caused him both to change his views and voice regret that he had not done so earlier.

A staunch isolationist in his youth and one who had vigorously opposed American assistance to Britain in its struggle against Nazi Germany, Buckley, as a grown man and World War II veteran, expressed gratitude that Franklin D. Roosevelt (whose administration he continued to detest for having increased the role the federal government came to play in so much of American life) had pressed the case for lend-lease and other efforts, even to the point of possibly violating American law. A committed anti-Communist until the end of his days, Buckley, as one of his most steadfast ideological adversaries in the 1950s and 1960s, Arthur M. Schlesinger Jr., noted, in the last decades of his life reached the point at which he stopped defending one of his early heroes, Senator Joseph McCarthy.[3]

In spite of these many changes of opinion and attitude, Buckley's core beliefs remained the same. Buckley made *National Review* a print form of a "town square" in which disparate elements of the conservative movement could engage with each other and rightward-leaning readers from all walks of life could see what the best conservative thinkers were saying as well as find validation for their opinions. He took pains to accommodate the differences of opinion within the movement he had steadily nurtured and, true to the spirit of "fusionism" that guided him, kept his magazine's pages open to economic conservatives, social conservatives, libertarians, traditionalists, and agrarians. In time, he made room for the religious Right, neoconservatives, and others.

All he welcomed were bound together by a common hatred of Communism abroad, an expanded welfare state at home, and moral equivalence, especially in intellectual life. His biographer would be remiss not to add the words "and a deep and abiding sense of loyalty to him." Yet Buckley sensed a need to impose boundaries on such pluralism. In his self-imposed role as "tablet keeper," he stood eternally vigilant against extremist elements whose views were so beyond the realm of acceptable public discourse that they threatened to cast a stain over the entire conservative movement he helped found. Buckley took special pride in the success he had in keeping that movement free of "kooks," "crack-pots," racists, and anti-Semites.

While mindful of the special place he occupied within the conservative movement, on occasion Buckley could take positions contrary to those of many of his ideological cohorts when his conscience pulled him in a different direction. Not a "knee-jerk" conservative, he took the positions he did not because they necessarily conformed to a particular conservative "canon," but because he thought they were correct. Much of the time, his positions aligned with those also thought to be "conservative," but not always. Buckley was never one to march in "lockstep." Yet, none of the deviations he occasionally made from what was thought to be the conservative position conflicted with the ancient truths he so revered, which continued to guide his actions.

Valuing his independence, Buckley took umbrage when a protégé working in the Nixon White House presumed to tell him to toe the line when the administration took a stand contrary to his merely because White House officials had lent assistance to Buckley's brother's campaign. Three administrations later, Buckley informed Reagan's Vice President that he would not temper his criticism of what the nation's second-highest-ranking official had said merely because Ronald Reagan agreed with his number two on the issue. Buckley was not the sort of man who could be "reined in." As much as it may have pained him to break ranks with Reagan, the President to whom he was closest both ideologically and personally, and on one of the administration's signature issues, the INF Treaty, Buckley stayed true to his beliefs—and did so without reducing the esteem in which Reagan held him.

Alongside his devotion to principle, Buckley placed the highest value on friendship and loyalty. An important part of his legacy is the mentorship he provided to countless others who went on to distinguished careers in the media, literature, public service, the arts, and other endeavors. Not all who benefited professionally and otherwise from their association with Buckley, including commentators Michael Kinsley and Jeff Greenfield, art critic John Leonard, and novelist Joan Didion, shared his ideological perspective. At the same time, a good many, such as George F. Will, whom Buckley retained to direct *National Review*'s Washington, DC, office and cover events transpiring in the nation's capital, did. In time, Will became a leading conservative syndicated columnist, appearing in even more daily newspapers than Buckley had during his heyday. Christopher Hitchens, who developed a transatlantic following among those on both the Left and the Right, made his first American television appearance on Buckley's *Firing Line*.

Always on the lookout for new and young talent, Buckley often recruited it in unconventional ways. While an undergraduate at the University of Chicago, future *New York Times* columnist and PBS commentator David Brooks wrote a satirical essay about Buckley, focusing on the columnist's purported inflated ego. When Buckley, sometime after reading it, spoke on campus, he made a rather unusual announcement from the podium: "David Brooks, if you're in the audience, I'd like to offer you a job."[4] Linda Bridges, future editor at large at *National Review,* was a student at the University of Southern California when she wrote a letter to the magazine in which she took exception to the translation of a French expression that had run in its "Notes and Asides" section. During a visit to Los Angeles, Buckley telephoned her home and explained to her mother that he wanted to take Linda out to dinner and offer her a job. Future senior editor and historian Richard Brookhiser began his long association with *National Review* when, as a high school student, he submitted to the magazine a parody of an antiwar demonstration at his school. After hearing nothing back for quite a while, he opened the mail one day to discover that his piece had made the magazine's cover.

Buckley gave advice and encouragement to others whose on-air styles differed from his own and who pitched their messages to more broad-based audiences than he reached. Talk show host Rush Limbaugh recalled being both honored and nervous to receive an invitation to an editorial meeting Buckley was having with his colleagues at the Buckleys' New York abode. From the time he was twelve years old, Limbaugh had been in awe of the conservative commentator. He recalled that as he reached Buckley's street on the day of the meeting, he ordered his driver to circle the block several times until he had summoned the courage to enter the building.[5] Limbaugh remembered Buckley chiding him, usually with a short note, whenever he thought that radio host had been "incorrect or whatever."[6]

Like Ronald Reagan, Buckley had an unshakable faith in his cause and remained eternally optimistic about his country's future. In 1970, when internal divisions over the war in Vietnam were at their height, the economy was fluttering, politicians were predicting "scarcity" of resources, and the media spoke about deep societal divisions, Buckley saw nothing but good days and spiritual and civic renewal ahead. He defiantly declared on CBS's *60 Minutes* that that the "full-time undertakers" were always "disappointed that America does not die on schedule."[7] He had no more use for predictions of America's decline than he had for previous assertions many had made during the 1950s that the United States would be better off "red than dead" (he deemed that it would be neither) or a decade later that "God was dead."

At Buckley's death, obituary writers and essayists unanimously wrote of his infinite capacity for friendship, often with people with whom he disagreed. Once he had forged intimate bonds with someone he held in high regard, Buckley went to extraordinary lengths to preserve them. A case in point was a misunderstanding that arose between Buckley and Henry Kissinger, his friend of fifty years. British-born writer Christopher Hitchens, a longtime Kissinger critic, had argued in *Harper's* and in a BBC documentary, *The Trials of Henry Kissinger*, that the former Secretary of State should be tried for war crimes. He argued that Kissinger's policies as National Security Adviser and Secretary of State had resulted in the deaths of innocents in Indochina, Bangladesh, Chile, Cyprus, and East Timor.

Not for the first time, Buckley rose to his friend's defense in his column. He noted the Left's "obsession" with Kissinger and described in detail images that appeared in the documentary that, he said, appeared to have been selected with the intent of giving audiences an unfavorable impression of the former Secretary of State.[8] Buckley found these depictions of Kissinger anti-Semitic.

In advance of its publication, Buckley faxed his piece to Kissinger, and the former official took immediate offense at it. He wrote Buckley that in his intended defense of him, Buckley had repeated his most virulent critics' charges and assertions and had thereby supplied Kissinger's leftist detractors with "telling and unexpected material." He may also have objected to Buckley's description of the lurid and unflattering caricatures of him that were in the documentary. Kissinger said that he regretted that "fifty years of friendship would yield such a sour assessment" of his career.[9] He then supplied a detailed refutation of Hitchens's allegations. "In the fifty years of our friendship," Buckley responded, "I have probably written fifty times acclaiming you and your work. It is discouraging that in my 51st sally, you should think that I suddenly changed my mind about you."[10] Kissinger was not mollified.

Not ready to give up on the friendship, Buckley reached out to the one person he thought could turn Kissinger around, Nelson A. Rockefeller's widow.

After having paid Happy Rockefeller a visit at her home, Buckley followed up by sending her the column in question, a copy of the letter Kissinger had written him, his reply, and his most recent novel. He wrote in his thank-you note for her hospitality how glad he was that Mrs. Rockefeller agreed that his piece was "admiring as always of Henry."[11] One can only surmise that in the time that had elapsed between Buckley's visit with her and her letter to him acknowledging his note to her, Mrs. Rockefeller had undertaken some Kissingerian "shuttle diplomacy" of her own

On previous occasions, Kissinger had acted as go-between for Buckley and Mrs. Rockefeller's husband; and Buckley had acted as go-between for Kissinger with Richard Nixon's transition team and with Ronald Reagan. Now in need of a go-between to help repair his relationship with Kissinger, Buckley enlisted the aid of the wife of the man whose presidential ambitions he had thrice helped torpedo. Apparently, Mrs. Rockefeller performed her mission ably, and the Buckley-Kissinger friendship endured.

Kissinger and Buckley's son, Christopher, were the only speakers at Buckley's funeral in New York's Saint Patrick's Cathedral. Summarizing the feelings of all assembled, Kissinger described Buckley as a "noble, gentle and valiant man who was truly touched by the grace of God."[12]

Notes

Chapter 1. In the Shadow of Woodrow, Lindbergh, and Franklin D.

1. Reid Buckley, *The Buckleys: An American Family* (New York: Threshold, 2008).
2. Ibid.
3. Ibid., 197.
4. Usually celebrated on July 12, this holiday commemorates the victory of Protestant forces loyal to Prince William of Orange over those of King James II of England, to whom Catholics throughout the British Isles rallied, at the battle of the Boyne. Fought in 1690 on the eastern coast of Ireland, the battle established William as Great Britain's king and Protestantism as the official religion of his kingdom.
5. John B. Judis, *William F. Buckley, Jr.: Patron Saint of the Conservatives* (New York: Simon and Schuster, 1988), 19; and Buckley, *The Buckleys*, 57.
6. The Irish Prison Record for County Cork, contained in the National Archives, Dublin, furnished this author with evidence that a John Buckley was arrested for assault on July 6, 1843, fined, and released. Whether this was the John Buckley in question is unclear.
7. Buckley, *The Buckleys*, 58.
8. Ibid., 42.
9. Reid Buckley, "Retold Tale," in *W.F.B.: An Appreciation*, ed. Priscilla L. Buckley and William F. Buckley Jr. (New York: Privately published, 1979), 5.
10. Buckley, *The Buckleys*, 42.
11. Sheriff John was not the only Buckley to take an active role in Texas politics. His granddaughter Beryl Milburn (daughter of his son Edmund) was for many years active in the then nascent Texas Republican Party. She founded the Texas Federation of Republican Women, sought public office, was a delegate to Republican National Conventions, and served as a regent of the University of Texas.
12. James L. Buckley, *Gleanings from an Unplanned Life: An Annotated Oral History* (Wilmington, DE: Intercollegiate Studies Institute, 2006), 4–10.
13. Buckley, *The Buckleys*, 50.

14. See Elliott Young, *Catarino Garza's Revolution on the Texas-Mexico Border* (Durham, NC: Duke University Press, 2004), 157, 172–73.
15. Quoted in Buckley, *Gleanings from an Unplanned Life*, 12; and Buckley, *The Buckleys*, 44.
16. Buckley, *The Buckleys*, 81.
17. Walter S. Pope, "College Days," in Buckley and Buckley, *W.F.B.: An Appreciation*, 14–15.
18. Ibid., 15–16.
19. Buckley, *The Buckleys*, 121.
20. FBI file on William F. Buckley Jr., March 27, 1951, accessed through the Freedom of Information Act; and Pope, "College Days," 19.
21. John Milton Cooper Jr., *Woodrow Wilson: A Biography* (New York: Vintage Books, 2011), 14.
22. Nemesio Garcia Naranjo, "A Friend of Mexico," in Buckley and Buckley, *W.F.B.: An Appreciation*, 46–50.
23. Ibid.
24. Ibid., 48.
25. Charles Lam Markmann, *The Buckleys: A Family Examined* (New York: Morrow, 1973), 12.
26. Judis, *William F. Buckley, Jr.*; Markmann, *The Buckleys*, 24.
27. William F. Buckley Jr., "Middle Class Values," On the Right, March 27, 1969.
28. William F. Buckley Jr., *Miles Gone By: A Literary Biography* (Washington, DC: Regnery, 2004), 27.
29. James L. Buckley, conversation with author.
30. Judis, *William F. Buckley, Jr.*, 27.
31. Buckley, *The Buckleys*, 339–40.
32. William F. Buckley Jr., *In Search of Anti-Semitism* (New York: Continuum, 1992), 6. Buckley did not specify how his father reacted to similar assertions Protestants made about Catholics.
33. Ibid.
34. See Judis, *William F. Buckley, Jr.*, 36.
35. Or so he recalled in at least one interview. See David Remnick, "Buckley: The Lion in Autumn," *Washington Post*, December 5, 1985. His brother James believes that Billy learned English at the same time as Spanish, as it was spoken in his home. If his Spanish was more developed, it may be because the Mexican nurses in his parents' employ spoke it to him.
36. "Memorandum" (excerpts from memoranda Will Buckley sent his children), chapter 2 in "Part Four—Connecticut," in Buckley and Buckley, *W.F.B.: An Appreciation*, 243. Billy's mother said that he was seven at the time. See Israel Shenker, "450 Celebrate 15th Year of *National Review*," *New York Times*, November 14, 1970. This author made several unsuccessful attempts to retrieve the letter in the Royal Archives, Windsor.
37. Buckley, *Miles Gone By*, 19.
38. Joseph Crespino, *Strom Thurmond's America* (New York: Hill and Wang, 2012), 10.

39. Buckley, *Miles Gone By*, 19–20. Will's sister had taken a second residence near Sharon so she could be near Will and his family for part of the year.
40. Ibid., 23. Chamberlain's plane landed at the Heston Aerodrome, west of London. The airport was in operation from 1929 to 1947.
41. William F. Buckley Jr., "God and Boys at Millbrook," *New York Times Magazine*, October 4, 1981.
42. Buckley, *Miles Gone By*, 33.
43. See *National Review*, April 22, 1961, and December 4, 1961.
44. William F. Buckley Jr., interview with James Rosen, *Fox News*, October 26, 2000.
45. After Buckley began courting Waugh for *National Review*, the novelist complained to British journalist and politician Tom Driberg that Buckley had shown him "great and unsought attention." Waugh dismissed *National Review* as a "neo-McCarthy magazine" and pronounced Buckley's book *Up from Liberalism* "unreadable." Yet in a letter to Buckley a year later, Waugh praised Buckley's writings in *Rumbles Left and Right* as reminiscent of Hilaire Belloc. See William F. Buckley Jr., *Cancel Your Own Goddam Subscription* (New York: Basic Books, 2007), 139–45.
46. Buckley, interview with Rosen.
47. Report card for William F. Buckley Jr. at St. John, Beaufort, March 5, 1939, William F. Buckley, Jr. Papers, (MS 576), Manuscripts and Archives, Yale University Library, New Haven, CT.
48. Transcripts and grades St. John's, Beaumont, January 14, 1939, and March 5, 1939, William F. Buckley, Jr. Papers.
49. "Millbrook School," *Wikipedia*.
50. Judis, *William F. Buckley, Jr.*, 32.
51. Ibid., 40.
52. Ibid., 38
53. Ibid., 39.
54. Anne Morrow Lindbergh, *The Wave of the Future: A Confession of Faith* (New York: Harcourt Brace, 1941).
55. Robert Gale Woolbert, review of *The Wave of the Future*, *Foreign Affairs*, July 1941, www.foreignaffairs.com/articles/anne-morrow-lindbergh/wave-of- the future.
56. Markmann, *The Buckleys*, 50.
57. Ibid.
58. Buckley, *Miles Gone By*, 5
59. Alistair Horne, A *Bundle from Britain* (New York: St. Martin's, 1993), 267. See also Buckley and Buckley, *W.F.B.: An Appreciation*, 244.
60. Buckley and Buckley, *W.F.B.: An Appreciation*, 244.
61. William F. Buckley Sr. to William F. Buckley Jr., January 7, 1941, William F. Buckley, Jr. Papers.
62. William F. Buckley Sr. to William F. Buckley Jr., March 14, 1941, William F. Buckley, Jr. Papers.
63. Nathaniel B. Abbott to William F. Buckley Sr., April 30, 1942, William F. Buckley, Jr. Papers.
64. Horne, *A Bundle from Britain*, 175.

65. Ibid.
66. Ibid., 207.
67. Ibid., 248.
68. William F. Buckley Jr. to Charles Lindbergh, January 10, 1942, William F. Buckley, Jr. Papers.
69. Horne, A *Bundle from Britain*, 248.
70. Ibid., 249.
71. Judis, *William F. Buckley, Jr.*, 43.
72. Ibid., 44.
73. Horne, A *Bundle from Britain*, 249.
74. Ibid.
75. Buckley, "God and Boys at Millbrook."
76. Ibid.
77. Nathaniel Abbott to William F. Buckley Sr., April 30, 1942, William F. Buckley, Jr. Papers.
78. Buckley, "God and Boys at Millbrook."
79. William F. Buckley Jr., *Gratitude: Reflections on What We Owe to Our Country* (New York: Random House, 1990).
80. Horne, A *Bundle from Britain*, 285.
81. Buckley "God and Boys at Millbrook."
82. Alfred Jay Nock, *Memoirs of a Superfluous Man* (New York: Harper and Brothers, 1943).
83. School essay by William F. Buckley Jr., March 1943, William F. Buckley, Jr. Papers.
84. Presumably, Buckley considered voters Mark Hanna's Ohio machine turned out for McKinley more "informed" and "qualified" than those Tammany Hall turned out.
85. Frances Bronson to Edward Pulling, November 5, 1981, William F. Buckley, Jr. Papers.
86. Buckley, "God and Boys at Millbrook."
87. William F. Buckley Jr. to Edward Pulling, September 5, 1988, William F. Buckley, Jr. Papers.
88. Edward Pulling to William F. Buckley Jr., September 13, 1988, William F. Buckley, Jr. Papers.
89. William F. Buckley Jr. to Edward Pulling, September 5, 1988.
90. Edward Pulling to William F. Buckley Jr., September 13, 1988.
91. William F. Buckley Jr. to Henry Callard, June 20, 1943. This letter was provided to the author by Paul E. Sigmund, who went on to become a distinguished medievalist and specialist on Latin American politics. Both he and his brother Peter recalled that in their discussions with Buckley, they also debated more contemporary issues such as racial segregation, which Buckley defended. Callard later became headmaster of the Gilman School in Baltimore. The *Quiz Kids* was a popular radio game show of the period in which high school students competed against each other in answering questions on multiple subjects. Buckley's brother Reid makes reference to his family's 1943 visit to Mexico but not to the Austin stopover in *The Buckleys*, 168.
92. William F. Buckley Jr. to Henry Callard, June 20, 1943.
93. Judis, *William F. Buckley, Jr.*, 46.

94. Ibid., 47.
95. Ibid., 46.
96. Ibid., 49.
97. Ibid.
98. William F. Buckley Jr. to William F. Buckley Sr., undated, probably 1944, William F. Buckley, Jr. Papers.
99. These quotations are from undated letters from William F. Buckley Jr. to William F. Buckley Sr., probably in late 1944 and early 1945, William F. Buckley, Jr. Papers.
100. Buckley, *Miles Gone By*, 115.
101. "Memorandum," 244.
102. Judis, *William F. Buckley, Jr.*, 50.
103. The paper, "Sam Houston: An American Paradox," dated May 1946, "by Ella Verne Taylor," rests among term papers Buckley wrote at Yale in his papers stored at Yale University.
104. Judis, *William F. Buckley, Jr.*, 50.

CHAPTER 2. GOD AND BILL AT YALE

1. Dwight Macdonald, "On the Horizon: Scrambled Eggheads on the Right," *Commentary*, April 1956, 367–73.
2. Judis, *William F. Buckley, Jr.*, 53.
3. Sam Tanenhaus, "The Founder," *Yale Alumni Magazine*, May–June 2008.
4. Alistair Horne, *But What Do You Actually Do?* (London: Weidenfeld and Nicholson, 2011), 81. See also William F. Buckley Jr., "When Yale Was under Siege," *Dorm*, Spring 1985.
5. Tanenhaus, "The Founder."
6. Bourne Dempsey, "Buckley, Bozell Capture Decision in Socialism Fight: Yale Wins Unanimously over Oxford Debaters Before Overflow House," *Yale Daily News*, October 19, 1949; and Judis, *William F. Buckley, Jr.*, 54–56, 74.
7. Dempsey, "Buckley, Bozell Capture Decision in Socialism Fight"; and Judis, *William F. Buckley, Jr.*, 54–55, 74. Robin Day would go on to be a well-known media personality, interviewer, and originator of the long-running British public affairs television program *Question Time*. Johnson-Smith would become a Conservative MP representing Scotland in the British Parliament, and would hold cabinet posts in Conservative governments. In his 1988 biography of Buckley, John Judis misidentified Day's debating partner as Anthony Wedgwood-Benn, who also later served in Parliament, but as a Labour MP. Known as Tony Benn, he became identified in the public mind as the leader of the most left-leaning faction of his party during the Thatcher era. See Judis, *William F. Buckley, Jr.*,74–75.
8. *Yale Class Book of 1950*, 150.
9. Judis, *William F. Buckley, Jr.*, 75.
10. Markmann, *The Buckleys*, 64.
11. Ibid., 65.
12. Ibid.

13. Ibid., 60.
14. Raymond Price, *With Nixon* (New York: Viking, 1977), 90.
15. Raymond Price, interview with author, June 17, 2009.
16. Markmann, *The Buckleys*.
17. Tanenhaus, "The Founder."
18. Judis, *William F. Buckley, Jr.*, 55.
19. Ibid., 65.
20. Ibid., 59; Tanenhaus, "The Founder."
21. Judis, *William F. Buckley, Jr.*, 59.
22. Buckley, *In Search of Anti-Semitism*, 7.
23. Ibid., 6–8.
24. Judis, *William F. Buckley, Jr.*, 58.
25. Art Milam, "Dewey Favored by 63 Percent of the Student Body in Poll; Truman Follows with 21 Percent Backing," *Yale Daily News*, November 1, 1948.
26. Arthur M. Schlesinger Jr., "Not Left, nor Right, but a Vital Center," *New York Times*, April 4, 1948; and Arthur M. Schlesinger Jr., *The Vital Center: The Politics of Freedom* (Boston: Houghton Mifflin, 1949).
27. Judis, *William F. Buckley, Jr.*, 64.
28. William F. Buckley Jr., "Henry Wallace, R.I.P.," *National Review*, December 14, 1965.
29. Judis, *William F. Buckley, Jr.*, 60.
30. *Yale Class Book of* 1950, 120.
31. Judis, *William F. Buckley, Jr.*, 66.
32. *Yale Class Book of* 1950, 120.
33. "For a Fair Approach," *Yale Daily News*, March 9, 1949.
34. William F. Buckley Jr., "Moral Equivalency on Clinton," On the Right, March 5, 1999.
35. "Churchill Holds Atom Bomb Saved Europe from Soviet: Our Possession of New Weapon Deterred Communists, He Says in Boston," *New York Times*, April 1, 1949.
36. "For the Republican Conclave," *Yale Daily News*, April 30, 1949.
37. "The Veterans Organization and the AVC," *Yale Daily News*, March 7, 1949.
38. "President Truman's Complex," *Yale Daily News*, May 14, 1949.
39. "Needed: A Little Tolerance," *Yale Daily News*, October 12, 1949.
40. William F. Buckley Jr., "Harry Truman, R.I.P.," On the Right, December 6, 1972. For more on the debate surrounding Truman's Cold War policies and their origins, see Robert H. Ferrell, *Truman and the Cold War Revisionists* (Columbia: University of Missouri Press, 2006).
41. Judis, *William F. Buckley, Jr.*, 72; and *Harvard Crimson*, June 4, 1949.
42. See Judis, *William F. Buckley, Jr.*, 72–74.
43. Tanenhaus, "The Founder."
44. Judis, *William F. Buckley, Jr.*, 72–74; and correspondence between L. B. Nichols and M. A. Jones, October 20, 1950, October 24, 1950, and October 26, 1950; FBI file on William F. Buckley Jr., William F. Buckley, Jr. Papers.
45. "Lest We Forget," *Yale Daily News*, January 14, 1950. Buckley perhaps intended the reference to "the ingratiating voice and smile of a patent hypocrite" to evoke memories of FDR.

46. *Yale Daily News*, January 17, 1950. Massie would attain renown for his book *Nicholas and Alexandra.*
47. Judis, *William F. Buckley, Jr.*, 76.
48. Editorial, *Yale Daily News*, January 20, 1950.
49. Judis, *William F. Buckley, Jr.*, 12.
50. Ibid.
51. This figures are from Eugene H. Kone, *Yale Men Who Died in the Second World War: A Memorial Volume of Biographical Sketches* (New Haven, CT: Yale University Press, 1951), dedication and "Preface to Statistical Tables," 437.
52. *Yale Class Book of* 1950, 226.
53. Judis, *William F. Buckley, Jr.*, 78; and e-mail from James L. Buckley to the author, July 20, 2014.
54. *Yale Class Book of* 1950, 171.
55. Ibid., 90.
56. Arthur Wilson Milam, "The *Yale Daily News*," *Yale Class Book of* 1950.
57. William Hitchcock MacLeish, "Davenport College: Notes for a Time Capsule to Be Opened June 13, 3050," *Yale Class Book of* 1950, 87–88.
58. Donald Oberdorfer Jr., "Fabulous Yalie Blasts Eli, Calls for Alumni Awakening," *Daily Princetonian*, October 18, 1951.
59. Judis, *William F. Buckley, Jr.*, 79.
60. Ibid., 69.
61. Christopher Buckley, *Losing Mum and Pup* (New York: Twelve, 2008), 19–20.
62. Ibid.
63. Ibid, 70.
64. "Buckley-Taylor Rites Today Draw Interest Near and Far," *Vancouver Sun*, July 6, 1950. See also Bob Colacello, "Mr. and Mrs. Right," *Vanity Fair*, December 1, 2008.
65. Buckley, *Losing Mum and Pup*, 149.
66. Ibid., 56.
67. Austin Taylor died the day of the 1965 election.
68. Linda Bridges and John R. Coyne, *Strictly Right: William F. Buckley, Jr., and the American Conservative Movement* (New York: John Wiley and Sons, 2007), 21; and Judis, *William F. Buckley, Jr.*, 82.
69. William F. Buckley Jr. to E. Victor Milione, June 6, 1960, William F. Buckley, Jr. Papers.
70. In a footnote, Buckley defined "Christian" according to definitions supplied by the World Council of Churches and Dr. Reinhold Niebuhr, whose politics were decidedly liberal. He would come to use the terms *Christian* and *Judeo-Christian* interchangeably. See William F. Buckley Jr., *God and Man at Yale: The Superstitions of "Academic Freedom"* (Chicago: Regnery, 1951), 32.
71. For Buckley's crediting of Kendall, see *Miles Gone By*, 68.
72. Buckley, *God and Man at Yale*, foreword.
73. Buckley, *Miles Gone By*, 63–64.
74. Ibid. Still an active and intellectual force, the group is now known as the Intercollegiate Studies Institute.

75. Buckley, *God and Man at Yale*, 148.
76. Ibid., 157.
77. Ibid., 3.
78. William F. Buckley Jr., *Up from Liberalism* (New York: McDonnell, Obolensky, 1959), 148–49.
79. "Mike Wallace Asks William F. Buckley, Jr. 'Where Is the Right Wing?'" *New York Post*, January 15, 1958.
80. Buckley first used this phrase, often repeated in different forms by Buckley and others, in his essay "A Reply to Robert Hutchins," which he republished in his first collection of writings, *Rumbles Left and Right: A Book About Troublesome People and Ideas* (New York: Putnam, 1963), 134.
81. Buckley, *Miles Gone By*, 76.
82. Markmann, *The Buckleys*, 96.
83. John Chamberlain, introduction to Buckley, *God and Man at Yale*.
84. John Chamberlain, *A Life with the Printed Word* (New York: Regnery, 1982), 147.
85. Ibid.
86. William F. Buckley Jr., "The FBI Lists and Useful Idiots," On the Right, August 5, 1994.
87. G. G. Malmfeldt to T. E. Bishop, June 27, 1968, FBI file, "William F. Buckley, Jr," accessed through the Freedom of Information Act. See also "Special Issue of the *New York Times*," *National Review*, May 30, 1967.
88. William F. Buckley, Jr., "The Shocking Report of J. Edgar Hoover," On the Right, February 28, 1975.
89. Judis, *William F. Buckley, Jr.*, 98.
90. Howard Hunt to William F. Buckley Jr., June 29, 1961, William F. Buckley, Jr. Papers.
91. Willmoore Kendall authored this particular line. See Daniel McCarthy, "Willmoore Kendall, Man of the People," in *The Dilemmas of American Conservatism*, ed. Kenneth L. Deutsch and Ethan Fishman (Lexington: University Press of Kentucky, 2010), 182. See also Jeffrey Hart, "Willmoore Kendall: The Un-assimilable Man," *National Review*, December 31, 1985.
92. Judis, *William F. Buckley, Jr.*, 90.
93. Buckley, *Miles Gone By*, 60–63.
94. William Rogers Coe to William F. Buckley Jr., July 27, 1951, A. Whitney Griswold Papers, RU 22, group no. YRGA2A-16, box 43, folder 409, Yale University Archives.
95. Ibid.
96. Judis, *William F. Buckley, Jr.*, 90.
97. Bridges and Coyne, *Strictly Right*, 23.
98. Buckley, *Miles Gone By*, 59.
99. Dwight Macdonald, "God and Buckley at Yale," *Reporter*, May 27, 1952.
100. Lloyd G. Reynolds to A. Whitney Griswold, September 9, 1951, A. Whitney Griswold Papers, RU 22, group no. YRGA2A-16, box 43, folder 409.
101. Felix Frankfurter to A. Whitney Griswold, November 19, 1952, A. Whitney Griswold Papers, RU 22, group no. YRGA2A-16, box 43, folder 409.
102. Judis, *William F. Buckley, Jr.*, 93.

103. A. Whitney Griswold to A. Augustus Low, June 25, 1951, A. Whitney Griswold Papers, RU 22, group no. YRG2A-16, box 43, folder 406.
104. McGeorge Bundy to A. Whitney Griswold, September 24, 1951, A. Whitney Griswold Papers, RU 22, group no. YRG2A-16, box 43, folder 409.
105. Ibid.
106. McGeorge Bundy, "The Attack on Yale," *Atlantic Monthly*, November 1951.
107. See Buckley, *Miles Gone By*, 69; and Macdonald, "God and Buckley at Yale."
108. Macdonald, "God and Buckley at Yale," 35–58.
109. McGeorge Bundy, "The Attack on Yale," *Atlantic Monthly*, November 1951.
110. Henry Sloane Coffin to A. Whitney Griswold, September 19, 1951, A. Whitney Griswold Papers, RU 22, group no. YRG2A-16, box 42, folder 404.
111. McGeorge Bundy, "McGeorge Bundy Replies," *Atlantic Monthly*, December 1951.
112. William F. Buckley Jr., "The Changes at Yale," *Atlantic Monthly*, December 1961.
113. Kai Bird, *The Color of Truth: McGeorge Bundy and William Bundy, Brothers in Arms* (New York: Simon and Schuster, 1998), 119.
114. Arthur M. Schlesinger Jr., "God, Man and William F. Buckley, Jr.: Young Man with Old Ideas Lectures the Professors," *New York Post*, November 18, 1951.
115. Arthur M. Schlesinger Jr. to A. Whitney Griswold, December 1, 1951, and *New York Post*, November 18, 1951, A. Whitney Griswold Papers, RU2 2, group no: YRG2A-16, box 42.
116. Peter Viereck, "Conservatism under the Elms," *New York Times*, November 4, 1952.
117. Ibid.
118. John Davenport to A. Whitney Griswold, October 17, 1951, A. Whitney Griswold Papers, RU 22, group no. YRG2A-16, box 42.
119. John Davenport to George Van Santvoord, March 12, 1951, A. Whitney Griswold Papers, RU 22, group no: YRG2A-16.
120. "God and Socialism at Yale," *Life*, October 29, 1951, 32.
121. Frank Ashburn, "Isms and the University," *Saturday Review*, December 15, 1951, 44–45.
122. Buckley, *Miles Gone By*, 77.
123. Max Eastman, "Buckley vs. Yale: A Seasoned Iconoclast Considers a Young Campus Radical," *American Mercury*, December 1951, 22–29.
124. Markmann, *The Buckleys*, 120–21.
125. Ibid.

CHAPTER 3. STANDING ATHWART HISTORY

1. Bridges and Coyne, *Strictly Right*, 28–29; and Judis, *William F. Buckley, Jr.*, 108.
2. William F. Buckley Jr., "The Party and the Deep Blue Sea," *Commonweal*, January 25, 1952.
3. Ibid.
4. Ibid.
5. Text of radio advertisement written by William F. Buckley Jr., William F. Buckley, Jr. Papers.

6. Judis, *William F. Buckley, Jr.*, 104.
7. Ibid., 108–9.
8. William F. Buckley, ed., *Odyssey of a Friend: Whittaker Chambers, Letters to William F. Buckley, Jr.* (New York: Putnam, 1969), 48–52 (letter dated February 7, 1954).
9. Ibid. In explaining his reasons for selecting Richard Nixon as his vice presidential running mate in 1952, Eisenhower singled out Nixon's handling of the Hiss case: "Not once had he [Nixon] overstepped the limits prescribed by the American sense of fair play or American rules applying to such investigations. He did not persecute or defame." See Dwight D. Eisenhower, *Mandate for Change* (New York: Doubleday, 1963), 46.
10. Buckley, *Odyssey of a Friend*, 52–56.
11. Ibid., 52.
12. Ibid., 52–56.
13. Max Eastman, quoted in John P. Diggins, *Up from Communism* (New York: Columbia University Press, 1975) 217–18.
14. Buckley, *Odyssey of a Friend*, 58. The "helter-skelter" reference is from the Old Testament's book of Judges.
15. William F. Buckley Jr., *The Redhunter: A Novel Based on the Life of Senator Joe McCarthy* (Boston: Little, Brown, 1999), 340.
16. Harry S. Truman, "The President's News Conference," August 5, 1948, Gerhard Peters and John T. Woolley, *The American Presidency Project*,http://www.presidency.ucsb.edu/, 170. See also Richard M. Nixon, *Six Crises* (New York: Doubleday, 1962), chapter 1.
17. William F. Buckley Jr. and Brent Bozell, *McCarthy and His Enemies* (New York: Regnery, 1954), 272.
18. Ibid., 253.
19. Buckley, *The Redhunter*, 164.
20. Ibid., 259.
21. Ibid., 153.
22. *New Haven Journal Courier*, April 15, 1954.
23. "GOP Unit Hears Buckley Address: Talk Defending McCarthy Follows a Clash Among Club Women of Party," *New York Times*, April 27, 1954; and "Social Rot Fertilizes Jabs at Joe: Buckley," *New York Daily News*, April 27, 1954.
24. William S. White, "What the McCarthy Method Seeks to Establish," *New York Times*, April 4, 1954.
25. Arthur M. Schlesinger Jr., "The Pendulum of Dogma," *Saturday Review*, April 3, 1954.
26. Max Eastman, "Facts and Logic re: McCarthy," *Freeman*, April 19, 1954.
27. William F. Buckley Jr., "McCarthy to the Rescue," On the Right, April 22, 1968.
28. "GOP Unit Hears Buckley Address"; "Social Rot Fertilizes Jabs at Joe."
29. William F. Buckley Jr. to Daniel Bell, June 30, 1955, William F. Buckley, Jr. Papers.
30. Henry Regnery, *Memoirs of a Dissident Publisher* (New York: Harcourt Brace Jovanovich, 1979), 175.
31. See Bridges and Coyne, *Strictly Right*, 41.
32. Joseph E. Persico, *The Lives and Secrets of William J. Casey: From the OSS to the CIA* (New York: Penguin: 1991), 93.

33. William F. Buckley Jr., "Publisher's Statement," *National Review*, November 19, 1955.
34. William F. Buckley Jr. to Robert Donner, January 5, 1955, William F. Buckley, Jr. Papers.
35. William F. Buckley Jr., *Athwart History*, ed. Linda Bridges and Roger Kimball (New York: Encounter Books, 2010), 288.
36. Thomas W. Evans, *The Education of Ronald Reagan: The General Electric Years and the Untold Story of His Conversion to Conservatism* (New York: Columbia University Press, 2006), 106.
37. Judis, *William F. Buckley, Jr.*, 120.
38. Lee Edwards, *William F. Buckley, Jr.: The Maker of a Movement* (Wilmington, DE: ISI Books, 2010), 56.
39. Richard Norton Smith, *An Uncommon Man: The Triumph of Herbert Hoover* (New York: Simon and Schuster, 1984), 406.
40. William F. Buckley Jr. to Herbert Hoover, March 1, 1955, William F. Buckley, Jr. Papers.
41. Ibid.
42. Herbert C. Hoover to William F. Buckley Jr., November 28, 1958, William F. Buckley, Jr. Papers.
43. Buckley, *Miles Gone By*, 270.
44. Christopher Buckley, e-mail to author.
45. See Richard C. Weaver, *The Southern Tradition at Bay: A History of Post-bellum Thought* (New York, Regnery, 1968). He is better known for his *Ideas Have Consequences* (Chicago: University of Chicago Press, 1948). For a concise exposition of the traditionalist view, see Russell Kirk, *The Conservative Mind: From Burke to Santayana* (Chicago: Regnery, 1953).
46. Buckley, *Miles Gone By*, 288.
47. Judis, *William F. Buckley, Jr.*, 119.
48. Lee Edwards, *The Conservative Revolution: The Movement That Made America* (New York: Free Press, 1999), 80.
49. Arnold Foster and Benjamin R. Epstein, *Danger on the Right* (New York: Random House, 1966), 243.
50. William Loeb to Will and Aloise Buckley, December 30, 1957, William F. Buckley, Jr. Papers.
51. *National Review*, November 19, 1955.

CHAPTER 4. "READING DWIGHT EISENHOWER OUT OF THE CONSERVATIVE MOVEMENT"

Note on the title: Buckley wrote his future colleague Max Eastman that in order to attract investors to his magazine (many of whom liked Ike), he made "no mention [in his fund-raising appeal] of the fact that I intend, in an early issue, to read Dwight Eisenhower out of the conservative movement." Judis, *William F. Buckley, Jr.*, 119.

1. William F. Buckley Jr. to Dwight D. Eisenhower, February 9, 1950, pre-presidential papers, Eisenhower Presidential Library, Abilene, KS.

2. *National Review*, October 5, 1957.
3. Hague, who served as Mayor of Jersey City from 1917 to 1947, was known to use strong-arm tactics to impose his will. Truman, of course, owed his rise to the Pendergast machine of Kansas City.
4. Fred I. Greenstein, *The Hidden-Hand Presidency: Eisenhower as Leader* (New York: Basic Books, 1982), 50, 258.
5. Ibid.
6. Michael Barone, *Our Country: The Shaping of America from Roosevelt to Reagan* (New York: Collier Macmillan, 1990), 369.
7. Ralph de Toledano, *Notes from the Underground: The Whittaker Chambers–Ralph de Toledano Letters, 1949–1960* (Washington, DC: Regnery, 1997), 216.
8. Macdonald, "On the Horizon: Scrambled Eggheads on the Right." Coughlin was a Catholic priest and radio host who lent his voice to the isolationist cause in the 1930s. Long was a Louisiana "populist," given to demagoguery. McCarthy was a Senator from Wisconsin, widely believed to have shown little concern for civil liberties in the pursuit of security risks.
9. "Welcome Back," *National Review*, November 19, 1955.
10. William F. Knowland, "Peace—With Honor," *National Review*, November 19, 1955.
11. "Bloody but Still Bowed," *National Review*, November 19, 1955.
12. "Caesarism," *National Review*, November 26, 1955.
13. William F. Buckley Jr., "Mr. Eisenhower's Decision and the Eisenhower Program," *National Review*, March 21, 1956.
14. Ibid.
15. "Who Is Ahead?" *National Review*, June 20, 1956.
16. Among Eisenhower's reasons for expanding the nation's nuclear forces was that they were less costly to maintain than conventional forces. This allowed him to cut back on defense expenditures. He called the defense posture he put into place "the new look."
17. This was the "Secret Speech" Khrushchev delivered before the Twentieth Conference of the Communist Party on February 25, 1956.
18. James Burnham, "Containment or Liberation," *National Review*, September 29, 1956.
19. Whittaker Chambers to William F. Buckley Jr., October 4, 1959, in Buckley, *Odyssey of a Friend*.
20. William F. Buckley Jr., "Neutralization: Liberal Assumptions," *National Review*, February 23, 1957.
21. Ibid.
22. This account of the deterioration of the Buckley-Schlamm relationship is based on accounts provided by Linda Bridges and John Coyne in *Strictly Right* and from the author's conversations with the late Priscilla Buckley.
23. For an assessment of Rusher's career, see David B. Frisk, *If Not Us, Who? William Rusher, "National Review" and the Conservative Movement* (Wilmington, DE: ISI Books, 2012.)
24. See "night letter," William F. Buckley, Jr. Papers.
25. "Should Conservatives Vote for Eisenhower-Nixon?" *National Review*, October 20, 1956.

26. William F. Buckley Jr., "Reflections on Election Eve," *National Review*, November 3, 1956.
27. Judis, *William F. Buckley, Jr.*, 146.
28. "Why the South Must Prevail," *National Review*, August 24, 1957.
29. For more on the role LBJ played in passing the Civil Rights Act of 1957, see Rowland Evans and Robert Novak, *Lyndon Johnson and the Exercise of Power* (New York: New American Library, 1966), chapters 6 and 7; and Robert Caro, *Master of the Senate* (New York: Knopf, 2002).
30. "Why the South Must Prevail."
31. Ibid.
32. "Foul," *National Review*, April 18, 1956.
33. Taylor Branch, *Parting the Waters: America in the King Years* (New York: Simon and Schuster, 1988), 220–21.
34. "Mr. Bozell Dissents from the Views Expressed in the Editorial 'Why the South Must Prevail,'" *National Review*, September 7, 1957.
35. "A Clarification," *National Review*, September 7, 1957.
36. Quoted in Crespino, *Strom Thurmond's America*, 10.
37. "A Clarification."
38. William F. Buckley Jr., term paper written at the Millbrook School, March 17, 1943, William F. Buckley, Jr. Papers.
39. "The Lie to Mr. Eisenhower," *National Review*, October 5, 1957.
40. "How Much Is It Worth?" *National Review*, January 19, 1957.
41. "The Breathless General and the Honest Marshal," *National Review*, August 3, 1957.
42. William F. Buckley Jr., "Dwight Eisenhower," On the Right, August 24, 1968. For Kempton's view of Ike, see Murray Kempton, "The Underestimation of Dwight D. Eisenhower," *Esquire*, September 1967.
43. William F. Buckley Jr., "Ecce Ike," *National Review*, December 3, 1963.
44. Buckley, *Up from Liberalism*, 145.
45. William F. Buckley Jr., "Adlai Stevenson, R.I.P.," On the Right, July 20, 1965.
46. Ibid.
47. Buckley. "Dwight Eisenhower."
48. "William F. Buckley, Jr.: Conservatism Can Be Fun," *Time*, November 3, 1967.
49. "Who Obstructed Justice in the Case of Adam Clayton Powell?" *National Review*, May 24, 1958.
50. William F. Buckley Jr., "Ayn Rand: R.I.P.," On the Right, March 11, 1981.
51. Whittaker Chambers, "Big Sister Is Watching," *National Review*, December 28, 1957, 595.
52. Ibid.
53. Judis, *William F. Buckley, Jr.*, 161.
54. Buckley, "Ayn Rand: R.I.P."
55. William F. Buckley Jr., "Again, Ayn Rand," On the Right, May 8, 1981.
56. *National Review Bulletin*, November 1958. For a discussion of the book and its publication, see Peter Finn and Petra Couvee, *The Zhivago Affair: The Kremlin, the CIA, and the Battle over a Forbidden Book* (New York: Pantheon, 2014). For a discussion of

disagreement on the right over the significance of *Doctor Zhivago* and of the authenticity of the novel as an anti-Communist tract, see Ben Musachio, "*Doctor Zhivago* and American Conservatism," *National Review Online*, October 17, 2015.

57. "If You Want It Straight," *American Opinion*, February 1959.
58. See John Chamberlain, "A Judgment on Revolution," *National Review*, September 27, 1958; and Eugene Lyons, "Folklore of the Right," *National Review*, April 11, 1959.
59. William F. Buckley Jr. to Robert Welch, March 3, 1959, William F. Buckley, Jr. Papers.
60. Judis, *William F. Buckley, Jr.*, 195.
61. Robert Welch, "Dear Reader," *American Opinion*, May 1959.
62. Robert Welch to William F. Buckley Jr., April 28, 1958, William F. Buckley, Jr. Papers.
63. Jonathan M. Schoenwald, *A Time for Choosing: The Rise of American Conservatism* (New York: Oxford University Press, 2001), 41.
64. "The Damage We Have Done to Ourselves," *National Review*, September 26, 1959.
65. Judis, *William F. Buckley, Jr.*, 177.
66. For accounts of the Hiss case and of Chambers's role in it, see Whittaker Chambers, *Witness* (New York: Random House, 1952); Nixon, *Six Crises*; Allen Weinstein, *Perjury: The Hiss-Chambers Case* (New York: Random House, 1999); Sam Tanenhaus, *Whittaker Chambers, A Biography* (New York: Random House, 1997); Ralph de Toledano, *Seeds of Treason* (New York: Funk and Wagnalls, 1950); and Alistair Cook, *A Generation on Trial* (New York: Knopf, 1950).
67. Chamberlain, *A Life with the Printed Word*, 160.
68. See William F. Buckley Jr., "The Tranquil World of Dwight D. Eisenhower," *National Review*, January 4, 1958. Nixon or his staff checked certain phrases in the margins and underlined others.
69. William F. Buckley Jr. to Richard Nixon, December 26, 1957, William F. Buckley, Jr. Papers.
70. Ibid.
71. Buckley, *Odyssey of a Friend*, 79.
72. William F. Buckley Jr., "Towards an Empirical Definition of Conservatism," in *The Jeweler's Eye*, ed. William F. Buckley Jr. (New York: Putnam, 1968), 16. In a letter to Buckley, Chambers made reference to the papered-over split between Burnham (the champion of realpolitik) and Bozell (and, to a lesser extent, Meyer) and made clear his aversion for the uncompromising stances he saw creeping into the magazine.
73. Buckley, *Up from Liberalism*. At the time Buckley wrote this book, the *New York Post* was owned by Dorothy Schiff, a pillar of the liberal establishment in her own right.
74. Ibid.
75. Ibid., 194.
76. William F. Buckley Jr., "A Relaxing View of Ronald Reagan," November 28, 1967, in Buckley, *The Jeweler's Eye*, 97. Buckley cited Chambers's reflection that a conservatism that "cannot find room in its folds for the actualities [of maneuver] is a conservatism that is not a political force, or even a twitch: it has become a literary whimsy."

77. Arthur M. Schlesinger Jr., "Inside Conservative Looking Out," *New York Times*, October 4, 1959.
78. Whittaker Chambers to William F. Buckley Jr., May 16, 1960, in Buckley, *Odyssey of a Friend*, 285–87.
79. Barry Goldwater, *The Conscience of a Conservative* (Shepherdsville, KY: Victor, 1960), 23–24.
80. Lee Edwards, *Goldwater: The Man Who Made a Revolution* (Washington, DC: Regnery, 1995), 134.
81. Theodore H. White, *The Making of the President, 1960* (New York: Atheneum, 1961), 388–90.
82. Bird, *The Color of Truth*, 159–60.
83. William F. Buckley, Jr., "Why Not Teddy?" On the Right, September 30, 1962. See also *National Review*, October 9, 1962.
84. Thomas J. Whalen, *Kennedy Versus Lodge: The 1952 Massachusetts Senate Race* (Boston: Northeastern University Press, 2000), 121–26.
85. In *Profiles in Courage*, Kennedy singled out Taft for the "courage" he exhibited in opposing the Nuremberg war crimes trials, which he believed were unconstitutional because they were conducted under ex post facto laws intended to hold to account perpetrators of genocide. See John F. Kennedy, *Profiles in Courage* (New York: Harper and Brothers, 1956). Buckley would later oppose the trial of Adolf Eichmann on similar grounds and question why the trial was taking place in Israel rather than Europe, where Eichmann had committed his crimes, especially since Israel as a nation did not exist until 1948.
86. Robert Alan Goldberg, *Barry Goldwater* (New Haven, CT: Yale University Press, 1995), 147.
87. Marvin Liebman, *Coming out Conservative* (San Francisco: Chronicle Books, 1992), 150.
88. *National Review*, September 24, 1960.
89. "*National Review* and the 1960 Election," *National Review*, October 22, 1960.
90. Frank S. Meyer, "Principles and Heresies: Only Four Years to 1964," *National Review*, December 3, 1960.
91. Ibid.
92. "*National Review* and the 1960 Election."
93. Judis, *William F. Buckley, Jr.*, 179.
94. Ibid., 178. See also Kevin J. Smant, *How Great the Triumph: James Burnham, Anti-Communism, and the Conservative Movement* (Lanham, MD: University Press of America, 1992), 74.
95. "So Long, Ike," *National Review*, January 14, 1961.
96. Eisenhower revisionism of the kind Buckley rejected received a boost from Garry Wills in *Nixon Agonistes: The Crisis of the Self-Made Man* (1970) and from New Left historian William Appleman Williams in *Some Presidents from Wilson to Nixon* (1972).
97. William F. Buckley Jr., "A New Preface," in *Up from Liberalism* (New York: Bantam, 1968,) xxvii–xxviii.
98. *National Review*, January 14, 1961.

CHAPTER 5. THE EDITOR, THE COLOSSUS, AND THE "ANTI-COMMUNIST AT HARVARD"

1. Buckley, "The Party and the Deep Blue Sea."
2. For a discussion of Dewey's career, see Richard Norton Smith, *Thomas E. Dewey and His Times* (New York: Norton, 1982).
3. The two led the dominant faction within the state Young Republicans, which they named the "Syndicate." White served as the Young Republicans Chairman. Dewey named him head of the politically sensitive and patronage-rich Department of Motor Vehicles.
4. Javits wrote two books describing his political career and his identity as a liberal Republican. See Jacob K. Javits, *Order of Battle* (New York: Atheneum, 1964); and Jacob K. Javits and Rafael Steinberg, *Javits: The Autobiography of a Public Man* (Boston: Houghton Mifflin, 1982).
5. William F. Buckley Jr., "The Agony of Richard Nixon," On the Right, December 19, 1967.
6. See George J. Marlin, *Fighting the Good Fight: A History of the New York Conservative Party* (South Bend, IN: St. Augustine's, 2002).
7. Ibid., 28.
8. William F. Buckley Jr. to Nelson A. Rockefeller, January 3, 1956, "Magazines: *National Review*," Rockefeller Family Archives, record group 4, Nelson A. Rockefeller, Personal Papers, Tarrytown, NY.
9. Francis A. Jamieson to Nelson A. Rockefeller, January 23, 1956, and February 2, 1956, "Magazines: *National Review*," Rockefeller Family Archives.
10. See Marlin, *Fighting the Good Fight*. The "listening tour" comparison was a reference to Hillary Clinton's activities in the run-up to her campaign for the U.S. Senate in New York in 2000.
11. "The Week," *National Review*, February 15, 1958.
12. William F. Buckley Jr., foreword to J. Daniel Mahoney, *Actions Speak Louder: The Story of the New York Conservative Party* (New Rochelle, NY: Arlington House, 1969), 12.
13. White, *The Making of the President, 1960*, 182.
14. Persico, *Lives and Secrets of William J. Casey*, 114.
15. See J. P. McFadden, "The Royal Road to Albany: When a Rockefeller Needs a Friend," *National Review*, August 2, 1958.
16. The talking points Rockefeller's staff prepared for the candidate's use in possible response to *National Review*'s criticisms of him can be found at the Rockefeller Family Archives.
17. "Rockefeller It Is—But Can They Be So Sure?" *National Review*, August 30, 1958.
18. See James Desmond, *Nelson Rockefeller: A Political Biography* (New York: Macmillan, 1964), 197–98.
19. The concept of "moral obligation bonds" originated with future Attorney General John Mitchell, bond counsel and occasional Rockefeller attorney.
20. For assessments of Rockefeller's record as Governor, see Richard Norton Smith, *On His Own Terms: A Life of Nelson Rockefeller* (New York: Random House, 2015); Robert

H. Connery and Gerald Benjamin, *Rockefeller of New York: Executive Power in the State House* (Ithaca, NY: Cornell University Press, 1979); Gerald Benjamin and T. Norman Hurd, *Rockefeller in Retrospect* (Albany: Rockefeller Institute of Government, 1984); and Peter Collier and David Horowitz, *The Rockefellers: An American Dynasty* (New York: Holt, Rinehart and Winston, 1976).

21. "How're You Getting on with D.F.B.?" *National Review*, January 19, 1963.
22. Buckley, *The Unmaking of a Mayor*, 52.
23. Ibid.
24. George J. Marlin, *Fighting the Good Fight: A History of the New York Conservative* Party (South Bend, IN: St. Augustine's Press, 2002), 39.
25. Timothy J. Sullivan, *New York State and the Rise of Modern Conservatism: Redrawing Party Lines* (Albany: SUNY Press, 2009), 16.
26. David Rogers, financial editor of the *New York Herald Tribune*, was ordered to resign as Conservative Party official or face unemployment. LeMoyne University Professor Anthony Bouscaren, considering a run for state office, declined after being pressured by the Syracuse Republican organization. See Marlin, *Fighting the Good Fight*, 84.
27. James Desmond, "Bob Aims Own Knife at Split-up of State Pie," *New York Daily News*, November 16, 1961. See also Buckley, *The Unmaking of a Mayor*, 54.
28. Desmond, *Nelson Rockefeller.*
29. Marlin, *Fighting the Good Fight*, 57.
30. See Desmond, *Nelson Rockefeller*, 312.
31. Marlin, *Fighting the Good Fight*, 63.
32. Sullivan, *New York State and the Rise of Modern Conservatism*, 29.
33. Ibid.
34. Buckley, *The Unmaking of a Mayor*, 57.
35. Sullivan, *New York State and the Rise of Modern Conservatism*, 29.
36. Buckley, *Miles Gone By*.
37. Ibid.
38. For a discussion of Kissinger's journal *Confluence*, see Walter Isaacson, *Kissinger: A Biography* (New York: Simon and Schuster, 1992), 72–74, 86.
39. Henry A. Kissinger, *Nuclear Weapons and Foreign Policy* (New York: Westview Press, 1957).
40. William F. Buckley Jr., "Enter Rockefeller," On the Right, April 13, 1968.

CHAPTER 6. SAILING AGAINST THE NEW FRONTIER

1. James MacGregor Burns, *John F. Kennedy: A Political Profile* (New York: Harcourt, Brace, 1960), 81.
2. Reeves, *The Life and Times of Joe McCarthy*, 444.
3. Burns, *John F. Kennedy*, 134–35.
4. Arthur M. Schlesinger Jr., *Kennedy or Nixon: Does It Make a Difference?* (New York: Macmillan, 1960). Schlesinger intended his book as a response to a statement CBS commentator Eric Sevareid had made that the two candidates were so similar in outlook and policy orientation that it mattered little which was elected.

5. "A Little Positive Thought for Norman Peale," *National Review*, September 29, 1960. Peale had said that the election of a Catholic would put the nation's "culture" at risk and could usher in the end of "free speech." See "The Religious Issue Is Getting Hotter and Hotter," *Newsweek*, September 19, 1960. Peale had won national acclaim for his best-selling book *The Power of Positive Thinking* (New York: Fireside Books, 1952). The "apology" reference pertained to Kennedy's reaction when the USSR shot down an American U-2 reconnaissance plane over Soviet air space. The Democrat had called upon Eisenhower to apologize for having ordered the flight.
6. Ken Burns, *The Roosevelts: An Intimate History*, PBS, September 14, 2014.
7. Markmann, *The Buckleys*, x, 23, 53.
8. "The Buckleys: A Gifted American Family," *Life*, December 18, 1970.
9. Buckley, "Why Not Teddy?" On the Right, September 30, 1962.
10. Kenneth P. O'Donnell and David F. Powers, *Johnny, We Hardly Knew Ye* (Boston: Little, Brown, 1972), 129.
11. John F. Kennedy, speech before the Houston Ministerial Association, September 9, 1960.
12. William F. Buckley Jr., "JFK and Catholicism" (review of *John F. Kennedy and American Catholicism*, by John Fuchs), reprinted in William F. Buckley Jr., *The Governor Listeth* (New York: Putnam, 1970), 254.
13. Ibid. See also William F. Buckley Jr.,"Why We Need a Black President in 1980," *Look*, January 13, 1970.
14. "Lion of Conservatism," *Newsweek*, May 13, 1963.
15. William F. Buckley Jr., "The Violation of Arthur," On the Right, March 30, 1963.
16. Ibid.
17. Buckley, *Rumbles Left and Right*.
18. Buckley, "The Violation of Arthur."
19. Transcript, *60 Minutes*, CBS broadcast, September 29, 1970.
20. Arthur M. Schlesinger Jr., *Journals, 1952–2000*, ed. Andrew Schlesinger and Stephen Schlesinger (New York: Penguin, 2007), 781.
21. William F. Buckley Jr., "Arthur Schlesinger, R.I.P.," On the Right, March 2, 2007.
22. Judis, *William F. Buckley, Jr.*, 274.
23. "The Federal Way," *National Review*, January 14, 1961; "Are There Other Ways to Speed Research?" *National Review*, February 11, 1961; and William F. Buckley Jr., "JFK Cloying," *National Review*, April 8, 1961.
24. "Cuba, R.I.P.," *National Review*, May 6, 1961.
25. Dan Wakefield, "William F. Buckley, Jr.: Portrait of a Complainer," *Esquire*, January 1961.
26. "Berlin: Score at the Half," *National Review*, December 16, 1961.
27. Ibid.
28. Jason Duncan, *John F. Kennedy and the Spirit of Cold War Liberalism* (New York: Routledge, 2014) 95.
29. "The Collapse of the GOP," *National Review*, May 8, 1962.
30. William F. Buckley Jr., "Disorganized We March," On the Right, February 3, 1963.
31. John F. Kennedy, "Government and Business: The True Dialogue," commencement speech, Yale University, June 11, 1962.

32. Arthur M. Schlesinger Jr. to McGeorge Bundy, June 29, 1962, "Remarks for the President: Address at Yale University," 6/11/62 file unit, box WH67, folder 1, John F. Kennedy Presidential Library, Boston.
33. Kennedy had covered the San Francisco United Nations conference as a reporter for the Hearst newspaper chain.
34. William F. Buckley Jr., "Are Liberals Afraid of Truth?" *Salt Lake Tribune*, December 10, 1961.
35. Gore Vidal, "Liberals? There Aren't Any," *Salt Lake Tribune*, December 10, 1961.
36. Fred Kaplan, *Gore Vidal* (London: Bloomsbury,2000), 496.
37. Judis, *William F. Buckley, Jr.*, 203. For more on the genesis of Buckley's column, see William F. Buckley Jr., *Cruising Speed* (New York: Putnam, 1971), 114–21.
38. William F. Buckley Jr., "An Evening with Jack Paar," in Buckley, *Rumbles Left and Right*, 153–69.
39. Ibid.
40. Ibid.; William F. Buckley Jr., "On Experiencing Gore Vidal," *Esquire*, August 1969; and Buckley, "Why Not Teddy?"
41. William F. Buckley Jr., "A 24th Amendment," On the Right, July 8, 1962.
42. William F. Buckley Jr., "The Moon *and* Bust," On the Right, June 1, 1963.
43. John Kenneth Galbraith, *The Affluent Society* (New York: Houghton Mifflin, 1958).
44. For a discussion of the Kennedy tax cuts, see Alvin S. Felzenberg, *The Leaders We Deserved (and a Few We Didn't): Rethinking the Presidential Rating Game* (New York: Basic Books, 2011).
45. "The Coming Tax Cut," *National Review*, December 31, 1962.
46. Felix Belair Jr., "Eisenhower Would Limit Withholding to 50% Tax," *New York Times*, January 3, 1963.
47. William F. Buckley Jr., "The Mess in Mississippi," On the Right, October, 7 1962.
48. William F. Buckley Jr., "Saying Good-bye to Aloise Steiner Buckley, R.I.P.," *National Review*, April 19, 1985.
49. Ibid.
50. Michael Beschloss, *Presidential Courage: Brave Leaders and How They Changed America, 1789–1989* (New York: Simon and Schuster, 1007), 235–79.
51. William F. Buckley Jr., "Worshipping JFK," On the Right, November 21, 2004.
52. William F. Buckley Jr., "Birmingham and After," On the Right, May 5, 1963.
53. William F. Buckley Jr., "Count Me Out," On the Right, August 17, 1963. See also John F. Kennedy, "Address to the Nation on Civil Rights," June 11, 1963.
54. *National Review Bulletin*, October 1, 1963.
55. Ibid.
56. See Graham Allison and Philip Zelikow, *Essence of Decision: Explaining the Cuban Missile Crisis* (New York: Longman, 1999.)
57. William F. Buckley Jr., "We Have Had It, Amigos," On the Right, September 16, 1962.
58. William F. Buckley Jr., "Quiet, Conspiracy at Work," On the Right, January 6, 1963.
59. For a detailed analysis of the collective mindset of Kennedy's advisers, see Geoffrey Kabaservice, *The Guardians: Kingman Brewster, His Circle and the Rise of the Liberal*

Establishment (New York: Henry Holt, 2004); and David Halberstam, *The Best and the Brightest* (New York: Simon and Schuster, 1972).

60. William F. Buckley Jr., "The Decline of Mr. Kennedy," On the Right, July 13, 1963.
61. William F. Buckley Jr., "On the Treaty of Moscow," On the Right, August 24, 1963.
62. "Notes on the Grand Tour," *National Review*, July 16, 1963.
63. William F. Buckley Jr., "The Secret Memorandum," On the Right, October 5, 1963.
64. John F. Kennedy, speech delivered at the University of Washington, November 16, 1961.
65. John F. Kennedy, address at a Democratic Party dinner in Los Angeles, November 18, 1961.
66. Quoted in David Burnham, *A Law unto Itself: The IRS and the Abuse of Power* (New York: Vintage Books, 1989), 270. See also transcript, presidential news conference, November 29, 1961, www.jfkl.org.
67. Burnham, *A Law unto Itself.*
68. James Bovard, "A Brief History of IRS Political Targeting," *Wall Street Journal*, May 14, 2013.
69. William F. Buckley Jr., "The Secret Memorandum," On the Right, October 5, 1963.
70. See Tom Wicker, "Kennedy Asserts Far-Right Groups Provoke Disunity," *New York Times*, November 24, 1961; "Thunder on the Right," *Time*, November 24, 1961; "Crackpots: How They Help Communism," *Life*, December 1, 1961.
71. James Reston, "The Conservative Battle in the G.O.P.," *New York Times*, February 2, 1961. Before becoming national party Chairman, Bailey headed the Democratic Party in Connecticut.
72. Buckley, "The Secret Memorandum."
73. Myer Feldman, "Memorandum for the President. Subject: Right Wing Groups," August 15, 1963, President's Office Files, box 196, folder "Right Wing Movements, Part 1," JFKL, Papers of John F. Kennedy, John F. Kennedy Presidential Library. Entities and individuals singled out for special attention were the John Birch Society, Texas billionaire H. L. Hunt, the Reverend Carl McIntire, *Human Events*, and certain radio stations. The next day, Myer sent the President Senator Gale McGee's (D-WY) own assessment of the situation.
74. Burnham, *A Law unto Itself*, 272.
75. See James Bovard, "A Brief History of IRS Political Targeting," *Wall Street Journal*, May 14, 2013; and Burnham, *A Law unto Itself.*
76. Of the founding of ISI, Feldman wrote: "The ISI's first president was William F. Buckley, Jr. In addition to its publications, ISI promotes campus discussion groups or conservative clubs, and arranges lecture tours for such conservatives as L. Brent Bozell, Frank Meyer, Russell Kirk, and Frank Chodorov, all of whom are writers for *National Review.*" Young Americans for Freedom, Feldman noted, "was founded at the Sharon, Connecticut home of *National Review* editor, William F. Buckley, Jr., in September, 1960, when more than one hundred delegates responded to a call by the executive committee of a group calling itself Youth for Goldwater." See Feldman, "Memorandum for the President."
77. Gale McGee to Myer Feldman, August 14, 1963, Papers of John F. Kennedy. According to one account, the administration had initially considered monitoring, if only for

political cover, two liberal-learning organizations, the Anti-Defamation League of B'nai B'rith and the League for Industrial Democracy, as well as one further on the left, Fair Play for Cuba. One agitator affiliated with the latter group was Lee Harvey Oswald, JFK's accused assassin. See Burnham, *A Law unto Itself*, 272.

78. Foster and Epstein, *Danger on the Right*, 247.
79. Ibid.
80. Gerald L. K. Smith to William F. Buckley Jr., November 21, 1964, William F. Buckley, Jr. Papers.
81. William F. Buckley Jr. to Gerald L. K. Smith, December 16, 1964, William F. Buckley, Jr. Papers.
82. William F. Buckley Jr. to Gerald L. K. Smith, September 15, 1961, and November 29, 1971, William F. Buckley, Jr. Papers.
83. Charles A. Johnson, "Producer Regards Backlash as Anti-Rights Rationalization," *Red Bank Register*, April 13, 1967.
84. John T. McNamara to the editor of the *Red Bank Register*, April 20, 1967.
85. William F. Buckley Jr. to Dore Schary, June 27 1967, William F. Buckley, Jr. Papers.
86. Transcript, Firing Line, August 18, 1966.
87. William F. Buckley Jr., "Nathan Perlmutter, R.I.P.," *National Review*, August 14, 1987.
88. Abraham H. Foxman, *Never Again* (San Francisco: Harper San Francisco, 2003), 58. While campaigning for President in 1988, Jackson was widely criticized for referring to New York City as "hymie-town." Many, including the Anti-Defamation League, considered a speech Sharpton gave eulogizing an African American youth who had been struck by a car in a motorcade in the Crown Heights section of Brooklyn a factor that contributed to the retaliatory murder of a rabbinical student at the hands of a gang. See William Saletan and Avi Zenilman, "The Gaffes of Al Sharpton," *Slate*, October 7, 2003.
89. William F. Buckley Jr., "The Guilt Is Personal," On the Right, November 25, 1963.
90. Ibid.
91. William F. Buckley Jr., "Do They Really Hate to Hate?" On the Right, December 14, 1963.
92. Bill Minutaglio and Steven L. Davis, *Dallas 1963* (New York: Twelve, 2013).
93. William F. Buckley Jr., "JFK: The Morning After," On the Right, December 7, 1963.
94. Lyndon B. Johnson, address to a joint session of Congress, November 27, 1963.
95. Buckley, "JFK: The Morning After."
96. William F. Buckley Jr., "Bobby for King," On the Right, June 2, 1966.
97. Rose Kennedy to William F. Buckley Jr., December 15, 1966, William F. Buckley, Jr. Papers.
98. William F. Buckley Jr. to Rose Kennedy, December 28, 1966, William F. Buckley, Jr. Papers.
99. "William F. Buckley, Jr.: Conservatism Can Be Fun." See also "The Bill and Bobby Show," *Time*, April 8, 1966. In that earlier issue of the magazine Buckley is quoted as saying, "Why does baloney reject the grinder?"

100. Barbara Leaming, *Jacqueline Kennedy Onassis: The Untold Story* (New York: St. Martin's, 2014), 267–68.
101. William F. Buckley Jr., "Jacqueline Onassis, R.I.P.," On the Right, June 13, 1994.
102. William F. Buckley Jr., "Impeach the Speech, Not the President," *New York Times Magazine*, May 10, 1973.
103. William F. Buckley Jr. to Edward M. Kennedy, October 15, 1969, William F. Buckley, Jr. Papers.
104. Edward M. Kennedy to William F. Buckley Jr., October 23, 1969, William F. Buckley, Jr. Papers.
105. Judis, *William F. Buckley, Jr.*, 386.
106. Ibid. There are several iterations of this story. In *Strictly Right*, Bridges and Coyne have Pat Buckley say that there were three bridges. In *Miles Gone By*, Buckley told of only one bridge.
107. See Richard Reeves, *President Kennedy: Profile in Power* (New York: Simon and Schuster, 1993); and William F. Buckley Jr., "Reeves' Kennedy," *National Review*, December 31, 1994.
108. Buckley, "Worshipping JFK."

CHAPTER 7. BILL, BARRY, AND THE BIRCHERS

1. Judis, *William F. Buckley, Jr.*, 165.
2. "Toward a More Responsible Two Party System," *American Political Science Review* 44 (September 1950).
3. James MacGregor Burns, *The Deadlock of Democracy: Four Party Politics in America* (New York: Prentice Hall, 1963).
4. Kennedy won reelection that year by over 1 million votes.
5. Barry Goldwater, *Pure Goldwater*, ed. John W. Dean and Barry M. Goldwater Jr. (New York: Palgrave, 2008), 115.
6. For a fuller discussion of Milliken's rising influence within the GOP during this period, see Jonathan Katz, "The Man Who Launched the GOP's Civil War," *Politico* October 1, 2015.
7. Lee Edwards, *Goldwater*, 110.
8. Manion arranged for publication of the 127-page book through a nonprofit company he established for this purpose. After an initial printing of fifty thousand copies, *The Conscience of a Conservative* appeared in tenth place on *Time*'s best-seller list and at fourteenth on that of the *New York Times*. See Rick Perlstein, *Before the Storm: Barry Goldwater and the Unmaking of the American Consensus* (New York: Hill and Wang, 2001), 62–63; and Goldberg, *Barry Goldwater*, 138–39.
9. "Goldwater Here, There, Everywhere," *National Review*, April 9, 1960.
10. Goldwater, *The Conscience of a Conservative*, 15.
11. Goldberg, *Barry Goldwater*, 144.
12. Ibid.
13. Ibid.
14. Barry Goldwater, "Declaration of Presidential Candidacy," Goldwater for President, press release, January 3, 1964.

15. Goldberg, *Barry Goldwater,* 371.
16. Ibid., 148.
17. William F. Buckley Jr. to Barry Goldwater, January 11, 1961, William F. Buckley, Jr. Papers.
18. Ibid.
19. Barry Goldwater to William F. Buckley Jr., January 21, 1961, William F. Buckley, Jr. Papers.
20. Barry Goldwater to William F. Buckley Jr., February 21, 1961, William F. Buckley, Jr. Papers.
21. William F. Buckley Jr. to Barry Goldwater, June 14, 1961, William F. Buckley, Jr. Papers. See also Barry Goldwater to William F. Buckley Jr., March 8 and March 22, 1961, William F. Buckley, Jr. Papers.
22. Judis, *William F. Buckley, Jr.,* 221.
23. William F. Buckley Jr. to Barry Goldwater, June 7, 1961, William F. Buckley, Jr. Papers.
24. Barry Goldwater to William F. Buckley Jr., May 31, 1961, William F. Buckley, Jr. Papers.
25. William F. Buckley Jr. to Barry Goldwater, June 7, 1961, William F. Buckley, Jr. Papers.
26. Barry Goldwater to J. O. McCurray, July 5, 1961, William F. Buckley, Jr. Papers.
27. E. J. Dionne, "Buckley Retires as Editor; *National Review* Founder Steps Down After 35 Years," *Washington Post,* October 6, 1990. Welch, in Buckley's eyes, certainly qualified as a "kook." He did not, however, traffic in anti-Semitism or racism. One who did, with whom Buckley tangled often, was Liberty Lobby founder Willis Carto who, Buckley said, "epitomized the fever swamps of the right." See Douglas Martin, "Willis Carto, Far Right Figure and Holocaust Denier, Dies at 89," *New York Times,* November 1, 2015.
28. William F. Buckley Jr. to Paul H. Talbert, March 29, 1961, William F. Buckley, Jr. Papers.
29. Regnery published Welch's *May God Forgive Us* (1952), a critical account of U.S. policy regarding China in the first half of the twentieth century, and his *The Life of John Birch* (1960).
30. Judis, *William F. Buckley, Jr.,* 193.
31. Robert Welch to William F. Buckley Jr., May 20, 1958, William F. Buckley, Jr. Papers.
32. William F. Buckley Jr. to Robert Welch, March 3, 1959, William F. Buckley, Jr. Papers.
33. William F. Buckley Jr., "Goldwater, the John Birch Society, and Me," *Commentary,* March 2008.
34. Robert Welch to William F. Buckley Jr., April 28, 1958, William F. Buckley, Jr. Papers.
35. William F. Buckley Jr., *Flying High: Remembering Barry Goldwater* (New York: Basic Books, 2008).
36. Buckley, "Goldwater, the John Birch Society, and Me."
37. Ibid.
38. Goldberg, *Barry Goldwater,* 137.
39. Robert W. Welch, *Blue Book* (Belmont, MA: Western Islands, 1959), 146. For a fuller discussion of Welch's tactics, see Schoenwald, *A Time for Choosing,* chapter 3.
40. Schoenwald, *A Time for Choosing,* 64. See also Foster and Epstein, *Danger on the Right,* 11.

41. Foster and Epstein, *Danger on the Right*, 24–26.
42. Ibid.
43. Jane Buckley Smith to Miss Page Garrity, St. Timothy's School, William F. Buckley, Jr. Papers.
44. William F. Buckley Jr., "How Does It Go with the John Birch Society?" On the Right, November 14, 1967.
45. Ibid.
46. William F. Buckley Jr. to Robert Welch, March 3, 1959, William F. Buckley, Jr. Papers.
47. William F. Buckley Jr. to Robert Welch, October 21, 1960, and William F. Buckley Jr. to Cap Breezley, November 7, 1960, William F. Buckley, Jr. Papers.
48. Robert Welch to William F. Buckley Jr., October 24, 1960, William F. Buckley, Jr. Papers.
49. Unsigned memo to William F. Buckley Jr. by a member of *National Review*'s staff, March 28, 1961, William F. Buckley, Jr. Papers.
50. Unsigned memo to William F. Buckley Jr. by a member of *National Review*'s staff, March 28, 1961.
51. Neil McCaffrey to William F. Buckley Jr., April 3, 1961, William F. Buckley, Jr. Papers.
52. Paul H. Talbert to William F. Buckley Jr., March 29, 1961, William F. Buckley, Jr. Papers.
53. James J. Kilpatrick to William F. Buckley Jr., March 27, 1961, William F. Buckley, Jr. Papers.
54. "Senator Scores Group Calling Eisenhower a Red: Young Deplores Growth of John Birch Society," *New York Times*, March 9, 1961; and "Storm over Birchers," *Time*, April 7, 1961.
55. Scott Farris, *Almost President: The Men Who Lost the Race, but Changed the World* (Lanham, MD: Lyons, 2013), 195.
56. William F. Buckley Jr. to Barry Goldwater, March 13, 1961, William F. Buckley, Jr. Papers.
57. "The Uproar," *National Review*, April 22, 1961.
58. Geoffrey Kabaservice, "What William F. Buckley, Jr. Would Think of Today's GOP," *New Republic*, April 2, 2012.
59. William F. Buckley Jr., April 12, 1961, William F. Buckley, Jr. Papers (Birch file).
60. William F. Buckley Jr., April 18, 1961, William F. Buckley, Jr. Papers (Birch file).
61. William Rusher to William F. Buckley Jr., February 5, 1963, William F. Buckley, Jr. Papers.
62. Barry Goldwater and Jack Casserly, *Goldwater* (New York: Doubleday, 1988), 139.
63. Theodore H. White, *The Making of the President, 1964* (New York: Atheneum, 1965), 125.
64. Buckley, "Goldwater, the John Birch Society, and Me."
65. Stephen Shadegg, *What Happened to Goldwater?* (New York: Holt, Rinehart, and Winston, 1965), 105.
66. Buckley, "How Does It Go with the John Birch Society?"
67. Buckley, *Flying High*, 69–70.
68. William F. Buckley Jr. to Barry Goldwater, January? 1962, William F. Buckley, Jr. Papers.

69. William F. Buckley Jr. to Robert Welch, January 29, 1962, William F. Buckley, Jr. Papers.
70. William F. Buckley Jr., "The Question of Robert Welch," *National Review*, February 13, 1962.
71. Ibid.
72. Ibid.
73. Ibid.
74. Ibid.
75. William F. Buckley Jr. to Ronald Reagan, February 1, 1962, William F. Buckley, Jr. Papers.
76. Ronald Reagan, "Robert Welch," letter to the editor, *National Review*, March 13, 1962. Reagan praised *National Review* for "giving a voice to the conscience of conservatism" and said that he eagerly awaited "a Liberal definition of Left and far Left."
77. Judis, *William F. Buckley, Jr.*, 199.
78. Ibid.
79. William Rusher to William F. Buckley Jr., May 23, 1963, William F. Buckley, Jr. Papers.
80. William F. Buckley Jr., "Goldwater and the John Birch Society," On the Right, November 2, 1963.
81. William F. Buckley Jr. to James Burnham, July 25, 1963, William F. Buckley, Jr. Papers.
82. James Reston, "The Conservative Battle in the G.O.P.," *New York Times*, February 7, 1961.
83. "Uproar on the Right," *Washington Post*, February 2, 1962.
84. "Thunder on the Right," *Time*, February 16, 1961.
85. William F. Buckley Jr. to Robert Welch, April 10, 1963, William F. Buckley, Jr. Papers.
86. Shadegg, *What Happened to Goldwater?* 68–69.
87. "Random Notes from All Over: Goldwater Aides Counter Right, Rebuff Overture by Buckley, Ultra-Conservative Editor," *New York Times*, September 16, 1963.
88. See Goldwater and Casserly, *Goldwater*, 147–48; Goldberg, *Goldwater*, 179; Shadegg, *What Happened to Goldwater?*; and J. William Middendorf II, A *Glorious Disaster: Barry Goldwater's Presidential Campaign and the Origins of the Conservative Movement* (New York: Basic Books, 2006), 50–52.
89. Judis, *William F. Buckley, Jr.*, 223.
90. Edwards, *Goldwater*, 148.
91. Ibid., 184.
92. Judis, *William F. Buckley, Jr.*, 226.
93. Ibid.
94. Ibid., 221.
95. William F. Buckley Jr., "Goldwater for President? Are You Mad? No," On the Right, April 7, 1963.
96. William F. Buckley Jr. to Dwight D. Eisenhower, January 9, 1964, box 30, William F. Buckley, Jr. Papers.
97. Ibid. and enclosure.
98. William F. Buckley, Jr. to Walter N. Thayer, June 15,1964, William F. Buckley, Jr. Papers.

99. Walter Thayer to William F. Buckley Jr., Papers of William F. Buckley, Jr., June 22, 1964.
100. See "Ike for VP?" *National Review*, June 30, 1964; and "Ike for VP, Continued," *National Review*, July 14, 1964, James Kilpatrick, "The Ike Plan Cometh," *National Review*, June 16, 1964.
101. William F. Buckley Jr., "Lodge?" On the Right, April 11, 1964.
102. William F. Buckley Jr. to John Davis Lodge, May 4, 1964, William F. Buckley, Jr. Papers.
103. William F. Buckley Jr., "Why Doesn't Rockefeller Quit?" On the Right, May 5, 1964.
104. Barry Goldwater to William F. Buckley Jr., May 15, 1964, William F. Buckley, Jr. Papers.
105. William F. Buckley Jr., "California: The End of the Road," On the Right, May 30, 1964. This was the second time Buckley had discussed Rockefeller's divorce and remarriage in his column. See William F. Buckley Jr., "Is Mrs. Murphy Everybody's Business?" On the Right, May 3, 1963.
106. William F. Buckley Jr., "Notes the Morning After," On the Right, June 6, 1964.
107. Ibid.
108. William F. Buckley Jr., "Goldwater: Profile in Courage," On the Right, June 25, 1964.
109. Kennedy, *Profiles in Courage*.
110. William F. Buckley, "Why Goldwater Will Lose, Maybe," On the Right, July 2, 1964.
111. Judis, *William F. Buckley, Jr.*, 229.
112. Kevin M. Schultz, *Buckley and Mailer: A Difficult Friendship That Shaped the Sixties* (New York: Norton, 2015), 81.
113. Judis, *William F. Buckley, Jr.*, 229.
114. Gore Vidal, "A Distasteful Encounter with William F. Buckley, Jr.," *Esquire*, September 1969.
115. Terrence O'Flaherty, "Talent Scouts," *San Francisco Chronicle*, July 15, 1964.
116. Edwards, *William F. Buckley, Jr.*, 107.
117. Judis, *William F. Buckley, Jr.*, 230.
118. Barry Goldwater, speech accepting the Republican Party nomination for President, July 16, 1964, San Francisco, Washington Post.com. These two lines in Goldwater's speech had been the suggestion of historian Harry Jaffa, a scholar at the Claremont Institute. See Robert McFadden, "Harry V. Jaffa, Conservative Scholar and Goldwater Muse, Dies at 96," *New York Times*, January 12, 2015.
119. William F. Buckley Jr., untitled article, On the Right, July 23, 1964.
120. White, *The Making of the President*, 1964, 336–37.
121. *National Review*, July 14, 1964.
122. See Middendorf, *A Glorious Disaster*, 207–9.
123. William F. Buckley Jr. to Denison Kitchel, September 28, 1964, William F. Buckley, Jr. Papers.
124. Denison Kitchel to William F. Buckley Jr., September 18, 1964, William F. Buckley, Jr. Papers.
125. Denison Kitchel to William F. Buckley Jr., September 25, 1964, William F. Buckley, Jr. Papers.

126. Denison Kitchel to William F. Buckley Jr., October 26, 1964, William F. Buckley, Jr. Papers.
127. William F. Buckley Jr., "The Impending Defeat of Barry Goldwater," September 11, 1964, in William F. Buckley Jr., *Let Us Talk of Many Things* (Roseville, CA: Prima, 2000), 74–78.
128. William F. Buckley Jr., "The Vile Campaign," On the Right, September 22, 1964.
129. "The Compleat Goldwater," *Ramparts*, 1964. Maxwell Geisner, Louis E. Lomax, Jules Feiffer, Sidney Michaels, Neal Ascherson, Judd Teller, and Terrence Prittie all submitted pieces.
130. "1189 Psychiatrists Say Goldwater Is Psychologically Unfit to Be President!" *Fact*, September–October 1964; "Voices of Moderation," *National Review*, November 3, 1964.
131. Edward C. Burke, "Goldwater Awarded $75,000 in Damages in His Suit for Libel," *New York Times*, May 25, 1968.
132. Richard Hofstadter, "The Paranoid Style in American Politics," *Harper's*, November 1964, and *The Paranoid Style in American Politics and Other Essays* (New York: Random House, 1965).
133. David Hackett Fischer, *Historians' Fallacies: Toward Logic of Historical Thought* (New York: Harper Torchbooks, 1970), 195.
134. "The Election," *National Review*, November 17, 1964. James Reston in the *New York Times* was representative of the prevailing mainstream opinion, which took the opposite view. See James Reston, "What Goldwater Lost: Voters Rejected His Candidacy, Conservative Cause and the GOP," *New York Times*, November 4, 1964. Buckley's analysis proved more accurate. Before long, political scientists would be referring to the election of 1964 as a "realigning" election. See James L. Sundquist, *The Dynamics of the Party System: Alignment and Realignment of Political Parties in the United States* (Washington, DC: Brookings Institution Press, 1973).
135. Buckley, *Let Us Talk of Many Things.*
136. Ronald Reagan to William F. Buckley Jr., November 5, 1964, William F. Buckley, Jr. Papers.
137. Ibid.
138. Ronald Reagan, contributor, "The Republican Party and the Conservative Movement," *National Review*, December 1, 1964. Other contributors were George H. W. Bush, John Davis Lodge, Gerhard Niemeyer, and Russell Kirk.

CHAPTER 8. PART OF THE WAY WITH LBJ

1. "The Week," *National Review*, December 17, 1963.
2. The impetus for the War on Poverty was Michael Harrington's *The Other America*, published at the outset of the Kennedy administration. In his campaign for the Democratic presidential nomination, Kennedy visited West Virginia, where he purportedly saw poverty up close for the first time. Advisers saw in Harrington's book strategies they might use in reducing poverty and its effects.
3. Judis, *William F. Buckley, Jr.*

4. William F. Buckley Jr., "The Strength of President Johnson," On the Right, February 13, 1964.
5. Ibid.
6. William F. Buckley Jr., "Johnson at High Tide," On the Right, August 22, 1964.
7. William F. Buckley Jr., "Lyndon Johnson, Rex," On the Right, May 19, 1964.
8. Ibid.
9. Ibid.
10. William F. Buckley Jr., "The Case for Bobby," On the Right, November 17, 1964.
11. William F. Buckley Jr., "Georgia and Bo Callaway," On the Right, November 3, 1966.
12. See William F. Buckley Jr., "They Are Going to Do It," On the Right, November 6, 1969.
13. Ibid.
14. William F. Buckley Jr., "Half-Thoughts on Mississippi," On the Right, July 4, 1964.
15. William F. Buckley Jr., "The Issue at Selma," On the Right, February 18, 1965.
16. "The American Dream and the American Negro," *New York Times Magazine,* March 7, 1965.
17. "Mr. Buckley vs. Mr. Mailer," *Guardian,* February 19, 1965.
18. "Government Unlimited," *National Review,* August 24, 1965.
19. William F. Buckley Jr. to Kevin J. Smant, April 1, 1995, quoted in Kevin J. Smant, *Principles and Heresies: Frank S. Meyer and the Shaping of the American Conservative Movement* (Wilmington, DE: ISI Books, 2002), 369.
20. "Greenfield at Large," transcript, September 3, 2001.
21. James Carney, "10 Questions for William F. Buckley," *Time,* April 12, 2004.
22. William F. Buckley Jr., "The Leftward March of the Negro Movement," On the Right, January 4, 1964.
23. William F. Buckley Jr., "Understanding Hoover via Rowan," On the Right, January 3, 1976.
24. William F. Buckley Jr., "The Decline of Dr. King," On the Right, April 11, 1967. See also Buckley, "Understanding Hoover via Rowan."
25. William F. Buckley Jr., "Time for a Hiatus," On the Right, October 4, 1966.
26. William F. Buckley Jr., "Revolt with Humphrey," On the Right, June 25, 1966.
27. Hubert H. Humphrey to William F. Buckley Jr., July 25, 1966, William F. Buckley, Jr. Papers.
28. William F. Buckley Jr. to Hubert H. Humphrey, July 29, 1966, William F. Buckley, Jr. Papers.
29. Hubert H. Humphrey to William F. Buckley Jr., March 13, 1968, William F. Buckley, Jr. Papers.
30. William F. Buckley Jr. to Hubert H. Humphrey, March 20, 1968, William F. Buckley, Jr. Papers.
31. William F. Buckley Jr., "The Report on Riots," On The Right, March 16, 1968.
32. William F. Buckley Jr., "The End of Martin Luther King," On the Right, April 9, 1968.
33. William F. Buckley Jr., "A Memorial for Dr. King," On the Right, October 9, 1969. Kennedy was assassinated two months after King.
34. Ibid.

35. William F. Buckley Jr., "Martin Luther King Day?" On the Right, January 23, 1979.
36. William F. Buckley Jr., "The Doves Gird Their Loins," On the Right, March 27, 1965.
37. Ibid.
38. Ibid.
39. William F. Buckley Jr., "Why Must We Use American Soldiers?" On the Right, June 19, 1965.
40. William F. Buckley Jr., "The President's Dilemma," On the Right, March 24, 1966.
41. William F. Buckley Jr., "Johnson & Vietnam," On the Right, July 31, 1965.
42. William F. Buckley Jr., "Beware the Negotiating Table," On the Right, September 4, 1965, and "Counter Demonstration Coming Up," On the Right, November 20, 1965.
43. William F. Buckley Jr., "Enter the GOP," On the Right, December 25, 1965.
44. William F. Buckley Jr., "Vietnam Dissent," On the Right, April 16, 1966.
45. William F. Buckley Jr., "Pity LBJ," On the Right, February 15, 1966.
46. Ibid.
47. William F. Buckley Jr., "Johnson's Next Step," On the Right, May 28, 1966.
48. William F. Buckley Jr., "The National Conference for Surrender," On the Right, June 4, 1966.
49. William F. Buckley Jr., "The Silence of LBJ," On the Right, April 25, 1967.
50. William F. Buckley Jr., "More Troops?" On the Right, March 19, 1968.
51. Ibid.
52. Buckley, "The Doves Gird Their Loins."
53. William F. Buckley Jr., "L—YND—N J—HNS—N," On the Right, April 2, 1968.
54. Ibid. See also Jules Feiffer, *LBJ Lampooned* (New York: Cobble Hill, 1968), 9.
55. William F. Buckley Jr., "The Withdrawal of Johnson," On the Right, April 4, 1968.
56. Ibid.
57. The final count showed that McCarthy had polled 42 percent.
58. William F. Buckley Jr., "The Unseating of Johnson," On the Right, April 6, 1968.
59. Ibid.
60. Lady Bird Johnson to William F. Buckley Jr., July 29, 1968, William F. Buckley, Jr. Papers. See William F. Buckley Jr., "Come to the Fair," On the Right, July 24, 1968.
61. William F. Buckley Jr., "LBJ Packs Up," On the Right, December 12, 1968.
62. Ibid.
63. William F. Buckley Jr., "Lyndon B. Johnson, R.I.P.," On the Right, January 24, 1973.
64. Ibid.
65. Lyndon B. Johnson, "Peace Without Conquest," speech delivered at Johns Hopkins University, April 7, 1965.
66. Buckley, "Lyndon B. Johnson, R.I.P."

CHAPTER 9. "DEMAND A RECOUNT"

1. Judis, *William F. Buckley, Jr.*, 255.
2. Buckley, *The Unmaking of a Mayor*, 14.
3. Ibid.
4. Ibid.

5. Ibid., 9–17.
6. Ibid., 14–15. See also *National Catholic Reporter*, May 12, 1965.
7. Buckley, *The Unmaking of a Mayor*, 11, 15, 20–23.
8. Judis, *William F. Buckley, Jr.*, 237.
9. Buckley, *The Unmaking of a Mayor*, 65.
10. Vincent J. Cannato, *The Ungovernable City: John Lindsay and His Struggle to Save New York* (New York: Basic Books, 2001).
11. William F. Buckley Jr., "Mayor Anyone?" On the Right, May 22, 1965. The "crisis" reference was to a series of articles the *Herald Tribune* ran under the heading "A City in Crisis."
12. Ibid. In subsequent years, at least one scholar suggested that Buckley's taxi idea anticipated the advent of Uber. See Michael J. Flamm, "Did Bill Buckley Dream Up Uber Before There Even Was an Uber?" *History News Network*, July 5, 2015.
13. Buckley, "Mayor Anyone?"
14. Judis, *William F. Buckley, Jr.*, 238.
15. Oliver Pilat, *Lindsay's Campaign: A Behind the Scenes Diary* (Boston: Beacon, 1968), 95. The previous year, Kennedy, a Massachusetts resident and voter, moved into New York months preceding his election to the U.S. Senate.
16. Cannato, *The Ungovernable City*, 39.
17. Buckley, *The Unmaking of a Mayor*, 98.
18. Cannato, *The Ungovernable City*, 68.
19. Buckley, The *Unmaking of a Mayor*, 98; and *New York Herald Tribune*, June 6, 1965.
20. Schultz, *Buckley and Mailer*, 145.
21. Buckley, *The Unmaking of a Mayor*, 123.
22. Ibid., 112, 123.
23. Pilat, *Lindsay's Campaign*, 149.
24. Buckley, *The Unmaking of a Mayor*, 120.
25. Cannato, *The Ungovernable City*, 40.
26. Buckley, *The Unmaking of a Mayor*, 120.
27. Barry Goldwater to William F. Buckley Jr., July 20, 1965, William F. Buckley, Jr. Papers.
28. Sam Tanenhaus, "The Buckley Effect," *New York Times Magazine*, October 2, 2005.
29. Ibid.
30. Buckley, *The Unmaking of a Mayor*.
31. Pilat, *Lindsay's Campaign*, 163–64.
32. "Lindsay Is Chided on 10-Point Plan," *New York Times*, August 20, 1965.
33. Pilat, *Lindsay's Campaign*, 189.
34. Mahoney, *Actions Speak Louder*, 286.
35. Buckley, *The Unmaking of a Mayor*, 94–96; and Joe Leo, "Very Dark Horse in New York," *New York Times Magazine*, September 5, 1965.
36. Judis, *William F. Buckley, Jr.*, 237.
37. Kabaservice, *The Guardians*, 334.
38. William Borders, "Buckley Opposed by Cyrus Vance in Yale Election," *New York Times*, March 9, 1968.

39. James Reston, "The Fable of the Pygmies," *New York Times*, October 29, 1965.
40. Buckley, *The Unmaking of a Mayor*, 262.
41. Ibid.
42. Sydney H. Schanberg, "Lindsay and Buckley Duel," *New York Times*, October 12, 1965. See also Buckley, *The Unmaking of a Mayor*, 261–64.
43. Pilat, *Lindsay's Campaign*, 283.
44. Ibid., 284. The insult may have originated in a quip Dorothy Parker allegedly uttered in 1932 upon being told that former President Calvin Coolidge had died. "How can they tell?"
45. Buckley, *The Unmaking of a Mayor.*
46. Pilat, *Lindsay's Campaign*, 246.
47. Buckley, *The Unmaking of a Mayor*, 284.
48. Pilat, *Lindsay's Campaign*, 33–34.
49. Buckley, *The Unmaking of a Mayor*, 276–78.
50. See Rowland Evans and Robert Novak, "Fifty Bucks from Buckley," Inside Report, *Washington Post*, October 14, 1965. (The $50 reference was to a contribution Buckley had made the previous year to a Yale classmate who was running for Congress as a Democrat.)
51. See William F. Buckley Jr., "The Birch Society," On the Right, August 5, 1965; "More on Birch," On the Right, August 17, 1965; and "And Finally on John Birch," On the Right, August 21, 1965. (These three pieces were republished in *National Review* on October 19, 1965.)
52. Buckley, "The Birch Society."
53. Ibid.
54. Ibid.
55. "Bill Buckley, Candidate: The Conservative Runs a Tongue-in-Cheek Race for Mayor of New York," *Life*, September 17, 1965.
56. Buckley, "And Finally on John Birch."
57. James J. Kilpatrick, "Birchers' Barrage Inundates Buckley," *Philadelphia Inquirer*, September 9, 1965.
58. Pilat, *Lindsay's Campaign*, 234, 243.
59. Buckley, *The Unmaking of a Mayor*, 280.
60. Pilat, *Lindsay's Campaign*, 265.
61. Ibid., 252.
62. *Village Voice*, October 28, 1965.
63. Pilat, *Lindsay's Campaign*, 269, 274, 299, 311.
64. Ibid., 284; and Buckley, *The Unmaking of a Mayor*, 183.
65. Sydney H. Schanberg, "Lindsay and Buckley Duel," *New York Times*, October 12, 1965.
66. Buckley, *The Unmaking of a Mayor*, 162. Buckley referenced the *New York Times* of October 19 and October 29, in which Javits was quoted as saying that Buckley wanted to send people to "concentration camps." He also referenced a *New York Post* story of October 31 in which Lindsay used the identical term in characterizing Buckley's proposal.

67. Pilat, *Lindsay's Campaign*, 322.
68. Sam Tanenhaus, "The Buckley Effect," *New York Times Magazine*, October 2, 1995.
69. Buckley, *The Unmaking of a Mayor*, 163.
70. Homer Bigart, "Buckley a Clown, Beame Declares," *New York Times*, October 30, 1965.
71. Buckley, *The Unmaking of a Mayor*, 168. The "Lords Spiritual of the Community" were aristocrats charged with the maintenance of civilized standards during the Middle Ages. Critics charged that Buckley sought to restore the medieval establishment. See Pilat, *Lindsay's Campaign*, 149.
72. Buckley, *The Unmaking of a Mayor*, 226.
73. Tanenhaus, "The Buckley Effect."
74. Pilat, *Lindsay's Campaign*, 96.
75. Schultz, *Buckley and Mailer*, 154.
76. Nathan Glazer and Daniel Patrick Moynihan, *Beyond the Melting Pot: The Negroes, Puerto Ricans, Jews, Italians and Irish of New York City* (New York: Cambridge, MA: MIT Press, 1963).
77. Daniel P. Moynihan, *The Negro Family: The Case for National Action* (Washington, DC: Office of Policy Planning and Research, U.S. Department of Labor, 1965).
78. Buckley, *The Unmaking of a Mayor*, 152–53. Buckley reminded his readers and listeners that it is not plagiarism to quote someone with attribution, which he said he had repeatedly done in the case of Moynihan.
79. James Q. Wilson, *The Amateur Democrat: Club Politics in Three Cities* (Chicago: University of Chicago Press, 1966).
80. Buckley, *The Unmaking of a Mayor*, 109.
81. Ibid.
82. Ibid., 182–83.
83. Joseph Kraft, *New York Post*, October 29, 1965, quoted in Buckley, *The Unmaking of a Mayor*, 122.
84. Cannato, *The Ungovernable City*, 62.
85. Tanenhaus, "The Buckley Effect."
86. Sullivan, *New York State and the Rise of Modern Conservatism*, 69.
87. Judis, *William F. Buckley, Jr.*, 250.
88. Tanenhaus, "The Buckley Effect."
89. Buckley, *The Unmaking of a Mayor*, 107–8.
90. Ibid., 145–48.
91. Ibid., 145.
92. Ibid.
93. Ibid.
94. "Buckley Outlines Plan for Harlem," *New York Times*, October 23, 1965. Five years later in a primary election, the voters in Powell's district elected Assemblyman Charles Rangel over the long-serving incumbent.
95. Richard Witkin, "Bircher Sends Letters," *New York Times*, October 25, 1965.
96. Ibid.
97. Cannato, *The Ungovernable City*, 55.
98. Ibid.

99. Ibid.
100. Buckley, *The Unmaking of a Mayor*, 229.
101. Cannato, *The Ungovernable City*, 59. See also Buckley, *The Unmaking of a Mayor*, 122–29, and *New York Times*, October 28, 1965.
102. Buckley, *The Unmaking of a Mayor*, 301.
103. Buckley, *Miles Gone By*, 542. When *The Unmaking of a Mayor* was published in 1966, Buckley had not yet identified Moses as his source. For an examination of Moses's career, see Robert Caro, *The Power Broker: Robert Moses and the Fall of New York* (New York: Knopf, 1974).
104. William J. Quirk, "A Look Back at John Lindsay: Remembrances of Things Trashed," *New York Magazine*, September 7, 1977.
105. Buckley, *Miles Gone By*, 542.
106. Ibid.
107. Judis, *William F. Buckley, Jr.*, 255.
108. Richard Witkin, "Seesaw Contest: Vote Is Tightest Here in Quarter Century—13% for Buckley," *New York Times*, November 3, 1965.
109. Buckley, *The Unmaking of a Mayor*, 285.
110. Cannato, *The Ungovernable City*, 71.
111. Buckley, *The Unmaking of a Mayor*, appendix.
112. Remnick, "Buckley: The Lion in Autumn."
113. Neal B. Freeman, "Bill Buckley's Lesson for Today's Conservatives," *Wall Street Journal*, February 27–28, 2016.
114. Remnick, "Buckley: The Lion in Autumn."
115. Buckley, interview with Rosen.
116. Marlin, *Fighting the Good Fight*, 113.

CHAPTER 10. BUCKLEY AND NIXON: MUTUAL SUSPICIONS

1. Wallace served as Governor from 1963 to 1967 and again from 1971 to 1979 and from 1983 to 1987.
2. "The Future of the GOP," *Firing Line* (Richard Nixon, guest), September 14, 1967. See also William F. Buckley Jr., "Richard Nixon, R.I.P.," On the Right, May 16, 1994.
3. William F. Buckley Jr. to Victor Lasky, October 9, 1962, William F. Buckley, Jr. Papers.
4. Bill Barry, "A Trip into Idea Land with Bill Buckley," *Miami News*, April 18, 1967.
5. "William F. Buckley, Jr.: "Conservatism Can Be Fun."
6. Ibid.
7. Patrick J. Buchanan, *The Greatest Comeback: How Richard Nixon Rose from Defeat to Create the New Majority* (New York: Crown, 2014), 39.
8. Judis, *William F. Buckley, Jr.*, 299.
9. Rowland and Evans, "Fifty Bucks from Buckley."
10. "Answer Please, Mr. Nixon," *National Review*, March 8, 1966.
11. Patrick J. Buchanan, "Nixon and the 'Buckleyites,'" *National Review*, April 5, 1966. See also Patrick J. Buchanan to William F. Buckley Jr., March 8, 1966, William F. Buckley, Jr. Papers; and Buchanan, *The Greatest Comeback*, 37–39.

12. Buchanan, *The Greatest Comeback*, 38.
13. Richard Nixon to William F. Buckley Jr., April 8, 1968, and Richard Nixon to William F. Buckley Jr., October 23, 1967, William F. Buckley, Jr. Papers.
14. "The son of an alumnus, who attends private preparatory school, now has less of a chance of getting in than some boy from P.S. 109 somewhere," he complained. See William Borders, "Buckley Runs at Yale to Combat Liberals," *New York Times*, October 21, 1967.
15. Richard Nixon to William F. Buckley Jr., August 23, 1961, William F. Buckley, Jr. Papers.
16. William F. Buckley Jr. to Richard Nixon, August 27, 1961, William F. Buckley, Jr. Papers.
17. Judis, *William F. Buckley, Jr.*, 280.
18. Ibid.
19. William F. Buckley Jr. to Patrick J. Buchanan, January 19, 1967, William F. Buckley, Jr. Papers.
20. William F. Buckley Jr. to Patrick J. Buchanan, September 3, 1967, William F. Buckley, Jr. Papers.
21. "The Future of the GOP."
22. William F. Buckley Jr. to Richard Nixon, November 22, 1967, William F. Buckley, Jr. Papers.
23. William F. Buckley Jr., "Rockefeller, Nixon, and Vietnam," On the Right, April 28, 1968.
24. Judis, *William F. Buckley, Jr.*, 305.
25. William F. Buckley Jr., The Lesson of Mr. Romney," On the Right, March 7, 1968.
26. William F. Buckley Jr., "Enter Rockefeller," On the Right, April 13, 1968. Buckley used the term "anti-Communist at Harvard" to characterize Kissinger again in an editorial in *National Review* entitled "Rockefeller on Vietnam," July 30, 1968.
27. William F. Buckley Jr., "Sherlock Buckley Rides Again," On the Right, September 10, 1968.
28. Ibid.
29. William F. Buckley Jr., *United Nations Journal: A Delegate's Odyssey* (New York: Putnam, 1974,), 38–39.
30. William F. Buckley Jr. to Henry A. Kissinger, February 20, 1968, William F. Buckley, Jr. Papers.
31. See Buckley, "Is Mrs. Murphy Everybody's Business?"; and Buckley, "California."
32. Buckley, *Miles Gone By*, 260.
33. Henry A. Kissinger to William F. Buckley Jr., August 14, 1968, William F. Buckley, Jr. Papers.
34. William F. Buckley Jr. to Henry A. Kissinger, August 27, 1968, William F. Buckley, Jr. Papers.
35. Ibid.
36. William F. Buckley, Jr., "The Doubts about Agnew," On the Right, October 22, 1968.
37. For a full account of the ten debates Buckley had with Vidal, see the documentary *Best of Enemies* (Magnolia Pictures, 2015).

38. Buckley, "On Experiencing Gore Vidal."
39. Vidal's second novel, *The City and the Pillar,* published in 1948, took as its theme the protagonists' romantic homosexual yearnings. Twenty years later, in *Myra Breckinridge,* Vidal turned his attention to bisexuality and transgender-related issues.
40. Kaplan, *Gore Vidal,* 594.
41. Nancy Reagan to William F. Buckley Jr., August 21, 1968, William F. Buckley, Jr. Papers.
42. William F. Buckley Jr. to Nancy Reagan, August 27, 1968, William F. Buckley, Jr. Papers. In his book *The Reagan I Knew,* Buckley published his response to Nancy Reagan but omitted the "pink queer" reference.
43. Judis, *William F. Buckley, Jr.,* 291.
44. Ibid.
45. Ibid., 291.
46. Transcript, *ABC News,* August 28, 1968.
47. Ibid.
48. Judis, *William F. Buckley, Jr.,* 292.
49. Buckley, "On Experiencing Gore Vidal."
50. Ibid.
51. Ibid.
52. Gore Vidal, "Tennessee Williams: Someone to Laugh at the Squares With," *New York Review of Books,* June 13, 1985, reprinted in Gore Vidal, *At Home: Essays, 1982–1988* (New York: Random House, 1988).
53. Buckley, "On Experiencing Gore Vidal."
54. Vidal, "A Distasteful Encounter with William F. Buckley, Jr."
55. Judis, *William F. Buckley, Jr.,* 294.
56. Meadows had been out of town on tour with the USO when her father's church was vandalized. Fifteen years after the incident, learning that Meadows was widely broadcasting her understanding of what had occurred, Buckley wrote her, inquiring how long she intended to publicize misdeeds that had been acknowledged and atoned for. See William F. Buckley Jr. to Jayne Meadows, March 30, 1959, William F. Buckley, Jr. Papers (file marked "Vidal Case").
57. For documentation of that incident and to view a photograph of the protest, see Maurice Obstfeld, "Repression of Rebels Defended by Buckley," *Daily Pennsylvanian,* December 15, 1970.
58. "Buckley Drops Vidal Suit, Settles with *Esquire,*" *New York Times,* September 26, 1972.
59. See Gore Vidal, *Burr* (New York: Random House, 1973); and Christopher Bram, *Eminent Outlaws: The Gay Writers Who Changed America* (New York: Twelve, 2012), 127–29.
60. Henry A. Kissinger, *White House Years* (Boston: Little Brown), 1979.
61. Ibid., 10.
62. "The Wallace Crusade," *Firing Line* (Governor George Wallace, guest), January 24, 1968.
63. Ibid.

64. Buckley, *United Nations Journal*, 38.
65. William F. Buckley Jr. to Nancy Reagan, February 12, 1968, William F. Buckley, Jr. Papers.
66. William F. Buckley Jr., "What George Wallace Means to Me," *Look*, October 29, 1968.
67. William F. Buckley Jr. to James L. Buckley, October 30, 1968, William F. Buckley, Jr. Papers.
68. William F. Buckley Jr. to John Mitchell, William F. Buckley, Jr. Papers.
69. William F. Buckley Jr., "Mr. Nixon's Cabinet," On the Right, November 16, 1968.
70. William F. Buckley Jr., "Overthrow Thieu?" On the Right, November 21, 1968.
71. Judis, *William F. Buckley, Jr.*, 302.
72. Isaacson, *Kissinger*, 133–36.
73. Richard Nixon, *RN: The Memoirs of Richard Nixon* (New York: Grosset and Dunlap, 1976), 340–41.
74. "Mr. Kissinger," *National Review*, December 16, 1968.
75. Undated note from William F. Buckley, Jr. to Henry A. Kissinger, William F. Buckley, Jr. Papers.
76. Jeff Bell to William F. Buckley Jr., February 16, 1969, William F. Buckley, Jr. Papers
77. William F. Buckley Jr. to Jeff Bell, March 13, 1969, William F. Buckley, Jr. Papers.
78. Judis, *William F. Buckley, Jr.*, 388.
79. Ibid.
80. Ibid., 304.
81. "Interview with William F. Buckley Jr.," *Playboy*, May 1970.
82. William F. Buckley Jr. to Henry A. Kissinger, January 28, 1969, and Henry A. Kissinger to William F. Buckley Jr., March 4, 1969, William F. Buckley, Jr. Papers.
83. William F. Buckley Jr. to Henry A. Kissinger, April 21, 1969, and Henry A. Kissinger to William F. Buckley Jr., April 26, 1969, William F. Buckley, Jr. Papers.
84. William F. Buckley Jr., "Washington, DC, Tour's End," On the Right, June 3, 1969.
85. Ibid.
86. Buckley, "Why We Need a Black President in 1980."
87. Ibid.
88. Ibid.
89. See "In Egypt Land (Marian Anderson)," *Time*, December 30, 1946. The positive reaction Chambers's story on Anderson produced led *Time*'s publisher Henry Luce to break with his long-standing practice and reveal the identity of the article's author. See Whittaker Chambers, *Witness*, 50th anniversary edition (Washington, DC: Regnery, 2002), 505. The subject of Chambers's cover story had been no stranger to racial discrimination. In 1939, the Daughters of the American Revolution had denied Anderson the opportunity to perform in its auditorium because of her race. Through the intervention of First Lady Eleanor Roosevelt, who resigned her membership in the DAR in protest, Anderson performed on the steps of the Lincoln Memorial. She rendered a repeat performance at this site during the 1963 March on Washington for Jobs and Freedom. She later sang many times before the DAR after the organization altered its policy.
90. William F. Buckley Jr., "Mississippi on My Mind," On the Right, December 19, 1972. Also see William F. Buckley Jr., "They Are Going to Do It," On the Right, November 6, 1969.

91. Patrick J. Buchanan to William F. Buckley Jr., October 29, 1969, William F. Buckley, Jr. Papers.
92. Richard Nixon to William F. Buckley Jr., November 23, 1969, William F. Buckley, Jr. Papers.
93. William F. Buckley Jr., "The Speech," On the Right, November 8, 1969.
94. Richard Nixon to William F. Buckley Jr., November 20, 1969, William F. Buckley, Jr. Papers.
95. William F. Buckley Jr. to Patrick J. Buchanan, May 7, 1970, William F. Buckley Jr. to Patrick J. Buchanan, September 16, 1971, Patrick J. Buchanan to William F. Buckley Jr., May 18, 1970, and Richard Nixon to William F. Buckley Jr., September 29, 1971, William F. Buckley, Jr. Papers.
96. Edith Efron, *The News Twisters* (New York: Manor Books, 1971).
97. Judis, *William F. Buckley, Jr.*, 303.
98. Charles L. Ponce De Leon, *That's the Way It Is: A History of Television News in America* (Chicago: University of Chicago Press, 2015), 103–4.
99. Transcript of *Laugh-In*, broadcast on NBC, December 27, 1970.
100. "Interview with William F. Buckley Jr."
101. Judis, *William F. Buckley, Jr.*, 311; and William F. Buckley Jr. to James L. Buckley, August 9, 1968, and *William F. Buckley Jr.* to James L. Buckley, October 30, 1968, William F. Buckley, Jr. Papers.
102. Judis, *William F. Buckley, Jr.*, 311.
103. Ibid.
104. Ibid., 312.
105. The Conservative Party's candidate for Governor in 1966, an obscure college professor named Paul Adams, had polled 500,000 votes. That same year, Rockefeller's winning margin fell to 392,263, from 529,169 in 1962. But for the presence of Franklin D. Roosevelt Jr. on the Liberal line, where he drew 507,234 votes that might otherwise have gone to Democrat Frank O'Connor, Rockefeller might well have lost.
106. Sullivan, *New York State and the Rise of Modern Conservatism*, 122.
107. Henry A. Kissinger to William F. Buckley Jr., February 26, 1970, William F. Buckley, Jr. Papers.
108. Memo of staff meeting of Nelson A. Rockefeller, staffer Burdell Bixby, Robert R. Douglass, Alton G. Marshall, Hugh Morrow, and pollster Samuel Lubell, August 21, 1970, Rockefeller Family Archives.
109. Carter B. Horsley, "L.I. Conservatives Back Republican," *New York Times*, May 16, 1970.
110. "5 New York G.O.P. Men at Buckley Reception," *New York Times*, June 3, 1970.
111. Tom Wicker, "Three-Ring Show in New York," *New York Times*, October 1, 1970.
112. Richard Reeves, "Buckley: Serious Contender in Three-Way Race," *New York Times*, July 12, 1970.
113. Leonard Buder, "Rockefeller and Buckley Supported by Group Made Up of Principals and Others in City Schools," *New York Times*, October 29, 1970.
114. Ibid.
115. "The Alternative Is Goldberg," *National Review*, October 20, 1970.

116. Smith, *On His Own Terms*, 572.
117. Richard Phalon, "Buckley Outspends 2 Rivals for Senate," *New York Times*, October 27, 1970.
118. Smith, *On His Own Terms*, 572.
119. See Sullivan, *New York State and the Rise of Modern Conservatism*, chapter 5.
120. Clayton Knowles, "Dr. Adams Asserts Agnew's Attack Has Aided Buckley," *New York Times*, October 13, 1970.
121. Sullivan, *New York State and the Rise of Modern Conservatism*, 133.
122. Ibid.
123. Clayton Knowles, "Buckley Predicts a Triumph for 'Silent Majority,'" *New York Times*, October 13, 1970.
124. Ibid.
125. William F. Buckley Jr., *Inveighing We Will Go* (New York: Putnam, 1971), 344–45.
126. McCandlish Phillips, "A Polite Whoop of Victory on East 73rd St.," *New York Times*, November 4, 1970.
127. Robert B. Semple Jr., "President Meets 3 State Leaders of Conservatives: William Buckley, Brother of New Senator, and 2 Others at Bahamas Conference," *New York Times*, November 9, 1970.
128. Sullivan, *New York State and the Rise of Modern Conservatism*, 138; and Dan Mahoney to John Mitchell, December 22, 1970, William F. Buckley, Jr. Papers.
129. "The Buckleys: An Extraordinary Family," *Newsweek*, November 16, 1970; and "The Buckleys: A Gifted American Family." See also "How Buckley Won New York," *Newsweek*, November 16, 1970; "New York's James Buckley," *Time*, November 16, 1970; and L. C. Dubois, "The Buckleys: First Family of Conservatism," *New York Times Magazine*, September 6, 1970.

CHAPTER 11. "LET THE MAN GO DECENTLY"

1. William F. Buckley Jr., "Will Price Controls Be Next?" On the Right, July 29, 1971.
2. William F. Buckley Jr., "A Home of Terror, but Liberals Clap," On the Right, July 23, 1971.
3. "Notes on People," *New York Times*, August 29, 1971; and Linda Charlton, "Buckley Admits 'Secrets' Hoax; Many in Media Taken In," *New York Times*, July 22, 1971.
4. In attendance were Meyer, Burnham, and Rusher from *National Review;* Allan Ryskind and Tom Winter of *Human Events*; John Jones and Jeff Bell of the American Conservative Union; Randy Teague of YAF; Stan Evans of the *Indianapolis News;* Neil McCaffrey (formerly with *National Review)* of Arlington House; Daniel Mahoney of the New York Conservative Party; and Buckley adviser Neal Freeman.
5. Judis, *William F. Buckley, Jr.*, 330.
6. *Human Events*, August 7, 1971.
7. Transcript of White House telephone conversations between Kissinger and Buckley, July 28, 1971.
8. William B. Buckley Jr. "Is Nixon One of Us?" *New York Times Magazine*, August 1, 1971.

9. Ibid.
10. Ibid.
11. "In Re New Hampshire," *National Review,* December 31, 1971.
12. William F. Buckley Jr. to Peter Flanagan, January 3, 1972, William F. Buckley, Jr. Papers.
13. Ibid.
14. William F. Buckley Jr. to Peter Flanagan, February 16, 1972, William F. Buckley, Jr. Papers.
15. Buckley, *Inveighing We Will Go,* 87.
16. Ibid., 88.
17. Ibid., 96.
18. Telephone conversation between Nixon and Kissinger, February 28, 1972.
19. Ibid.
20. David Halberstam, *The Powers That Be* (New York: Dell Books, 1979), 845.
21. "The Morning After," November 9, 1972, in William F. Buckley Jr., *Execution Eve and Other Contemporary Ballads* (New York: Putnam, 1975), 100.
22. William F. Buckley Jr., preface to *Execution Eve,* 14–15.
23. Bridges and Coyne, *Strictly Right,* 147–48.
24. Buckley, *Execution Eve,* 14–15.
25. Judis, *William F. Buckley, Jr.,* 345.
26. Ibid. See also Buckley, *Execution Eve,* 15.
27. Buckley, *Losing Mum and Pup,* 231.
28. For more on Hunt's role in the plot against Anderson, see Mark Feldstein, *Poisoning the Press: Richard Nixon, Jack Anderson and the Rise of Washington's Scandal Culture* (New York: Farrar, Straus and Giroux, 2010), 282–90.
29. Buckley, *Losing Mum and Pup,* 231.
30. Buckley, *Execution Eve,* 15.
31. Bridges and Coyne, *Strictly Right,* 148.
32. Buckley, *Losing Mum and Pup,* 232.
33. Judis, *William F. Buckley, Jr.,* 358
34. William F. Buckley Jr., "Is Nixon a Fool?" On the Right, April 28, 1973.
35. William F. Buckley Jr., "Nixon's Mistake," On the Right, May 2, 1973
36. William F. Buckley Jr., "Reflections on Nixon and Impeachment After Listening to the Speech," May 10, 1973, in *Execution Eve,* 112–22.
37. Ibid.
38. Ibid., 121.
39. Ibid., 116.
40. William F. Buckley Jr., "One Down for Senator Buckley," On the Right, May 12, 1973.
41. William F. Buckley Jr., "As It Might Have Gone," On the Right, May 15, 1973.
42. William F. Buckley Jr. "Democratic Strategy," On the Right, May 19, 1973.
43. William F. Buckley Jr., "The Dean Memorandum," On the Right, July 6, 1973.
44. Ibid.
45. Gore Vidal, among others, used the term to slander Buckley.
46. Buckley, "The Dean Memorandum."

47. William F. Buckley Jr., "The Presidential Tapes," On the Right, July 21, 1973.
48. Eric Redman, "William Buckley Reports on a Tour of Duty," *New York Times*, October 6, 1974.
49. William F. Buckley Jr., *United Nations Journal: A Delegate's Odyssey* (New York: Putnam, 1974), 143–44.
50. William F. Buckley Jr., "Nixon and Resignation," On the Right, January 14, 1974.
51. James L. Buckley, "Why Richard Nixon Should Resign the Presidency," *National Review*, April 12, 1974 (speech delivered in the Senate, March 19, 1974). See also Martin Tolchin, "Senator Buckley Bids Nixon Quit," *New York Times*, March 20, 1974.
52. William F. Buckley Jr., "Let Him Go," On the Right, August 7, 1974.
53. Ibid.
54. Buckley, "Richard Nixon, R.I.P."; William F. Buckley Jr., *Athwart History: Half a Century of Polemics, Animadversions, and Illuminations*, ed. Linda Bridges and Roger Kimball (New York: Encounter, 2010), 318–21.
55. Nixon, *Six Crises*, section 1, "The Hiss Case."
56. Buckley, "Richard Nixon, R.I.P.."

CHAPTER 12. BILL AND RONNIE: PREPARING A PRESIDENT

1. Ronald Reagan, speech delivered December 5, 1985, upon the occasion of *National Review*'s thirtieth anniversary, Speechwriting, White House Office of: Speech Drafts, box 242, folder National Review Anniversary Dinner (Dolan) (Itchon), 1–4, Ronald Reagan Presidential Library, Simi Valley, CA.
2. See Evans, *The Education of Ronald Reagan*, 104–6.
3. Associated Press, July 18, 1961.
4. William F. Buckley Jr., *The Reagan I Knew* (New York: Basic Books, 2008), 4.
5. Buckley recounted this story in multiple places, including in his books *The Reagan I Knew*, 3–7, and *Miles Gone By*, 258–60. Buckley referred to himself not only as Reagan's friend but also as his "tutor." See *The Reagan I Knew*, 1.
6. Buckley, *Losing Mum and Pup*, 175.
7. Nancy Reagan wrote of her husband, "He lets me closer than anyone else, but there are times when even I feel that barrier." See Nancy Reagan, *My Turn* (New York: Random House, 1989), 106.
8. Peggy Noonan, *When Character Was King* (New York: Viking, 2001), 258.
9. Judis, *William F. Buckley, Jr.*, 229.
10. William F. Buckley Jr. to Ronald Reagan, November 11, 1964, William F. Buckley, Jr. Papers.
11. William F. Buckley Jr., "How Is Reagan Doing?" On the Right, December 16, 1965.
12. Buckley, *The Reagan I Knew*, 128.
13. Christopher had changed parties several times.
14. William F. Buckley Jr. to Nancy Reagan, February 18, 1966, William F. Buckley, Jr. Papers.
15. William F. Buckley, Jr., On the Right, April 19, 1966.
16. William F. Buckley Jr., "The Travail of the GOP," On the Right, May 5, 1966.

17. William F. Buckley Jr., "The Reagan Primary," On the Right, May 7, 1966.
18. William F. Buckley Jr., "1968," On the Right, June 25, 1966.
19. William F. Buckley Jr. to Nancy Reagan, October 19, 1966, William F. Buckley, Jr. Papers.
20. "Is It Possible to Be a Good Governor?" *Firing Line* (Ronald Reagan, guest), July 6, 1967.
21. Buckley, *The Reagan I Knew*, 35.
22. Ibid. "The "brainwash" comment was a reference to one Romney had made about how the Pentagon had dissuaded him from opposing a continued U.S. presence in South Vietnam when he visited the region.
23. William F. Buckley Jr., "The Troubled Conscience of Adam Parry," On the Right, November 16, 1967.
24. Ibid.
25. Donald MacGillis, "Is Ronald Reagan Welcome at Yale?" *Yale Daily News*, November 7, 1967.
26. Douglas W. Rae and Peter A. Lupsha, "Politics as Theater: Ronald Reagan at Yale," *Yale Alumni Magazine*, January 1968.
27. Ibid.
28. William F. Buckley Jr., "Reagan: A Relaxing View," in Buckley, *The Jeweler's Eye*, 85. Originally published in *National Review*, November 28, 1967.
29. Ibid.
30. Ibid. See also James Q. Wilson, "A Guide to Reagan Country: The Political Culture of Southern California," *Commentary*, May 1, 1967. In subsequent years, Wilson would come to identify as a conservative or "neoconservative."
31. Ronald Reagan to William F. Buckley Jr., March 13, 1968, and William F. Buckley to Ronald Reagan, March 27, 1968, William F. Buckley, Jr. Papers.
32. Ronald Reagan to William F. Buckley Jr., November 2, 1972, William F. Buckley, Jr. Papers.
33. Buckley, "Reagan: A Relaxing View," 86.
34. Buckley made the same point when he ran for Mayor of New York. When he defended his proposal at Queens College, his audience, which had been friendly up to that point, booed him. See Buckley, *The Unmaking of a Mayor*, 185.
35. Buckley, "Reagan: A Relaxing View," 86.
36. William F. Buckley Jr. to Ronald Reagan, November 23, 1971, William F. Buckley, Jr. Papers.
37. At the time Buckley was urging conservatives to be patient with Reagan, the Governor was in the throes of a major tax increase as a means of addressing California's budgetary crisis and meeting its constitutional requirement to balance the state's budget. For an assessment of Reagan's governorship, see Lou Cannon, *Governor Reagan: His Rise to Power* (New York: Public Affairs, 2003).
38. William F. Buckley Jr. to Nancy Reagan, February 12, 1968, William F. Buckley, Jr. Papers. Buckley did not state in this letter what his suggestion was. Reed made no mention of his meeting with Buckley in his memoir of his activities on Reagan's behalf. See Thomas C. Reed, *The Reagan Enigma, 1964–1980* (New York: Figueroa, 2014).

39. Cannon, *Governor Reagan*, 245–46; and Reed, *The Reagan Enigma*.
40. Drew Pearson, "Governor Reagan Faces His First Acid Test: Homosexuals Discovered in His Office; His Staff Considers Themselves Certain to Serve in White House," Washington Merry-Go-Round, October 31, 1967.
41. Ibid.; Cannon, *Governor Reagan*, 245–46.
42. Cannon, *Governor Reagan*, 248–51.
43. Ibid, 250.
44. Pearson, "Governor Reagan Faces His First Acid Test." In his diaries, Pearson related a conversation in which he told a friend that homosexuals in the office of the Governor of California were security risks because the Governor was privy to intelligence information regarding the nation's defense on the West Coast. See Drew Pearson, *Washington Merry-Go-Round: The Drew Pearson Diaries, 1960–1969*, ed. Peter Hannaford (Lincoln: University of Nebraska Press, 2015), 511.
45. William F. Buckley Jr., "The Sacramento Scandal," On the Right, November 7, 1967.
46. See Lou Cannon, *Governor Reagan*, 241–69.
47. Theodore H. White, *The Making of the President, 1968* (New York: Atheneum, 1969), 239–40.
48. Judis, *William F. Buckley, Jr.*, 280.
49. William F. Buckley Jr. to Nancy Reagan, August 13, 1968, William F. Buckley, Jr. Papers.
50. William F. Buckley, Jr., "What Was Reagan Doing?" On the Right, August 8, 1968.
51. Buckley, *The Reagan I Knew*, 43.
52. William F. Buckley Jr. to Nancy Reagan, August 27, 1968, William F. Buckley, Jr. Papers.
53. William F. Buckley Jr. to Ronald Reagan, July 8, 1970, William F. Buckley, Jr. Papers.
54. William F. Buckley Jr., "Reagan the Revolutionary," On the Right, September 4, 1971; William F. Buckley Jr., "Reagan and Nixon," On the Right, December 18, 1971.
55. Buckley, "Reagan the Revolutionary."
56. Buckley, "Reagan and Nixon."
57. Ibid.
58. William F. Buckley Jr., "Nixon and the Conservatives," On the Right, March 25, 1972.
59. Buckley, *The Reagan I Knew*, 53.
60. William F. Buckley Jr. to Ronald Reagan, November 2, 1971, and Ronald Reagan to William F. Buckley Jr., December 2, 1971, William F. Buckley, Jr. Papers. Buckley noted that they discussed the idea over the telephone.
61. Ronald Reagan to William F. Buckley Jr., August 3, 1971, William F. Buckley, Jr. Papers.
62. William F. Buckley Jr. to Ronald Reagan, October 24, 1973, William F. Buckley, Jr. Papers.
63. Ibid.
64. Ibid.
65. Ibid.
66. William F. Buckley Jr. to Ronald Reagan, January 25, 1974, William F. Buckley, Jr. Papers.

67. Ibid.
68. Ronald Reagan to William F. Buckley Jr., February 6, 1974, William F. Buckley, Jr. Papers.
69. William F. Buckley, Jr. to Ronald Reagan, July 29, 1974, in Buckley, *The Reagan I Knew*, 65. Buckley began attending meetings of the prestigious Bohemian Grove in the mid-1960s as the guest of California Senator George Murphy. He later became a member.
70. William F. Buckley Jr., "Half-Nelson," On the Right, August 24, 1974.
71. Ibid.
72. William F. Buckley Jr., "Ford and Conservatism," On the Right, September 3, 1974.
73. See William Rusher, *The Making of a New Majority Party* (New York: Sheed and Ward, 1975); William F. Buckley Jr., "How to Approach the Wallaceite," On the Right, December 4, 1974, and William F. Buckley Jr., "Thunder on the Right," On the Right, May 29, 1975.
74. William F. Buckley Jr., "Reagan for Challenger," On the Right, August 19, 1975.
75. Buckley, "How to Approach the Wallaceite."
76. Judis, *William F. Buckley, Jr.*, 379.
77. Ibid.
78. William F. Buckley Jr. to Ronald Reagan, January 16, 1974, William F. Buckley, Jr. Papers.
79. William F. Buckley Jr., *Four Reforms: A Program for the Seventies* (New York: Putnam, 1973).
80. Ronald Reagan, address to Young Americans for Freedom, July 20, 1974.
81. William F. Buckley Jr., "What Reagan Might Say," On the Right, October 7, 1975.
82. Buckley, "Reagan for Challenger."
83. William F. Buckley Jr., "Reagan: The Rout Begins?" On the Right, December 18, 1975.
84. Ibid.
85. William F. Buckley Jr., "Opening up Détente," On the Right, February 19, 1976.
86. Ibid.
87. William F. Buckley Jr. "Rhodesia Briefing," On the Right, May 19, 1976.
88. William F. Buckley Jr. to Ronald Reagan, telegram, June 2, 1976, William F. Buckley, Jr. Papers.
89. William F. Buckley Jr. to Nancy Reagan, June 10, 1976, William F. Buckley, Jr. Papers.
90. William F. Buckley Jr. to Ronald Reagan, May 11, 1976, William F. Buckley, Jr. Papers.
91. William F. Buckley Jr., "Reagan and the Right," On the Right, July 31, 1976
92. William F. Buckley Jr. "Closing Night," On the Right, August 24, 1976.
93. Ronald Reagan, speech before the 1976 Republican National Convention, August 19, 1976.
94. Buckley, "Closing Night."
95. See "Proposals for Welfare," *Firing Line*, April 23 1973; and William F. Buckley Jr., "New Boy in Town," On the Right, June 29, 1976.
96. For an account of Moynihan's time at the United Nations, see Gil Troy, *Moynihan's Moment: America's Fight Against Zionism as Racism* (New York: Oxford University Press, 2012).

97. William F. Buckley Jr. to Ronald Reagan, August 30, 1976, William F. Buckley, Jr. Papers.
98. Judis, *William F. Buckley, Jr.*, 391.
99. William F. Buckley Jr., "Manmade in Manhattan," On the Right, August 15, 1978.
100. William F. Buckley Jr., "An Evening with Castro," On the Right, October 12, 1976.
101. Ronald Reagan to William F. Buckley Jr., January 27, 1977, William F. Buckley, Jr. Papers.
102. William F. Buckley Jr. to Ronald Reagan, September 12, 1977, William F. Buckley, Jr. Papers.
103. William F. Buckley Jr. to Ronald Reagan, February 17, 1977, William F. Buckley, Jr. Papers.
104. Ronald Reagan to William F. Buckley Jr., March 8, 1977, William F. Buckley, Jr. Papers; and William F. Buckley Jr., "For the Record," On the Right, January 31, 1978.
105. "The Panama Canal Treaties," *Firing Line*, January 13, 1978.
106. Buckley, *The Reagan I Knew*, 111.
107. William F. Buckley Jr., "Why Can't I Play?" On the Right, January 14, 1978.
108. William F. Buckley Jr., "Republican Manners," On the Right, April 3, 1979.
109. Ibid.
110. "Presidential Hopeful: Ronald Reagan," *Firing Line*, January 14, 1980. See also Buckley, *The Reagan I Knew*, 115–25.
111. William F. Buckley Jr. to Ronald Reagan, May 31, 1979, William F. Buckley, Jr. Papers.
112. William F. Buckley Jr., "Visiting with the Entrails," On the Right, March 1, 1980.
113. Theodore H. White, *America in Search of Itself* (New York: Harper and Row, 1982), 146.
114. Judis, *William F. Buckley, Jr.*, 417.
115. William F. Buckley Jr. to Ronald Reagan April 2, 1980, William F. Buckley, Jr. Papers.
116. Judis, *William F. Buckley, Jr.*, 418.
117. Ibid., 414.
118. William F. Buckley Jr., "Day Four," On the Right, July 22, 1980.
119. Ibid.
120. Ronald Reagan, speech accepting the Republican presidential nomination, July 17, 1980.
121. William F. Buckley Jr., "The Left Discovers Reagan," On the Right, March 15, 1980.
122. William F. Buckley Jr., "On Reagan's Slips," On the Right, September 16, 1980.
123. Judis, *William F. Buckley, Jr.*, 421.
124. Ibid.
125. William F. Buckley Jr. to Ronald Reagan, September 2, 1980, William F. Buckley, Jr. Papers.
126. Ibid.
127. Ronald Reagan to William F. Buckley Jr., September 19, 1980, William F. Buckley, Jr. Papers.
128. Ibid.

129. William F. Buckley Jr. to Ronald Reagan, September 2, 1980, William F. Buckley, Jr. Papers. Buckley used "the governor listeth" as the title of his second published collection of columns in 1970.
130. William F. Buckley Jr., "Who Will Win the Debate," On the Right, September 13, 1980.
131. Ibid.
132. William F. Buckley Jr., "The Debate," On the Right, November 1, 1980.
133. Ibid.
134. William F. Buckley Jr. to Ronald Reagan, November 5, 1980, William F. Buckley, Jr. Papers.
135. Ibid.
136. Ibid.
137. Judis, *William F. Buckley, Jr.*, 423–24.
138. William F. Buckley Jr. to Ronald Reagan, April 28, 1980, William F. Buckley, Jr. Papers.
139. Ibid.
140. Ronald Reagan to William F. Buckley Jr., May 28, 1980, William F. Buckley, Jr. Papers.
141. William F. Buckley Jr. to Ronald Reagan, October 13, 1980, William F. Buckley, Jr. Papers.
142. Henry Allen, "National Review at 25," *Washington Post*, December 8, 1980.
143. Judis, *William F. Buckley, Jr.*, 424.
144. Ibid., 425.
145. Buckley, *The Reagan I Knew*, 129.
146. Ronald Reagan to William F. Buckley Jr., December 9, 1980, William F. Buckley, Jr. Papers.
147. Buckley, *The Reagan I Knew*, 129.
148. Ibid.
149. William F. Buckley Jr. to Ronald Reagan, December 16, 1980, William F. Buckley, Jr. Papers.
150. Ronald Reagan to William F. Buckley Jr., December 30, 1980, William F. Buckley, Jr. Papers.

CHAPTER 13. BILL AND RONNIE: ADVISING A PRESIDENT

1. William F. Buckley Jr., "Reagan the Pragmatist," On the Right, December 6, 1980.
2. Ibid.; and William F. Buckley Jr., "Reagan and Busing: A Proposal," On the Right, December 9, 1980.
3. Ibid. Buckley voiced the same concern in a letter to Reagan dated January 9, 1982, William F. Buckley, Jr. Papers.
4. William F. Buckley Jr., "The Failure of Ronald Reagan," On the Right, February 10, 1984.
5. William F. Buckley Jr., "Say Again?" On the Right, March 17, 1981.
6. William F. Buckley Jr., "Don't Forget, Blame Reagan," On the Right, January 13, 1983.

7. William F. Buckley Jr., "Better Than Ever," On the Right, April 4, 1981.
8. Buckley, *The Reagan I Knew*, 134–35.
9. William F. Buckley Jr. to William Draper, May 13, 1981, William F. Buckley, Jr. Papers.
10. Ronald Reagan to William F. Buckley Jr., July 15, 1981, in *Reagan: A Life in Letters*, ed. Kiron Skinner, Annelise Anderson, and Martin Anderson (New York: Simon and Schuster, 2004), 63.
11. Ibid.
12. William F. Buckley Jr. to Ronald Reagan, July 31, 1981, William F. Buckley, Jr. Papers.
13. William F. Buckley Jr. to Ronald Reagan, November 9, 1982, William F. Buckley, Jr. Papers.
14. Ronald Reagan to William F. Buckley Jr., November 12, 1982, William F. Buckley, Jr. Papers.
15. "'Freeze' Leader Caldicott Cites 75-Minute Talk with Reagan," *Washington Post*, May 23, 1983.
16. Buckley, *The Reagan I Knew*, 78–79.
17. Ibid., 82.
18. William F. Buckley Jr. to Ron Reagan, January 3, 1986, William F. Buckley, Jr. Papers.
19. William F. Buckley Jr. to Ronald and Nancy Reagan, August 11, 1986, William F. Buckley, Jr. Papers.
20. Ronald Reagan to William F. Buckley Jr., July 15, 1981, in Buckley, *The Reagan I Knew*, 144. Reagan nominated Bork for a vacancy on the Supreme Court in 1987 and the Senate rejected his confirmation.
21. William F. Buckley Jr., "How to Think about Sandra Day O'Connor," On the Right, July 11, 1981.
22. Ibid.
23. See Buckley, *The Reagan I Knew*, 147–50; and William Greider, "The Education of David Stockman," *Atlantic*, December 1981.
24. William F. Buckley Jr. to Ronald Reagan, November 15, 1981, William F. Buckley, Jr. Papers.
25. Ronald Reagan to William F. Buckley Jr., February 2, 1982, William F. Buckley, Jr. Papers.
26. Buckley, *The Reagan I Knew*, 163. Buckley had first met Nixon late in 1957.
27. Ibid., 163–65.
28. Ibid., 151–52. (From a commencement address Buckley delivered at Cornell University Graduate School of Business, June 13, 1981.)
29. Ibid., 152–54.
30. Transcript published in *National Review*, April 1, 1983.
31. Ronald Reagan, address to the nation, September 5, 1983.
32. William F. Buckley Jr., "The US Response," On the Right, September 10, 1983.
33. Ibid.
34. William F. Buckley Jr., "Missing the Point on Grenada," On the Right, November 5, 1983.
35. William F. Buckley Jr. to Ronald Reagan, July 20, 1982, William F. Buckley, Jr. Papers.
36. Lou Cannon, *President Reagan: The Role of a Lifetime* (New York: Public Affairs, 1991), 363.

37. Reagan considered replacing Clark, who became Secretary of the Interior, with his Chief of Staff, James Baker. Reagan biographer Lou Cannon speculates that, had he done so, the Iran-Contra scandal (the trading of arms for hostages), might have been averted. See ibid., 380–81. Reagan took a similar view. See Ronald Reagan, *An American Life* (New York: Simon and Schuster, 1990), 448. "My decision not to appoint Jim Baker as national security adviser, I suppose, was a turning point for my administration," Reagan said, "although I had no idea at the time how significant it would prove to be."
38. Cannon, *President Reagan*, 380–81.
39. William F. Buckley Jr., "Caution: Soldiers at Work," On the Right, December 8, 1983.
40. William F. Buckley Jr., "Go Home," On the Right, December 18, 1984.
41. Ronald Reagan to William F. Buckley Jr., December 19, 1983, William F. Buckley, Jr. Papers.
42. Ronald Reagan to William F. Buckley Jr., January 5, 1984, William F. Buckley, Jr. Papers.
43. William F. Buckley Jr. to Ronald Reagan, March 10, 1981, William F. Buckley, Jr. Papers. In his letter to Reagan, Buckley referred to Niven's ailment as "the same disease Jack Javits has." His use of the ex-Senator's preferred nickname suggests that his sense of empathy had trumped any lingering animosities, whether personal or ideological, between him and the liberal Republican Senator from New York.
44. William F. Buckley Jr. to Nancy Reagan, July 27, 1984, William F. Buckley, Jr. Papers.
45. William F. Buckley Jr. to Ronald Reagan, April 19, 1982, William F. Buckley, Jr. Papers. Talbott was a former student of Sokolov's. He later served as Undersecretary of State in the Clinton administration and as President of the Brookings Institution.
46. William F. Buckley Jr. to Lyn Nofziger, August 17, 1981, William F. Buckley, Jr. Papers.
47. William F. Buckley Jr. to Alexander Haig, June 8, 1981, William F. Buckley, Jr. Papers.
48. Tony Dolan to William F. Buckley Jr., July 16, 1982, William F. Buckley, Jr. Papers.
49. Ronald Reagan to William F. Buckley Jr., November 6, 1985, William F. Buckley, Jr. Papers. Bork retired from this post in 1986. One year later, Reagan nominated him to the Supreme Court. The Senate denied him confirmation in a vote of 58 to 42.
50. William F. Buckley Jr. to Ronald Reagan, November 6, 1985, William F. Buckley, Jr. Papers.
51. Ronald Reagan to William F. Buckley Jr., October 21, 1985, William F. Buckley, Jr. Papers.
52. See Alden Whitman, "Reagan Echoes Hitler's Strident Anti-Communism," *National Catholic Reporter*, July 4, 1984. Reagan's assistant Kathy Osborne, at the President's direction, sent the piece to Buckley.
53. William F. Buckley Jr. to Ronald Reagan, undated, 1984, William F. Buckley, Jr. Papers.
54. Ronald Reagan to William F. Buckley Jr., September 25, 1990, William F. Buckley, Jr. Papers. See also Buckley, *The Reagan I Knew*, 128.
55. Buckley, *The Reagan I Knew*, 128.
56. William F. Buckley Jr. to Ronald Reagan, September 1, 1984, William F. Buckley, Jr. Papers.

57. Ibid.
58. Jeane Kirkpatrick, "Dictatorships and Double Standards," *Commentary*, November 1979.
59. Jeane Kirkpatrick, keynote address before the Republican National Convention, August 20, 1984, Dallas.
60. Jeane Kirkpatrick to William F. Buckley Jr., August 30, 1984, William F. Buckley, Jr. Papers.
61. "New Question in Race: Is Oldest U.S. President Now Showing His Age?" *Wall Street Journal*, October 9, 1984.
62. William F. Buckley Jr., "Split Decision," On the Right, October 11, 1984.
63. Ibid.
64. William F. Buckley Jr. to Nancy Reagan, October 15, 1984, William F. Buckley, Jr. Papers.
65. Transcript, presidential debate between Ronald Reagan and Walter Mondale, October 21, 1984.
66. William F. Buckley, Jr. to Nancy Reagan, January 22, 1985, in Buckley, *The Reagan I Knew*, 171.
67. William F. Buckley Jr., "Nancy and Ronald Reagan," On the Right, June 1985.
68. See Cannon, *President Reagan*, 306–7, 506–17.
69. Ibid., 513.
70. Ibid., 514.
71. Reagan was said to have been profoundly affected by footage of what the Fourth Armored Division of the Third Army encountered after liberating the Buchenwald death camp. See Cannon, *President Reagan*.
72. President Ronald Reagan, speech delivered at Bergen-Belsen, May 6, 1985.
73. William F. Buckley Jr., "One Last Try," On the Right, May 5, 1985.
74. William F. Buckley Jr. to Ronald Reagan, May 20, 1985, William F. Buckley, Jr. Papers.
75. See *New Republic*, August 9, 1986.
76. "In Re: Joe Sobran and Anti-Semitism," Notes and Asides, *National Review*, July 4, 1986.
77. Judis, *William F. Buckley, Jr.*, 459–60.
78. Buckley, *In Search of Anti-Semitism*, 13.
79. Ibid.; also see Judis, *William F. Buckley, Jr.*, 458–60.
80. Joseph A. Sobran, "How I Was Fired By Bill Buckley," *Voice of Reason*, October 2, 2110, http://reasonradionetwork.com/20101002/how-i-was-fired-by-bill-buckley-joe-obran.
81. Bentley T. Elliott to William F. Buckley Jr., November 25, 1985, William F. Buckley, Jr. Papers. Peggy Noonan, whom Elliott had hired at the White House, described the role he played in advancing Reagan's conservative agenda: "Ronald Reagan said a lot of famous things, and he said them in part because Ben Elliott got them past the bureaucracy, past the powerful so-called pragmatists, so Reagan could consider them, rewrite them, underscore them. But Ben is the one who got the draft to him." See Peggy Noonan, "The Ben Elliott Story: What I Saw at the Funeral," *Wall Street Journal*, June 14, 2004.

82. Buckley, *The Reagan I Knew*, 177.
83. Ibid., 184.
84. Reagan, speech delivered December 5, 1985, upon the occasion of *National Review*'s thirtieth anniversary.
85. William F. Buckley Jr., "Oh, It's Just Politics," On the Right, August 12, 1986.
86. William B. Buckley Jr. to Ronald Reagan, August 21, 1986, William F. Buckley, Jr. Papers.
87. Ibid.
88. William F. Buckley Jr. to Ronald Reagan, September 4, 1986, William F. Buckley, Jr. Papers.
89. Buckley, "The Strange Turn of Warren Rudman," On the Right, September 9, 1986.
90. William F. Buckley Jr. to Ronald Reagan, April 21, 1986, William F. Buckley, Jr. Papers.
91. Ibid. See also William F. Buckley Jr., "Steps in Combating the AIDS Epidemic: Identify All the Carriers," *New York Times*, March 18, 1986.
92. Judis, *William F. Buckley, Jr.*, 455.
93. Ibid.
94. Buckley, *The Reagan I Knew*, 196.
95. William F. Buckley Jr. to Ronald Reagan, April 24, 1986, William F. Buckley, Jr. Papers.
96. "A Conservative Speaks Out for Gay Rights," *National Review*, September 12, 1986. See also Liebman, *Coming Out Conservative*, 257–61.
97. Deborah Solomon, "Conservatively Speaking: Questions for William F. Buckley, Jr.," *New York Times*, July 11, 2004.
98. William F. Buckley Jr., "Understanding Dr. Koop," On the Right, October 24, 1986.
99. See Jennifer Brier, *Infectious Ideas: U.S. Political Response to the AIDS Crisis* (Chapel Hill: University of North Carolina Press, 2009), chapter 3.
100. Holcomb B. Noble, "C. Everett Koop, Forceful U.S. Surgeon General, Dies at 96," *New York Times*, February 25, 2013.
101. Philip M. Boffey, "Reagan Urges Wide AIDS Testing, but Does Not Call for Compulsion," *New York Times*, June 1, 1987.
102. Carl M. Cannon, "Reagan and AIDS: Correcting the Record," *Real Clear Politics*, June 1, 2014. Several AIDS activists maintained that Reagan did not mention the disease by name until the seventh year of his presidency. The record shows that he referred to it at a press conference on September 17, 1985, and again when he officially commissioned the Koop report. For a balanced view of Reagan's record on AIDS, see Brier, *Infectious Ideas*.
103. Boffey, "Reagan Urges Wide AIDS Testing."
104. William F. Buckley Jr., "Eight Down? To Go?" On the Right, October 8, 1991.
105. Solomon, "Conservatively Speaking."
106. William F. Buckley Jr., "The Repeal of the Homosexual Laws," On the Right, March 3, 1966.
107. Carl M. Cannon, "Reagan and AIDS: Correcting the Record," *Real Clear Politics*, June 1, 2014.

108. William F. Buckley Jr., "The Ordeal of Robert Bauman," On the Right, October 9, 1980.
109. Robert Bauman, *Gentleman from Maryland: The Conscience of a Gay Conservative* (New York: William Morrow, 1986), 257–61.
110. William F. Buckley Jr., "Americans Press for Soviet Position," On the Right, August 19, 1986.
111. William F. Buckley Jr., "The Grand Design," On the Right, August 29, 1986.
112. William F. Buckley Jr., "Saved from the Brink," On the Right, October 14, 1986.
113. William F. Buckley Jr. to Ronald Reagan, October 13, 1986, William F. Buckley, Jr. Papers. For a fuller account of the Reykjavik summit, see Ken Adelman, *Reagan at Reykjavik: Forty-Eight Hours That Ended the Cold War* (New York: Harper Collins), 2014.
114. Ronald Reagan to William F. Buckley Jr., October 22, 1986, William F. Buckley, Jr. Papers.
115. William F. Buckley Jr., "Hangover," On the Right, October 23, 1986.
116. Ronald Reagan to William F. Buckley Jr., December 2, 1986, William F. Buckley, Jr. Papers.
117. William F. Buckley Jr., "Playing with Common Sense," On the Right, December 5, 1986.
118. William F. Buckley Jr. to Ronald and Nancy Reagan, November 13, 1988, William F. Buckley, Jr. Papers.
119. Evan Thomas, *The Man to See* (New York: Touchstone, 1991), 21, 471–72.
120. Ibid., 471–72.
121. William F. Buckley Jr., "The Unexamined Side of Edward Bennett Williams," *National Review*, July 31, 1962.
122. "Buckley Replies Sharply to Recent Williams Slur," *Yale Daily News*, October 24, 1962.
123. Ibid.
124. Thomas, *The Man to See*, 139. The convict was Edgar Smith. While in prison, Smith maintained his innocence in *Brief Against Death*, a book he published in 1968, to which Buckley had written the foreword.
125. William F. Buckley Jr. to Ronald Reagan, January 19, 1987, William F. Buckley, Jr. Papers.
126. Thomas, *The Man to See*, 75.
127. Cannon, *President Reagan*, 696.
128. See Hedrick Smith, "The Right Against Reagan," *New York Times Magazine*, January 17, 1988.
129. William F. Buckley Jr. to Ronald Reagan, April 29, 1987, William F. Buckley, Jr. Papers.
130. John P. Roche, "Reagan's Suicide Pact: From Reykjavik All Roads Led Down," *National Review*, May 22, 1987.
131. William F. Buckley Jr. to Ronald Reagan, April 27, 1987, William F. Buckley, Jr. Papers.
132. Ronald Reagan to William F. Buckley Jr., April 27, 1987, William F. Buckley, Jr. Papers.
133. William F. Buckley Jr., "The Harm Is Done," On the Right, October 8, 1987.

134. William F. Buckley Jr., "Reagan Outwitted," On the Right, November 26, 1987.
135. William F. Buckley Jr. to Ronald Reagan, October 18, 1987, William F. Buckley, Jr. Papers.
136. William F. Buckley, Jr., "Peace Drunk," On the Right, September 22, 1987.
137. William F. Buckley Jr. to Ronald Reagan, August 11, 1987, William F. Buckley, Jr. Papers.
138. William F. Buckley Jr. to Ronald Reagan, January 24, 1988, William F. Buckley, Jr. Papers.
139. Ronald Reagan to William F. Buckley Jr., February 1, 1988, William F. Buckley, Jr. Papers.
140. William F. Buckley Jr., "Reagan's Spooky Revelations," On the Right, May 12, 1988.
141. Buckley, *The Reagan I Knew*, 206.
142. William F. Buckley Jr. to Ronald Reagan, January 24, 1988, William F. Buckley, Jr. Papers.
143. Ronald Reagan to William F. Buckley Jr., February 1, 1988, William F. Buckley, Jr. Papers.
144. William F. Buckley Jr. to Nancy Reagan, May 17, 1988, William F. Buckley, Jr. Papers.
145. Cannon, *President Reagan*, 699.
146. William F. Buckley Jr., "A Farewell to the Reagans," On the Right, January 17, 1989.
147. Buckley, *The Reagan I Knew*, 224.
148. William F. Buckley Jr. to Ronald Reagan, April 1, 1991, William F. Buckley, Jr. Papers.
149. William F. Buckley Jr. to Ronald Reagan, November 6, 1989, William F. Buckley, Jr. Papers. See also Reagan, *My Turn*.
150. Buckley to Reagan, November 6, 1989.
151. Kitty Kelly, *Nancy Reagan: An Unauthorized Biography* (New York: Simon and Schuster, 1991. Kelly referenced articles Buckley had written and interviews published in magazines and newspapers.
152. Buckley to Reagan, November 6, 1989.
153. William F. Buckley Jr., "The Democrats Win with a Sweep," On the Right, April 9, 1991. Buckley was referring to the coverage of the rape trial of Kennedy's nephew William Kennedy Smith, who was subsequently acquitted, and to reports of the Senator's drinking habits and other behavior over the 1991 Easter weekend.
154. Buckley, *The Reagan I Knew*, 229.
155. Ibid, 216.
156. Ibid., 230.
157. See Ronald Reagan, letter to the American people, November 5, 1994; and Edmund Morris, *Dutch: A Memoir of Ronald Reagan* (New York: Random House, 1999).
158. Buckley, *The Reagan I Knew*, 221–23.

CHAPTER 14. DISAPPOINTED WITH G. H. W. BUSH; UNSOLD ON CLINTON

1. "*Chronicle* Poll Sees Goldwater over Kennedy; Conservatism Would Carry Republican in Critical Texas Areas," *Houston Chronicle*, November 22, 1963.

2. George Bush, contributor,, "The Republican Party and the Conservative Movement," *National Review*, December 1, 1964. Other contributors were John Davis Lodge, Ronald Reagan, Russell Kirk, and Gerhard Niemeyer.
3. George H. W. Bush to William F. Buckley Jr., July 20 1964, and November 12, 1964, William F. Buckley, Jr. Papers.
4. Lindsay met his future bride, Mary Harrison, at the wedding of Bush's sister Nancy to John Ellis.
5. William F. Buckley Jr. to David Clark, March 13, 1968, William F. Buckley, Jr. Papers.
6. William F. Buckley Jr. and Patricia Buckley to George H. W. Bush, November 4, 1970, William F. Buckley, Jr. Papers.
7. George H. W. Bush to William F. Buckley Jr., November 16, 1970, William F. Buckley, Jr. Papers.
8. William F. Buckley Jr. to George H. W. Bush, September 8, 1972, William F. Buckley, Jr. Papers.
9. William F. Buckley Jr. to George H. W. Bush, August 20, 1974, William F. Buckley, Jr. Papers.
10. William F. Buckley Jr., "The Council on Foreign Relations and Ideology," On the Right, October 2, 1979.
11. George H. W. Bush to William F. Buckley Jr., November 15, 1980, William F. Buckley, Jr. Papers.
12. The article Christopher Buckley had written that captured Bush's attention was "Mexico's Oil Boom and What's in It for Us," *Esquire*, December 19, 1978.
13. William F. Buckley Jr. to George H. W. Bush, undated, William F. Buckley, Jr. Papers. At the time, Bush's brother Prescott was challenging incumbent Lowell Weicker for the Connecticut Republican senatorial nomination.
14. William F. Buckley Jr. to George H. W. Bush, February 2, 1984, William F. Buckley, Jr. Papers.
15. Barbara Bush to William F. Buckley Jr., April 15, 1985, William F. Buckley, Jr. Papers.
16. Ibid.
17. William F. Buckley Jr. to George H. W. Bush, May 5, 1986, William F. Buckley, Jr. Papers.
18. William F. Buckley Jr., "Bush Has Got It Wrong," On the Right, May 9, 1986.
19. Buckley to Bush, May 5, 1986.
20. Ibid.
21. George H. W. Bush to William F. Buckley Jr., September 9, 1987, William F. Buckley, Jr. Papers.
22. Ibid.
23. William F. Buckley Jr. to George H. W. Bush, August 25, 1987, William F. Buckley, Jr. Papers.
24. See "Bush Battles the Wimp Factor," *Newsweek*, October 19, 1987; and George F. Will, "The Sound of the Lapdog," *Washington Post*, January 30, 1988.
25. William F. Buckley Jr., "George Bush, Reborn," On the Right, March 3, 1988.
26. William F. Buckley Jr., "Thursday Night with the GOP," On the Right, August 19, 1988.

27. See William Safire, "Bush's Gamble," *New York Times Magazine*, October 18, 1992; and William Safire, "Kinder Than Who?" On Language, *New York Times Magazine*, November 15, 1992. Safire added that Mrs. Reagan "knew when the cord was being cut, despite her grammatical lapse." Of the grammatical controversy her remarks purportedly generated, he noted that she had a "legion of who-whomnicks to support her grammar."
28. William F. Buckley Jr., "What's Going On?" On the Right, August 26, 1988; and William F. Buckley Jr., "Bush Scores," On the Right, October 14, 1988.
29. William F. Buckley Jr., "Conservatives and George Bush," On the Right, October 13, 1988; and Buckley, "Bush Scores."
30. William F. Buckley Jr., "The Challenger's Plight," On the Right, September 1, 1988.
31. William F. Buckley Jr. to Ronald Reagan, January 19, 1988, William F. Buckley, Jr. Papers.
32. William F. Buckley Jr., "The Birth of BuckPac," On the Right, August 16, 1988.
33. "Buck-Pac Kills!" *National Review*, December 9, 1988.
34. William F. Buckley Jr., "Bush and the Hundred Days," On the Right, May 2, 1989.
35. William F. Buckley Jr., "Sleaze, 18 Karat," On the Right, June 15, 1989; and William F. Buckley Jr., "The Indelicate Question," On the Right, July 11, 1989.
36. William F. Buckley Jr. to George H. W. Bush, May 12, 1989, William F. Buckley, Jr. Papers.
37. William F. Buckley Jr., "Penny-Wise," On the Right, September 29, 1989.
38. William F. Buckley Jr. to George H. W. Bush, November 8, 1989, William F. Buckley, Jr. Papers.
39. George H. W. Bush to William F. Buckley Jr., December 22, 1989, William F. Buckley, Jr. Papers.
40. William F. Buckley Jr., "The Parted Lips," On the Right, May 10, 1990.
41. William F. Buckley Jr., "Pledge Anyone?" On the Right, January 1, 1991.
42. Ibid.
43. Eric Pace, "*National Review* Losing Buckley as Its Chief Editor," *New York Times*, October 6, 1990.
44. William F. Buckley Jr., "Bush and the Constitutional Question," On the Right, January 3, 1991.
45. Ibid.
46. William F. Buckley Jr., "The Persian Gulf: Should We Be Prepared to Go?" On the Right, December 11, 1990. Buckley was quoting columnist Charles Krauthammer.
47. William F. Buckley Jr., "The End of America as Superpower?" On the Right, January 10, 1991.
48. William F. Buckley Jr., "Bravo Bush," On the Right, February 26, 1991.
49. Transcript, *The McLaughlin Group*, August 26, 1990. See also Patrick Buchanan, "Rupture on the Right," *Washington Times*, August 27, 1990.
50. Charles Lindbergh, speech in Des Moines, Iowa, September 11, 1941.
51. Transcript, *The McLaughlin Group*, June 15, 1990.
52. Pat Buchanan, *Washington Times*, August 29, 1990.
53. A. M. Rosenthal, "In Search of Buckley," *New York Times*, January 21, 1992.

54. William F. Buckley Jr., "Rosenthal Think," On the Right, March 10, 1992
55. Buckley, *In Search of Anti-Semitism*, 27.
56. Paul Berman, "Gentlemen's Disagreement," *New Yorker*, October 12, 1992.
57. Richard Cohen, "Buchanan's Offensive Language," *Washington Post*, December 17, 1991.
58. William Safire, "Buchanan's Campaign," *New York Times*, December 16, 1992.
59. William F. Buckley Jr. to Ronald Reagan, December 18, 1991, William F. Buckley, Jr. Papers.
60. See William F. Buckley Jr., "In Search of Anti-Semitism," *National Review*, December 31, 1991; and Buckley, *In Search of Anti-Semitism*.
61. William F. Buckley Jr., "Step Down, Dick," On the Right, September 23, 1991.
62. William F. Buckley Jr., "Bush's Man at Dem HQ," On the Right, November 27, 1992.
63. William F. Buckley Jr., "Campaign Manners," On the Right, January 17, 1992.
64. William F. Buckley Jr., "Bush Is Going, Going . . . Gone?" On the Right, January 23, 1992.
65. William F. Buckley Jr., "His Supreme Preppiness," On the Right, February 14, 1992. His references were to a popular prime-time soap opera series of the 1980s, comedian Roseanne Barr, tabloid celebrity journalist Geraldo Rivera, and talk show social arbiter Oprah Winfrey. At age sixty-eight, Buckley attended his first and only baseball game as the guest of Ira Glasser of the New York ACLU, who took Buckley to see the New York Mets play. Their excursion also marked Buckley's first "serious" ride on the New York City subway. Buckley declined to attend a second game on the grounds that he had already had the experience.
66. William F. Buckley Jr., "Thunder on the Right," On the Right, February 20 and 21, 1992. Buchanan actually pulled 47 percent of the vote, a major symbolic victory over a President whose standing in the polls a year earlier had reached 91 percent.
67. William F. Buckley Jr., "St. Crispin's Day for the Dems," On the Right, July 17, 1992. In 1992, Democrats were pressing for mandated "family leave." It was enacted during the Clinton administration. By 2016, they were arguing in favor of mandated "paid family leave."
68. William F. Buckley Jr., "Bush at Bat," On the Right, April 3 1992. Clinton had sought to take advantage of Bush's perceived lethargic response to economic hardships within the Soviet Union, for which Richard Nixon, among others, had criticized him.
69. William F. Buckley Jr., "Quayle Out?" On the Right, July 23, 1992.
70. William F. Buckley Jr., "Houston, Day One," On the Right, August 18, 1992. See also Ronald Reagan, address before the Republican National Convention, August 17, 1992.
71. William F. Buckley Jr., "Yes, Bush," On the Right, October 30, 1992.
72. Ibid.
73. Ibid.
74. William F. Buckley Jr., "Bill the Pothead," On the Right, April 2, 1992; William F. Buckley Jr., "On the Patriotism of Clinton," On the Right, October 13, 1992; and William F. Buckley Jr., "Was Clinton Dishonorable?" On the Right, September 17, 1992. See also "The 1992 Campaign: A Letter by Clinton on His Draft Deferment; 'A War I Opposed and Despised.'" *New York Times*, February 13, 1992 (letter dated December 3, 1969.)

75. William F. Buckley Jr., "Bill Clinton's Other Life," On the Right, January 1, 1992.
76. William F. Buckley Jr., "The Questions of Public Character," On the Right, September 22, 1992.
77. Buckley, "Bill the Pothead."
78. Ibid.
79. William F. Buckley Jr., "The Untroubled Political Conscience of Bill Clinton," On the Right, April 7, 1992.
80. Writer Christopher Hitchens's observation that at Oxford Clinton "preferred, like many another marijuana enthusiast, to take his dope in the form of large handfuls of cookies and brownies," if true, might have provided Buckley with another example. See "Christopher Hitchens: Bill Clinton Liked Pot Brownies," *Huffington Post*, May 25, 2011.
81. William F. Buckley Jr., "The Struggle to Understand Clinton," On the Right, March 3, 1993.
82. William F. Buckley Jr., "Clinton's National Service," On the Right, May 21, 1993.
83. Ibid.
84. "NAFTA, Yes," *National Review*, November 29, 1993.
85. William F. Buckley Jr., "The Data Pour In," On the Right, November 11, 1993.
86. William F. Buckley Jr., "Clinton's First Day," On the Right, January 21, 1993.
87. William F. Buckley Jr., "The Lotus Maker," On the Right, February 25, 1993.
88. William F. Buckley Jr., "Gingrich Thought," On the Right, May 7, 1996.
89. Ibid.
90. William F. Buckley Jr., "Thank-you, Thank-you Very Much," On the Right, August 15, 2000.
91. William F. Buckley Jr., 'What Would We Do to Clinton?" On the Right, March 7, 1994.
92. William F. Buckley Jr., "Inside Whitewater," On the Right, March 25, 1994; Buckley, "What Would We Do to Clinton?" and William F. Buckley Jr., "Poor Paula Jones," On the Right, January 14, 1997.
93. William F. Buckley Jr., "Oh What a Beautiful Morning," On the Right, November 1, 1994; and William F. Buckley, interview with Charlie Rose, PBS, January 9, 1995.
94. Buckley, interview with Rose.
95. William F. Buckley Jr., "Junk Analysis," On the Right, October 20, 1995. For an account of the Clinton-Gingrich relationship, see Steven M. Gillon, *The Pact: Bill Clinton, Newt Gingrich, and the Rivalry That Defined a Generation* (Oxford: Oxford University Press, 2008).
96. William F. Buckley Jr., "He's Guilty or I Am Blind," On the Right, August 11, 1998.
97. William F. Buckley Jr., "Orderly Thought on Clinton," On the Right, January 27, 1998.
98. William F. Buckley Jr., "The Plight of the Friends of Bill," On the Right, February 6, 1998.
99. William F. Buckley Jr., "The Difficulties of Mr. Starr," On the Right, February 27, 1998; and William F. Buckley Jr., "The Final Word on Lewinsky," On the Right, September 15, 1998.

100. William F. Buckley Jr., "What Are the Alternatives?" On the Right, August 8, 1998.
101. Buckley, "The Final Word on Lewinsky."
102. Ibid.
103. William F. Buckley Jr., "What Can Clinton Do?" On the Right, May 30, 1997. Hubbell and Foster, associates of the Clintons in Arkansas, were the subjects of various investigations. Foster committed suicide while a White House aide. Johnny Huang was convicted for funneling illegal contributions to Clinton's reelection campaign.
104. William F. Buckley Jr., "Notes and Asides," *National Review*, October 12, 1998.
105. Ibid.
106. William F. Buckley Jr., "Countdown on U.S. History," On the Right, December 8, 1998.
107. William F. Buckley Jr., "The End of the Affair?" On the Right, November 11, 1998.
108. William F. Buckley Jr., *Commentary*, January 1999.
109. William F. Buckley Jr., "What Next in USA vs. Clinton," On the Right, December 2, 1998.
110. William F. Buckley Jr., "Clinton Has Loved Every Minute," On the Right, November 11, 2000. See also Joe Eszterhas, *American Rhapsody* (New York: Vintage, 2001).
111. Buckley, "Clinton Has Loved Every Minute."
112. William F. Buckley Jr., "Where Do We Go Now with Clinton?" On the Right, February 23, 2001. Marc Rich had been sentenced to prison in absentia for tax evasion, wire fraud, racketeering, and violating the U.S.-imposed oil embargo on Iran during the 1979 Iranian hostage crisis. He had fled the country to avoid serving his sentence.
113. Heidi Przybyla and Judy Woodruff, "Buckley Says Bush Will Be Judged on Iraq War, Now a Failure," *Bloomberg News*, March 31, 2006.

CHAPTER 15. W: "COUNTING THE SILVER"

1. *Public Statements of the Presidents*, "Administration of George W. Bush," 1527–29.
2. William F. Buckley Jr., "The Rush to Bush," On the Right, June 10, 1999.
3. William F. Buckley Jr., "How Much Do We Like 'W'?" On the Right, July 11, 2000.
4. William F. Buckley Jr., interview with Charlie Rose, PBS, June 10, 1999.
5. Safire, "Bush's Gamble"; and Safire, "Kinder Than Who?"
6. Buckley, interview with Rose, June 10, 1999.
7. Buckley, "How Much Do We Like 'W'?"
8. William F. Buckley Jr., "Fun and Games in New York City," On the Right, October 20, 1999.
9. Transcript, Al Smith dinner, October 19, 2000, C-SPAN archives. This was a reference to Bush's three performances against Gore.
10. William F. Buckley Jr., "Aching to Be President," On the Right, October 31, 2000.
11. William F. Buckley Jr., "Confidential Memo—Eyes Only," On the Right, November 11, 2000. Chads were perforated pieces of paper voters used to indicate their preferred candidate.

12. William F. Buckley Jr., "Reflections at 0600," On the Right, November 8, 2000.
13. William F. Buckley Jr., "How to Practice Disrespect," On the Right, January 12, 2001.
14. William F. Buckley Jr., "The Paul O'Neill Hour," On the Right, February 9, 2001; William F. Buckley Jr., "Capitalist Unction," On the Right, February 16, 2001; William F. Buckley Jr., "O'Neill Hits the What-ifs on Tax," On the Right, March 2, 2001; and William F. Buckley Jr., "A Parable: The Tenth Man," On the Right, April 27, 2001.
15. Buckley, "O'Neill Hits the What-ifs on Tax."
16. William F. Buckley Jr., "Trial Lawyers vs. Sanity," On the Right, June 8, 2001. See also William F. Buckley Jr., "'W's Strange Flirtation," On the Right, July 17, 2001; and William F. Buckley Jr., interview with Charlie Rose, PBS, July 20, 2001.
17. Buckley, interview with Rose, July 20, 2001.
18. William F. Buckley Jr., "Bush Has Problems," On the Right, July 15, 2003.
19. William F. Buckley Jr., "Is Democracy Pork?" On the Right, December 2, 2003.
20. William F. Buckley Jr., "Post Katrina Doubletalk," On the Right, September 9, 2005.
21. Peggy Noonan, "Hey, Big Spender," *Wall Street Journal* March 16, 2006. See also Peggy Noonan, "Whatever It Takes: Is Bush's Big Spending a Bridge to Nowhere?" *Wall Street Journal*, September 22, 2005.
22. Buckley, "Bush Has Problems."
23. William F. Buckley Jr., "The Target: Bin Laden," On the Right, September 12, 2001.
24. Ibid.
25. William F. Buckley Jr., "Loss of Freedom Ahead?" On the Right, November 30, 2001. The number of terrorists involved in the attacks of 9/11 was actually nineteen.
26. William F. Buckley Jr., "Evidence Against Iraq," On the Right, October 9, 2001. See also Laurie Mylroie, *Study of Revenge: Saddam Hussein's Unfinished War Against America* (Washington, DC: American Enterprise Press, 2000).
27. William F. Buckley Jr., "High Noon in Europe," On the Right, January 24, 2003.
28. William F. Buckley Jr., "Forrest Gump Abroad?" On the Right, February 2, 2002.
29. William F. Buckley Jr., "Iraq: Question Closed?" On the Right, August 27, 2002.
30. William F. Buckley Jr., "Thoughts Said and the UN Said," On the Right, September 13, 2002.
31. William F. Buckley Jr., "The Parlous State of the Union," On the Right, January 29, 2003.
32. Ibid.
33. William F. Buckley Jr., "No Smile on His Face," On the Right, February 7, 2003.
34. William F. Buckley Jr., "POTUS to the Press," On the Right, March 7, 2003.
35. William F. Buckley Jr., "What Mr. Bush Left Out," On the Right, March 3, 2003.
36. William F. Buckley Jr., "Great Words from W," On the Right, May 2, 2003.
37. William F. Buckley Jr., "Who Screwed Up," On the Right, June 3, 2003.
38. William F. Buckley Jr., "No on Liberia," On the Right, July 8, 2003.
39. William F. Buckley Jr., "Vote for Me: Here's Why," On the Right, January 13, 2004.
40. William F. Buckley Jr., "How Long, How Long?" On the Right, March 19, 2003.
41. William F. Buckley Jr., "Leadership, Front and Center," On the Right, April 6, 2004.
42. William F. Buckley Jr., "Press Conference Aweigh," On the Right, April 16, 2004. In the print edition, the editorial ran on May 4.

43. "An End to Illusion," *National Review*, April 16, 2004.
44. David D. Kirkpatrick, "Lack of Resolution in Iraq Finds Conservatives Divided," *New York Times*, April 19, 2004.
45. George F. Will, "Time for Bush to See the Realities of Iraq," *Washington Post*, May 4, 2004.
46. Franklin Foer, "Once Again, America First," *New York Times*, October 10, 2004.
47. Bruce Bartlett, "The Growing Chorus of Antiwar Conservatives," *New York Times* blog, January 29, 2007.
48. William F. Buckley Jr., "Exit Rumsfeld," On the Right, May 11, 2004.
49. William F. Buckley Jr., "Did We Do War Crimes?" On the Right, June 11, 2004.
50. David D. Kirkpatrick, "*National Review* Founder Says It's Time to Leave Stage," *New York Times*, June 29, 2004.
51. William F. Buckley Jr., "Who's Paying for the War," On the Right, July 20, 2004.
52. William F. Buckley Jr., "The War We Are In," On the Right, August 20, 2004.
53. William F. Buckley Jr., "Killer Debate Ahead," On the Right, September 28, 2004.
54. William F. Buckley Jr., "We Didn't Tell You So," On the Right, November 3, 2004.
55. William F. Buckley Jr., "Algeria Warned Us," On the Right, October 26, 2004.
56. William F. Buckley Jr., "Thinking Out Iraq," On the Right, January 14, 2005.
57. William F. Buckley Jr., "State of the Nation," On the Right, November 23, 2004.
58. George W. Bush, Second Inaugural Address, January 20, 2005.
59. William F. Buckley Jr., "What Is Bush Saying?" On the Right, January 21, 2005.
60. Robert F. Kennedy, *To Seek a Newer World* (New York: Bantam Books, 1968), 163. Kennedy had quoted from Sophocles' play *Antigone:* "All men make mistakes, but a good man yields when he knows his course is wrong, and repairs the damage. The only sin is pride."
61. William F. Buckley Jr., "The Mounting Protests," On the Right, June 17, 2005.
62. Joseph Rago, "Weekend Interview: 'Old School,'" *Wall Street Journal*, November 12, 2005.
63. George F. Will, "Can This Nomination Be Justified?" *Washington Post*, October 5, 2005.
64. This was the second time Bush alluded to his undistinguished academic record at Yale in a talk in which he also referenced Buckley's erudition.
65. Matt Latimer, *Speech-Less: Tales of a White House Survivor* (New York: Crown, 2009), 250.
66. William F. Buckley Jr., "It Didn't Work," On the Right, February 24, 2006.
67. William F. Buckley Jr., "Next Step," On the Right, March 1, 2006.
68. Przybyla and Woodruff, "Buckley Says Bush Will Be Judged On Iraq War."
69. Ibid.
70. George F. Will, "Bleakness in Baghdad," *Washington Post*, March 19, 2006. See also George F. Will, "Rhetoric of Unreality," *Washington Post*, March 2, 2006.
71. Francis Fukuyama, "After Neo-conservatism," *New York Times*, February 19, 2006.
72. David E. Sanger, "Bush, Conceding Problems, Defends Iraq War," *New York Times*, March 14, 2006.
73. Peter Wehner, "The Wrong Time to Lose Our Nerve," *Wall Street Journal*, April 4, 2006.
74. George W. Bush, speech at the American Enterprise Institute annual dinner, February 28, 2003.

75. Wehner, "The Wrong Time to Lose Our Nerve."
76. See Peter Baker, "Pundits Renounce the President," *Washington Post*, August 20, 2006.
77. For the argument that he had become precisely that, see Sam Tanenhaus, "Athwart History," *New Republic*, March 19, 2007.
78. Josh Gerstein, "Gingrich Criticized President on Iraq War and Wiretapping," *New York Sun*, April 12, 2006.
79. http://bartlett.blogs.nytimes.com/2007/01/29/the-growing-chorus-of-antiwar-conservatives/.
80. Joe Scarborough, "Is Bush an Idiot?" *Huffington Post*, August 14, 2006.
81. William F. Buckley Jr., "One Flag Too High," On the Right, July 14, 2006.
82. Amy Clark, "Buckley: Bush Not a True Conservative," *CBS News*, July 22, 2006. See also "Buckley Parting Ways with Bush," *CBS News*, July 23, 2006.
83. William F. Buckley Jr., "Tuesday's Ultimatum," On the Right, November 8, 2006.
84. The Tet Offensive was a simultaneous attack North Vietnam and the Viet Cong launched against U.S. occupied facilities throughout South Vietnam. It was considered a military defeat for Communist forces, but the surprise nature of the attacks and their severity helped turn public opinion in the United States against a continued U.S. presence there.
85. William F. Buckley Jr., "Yes or No to Bush?" On the Right, January 12, 2007.
86. Matt Latimer, "The Lady Was for Turning," *Washington Post*, April 11, 2013.
87. Pew Research Center, "Republican Support for the War at an All Time Low: A Decade Later/Iraq War Divides the Public," March 18, 2013.
88. William F. Buckley Jr., "Inside Obama," On the Right, January 11, 2008.

CHAPTER 16. THE ANCIENT TRUTHS

1. Douglas Martin, "William F. Buckley, Jr. Is Dead at 82," *New York Times*, February 27, 2008.
2. Usually, Buckley let others comment on his lasting achievements. In a television interview, Buckley granted that in its early years, *National Review* became the "only voice for intelligent conservatism," that the quality of its writing affected several "critical" people such as Ronald Reagan, and that the thinking that undergirded the Goldwater campaign would never have happened in the absence of *National Review*. See Buckley, interview with Rosen.
3. Arthur M. Schlesinger Jr., *Journals, 1952–2000*, ed. Andrew Schlesinger and Stephen Schlesinger (New York: Penguin, 2007).
4. David Brooks, "Remembering the Mentor," *New York Times*, February 29, 2008.
5. Rush Limbaugh, "Buckley Was My Greatest Inspiration," Newsmax.com, February 27, 2008.
6. Evan Thomas, "Mr. Right, R.I.P.," *Newsweek*, March 1, 2008.
7. Transcript, *60 Minutes*, CBS broadcast, September 29, 1970.
8. William F. Buckley Jr., "The War on Henry Kissinger," On the Right, October 22, 2002.
9. Henry A. Kissinger to William F. Buckley Jr., October 22, 2002, William F. Buckley, Jr. Papers.

10. William F. Buckley Jr. to Henry Kissinger, October 22, 2002, William F. Buckley, Jr. Papers.
11. William F. Buckley Jr. to Happy Rockefeller, October 27, 2002, William F. Buckley, Jr. Papers.
12. http://www.henryakissinger.com/eulogies/040408.html.

ACKNOWLEDGMENTS

Writing books, as every author can attest, is not a team sport. Nevertheless, a number of people gave generously of themselves to help me along my way. This is my opportunity to thank them.

I begin by expressing my appreciation to the subject of this book, the late William F. Buckley Jr., for providing me such lively material upon which to draw. Ben Franklin advised his readers to "write things worth the reading or do things worth the writing." Bill Buckley did both. Telling his story proved almost as exhilarating as was watching him live it the first time around.

I thank Christopher Buckley for granting me access to his father's papers, housed at Yale University's Sterling Memorial Library. William R. Massa Jr., Yale University Library Archivist, and his able staff helped me navigate my way through the voluminous Buckley collection with good cheer. I thank them all. The Earhart Foundation, the Achelis and Bodman Foundations, the Lynde and Harry Bradley Foundation, and the William F. Buckley, Jr. Program at Yale provided me with support to defray expenses and to retain research assistance. I thank them for the confidence they placed in me and in this project from its early stages. I also want to note my deep personal appreciation to Montgomery Brown of the Earhart Foundation, John B. Krieger of the Achelis and Bodman Foundations, Daniel P. Schmdt of the Lynde and Harry Bradley Foundation, and Lauren Noble of the William F. Buckley, Jr. Program at Yale for their assistance, patience, and moral support.

Michael Delli Carpini, Dean of the Annenberg School for Communication at the University of Pennsylvania, was a source of continued encouragement and support, for which I remain grateful. Hermon Mebrahtu of the University of Pennsylvania put her extraordinary administrative talents to work helping me keep track of expenses and meet reporting requirements. Kelly Fernández was a steady source of encouragement and good cheer, while Alison J. Feather, Richard Cardona, Kelly Anderson, and Rose Halligan keep me going. All make Annenberg the special place it is.

While researching this book, I had ample opportunities to interact with so many of the extraordinary people who make Yale University such a special place. I came away greatly enriched from my interactions with so many of its students and faculty. In the fall of 2010, under the sponsorship of Branford and Davenport Colleges, I had the honor of directing a student-initiated seminar on William F. Buckley Jr. The experience brought home to me why Bill Buckley retained throughout his life a special place in his heart for Yale undergraduates. I am grateful that the spirit of that seminar lives on in the William F. Buckley, Jr. Program at Yale, which alumni of that seminar founded and continue to direct.

I am grateful to Yale University's extraordinary political science department for also allowing me to teach a seminar on Congress in the spring of 2011. I thank Professor Steven Smith of the department for helping me transition into Yale's academic community and for sharing with me his encyclopedic knowledge of Yale's history and Buckley's contributions to it. Professors Harry Blair, Charles Hill, and Donald Kagan were delightful lunch companions and steady sources of intellectual stimulation.

The late Dr. Paul Hudak, while Master of Saybrook College, afforded me the opportunity to serve as Resident Fellow at the Residential College during the 2010–11 academic year. He and Associate Master Cathy Van Dyke and Saybrook's staff and students made me feel at home from the instant I arrived. I thank all I encountered there for wonderful memories, enduring friendships, and yes, the shortest commute to work I ever had. (Buckley's papers are housed a mere half block away!)

I express my deep appreciation to the staffs of the Library of Congress; the Rockefeller Archives in Tarrytown, New York; the Hoover Institution Archives at Stanford University; the Mudd Library at Princeton University; and the Herbert Hoover, Franklin D. Roosevelt, Dwight D. Eisenhower, John F. Kennedy, Lyndon B. Johnson, Richard Nixon, Gerald R. Ford, Ronald Reagan, G. H. W. Bush, and G. W. Bush Presidential Libraries for their kind assistance as I made my way through their collections. I am indebted to Hillsdale College for making available online Buckley's newspaper columns, articles, reviews, and speeches. I also benefited from the meticulous care with which the Hoover Institution at Stanford University has preserved and makes available to researchers Buckley's *Firing Line* programs and associated documents and photographs.

Special shout-outs go to Tim Rives of the Dwight D. Eisenhower Presidential Library; Abigail Malangone and Stephen Plotkin of the John F. Kennedy Presidential Library; Jennifer Mandel, Michael Pinckney, and Steve Branch of the Ronald Reagan Presidential Library; Joanne Drake, Wren Powell, and Alison Borio, all with the Ronald Reagan Presidential Foundation; Rachel E. Bauer and Stephanie Stewart of the Hoover Institution at Stanford University; and Andrew Riley of the Churchill Archives Center, Cambridge University. All extended themselves many times on my behalf.

I thank Magnolia Pictures and Participant Media for making available to me their documentary *Best of Enemies*, the story of William F. Buckley Jr.'s 1968 televised exchanges with Gore Vidal, and for granting me permission to use still photographs from it. Caryn Capotosto was particularly helpful in this regard, as were her colleagues at Tremolo Productions. I also acknowledge the generosity of Morgan Neville and Robert Gordo. I am grateful to Paul Needham and Isheta Salgacar for their assistance in helping me obtain complete transcripts of all Charlie Rose's interviews with William F. Buckley Jr. and to James Rosen of Fox News, who furnished me with the interview he conducted with Buckley as he neared his seventy-fifth birthday and prepared to terminate his long-running television program, *Firing Line*. Michael Callahan and Nicole Eno of Bloomberg News were also of great assistance.

Several individuals who knew Buckley exceptionally well were exceedingly generous with their time and patience. I express my deepest appreciation to Linda Bridges, Richard Brookhiser, Christopher Buckley, the Honorable James L. Buckley, John Buckley, the late Priscilla Buckley, Richard Coulson, Tony Dolan, Lee Edwards, Jack Fowler, Neal Freeman, Sir Alistair Horne, David Keene, the Honorable Henry A. Kissinger, Richard Lowry, the late Frank Shakespeare, and George F. Will. Cameron O. Smith and Liza Vann Smith entrusted me with precious Buckley family photographs, and Linda Bridges helped me track down the owners of rights to other photographs. I greatly benefited from Linda's institutional knowledge of *National Review* and from her familiarity with many past Buckley endeavors. The Honorable James L. Buckley answered countless questions I put to him. I thank them both again.

Colleagues and friends provided me with invaluable insights and special takes on subjects this book covers. Some provided valuable suggestions. Others guided me to sources. Others consulted their own files and personal recollections to answer questions. Special thanks go to the Honorable James A. Baker, the Honorable James H. Billington, Patrick J. Buchanan, Professor Robert Dallek, Dayton Duncan, Lee Edwards, David Eisenhower, Professor James K. Galbraith, Julian Gingold, Professor David Allen Grier, Kathleen Hall Jamieson, the Honorable Thomas H. Kean, Roger Kimball, Chris Matthews, Mark McKinnon, Mike McCurry, Robert P. O'Quinn, the late Mrs. Nancy Reagan, Alfred S. Regnery, Cokie Roberts, James Rosen, the late Professor Paul E. Sigmund, the Honorable George P. Shultz, Richard Norton Smith, R. Emmett Tyrrell, George F. Will, Judy Woodruff, and Professor Elliott Young.

My friend Richard E. Cohen reviewed the entire manuscript and made suggestions as to how it might be improved and, especially, shortened! Lee Edwards, Lee D. Evans, Alex Gray, Steven E. Johnson, Joann Lynch, Ben Musachio, Robert O'Quinn, Emil Pitkin, and Rahul Prabakar read all or part of the manuscript and offered helpful comments and perspective.

I benefited enormously from the diligence, enthusiasm, and skills of several extraordinary individuals who provided me with invaluable research assistance. They scoured through archives, wrestled with microfilm and copiers, helped obtain rights to previously published materials, and tracked down obscure items. Alex Gray was the first of several who picked up the baton. Joshua Altman, Elizabeth Aslinger, Ryan Boone, Adam Erickson, Adam Humayun, Helen Knight, John Masko, Ben Musachio, Lauren Noble, Danilo Petrovich, Murphy Temple, and Nathaniel Zelinsky all subsequently assisted, and quite ably.

Dr. Emil Pitkin put his extraordinary technical know-how, inexhaustible energy, and good humor to work on my behalf as this manuscript took shape. He received able assists from Katie Miskill, Jonny Xu, and Barry Chiu. Ben Musachio brought to this enterprise his own familiarity with the history and politics of Buckley's times. Repeatedly, he came to my rescue by checking citations and sources from wherever he happened to be, whether in Baltimore, Palo Alto, Oxford, or Latvia.

I express my appreciation to Yale University Press for what has proved to be an extraordinary partnership. My editor, William Frucht, drew upon his significant knowledge of American history and politics to help me make this a better book than it would otherwise have been. I also thank his colleagues Mary Pasti and Karen Olson for their help and support. I had the good fortune to be assigned to Robin DuBlanc, one of the best copy editors in the business. The same good fortune prevailed in the choice of my indexer and proofreader, Fred Kameny. My agent, Alexander C. Hoyt, proved a ready and steady source of support and humor when both were needed. Any mistakes that appear on these pages are mine and mine alone.

Index